1996

TEACHING SECONDARY
SCHOOL SCIENCE

1996

SIXTH EDITION

TEACHING SECONDARY SCHOOL SCIENCE

Strategies for Developing Scientific Literacy

Leslie W. Trowbridge
Professor Emeritus of Science Education
University of Northern Colorado

Rodger W. Bybee
Associate Director
Biological Sciences Curriculum Study
The Colorado College

Merrill,
an Imprint of Prentice Hall

Englewood Cliffs, New Jersey   Columbus, Ohio

Library of Congress Cataloging-in-Publication Data

Trowbridge, Leslie W.
    Teaching secondary school science: strategies for developing scientific literacy/Leslie W. Trowbridge, Rodger W. Bybee.—6th ed.
        p. cm.
    Includes bibliographical references and index.
    ISBN 0-02-421581-9
    1. Science—Study and teaching (Secondary)—United States.
  2. Science teachers—United States.   I. Bybee, Rodger W.
  II. Title.
  Q183.3.A1T76 1996
  507.1'273—dc20   95-23327
                                              CIP

Cover photo: © J. Myers/H. Armstrong Roberts
Editor: Bradley J. Potthoff
Production Editor: Julie Anderson Tober
Production Coordination: WordCrafters Editorial Services, Inc./Ann Mohan
Photo Editor: Anne Vega
Design Coordinator: Jill E. Bonar
Text Design: WordCrafters
Cover Design: Proof Positive/Farrowlyne Associates, Inc.
Production Manager: Laura Messerly

This book was set in Utopia by Carlisle Communications, Ltd. and was printed and bound by Quebecor Printing-Semline. The cover was printed by Phoenix Color Corp.

The fourth and fifth editions of this book were entitled *Becoming a Secondary School Science Teacher,* © 1990 by Macmillan Publishing Company, © 1981 and 1981 by Merrill Publishing Company. The first and second editions of this book were published under the title *Teaching Science by Inquiry in the Secondary School,* © 1973, 1967 by Bell & Howell Company.

Photo credits: Scott Cunningham/Prentice Hall/Merrill, pp. 85, 150, 154, 166, 186, 327, 348, 366, 377, 384 (top), 387; Anne Vega/Prentice Hall/Merrill, pp. 139, 157, 204, 347; Robert Vega/Prentice Hall/Merrill, p. 365; Tom Watson/Prentice Hall/Merrill, p. 343; Todd Yarrington/Prentice Hall/Merrill, pp. 332, 384 (bottom).

Printed in the United States of America

10 9 8 7 6 5 4 3 2 1

ISBN: 0-02-421581-9

Prentice-Hall International (UK) Limited, *London*
Prentice-Hall of Australia Pty. Limited, *Sydney*
Prentice-Hall of Canada, Inc., *Toronto*
Prentice-Hall Hispanoamericana, S. A., *Mexico*
Prentice-Hall of India Private Limited, *New Delhi*
Prentice-Hall of Japan, Inc., *Tokyo*
Simon & Schuster Asia Pte. Ltd., *Singapore*
Editora Prentice-Hall do Brasil, Ltda., *Rio de Janeiro*

PREFACE

The Sixth Edition of *Teaching Secondary School Science: Strategies for Developing Scientific Literacy,* previously titled *Becoming a Secondary School Teacher,* is primarily designed for the undergraduate preservice science teacher. Many of the text's features, however, make it valuable for graduate students and experienced teachers in courses dealing with instructional problems, trends in science teaching, curriculum development, and assessment in science classes. Workshops and institutes designed to develop pedagogical topics for science teachers can also profit from material in this book.

■ FOCUS OF THE TEXT

The strong features of previous editions of this textbook for preservice middle school and high school teachers has been continued in this edition. Among these are emphases on active pupil involvement in their own learning, use of investigative and inquiry teaching strategies to provide experiences in solving real problems and gathering data to support hypotheses, and an explication of "constructivism" as it applies to how secondary students form scientific concepts and understandings of the world. Many practical examples are given of teaching strategies that work, based on the extensive teaching experience of the authors.

Throughout the text, the theme of developing scientific literacy is stressed to assist teachers and students in becoming aware of the many interrelationships between science teaching and national standards.

■ NEW TO THIS EDITION

This edition has undergone a number of important changes.

- Several chapters have been extensively revised. For example, Chapter 18, New Models for Assessment, describes new methods of assessment adapted to current methods of teaching that involve pupil activities and investigations. Chapter 20, Individual and Cultural Differences in Science Classrooms, makes clarifications on the inclusion of exceptional students under the law and guidelines for dealing with advantaged and disadvantaged students in science classrooms. Chapter 22, Computers in Science Classes, reflects the rapidly changing classroom use of computer technology.
- Reports and recommendations of the National Research Council concerning the *National Science Education Standards* formulated in 1995 have been given a strong emphasis in this edition. Every effort has been made to illustrate for teachers how to incorporate these recommendations into their everyday science teaching.
- A new chapter, Chapter 16, titled Controversy in the Classroom, provides suggestions for handling discussion and class activities on controversial science topics of current concern, including the use of ethical dilemmas as topics for discussion.

Acknowledgments

Robert B. Sund, to whom this book is dedicated, was senior author on the first two editions. He died in the planning stages of the third edition. His influence on teaching methods and philosophy remains strong in this edition. We wish to acknowledge his valuable contributions to this textbook in particular and to science education in general.

A special word of thanks is given to Dr. Joel Bass, Sam Houston State University, for his part in writing Chapter 22, Computers in Science Classes. We also wish to thank the reviewers who provided suggestions for this revision: George J. Frangos, California University of Pennsylvania; James J. Gallagher, Michigan State University; Cheryl L. Mason, San Diego State University; Dr. Gilbert D. Starks, Central Michigan University; Herbert H. Stewart, Florida Atlantic University.

Leslie W. Trowbridge
Rodger W. Bybee

CONTENTS

....

TEACHING SECONDARY SCHOOL SCIENCE

UNIT 1

....

INTRODUCTION

As she worked late into the night on her first lesson, Maria Romero questioned her effectiveness as a science teacher. The next day, Ms. Romero began her lesson by asking the students to describe some genetic concepts: *genes, chromosomes, and mutations.* Since Ms. Romero assumed students had learned these concepts in elementary school, she was surprised when they expressed a wide range of responses, mostly incorrect. As she thought about it, she realized that most students recognized the terms as scientific, even biological, but that they consistently responded incorrectly. For example, students indicated that genes were different layers of skin, something in one's blood, things that indicate one's age, a reproductive part of the body; that chromosomes were things that clogged one's arteries, a plant-eating animal; and that mutations were changes that occurred as one got older, a sickness caused by bacteria, and little structures in plants.

Ms. Romero thought that certainly other teachers had taught some biology and even introduced some of these same ideas about genetics, but that the students had not developed an understanding of the information, and the terms had no meaning or importance to them. Ms. Romero wondered about her role in helping students develop scientific literacy especially in connection with teaching secondary school science.

After a little library research, Ms. Romero discovered that the students displayed what contemporary learning theorists referred to as *misconceptions* or *naive theories.* As she investigated further, she found that psychologists had proposed explanations for student misconceptions and the learning process. Ms. Romero found that the model was referred to as *constructivism,* a term that expresses a dynamic and interactive view of learning. In the constructivist view of learning, students continually revise, redefine, and reorganize concepts through interactions among themselves, natural phenomena, science lessons, discussions with other individuals, and the introduction of information from other sources, such as science textbooks. Students first interpret objects and events in terms of their prior experiences, which, from the perspective of the science teacher, may be incorrect or a misconception. In order to change the misconceptions, someone (for example, teachers or students) or something (for example, observations of natural phenomena, textbooks, laboratory experiences) have to challenge the students' conceptions by showing them that their current ideas are inadequate. Further, students must have time and experiences to reconstruct a more adequate conception.

The results of this brief review of research provided Ms. Romero with insights about teaching secondary school science and strategies for developing scientific literacy. When science teachers discover new and better ways to teach, they experience the excitement of education, and the extension of these insights to students' learning science can be the most exhilarating of a teacher's career.

A life in science teaching can entail frustrations and disappointments, but it also involves satisfactions and achievements that promise to outweigh the problems. This unit introduces you to some of the ideas and issues that you will have to consider as a science teacher. Ms. Romero's story about the connections between student learning and science teaching is only one of many that could be told, but more importantly, that you will experience as you become a science teacher with the goal of developing scientific literacy.

Chapter 1

BECOMING A SCIENCE TEACHER

If you are reading this sentence, you are in the process of becoming a science teacher. As with other important issues in your life, you no doubt struggled with this decision. While deciding, you probably gathered information on the options—you might have explored the science major, talked to friends and parents, conferred with your college advisor, and even visited your high school science teacher. With all the facts in mind, you decided to become a science teacher. Thinking all was settled, you went to work on your science major and began taking education courses. For a time, most aspects of your career choice seemed resolved. Now you are taking a course to learn about science teaching; soon you will be student teaching; in the foreseeable future, you will have your first job as a science teacher.

All of this is exciting. But now you have an entirely new set of questions about your career. "How do I teach science?" "Am I qualified to teach science?" "What do I need to know about science and technology?" "What science do I teach to middle school or high school students?" "What is science teaching like?" "What are the problems facing science teachers today?" Constantly emerging questions and concerns regarding science teaching are part of becoming a science teacher.

Some of your questions have answers; others depend on your specific talents, personality, knowledge, enthusiasm, and other important, but elusive, qualities. Obviously, we cannot answer all of these questions in this chapter or this book. We can provide some information and direction and can suggest activities to help clarify your strengths and weaknesses and the realities and possibilities of science teaching. The best way to begin is by completing Activity 1–1 "How I See Myself as a Science Teacher" at the end of this chapter.

■ AM I QUALIFIED TO TEACH SCIENCE?

This question is difficult to answer with a simple yes or no because of the adjective *qualified*. Traditionally, persons have qualified as science teachers by completing a set of educational requirements. In this sense, most individuals can be qualified for teaching. There is more to teaching science than fulfilling a set of requirements and more to teaching science than being able to talk about science. Some of the dimensions of science teaching addressed in Activity 1–1 are identifiable in the following discussion.

Understanding Science and Technology

You should have a background in science, including a broad general knowledge and specific knowledge in your major. These statements seem obvious. In the 1990s, however, you will also need to have an understanding of technology because our society and the experiences of your students are extensively oriented toward technology. You should be aware of the many relationships between science and technology. In the past, science teachers and textbooks presented technology as *applied science;* that is, the enterprise of science resulted in knowledge that was applied to human problems. Although this statement is generally accurate, in some cases scientific advances must wait until technology is developed. Technology can also be viewed as an area of study. As with science, technology also has products and processes that form the basis of study.

In addition to having scientific and technological knowledge, you should apply this knowledge in new situations, use basic science concepts to analyze problems presented by students, and synthesize knowledge so that you may answer questions accurately. You should be well-informed and be able to use your scientific knowledge in many ways. An understanding of science and technology does not automatically qualify you to teach science; other understandings and skills are necessary.

Understanding the Purpose of Science Teaching

You have already encountered the term *scientific literacy* in the title of this book. Most individuals in the science education community use this term to express the major purposes of science education. To begin with, the term refers to your role in advancing individual development of students and achieving society's aspirations within the context of the science curriculum and your classroom. You certainly recognize that scientific literacy expresses the highest and most admirable purposes of science teaching. But we can be a little more concrete and practical.

What do you think the scientifically and technologically literate person should know, value, and do—as a citizen? As you think about this question, we ask that you recognize that the final phrase—*as a citizen*—is a controlling orientation for your answer. An answer that focuses on acquiring knowledge about biology, chemistry, physics, and the earth sciences should be mediated by the question, "What is it about the knowledge from these disciplines that a student should develop?" How do you justify that knowledge in terms of your student's future role as a citizen? What about values and skills? What are those values, attitudes, and habits of mind based on the science and technology that your teaching should help students develop?

A very close connection exists between the purpose of developing scientific literacy and other books you will encounter. Both the *National Science Education Standards*[1] and the *Benchmarks for Science Literacy*[2] address the question of exactly what is meant by scientific literacy. We discuss these and other reports in later chapters. For now, we would have you think about the following statement on the purpose of science teaching:

Science teaching should facilitate students' learning about science and technology as they need to understand and use them in their personal lives and as future citizens. Science teaching should sustain students' natural curiosity; develop their skills in inquiry and design; improve their scientific explanations; help them develop an understanding and use of technology; contribute to their understanding of the role, limits, and possibilities of science and technology in society; and inform the choices they must make in their personal and social lives.

Indeed this statement about science teaching is tightly packed with ideas. As you proceed through this book, we will unpack this statement and provide more concrete and practical ideas for your use as a science teacher. We will discuss scientific literacy in the next chapter.

Organizing Science Instruction

You should be prepared, organized, and have a direction and purpose in your teaching. There is no substitute for a well-prepared lesson. At one time or another, most science teachers have tried to teach without preparation. More often than not, the lesson was not very effective. As you begin organizing your science program, try to establish the big picture by determining the sequence of your program for the year. You may wish to divide the year into units and the units into individual lessons. This simple procedure will give you a sense of overall organization. However, there is more to teaching methods than organization.

Effective science teachers use a variety of teaching methods, choosing the best for each lesson. Always keep in mind the following simple questions: "What do I want to teach?" and "How can I best teach it?" The answers to these questions will direct you to different teaching methods. Complete Activity 1–2

"The What and How of Science Lessons" at the end of this chapter.

Understanding Student Learning

Imagine that you are ready to begin your first science lesson. The students are sitting at their desks, waiting for you to teach them. Do the students in front of you already understand any science concepts? The answer is yes. The students you will be teaching have lived twelve to sixteen years. Through formal and informal experiences the students have developed ideas about the events, objects, and organisms in their world. They have also placed labels on many of those events, objects, and organisms. In this regard you should remember three points: (1) students have concepts about their world, (2) many of these concepts are inadequate when compared to scientific explanations or concepts, and (3) these concepts of the natural world influence what and how students will learn about science.[3] David Ausubel summarized this when he wrote: "If I had to reduce all of educational psychology to just one principle, I would say this: The most important single factor influencing learning is what the learner already knows. Ascertain this and teach him accordingly."[4]

Many science teachers approach instruction as though students are empty vessels to be filled with facts, information, and concepts about the world. This perception of how students learn is inaccurate. It is more accurate to say that students construct their explanations of the world through a personal process in which sensory data are given meaning in terms of prior knowledge. In order for learning to occur, the adequacy of students' current conceptions must be challenged, and appropriate time and opportunities must be provided so students can reconstruct newer and more adequate explanations. Ways to facilitate this process of learning will be explored in later chapters. How is this process of learning different from what you currently understand about student learning? Review your response to Activity 1–2 "The What and How of Science Lessons" at the end of this chapter.

Recognizing Personal Meaning in Teaching and Learning

Imagine two middle school lessons about the life cycles of organisms. In the first lesson, the students individually read about mealworms. In the second, a container of mealworms is given to small groups of students, and they are allowed to explore the tiny organisms. There are numerous exclamations of "Ooh," "Ahh," "I can't touch this," "It squirmed," "Look at my worm back up!" and other utterances that indicate the students' feelings about the experience.

The second lesson provides an experience that is physically close, is less abstract, and is emotionally connected to the subject. There is little problem in extending this exercise into areas such as designing experiments, reaction to stimuli, and the life cycle of mealworms. Both lessons convey the material; however, the second would probably be more effective in teaching the concepts because it offers physical and psychological involvement and social interactions, all of which contribute to personal meaning for the students.

Many contemporary science curricula are inquiry oriented. For the most part, the inquiry centers on science facts and concepts; physical involvement with materials through laboratory activities provides the primary teaching method for presenting these facts and concepts. The next step in the teaching task is incorporating the affective dimension of inquiry; that is, the discovery of the personal meaning of these facts and concepts for the individual. Obviously, learning science is easier when students are interested and involved. For example, you have been motivated to read this chapter because it has some personal meaning: You are becoming a science teacher and you want to be as effective as possible. What is said in this book, then, has personal meaning for you.

Personal meaning has three aspects: (1) the physical closeness of the materials, (2) the psychological interest that the individual has in the materials, and (3) the social relevancy of the material or topic. To state this idea succinctly: learning science is enhanced when there is personal involvement with materials and organisms that have some direct importance to students. Usually, science teachers have started with content and assumed that personal meaning would emerge. This progression, as it turns out, may or may not occur. It is also possible to begin with interest, motivation, and personal meaning, and structure the content on these experiences while still teaching scientific concepts. Feelings and emotional involvement can be used to the teacher's advantage in developing science concepts and processes.

Personalizing Science Teaching

The effective science teacher realizes the importance of interpersonal relations. One of the important findings in regard to helping others is that objectivity has a negative correlation with effectiveness; that is, if students are treated as objects, the relationship becomes impersonal. No one becomes significant to someone else, whether student, fellow teacher, or friend, if he or she is made to feel insignificant. You become significant to others by treating them with integrity, sincerity, and openness.[5] Some of the best science teachers make a conscious effort to regard all students positively, to understand them as human beings, and to help them grow in every way possible. In these situations, students learn science; in fact, they probably learn more science because of the interpersonal rapport. If you become a significant person to your students, the final reward is yours; you cannot help another person without becoming a better science teacher in the process.

Personalizing your relationship with students can include many things, such as, a greater understanding of the pupils, devising different tasks for different students, individual assessment, varied questioning, or the use of different materials and equipment. Effective communication is the idea that covers, in one way or another, most of the important aspects of personalizing science teaching.

Talking and listening to students is a subtle and important way of recognizing adolescents' growing need for identity. It also enhances the learning relationship and increases the teacher's efficiency in facilitating students' understanding of science.

Realizing the Decisions You Make in Science Teaching

Imagine that you are about to begin a chemistry lesson on pollution. Your plan is to demonstrate how the common air pollutants sulfur dioxide (SO_2) and sulfur trioxide (SO_3) are produced when coal and oil containing sulfur are burned. You plan to then show how sulfur trioxide can react with water vapor (H_2O) to form sulfuric acid. You have some sulfuric acid on the demonstration desk so that you can show the students the corrosive power of this acid. As you begin your demonstration, you accidentally knock over the beaker containing the acid, which spills onto papers and books. Take a moment and think about the situation. What would you do?

Suppose you have just finished an activity investigating the effects of continental glaciers. You begin a video on the subject. As soon as you turn off the lights, Melvin, the class clown, starts his act. You are fairly (but not absolutely) certain it is Melvin making funny noises and muffled comments. Take a moment to think about this situation. What would you do?

You could consult this textbook for answers. You could call your methods teacher for answers. You could ask the science supervisor in your district for answers. You could do any number of things, most of which would help only in the unlikely event that the same situation recurred. The one certainty in these and all other real classroom situations is that you will have to decide what to do and respond in the best way possible. Your role as a science teacher will be to combine your knowledge and perceptions of classroom situations with your understanding of the students and then to decide on appropriate action. Many science teachers do not realize this central role of decision making. You must adapt the textbook, the curriculum, and the inquiry method to the events that occur in actual teaching situations.

Look back to the opening question, "Am I qualified to teach science?" This question still cannot be answered with a direct yes or no. But you have begun thinking about what it means to become a science teacher. How well do you understand science? How do you incorporate the purposes of science education? How are you at organizing instruction in science? What ideas do you have about student learning? Can you personalize science teaching? How can you include personal meaning as a part of science lessons? Do you realize what your role will be in the science classroom? These questions and many more will emerge as you continue the process of becoming a science teacher. It is not our purpose, nor should it be yours, to try to answer these questions now. Let us go on to another important question.

■ WHAT IS SCIENCE TEACHING LIKE?

Most individuals entering the teaching profession are concerned about daily happenings in the school. In one form or another they inquire, "What is science teaching like?" When asked to further clarify the question, they want to know what the science programs are like, what teachers talk about, what it is like actually being in front of a class, and the concerns of other science teachers. If you complete Activity 1–3, "A First Lesson," at the end of this chapter, some of these questions will be answered. In addition, the next sections give glimpses into different schools, science programs, and science teachers. We have adapted these vignettes from case studies funded by the National Science Foundation (NSF) and completed as part of a larger evaluation of science education. The case studies were completed by individuals who spent time at different schools, observing and participating in the various activities of science teachers.[6] Our adaptations have maintained the ideas of the original case studies while updating some of the ideas, language, and issues of contemporary science teaching. Although we realize that schools, science programs, and teachers differ, the case studies present some perspectives of actual science programs, some insights into teacher conversations, and some perception of the reality of science teaching.

Middle School Science Programs

This section characterizes two middle school science programs from the same science district. The district is located in mid-California (Western City is the name used in the case study), a region where much of the population is involved in agriculture. Student backgrounds and interests are diverse due to the large African American and Hispanic American populations. This comparison of middle school science programs points out how differently science can be taught at the same grade level and within the same district.[7]

Case Study 1
    Science instruction at both schools is offered at the discretion of the building principal. If the principal had no interest in science, the science program at either school would fail to exist. As a consequence, the science program at both schools is a minimal program and is only as complete and thorough as the teachers who instruct in the program make it. The following observations (made during site visits) tell the story.

At Middle School I, the "science room" is almost bare. There are some bulletin boards but they, too, have only a few items about earth tacked on them. The storeroom is badly supplied. There are three microscopes that are in semioperable condition, a few unlabeled chemicals, a few pieces of broken glassware (thistle tubes, test tubes), a Fisher burner, and a Bunsen burner. There is no evidence of any packaged kits (such as Introductory Physical Science [IPS] kits) or other pieces of equipment that would indicate that the students would have some experience with hands-on equipment. The desks and only a few tables are available in the room. The principal is making a great effort to upgrade this area.

The "science room" at Middle School II is not in the same condition as the science room at Middle School I. Although the walls are still relatively bare, the closets are filled with Intermediate Science Curriculum Study (ISCS) (Florida State University Science Program) packaged kits. There are ample supplies of glassware, hardware, and chemicals normally used in a middle school science class. The collection of rocks and minerals is minimal, as is the preserved animal collection. Relatively speaking, the science room is much better supplied and organized at Middle School II than the science room at Middle School I.

The science program at Middle School II has been well established by the instructor (one of the participants in the Florida State University Project), who has been at Middle School II for three years. He follows a course of study that he has developed over the years and continues to modify it, utilizing the ISCS materials as time goes on. His counterpart at Middle School I, on the other hand, appears to flounder in the science

■■■■■■■■■■■■■■■■■ **GUEST EDITORIAL** ■■■■■■■■■■■■■■■■■

Who Me?! A Science Teacher?

Laurel Hall
Science Education Student—Geology
Carleton College, Northfield, Minnesota

"Teaching science? Me? You've got to be nuts." This would have been my reaction a few months ago; however, today my response is just the opposite: science teaching is a plausible career for me. Why the change of opinion in such a short time? The answer is simple: After seriously evaluating my interests and goals, with respect to possible careers, I found that teaching would allow me to incorporate and use more of them. The next step was to discover what education is and what methods are used. This step was achieved through a science methods course where I actually observed and participated in various teaching activities of a class at a local school. The career experience in this field has had an important positive effect on my knowledge and opinions of the educational system, besides showing me some of the realities of science teaching.

I have always been interested in helping people learn; my past working experience as a camp counselor, recreational leader, and YMCA swimming instructor and coach is evidence of this interest. However, teaching in the educational system did not appeal to me; I felt that I would become very bored with teaching the same thing to several classes year after year. Yet, with my recent finding that education was a career possibility and that many of my goals and interests could be combined with it, I began to take a new look at education and saw it as a challenge as long as I could eradicate my adolescent biases toward the educational system.

I entered the education program still unsure of what teaching science entailed. I soon found out that my preconceived biases toward the educational system, based on my own public school experiences, were not universally true. The elimination of these biases was the major factor in altering my opinion of the system. Now, instead of looking at the system as hopeless, I see myself as an agent of change: I can set an example and hope others will follow. I can challenge myself to improve, change, and alter lessons, activities, and methods to counteract any boredom in myself and in the students and to communicate with more students.

Through a science methods course, I learned about education, the variety of methods that can be used to attain objectives, and some of the realities of teaching. From these new views, I can see that teaching can be a much tougher occupation than I had previously expected. It involves many time-consuming activities, such as developing new units, changing lesson plans, improving activities, keeping up to date on recent developments in the specific area of science, and keeping enthusiasm at a high level. Yet, it is through these same time-consuming processes that the rewards of teaching are to be found: for example, communicating with those who previously did not understand or care, introducing students to new and interesting ideas and techniques, developing within the students an enthusiasm for continued learning, and watching them develop as individuals.

area. At Middle School I, a considerable amount of time is spent studying earthquakes. ("Since we live in an area that is earthquake-prone, I feel the students should spend some time studying earthquakes.") Besides earthquakes, there is not much evidence of other science topics being discussed, nor is there any evidence of students having an opportunity to get their hands on any equipment.

Because the science program at the middle school level is left up to the individual school and the respective science teachers, there is a wide range of areas and approaches that are used by the science teachers. Some science teachers in Western City have attended NSF institutes and are well versed in a variety of pro-

grams (IPS, BSCS, ISCS) but do not use the materials exclusively. A great number of science teachers in the district are not aware of these planned science curricula and their packaged equipment and, as a consequence, do not use them.

The teachers, when asked about their major concerns about the science program at their respective schools, responded accordingly:

Middle School I
    The students lack discipline. They make little or no effort to learn. They would rather talk and delay the teaching process. They are the ones that will suffer the most.

Middle School II

The biggest problem at the school is absences. The students don't seem to care. They would much rather be somewhere else. Discipline is not as much of a problem here as is the lack of supplies and equipment. I always have to be on the lookout for equipment.

These expressed concerns by two faculty members from different schools are not necessarily the two most pressing concerns in the district. Other teachers in the same schools have voiced concern about such things as:

1. lack of administrative support for their programs,
2. lack of supplies and equipment,
3. the continued use of outdated books,
4. large classes,
5. lack of student motivation,
6. lack of parental interest in their children, and
7. lack of adequate facilities to conduct their programs.

When the science teachers were asked to describe a typical day in their science classes, the following is typical of their comments:

The kids come into class as soon as the bell rings. We check their homework (this is done for purposes of reinforcement). We present a short lecture (at least twenty minutes) on a given topic. We make an assignment for the following day. On Fridays, we schedule quizzes based on the last four days of work.

High School Science Programs

This case study was completed in a small city on the plains east of the Rocky Mountains. The name used for the school was Fall River.[8]

Case Study 2

The high school science program consists of eighteen courses. Despite lenient graduation requirements, enrollments are high. The courses are staffed with an impressive group of teachers, most of whom have advanced degrees in the disciplines and have attended National Science Foundation institutes.

The biology program has the largest enrollment and staff. All students who elect biology take a one-semester introductory course, after which they can choose one or more follow-up courses in ecology, plant structure and function, social biology, microbiology, heredity, and animal anatomy. Some students fail or opt out of biology after the introductory course. An advanced placement course in biology is also offered.

The content of the introductory course is largely the same, regardless of who teaches it. The text used is from the Biology Sciences Curriculum Study (BSCS) (green version). The instructional methods are largely lectures, laboratory investigations, review sheets, and occasionally films and guest speakers. Although the BSCS text emphasizes developing students' interest and heuristic inquiry, the classroom instruction at Fall River High tends to be formal, didactic, and organized. Almost the entire text is covered. This is a large quantity of material for one semester, but it provides the background needed for the more specialized follow-up courses. In the ecology course, for example, the students review the relevant BSCS chapters and then go on to more specialized texts. They participate in simulations designed to show the relationship between values and environmental processes. Topics covered include ecology and the law, mountain ecosystems, and the food chain. Laboratory investigations are conducted on photosynthesis and chromatography, as are field investigations in small ecosystems near the school building. The students conduct independent research on biomes.

Although the other follow-up courses are not so directly related to the environment, a strong environmental consciousness pervades the entire department and has been adopted by many of the students who participate in Earth Club. When asked about the principles that underlie the program, three teachers made the following statements:

The purpose is to make them better citizens, help them understand the issues in society that are related to science, help them make better decisions. Like, I ask them how much longer they're going to be able to drive up and down Main Street. I don't try to impose my own view on them, but I do try to make them think.

You can't separate our values and science anymore. When we talk about population growth or genetics, controversial issues come in. I tell them they should learn the material, if only so they can determine their own futures.

The person just can't be an effective citizen unless he can read and understand political issues that have scientific overtones. . . . The average citizen has to have the awareness and appreciation of how his actions affect the environment and what is likely to happen, depending on the choices he makes now.

In addition to the notion of developing environmental consciousness, the teachers believe their purpose is to provide a strong and diverse academic experience that puts the students in touch with the major body of knowledge in biology and the processes used to arrive at it. One teacher reported, "Any systematized body of knowledge is part of the foundation of civilization. It's part of their responsibilities as citizens to be aware of it. Science has applications in all their lives."

The biology program is not without its rough edges. Students in the introductory course fail in higher proportions than from other courses. Most teachers are determined to hold to their standards, however. Based on previous experience, they are convinced that students will take the easiest possible path, dilute the content of the course, and make the follow-up course structure impossible. The teachers feel that any student who makes the effort can pass.

Another serious problem is lack of space and facilities. There are two well-equipped laboratories, but sometimes four sections must share them in a single class period. Therefore, the teachers have to coordinate classes so that while one section is doing lab work, the other teacher must lecture in a classroom designed for physics. No space is available for advanced laboratory preparations. They look back wistfully on the year they had a teacher's aide.

> *Not having the facilities lowers my interest and energy and influences what I teach. The situation has discouraged every bit of open-ended inquiry I've got. A question comes up from the class and I think of an investigation that would be related, but there we are in the physics room, so I lecture.*

About 40 percent of each graduating class go to college. A greater proportion of students follow a traditional college-preparatory course of study. Most of this group take chemistry in the junior year. The chemistry classes are packed, but it is unclear whether the high enrollment is due to students' scientific curiosity, the genial personality and showmanship of the teacher, or the abundance of A grades. Although there was some complaint from the best students that the class "wasn't tough enough . . . didn't go too deep into chemistry," the instructor primarily wants

> *them to be interested in science and to master the basic material in the field. I feel like anybody can learn at the level I teach them. The kids who are really interested then can go off on their own and learn more.*

The text *Modern Chemistry* is used, and the approach is traditional. The greatest amount of class time is spent in lectures and laboratory experiments. The laboratory areas are well-equipped for a basic program, but the teacher longs for materials that would support more advanced work. The laboratories are terribly overcrowded, and the teacher worries that someone will be injured in an accident.

The physics course is taught by a man with experience and impressive credentials—advanced degrees in physics and math, several NSF training institutes, including training in the use of both Physical Science Curriculum Study (PSCS) and Harvard Project Physics (HPP). His laboratory is well equipped, and under his leadership the science program has always received a healthy share of the school budget. He now uses HPP in his three sections of physics. For several years, PSSC was used, but "NSF backed a real loser with that one." He found that few students were capable of learning the PSSC materials, enrollment dropped, and the physics program was jeopardized. He decided to change over to the HPP course and textbook, which are somewhat less theoretically and mathematically rigorous and more appealing to larger segments of the

school population. A few students and parents complained. One parent stated:

> *I've been very disappointed with the district for watering down the courses. There used to be a really strong physics program (under PSSC), but then [the teacher] decided he needed to accommodate the low to middle achiever so he threw out the good program and came up with this other one that is less comprehensive. It really hurts the well-motivated kids.*

In answering a question about the purpose of science education, the physics teacher spoke of his own philosophy:

> *In recent years, I've wondered if you could justify it. Earlier I would have said that physics was a part of cultural knowledge, something enormously practical, like all science having something philosophically to offer the public, and intellectual integrity which would carry over into politics and society.*
>
> *Now I don't know. We live in a technological society, so it is necessary to propagate information to some parts of the society. But for the general person in high school who will eventually go into business or become a homemaker they really don't need to know about physics, except in a very superficial way. If you want a kid to know how to change a tire, you teach him about levers. . . . I'm a good sailor and I apply my knowledge of physics, but other people are better sailors and have no physics background.*
>
> *That is too pessimistic. Let me state it this way. Everyone deals with nature. Every high school student knows a great deal of physics, and the teacher merely encourages him to abstract his knowledge to form more general and sometimes more useful patterns of thought. If the student can deal with ideas in the abstract, he learns this before going to college and can thereby make a sounder choice of careers. He may not do better than another competent college student, but he has had the benefit of guidance and proven academic discipline. Finally, and this is important for all ability ranges of students, a sense of being at home in the universe must be transmitted. The physical world and the technology of man must be dealt with as an important part of the total culture he is to inherit.*

In addition to the more traditional track of three courses, the science program includes a great variety of offerings: astronomy, archaeology, geology, conceptual physics, electronics (less mathematical than the physics course), introduction to chemistry (a student-centered laboratory program using discovery techniques and emphasizing the process of science), and space science (a rather easy course for students who have a previous failure or little interest in science).

The man responsible for several of these courses is a former geologist who runs his classes very informally, trying to structure each one around the interests and questions of the students. Environmental consciousness appears strongly in his course as well. In the course description for geology, he wrote:

> *Our study of geology will be centered around the following concepts. Geology, the study of the earth, is essentially an environmental science. . . . Man . . . must learn to function in harmony with the earth environment. . . . Citizen roles dictate an understanding of the environmental problems confronting man, solutions to these problems, and the responsibilities of citizens and government to work toward their solutions.*

These objectives are not mere educational cant. During his classes this philosophy is never far off, injected even into a presentation on the physical properties of minerals.

In his courses, perhaps more than those of others, scientific methods are given prominent attention. One of his science courses centers on the following objectives:

> *Demonstrates an understanding of the process of identifying and defining a scientific problem or question to be investigated . . . of proposing a logical test of a hypothesis . . . of testing the effects of variables and controlling relevant variables . . . the ability to synthesize data from several sources to arrive at generalizations or conclusions . . . withhold judgments or conclusions until adequate information has been validated.*

The following is a second view of high school science. This program is from a large high school in a major city in the Pacific Northwest. The name used to identify the school is Hardy.[9]

The natural science program at Hardy is strong. It is paced by an active biology program team-taught by three full-time and one part-time teacher. Currently 472 students (93 percent of sophomore enrollment)[10] are enrolled in a laboratory course led by the department chairman. The classrooms are filled with science artifacts (birds, weather maps, rocks, specimens, snakes, etc.), and the spirit of the group can be portrayed by two episodes: an open session with students one day after school to discuss the implications for science of the presidential election and a weekend assault on the walls separating the three biology rooms, resulting in open portals that central administration had stalled on for nearly two years.

Probably 80 percent of the class time is spent by students working on experiments, and three tracks (developed locally) are provided, depending on student ability. The course is patterned after college science courses and seems difficult for many of the students. However, teacher enthusiasm and interest seem to rub off on students, and they rate the course as very good. Marine biology, human physiology, mushrooms, and wildflowers are other courses offered as part of this strong program. Exactly which courses will be offered during a given semester depends a great deal

on student interest. A college-style registration procedure is used, and if a given course doesn't fill (i.e., isn't selected by more than 25 students), then it may not be offered. Conversely, sections are added if student interest is high.

During the semester following the site visit, the life science enrollment was as follows:

Biology II	250
Molecular Biology	29
Marine Biology	53
Wild Flowers/Edibles	34
Human Physiology	53

Apparently, some of those students in the first semester of biology opt for more specialized courses the second semester.

The first year of chemistry is currently taken by 146 students (27 percent of junior enrollment) and is taught as a laboratory science. The five sections of chemistry are handled by the physics teacher and a chemistry teacher who also teaches biology. The CHEM Study texts are used, and the course is viewed by students and teachers as primarily a college-preparatory course. A third semester of general chemistry and a semester of organic chemistry are offered if enough students register for these courses.

Physics may be taken in either the junior or senior year, and currently 68 students (13 percent of senior enrollment) are enrolled. About half of the group are girls, which is seen by students and teachers as a result of changing female roles. Counselors, parents, and friends are relaxing their attitude that advanced science is only for males. The course has some laboratory components, but in general is taught more like a mathematics class—that is, explain concepts, assign problems, correct problems, discuss difficulties. This routine is interrupted occasionally by exams or experiments, but the doing of problems is predominant over the doing of science found in the other classes. The class is clearly for the academically elite, and the teacher sees no need to try to increase enrollments. At one time the PSSC and the Engineering Concepts Curriculum Project (ECCP) courses were used, but this year the Holt-Rinehart-Winston book *Modern Physics* is being tried and will probably become the district-wide text for next year.

The rest of the science program includes a semester of geology and a science seminar. The geology situation portrays quite well some of the current problems in the school. Because of staff cutbacks, the assistant principal [had been] teaching one section of geology [in the] fall. After two weeks of school, a displaced junior high teacher was assigned by the district office to teach mathematics and science. He took over the geology class along with several mathematics classes, and the assistant principal returned to full-time administration. The new teacher . . . [encountered] some difficulties in the class because students were irritated by the changes. In fact, in one class, there were four teachers during the first month of school.

An adjunct to the science program is a popular horticulture program offered in the industrial arts department. In a temporary building and greenhouse located about two blocks from the main building, 113 students were enrolled in environmental horticulture. The course meets the state requirements for a laboratory science, but although it is considered a strong program by the science teachers, there seems to be very little interaction between it and the rest of the science program. It has grown through the efforts of an active teacher whose academic home is industrial arts.

The science program is strong and surviving, but it is being subjected to many challenges: transfer of teachers, declining budgets for texts and equipment, and competition from the basics. It may be seriously affected if subjected to many more problems.

Conversations with Science Teachers

In this section, comments from the teachers' lounge are used to point out some issues in science education. The observations are from a case study made in a greater Boston high school.[11]

The Role of the Experiment in Science Teaching
STEVE: (Looking through a workbook of experiments David has been using in his class) The trouble with a lot of this stuff is that it is so obvious. Even when you have done the experiment, you only know what you knew already.
DAVID: Maybe it's obvious to you, but it isn't always obvious to these kids. To some of them maybe, but not to all of them. Sometimes they do know what is going to happen in the experiment, but they only know it vaguely; they haven't really thought it out.

Like this morning we were talking about that experiment where you float a cork in water, then push an upturned glass down on top of it. They did the experiment and saw what happened. When I asked why the cork went down, one girl just said "gravity." Well, you can see what she means; it does involve gravity, but that's not an explanation of what you see happening.
STEVE: Yes, but you can't say that's exciting. Floating corks in water. I want to get these kids interested in science. I want experiments you can do that set them all off saying, "Wow! How did that happen?" Something that really challenges and excites them. (Looking at the book) Finding out 20 percent of the air is oxygen, that's no challenge. Why not just tell them. You shouldn't just have to do an experiment for everybody, only if it excites them or triggers them off.
DAVID: But before you can work on these dramatic experiments they have got to know scientific procedures and appreciate the methods. All this week I've been emphasizing the five stages of writing a lab report and getting them to appreciate the difference between observation and explanation. You have to do it several times, and it takes practice. And for most of them,

writing a scientific report is not something they are used to doing; in fact, some of them have got so used to multiple-choice tests that it is an effort for them to write complete sentences.
STEVE: Maybe you are right. I think teaching them rigor and method is a useful thing to do. The danger, though, is that you end up just pacifying them. The science that is going to affect their lives isn't the five stages of writing a lab report. It is nuclear power, pollution, recombinant DNA research. Those are the things I want them to know about, and I want them to be able to pursue things for themselves, not just because they are in a course or a textbook.

Methods of Teaching

Teaching methods is an issue that emerged in several conversations among members of the cluster teams. The conversation reported here has been assembled from various fragments and so lacks the authenticity of others reported in this section. We hope it is no less true. We have done our best to illustrate accurately what we think is an important emerging issue.

CIVICS TEACHER: I feel constrained by the forty-minute period and the pressures of working in a building that is really only a heap of classrooms. I'd like to be able to get out more with the students and get to do more things.
SCIENCE TEACHER: I don't agree. I think almost the most important thing for the students to learn is the discipline of working in the classroom. When they come here at the beginning of the year, they are all up in the air and we have got to bring them down. You've got to get order and discipline before you can give it up.
CIVICS TEACHER: By this time of year [March], they should have learned some sort of classroom discipline. The problem is that enforcing it starts to become an end in itself. You begin to forget about what you are trying to teach and just think about keeping a neat, orderly class.
SCIENCE TEACHER: I don't just think of discipline as keeping an island of sanity in my class, whatever happens in the rest of the school. I don't think you can separate discipline in class from the discipline of the subject. In science especially, where you have expensive equipment and valuable things around, you have to learn certain ways of behaving, and learning those ways of behaving are [sic] part of learning the subject.
SECOND SCIENCE TEACHER: I'd like to get out of the classroom more because there are a lot of things I want to do that you can't very easily do in school. I think really the only way to get students to appreciate the significance of things like environmental pollution is to get them out of the classroom [and] looking at it.
ENGLISH TEACHER: My classroom is important to me. I can't imagine a better place for doing the kind of teaching I want to do. Going outside the classroom on

some occasions might have advantages. I'd like to have students going out to interview people, for example. But what they do in the classroom (which is mainly writing) has got to remain at the center of everything else for me.

CIVICS TEACHER: Sometimes I feel limited by the expectations the students have of me as their teacher. For most of them, the range of things they will allow in a teacher is very limited, and this makes it very hard to start anything new or different. The experience I have had in the past of working a lot outside school has shown me that you can have quite a different kind of relationship with students once you get them out of the school building.

ENGLISH TEACHER: I don't want a different kind of relationship. I want to be the kind of teacher I am.

Motivating Students

Most teachers agree that the key problem is motivation. "In every class, there are one or two [students], perhaps sometimes it's more, who just sit there, and whatever you do, however hard you try, it's just really difficult to reach them."

One of the guidance counselors sees the problem as being a general one:

Motivation really is the big problem here. I don't understand why it is, but looking at it rationally, students in the Northeast of the United States consistently score higher on tests of academic motivation than students in the South. Yet, I am sure our students are just as able.

How would you design a program that would motivate students to study science? What would you do, as a teacher, if you were going to have a particularly difficult group next year? These are some of the questions that you might think about since you may have to answer them yourself in the future.

We return to the Fall River Case Study. The following summary is, perhaps, the most succinct answer to our question, "What is science teaching like?" We use this as a conclusion because it could have been written for any of the case study reports and probably for any school district.

A Conclusion About Science Teaching

Three statements conclude four months of watching the teachers of Fall River: probing their motives; listening to students, parents, and administrators; reading the records and studying the evidence.

Virtually nothing meaningful can be said about the Fall River science program in general. The district has developed a science curriculum packed with articulated objectives and brimming with specified content; yet there remain differences in content, method, and sense of purpose from one grade level to the next, among schools, among departments within schools, even from teacher to

teacher. This diversity and complexity suggest why national efforts to reform the curriculum become transformed, attenuated, or lost entirely before they reach the classroom. The schools have lives of their own, existing as organisms exist, to "be on with it," perpetuating themselves and protecting against assault from without.

People in schools are conscientiously doing the jobs they have defined: tutor, scholar, but also at times, counselor, steward, custodian, and social director.

Teachers must juggle the expectations of the invisible, distant, and mostly impersonal profession of science education and the local, powerful, and relentless demands of teaching. The two roles do not necessarily conflict, but the latter usually overpowers and preempts the former.[12]

Complete Activity 1–4 "An Interview with a Science Teacher."

■ HOW CAN I BECOME AN EFFECTIVE SCIENCE TEACHER?

We assume that you have the normal concerns of beginning teachers. Alongside these fears, we also assume that you are motivated to become an effective science teacher. Three things that will help reduce these fears and increase effectiveness are time, experience, and preparation. Remember that this is only the beginning of your career as a science teacher and you cannot accomplish everything you wish, learn everything you need, or do everything you would like during the science methods course or even during the first year of teaching. Becoming an effective science teacher and comfortable in your role takes time.

The corollary to time is experience. There is no substitute for the actual experience of teaching science. It is the one sure way that will help you detect strengths and weaknesses in yourself as a teacher. You will learn more about yourself and science teaching in the first year than you can now imagine. It will not be easy, but it will be interesting and challenging. Every day will involve you in experiences that contribute to your effectiveness.

There is something specific and immediate that can be done to help you reduce your concerns and develop your effectiveness. *Be prepared.* This message is crucial. Some teachers equate preparation with knowledge of their scientific discipline. Although this is important, there is much more implied by the words "Be prepared." We have mentioned some ideas, such as plans and procedures in the classroom, adequate relationships with students, enthusiasm for teaching science, and strategies and models of science teaching. Since these are the topics of this book, there is little need to develop them now. One thing we can do is turn to you and ask about your concerns, apprehensions, and needs concerning science teaching. We do this in the form of Activity 1–5 "My Concerns" at the end of this chapter.

■ BECOMING A SCIENCE TEACHER: SOME CLOSING REFLECTIONS

One of the premises of this chapter (and of this book) is that you do not have to be a bad science teacher to become a better science teacher. Students entering science teaching and those already in the profession are concerned about improving the quality of instruction in science. There is ample evidence for this statement. Your own concerns and activities in studying this book and taking the methods course have already demonstrated your willingness to learn more about science teaching. Once you obtain a teaching position, there will be workshops, curriculum revision, and continuing education courses. Participation in all of these programs indicates a desire to become a better science teacher.

A second premise is that you are the one person who best knows what is necessary for you to become an effective teacher. This is the reason for the self-evaluation exercises. There will also be feedback from your college supervisor, methods professor, and perhaps classroom teachers. This feedback will help, especially when you combine it with your own insights and act on the information. That is, you have many personal choices in the process of becoming a science teacher.

Ultimately, the responsibility for becoming an effective science instructor is yours. There are many individuals and an abundance of programs to aid you. Finally, however, you are the person who must combine all of the elements to facilitate science education for your students.

We can suggest several goals that are related to the process of becoming a science teacher. Becoming a science teacher means continually

1. Demonstrating an adequate understanding of scientific knowledge. This goal includes an in-depth understanding of specific disciplines, as well as a broad understanding of science in general. It also includes a comprehension of the role of science in our society and in the world.
2. Demonstrating an adequate understanding of scientific inquiry. Specifically, this understanding includes the attitudes and skills of inquiry and the application of scientific philosophies to classroom instruction.
3. Demonstrating an adequate awareness of educational foundations and the place of science education as a discipline in the larger framework of education.
4. Demonstrating an adequate understanding of teaching methods. This goal includes the ability to plan and organize activities for the classroom, to carry out standard classroom procedures, to use a variety of techniques and equipment in teaching science lessons, and to evaluate student progress.
5. Demonstrating adequate interpersonal relations and an enthusiasm for working with secondary-level students.
6. Demonstrating the synthesis of these five goals into the actual practice of teaching science in the secondary school.

■ SUMMARY

The experience of becoming a science teacher is identifiable through the questions one asks. Here we have asked, "Am I qualified to teach science?" Although it is impossible to answer, several activities were presented, each allowing you to investigate this question. We also described some of the attributes essential for science teaching: understanding science, understanding students, organizing materials for science instruction, personalizing your interaction with students, recognizing personal meaning as a part of learning, and very importantly, realizing your own role as decision maker in the science classroom.

After discussing the first question, we turned to a second: "What is science teaching like?" To answer this we used a series of vignettes drawn from case studies of schools from all over the country. They represented a variety of schools and science programs.

Next, we turned to the question of becoming an effective science teacher. The question seems to be a part of the natural sequence of questions asked by students as they enter teaching. Once the initial anxiety of becoming a science teacher has been overcome, individuals turn to the problem of becoming a better teacher. Time, experience, and preparation contribute to the increasing effectiveness of the beginning teacher. One way of helping to overcome apprehension is to identify concerns and act on reducing them. In this case, the investigation of science teaching is a self-examination and a personal response to the question, "What are my concerns?"

The chapter ends with some goals related to the process of becoming a science teacher. The goals are summarized as demonstrating an understanding of scientific knowledge and inquiry, of science education as a discipline, and of teaching methods; adequate interpersonal relationships with students; and a synthesis of these goals into actual teaching of science in the secondary school.

■ REFERENCES

1. National Research Council, *National Science Education Standards* (Washington, DC: Author, 1995).

2. American Association for the Advancement of Science, *Benchmarks for Science Literacy* (Washington, DC: Author, 1993).

3. Joseph D. Novak, "Learning Science and the Science of Learning," *Studies in Science Education, 15* (1988): 77–101.

4. David Ausubel, *The Psychology of Meaningful Verbal Learning* (New York: Grune & Stratton, 1963).

5. Arthur W. Combs, Donald L. Avila, and William W. Purkey, *Helping Relationships: Basic/Concepts for the Helping Professions* (Boston: Allyn and Bacon, 1978).

6. The project, titled "Case Studies in Science Education," was directed by Robert Stake and Jack Easley at the Center for Instructional Research and Curriculum Evaluation at the University of Illinois at Urbana-Champaign, in 1977.

7. Rodolfo G. Serrano, *The Status of Science, Mathematics, and Social Science in Western City, U. S. A., Case Studies in Science Education, Booklet 7* (Urbana-Champaign: University of Illinois, June 1977), pp. 10–13.

8. Mary Lee Smith, *Teaching and Science Education in Fall River, Case Studies in Science Education, Booklet 2* (Urbana-Champaign: University of Illinois, May 1977), pp. 5–9.

9. Wayne Welch, *Science Education in Urbanville: A Case Study, Case Studies in Science Education, Booklet 5* (Urbana-Champaign: University of Illinois, April 1977), pp. 4–5.

10. This figure is obtained by dividing the total biology enrollment by the number of sophomores. Some juniors and seniors, however, take biology, and some sophomores take other sciences.

11. Rob Walker, *Case Studies in Science Education: Boston, Booklet 11* (Urbana-Champaign: University of Illinois, April 1977), pp. 6, 7, 15, 25.

12. Smith, *Fall River,* p. 23.

INVESTIGATING SCIENCE TEACHING

Activity 1–1

HOW I SEE MYSELF AS A SCIENCE TEACHER

The statements in this exercise allow you to examine your perceptions about yourself as a science teacher. The exercise is designed for your personal knowledge and need not be shared with others. Read the statement and decide if you strongly agree, moderately agree, agree, are neutral, slightly disagree, moderately disagree, or strongly disagree. Then place the appropriate number in the space to the left of the statement.

Strongly agree	Moderately agree	Slightly agree	Neutral	Slightly disagree	Moderately disagree	Strongly disagree
7	6	5	4	3	2	1

_____   1. I am well informed about science and technology.
_____   2. Students can generally take care of themselves.
_____   3. I identify with people.
_____   4. My task as a science teacher is one of assisting students to learn.
_____   5. The meaning of science and technology for our society is more important than the facts and events of science and technology.
_____   6. Science and technology are meaningful in my personal life.
_____   7. For the most part, other people are friendly.
_____   8. Basically, I am an adequate science teacher.
_____   9. I see my purpose as concerned with larger issues of science, technology, and society.
_____ 10. I try to understand how my students perceive things.
_____ 11. I have a commitment to the field of science and technology.
_____ 12. Students have their own worth and integrity.
_____ 13. I am a dependable and reliable science teacher.
_____ 14. I usually do not conceal my personal feelings and shortcomings from students.
_____ 15. Teaching science is best done by encouraging personal development of students.
_____ 16. Science and technology are essential in our society.
_____ 17. People are basically trustworthy and dependable.
_____ 18. Students generally see me as personable and likable.
_____ 19. I am personally involved with my students.
_____ 20. I am accepting of individual differences in my students.
_____ 21. My understanding of science and technology is adequate.
_____ 22. Students are important sources of personal and professional satisfaction for me.
_____ 23. As a science teacher, I am worthy of respect.
_____ 24. The process of learning science is important for our culture.
_____ 25. My orientation is toward people more than things.

The items in this list are keyed to five important dimensions of science teaching as a helping profession. If you would like to see how you perceive yourself on these dimensions, complete the following section. Add your response for the items in the left column. Divide that number by five. The result should be a number between seven and one for each of the dimensions of science teaching listed. The numbers give some indication of your perceptions of yourself as related to the different categories.

Items		*Average*	*Dimensions of Science Teaching*
1, 6, 11, 16, 21	=	_____	Perceptions about science subject matter
2, 7, 12, 17, 22	=	_____	Perceptions of students
3, 8, 13, 18, 23	=	_____	Perceptions of yourself as a science teacher
4, 9, 14, 19, 24	=	_____	Perceptions of your purpose as a science teacher
5, 10, 15, 20, 25	=	_____	Perceptions of the teaching task

Activity 1–2

THE WHAT AND HOW OF SCIENCE LESSONS

In this activity you are presented with a teaching situation on the left and asked to match a method from the right to achieve your teaching goal. In each case you should be able to give a rationale for your choice of method. Complete the activity alone. Then share your responses with several other students in the class.

What you want to accomplish—the goal	How you would accomplish your goal—the method		Methods of teaching
1. Introduce the concept of acids and bases.	_____	A.	Bulletin board
		B.	Demonstration
2. Clarify the effects of air pollution.	_____	C.	Discussion
		D.	Field Trip
3. Summarize the effects of erosion.	_____	E.	Film
		F.	Film loop (single concept)
4. Show the interrelationships of organisms in a community.	_____	G.	Filmstrip
		H.	Guest speaker
5. Evaluate the students' understanding of pulleys.	_____	I.	Laboratory investigation
		J.	Library research
		K.	Lecture
6. Differentiate the phylum Echinodermata from the phylum Chordata.	_____	L.	Projects
		M.	Questioning
		N.	Quiz
7. Realize the ethical decisions involved in scientific research.	_____	O.	Reading records
		P.	Role playing
		Q.	Slides (35 mm) presentation
8. Introduce the structure of DNA.	_____	R.	Simulation game
		S.	Television
9. Show the dynamic qualities of weather.	_____	T.	Test
		U.	Chalkboard
10. Expand the students' understanding of the systems concept.	_____	V.	Computer
		W.	Calculator (hand-held)
		X.	Records
11. Review the concept of force.	_____		
12. Teach students to handle the microscope correctly.	_____		
13. Outline safety procedures for the chemistry laboratory.	_____		
14. Introduce students to careers in science.	_____		
15. Help students understand the role of science and technology in society.	_____		

Activity 1–3

A FIRST LESSON

It is strongly recommended that you teach a short science lesson early in the methods course. Preferably, this lesson should be taught in a local science class; however, it may be taught to your peers in the methods class. An important objective of this lesson is to help you answer two questions: "Can I teach science?" and "What is science teaching like?" There is no better way to answer these questions than to actually teach a science lesson.
Here are some guidelines to help you prepare your first lesson.

1. Keep the lesson simple,. Try to present a single concept, single process, or single skill.
2. What do you hope to accomplish by the end of the lesson? What should the students know or be able to do that they could not do before the lesson?
3. What experiences will best achieve the goals and be interesting and motivating for the students?
4. What is the most effective way to organize the materials or experiences of the lesson? What is its conceptual structure and instructional sequence?
5. Use the following format as the basis of your lesson plan.

Title of Lesson	
Goal of lesson (See item 2 above)	
Procedures (outline the progress and methods of the lesson)	
What do you want to teach?	*How* do you plan to teach it?
1.	1.
2.	2.
3.	3.
4.	4.
5.	5.
6.	6.
What is your plan for starting the lesson?	
What is your plan for ending the lesson?	
Materials needed for lesson:	
Length of lesson in minutes:	

SELF-CRITIQUE OF YOUR FIRST LESSON

1. Rate the following:

	Poor	Fair	Good	Excel-lent	Comments
Voice quality and articulation	___	___	___	___	_____
Poise	___	___	___	___	_____
Adaptability and flexibility	___	___	___	___	_____
Use of English	___	___	___	___	_____
Procedure	___	___	___	___	_____
Enthusiasm	___	___	___	___	_____
Continuity	___	___	___	___	_____
Maintenance of good class control	___	___	___	___	_____
Provision for individual differences	___	___	___	___	_____
Ability to interest students	___	___	___	___	_____
Ability to involve students	___	___	___	___	_____
Ability to ask questions	___	___	___	___	_____
Ability to answer questions	___	___	___	___	_____
Use of instructional methods	___	___	___	___	_____
Provision of adequate summaries	___	___	___	___	_____
Budgeting of time	___	___	___	___	_____
Organization of the lesson	___	___	___	___	_____
Knowledge of subject	___	___	___	___	_____

2. Did you achieve your goals?

3. What were the strengths of the presentation?

4. What were the weaknesses of the presentation?

5. What would you change if you were to teach this lesson again?

6. Give your personal answer to the question, "Can I teach science?"

7. Overall, how well do you think you did on the lesson?

8. Based on this experience, answer the question, "What is science teaching like?"

Activity 1–4

AN INTERVIEW WITH A SCIENCE TEACHER

One way to find out what science teaching is like is to interview a science teacher. Tell the teacher the reason for the meeting and the general topics of discussion. If at all possible, make arrangements to observe a class period before the interview. This visit will give you some insights concerning the teacher's style and approach to science instruction. It will also provide some bases of discussion. You may wish to ask the following questions to get the conversation started.

1. What is the science program in your school?
   How many courses are offered?
   What is the enrollment in life science? Earth science? Physical science?
   What textbook is used?
   How does the science program in your school relate to the rest of the science program in the district?
   Do you offer any special science courses?
   Has the science program changed in the last five years?

2. What do you see as the important trends and issues in science teaching?
   Have enrollments in science increased? Decreased?
   Has the science budget increased? Decreased?
   How much do you use the laboratory in science teaching?
   Do you introduce any science-related social issues?

3. What are your concerns as a science teacher?
   Are your facilities adequate?
   Do you have materials for your program?
   Is student interest high? Low?
   Is maintaining discipline a problem?

4. What are your greatest rewards as a science teacher?
   Seeing students learn?
   Helping other people?
   Working with interesting and exciting colleagues?
   Contributing to the public's scientific literacy?

5. Why is science important?

Activity 1–5

MY CONCERNS

Listed below are several statements that are commonly expressed by students entering teaching. Indicate your present concern about the problem by placing an X in a space provided on the continuum: Number 1 indicates little concern, whereas number 9 indicates a high degree of concern.

1. Developing short- and long-term purposes, goals, and objectives for science instruction
   1 2 3 4 5 6 7 8 9
2. Understanding the scientific enterprise, the processes of science, and different philosophies of science
   1 2 3 4 5 6 7 8 9
3. Motivating students to learn science
   1 2 3 4 5 6 7 8 9
4. Designing programs to increase the learning of science
   1 2 3 4 5 6 7 8 9
5. Recognizing and responding to different developmental levels of students
   1 2 3 4 5 6 7 8 9
6. Understanding the dynamics of student groups
   1 2 3 4 5 6 7 8 9
7. Adapting to the needs, interests, and abilities of pupils, including special and gifted students
   1 2 3 4 5 6 7 8 9
8. Designing programs for the individual needs of students
   1 2 3 4 5 6 7 8 9
9. Knowing about science-curriculum programs and instructional materials
   1 2 3 4 5 6 7 8 9

10. Incorporating other disciplines, such as mathematics or social science, into the science program

    1 2 3 4 5 6 7 8 9

11. Understanding and using different instructional strategies

    1 2 3 4 5 6 7 8 9

12. Planning and organizing science activities

    1 2 3 4 5 6 7 8 9

13. Evaluating student progress

    1 2 3 4 5 6 7 8 9

14. Handling problems of classroom management, pupil control, and student misbehavior

    1 2 3 4 5 6 7 8 9

15. Preparing for practice teaching

    1 2 3 4 5 6 7 8 9

16. Budgeting time and judging the flow of science lessons

    1 2 3 4 5 6 7 8 9

17. Handling routines such as making out reports, attendance, and keeping records

    1 2 3 4 5 6 7 8 9

18. Lack of an adequate background in science

    1 2 3 4 5 6 7 8 9

19. Lack of self-confidence to teach science

    1 2 3 4 5 6 7 8 9

20. Presenting science demonstrations, questioning, and guiding student discussions

    1 2 3 4 5 6 7 8 9

21. Adapting to the unique problems of school facilities, materials, and equipment

    1 2 3 4 5 6 7 8 9

22. Understanding and using special school services such as counseling and testing

    1 2 3 4 5 6 7 8 9

23. Knowing how to obtain a science teaching job

    1 2 3 4 5 6 7 8 9

24. Understanding the place and importance of science education

    1 2 3 4 5 6 7 8 9

25. Other concerns

    1 2 3 4 5 6 7 8 9

These statements constitute a personal inventory of concerns. Many of them are addressed in this book and will be included as part of the methods course. Identifying and clarifying your concerns will better enable you to direct your work, study, and activities during this preparation for science teaching.

Chapter 2

BEGINNING YOUR INSTRUCTIONAL THEORY

In this chapter we introduce some practical aspects of science teaching. The last chapter focused on questions, such as, "Am I qualified to teach science?" and "What is science teaching like?" The questions for this chapter might well be "What do I have to know in order to teach science?" and "What do I have to be able to do to teach science?" and "How do I put it all together for effective science teaching?" In order to begin answering these questions, we use the idea of an *instructional theory* to introduce some ideas about science teaching and begin answering your questions. Further, you will not just read about science teaching in the abstract, for we try to facilitate your synthesizing an approach to science teaching.

Teaching science requires continual decision making. How do I respond to students' misconceptions in science? The light burned out on the overhead projector—what should I do? Where should I use this new piece of software? Is this laboratory safe? Indeed, you will have to consider many variables from moment to moment and day to day. One characteristic of effective science teachers is their ability to act efficiently and respond constructively to numerous classroom situations. Before continuing in this chapter, you should complete Activity 2–1 "What Would You Do?" By considering different answers and reflecting on what you would do and why, you begin the process of constructing your instructional theory.

WHY DEVELOP AN INSTRUCTIONAL THEORY?

Scientists use theories to guide their research and to help them develop new insights into the intricacies of nature. A theory is an effective intellectual tool that integrates many of the mind's processes. Through knowing relatively little—a theory—the individual actually knows a great deal. A theory has three fundamental attributes. It (1) organizes observations and data, (2) provides explanations for phenomena, and (3) helps predict events and therefore provides direction. Through theoretical understanding we can interpret and synthesize volumes of information.

As a science teacher your effectiveness can be enhanced by your ability to organize observations of students, explain behaviors, and predict what will happen as a result of your activities and actions in the classroom. Although an instructional theory may not have the power and utility of a scientific theory, it will certainly help you bring consistency to the variety of decisions you make in the process of teaching.

WHAT ARE THE FOUNDATIONS OF AN INSTRUCTIONAL THEORY?

There are several bases for an instructional theory in science education. One essential foundation is your sense of the purposes for science education. Principles of learning, motivation, development, and social psychology should be included, as well as attitudes and values of the scientific enterprise, curriculum materials, and instructional techniques. All of these elements must be combined in a way unique to the individual science teacher.

CHARACTERISTICS OF AN INSTRUCTIONAL THEORY

Some years ago, Jerome Bruner outlined the characteristics of an instructional theory in a book entitled *Toward a Theory of Instruction.*[1] According to Bruner, a theory of instruction is *prescriptive*. It gives direction and provides guidelines for effective instruction and enables the teacher to evaluate teaching techniques and procedures. A theory of instruction is also *normative;* it is general rather than specific. For example, a theory of instruction would give some criteria for a chemistry lesson on acids and bases but would not give specific guidelines for the lesson.

What help does a theory of instruction provide? What questions will it answer? An instructional theory has four important characteristics. It should help the science teacher specify:

1. *The experiences that will most effectively motivate the learner.* An instructional theory helps you answer the question: What activities will encourage learning?
2. *The most effective way in which knowledge can be structured to enhance learning.* An instructional theory helps you answer the question: What is the best way to structure the knowledge and skills of my lesson?
3. *The best sequence in which to present material.* An instructional theory helps you answer the

■■■■■■■■■■■■■■■■■■ **GUEST EDITORIAL** ■■■■■■■■■■■■■■■■■■

Anticipating Student Teaching

Mary McMillan
Science Education Student–Geology
Carleton College, Northfield, Minnesota

As I anticipate my student teaching placement in the fall, I am beginning to formulate my definition of a successful teacher. The ideal teacher is organized, energetic, and confident. He or she uses subject matter as a 2means of helping students to develop an appreciation of themselves, others, and society. During my student teaching placement, I hope to develop the skills of an "ideal" teacher. As I work toward my goal, student teaching will have a dual purpose for me. I want to help my students appreciate their own abilities, and I hope to learn more about myself as a science teacher.

To recognize students' abilities, I will need to become acquainted with them and their interests. As I search for topics that interest them, I will hope for interesting moments and sparks of thoughtful questions. It will be necessary to appreciate diversity. Some students will have trouble with analytical skills, but they may demonstrate the ability to lead others, to communicate, or to be creative. To provide each student with the opportunity for success and enthusiasm, I will have to include a broad range of activities.

As I envision activities for students, I recognize one of the causes of my own enthusiasm. I believe that science classes provide a means of understanding the earth and its resources. Such understanding is essential if we hope to protect and improve the environment. The science courses I most enjoyed were those that increased my awareness of the environment and my perceptions of change. As a teacher, the opportunity to select materials and topics will be very important to me. I hope to teach about general principles by providing a background of specific examples. I plan to infuse a good deal of environmental education in my classes, and I hope that my enthusiasm for science will be shared.

As I try to share my interests and concerns with others, I also will be learning about myself. A cooperating teacher will probably provide both criticism and praise. Students' actions and reactions in the classroom will challenge my assumptions as well as my creativity. There will be times when I cannot select the exact subject matter I would like to teach. Unless I demonstrate my willingness to take risks and correct mistakes, however, I will not learn the ways in which I need to change. To succeed as a student teacher, I will need to be persistent, open, and energetic. I want to help others value their own abilities and, by doing so, I hope to become better acquainted with myself.

---

question: How do you present the lesson so all students will further develop their understandings of science?

4. *The feedback and evaluation process.* An instructional theory helps you answer the questions: How and when should feedback be given? When should instruction be assessed? What is the most appropriate form to obtain and return feedback? How should instruction be modified?

One of the most important conditions for learning is *active participation by students.* Science teachers often ask, "How can I motivate students?" You will slowly accumulate ideas and activities that encourage within your students a predisposition toward learning. Engaging the learner is difficult for even the most experienced science teacher. Recall your own

response to the problems in Activity 2–1 "What Would You Do?" Ideally, the problems engaged your interest. One response you could have made was the exploration of alternative solutions to the problem. Another was a curiosity concerning details of the situation. Both of these responses originated in the uncertainty and the ambiguity of the problems. There is an optimal level of uncertainty and ambiguity: too little and the problem is easily resolved; too much and there is confusion, anxiety, and lack of resolution. Part of your task as a science teacher is to help learners stay within the optimal range of their curiosity.

Once you have engaged the learners, they must continue to work on the problem. To stimulate continued interest the rewards of the exploration must be greater than the risks. Was this true with your work on the problems in "What Would You Do?" Giving or receiving instruction should increase the rewards and decrease risks: If such is not the case, your instruction is not as effective as it should be.

Finally, you need a direction or goal. From the alternatives provided you were asked to resolve the classroom problems in the best way that you could. The question—"What would you do?"—helped define the direction and goal.

A second condition for effective instruction is the *optimal structure of the knowledge.* In most cases this condition is provided by the science curriculum. The body of knowledge should be presented in a form simple enough to be understood by the learner. The fact that the material is in a textbook means that the science teacher will have to adapt the structure of knowledge to accommodate the needs and interests of students.

A third condition for learning is the *optimal sequence of knowledge.* As science instruction progresses, ideas, processes, and skills are presented and related. The sequence should increase the probability that at each step the learner understands, transforms, and applies these ideas, processes, and skills. Here again you may encounter the problem of steps that are too small, resulting in boredom, or steps that are too large, resulting in frustration. In part, the purpose of your instructional theory is to help you bridge the gap between the structural and sequential logic of the curriculum and the social and psychological needs of the students.

A fourth condition essential to the earlier three is your ability to receive, respond, and give *feedback in the teaching environment.* Motivating, structuring, and sequencing of instruction are contingent on your ability to receive and respond to cues from the students. Student feedback should in turn influence your instruction and your response to student achievement.

■ PURPOSE, GOALS, AND OBJECTIVES

Like any journey, in science teaching you have to know where you are going. What is it that you perceive as the destination for your students? What do you see as the stops along the way to this final destination? In the first chapter we suggested that the term *scientific literacy* expresses the destination for all students. Translating scientific literacy into concrete goals of knowledge, skills, and values of curriculum and instruction is an important process for science teachers because the translation has to be fairly consistent with the overall purpose. Finally, the specific objectives of lessons have to be consistent with the purpose of developing scientific literacy. Separate chapters are devoted to these topics. Before

continuing, complete Activity 2–3, "My Aims and Preferences." You should review your responses on this investigation after completing the chapter.

The national standards for science education also provide purpose, goals, and objectives for science teaching. They give a valuable description of your destination, and they outline the territory for your travels. But they do not have specific, detailed maps for the trip. You will have to create your own maps for your curriculum and instruction, helped by your instructional theory. Other chapters provide more information and details about the national standards.

■ LEARNING AND INSTRUCTION

Research on student learning has long been an important factor in any teacher's instructional theory. In the 1960s and 1970s, science teachers looked to Jean Piaget's theory of cognitive development.[2] The research focused on two major features of Piagetian theory. First, Piaget proposed that learning occurs through an individual's interaction with the environment. This interaction is described by a student assimilating new information and ideas from various educational experiences and the accommodation of the new information with previously held information, thus establishing a consistency between the individual's cognitive structure and everyday experience. Second, each individual passes through different stages of development, each characterized by the ability to perform various cognitive tasks.

The most relevant stages for science education are concrete reasoning and formal reasoning. Simply put, a formal reasoner can manipulate abstract ideas and concepts, while a concrete reasoner requires tangible objects and their observable relations in order to reason logically.

Piaget's notion of learning as an interaction with the environment has been generally supported[3,4] and, in fact, is a key element in current constructivist explanations of students' conceptual understanding and change. The concept of stages of concrete and formal reasoning, however, has been criticized and revised. Several studies[5,6,7] have demonstrated that, as measured by performance on cognitive tasks, the majority of secondary students are at the concrete stage of reasoning. There is also mounting evidence that performance on such tasks is strongly influenced by context, mode and language of task presentation, and subject matter.[8,9] Other studies have demonstrated that even young children are capable of abstract thought in certain situations.[10]

What conclusions can you draw from these results? Because most secondary students engage primarily in concrete reasoning, you should be careful about introducing tasks that primarily require formal thought. For example, most texts of secondary science implicitly assume that the reader can reason at the formal level. A statement about where students are in their reasoning ability does not, however, place limitations on where they can be. Students much younger than secondary students are capable of formal thought under certain conditions. Appropriate contexts and experiences that progress from concrete to formal could foster the formal reasoning abilities necessary for understanding many science concepts.

In recent years science educators have used a model termed *constructivism* to help understand students' learning. The theoretical basis for constructivist research comes from several sources, including David Ausubel.[11] We have introduced the essence of Ausubelian theory[12] earlier: a learner's prior knowledge is an important factor in determining what is learned in a given situation. L. S. Vygotsky[13] is a second important source for constructivism. He wrote of student conceptions and teacher conceptions, and how students and teachers might use similar words to describe concepts, yet have different personal interpretations of those concepts. Vygotsky's work implies that science instruction should take into account the differences between teacher and student conceptions and should provide a great deal of student-student interaction so that learners can develop concepts from those whose understandings and interpretations are closer to their own.

Early work in constructivist research focused on identifying students' conceptions about scientific phenomena and how those student conceptions differ from scientific conceptions. These student conceptions have been referred to by various unfortunate labels, such as misconceptions, alternative conceptions, alternative frameworks, and naive theories. We think it is much more useful to simply recognize students' *current* conceptions and emphasize your role in changing those conceptions so they are more aligned with those recognized as scientific. Several good reviews of this so-called misconceptions research exist.[14,15,16] We recommend that you review these or other summaries of students' understanding of scientific concepts.

In the constructivist model, students construct knowledge by interpreting new experiences in the context of prior knowledge, experiences, episodes, and images. Students' construction of knowledge begins at an early age so that by the time students encounter formalized study of science, they have developed stable and highly personal conceptions for the natural phenomena they experience. Given this view, one goal of your approach to instruction must be to facilitate change in students' conceptions of the world. Some researchers[17,18] have likened this process of conceptual change to the process by which scientific theories undergo change and restructuring. In fact, studies have demonstrated that student beliefs and conceptions often parallel early scientific theories, dating back to Aristotle and Larmarck.[19,20,21] However, other research cautions against drawing a parallel between student conceptions and the history of science, largely because student conceptions are not nearly as comprehensive as, say, Aristotelian theories.

G. J. Posner and others[22] have proposed four conditions for conceptual change that should be recognized as you formulate your instructional theory. First, in order for students to change their conceptions of a given phenomenon, they must be *dissatisfied* with their current conception. This dissatisfaction presumably comes about through repeated exposure to experiences they cannot explain by using current conceptions. Second, the new conception must be *intelligible* in terms of prior experiences and knowledge. Third, the new conception must be *plausible* in that it can explain a number of prior experiences and observations. Finally, the new conception must be *fruitful* in that it opens up new areas of inquiry, primarily through predictions about future events.

Other strategies to promote conceptual change are also suggested by constructivist research. You should be aware that students have conceptions of the world and that those conceptions often do not differentiate concepts.[23] Students need time to make their ideas explicit, and they should have a chance to apply their conceptions of the world in different contexts.[24]

The research associated with cognitive sciences and constructivism has had an important influence on science teaching. When considering your approach to instruction you should recognize that your students probably already have explanations or conceptions for many phenomena. Stated another way, your students are not empty vessels into which you can pour scientific facts, information, and concepts. Your challenge as a science teacher is demonstrating the inadequacy of students' current conceptions and providing the time and opportunity for them to construct more scientifically accurate concepts. In later chapters we will return to the theme of constructivism and your role in providing linkages between students' explanations and scientific explanations of the natural world.

■ EFFECTIVE RELATIONSHIPS WITH STUDENTS

For many years Arthur Combs and others[25] have investigated the characteristics of effective helping relationships, including teaching. Their research indicates that a teacher's perceptions of self, students, and the teaching task are critical to effective instruction.

Effective teachers perceive other people, particularly their students, as able, friendly, worthy, intrinsically motivated, dependable, and helpful. In the same manner, effective teachers see themselves as good teachers who are needed, trustworthy, and relate well to other people.

The roles of teachers also play an important role in their effectiveness. Better teachers see themselves assisting and facilitating rather than coercing and controlling. They identify with larger issues, are personally involved with issues, problems, and other people, and view the whole process of education as important. In addition, they tend to be altruistic and self-revealing. Effective teachers see their task as helping people rather than dealing with objects. And, generally, they try to understand the perceptions and backgrounds of their students.

Combs' studies delineated the perceptions of effective teachers. What about the students' percep-

tions of the science teacher? Rodger Bybee conducted research on the perceptions of the ideal science teacher.[26,27,28] The results of these studies are summarized in Table 2–1, which shows that adequate personal relations with students and enthusiasm in working with them consistently rank as the most important characteristics for science teachers. With only one exception these two categories were ranked first or second by all the groups studied.

Although this research indicates that personal qualities are perceived as important dimensions of science instruction, knowledge, personal relations, planning, enthusiasm, and methods are all important for effective science teaching. An instructional theory should incorporate these elements, adapting them individually and in toto to the situation in the science classroom.

Lee Shulman of Stanford University reported the role and development of teachers' knowledge in relation to teaching.[29] Shulman identified three categories of content knowledge: (1) subject matter, (2) pedagogical, and (3) curricular.

TABLE 2–1
Science educators' grand mean ranking compared with other populations' data reported by rank

Category	Science Educators N=172	In-Service Teachers N=76	Preservice Elementary Majors N=58	High School Students Average N=44	High School Students Disad- vantaged N=106	High School Students Advantaged N=31	Elementary School Children Grade 6 N=25	Elementary School Children Grades 4-5-6 N=18
Knowledge of subject matter	4	4	4	3	4	3	3	3
Adequate personal relations with students	1	1	1	1	1	2	1	1
Adequate planning and or- ganization	5	5	5	4	3	4	5	4
Enthusiasm in working with students	2	2	2	2	2	1	2	2
Adequate teaching methods and class procedures	3	3	3	5	5	5	4	5

Subject Matter

For science teachers subject matter is more than information and facts about a discipline or disciplines. Content knowledge of a subject includes what Joseph Schwab called the "substantive and syntactic structures" of a discipline. That is, substantial knowledge is an understanding of the different ways the basic concepts and principles of a discipline are organized. Do you know the major conceptual schemes in your discipline? If you had to organize the information and facts of physics, chemistry, biology, or the earth sciences, what major ideas would you identify as basic structures of these disciplines? In biology, for example, one can use the levels of organization approach, studying biology from the smallest particles to larger domains, and explaining living processes in terms of molecular activities. One also can use an ecological approach in which the ecosystem is the basic level of study and individual activities are studied in terms of the systems in which they live and interact. Using either of these structures you can develop basic conceptual schemes of biology, such as energetics, genetics, diversity, and evolution.

The syntax of a discipline is the set of ways scientists establish the truth or falsehood, validity, or invalidity of new or extant knowledge claims. Science teachers' use of inquiry introduces students to the processes of obtaining new knowledge, such as observation, hypothesis, and experimentation. There is the additional understanding that knowledge must be evaluated. By what criteria do biologists, geologists, or astronomers evaluate the worth of different theories?

Pedagogical Content Knowledge

Pedagogical content knowledge describes the depth and breadth of knowledge a teacher has about teaching a particular subject. Examples of pedagogical knowledge include forms of representing concepts such as use of analogies, examples, illustrations, and demonstrations. Pedagogical content knowledge is the capacity to formulate and represent science in ways that make it comprehensible to learners. Effective science teachers have a variety of ways and means of representing such ideas as ionic bonding, density, recombination of DNA, or stellar evolution.

Another dimension of pedagogical content knowledge is the understanding of what makes a concept easy or difficult for a learner to grasp. What misconceptions might students have about phenomena, such as heat and temperature,[30] position and velocity,[31] or living and nonliving?[32,33] What preconceptions do students have for objects and events in the natural world? The science teacher's instructional

theory helps establish links between new concepts and the students' current understanding.

Curricular Knowledge

One goal of this book and your course is to introduce you to the many methods and materials used in science teaching. The science curriculum includes a full range of materials with which science teachers should be familiar. Materials are designed for a particular subject, at a particular level, to be used with particular students. Each discipline has its own textbooks, kinds of laboratory equipment and educational software, films, filmstrips, and demonstrations.

In addition to knowledge of curricular materials and how best to use them, curricular knowledge extends to science teachers' abilities to relate topics of study to the curricula their students may be studying in other disciplines. Curricular knowledge encompasses a horizontal and vertical understanding of both school and science curricula.

The discussion of teacher knowledge as it relates to content, pedagogy, and curriculum is obviously important, even essential, but you will need more than an adequate knowledge base for your instructional theory; you will also have to make many instructional decisions. David Berliner reviewed research on teaching and provided some valuable insights about these decisions, using the categories of preinstructional decisions, instructional decisions, and post-instructional decisions.

Preinstructional Decisions

Before you begin teaching a science lesson, you should be aware of the effect of certain decisions on student achievement, attitudes, and behaviors. You must make *content decisions*. What is the content of your science lesson? You must consider not only national standards and state and local guidelines, but also your judgments about issues, such as the effort required to teach a subject and the problems that you perceive the students will have with the subject. Finally, you must take into account the subjects you enjoy teaching. Which are the areas within your discipline that you really like? Are you excited about introducing students to the nature and history of science? Do you think it most important to have students recognize science-related social issues?

Science teaching involves groups of students. *Grouping decisions* are part of your preparation for a lesson. What is the best size of a group? How much laboratory equipment do you have? Who should (or should not) work together? Should you use cooperative groups? What criteria do you have for forming a particular group? Whether you lecture to the entire

class or work in the laboratory, you will usually make grouping decisions. Even when assigning individual work on projects, experiments, and tests, a group in some sense still exists.

Finally, you will have *decisions about activities*. Laboratory work, for example, has specific functions; that is, it is used to achieve certain goals. In a laboratory students may learn to design an experiment, manipulate equipment, and use computers. Operations—the rules or norms of conduct for the activity—are also important. Is it okay to be out of one's seat? What type of conversation is acceptable? What rules *must* be followed for safety reasons?

The importance of these kinds of decisions cannot be overstated. An instructional theory will help you review these decisions. Just reading this section should make you aware of the many and varied decisions you must make *before you begin teaching even the simplest lesson*.

Instructional Decisions

Once you begin teaching a lesson, numerous factors determine what your students learn. The amount of time students spend on a task—*engaged time*—is directly related to how much students will learn. You should recognize that *engaged* can mean physically (hands-on), mentally (minds-on), or both. Although this seems obvious, the amount of engaged time varies from class to class. You should be aware of the amount of time students are actually working. Engaged time is especially important for under-achieving and low-ability students. These students will benefit most from time *on task*, and they also are the students who are most likely to be *off task*.

The *success rate* of students is related to continued achievement. Success in the early stages of learning new concepts or skills is especially important for unsuccessful and low-ability students. If students do not experience some success in the early stages of lessons, their frustration and lack of understanding can contribute to the cycle of low achievement and failure.

Decisions you make about *questioning* will also influence your teaching effectiveness. Science teachers in particular should ask many questions—questions about the natural world are the foundation of science. The first thing to consider is the cognitive level of the question. Most teachers ask low-level questions, such as, "What do the letters DNA stand for?" "What is the second law of thermodynamics?" or "What is a silicon oxygen tetrahedron?" Although questions of this nature have some benefit, you should remember that higher level questions facilitate thinking and learning. Questions that require

students to analyze and synthesize will produce higher levels of student achievement. You could, for example, provide data in graph form and ask the students to analyze the results and form an explanation based on the evidence. Or, you could provide information from two separate but related experiments and ask students for their predictions of possible outcomes.

The second point about questioning concerns the importance of *waiting* after you have asked a question. Research by Mary Budd Rowe[34] confirms the importance of wait time. Longer waits (most teachers wait less than one second after asking a question) result in increases in the appropriateness, confidence, variety, and cognitive level of responses. A two- to three-second adjustment in your teaching style can result in a much higher return for you and your students.

Postinstructional Decisions

Now that the lesson unit or semester is over, how much did the students learn? Science teachers usually arrive at an answer through the assessments, grades, and feedback given to students.

Assessment is not the central issue. You should ask yourself how closely the assessment is correlated with your aims and the nature of the subject matter. Should you use a standardized test? How can you construct an assessment that accurately represents the content and skills that students had an opportunity to learn? You do not want to emphasize higher levels of cognitive thinking during instruction and then undermine that with lower level questions, or vice versa.

Grades do motivate students to achieve. However, the overuse of grades or their use as coercion can have detrimental effects. Corrective *feedback*, if properly given, results in positive achievement and attitudes on the part of students. Your decisions to give praise for correct work, recognition for proper behavior, and personally neutral criticism (as opposed to sarcasm) for incorrect responses can all influence student learning.

By now you must be overwhelmed at the number of decisions that go into science teaching. We think the early introduction of these ideas will prepare you for the topics and activities to come. For the time being, only an awareness of these decisions is necessary. Remember that you are just beginning to form your instructional theory.

Research on Effective Teaching

Research on good teaching provides some insights that may help you synthesize the ideas in this sec-

FIGURE 2–1
Highlights of research on good teaching. (Source: Andrew Porter and Jere Brophy, "Synthesis of Research on Good Teaching: Insights from the Work of the Institute for Research on Teaching," *Educational Leadership* **(May 1988): 75.)**

Good teaching is fundamental to effective schooling. From the studies of the Institute for Research on Teaching and from other studies conducted over the last 10 years, there is a picture of effective teachers as semiautonomous professionals who

- are clear about their instructional goals,
- are knowledgeable about lesson content and strategies for teaching it,
- communicate to their students what is expected of them—and why,
- make expert use of existing instructional materials in order to devote more time to practices that enrich and clarify lesson content,
- teach students meta-cognitive strategies and give them opportunities to master them,
- address higher as well as lower level cognitive objectives,
- monitor students' understanding by offering regular and appropriate feedback,
- integrate their instruction with that of other subject areas,
- accept responsibility for student outcomes,
- are thoughtful and reflective about their practice.

tion. After reviewing the research on good teaching, Andrew Porter and Jere Brophy concluded that the concept of good teaching is changing.[35] In the past, teachers were sometimes viewed as technicians who had to apply how-to lessons, or as weak links in the education system who had to be circumvented with a teacher-proof curriculum. Those approaches did not work. The current concept of effective teaching deals with empowering teachers. How are teachers empowered? A short-term answer is through the application of research on teaching, and a long-term answer is through the continuous development of an instructional theory. Our discussion assumes that student learning within science classes requires good teaching, and good teaching requires science teachers who make appropriate decisions about how to educate students.

A contemporary image of the good teacher is that of a thoughtful professional who works purposefully toward educational goals. According to Porter and Brophy:

- Effective teachers are clear about their instructional goals. They inform their students of these goals and keep them in mind as they design lessons and communicate with students.
- Effective instruction provides students with strategies they can use for their own learning.
- Effective instruction creates learning situations in which students are expected to learn information, solve problems, and organize that information in new ways.
- Effective teachers continually monitor student understanding and adjust instruction accordingly.
- Effective teachers frequently integrate other subjects and skills into their lessons.

- Effective teachers design instruction so that what is learned can be used in the future.
- Effective teachers are thoughtful and reflective about their instruction.

Figure 2–1 summarizes these points.

Science teachers have been depicted as individuals who can do almost everything or practically nothing. In reality, science teachers are continually developing and improving their approach to instruction—what we call an instructional theory. The feature that mediates between the instructional theory and teaching practice is decision-making as it applies to different teaching situations. In the next section, we introduce many of the teaching methods that you will apply in different classroom situations. We have provided background in research and theory for your consideration.

■ SOME METHODS TO CONSIDER IN FORMING YOUR INSTRUCTIONAL THEORY

When science teachers lecture, show a film, take a field trip, have students work in the laboratory, or guide a discussion, they are using instructional methods that will develop understanding, skills, or values relative to science and technology. The assumption underlying an instructional method is that it is the most effective and efficient means of presenting the material. A method should also be appropriate for the subject and students.

In this section, we introduce a variety of teaching methods. They are listed in alphabetical order along with a brief description and guides for effective use.

Assessment

Purpose: To provide feedback to both the students and teacher about student understanding of concepts and ability to use skills.
Predominate Learning Modes: Visual and Kinesthetic.
Group Size: Individual, Occasionally Small.

Tests, quizzes, performance-based assessments, and portfolios used frequently in science classes should be designed to provide accurate feedback concerning student progress. Appropriate and effective use of assessment includes the following.

- Assess what was taught.
- Use performance-based assessments to evaluate the scientific inquiry and technological design.
- Provide students feedback about their strengths and weaknesses.
- Use questions and situations that require critical thinking and problem solving at different cognitive levels: that is, recall, comprehension, application, analysis, synthesis, and evaluation.

Chalkboard/Marker Board

Purpose: To illustrate, outline, or underscore ideas in written or graphic form.
Predominate Learning Mode: Visual.
Group Size: Small to Large.

Chalkboards/marker boards are used extensively in science classrooms. Their uses vary, as does their effectiveness. Most science teachers use the chalkboard/marker board with some skill; here are a few helpful hints.

- Say what you are going to write before writing it on the board.
- Use key words or concepts.
- Write legibly and spell correctly.
- Stand to the side of the material so the students can see the board and you can see the students.
- Erase the board before writing a new concept, idea, or diagram.

Debate

Purpose: To allow students to gain information and discuss different sides of an issue.
Predominate Learning Mode: Auditory.
Group Size: Medium—10 to 15 students.

Debate is an effective way to introduce different sides of science-related issues. The debate can continue over several days and involve several teams in various aspects of a topic. Students will have to understand information concerning their position and develop the skills of analysis and evaluation concerning their opponent's position. Debate is an excellent method to encourage students to take a different perspective and engage in ethical discussion of issues. Here are some guidelines for using debate.

- Be sure the debate topic has clear pro/con sides.
- Use teams of 3 to 4 students per side for an issue.
- Set clear time limits for opening statements, rebuttals, and closing statements.
- Make it clear that there are to be no interruptions while a speaker has the floor.
- Let the class audience vote on the outcome.

Demonstrations

Purpose: To provide students the opportunity to see a phenomenon or event that they otherwise would not observe.
Predominate Learning Modes: Visual, Auditory.
Group Size: Medium to Large.

Demonstrations can be used to teach concepts or skills directly, or to prepare students for work in the laboratory. Demonstrations are often used due to safety concerns or lack of equipment. The best demonstrations have a theatric quality and usually deal with something that is puzzling to the students. Here are a few helpful hints.

- Present demonstrations so students can see them and hear you.
- Do the demonstration *before* trying it in class.
- Take all necessary safety precautions.
- Plan your demonstration so it clearly shows the intended concepts or skills.

Discussion

Purpose: To promote an exchange of information and ideas among members of a group or class.
Predominate Learning Mode: Auditory.
Group Size: Small to Medium—2 to 8 students.

Discussions are used frequently in science instruction. To be effective, discussions must be carefully designed and facilitated. The teacher must plan the discussion so information is accurate and students stay on the topic. Some suggestions follow.

- Think carefully about the topic and initial questions.
- Prepare students for the discussion through reading or a laboratory experience.
- Provide a sheet of topics and/or questions that help guide the discussion.
- Facilitate discussions through planning, questioning, and summarizing. Avoid using the discussion method as a means of lecturing.

Educational Software/Computers

Purpose: To allow students the opportunity to review, record, model, and acquire concepts and skills.

Predominate Learning Modes: Visual and Auditory.
Group Size: Individual to Small—2 to 4 students.

Educational software/computers are being used in many science classrooms. Initial use centers on individual pieces of software that are predominately tutorial. Examples of this technology in the science classroom include word processing, computer-assisted instruction, microcomputer-based laboratories, HyperCard, simulations, and modeling. Suggestions for use of software include the following.

- Select software aligned with the learning task.
- Use the software as part of the planned instruction.

Field Trip

Purpose: To provide a learning experience that is unique and cannot be accomplished in the classroom.
Predominate Learning Modes: Kinesthetic, Visual, Auditory.
Group Size: Large.

Field trips can be an exciting complement to the science program. They also can be a disaster. The difference between a learning experience and a disaster lies in the preparation for and appropriateness of the trip. As a science teacher, you will have to decide the appropriateness of the timing, destination, and place of the trip in the instructional sequence. Concerning preparation, here are some guidelines.

- Take the trip yourself before making the trip with students.
- Prepare the students for the trip by informing them of the objectives, activities, and expected behaviors.
- Make sure transportation arrangements have been made and are safe and adequate.
- Confirm any prior arrangements for admission and guides at your destination.
- Obtain permission slips from parents.
- Arrange for additional adults (teachers and/or parents) to go on the trip.

Films/Video/CD-ROM

Purpose: To present information in an interesting and efficient manner.
Predominate Learning Modes: Auditory and Visual.
Group Size: Small to Large.

Most students are interested in films and video. Science teachers need to use films in a manner that will attain the established objectives. Placement of a film or video in the instructional sequence is critical. These are some recommendations for effective use of films and videos.

- Preview the film or video before showing it.
- Decide where the film can best fit in the curriculum.

- Outline some introductory remarks.
- Prepare questions and distribute them to the students.
- Identify one or two places to stop the film or video and have a brief discussion.
- Conduct a discussion after the film. You can evaluate the students' understanding of key concepts. Answer questions and make connections between the film and students' previous knowledge and/or future topics of study.

Games

Purpose: To give the students an opportunity to learn in an enjoyable, stimulating manner.
Predominate Learning Mode: Kinesthetic.
Group Size: Small to Medium.

Use of games can provide students with a variation on the usual classroom procedures. If used wisely, they can be valuable for developing concepts and ideas not generally conveyed by other methods. There are many commercial games available for science teaching. Here are some guides to the use of games.

- Consider the difficulty of the game.
- Consider the appropriateness of the game for your objectives.
- Provide clear rules for the game.
- Conduct pre- and postgame discussions.

Inquiry/Design

Purpose: To give students experience in the actual use of equipment and materials as they develop knowledge, skills, and values related to science (inquiry) and technology (design).
Predominate Learning Mode: Kinesthetic.
Group Size: Individual to Small.

Inquiry and design have become important aspects of science teaching. Methods related to use of inquiry and design include asking questions, using technology, designing experiments, analyzing data, formulating explanations, thinking about the relationship between evidence and explanation, and communicating explanations and methods. Here are some introductory guides.

- Select the inquiry activity that best illustrates the concepts or skills you have as objectives.
- Make any necessary changes in the physical arrangement of the room.
- Be sure materials are available and functional.
- Check any equipment to be sure it works.
- Give clear, succinct directions including safety precautions, how to handle equipment, where to obtain materials, assignment of groups, and your expectations of conduct and reporting.

Laboratory Report

Purpose: To have students formalize their experiences and make connections between prior and present knowledge.
Predominate Learning Mode: Visual.
Group Size: Individual to Small.

Laboratory reports can be valuable means to bring different ideas into focus, to have students consider the context of concepts, and to reflect on the meaning of the laboratory experience. In order for the laboratory report to be effective, we recommend the following guidelines.

- Provide a purpose for the report.
- Outline your expectations in terms of content, length, and format.
- Review the reports.
- Have all members of groups sign the report, indicating they contributed.

Lecture

Purpose: To present a large body of information in an efficient manner.
Predominate Learning Mode: Auditory.
Group Size: Large.

Lecturing is one of the most frequently used methods of teaching science in secondary schools. Unfortunately, it is used more often than is effective, especially for middle students. Here are some suggestions for effective lecturing.

- Use an outline and either distribute it before the lecture or place it on the overhead projector.
- Supplement the lecture with slides, overheads, or charts to illustrate concepts and ideas.
- Monitor student attention and understanding.
- Talk clearly and in a manner that identifies key points and facilitates note taking.

Oral Reports

Purpose: To allow students to demonstrate their understanding of a subject.
Predominate Learning Mode: Auditory.
Group Size: Individual to Small.

Oral reports are the students' equivalent of the teacher's lectures. Students, individually or in small groups, research information, organize material, and present a report. In effect, students teach other students. Here are some helpful hints.

- Coordinate topics so there is an organized sequence of presentations that are aligned with the science program objectives.
- Allow students to report on topics of interest to them or that they have selected.

- Organize presentations as if they were to take place at a professional scientific meeting.
- Help students with audiovisual aids.
- Set clear time limits for the preparation and presentation of reports.
- Provide a formal evaluation in advance.

Problem Solving

Purpose: To give students experience in identifying and resolving a problem.
Predominate Learning Mode: Visual.
Group Size: Individual to Small.

Problem solving is a continuing objective of science teaching but is not used as often as one would expect. Basically, the method is to place the students in a situation where they must take some action that is not immediately obvious. Problem solving is closely related to technological design and provides opportunities for students to encounter concepts such as criteria, constraints, costs, risks, benefits, and trade-offs. Since students usually have not had much experience in problem solving, it is helpful to do some of the following:

- Identify general problems for study and resolution.
- Help students narrow their problems.
- Provide an opportunity to brainstorm possible solutions to the problem.
- Select and try reasonable solutions for the problem.
- Evaluate the tested solutions.
- Prepare a formal report using the protocol of professional papers.

Projects

Purpose: To give students knowledge, skills, and understanding related to a unique problem.
Predominate Learning Mode: Kinesthetic.
Group Size: Individual to Small.

Many science teachers like to have students work on projects and participate in local or regional science fairs. We believe projects are a wonderful way to give students a real sense of science. Here are some things to consider.

- Develop a list of project ideas for students.
- Provide written guidelines concerning the purpose and nature of the project, the final product, time limits, and any special expectations.
- Provide time and assistance as the students work on their projects, particularly in locating resources and designing experiments.

Questioning

Purpose: To stimulate thinking by engaging the learner.
Predominate Learning Mode: Auditory.

Group Size: Individual, or Small, Medium, and Large.

Questioning is one of the primary means teachers use to engage learners. Asking questions can be one of the most effective and efficient means of stimulating students to think about the topic. Here are some suggestions on questioning.

- Use both convergent and divergent questions.
- Provide time for students to think about the answer.
- Use questions that require thinking at different levels: that is, recall, comprehension, application, analysis, synthesis, and evaluation.

Reading

Purpose: To present information that is uniform and consistent.
Predominate Learning Mode: Visual.
Group Size: Individual.

Reading is central to effective instruction. Though reading should be used in science classes, it should not be the *exclusive* learning method. We also encourage reading of materials other than the textbook. Some guidelines follow.

- Use reading materials that are appropriate to the students' abilities and your program objectives.
- Assign a variety of readings (for example, textbook, science books, popular magazines, and articles or tracts of historical significance).
- Make available a variety of reading materials in the classroom.

Simulations

Purpose: To increase students' abilities to apply concepts, analyze situations, solve problems, and understand different points of view.
Predominate Learning Modes: Visual and Auditory.
Group Size: Small to Medium—5 to 15 students.

Simulations provide teachers with a means of presenting situations, concepts, and issues in a condensed and simplified form. Simulations are especially useful for involving students in science-related social issues. Use of simulations can be enhanced by doing the following:

- Select a problem or issue of interest to the students with at least two different viewpoints.
- Include key issues and concepts in a realistic way.
- Make procedures clear, including expected behaviors, roles to be played, time limits, and guidelines.
- Use lifelike materials and situations.
- Conclude the simulation with a discussion of different perceptions of the issue, how the students felt about the issue, how the conflict was resolved, and what actions might be taken in the future.

This description of methods is intentionally brief; complete chapters are devoted to some of them later in this book. You will use the methods described in this section in Activity 2–2 "Applying the Best Method."

■ A FINAL NOTE

Developing your personal instructional theory will be one of the most helpful and rewarding accomplishments of your preparation for science teaching. The result will be consistency in your teaching and the ability to transcend the minor day-to-day difficulties that are major problems for some teachers. The preceding process will help you build your instructional theory and improve your effectiveness.

Education has fractionated, divided, and isolated many of the important components of successful teaching. Unfortunately, many teacher preparation programs emphasize these ad hoc components: "If you are well planned. . . ," "If you use this curriculum. . . ," "If you understand the child's cognitive stages. . . ," and "If you know your subject. . . ." Planning, classroom procedures, methods, and subject matter are obviously important, but they are means, not ends. This educational view has shifted the emphasis of programs away from the primary and crucial variable in the classroom—the teacher as a person. Science teachers with an adequate instructional theory have knowledge, plans, methods, and curricular materials. In addition, they have larger goals for their interaction with students and the added dimension of a personalized approach to education.

When the goals, theories, techniques, plans, and materials are combined, you are ready to interact with students. The *way* in which science teachers combine these elements and build a helping relationship with students is crucial. An instructional theory will help provide the needed direction. Science teaching is characterized by situations that require the teacher to react immediately. The creative, insightful, and prepared science teacher will effectively respond to the instantaneous needs of the students and school.

■ SUMMARY

An instructional theory will help the science teacher make predictions, explain different strategies that will enhance learning, and organize instruction. It increases instructional effectiveness by prescribing motivation, structure, sequence, and feedback.

■■■■■■■■■■■■■■■■■ **GUEST EDITORIAL** ■■■■■■■■■■■■■■■■■

Teaching Science

Caryl E. Buchwald
Professor of Geology and Director of the Arboretum
Carleton College, Northfield, Minnesota

Science is important to all of us. The world is in desperate need of more and better science precisely because it has been one of the dominant forces in our lives and the life of the world for several hundred years. Science and its derivative, technology, have increased the life expectancy and material well-being of Western people but at the same time have led us to the brink of disaster through ecological catastrophe or nuclear war. Science raises the hope that we can truly progress to a higher understanding of ourselves and our interrelationships with nature.

There can scarcely be a higher calling or more honorable occupation than teaching science to young people. It is important because, when well taught, science leads us to discover two characteristics that are important not only to our own lives but to the future of humanity. Science should help us to discover humility on the one hand and the ability to affect our own futures on the other.

Humility comes from studying science, for the obvious reason that we learn about our own place in nature. That we are minuscule in the universe, but domineering in the biosphere, is a position not always easy to grasp. That we are a part of the very biosphere that we dominate should lead us to realize that we cannot deny the integration of our own lives with nature.

Science is often portrayed as possessing facts and laws. Yet, when we attempt explanation in our own research, most of the time we discover that facts are contextual in time and place. Because science is really explanation and not discovery, the explanations change as we learn more or see causal relations that were previously unsuspected. When reflecting on my own career as a teacher, I am constantly amazed by how the so-called facts have changed. What has not changed is the search for data and their meaning, the use of logic, the need for verification, and the consequences of knowledge.

The consequences of knowing are important. They lead us to moral dilemmas time and time again. Atomic research has given us improved medical treatment but also nuclear bombs. Better medical treatment has eased human suffering, extended our lifetimes, and contributed to the population explosion. It is hard to do one thing at a time. The reality remains: knowledge requires action.

What can we do with and for our students to improve their understanding of science? It seems to me that the best teachers possess two essential attributes: enthusiasm and patience. Enthusiasm stems from a love of what is being done, a belief that science is important and worth doing. Patience is needed because science is a process that must be internalized. Science is not a set of operating procedures that goes one, two, three . . . conclusions. Often it is difficult to figure out the steps that were actually taken in framing a question and seeking an explanation. To require a lockstep progression from data gathering through hypothesis to conclusion not only denies the reality of scientific activity but is likely to make students seek preconceived answers rather than to invent their own explanations.

Patience means letting students seek the relationships and explanations that fit their experience. If we insist that they hunt for the right answers, we end up teaching them the wrong thing; that is, that science is discovering the hidden. We want to teach them that science is a way to perceive nature. Seeking right answers also leads to the conclusion that science has answers entrusted to an elite and that is counter to the democratic idea.

So, we must be enthusiastic. This enthusiasm will flow from belief in what we are doing and our confidence with our subject. We must be patient because science is a complex way of thinking, and it takes time for it to develop and mature.

Research indicates that knowledge of subject matter, pedagogical content knowledge, and curricular knowledge are all important to effective teaching. This knowledge can be applied to specific decisions relative to preinstruction (content, time allocation, pacing, grouping activities), instruction (engaged time, success rate, questioning), and postinstruction (tests, grades, feedback). All of these ideas contribute to the goal of good teaching. Characteristics of good teachers include the following:

- Clarity of instructional goals.
- Knowledge of content and strategies to teach it.
- Adequate communication with students.
- Expert use of extant materials.
- Knowledge of student needs and development.
- Development of lower and higher order thinking in students.
- Monitoring of student learning with appropriate feedback.
- Integration of science instruction with other disciplines.
- Thought and reflection about their teaching.

Science teachers should consider their perceptions of themselves, students, the teaching task, and the subject before starting an instructional theory. Once this is done, they can begin to formulate such a theory by clarifying goals and preferences, understanding the theories and methods of science teaching, analyzing similarities and differences of theories and methods, and synthesizing their goals and preferences with appropriate theories and methods. Above all, science teachers should realize that they are the most important variable in the instructional theory.

■ REFERENCES

1. Jerome S. Bruner, *Toward A Theory of Instruction* (New York: W. W. Norton, 1968).
2. Rodger W. Bybee and Robert Sund, *Piaget for Educators* (Columbus, OH: Merrill, 1982).
3. E. A. Luzner, "Cognitive Development: Learning and the Development of Change," in *Cognitive Classroom Learning*, G. D. Phye and T. Andre, eds. (New York: Academic Press, 1986).
4. J. W. Renner, M. R. Abraham, and H. H. Birnie, "The Importance of the Form of Student Acquisition of Data in Physics Learning Cycles," *Journal of Research in Science Teaching, 23*(2) (1986): 121–143.
5. E. L. Chiapetta, "A Review of Piagetian Studies Relevant to Science Instruction at the Secondary and College Level," *Science Education, 60*(2) (1976): 253–261.
6. J. W. Renner, R. M. Grant, and P. Sutherland, "Content and Concrete Thought," *Science Education, 62*(2) (1978): 215–221.
7. M. J. Wavering, B. Perry, and D. Birdd, "Performance of Students in Grades 6, 9, and 12 on Five Logical, Spatial, and Formal Tasks," *Journal of Research in Science Teaching, 23* (1986): 321–333.
8. S. L. Golbeck, "The Role of Physical Content in Piagetian Spatial Tasks: Sex Differences in Spatial Knowledge," *Journal of Research in Science Teaching, 23* (1986): 321–333.
9. Paul Brandwein, "A General Theory of Instruction," *Science Education, 63*(3) (1979): 291.
10. M. T. H. Chi and R. D. Koeske, "Network Representation of a Child's Dinosaur Knowledge," *Developmental Psychology, 19* (1983): 29–39.
11. David P. Ausubel, *Educational Psychology: A Cognitive View* (New York: Academic Press, 1968).
12. David P. Ausubel, J. D. Novak, and H. Hanesian, *Educational Psychology: A Cognitive View (2nd edition)* (New York: Holt, Rinehart, and Winston, 1978).
13. L. S. Vygotsky, *Thought and Language*, trans. and ed. A. Kozulin (Cambridge, MA: MIT Press, 1968).
14. R. Driver, E. Guesne, and A. Tiberghien, eds., *Children's Ideas in Science* (Philadelphia, PA: Open University, Press, 1985).
15. R. J. Osborne and P. Freyberg, eds., "Concepts, Misconceptions, and Alternative Conceptions: Changing Perspectives in Science Education," *Studies in Science Education, 10* (1983): 61–98.
16. R. Duit, "Research on Students' Alternative Frameworks in Science: Topics, Theoretical Frameworks, Consequences for Science Teaching," *Proceedings of the Second International Seminar on Misconceptions and Educational Strategies in Science and Mathematics* (Ithaca, NY: 1987).
17. G. J. Posner, K. A. Strike, P. W. Hewson, and W. A. Gertzog, "Accommodation of a Scientific Conception: Toward a Theory of Conceptual Change," *Science Education, 66*(2) (1982): 211–227.
18. C. Smith, S. Carey, and M. Wiser, "On Differentiation: A Case Study of the Development of the Concepts of Size, Weight, and Density," *Cognition,* (1985): 177–237.
19. A. Caramazza, M. McCloskey, and B. Green, "Naive Beliefs in 'Sophisticated' Subjects: Misconceptions about Trajectories of Objects," *Cognition, 9* (1981): 117–123.
20. A. B. Champagne, L. E. Klopfer, and R. F. Gunstone, "Cognitive Research and the Design of Science Instruction," *Educational Psychologist, 17*(1) (1982): 31–53.
21. J. H. Wandersee, "Can the History of Science Help Science Educators Anticipate Students' Misconceptions?" *Journal of Research in Science Teaching, 23* (1986): 581–597.
22. G. J. Posner, K. A. Strike, P. W. Hewson, and W. A. Gertzog, "Accommodation of a Scientific Conception: Toward a Theory of Conceptual Change," *Science Education, 66*(2) (1982): 211–227.
23. D. E. Trowbridge and L. C. McDermott, "Investigation of Student Understanding of the Concept of Acceleration in One Dimension," *American Journal of Physics, 49* (1981): 242–253.

24. J. A. Minstrell, "Teaching Science for Understanding," in *Toward the Thinking Curriculum: Current Cognitive Research, 1989 Yearbook of the ASCD,* L. Resnick and L. Klopfer, eds. (Alexandria, VA: Association for Supervision and Curriculum Development, 1989).

25. Arthur Combs, Donald Avila, and William Parkey, *Helping Relationships: Basic Concepts for the Helping Profession* (Boston: Allyn and Bacon, 1978).

26. Rodger Bybee, "The Teacher I Like Best: Perceptions of Advantaged, Average, and Disadvantaged Science Students," *School Science and Mathematics, 73*(5) (May 1973): 384–390.

27. Rodger Bybee, "The Ideal Elementary Science Teacher: Perceptions of Children, Pre-service and In-service Elementary Science Teachers," *School Science and Mathematics, 75*(3) (March 1975): 229–235.

28. Rodger Bybee, "Science Educators' Perceptions of the Ideal Science Teacher," *School Science and Mathematics, 78*(1) (January 1978): 13–22.

29. Lee S. Shulman, "Those Who Understand: Knowledge Growth in Teaching," *Educational Researcher, 15*(2) (February 1986): 4–14.

30. M. Brumby, "Students' Perceptions of the Concept of Life," *Science Education, 66* (1982): 613–622.

31. David Berliner, "The Half-full Glass: A Review of Research on Teaching," in *Using What We Know About Teaching,* Philip Hosford, ed. (Alexandria, VA: Association for Supervision and Curriculum Development, 1984).

32. Mary Budd Rowe, "Wait Time and Rewards as Instructional Variables: Their Influence on Language, Logic, and Fate Control. Part One. Wait Time," *Journal of Research in Science Teaching, 11* (1974): 81–94.

33. Andrew Porter and Jere Brophy, "Synthesis of Research on Good Teaching: Insights from the Work of the Institute for Research on Teaching," *Educational Leadership* (May 1988): 74–85.

34. Mary Budd Rowe, "Wait Time and Rewards As Instructional Variables: Their Influence on Language, Logic, and Fate Control. Part One,. Wait Time," *Journal of Research in Science Teaching, 11* (1974): 81–94.

35. Andrew Porter and Jere Brophy, "Synthesis of Research on Good Teaching: Insights from the Work of the Institute for Research on Teaching," *Educational Leadership* (May 1988), 74–85.

INVESTIGATING SCIENCE TEACHING

Activity 2–1

WHAT WOULD YOU DO?

When you become a science teacher, you will continually be required to make decisions. An instructional theory helps you to make those decisions. This investigation directs your attention to sample situations that require decisions.

It is Monday morning. You have planned a lesson examining life in pond water. Over the weekend, the heating system failed and there is no life in your pond. What would you do? (Select the answer closest to what you think you would do. Then prepare a brief justification of your answer.)

1. Omit the section on "life in a pond."
2. Tell the students to read the section in their text entitled "life in a pond."
3. Have the students find other life to examine.
4. Say nothing, ask the students to find life in the water and, when they discover that there is none, have them determine what could have happened.

Justification:

As part of an environmental studies unit the class is to examine the possibility that a local mining operation is polluting the environment. The next day a group of parents asks you to describe your science program at the next PTA meeting. Their primary concern is that you are going to cause trouble for the community's major economic support. *What would you do?* (Select the answer closest to what you think you would do. Then prepare a brief justification of your answer.)

1. Decline the invitation.
2. Accept the invitation, take samples of the lesson, data sheets, and questions the students will be answering, and be prepared to explain your goals.
3. Accept the invitation on the condition that the parents come to class and complete the lesson with their sons and daughters.
4. Accept the invitation and plan the lesson in cooperation with the PTA.

Justification:

You are in the middle of a class discussion. You have noticed that for 20 minutes one student has not only paid no attention, but he has also been creating a disturbance. You reprimand him. The student merely looks at you, then continues to talk and disturb the class. *What would you do?* (Select the answer closest to what you think you would do. Then prepare a brief justification for your answer.)

1. Demand that the student stop talking.
2. Request that the student conform to the class rules.

3. Tell the other students that you cannot expect much more from such a person (hoping that public ridicule will terminate the disruptive behavior).
4. Tell the student that "we have a problem" and we will have to work it out. Then, ask the student to leave the room temporarily.

Justification:

All of the materials are ready for your first lesson in physical science. The lesson is on density. As you explain the procedures you notice that the students are sending nonverbal messages of "Oh, no—boring!" Then, several students say, "We did this same lesson last year—the answer is $D = m/v$." *What would you do?* (Select the answer closest to what you think you would do. Then prepare a brief justification of your answer.)

1. Have the students describe what they did in the experiment last year.
2. Skip this lesson and go on to the next, where students apply the concepts of density.
3. Do the activity as planned and try to extend each student's understanding of density through personal discussion.
4. At the end of the investigation, have the students answer questions to see if they understand density.

Justification:

Activity 2–2

APPLYING THE BEST METHOD

When planning a lesson, it is important to have in mind a variety of teaching methods to complement the many classroom situations you might encounter. In this activity you meet various situations, suggest a teaching method to accomplish your goal, and provide a short justification for the method you select. Your teacher may assign different situations to individuals or groups. The line to the left of the number is provided for you to indicate the suggested teaching method. The methods described in this chapter are listed below. Even if your teacher does not assign these, we recommend that you complete at least one situation in each category.

A. Chalkboards	G. Films	M. Problem Solving
B. Debate	H. Games	N. Projects
C. Demonstrations	I. Laboratory	O. Questioning
D. Discussion	J. Laboratory Report	P. Reading
E. Educational Software	K. Lecture	Q. Simulations
F. Field Trip	L. Oral Report	R. Tests

Situation	Method	Justification

Applications

_____ 1. A student has brought to class a newspaper clipping of a current scientific event.

_____ 2. You wish to use an everyday application as a review.

_____ 3. You wish to make your course particularly functional by relating it to a "do-it-yourself" experience.

Appreciations

_____ 4. You wish to bring about the realization that we have not exhausted the unsolved problems in science. On the contrary, the more we know the more we realize how much is still to be learned.

_____ 5. You wish to develop an appreciation for the work of scientists in the past.

_____ 6. You wish to apply scientific concepts just acquired to the home situation with particular emphasis on how lack of knowledge often leads to inadequate solutions.

_____ 7. You wish to relate scientific knowledge developed in class to intelligent consumer buying.

_____ 8. You decide to try to develop an appreciation for a truly unusual scientific phenomenon.

_____ 9. You decide to try to orient the group to an appreciation for the rapid advances of scientific knowledge through consideration of what new things the text might contain for students taking the course ten years from now.

Situation	Method	Justification

Attitudes

_____ 10. You wish to develop the proper attitude toward thorough observation and proper interpretation of what is observed.

_____ 11. You wish to guide the group in developing a sensible attitude toward those scientific problems or situations for which there is not, as yet, a definite answer.

Demonstrations

_____ 12. A demonstration experiment has just failed to produce the desired scientific results.

_____ 13. You wish to teach the proper method to use a scientific device.

_____ 14. You wish to demonstrate how the proper problem-solving approach can be used to answer a "why does it work" type of question.

_____ 15. You wish to make the teaching of a scientific principle more functional by demonstrating several everyday applications.

_____ 16. You wish to demonstrate a new scientific principle in a simple manner which the students themselves can try out at home.

Individual Differences

_____ 17. You wish to make a genuine effort in adjusting to differences by teaching one concept so that the slowest person will understand it and the most capable one will not be bored.

Situation	Method	Justification

_____ 18. You wish to familiarize students with new vocabulary at the beginning of a unit and convince them of the need for correct knowledge of new words.

_____ 19. You wish to emphasize the opportunities available in science careers in a manner that will appeal to students.

Knowledge

_____ 20. You wish to orient the students to the first unit of the course.

_____ 21. You wish to correct a prevalent misconception.

_____ 22. You wish to place a complex concept in a more concrete setting.

_____ 23. You wish to develop an understanding that our idea of what is "true" changes as we gain more knowledge.

_____ 24. You wish to bring about the realization that, through functional knowledge of a principle, we can group together many everyday applications.

Methods

_____ 25. You wish to emphasize the dangers of making quick decisions without enough supporting evidence.

_____ 26. You wish to use the inductive approach to teach a scientific principle.

Situation	Method	Justification

Review

_____ 27. You wish to conduct a drill experience but at the same time use a technique that will be enjoyable for the students.

_____ 28. You wish to use an instructional game as a means of developing new learning or review, or to lend variety to the class instruction.

_____ 29. You wish to give a demonstration using "common gadgets" as a means of reviewing material previously taught.**

You may wish to share your responses with other members of the class. These situations form a good basis for discussion.

**The original list of situations was provided courtesy of Lawrence Counrey, "Instructional Techniques," unpublished work. University of Michigan, Ann Arbor, Mich.

Activity 2–3

MY AIMS AND PREFERENCES

1. What do you wish to accomplish as a science teacher?
2. Which goals do you see as important outcomes of science instruction? Rank the following in order of importance.
   _____ Develop an understanding of fundamental knowledge of science.
   _____ Develop an understanding of and an ability to use the methods of science.
   _____ Prepare students to make responsible decisions concerning science-related social issues.
   _____ Fulfill the personal needs and development of students.
   _____ Inform students about careers in science.
3. What do you think is important for effective instruction in science? Rank the following in order of importance.
   _____ Knowledge of subject matter.
   _____ Adequacy of personal relations with students.
   _____ Planning and organization of classroom procedures.
   _____ Enthusiasm in working with students.
   _____ Adequacy of teaching methods and strategies.

UNIT 2

....

HISTORICAL PERSPECTIVES AND CONTEMPORARY TRENDS

You might perceive science teaching as a fairly clear and relatively simple process. First you must figure out what the students need to know and be able to do relative to life, earth, or physical science, and then teach them. If you have not already heard, contemporary science education is in the process of reform. We have established goals for all of education, and national, state, and local school districts are implementing standards to help guide the reform. Why should we reform science education and your science teaching if the process is simple and straightforward? Who determines why, when, and if science education should change? Are these decisions determined at the national level, or are they decided by the local school personnel? Teaching science in your classroom represents one small component of a system of science education. That system has a history that shows how it changes due to new scientific discoveries, new insights about students' development and learning, and new issues in society.

Although your primary responsibility as a science teacher rests in the daily organization and presentation of productive learning experiences in your classroom, you also have a professional responsibility to understand science education. In order to appreciate contemporary reform, it is best to develop some historical perspective and view of contemporary science education. In this unit, we present such information and offer a perspective on scientific literacy that you will find helpful as you design lessons and find strategies for teaching science and developing higher levels of scientific literacy among your students.

Developing students' scientific literacy means, in part, helping them to realize that throughout history philosophers and scientists have tried to clarify the process by which scientists generate scientific knowledge. In the seventeenth century, for example, individuals argued that the fundamental source of scientific knowledge was pure observations of nature. Scientists had the obligation to cleanse their minds of any ideas that might interfere with their observations. Thus, if scientists gathered facts and information without bias, they would eventually develop a correct theory. This may sound good until one asks if it is at all possible to observe nature with absolutely no preconceptions, no ideas, and no possible explanation for what is observed. The answer is no.

Over the years, scientists and science educators have proposed other formulations of *the scientific method*. For instance, there is the method often outlined in science textbooks. This method usually includes (1) stating the problem, (2) forming a hypothesis, (3) designing an experiment, (4) collecting data, and (5) forming a conclusion. Scientists generally view such a formula with suspicion. Perhaps this method helps organize the results of scientific investigation, but it does not express the actual process of doing science, which is, in fact, not as neat and orderly.

You can see that science teaching is more than the process of designing learning experience about life, earth, and physical science. It requires perspectives on science education, on science and technology, and on science and technology in society. This is but one example of what it means to help students become more scientifically literate. Chapter three reviews the history of science education and chapter four presents an introduction to the national standards for science education and an overview of scientific literacy.

Chapter 3

HISTORICAL PERSPECTIVES ON SCIENCE EDUCATION

Our society continues to change and science education is a part of that process. The need for change is underscored by the widespread concern about social policies—the debates over abortion, birth, and death; environment, cities, and wilderness; leisure, affluence, and poverty. Weaving through these issues one identifies the recurrent themes of science and technology, ethics and values, education and learning. Present social conditions mandate a rethinking and reformulation of science education policies. The changes that must occur in the next decades will be made by those who are entering the teaching profession as well as those already teaching science. Decisions you will make as a science teacher should be grounded in an understanding of the various forms and functions of science education in society. That is, you should be aware of the history of science education and the present situation in science, society, and science education. You must also realize that the decisions you make about your science curricula, instruction, classroom, and students help define the future.

This chapter has three parts. The first has sections on science teaching in our first and second centuries. In the second section, the golden age of science curriculum is covered. In the third, the view is toward the future and the role of science education in our changing national and global society.

■ THE FIRST TWO CENTURIES OF SCIENCE TEACHING

The First Century: 1776–1875, An Age of National Development

Even before the Declaration of Independence, the social institutions directed major efforts toward developing a nation. Ours was an agricultural society that later was to experience the tremors of industrial and civil revolutions.

In the decades after independence was declared, public education was slowly recognized as a necessary force for socialization. Education at this time was primarily religious and private. In 1779, Thomas Jefferson introduced a bill for educational reform in Virginia. The bill called for free public education for those of "worth and genius." At its base, however, in the Jeffersonian conception, education was designed to maintain social distinctions and a natural aristocracy between "the labour and the learned." In the late eighteenth and early nineteenth centuries, the government began granting land to each new state for public schools and to encourage universal free education. Although each state, county, and township had land, it generally lacked the necessary economic support and public enthusiasm to develop an adequate educational system.

Between 1820 and 1850, in the spirit of Jacksonian democracy, public schools received new support. By 1850, most elementary school children were receiving publicly supported education. The development of public high schools soon followed, so that, with the Jacksonian era, the social institution of public education was established. Later, the 1874 Kalamazoo Decision set the precedent for tax-supported public high schools.

During the late eighteenth and early nineteenth centuries, religious indoctrination decreased and utilitarian objectives increased in schools. With this change science education slowly gained a prominent place in American education.

The earliest forms of science instruction for children have been traced to the stories and didactic literature designed for home tutoring. These materials were based on the theories of John Locke and Jean Jacques Rousseau and emphasized the first-hand study of "things and phenomena" as well as Christian doctrine. Originating about 1750, these materials reached their peak from 1800–1825. With the rise of group instruction, books for home use evolved into textbooks designed for school use. Science was included in many of the lessons, all of which stressed the memorization of factual knowledge, usually supporting theological concepts.[1]

Object teaching, from approximately 1860–1880, was another movement in elementary science education. The primary aim of object lessons was personal development; science subject matter was of secondary importance. A method of teaching based primarily on the ideas of Johann Pestalozzi, this movement has had some impact on American education, but from its inception, it was strongly criticized and seldom fully implemented.

The mid-eighteenth to early nineteenth century marked the period of the academy in secondary level education. As religion ceased to dominate the instructional program, it was replaced with a more practical curriculum, which included some science, such as agriculture and navigation.

Next came the early high schools (circa 1820–1870). The principal objectives of science included learning practical arts and duties of citizenship. Sciences were firmly established in the curriculum during this period, although they were listed as natural philosophy (i.e., physics and chemistry) and natural history (i.e., biology and earth science).

After the Depression of 1873, American schools were severely criticized by citizens asking a question common to such periods: "What are we getting for our money?" As social and economic patterns changed, educators followed with clear demands for more science in the classroom. The aim of science education was to give the public greater understanding of science and technology, the framework of the emerging Industrial Revolution.

The Second Century: 1876–1976, An Age of Industrial Progress

In the first one hundred years of our nation, there were immense changes in the rate and direction of growth in American society. With the transition from an agricultural to an industrial economy, America became a new technological society. After World War II there was the further technological-industrial development of an atomic age. However, as social development continued, negative trade-offs of technological development emerged. Suburban development influenced urban decay; corporate conglomerates increased while small businesses decreased; and we became an affluent society with new minorities of organizational men, lonely crowds, and other Americans. By the 1960s, almost every aspect of public policy—both domestic and foreign—was being severely criticized as basic institutions, including education, were being called on to reform.

Periodically, throughout the century 1876–1976, the schools were asked to make changes that more accurately reflected the realities of our developing society. Committee reports often reveal the nature of these reformations; several from this period will serve as examples of the suggested changes in education.

In 1893, the Committee of Ten[2] stated that all students should be taught the same curriculum whether or not they planned to attend college. The committee detailed such matters as the subjects to be taught and the hours per week and weeks per year to be devoted to each subject. This report helped reduce the domination of colleges over high school programs and formed a stronger connection between high school and elementary school programs. It also stressed academic or intellectual goals.

In 1918, The Commission on the Reorganization of Secondary Education completed its work by publishing *The Cardinal Principles of Secondary Education*.[3] This report called for a shift in the goal of education from the narrower intellectual indoctrination to a broadened socialization of the student. The seven cardinal principles were health, command of fundamental processes, worthy home membership, vocation, civic education, worthy use of leisure, and ethics. School subjects were to be reorganized so that students would more effectively attain these objectives.

The slow but steady recognition of the role of science and technology in developing an industrial society inevitably resulted in a popular interest in science and subsequently in science education. Laboratory instruction was very popular because it contributed to a primary objective of the period: development of reasoning, observation, and concentration.

By 1915, the emphasis in science education shifted to goals broader than those for college entrance. A report of the Central Association of Science and Mathematics Teachers Committee on Unified High School Science Courses,[4] suggested that science should (1) give pupils such a knowledge of nature as will help them get along better in everyday life, (2) stimulate people to more direct purposeful activity, (3) help them choose intelligently for future occupations, (4) give students methods of obtaining accurate knowledge, and (5) enable students to achieve a greater, clearer, and more intelligent enjoyment of life.

College domination of the high school science program was further eroded in 1918 when the cardinal principles were published by the National Education Association, and a report on the reorganization of science in the secondary schools was also published by a subcommittee of the original commission. This report discussed the contributions that science teaching could make to the cardinal principles of secondary education. In general, it stressed the importance of organization and sequencing of secondary science, but it also pointed out social goals beyond the traditional knowledge goals usually stressed in secondary-school science.

By 1924, science teachers used the scientific process as a means to help students learn scientific knowledge. The Committee on the Place of Science in Education of the American Association for the Advancement of Science reported a study on the problems of science teaching. The report underscored the importance of scientific thinking as an objective of teaching. Science instruction, according to the committee, should be founded on scientific observation and experimentation for "a factual basis worthy of the spirit of science."[5]

In 1932, a national survey of secondary education reported on science teaching guides, courses of study, and syllabi. In general, the report stated that the knowledge taught lacked a coherent theoretical structure, that grade-level placement of courses was confusing, and that there was chaos concerning teaching methods. The report also indicated a variety of innovative practices to be considered when constructing new programs. Such considerations included problem methods of teaching, interpretation of the environment, use of illustrative materials, use of demonstrations, coordination of laboratory and textbook work, and greater use of visual aids.

These reports represent the change in values, as seen in science education, from the high ideals and social unity following World War I to the disillusionment of the economic depression of the late 1920s and 1930s.

The Great Depression raised doubts and questions concerning science education. There were two important publications in this period. The National Society for the Study of Education book, *A Program for Science Teaching*,[6] emphasized the importance of broad scientific principles which aid students in a fundamental understanding of nature. The Progressive Education Association publication, *Science in General Education*,[7] stressed progressive goals, such as personal-social relationships, personal living, economic relations, and reflective thinking. The general orientation of science programs was toward the more immediate needs of students; the content was of personal and social significance, and recommendations included programs in health, vocation, and consumerism. The greatest changes were in biology and general science courses, while physics and chemistry courses changed very little.

The period after the Depression was a relatively calm one for science education. The National Society for the Study of Education published *Science Education in American Schools*,[8] with general objectives for science teaching, such as functional information, concepts and principles, skills and attitudes aligned with the scientific method, and the recreational and social values of science. With World War II, America recovered a sense of national purpose, which was reflected in the literature of science education.

After World War II, reports on the American school system stressed life-adjustment education. Examples included the Educational Policies Commission, *Education for All American Youth*,[9] the Department of Secondary School Principals,

Planning for American Youth,[10] and *Life Adjustment Education for Every Youth* published by the Office of Education.[11]

In the 1950s, during another economic recession, schools were again criticized for lacking adequate academic goals.[12,13] The demand was for a return to the basics, emphasis on traditional subjects, and special attention to the gifted. This tide of criticism was aided by the October 1957 launching of Sputnik I, which became the symbol for a major reform in science education. The movement led to the most extensive period of curriculum revision and teacher education in American history. Reform of science curricula was based on a model described by Bruner in *The Process of Education*.[14] Scientific knowledge was the dominant aim, and students used inquiry as the process to acquire knowledge. In Bruner's model, knowledge involved the concepts that formed the structure of a science discipline. In the next section we describe the curriculum materials produced during this period.

By the middle of the 1960s, however, a new group of social critics appealed for a greater understanding of student alienation, identity, and self-concept. The focus in education had shifted from the space race to urban disgrace and by 1976 the tremors of a new reform were felt.

■ THE GOLDEN AGE: SCIENCE CURRICULUM: 1958–1988

In the late 1950s, numerous events contributed to a period in which society focused attention on the Cold War. One aspect included direct competition with the Soviet Union, especially in areas strongly associated with science and technology, for example, nuclear weapons and space exploration.

Although reform of the science curriculum began in the late 1950s, the movement was supported by the Soviet Union's launch of Sputnik I in October 1957. Several years later, in 1961, President John F. Kennedy articulated a national goal when, in a special message to a joint session of Congress, he stated, "I believe that this nation should commit itself to achieving the goal, before this decade is out, of landing a man on the moon and returning him safely to the earth." From the President, the symbol and purpose of this goal was translated into support for science programs that encouraged students to enter careers in science and engineering. The curriculum materials developed and implemented in this period have had tremendous influences on education in general and science education in particular. In the next sections we examine many of the programs developed for junior and senior high schools.

Science Curriculum for the Junior High School

Earth Science

Early in 1963, the American Geological Institute received a grant to implement the Earth Science Curriculum Project (ESCP) in the ninth grade. This course was interdisciplinary, involving geology, meteorology, astronomy, and oceanography. Its emphasis was on laboratory and field study, in which students actively participated in the process of scientific inquiry.

ESCP materials included a textbook, *Investigating the Earth*; the laboratory was augmented by the text, teacher's guide, films, laboratory equipment, maps, and a pamphlet series. After three years of testing and preparation of materials, the course was published commercially.

The Table of Contents from the first edition (1967) included the following chapters.

1. The Changing Earth
2. Earth Materials
3. Earth Measurement
4. Earth Motions
5. Fields and Forces
6. Energy Flow
7. Energy and Air Motions
8. Water in the Air
9. Waters of the Land
10. Water in the Sea
11. Energy, Moisture, and Climate
12. The Land Wears Away
13. Sediments in the Sea
14. Mountains from the Sea
15. Rocks within Mountains
16. Interior of the Earth
17. Time and Its Measurement
18. The Record in Rocks
19. Life—Present and Past
20. Development of a Continent
21. Evolution of Landscapes
22. The Moon: A Natural Satellite
23. The Solar System
24. Stars as Other Suns
25. Stellar Evolution and Galaxies
26. The Universe and Its Origin

The project continued its programs until 1969, when two offshoots, Environmental Studies (ES) and Earth Science Teacher Preparation Project (ESTPP), were initiated to deal specifically with the environmental problems and issues of teacher preparation in the earth sciences.

A serious problem first faced by the ESCP was the preparation of persons qualified to teach the course, but recent efforts in teacher preparation have narrowed the gap between supply and demand. The advances made in the design and implementation of *Investigating the Earth* have been commendable. The text design, integration of concepts from life and physical sciences, and the careful presentation of knowledge, process, and skills were unprecedented. Subsequent revisions of the text have replaced many topics and realigned the book with other standard earth science texts.

Physical Science

Another program developed for the junior high school was the Introductory Physical Science (IPS) program of Educational Services, Incorporated. This project, supported by the NSF, was to develop a one-year course in physical science. Laboratory work and equipment were designed in such a way that students performed the experiments in ordinary classrooms. The Table of Contents of the Introductory Physical Science (IPS) course included the following:

1. Introduction
2. Quantity of Matter: Mass
3. Characteristic Properties
4. Solubility and Solvents
5. The Separation of Substances
6. Compounds and Elements
7. Radioactivity
8. The Atomic Model of Matter
9. Sizes and Masses of Atoms and Molecules
10. Molecular Motion
11. Heat

The IPS course was tested in several centers throughout the United States, and the materials, which included textbooks, teachers' guides, laboratory notebooks, and comprehensive apparatus kits, were eventually made available through commercial sources.

The attractiveness of the IPS course to better-than-average junior high school students was made clear in the results of a test survey of representative IPS students in the 1965–1966 school year.

> In that year, 1,005 ninth-grade IPS students and 400 eighth-grade IPS students took the School and College Abilities Test (SCAT) survey Form, a test of verbal and mathematical ability. The results made it clear that the IPS students were more scholastically able on the average than typical junior high school students in the nation.[15]

As the success of a new course depends on well-qualified teachers, the National Science Foundation supported a program to locate qualified science teachers and to prepare them to instruct other teachers in the use of IPS. The program was quite successful; in IPS workshops, teachers were trained by their peers in the local environment.

Integrated Science

Several other junior high school courses were developed. Among them was the Intermediate Science Curriculum Study (ISCS) financed by the United States Office of Education and National Science Foundation and developed at Florida State University. "The fundamental assumption underlying the ISCS plan is that science at the junior high school level serves essentially a general education function."[16] Three levels were prepared, corresponding to the junior high school grades seven, eight, and nine. Level I for seventh grade was tightly structured. Its title, *Energy, Its Forms and Characteristics,* permitted students to delve into physical science principles by dealing with science in their environment. Level II put the students more on their own in designing experiments and recording and interpreting data. This level dealt with *Matter and Its Composition and Model Building.* Level III for the ninth grade dealt with biological concepts and was designed to use laboratory blocks six to eight weeks long as its basic plan of operation. The ninth grade student was expected to use the concepts and investigative skills acquired in the seventh and eighth grades. All of the class activity in the ISCS course was planned for individualized work, and the teacher's main duty was assisting students to work on their own. No formal lectures or information-dispensing sessions were planned for the course, unless needed on a short-term basis by a small group of students.

An innovative feature of the ISCS course was the production of a complete course on Computer-Assisted Instruction (CAI). Using behavioral objectives and a system of computer feedback, it was possible to obtain detailed information on the progress and problems encountered by each student. This information was used to modify and revise the trial versions of the course.

There were other smaller scale projects for revising junior high school science. Among them were the Interaction Science Curriculum Project (ISCP), Ideas and Investigations in Science (IIS), and a BSCS program *Patterns and Processes in Science.* Each was extensively field tested and met with certain elements of success. It is safe to say that the field of science teaching in the junior high school received an impetus similar to that enjoyed by senior high school teaching.

Science Curriculum for the High School

The high school science curriculum was subject to the forces of reform discussed in the first section of this chapter. That is, changes in society, science, and education all influenced the reform of curriculum. At the high school level, advances in science and technology have traditionally exerted the greatest influence on programs. In this section, we review traditional areas—physics, chemistry, and biology—in light of the major reform during the 1960s and 1970s.

Physics

Physics was first known as *natural philosophy* and appeared in the academies of the early 1700s. Content was organized into topics similar to those of our traditional courses today. Mechanics, fluids, heat, light, sound, magnetism, and electricity were taught, mainly by recitation. The Civil War and the advent of land-grant colleges in the 1860s placed emphasis on military and vocational aspects of science, and the course became known as physics. Laboratory instruction was emphasized. A list of standard experiments, called *The Descriptive List,* was circulated by Harvard in 1886 for use by the high schools. Candidates for admission to Harvard who had taken physics as a prerequisite were then tested by use of these experiments.

Physical Science Study Committee

In 1956, a group of university physicists at Cambridge, Massachusetts, looked at the secondary school physics curriculum and found that it did not present the content or spirit of modern physics. From this group, the Physical Science Study Committee (PSSC) was formed, with the objective of producing a new physics course for the high school level.

In four years this group developed a textbook, laboratory guide, teacher's guide, set of apparatus, monographs, and films. All of these aids were correlated closely with one another to produce an effective curriculum package. In addition, there were many summer institutes for upgrading teachers in physics and in the philosophy of the new course.

Some of the important differences between the PSSC physics course and traditional high school physics became apparent:

- fewer topics covered at greater depth,
- greater emphasis on laboratory work,
- more emphasis on basic physics,
- less attention to technological applications,
- development approach showing origins of basic ideas of physics, and
- increased difficulty and rigor of the course.

Teachers and administrators had conflicting opinions about the merits of the PSSC course. There was general agreement that it was a definite improvement over traditional courses, especially for better-than-average college-bound students. For average or below-average students, its merit was questionable.

In a 1971 study by John Wasik, PSSC students showed significantly higher performance than non-PSSC students in the process skills of application and analysis.[17] On the other hand, non-PSSC students performed at a higher level on the taxonomic process measure of knowledge. Wasik concluded that the results supported the position of new curriculum writers that the PSSC instructional materials were most effective in developing higher cognitive-process skills.

A 1983 analysis of the effects of new science curricula on student performance revealed that the physics curricula was second only to the biology curricula in terms of overall advances in student performances. Studies of achievement and analytic skills showed that students participating in the new physics courses gained at least a half-year more than students in traditional courses.[18] This result indicates that the new physics curricula was successful in achieving part of its stated goals. The goal generally not assessed was the students' perceptions of physics. This omission is unfortunate because it could have given some insights to help slow the long and steady decline in physics enrollments.

Project Physics

A second physics course was designed for the average student. Project Physics, a course produced at Harvard University, attempted to treat physics as a lively and fundamental science, closely related to achievements both in and outside the discipline itself.[19]

Financial support for the project was provided by the Carnegie Corporation of New York, the Ford Foundation, the National Science Foundation, the Alfred P. Sloan Foundation, the United States Office of Education, and Harvard University. Several hundred participating schools throughout the United States tested the course as it went through several revisions.

The philosophy of this course is emphasized in eight points.[20]

1. Physics is for everyone.
2. A coherent selection within physics is possible.
3. Doing physics goes beyond physics.
4. Individuals require a flexible course.
5. A multimedia system stimulates better learning.
6. The time has come to teach science as one of the humanities.
7. A physics course should be rewarding to take.
8. A physics course should be rewarding to teach.

Materials of Project Physics included a textbook, teacher's guide, student guide, experiments, films, transparencies, tests, film loops, readers, and other items. The chapter headings for the Project Physics course were[21]

Unit 1: Concepts of Motion
Unit 2: Motion in the Heavens
Unit 3: The Triumph of Mechanics
Unit 4: Light and Electromagnetism
Unit 5: Models of the Atom
Unit 6: The Nucleus

Several studies attempted to find reasons for the decreasing enrollments in high school physics. In a questionnaire sent by Raymond Thompson to 1,382 high school physics teachers, 79 percent believed that students stayed away because the course was too difficult.[22] Of these students, 40 percent ascribed their reluctance to fear of jeopardizing their grade average and 16 percent attributed it to fear of mathematics.

In a study of 450 physics students enrolled in Project Physics in 1966-1967, Wayne Welch concluded that students received lower grades in physics than in their other courses.[23] In the sample studied the median I.Q. was at the 82nd percentile, but the average grade received by these bright students was in the C+ to B− range. Thus, the students were dissatisfied with their experience.

The course was extensively evaluated during its development. Results were encouraging, both with respect to the performance of Project Physics students on standard tests such as the College Board Examinations and with respect to attracting increasing numbers of high school students to elect physics in their junior or senior years. The percentage of girls taking the course also appeared to have increased over PSSC or traditional physics courses.

Chemistry

The teaching of high school chemistry began in the early 1800s in girls' academies, while the Civil War years gave a stimulus to the course because of military and industrial applications. Laboratory work was increased during the late 1800s, and efforts were made to reproduce many of the classical experiments of early chemists such as Joseph Priestly and Antoine-Laurent Lavoisier. As with physics, Harvard in 1886 placed chemistry on the optional list for college entrance but controlled the quality of entering students by publishing *The Pamphlet*, containing sixty experiments, on which the prospective enrollee was tested in the laboratory. Influence of *The Pamphlet* was profound, and the high school chemistry course became highly standardized. Laboratory workbooks were developed, containing experiments that were mainly exercises in observation and manipulation of chemical reactions.

Chemical Bond Approach

In 1957, a summer conference of chemistry teachers at Reed College in Portland, Oregon, produced a plan for a new type of chemistry course and initiated the Chemical Bond Approach (CBA) Project. There followed a series of writing conferences, use of the new materials by trial schools, and the production of a commercial textbook in 1963. The major theme of this course was the chemical bond, and particular attention was given to *mental models* (conceptual schemes) of structure, kinetic theory, and energy.

The laboratory program and textbook paralleled and reinforced each other. No unusual chemicals or equipment were required, and the cost of conducting the CBA chemistry course was not significantly different from that of conducting conventional courses.

Chemical Education Materials Study

A second course-improvement project in chemistry was initiated at Harvey Mudd College in Claremont, California, in 1959. Called the Chemical Education Materials Study (CHEM), the project developed a course that was strongly based on experiment and included a text and laboratory manual, a teacher's guide, a score of excellent films, and a series of wall charts.

Both the CBA and CHEM Study chemistry programs received grants from the National Science Foundation, which supported numerous inservice and summer institutes for teachers.

Enrollment in CBA and CHEM chemistry classes increased initially. In 1968, approximately 40 percent of high school chemistry taught in the United States was the CHEM Study course.[24] Approximately 10 percent of the schools were using CBA.[25] At this time the CHEM project terminated its work, and commercial publishers were invited to prepare courses based on the philosophy and materials of the CHEM Study course. Several publishers produced high school chemistry textbooks influenced by the philosophies and pedagogies of the CHEM and CBA programs.

In a survey by Frank Fornhoff in 1970, in which 2,395 students were queried, the most widely used high school chemistry textbook was *Modern Chemistry; Chemistry—An Experimental Science* was second, and *Chemical Systems* was third.[26] The latter two texts were CHEM Study and CBA chemistry, respectively. Other information obtained in the study showed that most chemistry classes met five times per week for 40 to 59 minutes, and 13 percent of stu-

dents reported taking a college-level chemistry course in high school.

In a 1978 report it was estimated that fewer than 25 percent of chemistry teachers were using either CHEM Study, CBA approach, or a combination of the two.[27] The same study found that CHEM Study was used in 15 percent of school districts; yet, neither textbook appeared on the list of most commonly used textbooks. A 1983 report on the effects of new curricula found that the new chemistry curricula, both CBA and CHEM Study, produced the least impact in terms of student cognitive achievement and process skills.[28]

Interdisciplinary Approaches to Chemistry

In March 1972 a new chemistry course was developed by the University of Maryland. This was the Interdisciplinary Approaches to Chemistry (IAC). The IAC course approached the teaching of chemistry somewhat differently by using a group of modules dealing with special topics of an interdisciplinary nature. The titles of the modules were:

- Reactions and Reason (Introductory),
- Diversity and Periodicity (Inorganic),
- Form and Function (Organic),
- Molecules in Living Systems (Biochemistry),
- The Heart of the Matter (Nuclear),
- Earth and Its Neighbors (Geochemistry),
- The Delicate Balance (Environmental), and
- Communities of Molecules (Physical).

Among the goals of IAC was the

realization that a student's attitudes or feelings about chemistry are just as important in the long run as his acquisition of special chemical concepts.

Thus, in molding the IAC program, equal emphasis has been placed on providing the student with a sound background in those basic skills and concepts normally found in an introductory high school chemistry course as well as on developing the attitude that chemistry is not a dry, unrealistic science, but an exciting, relevant, human activity that can be enjoyable to study.[29]

There were several characteristics that made the IAC chemistry different from traditional chemistry or previous curriculum projects, with an emphasis on making chemistry more relevant and successful for the student. The program is modular, instead of being a single structured text. Each module is devoted to a different aspect of chemistry and its relationship to the other sciences and society. This format allows for many degrees of flexibility within the program.

A module consists of chemistry content and laboratory experiments integrated into a unified whole. The program includes suggested readings for students, problems and activities, safety precautions, and relevant chemical data, such as periodic tables and charts. Each module deals with a specific area of chemistry as indicated in the titles, relating chemistry to other sciences and phenomena encountered in the natural world.

IAC was revised in 1979 to update its content and teaching techniques in concepts and in laboratory experiments. It was well received by chemistry teachers who enjoy the freedom to experiment with different modules in their classes and to rearrange content in accordance with student and teacher interests.

Research by Robert Stevenson in 1977–1978 on the use of IAC chemistry in high school indicated that age, sex, and attitude had no effect on the achievement level of students; that cognitive-reasoning ability and grade-point averages were highly correlated with achievement success; and that achievement success on the introductory module tests could be used to predict success on subsequent modules.[30]

Biology

In school science programs, biology began in botany, physiology, and zoology courses and in the nineteenth century was patterned after college courses in these subjects. A course of study in biology appeared in New York in 1905, and the College Entrance Examination Board prepared an examination for the course in 1913. Biology was placed either in the ninth or tenth grade.

Of all the high school sciences, biology had the largest enrollment, due to a combination of factors. Placement in the ninth or tenth grade where the effect of school dropouts is less pronounced, the effect of compulsory education laws, the nonmathematical nature of the course, and the general requirement of a minimum of one science course for graduation from high school all combined to increase enrollments over the years. In 1958, approximately 68 percent of tenth-grade students enrolled in the biology course.[31]

Biological Sciences Curriculum Study

The American Institute of Biological Science organized the Biological Sciences Curriculum Study (BSCS) at the University of Colorado in 1958, with Arnold B. Grobman as director. In discussing the design of the course he said:

> A realistic general biology program must take into account a wider range of student ability, interests, and potential than exists in other high school science courses. It must be a course that most tenth-grade students can handle and at the same time prove challenging to the above-average student. For these reasons,

the committee thought it undesirable to limit the course to a single design.[32]

Three courses were developed, based on a molecular approach, a cellular approach, and an ecological approach, respectively. Although the courses differ in emphasis, nine common themes run through them:

1. Change of living things through time-evolution.
2. Diversity of type and unity of pattern of living things.
3. Genetic continuity of life.
4. Biological roots of behavior.
5. Complementarity of organisms and environment.
6. Complementarity of structure and function.
7. Regulation and homeostasis: the maintenance of life in the face of change.
8. Science as inquiry.
9. Intellectual history of biological concepts.[33]

Among the course materials were textbooks, laboratory guides, supplementary readings, and tests. Innovations include laboratory blocks consisting of a series of interlocking and correlated experiments on a special topic of biology. Eleven blocks were developed, including, for example, "Plant Growth and Development," "Microbes: Their Growth and Development," and "Interdependence of Structure and Function." A second-level course was prepared for advanced biology, and a simpler course called *Patterns and Processes in Science* was designed for unsuccessful learners.

Other supplementary materials included excerpts from historical papers, BSCS Invitations to Inquiry, discussion outlines for the laboratory, films on laboratory techniques, the *Biology Teacher's Handbook*, and the BSCS Pamphlet Series.

The BSCS biology courses received a generally favorable response throughout the country. Two versions of the course are still available, and it has been found that different versions are chosen in different regions. Several foreign countries are also using the course.

Research has been done on the effects of BSCS biology in the schools. In one study Kenneth George found that students taking Blue Version scored significantly higher on critical thinking, as measured by the Watson Glaser Critical Thinking Appraisal Form ZM, than did students taking conventional biology.[34] B. J. Adams found that there was no difference in the retention of biological information between BSCS students and those taking traditional biology.[35] However, there were significant relationships between retention and intelligence, reading scores, and teacher grading, with the BSCS students generally scoring higher. Charles Granger and Robert Yager[36] found no significant difference between students experiencing BSCS and non-BSCS backgrounds with respect to achievement in either high school or college-level biology. However, a significantly larger percentage of BSCS students felt their background was better in meeting individual needs, as well as preparing them for college-level biology.[37] Jack Carter and Alan Nakosteen, in a study with 8,500 college freshmen, found that BSCS students scored higher on inquiry and recall items on the BSCS Comprehensive Biology Tests than did students who did a non-BSCS course in high school.[38]

In a 1983 report, BSCS fared very well in the major review of curricula developed in the 1960s and 1970s. Biology curricula showed the greatest effect on student performance, particularly in the area of developing analytic skills. In a 1984 report on the BSCS programs, James Shymansky had this to say:

> We found the new science programs to be consistently more effective than their traditional counterparts. Moreover, we found Biological Sciences Curriculum Study (BSCS) to be the most effective of all the new high school programs.[39]

■ COMMON ELEMENTS OF GOLDEN AGE COURSES

A survey of various course materials developed in secondary school science during the 1960s and 1970s shows close similarity both in types of materials offered and in general objectives. The following common elements can be discerned:

1. There was less emphasis on social and personal applications of science and technology than in the traditional courses.
2. There was more emphasis on abstractions, theory, and basic science—the structure of scientific disciplines.
3. There was increased emphasis on discovery—the modes of inquiry used by scientists.
4. There was frequent use of quantitative techniques.
5. There were newer concepts in subject matter.
6. There was an upgrading of teacher competency in both subject matter and pedagogical skills.
7. There were well integrated and designed teaching aids to supplement the courses.
8. There was little emphasis on career awareness as a goal of science teaching.
9. There was primarily an orientation toward college-bound students.

10. There were similarities in emphasis and structure in the high school and junior high school programs.

■ AN ERA OF EDUCATIONAL REFORM: SCIENCE EDUCATION IN SECONDARY SCHOOLS: 1980–?

The early 1980s represent a turning point in science education. In 1981, Norris Harms and Robert Yager published the results of Project Synthesis, a major effort to evaluate the status of and make recommendations for the future of science education. In a larger context, publication of *A Nation at Risk* in 1983 symbolized the beginning of a wider and deeper national effort to reform education.

The history of American education had never witnessed such widespread calls for educational reform. By the late 1980s, more than 300 reports had admonished those within the educational system to reform. Depending on who published the report, recommendations emphasized such issues as updating scientific and technologic knowledge, applying learning theory and new teaching strategies, improving approaches to achieve equity, and providing better preparation for the workplace.

For science education at the secondary school level, there are significant differences between the 1960s and 1990s reforms. The 1960s reform began at the secondary level and progressed to the elementary level. In the 1990s, reports have generally addressed all levels, K–12, but the specific curriculum reform began at the elementary school level and progressed to secondary schools. The impetus for this sequential reform was initiated by funding from the NSF for new elementary and middle school programs. In the late 1990s educators can anticipate curricular changes at the secondary school level. The important point is that school science programs structured from the top down, from 12th grade physics to elementary programs, are quite different from school science programs that are structured from the bottom up, or when the science curriculum is viewed more holistically as a K–12 continuum.

A second difference between these two decades is that there are fewer curriculum projects at the national level. Reform efforts are being initiated through national standards and benchmarks, as well as state-level frameworks and guidelines, and are being completed through local development of materials. Such efforts have the advantage of higher levels of implementation and the disadvantage of lower levels of actual program reform. These lower levels of reform result from a lack of time and money to develop new materials so, subsequently, school districts adopt textbooks. Additionally, staff development programs to update teachers in science and technology content and innovative teaching strategies are not implemented. The result is a nationwide low level of reform in both quantity and quality.

Science Education in Secondary Science

The science curriculum in secondary schools is largely determined at the state and local levels by science teachers, science supervisors, administrators, and school boards.[40] Recent studies supported by the NSF have shown that even with significant autonomy there is considerable uniformity of science programs nationwide and curriculum and methods of instruction have not changed significantly.[41,42,43]

Science Courses

Typically, the science curriculum is general or earth science at the ninth grade, biology at the tenth grade, and chemistry and physics at the eleventh and twelfth grades, respectively. In 1978, the largest science enrollment in junior high schools was general science, with approximately 5 million students. Another 2 million students in schools with grades 7–12 or 9–12 were also enrolled in general science. Earth science enrollments were approximately 1.25 million. Enrollments did not change substantially in a decade, although they are currently changing more due to the emergence of middle schools.[44] General biology is offered to all students and enrolls approximately 3 million students each year. About 80 percent of graduating seniors have taken high school biology. However, this statistic is misleading and has an important bearing on reform of science education at the secondary level. For 50 percent of high school students who graduate each year, biology is their last experience with any science course. High school chemistry and physics courses are generally perceived as college preparatory, as are the majority of other courses offered in the high school curriculum.

Textbooks

The nature of the high school science curriculum can be determined by examining textbooks for the respective disciplines. The similarity among textbooks for a discipline—and even among textbooks for different disciplines—is remarkable. These characteristics include presenting a significant number of facts in simple and condensed form and an emphasis on extensive vocabulary and technical terms. In addition to being encyclopedic, science texts currently in use implicitly suggest a pedagogy of *inform, verify,* and *practice.* The NSF materials developed in

the 1960s and 1970s espoused goals of understanding conceptual schemes (the structure of disciplines) and using scientific processes (the modes of inquiry); changes in textbooks and, subsequently, teaching evolved in different directions. For example, recent reviews of the inquiry goal in science teaching found that teachers give little attention to inquiry and associated skills.[45]

Student Achievement

The need for contemporary reform is supported by poor student achievement in science. Results from the National Assessment of Educational Progress (NAEP) were summarized in *The Science Report Card.* Following are summaries of achievement for 17-year-olds, that is, those students leaving high school.

1. At age 17, students' science achievement remains well below those of students graduating in 1969. Steady declines occurred throughout the 1970s, followed by an upturn in performance between 1982 and 1986.
2. More than half of the nation's 17-year-olds appear to be inadequately prepared either to perform competently jobs that require technical skills or to benefit substantially from specialized on-the-job training. The thinking skills and science knowledge possessed by these high school students also seem to be inadequate for informal participation in the nation's civic affairs.
3. Only 7 percent of the nation's 17-year-olds have the prerequisite knowledge and skills to perform well in college-level science courses. Because high school science proficiency is a good predictor of whether a young person will elect to pursue postsecondary school studies in science, the probability that many more students will embark on future careers in science is low.

Current programs are not contributing to the two primary goals of science education: contribution to informed citizenship and development of future scientists and engineers. The NAEP results are supported by international assessments.[46,47]

Achievement of Underrepresented Groups

Social and economic realities have influences that far exceed the effect of school in general or a science program in particular. Still, the science program should contribute, in some small measure, to the future opportunities of all students. The NAEP data indicate continued and substantial disparities in science proficiency among groups of differing race, ethnicity, and gender. The following data related to achievement of underrepresented groups in secondary school science are from *The Science Report Card.*

1. Despite recent gains the average proficiency of 13- and 17-year-old black and Hispanic students remains at least four years behind that of their white peers.

2. Only about 15 percent of the black and Hispanic 17-year-olds assessed in 1986 demonstrated the ability to analyze scientific procedures and data, compared to nearly one half of the white students their age.

3. Average proficiency in 9-year-old-boys and girls was approximately the same—except in physical sciences—but the performance gap was evident at age 13 and had increased by age 17 in most science content areas. At age 17, roughly one half of the boys but only one third of the girls demonstrated the ability to analyze scientific procedures and data.

4. The marked edge in the physical sciences shown by boys in the 3rd grade increased in the 7th and 11th grades; by the 11th grade, the performance gap in physics was extremely large.

Causes of these disparities are many and varied; most are beyond the control of school science programs. At a minimum, science programs in secondary schools should not perpetuate initial inequities, and—ideally—curriculum, instruction, and assessment in science should ameliorate any inequities. Reform in textbook design, increased participation in hands-on activities, and use of cooperative learning strategies are three recommendations to improve achievement in underrepresented groups.

Trends in Secondary School Science

There is widespread support for reform of the educational system. The President of the United States and state governors have targeted U.S. science education as No. 1 in the world by the year 2000. Scientific and technological literacy is the main purpose of science education in K–12. This goal is for all students, not just those individuals destined for careers in science and engineering.

The curriculum for science education at the secondary school level is inadequate to the challenge of achieving scientific and technological literacy by the year 2000. Many scientists and science educators are urging a review of school personnel and science programs, a review that would affect millions of school personnel in thousands of autonomous school districts, but one that is necessary. Increasing the scientific and technological literacy of students also requires several fundamental changes in science curricula at the secondary school level. First, the amount of information presented must be replaced by key conceptual themes that are learned in some depth. Second, the rigid disciplinary boundaries of earth science, biology, chemistry, and physics should be softened; greater emphasis should also be placed on connections among the sciences and among disciplines generally thought of as outside of school science, such as technology, mathematics, ethics, and social studies.[48,49]

Achieving the goal of scientific and technological literacy requires more than understanding concepts and processes of science and technology. Indeed, there is some need for citizens to understand science and technology as an integral part of society. Science and technology are enterprises that shape, and are shaped by, human thought and social actions; aspects of this theme are discussed as STS.[50] The prevailing approach to STS is to focus on science-related social problems such as environmental pollution, resource use, and population growth. Our recommendation expands the STS theme to include some understanding of the nature and history of science and technology. There is recent and substantial support for this recommendation, though few curriculum materials. Including the nature and history of science and technology provides opportunities to focus on topics that blur disciplinary boundaries and show connections between such fields as science and social studies.

The substantial body of research on learning should be the basis for making instruction more effective. This research suggests that students learn by constructing their own meaning of the experiences they have.[51,52,53] A constructivist approach requires very different methods of science instruction in the secondary school.

Related to the implications of research on learning theory is the age-old theme that science teaching should consist of experiences exemplifying the spirit, character, and nature of science and technology. Students should begin with questions about the natural world (science) and problems about human beings adapting (technology). They should be actively involved in the processes of inquiry and problem solving. They should have opportunities to present their explanations for phenomena and solutions to problems and to compare their explanations and solutions to those concepts of science and technology. And, they should have a chance to apply their understandings in new situations. In short, the laboratory is an infrequent experience for secondary school students, but it should be a central part of their experience in science education. Extensive use of the laboratory is consistent with the other recommendations made in this section, and it has widespread support.

During the 1990s, the issue of equity must be addressed in science programs and by school personnel. For the past several decades, science educators at all levels have discussed the importance of changing science programs to enhance opportunities for historically underrepresented groups. Calls for scientific and technological literacy assume the inclusion of *all* Americans. Other justifications—if any are needed for this position—include the supply of future scientists and engineers, changing demographics, and prerequisites for work. Research results, curricula recommendations, and practical suggestions are available to those developing science curricula for the secondary school.[54–58]

Science education in middle schools is a special concern as educators look toward the year 2000. Numerous reports and commissions have addressed the need for education reform for high school science education, but few have specifically recognized the emergence of middle schools in the 1980s. Notable exceptions include the Carnegie Corporation report *Turning Points: Preparing Youth for the 21st Century*,[59] the California State Department of Education report *Caught in the Middle*,[60] the Maine Department of Educational and Cultural Services report *Schools in the Middle*,[61] and the National Association of Secondary School Principals report *An Agenda for Excellence at the Middle Level*.[62] The movement toward implementing middle schools, and phasing out junior high schools, is a significant trend in education. Yet, thus far, the middle school reform has not thoroughly addressed the particular issues of subject-matter disciplines—in this case, science and technology. Contemporary reform must not allow the science education of early adolescents to be overlooked or assumed to be part of either the elementary school or secondary school curriculum.

Improving curriculum and instruction by the year 2000 will be a hollow gesture without concomitant changes in assessment at all levels, from the local classroom to the NAEP. In general, the changes in assessment practices must reflect the changes described earlier for curriculum and instruction. Incongruities, such as teaching fewer concepts in greater depth but testing for numerous facts in fine detail, will undermine the reform of science education. New forms of assessment are available and being recommended by researchers, policymakers, and practitioners.[63–66]

Reform of science education at the secondary school level must be viewed as part of the general reform of education. Approaching the improvement of science education by changing textbooks, buying new computers, or adding new courses simply will not work. Fortunately, widespread educational reform, which includes science education, is under way. The improvement of science education in the secondary school must be part of the reconstruction

of science education for K–12 and include all courses and students, a staff development program, reform of science teacher preparation, and support from school administrators. This comprehensive or systemic recommendation is based on the research on implementation[67,68] and research literature on school change and restructuring.[69–72]

Looking toward the year 2000 leaves science educators viewing a system already in the process of reform. Though distinctly different from earlier reforms, this reform holds greater promise of accomplishing the goals of scientific and technological literacy for all Americans.

■ SUMMARY

The need for changes in high school science programs became increasingly evident mid-way through the twentieth century. A number of forces produced conditions that affected the curriculum. The rapid increase in scientific knowledge, the competitive nature of the race for space, technological advancements in teaching tools, a gradual dissatisfaction with the encyclopedic approach to the teaching of science, and new understandings of student learning and development combined to encourage changes.

The first secondary science curriculum course to react to these pressures was physics, followed by chemistry, biology, and junior high science, in that order. New courses for all these subjects appeared, stimulated by massive financial support from the National Science Foundation and other agencies.

Students of the investigative sciences were given opportunities for increased laboratory work and application of inquiry methods for learning. They were directed to better understandings of how scientists work and how knowledge is obtained.

The reform reached farther than the materials developed under National Science Foundation grants. Authors of popular science textbooks incorporated many aspects of the new science materials.

In the late 1960s and early 1970s, problems in urban environments began to influence science programs. By the middle 1970s, a new set of social forces redirected the attention of science educators: population, pollution, energy shortages, economic problems, and resource shortages.

This brief historical survey has shown the changes in science education resulting from the needs and demands of society. It seems that there is a clear relationship between social needs and the type of curricula and instruction that science educators are called on to provide in our schools. The major social pressures have been the early development of a nation, growth of an industrial-technological society, demands of a depressed economy, emergence of an atomic age, start of the space race, and the recent appearance of alienation and anxiety.

■ REFERENCES

1. O. E. Underhill, *The Origins and Development of Elementary-School Science* (New York: Scott Foresman, 1941).

2. Committee on Secondary School Studies, *Report of the Committee of Ten on Secondary Studies* (Washington, DC: National Education Association, 1983).

3. Commission on the Reorganization of Secondary Education, "Cardinal Principals of Secondary Education," *U.S. Bureau of Education Bulletin 35* (Washington, DC: U.S. Bureau of Education, 1918).

4. "Report of the Central Association of Science and Mathematics Teachers Committee on the Unified High School Science Course," *School Science and Mathematics 15*(4) (1915): 334.

5. O. Caldwell, "Report of the American Association for the Advancement of Science, Committee on the Place of the Sciences in Education," *Science 60* (1924): 536.

6. National Society for the Study of Education, *A Program for Science Teaching* (Chicago: University of Chicago Press, 1932).

7. Progressive Education Association, *Science in General Education* (New York: Appleton-Century-Crofts, 1938).

8. National Society for the Study of Education, *Science Education in American Schools* (Chicago: University of Chicago Press, 1947).

9. National Education Association and American Association of School Administrators, Educational Policies Commission, *Education for All American Youth: A Further Look* (Washington, DC: National Education Association and the American Association of School Administrators, 1952).

10. National Education Association, Department of Secondary School Principals, *Planning for American Youth* (Washington, DC: National Education Association, 1946).

11. United States Office of Education, *Life Adjustment Education for Every Youth* (Washington, DC: U. S. Government Printing Office, 1951).

12. A. Bestor, *Educational Wastelands: A Retreat from Learning in Our Public Schools* (Urbana: University of Illinois Press, 1953).

13. H. Rickover, *Education and Freedom* (New York: Random House, 1970).

14. Jerome Bruner, *The Process of Education* (New York: Vintage, 1960).

15. *Introductory Physical Science—Physical Science II: A Progress Report* (Newton, MA: IPS Group, Education Development Center, 1968), p. 16.

16. David D. Redfield and Stewart P. Darrow, *The Physics Teacher, 8* (April 1970,): 170–180.

17. John L. Wasik, "A Comparison of Cognitive Performance of PSSC and Non-PSSC Students," *Journal of Research in Science Teaching, 8*(1) (1971): 85–90.

18. James A. Shymansky, William Kyle, and Jennifer Alport, "The Effects of New Science Curricula on Student Performance," *Journal of Research in Science Teaching, 20*(5) (1983): 387–404.

19. Harvard Project Physics, Newsletter no. 1 (Cambridge: Harvard University Press).

20. Harvard Project Physics, Newsletter no. 7 (Cambridge: Harvard University Press).

21. Harvard Project Physics, Newsletter no. 10 (Cambridge: Harvard University Press).

22. Raymond E. Thompson, "A Survey of the Teaching of Physics in Secondary Schools," *School and Society, 98* (1970): 243–244.

23. Wayne W. Welch, "Correlates of Course Satisfaction in High School Physics," *Journal of Research in Science Teaching, 6* (1969): 54–58.

24. J. David Lockard, ed., *Seventh Report of the International Clearinghouse on Science and Mathematics Curricular Developments* (College Park: Science Teaching Center, University of Maryland, 1970), p. 305.

25. Gordon Cawelti, "Innovative Practices in High Schools: Who Does What—and Why—and How," *Nation's Schools, 79* (1968): 36–41.

26. Frank J. Fornoff, "Survey of the Teaching of Chemistry in Secondary Schools," *School and Society, 98* (1970): 242–243.

27. Iris Weiss, *Report of the 1977 National Survey of Science, Mathematics and Social Studies Education* (Washington, DC: U.S. Government Printing Office, March 1978).

28. Shymansky et al., "The Effects of New Science Curricula," pp. 387–404.

29. IAC Newsletter (College Park: Chemistry Department, University of Maryland) *2*(1) (January 1973): 3.

30. Robert Stephenson, "Relationships between the Intellectual Level of the Learner and Student Achievement in High School Chemistry" (Ph.D. dissertation, University of Northern Colorado, 1978).

31. Kenneth Brown and Ellsworth Obourn, *Offerings and Enrollments in Science and Mathematics in Public High Schools, 1958* (Washington, DC: U. S. Government Printing Office, 1961).

32. Quoted in American Association for the Advancement of Science, *The New School Science: A Report to School Administrators on Regional Orientation Conferences in Science*, Publication no. 63-6 (Washington, DC: 1963), p. 27.

33. *The New School Science*, p. 29.

34. Kenneth D. George, "The Effect of BSCS and Conventional Biology in Critical Thinking," *Journal of Research in Science Teaching, 3* (1965): 293–299.

35. B. J. Adams, "A Study of the Retention of Biological Information by BSCS Students and Traditional Biology Students" (Ed.D. dissertation, Colorado State College, 1968).

36. Charles R. Granger and Robert E. Yager, "Type of High School Biology Program and Its Effect on Student Attitude and Achievement in College Life Science," *Journal of Research in Science Teaching, 7* (1970): 383–389.

37. James Shymansky, "BSCS Programs: Just How Effective Were They?" *The American Biology Teacher, 4*(4) (1984): 54–57.

38. Jack L. Carter and Alan R. Nakosteen, "Summer: A BSCS Evaluation Study," *The Biological Sciences Curriculum Study, 42* (February, 1971).

39. Shymansky et al., "The Effects of New Science Curricula," pp. 387–404.

40. Rolf, 1989.

41. Ina V. Mullis and Lynn B. Jenkins, *The Science Report Card: Elements of Risk and Recovery* (Princeton, NJ: Education Testing Service, September 1988).

42. Iris Weiss, *Report of the 1977 National Survey of Science, Mathematics, and Social Studies Education* (Washington, DC: U. S. Government Printing Office, March, 1977).

43. Iris Weiss, *Report of the 1985–86 National Survey of Science and Mathematics Education* (Research Triangle Park, NC: Research Triangle Institute, 1987).

44. R. W. Bybee, C. E. Buchwald, S. Crissman, D. R. Heil, P. J. Kuerbis, C. Matsumoto, and J. D. McInerney, *Science and Technology Education for the Middle Years: Frameworks for Curriculum and Instruction* (Washington, DC: The National Center for Improving Science Education, 1990).

45. K. Costenson and A. Lawson, "Why Isn't Inquiry Used in More Classrooms?" *The American Biology Teacher, 48*(3) (1986): 150–158.

46. National Assessment of Educational Progress (NAEP), *Science Objectives: 1990 Assessment* (Princeton, NJ: Educational Testing Service, 1989).

47. International Association for the Evaluation of Educational Achievement (IEA), *Science Achievement in Seventeen Countries* (New York: Pergamon Press, 1988).

48. J. Confrey, "A Review of the Research on Student Conceptions in Mathematics, Science, and Programming," in *Review of Research in Education,* C. B. Cazden, ed. (Washington, DC: The American Educational Research Association, 1990): pp. 3–56.

49. F. M. Newmann, "Can Depth Replace Coverage in the High School Curriculum?" *Phi Delta Kappan, 69*(5) (1988): 345–348.

50. R. W. Bybee, "Science Education and the Science-Technology-Society (STS) Theme," *Science Education, 71*(5) (1987): 667–783.

51. R. Driver and V. Oldham, "A Constructivist Approach to Curriculum Development in Science," *Studies in Science Education, 13* (1986): 105–122.

52. T. P. Sachse, "Making Science Happen," *Educational Leadership, 47* (3) (1989): 18–21.

53. B. Watson and R. Konicek, "Teaching for Conceptual Change: Confronting Children's Experience," *Phi Delta Kappan, 71*(9) (1990): 680–685.

54. M. M. Atwater, "We Are Leaving Our Minority Students Behind." *The Science Teacher* (May 1986): 54–58.

55. A. L. Gardner, C. L. Mason, and M. L. Matyas, "Equity, Excellence, and 'Just Plain Good Teaching', " *The American Biology Teacher, 51*(2) (1989): 72–77.

56. M. C. Linn and J. S. Hyde, "Gender, Mathematics, and Science," *Educational Researcher, 18*(8) (1989): 17–19; 22–27.

57. S. M. Malcom, "Who Will Do Science in the Next Century?" *Scientific American, 262*(2) (1990): 112.

58. J. Oakes and the Rand Corporation, "Opportunities, Achievement, and Choice: Women and Minority Students in Science and Mathematics," in *Review of Research in Education,* C. B. Cazden, ed. (Washington, DC: The American Educational Research Association, 1990):, pp. 153–222.

59. Carnegie Council on Early Adolescents, *Turning Points: Preparing American Youth for the 21st Century* (New York: Carnegie Corporation of New York, 1989).

60. California State Department of Education, *Caught in the Middle* (Sacramento, CA: Author, 1987).

61. Maine Department of Educational and Cultural Services, *Schools in the Middle* (Augusta, ME: Author, 1988).

62. National Association of Secondary School Principals, *An Agenda for Excellence at the Middle Level* (Washington, DC: Author, 1985).

63. J. R. Frederiksen and A. Collins, "A Systems Approach to Educational Testing," *Educational Researcher, 18*(9) (1989): 27–32.

64. R. Murnane and S. Raizen, *Improving Indicators of the Quality of Science and Mathematics Education in Grades K–12* (Washington, DC: National Academy Press, 1988).

65. W. L. Roueche III, N. Sorensen, and C. Roueche, "Strategies to Verify the Essential Elements in Secondary Science. An alternative approach to involve students," *The Clearing House, 62*(2) (1988): 65–73.

66. R. J. Shavelson, N. B. Carey, and N. M. Webb, "Indicators of Science Achievement: Options for a Powerful Policy Instrument." *Phi Delta Kappan, 71*(9) (1990): 692–697.

67. M. Fullan, *The Meaning of Educational Change* (New York: Teachers College Press, Columbia University, 1982).

68. G. E. Hall, "Changing Practice in High School: A Process Not an Event," in *High School Biology: Today and Tomorrow,* W. G. Rosen, ed. (Washington, DC: National Academy Press).

69. P. Kloosterman, J. Matkin, and P. C. Ault, "Preparation and Certification of Teachers in Mathematics and Science" *Contemporary Education, 59*(3) (1988): 146–149.

70. D. A. Roberts and A. M. Chastko, "Absorption, Refraction, Reflection: An Exploration of Beginning Science Teacher Thinking," *Science Education, 74*(2) (1990): 197–224.

71. K. Tobin and M. Espinet, "Impediments to Change: Applications of Coaching in High School Science Teaching," *Journal of Research in Science Teaching, 26*(2) (1989): 105–120.

72. H. Yeany and M. J. Padilla, "Training Science Teachers to Utilize Better Teaching Strategies: A Research Synthesis," *Journal of Research in Science Teaching, 23*(2) (1986): 85–95.

Chapter 4

....

NATIONAL STANDARDS AND SCIENTIFIC LITERACY

In this chapter we introduce the National Science Education Standards Project.[1] We begin with background on the project and then review the project's major goals through a discussion of scientific literacy and the social orientation of national standards. We then summarize the components of the National Science Education Standards Project. Next, we review Project 2061 and reports on *Science for All Americans*[2] and *Benchmarks for Science Literacy*.[3] Both the standards and benchmarks have had, and will continue to have, a major influence on science education at national, state, and local levels. Your career as a science teacher will be affected by the national standards and by the Project 2061 documents.

■ BACKGROUND ON NATIONAL STANDARDS

The National Council of Teachers of Mathematics (NCTM) introduced the word *standards* into the public dialogue on education when they published the *Curriculum and Evaluation Standards for School Mathematics* in 1989. This statement of the profession's vision for what students ought to know and be able to do as a result of their mathematics education identified professional goals and provided a means of helping teachers of mathematics achieve them.

In the late 1980s and 1990s, politicians in the U. S. expressed their intense interest in improving education. This was symbolized by the National Education Goals created by President George Bush and the nation's governors, with leadership from then-governor Bill Clinton, in their unprecedented summit in 1989. The *National Education Goals* panel established the idea of standards in different subject matters and performance-based assessments. These bipartisan *National Education Goals* were the basis for the Goals 2000: Educate America Act signed by President Clinton in 1994 (see Figure 4–1 for a summary of these goals). As a science teacher, you will be especially interested in goals three and four.

When the National Council on Educational Standards and Testing (NCEST) reported on the merit and feasibility of national standards and assessments, the NCTM Standards provided the existence of proof that NCEST needed. National standards define high expectations, not minimal competencies; they set

FIGURE 4–1
The National Education Goals
In stressing quality education from early childhood through lifelong learning, the President and the Governors adopted the National Education Goals, which became law in 1994 when Congress passed the Goals 2000: Educate America Act

The Goals state that by the year 2000:
- All children in America will start school ready to learn.
- The high school graduation rate will increase to at least 90 percent.
- All students will leave grades 4, 8, and 12 having demonstrated competency over challenging subject matter, including English, mathematics, science, foreign languages, civics and government, economics, arts, history, and geography; and every school in America will ensure that all students learn to use their minds well, so they may be prepared for responsible citizenship, further learning, and productive employment in our nation's modern economy.
- United States students will be first in the world in mathematics and science achievement.
- Every adult American will be literate and will possess the knowledge and skills necessary to compete in a global economy and exercise the rights and responsibilities of citizenship.
- Every school in the United States will be free of drugs, violence, and the unauthorized presence of firearms and alcohol and will offer a disciplined environment conducive to learning.
- The nation's teaching force will have access to programs for the continued improvement of their professional skills and the opportunity to acquire the knowledge and skills needed to instruct and prepare all American students for the next century.
- Every school will promote partnerships that will increase parental involvement and participation in promoting the social, emotional, and academic growth of children.

focus and direction, not a national curriculum; they are national, not federal; they are voluntary, not mandatory; and they are dynamic, not static.

The National Science Education Standards Project

In the spring of 1991, Dr. Bonnie Brunkhorst, the President of the National Science Teachers Association (NSTA), acting on the basis of a unanimous vote of the NSTA Board, wrote to the Chairman of the National Research Council (NRC). She requested the NRC to convene and coordinate a process leading to national science education standards, K–12. This was seconded by the presidents of several leading science and science education associations, as well as the U. S. Secretary of Education, the Assistant Director of Education and Human Resources at the NSF, and the co-chairs of the *National Education Goals* panel. The NRC agreed to take the lead, and the U. S. Department of Education provided initial funding. Throughout that autumn the NRC developed a general design and time line for the project, and Dr. James Ebert, Vice President of the National Academy of Sciences, was designated chair of a National Committee on Science Education Standards and Assessment (NCSESA). His job was to oversee both development of science education standards and a nationwide critique and consensus process. In early 1994, Dr. Richard Klausner of the National Institutes of Health assumed Dr. Ebert's responsibilities.

As 1992 began, a Chair's Advisory Committee was formed. Consisting of representatives of several national science education organizations, it worked to assist in planning and directing the project. This group participated directly in the process of identifying and recruiting staff.

Early in the project, staff and committee members decided to develop an integrated volume containing content, teaching, and assessment standards, all displayed in mutually reinforcing ways. Another decision committed the working group chairs to function as a team throughout the project. A third decision involved a serious and extensive critique and consensus process, which would issue frequent updates on the project and materials suitable for intense critique by teachers, educators in colleges and universities, scientists, engineers, policy makers, and others interested in science education. The project released discussion and working papers in October and December of 1992, February 1993, and June 1993. The first integrated draft of content, teaching, assessment, program, and system standards appeared for extensive review in late 1994, and the *National Science Education Standards* were published in 1995.

■ NATIONAL SCIENCE EDUCATION STANDARDS: AN OVERVIEW

National standards in science education have several functions depending on who is using them and the purpose for which they are being used. For example, standards can serve as vision, aspiration, and attainment; they also can be used as measures to judge the quality of current science education and criteria to design school science programs.

The National Science Education Standards offer a coherent vision of what it means to be scientifically literate. The standards describe what *all* students must understand and be able to do as a result of their cumulative learning experiences. The standards also provide criteria for judgments regarding programs, teaching, assessment, policies, and initiatives that can provide opportunities for all students to learn in ways that are aligned with the standards. *National* means a nationwide agreement, not a federal mandate, on what defines successful science learning and the school practices that support the learning. National standards neither define a national curriculum nor are a form of national standardization.

The eight categories of content standards are displayed in Figure 4–2. The first seven categories have standards for grade levels K–4, 5–8, and 9–12. The final category crosses all grade levels. Within each of the areas represented in Figure 4–2, there are fundamental understandings. The content described in the standards does *not* represent a science curriculum. Curriculum includes not only the content, but also the structure, organization, balance, and presentation of the content. The selection of the fundamental concepts in these standards was based on the following criteria: it represents scientific ideas; it has rich explanatory power; it guides fruitful investigations; it applies to situations and contexts common to everyday experiences; it can be linked to meaningful learning experiences; and it is developmentally appropriate for students at the grade level specified. We elaborate the content in more detail in later chapters.

Unifying Concepts and Processes
Science as Inquiry
Physical Science
Life Science
Earth and Space Science
Science and Technology
Science in Personal and Social Perspectives
History and Nature of Science

FIGURE 4–2
National Science Education Standards: **Science Content**

Science as Inquiry should be recognized as a basic and controlling standard in the curriculum organization and in students' science education experiences. This standard highlights the ability to do inquiry and the fundamental concepts about scientific inquiry that students should develop. The emphasis on inquiry moves beyond the processes of science and emphasizes the students' cognitive development based on critical thinking and scientific reasoning required in the use of evidence and information to construct scientific explanations.

Physical, Life, and *Earth and Space Science* standards express the traditional subject matter of science. This subject matter focuses on those science concepts, principles, and theories that are fundamental for all students.

The *Science and Technology* standard establishes useful connections between the natural world and the designed world and offers essential decision-making abilities. This standard has two components. One emphasizes the development of abilities associated with technological design and problem solving. The second centers on developing understanding about the similarities and differences between science and technology, and their respective influences within society.

The standard on Science in Personal and Social Perspectives connects the students with their social and personal world. It helps students understand health, populations, resources, environments, and natural hazards that will enable them to fulfill their obligations as citizens.

The standard on the *History and Nature of Science* includes an understanding of the nature of science and uses history in school science programs to clarify different aspects of science in society, the human aspects of science, and how scientific advances occur.

The *Unifying Concepts and Processes* standard provides students with powerful ideas that help them understand the natural world. These conceptual and procedural schemes are integral to any school science program and students' learning experiences in science. The understanding and abilities associated with this standard should be developed over the entire K–12 continuum.

Teaching standards identify the characteristics of and provide a vision for good science teaching. Those standards are organized into two sections: The first centers on practice (teaching standards), and the second centers on how teachers master their practice (professional development standards). The teaching standards are criteria for judging the quality of teaching in the science classroom. They describe roles and responsibilities in the areas listed in Figure 4–3.

Science assessment standards identify essential characteristics of fair and accurate student assessments and provide criteria for judging the quality of assessment at the classroom, district, state, and national levels. The definition of assessment includes not only familiar tests but also a range of strategies for collecting and interpreting information about student attainment, teacher performance, and the work of educational institutions. Assessment standards are not tests, and they do not describe a single strategy to judge student learning or a school science program. Figure 4–4 displays standards for assessment in science.

Program standards describe how content, teaching, and assessment are coordinated in school practice over a range of school experience to provide all students the opportunity to learn science. They describe criteria for judging the quality of a K–12 science program.

System standards for science education guide the policies that must be implemented and the alignments that must be pursued by policy makers and others in order to support science learning described in the standards. System standards also address the essential functions that serve to build and sustain the capacities demanded by the standards of teachers and school communities.

■ NATIONAL STANDARDS, SOCIAL COMMITMENTS, AND SCIENTIFIC LITERACY

The National Science Education Standards define the level of understanding of science that all students, regardless of background, future aspirations, or interest in science, should develop. The standards embody the belief that all students can learn science. These standards encourage all students—including members of populations defined by race, ethnicity, economic status, gender, and physical and intellectual capacity—to study science throughout their school years and to pursue careers in science. By adopting the goal of science for all, the standards will promote the participation of all students in challenging opportunities to learn science. They will also define a level of necessary comprehension.

The standards forcefully advocate the inclusion of those who traditionally have not received encouragement and opportunities to learn science—women and girls, all racial and ethnic groups, the physically and educationally challenged, and those with limited proficiency in English—as well as those who have traditionally made achievements in science.

Various methods of learning and different sources of motivation are accommodated because the curriculum, teaching, and assessment standards take into account the diversity of the student population, disparate interests, motivation, experience, and ways of understanding science. The standards define criteria

FIGURE 4–3
Standards for Science
Teachers

- **Teachers of science plan an inquiry-based science program for their students.** In doing this, they:
  - develop a framework of year-long and short-term goals for students;
  - select science content and adapt and design curricula to meet the interests, knowledge, understanding, ability, and experiences of students;
  - select teaching and assessment strategies that support the development of student understanding and nurture a community of science learners; and
  - work together as colleagues within and across disciplines and grade levels.

- **Teachers of science guide and facilitate science learning.** In doing this, they:
  - focus and support inquiries as they interact with their students;
  - orchestrate discourse among students about scientific ideas;
  - challenge students to accept and share responsibility for their own learning;
  - recognize and respond to student diversity and encourage all students to participate fully in science learning; and
  - encourage and model the skills of scientific inquiry as well as the curiosity, openness to new ideas and data, and skepticism that characterize science.

- **Teachers of science should engage in ongoing assessment of their teaching and of student learning.** In doing this, they:
  - use multiple methods to systematically gather data about student understanding and ability;
  - analyze assessment data to guide teaching;
  - guide students in self-assessment;
  - use student data, and observations of teaching, and interactions with colleagues to reflect on and improve teaching practice; and
  - use student data, and observations of teaching, and interactions with colleagues to report student achievement and opportunities to learn to students, teachers, parents, policy makers, and the general public.

- **Teachers of science should design and manage learning environments that provide students with the time, space, and resources needed for learning science.** In doing this, they:
  - structure the time available so that students are able to engage in extended investigations;
  - create a setting for student work that is flexible and supportive of science inquiry;
  - ensure a safe working environment;
  - make the available science tools, materials, print, media, and technological resources accessible to students;
  - identify and use resources outside the school; and
  - engage students in designing the learning environment.

- **Teachers of science develop communities of science learners that reflect the intellectual rigor of scientific inquiry and the attitudes and social values conducive to science learning.** In doing this, they:
  - display and demand respect for the diverse ideas, skills, and experiences of all students;
  - enable students to have a significant voice in decisions about the content and context of their work, and require students to take responsibility for the learning of all members of the community;
  - nurture a collaboration among students;
  - structure and facilitate ongoing formal and informal discussion based on a shared understanding of rules of scientific discourse; and
  - model and emphasize the skills, attitudes, and values of scientific inquiry.

- **Teachers of science actively participate in the ongoing planning and development of the school science program.** In doing this, they:
  - plan and develop the school science program;
  - participate in decisions concerning the allocation of time and other resources to the science program; and
  - plan and implement professional growth and development strategies for themselves and their colleagues.

FIGURE 4–4
Standards for Assessment in Science

- **Assessments are consistent with the decisions they are designed to inform.**
  - Assessments are deliberately designed.
  - Assessments have explicitly stated purposes.
  - The relationship between the decisions and the data should be clear.
  - Assessments procedures are internally consistent.

- **Science achievement and opportunity to learn science must both be assessed.**
  - Achievement data collected focus on the science content that is most important for students to learn.
  - Opportunity-to-learn data collected focus on the most powerful indicators of the students' opportunity to learn.
  - Equal attention must be given to the assessment of opportunity to learn and to the assessment of student achievement.

- **The technical quality of the data collected is well matched to the consequences of the decisions and actions taken on the basis of their interpretation.**
  - The feature that is claimed to be measured is actually measured.
  - Assessment tasks are authentic.
  - An individual student's performance is similar on two or more tasks that claim to measure the same aspect of student achievement.
  - Students have adequate opportunity to demonstrate their achievements.
  - Assessment tasks and methods of presenting them provide data that are sufficiently stable to lead to the same decisions if used at different times.

- **Assessment practices must be fair.**
  - Assessment tasks must be reviewed for the use of stereotypes, for assumptions that reflect the perspectives or experiences of a particular group, for language that might be offensive to a particular group, and for other features that might distract students from the intended task.
  - Large-scale assessments must use statistical techniques to identify differential performance among subgroups that signal potential bias.
  - Assessment tasks must be appropriately modified to accommodate the needs of the students with physical disabilities, learning disabilities or limited English proficiency.
  - Assessment tasks must be set in a variety of contexts, engaging to students with different interests and experiences, and must not assume the perspective or experience of a particular gender, racial, or ethnic group.

- **The inferences made from assessments about student achievement and opportunity to learn must be sound.**
  - When making inferences from assessment data about student achievement and opportunity to learn science, explicit reference needs to be made to the assumptions on which the inferences are based.

for high-quality instructional experiences that engage all students in the full range of science content. These experiences teach the nature and processes of science. In addition to the subject matter they will reinforce the belief that people of diverse backgrounds can engage and participate in science. They will uphold the premise that all students have a claim on understanding science as a common human heritage.

The *National Science Education Standards* present an explicit definition of scientific literacy. School science education contributes to the broader goals of education by providing students with a scientific understanding of the natural world through knowledge of the basic concepts of science, scientific modes of inquiry, the nature of the scientific endeav-

or, and the historical, social, and intellectual contexts within which science is practiced. The ability to apply such scientific knowledge to aspects of one's personal and civic life is referred to as *scientific literacy*.

The goals of school science education include the preparation of students who understand

- a limited number of the basic concepts of science and the fundamental principles, laws, and theories that organize the body of scientific knowledge and can apply them,
- the modes of reasoning embodied in scientific inquiry and can use them,
- the nature of the scientific endeavor and its ways of knowing, laws, and theories,

- the history of scientific development; the relationships between science and technology; and the historical, cultural, and social contexts in which this relationship is embedded.

In order to support and develop the broad social goals of education, school science must attend to students' understanding of scientific knowledge and provide opportunities for them to practice using that knowledge. Therefore, school science programs must provide experiences that

- are personally and socially relevant;
- call for a wide range of knowledge, methods, and approaches to analyze personal and societal issues critically;
- encourage students to act in ways that reflect their understanding of the impact of scientific knowledge on their lives, society, and the world;
- encourage students' appreciation of the scientific endeavor and their excitement and pleasure in its pursuit; and
- develop in students an appreciation of the beauty and order of the natural world.

Few school science programs in the United States offer these experiences. Very few learners come close to demonstrating these understandings and abilities. Notice that these statements identify both goals and provide recommendations for achieving those goals, while allowing for a diversity in approaches and teaching styles. Eventually, science teachers such as you will have to transform these general policies into actual curriculum materials and teaching practices.

■ DEVELOPING SCIENTIFIC LITERACY

Your goal as a science teacher is developing scientific literacy. Most directly, this goal applies to your students, but it also applies to your professional colleagues, parents, and community. In this section, we first elaborate the idea of scientific literacy and then establish the connection between the general idea of scientific literacy and your specific need to teach students science in a manner that helps them to become more scientifically literate.

Background on Scientific Literacy

In the first chapter, we introduced *scientific literacy* as the term used to express the major purposes of science education. In fact, we went a step beyond this definition and suggested that you could define some aspects of scientific literacy by answering the question, "What should the scientifically and technologically literate person know, value, and do—as a citizen?" In answering this question you should note

several things. First, the question includes both science and technology. Second, the question includes knowledge, values, and skills. Third, and very important, the question directs one to justify the answer in terms of citizenship.

In the history of science education, many individuals have addressed the goals of science teaching and the idea of scientific literacy.[4, 5] In Tables 4–1, 4–2, and 4–3, we present discussions of scientific literacy so you can see what others have included in the translation of the idea to actual topics or themes for school science programs. These tables summarize various views of scientific literacy over a thirty-year period from 1960 to the 1990s.

Scientific literacy expresses general education purposes of a science education. The goal represents an orientation of the science curriculum and instructional practices that includes experiences and outcomes for all students. You should contrast the general education orientation with a specific or vocational education that would orient school science programs toward the knowledge, values, and skills required in scientific and technologic careers.

You should note the domains of scientific literacy described in Table 4–3. These domains parallel content in the *National Science Education Standards* and the *Benchmarks for Science Literacy*. In Table 4–4, we summarize the content from these two documents. This summary of two reports provides a contemporary description of the domains of scientific literacy.

The Domains of Scientific Literacy

Clearly, scientific literacy includes *more* than the knowledge, values, and skills associated with a specific discipline such as biology or chemistry. Concepts associated with scientific disciplines must be included, but students also should develop understandings and abilities associated with scientific inquiry and technological design, as well as understandings associated with personal and social aspects of science, the history and nature of science, and major unifying ideas of the sciences. In later chapters we provide more specific details of the national standards and benchmarks, including content information. Table 4–5 should help clarify the different domains of content associated with scientific literacy. We adapted the model for this framework from original work of Mortimer Adler and the *Paideia Proposal*.[6] Also note that the content parallels the *National Science Education Standards* and, with some modification of titles, *Benchmarks for Science Literacy*.

The framework for scientific literacy (see Table 4–5) depicts three columns, each with a distinctive orientation for content. As the elements of this

TABLE 4–1
Some characteristics of scientific literacy: the 1960s

National Science Teachers Association *Theory into Practice (1964)* *Conceptual Schemes*	*National Science Teachers Association* *Theory into Practice (1964)* *Processes of Science*	*Milton Pella (1967)*
(1) All matter is composed of units called *fundamental particles;* under certain conditions these particles can be transformed into energy and vice versa. (2) Matter exists in the form of units which can be classified into hierarchies of organizational levels. (3) The behavior of matter in the universe can be described on a statistical basis. (4) Units of matter interact. The basis of all ordinary interactions are electro-magnetic, gravitational, and nuclear forces. (5) All interacting units of matter tend toward equilibrium states in which the energy content (enthalpy) is a minimum and the energy distribution (entropy) is most random. In the process of attaining equilibrium, energy transformations or matter transformations occur; nevertheless, the sum of energy and matter in the universe remains constant. (6) One of the forms of energy is the motion of units of matter. Such motion is responsible for heat and temperature and for the states of matter: solid, liquid, and gaseous. (7) All matter exists in time and space, and since interactions occur among its units, matter is subject in some degree to changes with time. Such changes may occur at various rates and in various patterns.	(1) Science proceeds on the assumption, based on centuries-old experience, that the universe is not capricious. (2) Scientific knowledge is based on observation of samples of matter that are accessible to public investigation in contrast to purely private inspection. (3) Science proceeds in a piecemeal manner, even though it also aims at achieving a systematic and comprehensive understanding of various sectors or aspects of nature. (4) Science is not, and will probably never be, a finished enterprise, and there remains much more to be discovered about how things in the universe behave and how they are interrelated. (5) Measurement is an important feature of most branches of modern science because the formulation, as well as the establishment, of laws are facilitated through the development of quantitative distinctions.	(1) Interrelationships between science and society (2) Ethics of science (3) Nature of science (4) Conceptual knowledge (5) Science and technology (6) Science in the humanities

TABLE 4–2
Some characteristics of scientific literacy: the 1970s

Michael Agin *(1974)*	*Victor Showalter* *(1974)*	*Benjamin Shen* *(1974)*
(1) Science and Society (2) Ethics of Science (3) Nature of Science (4) Knowledge of the Concepts of Science (5) Science and Technology (6) Science and the Humanities	(1) Nature of Science (2) Concepts in Science (3) Processes of Science (4) Values of Science (5) Science and Society (6) Interest in Science (7) Skills Associated with Science	(1) Practical Science Literacy (2) Civic Science Literacy (3) Cultural Science Literacy

TABLE 4–3
Some characteristics of scientific literacy: the 1980s

National Science Teachers Association, Science-Technology- Society: Science Education for the 1980s (NSTA, 1982)	*National Commission on Excellence in Education, A Nation at Risk (NCEE, 1983*	*Improving Indicators of the Quality of Science and Mathematics Education in Grades K–12, (Murname & Raizen, 1988)*	*American Association for the Advancement of Science, Science for All Americans (AAAS, 1989)*
(1) Scientific and technological process and inquiry skills (2) Scientific and technological knowledge (3) Skills and knowledge of science and technology in personal and social decisions (4) Attitudes, values, and appreciation of science and technology (5) Interactions among science-technology-society via context of science-related societal issues	(1) Concepts, laws, and processes of physical and biological sciences (2) Methods of scientific inquiry and reasoning (3) Applications of knowledge to everyday life (4) Social and environmental implications of scientific and technological development	(1) The nature of the scientific world view (2) The nature of the scientific enterprise (3) Scientific habits of mind (4) Science and human affairs	(1) The nature of science (2) The nature of mathematics (3) The nature of technology (4) The physical setting (5) The living environment (6) The human organism (7) Human society (8) The designed world (9) The mathematical world (10) Historical perspectives (11) Common themes (12) Habits of mind

TABLE 4–4
Content summary for the *National Science Education Standards* and *Benchmarks for Science Literacy*

National Science Education Standards	*Benchmarks for Science Literacy*
Unifying Concepts and Processes Science as Inquiry Physical Science Life Science Earth and Space Science Science and Technology Science in Personal and Social Perspectives History and Nature of Science	The Nature of Science The Nature of Mathematics The Nature of Technology The Physical Setting The Living Environment The Human Organism Human Society The Designed World The Mathematical World Historical Perspectives Common Themes Habits of Mind

TABLE 4–5
A framework for the content of scientific literacy

Goal	Acquisition of Organized Knowledge	Development of Intellectual Abilities and Manipulative Skills	Enlarged Understanding of Ideas and Values
Domains of Content	*In the Areas of* Subject Matter Physical Science Life Science Earth Science Unifying Concepts Nature of Science and Technology	*In the Processes of* Scientific Inquiry and Technological Design	*In the Areas of* Personal Matters Social Challenges Historical Perspectives Cultural Perspectives

framework might be translated to curriculum and instruction, you should recognize that all three columns are essential to the development of scientific literacy. You might also note the parallel between the earlier question—"What should the technologically literate person know, value, and do as a citizen?"—and the three different columns. We suggest that the development of scientific literacy includes the acquisition of organized knowledge, the development of intellectual skills and manipulative abilities, and the enlarged understanding of ideas and values.

Column one centers on the acquisition of knowledge in five domains—physical sciences, life sciences, earth sciences, unifying concepts in the sciences, and the nature of science and technology. We emphasize the point that these are domains of knowledge and not necessarily the curriculum or courses of study for middle and high school science. In fact, the science curriculum should include content from all three columns and may have an emphasis on social challenges, inquiry, or an integrated approach to science content.[7]

Why these five domains of science content? There are several reasons. First, these domains, especially the physical, life, and earth sciences, have a tradition as branches of the sciences. These are generic in that more specific branches, such as particle physics and molecular biology, could be included but are not emphasized for educational purposes. Unifying concepts include scientific ideas, such as Isaac Newton's laws of force and motion, the laws of thermodynamics governing energy and entropy, and the atomic structure of matter that can provide connection among the traditional subject matter domains. Science teachers can use the unifying concepts to show the interconnectedness and interdependence among the sciences and to develop understanding of the larger theories of science. Unifying concepts become especially useful in many research studies and in developing explanations for such things as social challenges and health issues. Science education programs traditionally have not done very much to help students understand the nature of science and technology, yet this understanding (or lack of it) relates to many discussions of

---

- **Identify questions and concepts that guide scientific investigations.** Students should formulate a testable hypothesis and demonstrate the logical connections between the scientific concepts guiding a hypothesis and the design of an experiment. They should demonstrate procedures, a knowledge base, and conceptual understanding of scientific investigations.
- **Design and conduct scientific investigations.** This requires an introduction to conceptual areas of investigation, proper equipment, safety precautions, assistance with methodological problems, recommendations for use of technologies, clarification of ideas that guide the inquiry, and scientific knowledge obtained from sources other than the actual investigation. The investigation may also include such abilities as identification and clarification of the question, method, controls, and variables, the organization and display of data, the revision of methods and explanations, and the public presentation of the results and the critical response from peers. Regardless of the scientific investigations and procedures, students must use evidence, apply logic, and construct an argument for their proposed explanation.
- **Use technology to improve investigations and communications.** Students' ability to use a variety of technologies, such as hand tools, measuring instruments, and calculators, should be an integral component of scientific investigations. The use of computers for the collection, analysis, and display of data is also a part of this standard.
- **Formulate and revise scientific explanations and models using logic and evidence.** Student inquiries should culminate in formulating an explanation or model. In the process of answering the questions, students should engage in discussions and arguments that result in the revision of their explanations. These discussions should be based on scientific knowledge, the use of logic, and evidence from their investigation.
- **Recognize and analyze alternative explanations and models.** This standard emphasizes the critical abilities of analyzing an argument by reviewing current scientific understanding, weighing the evidence, and examining the logic, thus revealing which explanations and models are better and showing that although there may be several plausible explanations, they do not all have equal weight. Students should appeal to criteria for scientific explanations in order to determine which explanations are best.
- **Communicate and defend a scientific argument.** Students in school science programs should develop the abilities associated with accurate and effective communication, including writing and following procedures, expressing concepts, reviewing information, summarizing data, using language appropriately, developing diagrams and charts, explaining statistical analysis, speaking clearly and logically, constructing a reasoned argument, and responding to critical comments through the use of current data, past scientific knowledge, and present reasoning.

FIGURE 4–5
Abilities of scientific inquiry

- **Identify a problem or design an opportunity.** Students should be able to identify new problems or needs and have the ability to change and improve current technological designs.
- **Propose designs and choose between alternative solutions.** Students should demonstrate thoughtful planning for a piece of technology or technique.
- **Implement a proposed solution.** A variety of skills can be needed depending on the type of technology that is involved. The construction of artifacts can require the skills of cutting, shaping or forming, treating, and joining common materials, such as wood, metal, plastics, and textiles.
- **Evaluate the solution and its consequences.** Students should test any solution against the needs or criteria it was designed to meet. At this stage students may review new criteria not originally considered.
- **Communicate the problem, process, and solution.** Students should present their results in a variety of ways, such as orally to other students, in writing, and in a variety of forms, including models, diagrams, and demonstrations.

FIGURE 4–6
Abilities of technological design

the role, limits, and possibilities of science and technology in society.

Second, you will notice that these domains provide linkage between the national standards and benchmarks. Finally, we wish to underscore the importance of students acquiring scientific knowledge as a part of developing scientific literacy. Some educators have interpreted the constructivist approach as acceptance of students' explanations as scientific. This view fails to recognize the body of knowledge recognized as science and to view scientific literacy as the students' development of explanations more closely aligned with those we recognize as scientific.

Column two emphasizes the development of skills and abilities associated with scientific inquiry and technological design. If you examine the national standards for *Science as Inquiry* and *Science and Technology,* you will notice the specific cognitive abilities related to inquiry and design (see Figures 4–5 and 4–6).

Using science as the example, abilities include applying science processes (observing, inferring, experimenting, classifying, controlling variables), constructing scientific explanations (interpreting data, using critical thinking and logic to link evidence to explanation, formulating models, defining operationally), recognizing alternative explanations (maintaining an open mind, accepting the tentative nature of explanations, being skeptical), and communicating (reading, writing, speaking, listening).

If column one is know-about, column two is know-how. In column two, the learning outcomes indicate that students know how to do scientific investigations and technologic problem solving. The skills and abilities proposed in column two have very close connections with the domains of science outlined in column one. Developing scientific literacy includes developing the intellectual skills and abilities outlined in column two. If we wish students to acquire and use these skills, they must have experience doing investigations in science classrooms. That is to say, these skills must be practiced as a part of the students' science education. The method of teaching these skills cannot be lecture; rather, students must be engaged in investigations, and the science teacher should act as a coach, helping students to acquire the best techniques, pointing out strengths and weaknesses, giving directions, demonstrating the right moves, and sequencing actions to achieve a goal.

The innovative aspect of this domain consists of having students engage in inquiry and design. Most evidence indicates that students do not have many such experiences in their science education.[8] From your point of view as a science teacher, implementing the standards implies innovations through combinations of such teaching strategies as good coaching.

The content in column three provides important contexts for teaching and learning science. Recall that scientific literacy places science in the context of history, society, and individual decisions. The content of column three engages students in content that provides meaning for science knowledge and intellectual skills. It is here, as students encounter the personal and social contexts of science, that they will recognize the ideas and values of science and further develop, or enlarge, their own ideas and values. The development of understanding occurs because students have to use their knowledge and skills to respond to the proposed challenges of understanding science and technology in their own lives, in societal problems, in historical periods, and in different cultures.

The content of column three serves the purpose of developing scientific literacy because the topics require students to use the intellectual skills and scientific knowledge as they examine and analyze various positions. They become aware of their own ideas and values of science and technology. In order to help fulfill the requirements of citizenship, the content of column three requires students to correct misconceptions and improve their understanding of science and technology.

In this discussion we have tried to show you how the three columns represent an integrated approach to the development of scientific literacy. As you translate the content outlined in the framework to curriculum and instruction, you should implement all three columns.

The Dimensions of Scientific Literacy

You should recognize developing scientific literacy as a life-long goal for all individuals. Many discussions of scientific literacy use the terms and various domains we have described as a goal that one achieves or does not. It is the either/or, all-or-none position you so often hear. You will find it much more helpful to recognize that all of your students occupy positions somewhere on a continuum of literacy for various scientific concepts. It also seems clear that one can associate different levels of understanding with scientific concepts. For example, students might correctly spell and use the word *cell* in a simple sentence. However, the same students might not recognize several other important concepts about cells, for example that they convey information and reproduce. Further, what if you asked these students about the function of cells in cancer and they indicated that they had no idea about the relationship? Well, what would you say—are these students scientifically literate? If you look at the situation using a strict definition of literacy, one would have to say they are scientifically literate for this life science topic. What about the fact that the same students did not understand the structure and function of cells or the fact that cells have a role in cancer? It might be easier to use the either/or approach to scientific literacy, but it will probably not be very helpful deciding what to do to further these students' understanding of cells and other domains of science.

Your task as a science teacher is to help students to advance their scientific understandings and abilities. In order to help you, we provide a model of different dimensions of scientific literacy. In the following descriptions you should note that these dimensions are not developmental levels, nor do we intend to suggest that they represent a teaching sequence. We repeat, these are different dimensions of scientific literacy that you should be aware of, as they do relate to your decisions about how to structure lessons and units for your classes and how to respond to individual students who indicate a lack of understanding.

Scientific Illiteracy

In this model some individuals may be scientifically illiterate because of age, stage of development, or impaired cognitive abilities. These students are small in number, and for various reasons, will probably not be in your science classroom. The indicator of scientific illiteracy is the fact that they cannot relate to or respond to a reasonable question about science. They do not have the vocabulary, concepts, contexts, or cognitive capacity to identify the question as scientific.

Nominal Scientific Literacy

Suppose you begin a lesson on force and soon discover that students' statements about force indicate that they think force is a property of the moving object. They make statements such as, "A moving object has a force inside it, that is what makes it move." You try to introduce the idea that force is not a property of an object, but forces are characteristics of action between objects. Still, the students' ideas persist. These students exemplify nominal scientific literacy for the concept of force. The example is taken from *Making Sense of Secondary Science*.[9] The students understood the topic as scientific, but the level of understanding clearly indicates a misconception. You should recognize that such examples will be evident in your class and that they will usually express the students' current understanding.

Functional Scientific Literacy

Students may know scientific terms through other science classes, television, or reading. Students can memorize appropriate definitions of terms, and in this sense have some scientific knowledge, but they have limited knowledge and lack a full scientific understanding. Science textbooks and programs that exclusively emphasize rote memorization lead to functional levels of scientific literacy. Unfortunately, this has been the emphasis of many science textbooks and classrooms, and the result is emphasis on only one dimension of scientific literacy. Teaching that emphasizes functional scientific literacy leaves students with little or no understanding of the discipline, no experience with the excitement of inquiry, and probably little interest in science.

Conceptual and Procedural Scientific Literacy

In this dimension students develop some understanding of the conceptual schemes of a discipline related to the whole discipline. They begin to understand the central ideas of matter, energy, and motion in physical sciences and evolution in biological sciences.

FIGURE 4–7
Dimensions of scientific literacy

Nominal Scientific Literacy

- Identifies terms, questions, as scientific but demonstrates incorrect topics, issues, information, knowledge, or understanding.
- Misconceptions of scientific concepts and processes.
- Inadequate and inappropriate explanations of scientific phenomena.
- Current expressions of science are naive.

Functional Scientific Literacy

- Uses scientific vocabulary.
- Defines scientific terms correctly.
- Memorizes technical words.

Conceptual and Procedural Scientific Literacy

- Understands conceptual schemes of science.
- Understands procedural knowledge and skills of science.
- Understands relationships among the parts of a science discipline and the conceptual structure of the discipline.
- Understands organizing principles and processes of science.

Multidimensional Scientific Literacy

- Understands the unique qualities of science.
- Differentiates science from other disciplines.
- Knows the history and nature of science disciplines.
- Understands science in a social context.

Procedural abilities and understandings include the processes of scientific inquiry and technological design. Students actually have ability and understand that scientific inquiry includes asking questions, designing scientific investigations, using appropriate tools and techniques, developing explanations and models using evidence, thinking critically and logically about the relationship between evidence and explanation, recognizing alternative explanations, and communicating scientific procedures and explanations.

Multidimensional Scientific Literacy

This perspective of scientific literacy incorporates an understanding of science that extends beyond the concepts of scientific discipline and procedures of scientific investigation. It includes philosophical, historical, and social dimensions of science and technology. Here students develop some understanding and appreciation of science and technology as they have been and are a part of the culture. Students begin to make connections within scientific disciplines, between science and technology, and between science and technology and the larger issues of social challenges.

Although a number of individuals have presented frameworks for scientific literacy that incorporate the dimensions just described,[10, 11, 12, 13] two examples dominate the contemporary scene in science education, the *National Science Education Standards* and the *Benchmarks for Science Literacy*. Figure 4–7 summarizes the dimensions of scientific literacy.

■ SUMMARY

National Science Education Standards provides the qualitative criteria and framework for judging science programs (content, teaching, and assessment) and the policies necessary to support them. Among other things the standards define the understanding of science that all students, without regard to background, future aspirations, or prior interest in science, should develop; present criteria for judging science education content and programs at the K–4, 5–8, and 9–12 levels, including learning goals, design features, instructional approaches, and assessment characteristics; include all natural science sciences and their interrelationships, as well as the connections with technology, social science, and history; provide criteria for judging models, benchmarks, curricula, and learning experiences developed under the guidelines of ongoing national projects, or under state frameworks, or local district, school, or teacher-designed initiatives; and provide criteria for judging teaching, the provision of opportunities to learn (including such resources as instructional materials and assessment methods) and science education programs at all levels.

The national standards provide a broad view of scientific literacy, one that includes all students. Although the effort encompasses the entire nation, the *National Science Education Standards* honor the diversity of school districts, schools, and science teachers. Science teachers such as you can use many means to achieve the standards and the primary goals of developing higher levels of scientific literacy for all citizens.

■ REFERENCES

1. National Research Council (NRC), *National Science Education Standards* (Washington, DC: Author, 1995). Discussion of the national standards is based on a draft completed in 1995. The final document may have minor differences when compared with statements and figures in this and other chapters.
2. American Association for the Advancement of Science, *Science for All Americans: A Project 2061 Report on Goals in Science, Mathematics, and Technology* (Washington, DC: Author, 1989).
3. American Association for the Advancement of Science, *Benchmarks for Science Literacy* (Washington, DC: Author, 1993).
4. G. E. DeBoer, *A History of Ideas in Science Education* (New York: Teachers College Press, 1991).
5. R. W. Bybee and G. E. DeBoer, "Goals and the Science Curriculum." in *A Handbook of Research on Science Teaching and Learning*, Dorothy Gabel, ed. (Washington, DC: National Science Teachers Association, 1993).
6. Mortimer Adler, *The Paideia Proposal: An Educational Manifesto* (New York: Macmillan, 1982).
7. D. Roberts, Developing the Concept of "Curriculum Emphasis" in Science Education. *Science Education, 66*(2) (1982): 243–260.
8. K. Costenson, and A. E. Lawson, "Why Isn't Inquiry Used in More Classrooms?" *The American Biology Teacher,* 48(3) (1986): 150–158.
9. R. Driver, A. Squires, P. Rushworth, and V. Wood-Robinson, *Making Sense of Secondary Science: Research into Children's Ideas* (New York: Routledge, 1994).
10. M. O. Pella, G. T. O'Hearn and C. W. Gale, Referrents to Scientific Literacy. *Journal of Research in Science Teaching, 4*(1966): 199–208.
11. M. Agin, Education for Scientific Literacy: A Conceptual Frame of Reference and Some Applications. *Science Education, 58*(1974): 3.
12. V. Showalter, What Is Unified Science Education? Program Objectives and Scientific Literacy. *Prism II, 2*(1974): 1–6.
13. R. J. Murname and S. A. Raizen, eds., *Improving Indicators of the Quality of Science and Mathematics Education in Grades K–12* (Washington, DC: National Academy Press, 1988).

UNIT 3

GOALS AND OBJECTIVES

A thirty-year veteran science teacher, Jim Jefferson continually demonstrated the characteristics often associated with effective teaching. He knew the content of science, he used different instructional strategies, he efficiently managed the classroom, he was enthusiastic, and he had a good rapport with students. Jim's activity as a science teacher impressed everyone. He used discussions with students to gently challenge their ideas, he would help them formulate new ideas, and he always asked them to justify their ideas. Jim's teaching revealed a consistency that few noticed. It required extended observations in a variety of classrooms for even the careful observer to see the patterns. Jim's science teaching had an underlying framework that informed his pedagogical decisions.

We asked Jim about his approach to science teaching.

> I think of science education as consisting of knowledge and abilities related to science and the application of science to personal and social issues. These might be the big goals. I also think of scientific literacy as having several different dimensions. These goals provide frameworks that help me make decisions about the structure and content of my interaction with students. In teaching biology I keep major conceptual schemes from the *National Science Education Standards* and *Benchmarks for Science Literacy* in mind; for example, I try to keep ideas like evolution of living systems, genetic continuity, energetics, biosphere and interdependence in mind. I also know that students have to develop more specific terms and ideas, such as carrying capacity and limiting factors, gene regulation and DNA, and metabolism. Students need to know the terms *and* they need to see how the terms relate to big ideas in biology. Not only that, they need to see how the whole discipline of biology connects to other sciences and the student's life and social issues. I realize this is a lot, but you don't have to teach all of this at once, you teach a little at a time by making sure the students have meaningful experiences.
>
> Let me say that the same ideas apply when I emphasize scientific inquiry. I try to get students to clarify their questions, obtain data using the best methods they can, and then develop their answer to the question. I know this emphasis is different from just teaching biological knowledge. I cannot emphasize the importance of inquiry enough. Students should be able to formulate a testable hypothesis and demonstrate the connections between the science concepts that guide the investigation's design. At sometime in a student's experience in secondary school science, students should design and conduct a full scientific investigation. Every lesson does not have to be a full investigation, but I really think this is the best way to develop both the abilities of scientific inquiry and the understandings about scientific inquiry. In other lessons I try to incorporate different aspects of the inquiry goal. Sometimes it is as simple as asking a question about another student's explanation, sometimes it involves asking students to explain the connection between evidence and explorations, sometimes I ask students to explain what scientists have said about the topic. I think all of this contributes to students' understanding, and, for me, this emphasis on inquiry is one of the most exciting goals of science teaching.

Jim used this framework to help organize his science program and to guide his daily interactions with students. He also let the students know when he was emphasizing concepts or inquiry and when he was trying to get them to understand the nature of science or interaction between science and society. Whatever the goals, Jim seemed to know how to organize, emphasize, and present science. Even when students would take him off track, he returned to his goals and objectives.

Jim's teaching demonstrated constant variation, but there was a consistent structure. He knew his goals and what he was trying to accomplish with any individual lesson. Jim responded to the difficulty of concepts and the current conception of students with his repertoire of teaching strategies. We would say that, among other things, Jim Jefferson had a clear view of the goals of science education and the objectives of particular science lessons.

Chapter 5

THE GOALS OF SCIENCE TEACHING

You should begin this chapter by completing an activity concerning the goals of science teaching. Do Activity 5–1 "Goals of Science Teaching" at the end of this chapter.

Science teachers continuously reexamine the goals and objectives of their programs. "Which units will I teach this year?" "What new topics shall I introduce?" Questions such as these, and the answers, are the bases of revised goals and changes in science programs. Only the individual science teacher knows the variables that must be evaluated in the decision-making process. "What is my budget?" "What are the abilities and attitudes of my students?" "What are my interests?" "What was the students' response to last year's units?" "What new ideas did I get from the NSTA convention I attended?" There are, of course, other questions, but these examples illustrate how goals are revised by the individual.

In the next two chapters we are not using the terms *goals* and *objectives* synonymously. There is a clear distinction. Goals are broad statements that give a general direction to a science curriculum and classroom instruction. Because they are broad goals have the advantage of relating to many aspects of science, society, and education, and, simulta-neous-ly, of giving some direction to classroom planning and instruction. The disadvantage of goals is precisely that they are too broad for specific direction concerning grade levels, science subjects, and personal aims and preferences of science teachers. It is necessary to reformulate goals into objectives that are appropriate for each science teacher. Although goals and objectives differ, they are logically related in that objectives are derived from goals.

■ BASIC GOALS OF SCIENCE EDUCATION

As you found in the introductory activity, there are many goals of science teaching. By using the simple criteria listed below, most goals can be summarized into a few categories.

1. Goals should be comprehensive enough to include the generally accepted aims and objectives of science teaching.
2. Goals should be understandable for other teachers, administrators, and parents.

3. Goals should be neutral; that is, free of bias and not oriented toward any particular view of science teaching.
4. Goals should be few in number.
5. Goals should differ in concepts and abilities from each other.
6. Goals should be easily applicable to instructional and learning objectives.

Science teachers use a small number of goals when they construct lessons or design curricula. If you are interested in the role of goals in the history of science education, you may wish to read *A History of Ideas in Science Education*[1] and "Research on Goals for the Science Curriculum" by Rodger Bybee and George De Boer in *Handbook of Research on Science Teaching and Learning*.[2]

Using the aforementioned criteria, the following goals of science education have been identified: scientific knowledge, scientific methods, social issues, personal needs, and career awareness. You probably recognize many of the goals in the introductory activity as relating to these categories. Many objectives can be deduced from these goals, but keep in mind that at any time all of the goals are not equally important. Still, they have been the goals underlying science curriculum and instruction.

1. *Scientific Knowledge.* There is a body of knowledge concerning biological, physical, and earth systems. For over 200 years, our science education programs have aimed toward informing students of these natural systems. This goal has been, and will no doubt continue to be, of significant importance for science teachers. Stated formally, this goal is: *Science education should develop fundamental understandings of natural systems.*
2. *Scientific Methods.* A second goal has centered on the abilities and understandings of the methods of scientific investigation. Descriptions of the goal have changed; for example, the terms *inquiry* and *discovery* have been used to describe the scientific methods goal. The goal can be stated as: *Science education should develop a fundamental understanding of, and ability to use, the methods of scientific investigation.*
3. *Societal Issues.* Science education exists in society and should contribute to the maintenance and aspirations of the culture. This goal is especially important when there are social challenges

directly related to science. This goal is: *Science education should prepare citizens to make responsible decisions concerning science-related social issues.*

4. *Personal Needs.* All individuals have needs related to their own biological/psychological systems. Briefly stated this goal is: *Science education should contribute to an understanding and fulfillment of personal needs, thus contributing to personal development.*

5. *Career Awareness.* Scientific research, development, and application continue through the work of individuals within science and technology and through the support of those not directly involved in scientific work. Therefore, one important goal has been: *Science education should inform students about careers in the sciences.*

■ SCIENCE EDUCATION GOALS AND PROGRAMS: PRELUDE TO REFORM

In the late 1970s, three national surveys were conducted in an attempt to assess the status of science education: *The Status of Pre-College Science, Mathematics, and Social Science Education,*[3] *Report of the 1977 National Survey of Science, Mathematics, and Social Studies Education,*[4] and *Case Studies in Science Education.*[5] The following discussion is based on an extensive review of these studies.[6] In addition, Paul DeHart Hurd's review, "The Golden Age of Biological Education: 1960–1975," in *Biology Teachers Handbook* (3rd Edition)[7] and the *1976–1977 National Assessment of Education Progress—Science*[8,9] were used.

This review of goals is especially important in that it is a landmark in the history of science education. These studies present the first major national assessment of science education. We shall first describe a general review of science education and then discuss the specific goals outlined earlier.[10]

■ AN OVERVIEW OF GOALS FOR SCIENCE EDUCATION

We can get some understanding of science education by examining the longstanding goals described earlier: scientific knowledge, scientific methods, societal issues, personal needs, and career awareness. In the period 1955–1975, these goals were in transition. Between 1975 and 1995, the science education community reformed the goals. Publication of *Science for All Americans,*[11] *Benchmarks for Science Literacy,*[12] and the *National Science Education Standards*[13]

clearly sets new goals for science education. The following discussion describes the status of goals in 1975–1995 and suggests the direction of change.

Scientific Knowledge

Science programs are primarily oriented toward knowledge of the academic disciplines. In the classroom, knowledge goals become the scientific facts, concepts, and principles which reflect the structure of science. Science teachers report that they want their students to understand the subject matter of science. For example, they want the students to know scientific concepts and definitions of scientific words, and to develop problem-solving and critical thinking skills. Understanding science is generally interpreted as passing a test.

Scientific Method

There is little effort by science teachers to realize the goal of understanding and using the methods of science. For example, science teachers do not use questioning techniques or instructional procedures that facilitate systematic inquiry.

There is positive evidence indicating that students attain an understanding of scientific inquiry as a process, develop essential inquiry skills, and are able to use these skills to improve their ability to think critically about science-related problems.

There are several influencing factors in widespread implementation of the scientific methods goal. First, science teachers are neither *model inquirers* for their students, nor have they been educated in methodologies of scientific research. Second, most science teachers lecture for more than 75 percent of the classtime, leaving students few opportunities to ask questions. Third, inquiry as a goal of science teaching is generally not seen as productive and is not accepted by most science teachers. Fourth, teachers who are aware of scientific methods as a goal of teaching feel that only bright, highly motivated students can profit from inquiry teaching. Fifth, inquiry teaching is seen by teachers as time-consuming, thus reducing the time available for basics, that is, learning facts and getting so-called right answers. The current improvement of science education and national support for the goal of scientific inquiry should change the emphasis on this goal.

Societal Issues

Increasing interest in science literacy and societal goals is evident in science programs. Science teachers are including these goals to make science relevant to the concerns of all students.

The goals for teaching science indicate more emphasis on environmental concepts, world problems, decision making, and interdisciplinary studies—all areas related to the goal of teaching students how to deal with societal issues. *National Science Education Standards* are having a direct impact on state and local frameworks for science education. State departments of education are influencing changes in goals through their legislative and regulatory powers, such as specific requirements to include energy conservation, environmental problems, health, alcohol and drugs, nature study, and outdoor education in educational programs.

Personal Needs

School personnel and parents express their concerns about meeting the personal needs of students through science education. This rhetoric takes the form of life-and-work and school-to-work skills related to science, the preparation ethic, and vocational or career education. In response, science courses often emphasize things that are seen as useful in everyday living. It appears, however, that the goal of fulfilling personal needs is not generally emphasized.

Attempts to meet personal needs are made primarily through health or advanced placement courses. Some of the other goals, such as career awareness, overlap with these courses. Sometimes personal needs are met as a secondary effect of another goal. A socially relevant course on environmental education may provide fundamental knowledge that stimulates students to examine the life worth living.

The goal of meeting personal needs has always been subordinate in science education programs, especially when compared to goals such as knowledge. In the past ten years, the goal of fulfilling students' personal needs has become increasingly important. This goal is closely related to both career and societal goals.

Career Awareness

One of the currently important goals of science education is to provide information and training that will be useful in future employment. Recent increased emphasis on this goal is due in part to public opinion. The career-awareness goal was found to be constant across science programs, although not the primary goal of science education. What mattered most was the scientific and technological knowledge needed for the next course and whether all the courses were eventually related to one's future job.

There is some resistance to implementing the career goal in science education. There are several issues that emerge. Teachers and communities have questioned whether the school should serve labor needs; that is, whether the school should help prepare for work. They have questioned the apparent conflict between work of the school and the world of work. Science teachers are unwilling to sacrifice the scholastic program to help youth prepare for jobs. When teachers, parents, and science coordinators were asked about vocational goals of science courses, they all agreed that these goals should be included—however, the majority selected general education goals over vocational goals.

The inclusion of career goals in science programs has been increasingly important over the decades 1970–1990, undoubtedly because of continuing economic instability and associated realities of unemployment and underemployment. Resistance to this goal can be interpreted as science teachers' perceptions that their task is to teach pure science, not applied science or vocational training. Still, science textbooks clearly show that some information on scientific careers is being included in science programs. Although the career goal has been emphasized and is important, the preceding criticism indicates that it probably will not become a primary goal of science education in the latter part of the twentieth century. This is an excellent place to stop and complete Activity 5–2, "The Status of Goals and Programs," at the end of this chapter.

■ THE GOALS OF SCIENCE EDUCATION: A NEW REFORM MOVEMENT

The 1980s witnessed a flurry of reports calling for reform in American education.[14] Though varied in approach and recommendations, the national reports on education in the United States consistently identified science and technology as a vital area with a pressing need for reform. What brought about this national concern with science and technology education was a number of disturbing trends, including declines in the following:

- science enrollments in secondary schools,
- science education in elementary schools,
- achievement test scores,
- students entering science and engineering careers,
- qualified science teachers,
- public attitudes toward science education,
- the quality and quantity of American science education compared to that of other countries.[15-17]

As soon as discussions of reform in science education began, so did talk of rethinking goals. Obviously the direction of reform had to be guided by new goals. Anna Harrison called attention to the inadequacy of science education goals in an editorial in *Science*.[18] And Ronald Anderson asked the rhetorical question, "Are Yesterday's Goals Adequate for Tomorrow?"[19] He, too, called attention to the inadequacy of contemporary goals. In the 1980s these were only two instances of people who began directing science educators toward the reform of goals for science teaching.

Others began addressing the need and substance for new goals in more detail. In a short monograph entitled *Reforming Science Education: The Search for a New Vision*, Paul DeHart Hurd summarized the emerging vision of goals.

> The rationale and goals are derived from a consideration of how science and technology influenced social well-being and human affairs. The goals for teaching science are based on scientific and technological systems in social, cultural, and individual contexts. [Italics in original][20]

A major report issued by the National Science Board (NSB) in 1983 was titled *Educating Americans For the 21st Century*.[21] This report was quite comprehensive, including a section on goals for science and technology education. The report very clearly describes a vision that would eventually be set in place by the national standards and benchmarks. The list of general outcomes recommended by this report were:

- Ability to formulate questions about nature and seek answers from observation and interpretation of natural phenomena;
- Development of students' capacities for problem-solving and critical thinking in all areas of learning;
- Development of particular talents for innovative and creative thinking;
- Awareness of the nature and scope of a wide variety of science- and technology-related careers open to students of varying aptitudes and interests;
- The basic academic knowledge necessary for advanced study by students who are likely to pursue science professionally;
- Scientific and technical knowledge needed to fulfill civic responsibilities, improve the student's own health and life and ability to cope with an increasingly technological world;
- Means for judging the worth of articles presenting scientific conclusions.

The NSB report continues by saying that materials to achieve these outcomes must be developed and tests must be devised to measure the degree to which these goals are met. The section then concludes with a summary statement of the goals.

> In summary, students who have progressed through the Nation's school systems should be able to use both the knowledge and products of science, mathematics and technology in their thinking, their lives and their work. They should be able to make informed choices regarding their own health and lifestyles based on evidence and reasonable personal preferences, after taking into consideration short- and long-term risks and benefits of different decisions. They should also be prepared to make similarly informed choices in the social and political arenas. (p. 45)

The goal statement is finally extended to the curriculum:

> New science curricula that incorporate appropriate scientific and technological knowledge and are oriented toward practical issues are needed. They also will provide an excellent way of fostering traditional basic skills. The introduction of practical problems which require the collection of data, the communication of results and ideas and the formulation and testing of solutions or improvements would: (1) improve the use and understanding of calculation and mathematical analysis; (2) sharpen the student's ability to communicate verbally and to write precisely; (3) develop problem-solving skills; (4) impart scientific concepts and facts that can be related to practical applications; (5) develop a respect for science and technology and more generally for quantitative observation and thinking; and (6) stimulate an interest in many to enter scientific, engineering, and technical careers. (p. 45)

Developing a new reform for goals is based on the national standards that education in science and technology should be grounded on recent advances in scientific and technologic disciplines, needs and aspirations of society, and the interrelationship of science, technology and society.

First and foremost is the need to develop a contemporary perspective of goals for science and technology education. There have been tremendous advances in science, changes in social needs, and newly recognized interactions between science and society. These changes have been generally recognized in the goals expressed in the *National Science Education Standards* and *Benchmarks for Science Literacy*.

■ THE GOALS OF SCIENCE EDUCATION: NATIONAL STANDARDS AND BENCHMARKS

In contemporary reform the configuration of goals for science education should relate to the overall purpose of achieving scientific literacy. Thus, any review of national standards should assess the degree to which the standards incorporate the acquisition of scientific knowledge, development of inquiry abilities and understandings, and understanding of the applications of science (especially personal and social aspects of science and the history and nature of science and technology). Further, those implementing the standards, benchmarks, and frameworks should review the priorities and emphases suggested for the different goals. To what degree and in what form are the goals expressed? Do the standards suggest one orientation for the structuring of the goals, or do they suggest variations? Do the standards allow for a variety of curriculum materials and instructional approaches in order to achieve the goals? These questions should help focus your review of the national standards and the following discussion of science content in the standards.

The science content presented in the *National Science Education Standards* describes major concepts, as well as fundamental concepts and abilities for all students. Content only represents one component of a comprehensive view of science education expressed by the national standards. This comprehensive view includes teaching *and* assessment. As we mentioned in chapter 4, the national standards organize science content into eight categories, displayed in Figure 5–1.

Scientific Methods

The standard *Science as Inquiry* represents the goal we have discussed under Scientific Methods. The standard on inquiry has two features, the ability to *do* inquiry and the development of understandings *about* scientific inquiry. The inquiry standard emphasizes the students' *ability* to: ask scientific questions; plan and conduct investigations; use appropriate tools, techniques, and educational technologies; think critically and logically about the relationship between evidences and explanations; construct and analyze alternative explanations, and communicate scientific investigations and explanations.

Understandings about scientific inquiry generally parallel abilities. For example, the national standards encourage the student's development of knowledge about the types of questions scientists ask; the various reasons for conducting investigations; technology's role in inquiry; criteria for accept-

able scientific explanations; and the results and use of scientific inquiry.

The inquiry standard emphasizes the students' ability to think critically and to use observations and knowledge to construct scientific explanations. The national standards have moved science education a step beyond the *processes of science* which centered on students engaging in activities emphasizing skills such as observing, inferring, hypothesizing, experimenting, and controlling variables. The processes of science are obviously included in *Science as Inquiry,* but the national standards require students to use the processes, combined with existing knowledge, as a means to gather evidence used in their analysis, reasoning, and construction of other scientific understanding.

We also note that the national standards include *Science and Technology,* in which students would develop abilities of technological design as well as greater understanding of Science and Technology. The standard intentionally parallels the *abilities* outlined in *Science as Inquiry.* The difference between the standards is based in the difference between scientific inquiry and technological design. The latter includes: identifying a problem; proposing designs and selecting from alternative solutions; implementing a solution; evaluating the solution; and communicating the problem, process, and solution.

In the *National Science Education Standards* inquiry and design serve to: (1) assist students in the development of their understanding of scientific concepts; (2) help students answer the question "How do we know what we know in science?"; (3) introduce the nature of science; (4) develop abilities of critical thinking, scientific reasoning, and critical analysis; and (5) acquire the habits of mind associated with science and technology.

Scientific Knowledge

You should be aware that the national standards have defined a wide range of scientific knowledge and that the content of secondary-school science programs is not strictly confined to the *Physical, Life,* and *Earth Sciences.* However, three standards outline major concepts and fundamental understandings of *Physical, Life,* and *Earth Sciences,* three major divisions of the scientific disciplines. Figures 5–2, 5–3, and 5–4 present the conceptual organizers for these major divisions of science. Although you are most interested in secondary schools, we thought it important to present the conceptual organizers for grades K–4 so that you could review the overall development of concepts.

In the section on Scientific Methods we discussed the standards on *Science as Inquiry* and portions of the standard on *Science and Technology.* Both of these standards also elaborate fundamental

Unifying Concepts and Processes
Science as Inquiry
Physical Science
Life Science
Earth and Space Science
Science and Technology
Science in Personal and Social Perspectives
History and Nature of Science

FIGURE 5–1
National Science Education Standards: **Science Content**

FIGURE 5–2
Conceptual organizers for physical science standards

Physical Science K–4	Physical Science 5–8	Physical Science 9–12
• Properties of Objects and Materials • Position and Motion of Objects • Light, Heat, Electricity and Magnetism	• Properties and Changes in Properties of Matter • Motions and Forces • Transfer of Energy	• The Structure of Atoms • Structure and Properties of Matter • Chemical Reactions • Motion and Force • Conservation of Energy and the Increase in Disorder • Interactions of Energy and Matter

FIGURE 5–3
Conceptual organizers for life science standards

Life Science K–4	Life Science 5–8	Life Science 9–12
• Characteristics of Organisms • Life Cycles of Organisms • Organisms and Environments	• Structure and Function in Living Systems • Reproduction and Heredity • Regulation and Behavior • Populations and Ecosystems • Diversity and Adaptations of Organisms	• The Cell • The Molecular Basis of Heredity • Biological Evolution • The Interdependence of Organisms • Matter, Energy, and Organization in Living Systems • The Behavior of Organisms

FIGURE 5–4
Conceptual organizers for earth and space science standards

Earth and Space Science K–4	Earth and Space Science 5–8	Earth and Space Science 9–12
• Properties of Earth Materials • Objects in the Sky • Changes in Earth and Sky	• Structure of the Earth System • Earth's History • Earth in the Solar System	• Energy in the Earth System • Geochemical Cycles • The Origin and Evolution of the Earth System • The Origin and Evolution of the Universe

understandings for their respective areas. These understandings extend the goal of scientific knowledge from a narrow focus on the disciplines to a broader view that includes understanding scientific inquiry, science and technology, and the history and nature of science. We discussed some examples from understanding scientific inquiry in an earlier section. Generally, these understandings elaborate various aspects of scientific investigations. For example, scientific concepts guide investigations; technology enhances accuracy of data; scientific explanations use evidence, logically consistent arguments, and propose, modify, or elaborate principles, models, and theories in science; and science advances through legitimate skepticism.

In the standards on science and technology, understandings highlight the connections between science and technology and maintain a view of the scientific and technologic enterprise (that is, a larger and external view of science and technology in society). Examples of understandings include the similarities and differences between science and technology; the contributions of science to technology and technology to science; and the understanding that different people in different cultures have made, and continue to make, contributions to science and technology.

The scientific knowledge outlined in national standards also includes the *History and Nature of Science* (see Figure 5–5). This standard does not imply that students develop understandings of a complete history of science. Rather, science teachers can present history to clarify various aspects of scientific inquiry, the human dimensions of science,

FIGURE 5–5
Overview of the history and nature of science standards

History and Nature of Science K–4	*History and Nature of Science 5–8*	*History and Nature of Science 9–12*
• Science as a Human Endeavor	• Science as a Human Endeavor	• Science as a Human Endeavor
	• Nature of Science	• Nature of Scientific Knowledge
	• History of Science	• Historical Perspectives

Unifying Concepts and Processes K–12

- Systems, Order, and Organization
- Evidence, Models, and Explanation
- Constancy, Change, and Measurement
- Evolution and Equilibrium
- Form and Function

FIGURE 5–6
Overview of unifying concepts and processes

and the various roles science has played in Western and non-Western cultures. Science teachers might use case studies from history, classical experiments, and perspectives of normal and revolutionary science in order to provide students with opportunities to develop the understandings described in this standard.

The *National Science Education Standards* also includes *Unifying Concepts and Processes* within the goal of scientific knowledge. These standards present major conceptual and procedural schemes that unify science disciplines and, when understood, will provide students with very powerful ways of understanding the natural and designed world (see Figure 5–6). *Unifying Concepts and Processes* do not have specific grade level designations; rather, science teachers should continually bring these ideas to awareness in appropriate contexts, based on students' experiences. Specific understandings included in this standard are:

- Order and Organization—levels of organization, systems, prediction, and a statistical view of nature
- Evidence, Models, and Explanation—observations, data, models, hypothesis, law, and theory
- Change and Measurement—interactions, rate, scale, patterns, quantitative aspects of change, conservation of energy and matter
- Evolution and Equilibrium—gradual changes, present as connected to the past, descent from common ancestors, homeostasis, and energy content and distribution
- Form and Function—complimentarity, natural and designed world, and systems and subsystems.

Personal Needs and Societal Issues

As mentioned in the first section describing goals, one fundamental purpose of science teaching is to help students understand and act on various issues and challenges they will confront as individuals and as citizens. The national standards recognize this goal through inclusion of *Science in Personal and Social Perspectives* (see Figure 5–7).

These standards provide a context and topics for science curriculum and instructions. You should notice that the national standards include different aspects of health at each grade level, and that there is the implied development of understanding about population, resources, and environments at all grade levels. The standards at grades 5–8 and 9–12 include natural hazards, such as earthquakes, volcanoes, floods, and hurricanes. Finally, this standard recommends that students come to understand and act on science

FIGURE 5–7
Conceptual organizers for science in personal and social perspectives

Science in Personal and Social Perspectives K–4	*Science in Personal and Social Perspectives 5–8*	*Science in Personal and Social Perspectives 9–12*
• Personal Health	• Personal Health	• Personal and Community Health
• Characteristics and Changes in Populations	• Populations, Resources, and Environments	• Population Growth
• Types of Resources	• Natural Hazards	• Natural Resources
• Changes in Environments	• Risks and Benefits	• Environmental Quality
• Science and Technology in Local Challenges	• Science and Technology in Society	• Natural and Human-Induced Hazards
		• Science and Technology in Local, National, and Global Challenges

and technology challenges at local (grades K–4), social (grades 5–8), and global (grades 9–12) levels.

Career Awareness

The national standards do have an explicit goal supporting career awareness; however, they do not have a standard emphasizing careers. It should be clear that the experience implied by the understandings and abilities outlined in the standards would have a positive benefit on students' attitudes and inclinations toward careers in, for example, science, engineering, and the health professions.

The *National Science Education Standards* presents a fairly balanced approach to the goals of science education, with career awareness as the exception. Further, the national standards align quite well with the dimensions of scientific literacy described in chapter 4. The content standards form a complete set of outcomes for students. Development of students' understandings, attitudes, and abilities are grounded in scientific investigations, and they form a solid foundation in life, earth, and physical sciences and apply fundamental understanding and ability within various personal, social, and historical perspectives. Although balanced, thorough, and clearly aligned with long-standing goals of science education, the *National Science Education Standards* must be transformed in curriculum materials, instructional practices, and assessment strategies, all topics we take up in later chapters. You should complete Activity 5–3, "Goals of Science Textbooks," and Activity 5–4, "Reforming Goals to Align with National Standards and Benchmarks."

■ SUMMARY

This chapter provided an overview of five enduring goals of science education: scientific knowledge, scientific methods, societal issues, personal needs, and career awareness. We reviewed the status and changes of these goals in light of reports assessing science education for the period 1955–1975 and reform efforts of the 1980s.

In the 1990s, national standards have had, and will continue to have, a profound influence on the goals of science education. *National Science Education Standards* incorporates the enduring goals. Scientific knowledge includes the major divisions of *Physical, Life,* and *Earth Science* and other areas such as *Science and Technology,* the *History and Nature of Science,* and *Unifying Concepts and Processes.* The goal of scientific methods is expressed as the standard on scientific inquiry which includes both abilities and understandings associated with inquiry. Personal needs and societal issues are con-

solidated in the standard on *Science in Personal and Social Perspectives.*

The national standards provide a balanced and fairly thorough expression of traditional goals. It is clear that some areas, such as technology, personal and societal perspectives, the history and nature of science, and the unifying concepts and processes will extend science teachers' understanding on content. We do think it is significant that the aforementioned areas have the status of national standards.

■ REFERENCES

1. George E. DeBoer, *A History of Ideas in Science Education* (New York: Teachers College Press, 1991).

2. Rodger Bybee and George DeBoer, "Research on Goals for the Science Curriculum," in Dorothy Gabel, ed., *Handbook of Research on Science Teaching and Learning* (Washington, DC: National Science Teachers Association, 1993).

3. Stanley L. Helgeson, Patricia E. Blosser, and Robert W. Howe, *The Status of Pre-College Science, Mathematics, and Social Science Education: 1955-1975, Vol.1, Science Education* (SE 78–73 Vol. 1, Center for Science and Mathematics Education, Ohio State University, NSF Contract C762067) (Washington, D.C.: U.S. Government Printing Office, 1977).

4. Iris R. Weiss, *Report of the 1977 National Survey of Science, Mathematics, and Social Studies Education* (SE78–72, Center for Educational Research and Evaluation, Research Triangle Institute, NSF Contract C7619848) (Washington, DC: U.S. Government Printing Office, 1978).

5. Robert E. Stake and Jack Easley, et al., *Case Studies in Science Education, Vol. 1: The Case Reports* and *Vol. 2: Design, Overview and General Findings* (SE 78–74 Vol. 1. and SE 78–74 Vol. 2, Center for Instructional Research and Curriculum Evaluation, University of Illinois at Urbana-Champaign, NSF Contract C7621134) (Washington, DC: U.S. Government Printing Office, 1978).

6. Work on this review was completed as part of one author's (Rodger W. Bybee) participation on the National Science Foundation's "Project Synthesis," Dr. Norris Harms, Director. Dr. Paul DeHart Hurd, Dr. Jane Kahle, and Dr. Robert Yager also worked on the project. We wish to thank them for their comments, criticism, and discussion.

7. Paul DeHart Hurd, "The Golden Age of Biological Education: 1960–1975," in *Biology Teachers Handbook* (3rd ed.), William Mayer, ed. (New York: Wiley & Sons, 1978).

8. National Assessment of Educational Progress, *Science Achievement in the Schools, A Summary of Results from the 1976–1977 National Assessment of Science* (Science Report No. 08–01) (Denver, CO: Education Commission of the States, 1978).

9. National Assessment of Educational Progress, *Three National Assessments of Science: Changes in*

Achievement, 1969-1977 (Denver, CO: Education Commission of the States, 1978).

10. We have not footnoted each statement, fact, and statistic in this discussion in order to make reading the summary easier. All material is supported by the studies and reviews cited at the beginning of this section.

11. American Association for the Advancement of Science, *Science for All Americans: A Project 2061 Report on Goals in Science, Mathematics, and Technology* (Washington, DC: Author, 1989).

12. American Association for the Advancement of Science, *Benchmarks for Science Literacy* (Washington, DC: Author, 1994).

13. National Research Council, *National Science Education Standards* (Washington, DC: Author, 1995).

14. See The National Commission on Excellence in Education, *A Nation At Risk* (Washington, D.C.: U.S. Department of Education, April, 1983); Task Force on Education for Economic Growth, *Action for Excellence* (Denver, CO: Education Commission of the States, June 1983); John Goodlad, *A Place Called School* (New York: McGraw-Hill, 1984); Mortimer Adler, *The Paideia Proposal* (New York: Macmillan, 1982); Ernest Boyer, *High School* (New York: Harper and Row, 1983); and Theodore Sizer, *Horace's Compromise* (Boston: Houghton Mifflin Co., 1984).

15. Bill Aldridge and Karen Johnston, "Trends and Issues in Science Education," in *Redesigning Science and Technology Education*, 1984 NSTA Yearbook, Rodger Bybee, Janet Carlson, and Alan McCormack, eds. (Washington, DC: National Science Teachers Association, 1984).

16. Paul DeHart Hurd, "State of Precollege Education in Mathematics and Science," *Science Education*, 67 (1) (January 1983): 57–67.

17. Marjorie Gardner and Robert Yager, "How Does the U.S. Stack Up?" *The Science Teacher* (October 1983): 22–25.

18. Anna Harrison, "Goals of Science Education," *Science*, 217 (4555) (July 1982): 109.

19. Ronald Anderson, "Are Yesterday's Goals Adequate For Tomorrow?" *Science Education*, 67: 2 (1983): 171–176.

20. Paul DeHart Hurd, *Reforming Science Education: The Search For A New Vision* (Washington, D.C.: Council for Basic Education, 1984), p. 17.

21. The National Science Board Commission on Precollege Education in Mathematics, Science and Technology, *Educating Americans for the 21st Century* (Washington, D.C.: National Science Board, 1983).

INVESTIGATING SCIENCE TEACHING

Activity 5–1

GOALS OF SCIENCE TEACHING

Directions:

1. In the blank in front of the goal statements, you should indicate whether you agree (A) or disagree (D) with the goal or have no opinion (NO).
2. Review and discuss your individual responses in a group of three or four persons. At this step you can add new goals, combine, modify, or omit goals. As a group you should agree on the goal statements.
3. Compile the goals from the small groups into a class set of goals for science teaching.

Goals:

Science teaching should:

 ____   1. Make students aware of good health practices

 ____   2. Include contemporary social problems and solutions for those problems

 ____   3. Emphasize analytic skills more than the skills of synthesis

 ____   4. Prepare students for careers in science-related fields

 ____   5. Help individuals cope with their environment

 ____   6. Provide students with an understanding of the crucial role of science and technology in our society

 ____   7. Provide students with the ability to form a hypothesis and plan an experiment to test the hypothesis

 ____   8. Be more concerned with scientific facts than with broad generalizations since students cannot comprehend the generalizations

 ____   9. Develop skills basic to technical occupations and professions

 ____ 10. Be related to and clarify individual beliefs, attitudes, and values

 ____ 11. Make students aware of the fact that science is the only answer to our many social problems

 ____ 12. Help students organize concepts into broad conceptual schemes

 ____ 13. Make students aware of science-related careers

 ____ 14. Enable students to use the scientific method to solve daily problems

 ____ 15. Present fundamental knowledge and not contemporary, relevant information. If students understand the fundamentals, they can deal responsibly with personal and social issues

 ____ 16. Be future-oriented: the past and present should receive marginal emphasis

 ____ 17. Place more emphasis on the methods and processes of scientific investigation

 ____ 18. Train the intuitive, inventive, creative talents more than the rational, logical, and methodological; the former more than the latter talents are responsible for new knowledge

 ____ 19. Actually involve students in science activities

 ____ 20. Develop the following abilities: creative thinking, effective communication, and decision-making

 ____ 21. Demonstrate the aesthetic and ethical values of science

 ____ 22. Place great emphasis on recognizing the moral obligation of science and technology to the individual and to society

 ____ 23. Deal with broad, encompassing knowledge, since it is impossible to determine the best specific knowledge that most students will need

 ____ 24. Focus on the nature of scientific inquiry since this is the one aspect of the scientific enterprise that does not change

 ____ 25. Help students differentiate between facts and opinion and determine which is the best information available concerning problems

Activity 5–2

THE STATUS OF GOALS AND PROGRAMS

As you enter this profession, it is important to reflect on your goals of science teaching in comparison with our best estimate of what is actually happening in the field. To assist you in this process you might answer the following questions.

1. Why did the goals of science remain unchanged for approximately 20 years (1955–1975), then go into a period of transition?

2. What do you see as the direction of transition in goals for science teaching?

3. What is your position on teaching science by inquiry?

4. Why have science teachers shown little enthusiasm for teaching science by inquiry?

5. What do you think are the important goals of science teaching?

6. What is the best way of achieving those goals?

7. Do you think socialization should be a goal of science teaching? How would you justify your answer?

8. What is your reaction to the reported widespread socialization in science classrooms?

9. What is your reaction to the teaching of science as "a body of information to be learned as dogma and accepted on faith"?

10. What can you do about this situation in your own classroom?

Activity 5–3

GOALS OF SCIENCE TEXTBOOKS

You have seen that the goals of textbooks are, essentially, the goals for science programs. In this activity you will first compare the goals of three textbooks or curriculum programs in your discipline. In the second part of the activity you will observe a science class for several days to see if goals are recognizable aspects of daily science teaching.

First, select three textbooks in your discipline (e.g., physics, chemistry, biology, or earth science) and the level at which you plan to teach (e.g., junior high, middle, or high school). Next, examine the textbooks and teacher guides carefully and identify the goals of the program. Are they stated clearly? Did you have to derive the goals from the text materials? Complete the following information about goals:

	Text 1	Text 2	Text 3
1. Which goals were present and recognizable? (Y = yes, N = no, or M = marginal)			
Scientific knowledge	____	____	____
Scientific methods	____	____	____
Societal issues	____	____	____
Personal needs	____	____	____
Career awareness	____	____	____
2. Rank the importance of goals presented in the text. (1 = very important, 2 = important, 3 = somewhat important, 4 = marginally important, 5 = not important)			
Scientific knowledge	____	____	____
Scientific methods	____	____	____
Societal issues	____	____	____
Personal needs	____	____	____
Career awareness	____	____	____
3. Were the goals: (Y = yes, N = no, M = marginal)			
Comprehensive enough to include the generally accepted objectives of science teaching	____	____	____
Understandable to other teachers, administrators, and parents?	____	____	____
Free of bias toward a particular philosophy of science teaching?	____	____	____
Few in number?	____	____	____
Conceptually different?	____	____	____
Applicable to teaching and learning objectives?	____	____	____

Now that you have reviewed the goals of three texts:

1. Which text do you prefer?

2. How does the text reflect your own goals for science teaching?

3. What did you learn about the transfer of goals to the science classroom?

Activity 5–4

REFORMING GOALS TO ALIGN WITH NATIONAL STANDARDS AND BENCHMARKS

The initial task of redesigning science programs is to identify what it is about science and technology that has significance for students. This statement applies to national curriculum reform or the local development of a science program. Take a few minutes and answer the following questions.

1. What knowledge, values, skills and sensibilities relative to science and technology are important for citizens in the last decades of the twentieth century? How do the *National Science Education Standards* and *Benchmarks for Science Literacy* address this question?

2. What scientific and technologic knowledge do you think is important? Why?

3. What values of science and technology would you emphasize? Why?

4. What skills are important? Why?

5. What are the sensibilities required of citizens?

Chapter 6

THE OBJECTIVES OF SCIENCE TEACHING

One of the best ways to learn is to be actively involved in and with the material to be studied. To apply this principle, start by completing the exercise "Objectives of Science Teaching" at the end of this chapter.

Suppose you were going on a trip from New York City to a specific street and address in San Francisco, California. You have a goal and a road map of the United States which provides you with enough direction to get you to San Francisco. When you arrive in the San Francisco Bay Area, you would need another map with more specific directions in order to reach your destination. Some maps are better for your purposes than others; a topographic map may be interesting, but it would be of little help in locating San Francisco streets and addresses. What you need is a more detailed map of the area.

By now you have probably made the connection between the map analogy and goals and objectives for science teaching. In the last chapter, we described some of the larger purposes and directions of science education; now we will discuss some of the specific objectives for science teaching. Several points should be made about the analogy. General goals are related to specific objectives and both should be related to your purposes as a science teacher. Be sure you have the most appropriate objectives for your purposes.

■ NEW THRUST IN TEACHING OBJECTIVES

Today emphasis is being put on the development of scientific literacy, for a scientifically literate citizenry is essential in a highly technological society such as ours. Students in secondary schools form a preferred target group for developing this objective.

To realize success in their efforts to develop scientifically literate students, science teachers must have a clear idea of what comprises scientific literacy and proceed to formulate classroom objectives that emphasize appropriate activities and foster the desired learning and skill development.

The BSCS has explicated various levels of scientific literacy as they apply to biology. These levels have relevance to other areas of science teaching and are discussed below:

The lowest level of literacy is the nominal level. Students may enter a class with minimal recognition of science terms but may not be able to give ade-

quate or correct explanations of the scientific phenomena under discussion and may have misconceptions about them. A common problem in middle school classes is that students, when presented with a new topic to study, may believe they have already covered the material, thus diminishing their enthusiasm for the task ahead. In fact, they may have only name recognition of the topic and little or no understanding of the depth of the subject being proposed. A teacher's objective in this situation might be to develop a realization of the breadth and depth of the topic under consideration.

At a higher functional level students may be able to define science terms correctly from memory but have little understanding of purpose, interrelationships between parts, or organizational hierarchy of terms. Teachers may want to consider objectives that emphasize the role scientific terms play in classification, in organization, and in delineating scientific usage from everyday usage of some words.

Students may have reached structural literacy if they can construct appropriate explanations based on their experiences in class or out of school and can explain concepts in their own terms. Objectives and activities at this level should emphasize development of interrelationships between parts, applications of scientific phenomena to everyday experiences, and personal relevance of the newly learned material.

At the *multidimensional* level students can apply the knowledge they have gained and the skills they have developed to solve authentic problems that may require integration from other related disciplines, such as social studies, reading, and language arts. Objectives and activities at this level should provide many opportunities to work on real problems with alternate solutions that bring out the trade-offs that frequently are needed to make progress in the solutions of real-life problems.

■ OBJECTIVES FOR CONSTRUCTIVIST TEACHING

The recent emphasis on hands-on science has put constructivism squarely in the middle of learning theories relevant for teaching and learning science. "The basic premise of constructivism is that learners receive sensory input, compare it to existing ideas of what appears to be similar events, modify, if necessary, and construct explanations that seem to make sense."[1] What learners actually construct from a given learning experience varies from student to student and often deviates from what the teacher had intended. According to George Bodner of Purdue University:

> There is no conduit from one brain to another. All teachers can do is disturb the environment. Effective instruction depends on our ability to understand how students make sense of our 'disturbances' (stimuli) rather than how we make sense of those stimuli ourselves. Knowledge is constructed by the learner.[2]

Considering this, it becomes necessary to develop and refine classroom objectives in science. A highly effective instructional model based on constructivism is the *Learning Cycle.* Jay Hackett's modification of the learning cycle[3] as revised by Bybee in the late 1980s[4] (see chapter 14), employs four phases: Engagement, Exploration, Development, and Extension and Application. Working objectives for each of these phases are:

> *Engagement:* Mentally engage students in the big ideas or concepts of the lesson. Access prior knowledge and understandings. Whet interest and curiosity.
>
> *Exploration:* Investigate and explore ideas together to establish a common experience base and share prior understandings.
>
> *Development:* Put forth explanations based upon prior knowledge. Develop vocabulary. Provide experiences to reinforce and strengthen understandings.
>
> *Extension and Application:* Transfer and apply understandings of concepts to different situations. Make connections to other curriculum areas.

■ SELECTING OBJECTIVES FOR SCIENCE TEACHING

There are many objectives for science teaching, as you probably discovered during the introductory activity. Rather than giving our answers to your questions about objectives, we will clarify different types of science objectives and then discuss the preparation of objectives for science teaching. First, we examine six criteria that will help differentiate objectives from goals and give you a guide to selecting objectives for science teaching.

1. Science objectives should be general enough to be identifiably related to science goals and specific enough to give clear direction for planning and evaluating science instruction.
2. Science objectives should be understandable for students, teachers, administrators, and parents.
3. Science objectives should be few in number but comprehensive for any lesson, unit, or program.

4. Science objectives should be challenging yet attainable for your students.
5. Science objectives should differ conceptually from each other.
6. Science objectives should be appropriate for the subject you are teaching.

■ TYPES OF OBJECTIVES FOR SCIENCE TEACHING

Objectives can be stated in terms of instructional or learning results. In the first, the emphasis is on what the teacher does; in the second, it is on what the student does. Here are examples. Which is the teaching objective and which is the learning objective?

> To demonstrate to students how to use a barometer.
>
> To describe the steps in the proper use of a barometer.

The advantage of stating objectives as instructional results is that it gives you direction. The disadvantage is that you may not be clear as to whether the students learned anything. In general, we suggest that you concentrate on learning results when forming objectives. Doing so will help define the instruction sequence and set the stage for evaluation.

Objectives can be classified as either behavioral or nonbehavioral. Behavioral objectives state how the student will behave as a result of instruction. Behaviors are an observable indication that learning has occurred. Examples of behavioral objectives are:

The student should be able to

- Identify symbols on a weather map
- Describe predator and prey relationships
- Define the term energy

For contrast, examples of nonbehavioral objectives are:

The student should be able to

- Learn scientific names for common animals
- Comprehend the concept of work
- Know how to use the scientific method

All six of these examples could be objectives for science lessons, and they are all stated in terms of learning results for students. In the first set, the specific behaviors have been stated: if students can identify . . . , describe . . . , and define . . . , then they have learned. The second set is a little less clear as to how you will know whether or not students have learned . . . , does comprehend . . . , or does know. Are behavioral objectives better than nonbehavioral?

Here are some advantages and disadvantages of behavioral objectives.

Some of the advantages of behavioral objectives are:

1. They help the science teacher become more precise in her or his teaching.
2. They clarify exactly what is expected.
3. They provide performance criteria for student achievement and accountability for the teacher.
4. The teacher plans more carefully because she or he knows what performance the students should display after finishing a science lesson, unit, or course of study.
5. The teacher knows what materials are needed and is able to give more specific help to students in directing them to outside sources of information.
6. The teacher who prepares behavioral objectives finds them very helpful in evaluation. When preparing paper and pencil tests, the questions can be matched to the objectives and, by deciding on certain criteria of performance, questions can be phrased in such a way that the teacher has precise knowledge of the ability of the student to perform certain tasks.

Some disadvantages of behavioral objectives are:

1. They may tend toward an emphasis on trivial behaviors and ignore important objectives that are too difficult to define behaviorally.
2. They may inhibit the teacher's spontaneity and flexibility.
3. They may provide a precise measurement of less important behaviors, leaving more important outcomes unevaluated.
4. They may be used against teachers who are held accountable for the performance of students who do not learn.
5. They tend to focus the teacher's attention on the small, less significant aspects of teaching, leaving the larger picture unattended.
6. They represent only one particular psychology and philosophy of education.

■ DOMAINS OF OBJECTIVES FOR SCIENCE TEACHING

It is customary to think of objectives in three aspects: cognitive, affective, and psychomotor. These terms come from the work of Benjamin Bloom and others who developed taxonomies of educational objectives.[5–7] Cognitive objectives deal with intellectual results, knowledge, concepts, and understanding. Affective objectives include the feelings, interests, attitudes, and appreciations that may result from sci-

ence instruction. The psychomotor domain includes objectives that stress motor development, muscular coordination, and physical skills. Traditionally, cognitive objectives have received far more attention over the years than affective or psychomotor objectives. With increased attention to behavioral objectives and performance competencies, the cognitive area becomes fertile ground for writing objectives that stress performance in science knowledge and conceptual understanding. Still, science teachers should not omit important learning results in the affective and psychomotor domains.

Your understanding of the three domains will be one of the most helpful aids in formulating objectives for science teaching. We have used categories from the cognitive, affective, and psychomotor domains as the basis for tables summarizing instructional objectives in science (see Tables 6–1 through 6–7). The tables are based on the original work of Bloom et al., Krathwohl et al., and Norman Gronlund.[8] The domains are arranged in a hierarchical order, from simple to complex learning results.

The cognitive domain starts with acquiring simple knowledge about science and proceeds through increasingly more difficult levels: comprehension, application, analysis, synthesis, and evaluation. The categories are inclusive in that higher level results incorporate the lower levels. For example, students must *know* a science concept before they can *apply* it. Science teachers have usually concentrated on the cognitive domain and the lower levels of learning within the domain. Understanding the hierarchical nature of this and other domains will increase your awareness of higher levels of science objectives and,

A student teacher and his supervisor review objectives for science lessons.

■■■■■■■■■■■■■■■■■■ **GUEST EDITORIAL** ■■■■■■■■■■■■■■■■■■

Environmental Education and Science Teaching

Jeff Mow
Science Education Student
Environmental Education
Carleton College, Northfield, Minnesota

As a junior at Carleton College, I am just beginning my career in science education. Originally a Geology major, later I changed to Environmental Education. As I completed a science methods course, I realized that the informal teaching and educational opportunities found outdoors have the most meaning for me. I would like to be an outdoor educator or perhaps a visiting teacher and curriculum developer. One reason for this choice is that I have a strong interest in geology and would like to explore the career opportunities in this field. Another reason is that I have been teaching and developing curriculum materials for the U.S. Geological Survey. Because of this opportunity I have already been exposed to some novel approaches to environmental education. This experience, in conjunction with my own personal education and teacher training, has made me think about issues in environmental education.

The first question I have is, What is environmental education? A common conception of environmental education is that it is recreationally oriented. Also, environmental programs often offer such a different subject-matter focus that students are unable to relate the environmental activity to an everyday experience such as going to school. This lack of integration often results in an ineffective environmental program. Is environmental education going hiking in the woods, viewing a film on pollution, or hugging a tree? Or is environmental education calculating the rate of erosion on a poorly managed farm field or making physical measurements of the forest regeneration process? I think that environmental education should take the latter form, as it allows students to integrate concepts learned in the classroom with an actual life experience. I also think that it is important that the outdoor experience can and should be used as a laboratory; that is, a classroom without walls. I have developed and taught a map unit of the U.S. Geological Survey in which I have secondary students make detailed maps of their local environment. When I first taught this course, many of the students took the opportunity to run off. Since then, I have learned that for the exercise to be successful, I have to lay down some initial ground rules. The result of outlining my expectations of them is that I am able to focus the students' activity despite the loss of the classroom's physical constraints. I have found that the environmental activities I have taught have been successful, and I would hope that you might also try this approach.

A much larger issue is the role of science education in our society. My own education and what I have seen in the schools indicate a distinct gap or void between the science taught in the classroom and that encountered in life. As a future science educator, how can I help bridge this gap? For example, in your high school physics course, how much exposure did you have to daily scientific issues such as nuclear technology and electronic technology? A poll of my peers has revealed that these issues were not dealt with and realized, in hindsight, that they should have been. I believe it is important that, as a future science teacher, I try to relate classroom material to everyday science applications. I think that it is clear that science and technology will be an important factor in solving many of our world's problems and that, as a science teacher, I have the responsibility of creating an increased awareness of the importance of science in our society.

subsequently, higher levels of student achievement. (See Tables 6–1 and 6–5 for a summary of the cognitive domain and examples of general and specific instructional objectives in science.)

Affective objectives deal with feelings, interests, and attitudes. Science teachers are becoming increasingly concerned with this area in our schools today. Neglect or lack of attention to attitudes has produced some unexpected results. Students are often losing interest in science at a time when scientific advances are unparalleled in the history of humanity. Greater numbers of students and adults are questioning science, perhaps because of a poor understanding of its role in society or because of confusion over the relationships between science and technology.

············ REFLECTING ON SCIENCE TEACHING ············

BEHAVIORAL OBJECTIVES: PRO AND CON

You have read some of the advantages and disadvantages of behavioral objectives. What is your resolution of the problem?

1. Should you state your science objectives in behavioral terms?
2. Can you resolve the differences and find an appropriate position concerning the statement of objectives? What is your position?

TABLE 6–1
Cognitive domain for science teaching

Knowing

Knowledge represents the lowest level of science objectives. The definition of knowledge for this level is remembering previously learned scientific material. The requirement is to simply recall, i.e., bring to mind appropriate information. The range of information may vary from simple facts to complex theories, but all that is required is to remember the information.

Comprehending

Comprehension is the first step beyond simple recall. It is the first level, demonstrating and understanding of scientific information. It is the ability to apprehend, grasp, and understand the meaning of scientific material. Comprehension is shown in three ways: (1) translation of scientific knowledge into other forms, (2) interpretation of science knowledge by reordering and showing interrelationships and summarizing material, and (3) extrapolation and interpolation of science knowledge. Here the students can estimate or predict future trends or infer consequences between two points or items of data.

Applying

Application is the ability to show the pertinence of scientific principles to different situations. At this level students may apply scientific concepts, methods, laws, or theories to actual concrete problems.

Analyzing

Analysis requires more than knowledge, comprehension, and application. It also requires an understanding of the underlying structure of the material. Analysis is the ability to break down material to its fundamental elements for better understanding of the organization. Analysis may include identifying parts, clarifying relationships among parts, and recognizing organizational principles of scientific systems.

Synthesizing

Synthesis requires the formulation of new understandings of scientific systems. If analysis stresses the parts, synthesis stresses the whole. Components of scientific systems may be reorganized into new patterns and new wholes. A bringing together of scientific ideas to form a unique idea, place, or pattern could be a learning result at this level.

Evaluating

Evaluation is the highest level of learning results in the hierarchy. It includes all the other levels plus the ability to make value judgments based on internal evidence and consistency and/or clearly defined external criteria.

Writing affective objectives is usually more difficult than writing those in the cognitive area. It requires more care to formulate criteria for feelings, interests, and attitudes. It is impossible to peer inside the student's head and determine what attitudes lie there. However, certain behaviors are indicative of students' attitudes or interests. And students do have attitudes and values toward the scientific enterprise, an enterprise that is, of course, valuable in itself.

As science teachers we are as much obligated to present scientific attitudes and values as we are to present scientific facts and concepts. What are some of these attitudes and values? In Chapter 3 we described some scientific values. Others are curiosity, openness to different ideas, objectivity, precision, accuracy in reporting, perseverance in work, and questioning of ideas. Tables 6–2 and 6–6 should further clarify science objectives for the affective domain.

■ WRITING AFFECTIVE OBJECTIVES

Behaviorizing the student objectives in the affective domain requires attention to the use of action verbs that describe behavioral changes in such things as interest development, changes in attitudes, appreciations, and development of values. These are all legitimate objectives and important in the growth of understanding the essence of science and technology in society today.

TABLE 6–2
Affective domain for science teaching

Receiving

Receiving or attending to stimuli related to science is the lowest level of learning result in the affective domain. Receiving means that students are aware of the existence of and willing to attend to scientific phenomena. When students are paying attention in science class, they are probably behaving at this level. There are three levels of receiving: (1) awareness that science-related topics and issues exist, (2) willingness to receive information about science, and (3) selective attention to science topics.

Responding

Responding means that the learner does something with or about scientific phenomena. The student not only attends but reacts to science-related materials. Learning results can have three levels of responses: (1) acquiescence, meaning that the student does what is assigned or required, (2) willingness, meaning that the student does science study above and beyond requirements, and (3) satisfaction, meaning that the student studies science for pleasure and enjoyment.

Valuing

Valuing refers to consistent behavior which indicates the student's preference for science. The valuing level is based on internalized values related to science. Again there are three levels: (1) acceptance of scientific values, (2) preference for scientific values, and (3) commitment to scientific values. Instructional objectives related to attitudes and appreciation would be included at this level of the affective hierarchy.

Organizing

Organizing means that the student brings together different scientific values and builds a consistent value system. Learning results include the conceptualization of scientific values and the organization of a personal value system based on science. The student is organizing a philosophy of life based on scientific values.

Characterizing

Characterizing means that, in effect, the individual has developed a life style based on the preferred value system, in this case science. The individual's behavior is consistently and predictably related to scientific values. Learning results related to general patterns of behavior would be aligned with this level.

TABLE 6–3
Psychomotor domain for science teaching

Moving

The first level is generally referred to as gross body movements. It involves the coordination of physical actions or movements. In its most basic form, moving is a muscular response to sensory stimuli. There are movements of either upper of lower limbs and coordination of movements involving two or more large parts (limbs, head, torso) of the body. Learning results include physical coordination and smooth movements while in the science classroom.

Manipulating

Manipulating can include movement but adds fine body movements. Here, the activity includes coordinated patterns of movements involving body parts such as eyes, ears, hands, and fingers. Again there are movements of body parts such as hands, feet, fingers; coordination of movements involving two or more body parts, for example, hand-finger, hand-eye, ear-eye-hand; and finally, there is the combination of coordinated sequences of actions involving both moving and manipulating. Learning results include setting up laboratory equipment and handling and adjusting microscopes.

Communicating

Communicating is activity that makes ideas and feelings known to other persons or, conversely, makes the need for information known. This level is based on movement and manipulation and extends these levels in that something that is known, felt, or needed as a result of movement or manipulation is communicated to others. At the most basic level there are signals involving nonverbal messages through facial expression, gestures, or body movements; speech, the verbal communication, starting with sounds and progressing to word-gesture coordinations; and finally, symbolic communication through the use of pantomime, writing, pictures, and other abstract forms. Science teachers are usually interested in learning results at this level.

Creating

Creating is the process and performance that results in new ideas. Creative products in science or the arts usually require some combination of moving, manipulating, and communicating in the generation of new and unique products. Here the cognitive, affective, and psychomotor are coordinated in efforts to solve problems and create new ideas.

Because the observation and evaluation of behavioral changes among students in the affective areas is somewhat more difficult than in cognitive and psychomotor domains, it is important to design objectives that are carefully thought out and stated with precision. The teacher can observe many affective changes in behavior during the course of instruction. These might be called overt behavioral changes. Others, more subtle, may not be directly observable and, therefore, can be called covert.

Here are some examples of overt and covert behavioral objectives in the affective domain.

TABLE 6–4
Alternative view of psychomotor domain for science teaching

Simple

This initial state of psychomotor behavior is one which confirms positive readiness and mental set for the learner's further development in this skill area. It is not to be viewed as an objective in "performance" terms. Learner objectives need not be written at this level. However, if the teacher is keenly observing the learner's imitative activity, and reads the learner's need accurately, the teacher can, at this point, identify appropriate objectives(s) to move the learner through the succeeding stages (manipulation, etc.).

Imitation

Perceptual readiness (eyes, touch, muscle sense, etc.) When learners are exposed to an observable action they begin to make covert imitation of that action. Such covert behavior appears to be the starting point in the growth of psychomotor skill. This is then followed by overt performance of an act and capacity to repeat it. The performance, however, lacks neuromuscular coordination or control and hence is generally in a crude and imperfect form. This level is characterized by impulse, crude reproduction, and repetition. There is a low degree of learner control, accuracy and confidence.

Manipulation

Emphasizes the development of skill in following directions, performing selected actions, and fixation of performance through necessary practice. At this level learners are capable of performing an act according to instruction rather than just on the basis of observation as is the case at the level of imitation. They are able to follow directions, give attention to form, and begin to integrate their motor responses.

Precision

The proficiency of performance reaches a higher level of refinement in reproducing a given act. Here, accuracy, proportion and exactness in performance become significant. The actions are characterized by minimal errors, higher degree of control and increased self-confidence.

Articulation

Emphasizes the coordination of a series of acts by establishing appropriate sequence and accomplishing harmony or internal consistency among different acts. There is accurate, controlled performance which incorporates elements of speed and time. Learners' responses become habitual, yet are capable of being modified.

Naturalization

A high level of proficiency in the skill or performance of a single act is required. The behavior is performed with the least expenditure of psychic energy. At this level, the performance is smooth and natural. It is routinized, automatic and spontaneous, and performed with a high degree of learner confidence.

OVERT: "Students should be able to give evidence of behavioral change in the development of interest in the study of crystals by voluntarily selecting three or more books from the library and reading them for their own understanding of crystals."

Note that in the statement of this behavioral objective, the word "voluntarily" is included. This is important because evidence of behavioral change in interest development can only be credible if the student shows a voluntary response. If it is in the form of a teacher assignment, extra credit, or some other structured request, there is doubt about whether the response represents a true behavioral change.

COVERT: "Students will give evidence of behavioral change in development of a set of values in classroom demeanor by voluntarily self-reporting that they plan to assist other students to improve their skills of sharing with other classmates."

In this statement, note the addition of the words "self-reporting." In a covert objective there can be no outward sign of the behavioral change, although such change may have taken place in the student. Therefore, the teacher must rely on the student's own statement of intent. While this may not insure complete validity, it is an improvement over complete lack of observable evidence. Many covert objectives involving feelings, likes and dislikes, and valuing fall into this category.

In science, psychomotor objectives concern learning results which involve physical manipulation of apparatus, skill development, and proficiency in using tools, such as scientific instruments and devices. Many of these desired behaviors are not ends in themselves but are means for cognitive and affective learning. This observation points out the interrelation of the three domains and stresses the importance of total learning by the individual. Since one of the goals of education is to produce fully competent individuals who are self-reliant and capable of pursuing learning on their own throughout their lives, the psychomotor objectives occupy an important place in the overall educational endeavor. Although psychomotor objectives play a major role in physical activities, their importance in science classes should not be overlooked, especially since much of science instruction involves laboratory work requiring the physical handling and manipulation of materials.

The taxonomy of psychomotor objectives is not as well organized as are the cognitive and affective domains. In Tables 6–3 and 6–7, we have relied on our own experience and understanding of psychomotor skills required for learning science. The cognitive, affective, and psychomotor domains have been out-

TABLE 6–5
Examples of general objectives, behavioral objectives, and terms for specifying objectives for science instruction in the cognitive domain

	General Objectives	Behavioral Objectives	Terms for Objectives
Knowing	Knows scientific facts Knows scientific methods Knows basic principles of earth science, biology, chemistry, physics Knows the conceptual schemes of science	To label the parts of a frog To list the steps in the scientific method To state the second law of thermodynamics	Define, describe, identify, label, list, name, select, state
Comprehending	Understands scientific facts Interprets scientific principles Translates formulas to verbal statements Estimates the consequences of data Justifies procedures of scientific investigation	To distinguish between scientific facts and theories To explain Newton's laws To give examples of density To infer the results of continued population growth To defend procedures in problem solving	Convert, defend, interpolate, estimate, explain, extrapolate, generalize, infer, predict, summarize
Applying	Applies scientific concepts to new situations Applies theories to practical events Constructs graphs from data Uses scientific procedures correctly	To apply the theory of natural selection to new data To predict the results of fossil fuel depletion To prepare a graph of temperature changes of ascending and descending air masses	Apply, compute, discover, modify, operate, predict, prepare, relate, show, use
Analyzing	Identifies stated and unstated assumptions of a scientific theory Recognizes logical fallacies in arguments Differentiates between facts and inferences Evaluates the appropriateness of data Analyzes the structure of a scientific inquiry	To identify the assumptions of Newtonian physics To point out logical connections in the reasoning of scientific principles applied to practice To distinguish fact from assertion To select relevant data for the solution of a problem	Analyze, diagram, differentiate, discriminate, divide, identify, illustrate, infer, relate, select
Synthesizing	Gives an organized account of two theories applied to a problem Proposes procedures for solving a problem Integrates principles from meteorology, biology, and chemistry in a discussion of pollution Formulates a scheme for resolving an interdisciplinary problem	To combine the second law of thermodynamics and principles of supply and demand in discussing energy To solve an original scientific problem To relate different scientific principles To design procedures for classifying unrelated objects	Arrange, combine, compile, compose, construct, devise, design, generate, organize, plan, relate, reorganize, summarize, synthesize
Evaluating	Judges the adequacy of a theory to explain actual phenomena Judges the value of a solution by use of internal and external criteria	To criticize the theory of continental drift To evaluate the Green Revolution as a solution to world food problems	Appraise, compare, conclude, contrast, discriminate, explain, evaluate, interpret, relate, summarize

lined for your use in preparing instructional objectives for science teaching. Each domain has a hierarchical order that goes from simple to complex learning results. As you prepare objectives for science teaching, we suggest that you use Tables 6–1 to 6–7 as guides to the levels of learning and the formulation of general and specific objectives. The tables should help you:

1. Clarify objectives for an instructional unit.
2. Identify appropriate levels for instructional objectives.
3. Define objectives in meaningful terms.
4. Prepare comprehensive lists of objectives for instruction.
5. Integrate the cognitive, affective, and psychomotor domains in your teaching.
6. Communicate intentions, levels, and nature of learning, relative to your instructional unit.

Don't be a slave to the classification systems. You may have some objectives that do not fit in any domains and others that fit all three. Be less concerned about classifying your objectives and more concerned about how they will contribute to making you more effective as a science teacher so that your students will become better learners.

■ PREPARING OBJECTIVES FOR SCIENCE TEACHING

The task of writing objectives can be simplified by following these steps.

1. *Have your overall instructional objectives in mind.* What are your general objectives for the lesson or unit you are going to teach? Is it improvement of a skill? Developing the understanding of a concept? Stimulating interest in a new area of science? A combination of these objectives? Are your objectives cognitive? Affective? Psychomotor? Is there a congruence between the levels of objectives and your instructional aims? For example, your instructional objective may be: To teach problem solving.
2. *Select the content desired to achieve the objectives of the unit.* In many teaching situations unit goals may depend on the sequence of topics found in a science textbook or curriculum guide. However, the presence of a topical outline should not influence your teaching objectives. After all, you are trying to achieve certain objectives for a unique group of students. The topics chosen should be vehicles to achieve these objectives. Usually, several subject-matter topics can be used to accomplish the task. Select those that are appropriate in terms of student interests and needs, your interest, suitability to the background of the students, and other factors. If you

live in a mountainous area, use mountain terrain and topography to teach about variations of weather in different locations. Adapt your teaching to local situations. If brachiopods and trilobites can be found in a local limestone quarry, use that resource to teach about fossils rather than discussing forms that can be found only as pictures in books or in exotic collections from laboratory supply houses. Selection of content is very important. Try to find content that is both appropriate to your objectives and personally meaningful to your students. An example could be: Each student has a predator-prey problem.

3. *Write general statements describing how the student should perform.* Begin these statements with a verb (knows, defines, responds, calibrates, etc.), and then state what it is you intend to accomplish. It is helpful to write these statements in terms of learning results for the students. Be sure you have stated only one learning result per objective. Three or four general objectives should be sufficient for any lesson and six to eight for sets of lessons or units. When the general objectives are completed, you should be able to relate them to the general goals of science education and to identify an instructional plan or sequence for your lesson. (See the first column of Tables 6–5, 6–6, and 6–7.) For example: Understands the process of scientific inquiry.

4. *Write specific objectives under the general statements.* Again, the objective should start with a verb and state a learning result that is related to the general objective. Usually two or three specific objectives will be sufficient to describe the specific learning results. You may wish to change general and/or specific objectives after the closer analysis provided by this step. (See the second and third columns of Tables 6–5, 6–6, and 6–7.) Following is an example using the general objective stated in step 3. Understands the process of scientific inquiry:

   a. Applies the process to his or her own problem.
   b. Summarizes the process in his or her own words.
   c. Identifies correct and incorrect problem-solving procedures in the work of others.

Note that the conditions for good objectives are clear in the example; that is, both the general and specific objectives are clear, since they use a verb and they define observable learning results. Satisfactory performance of the task can be shown by the student's ability to apply the inquiry process to his or her own problem, to summarize the process, and to identify correct and incorrect procedures in the work of other students. Certainly there could be other learning results for this problem, but this one should serve as an example.

TABLE 6–6
Examples of general objectives, behavioral objectives, and terms for specifying objectives for science instruction in the affective domain

	General Objectives	*Behavioral Objectives*	*Terms for Objectives*
Receiving	Attention to activities in science Awareness of the importance of science Sensitivity toward science-related social issues	To listen during chemistry class To ask questions about physics To select a book on geology to read	Ask, attend, choose, follow, identify, listen, locate, look, select, tell
Responding	Completes assignments in science Participates in science class Discusses science Shows an interest in science Helps other students with science	To respond to questions related to photosynthesis To complete a report on glaciers To discuss the limitations and potential of science in social issues	Answer, assist, complete, discuss, do, help, perform, practice, read, recite, report, select, tell, watch, write
Valuing	Demonstrates confidence in science and technology Appreciates the role of science and technology Demonstrates the values of scientific problem-solving Prefers science over other subjects	To initiate further study in ecology To work on community projects relating to recycling To complete a science project To accept leadership in the science club	Accept, argue, complete, commit, describe, do, explain, follow, initiate, invite, join, prefer, propose, read, report, study, work
Organizing	Recognizes the responsibility of science and technology to society Develops a rationale for the place of science in society Bases judgments on evidence Accepts scientific values as personal values	To present scientific values as one's own To defend the right of scientists to do research To argue using fact, evidence, and data	Adhere, alter, argue, combine, defend, explain, integrate, modify, organize, synthesize
Characterizing	Uses problem solving for daily problems in work Displays scientific values Shows a consistent philosophy of life based on scientific values	To solve problems objectively To verify knowledge To display scientific attitudes	Act, confirm, display, influence, perform, practice, propose, question, refute, serve, solve, use, verify

5. *Review and evaluate objectives in terms of their comprehensiveness, coherence, and contribution to the science lesson unit or program.* The evaluation should identify any imbalance between levels of objectives or domains. Are all your objectives at the lower levels of the cognitive domain? We hope not. (Use Tables 6–5, 6–6, and 6–7 to help in the review.)

■ SUMMARY

It is important to have good objectives for science teaching. Without objectives, teaching becomes a confused and directionless experience, frustrating to the teacher and ineffective for the students.

Recent years have seen increased attention to stating objectives in performance terms. Good objec-

tives include a statement that uses action verbs, signifies learning results in observable or measurable terms, describes the conditions under which the performance can be expected, and indicates the level of attainment needed to satisfy the objective. Objectives are often divided into cognitive, affective, and psychomotor types. The first pertains to conceptual understandings or knowledge objectives. The second refers to attitudes, feelings, interests, and appreciations. Psychomotor objectives refer to skills and competencies that involve manipulation, muscular coordination, or sensory achievements.

The steps in preparing objectives are as follows: (1) review your general intentions; (2) select the content; (3) write general objectives; (4) write specific objectives; and (5) review your objectives for comprehensiveness, coherence, and contribution to the lesson.

TABLE 6–7
Examples of general objectives, behavioral objectives, and terms for specifying objectives for science instruction in the psychomotor domain

	General Objectives	*Behavioral Objectives*	*Terms for Objectives*
Moving	Walking smoothly in science class Moving around the science class without problems Keeping up with the class on science field trips	To clean and replace science materials To carry a microscope properly To obtain and carry materials for laboratory activities	Adjust, carry, clean, follow, locate, move, obtain, store, walk
Manipulating	Manipulating science materials without damaging them Coordinating several activities during laboratory periods Performing skillfully in the science laboratory Operating science equipment safely	To set up science laboratory equipment quickly To adjust a microscope so that the image is clear To dissect with precision To operate scientific instruments correctly To assemble science apparatus To pour chemicals safely	Adjust, assemble, build, calibrate, change, clean, connect, construct, dismantle, fasten, handle, heat, make, mix, repair, set, stir, weigh
Communicating	Informing the teacher of problems Communicating results of science activities Drawing accurate reproductions of microscopic images Talking and writing clearly and logically Explaining science information clearly	To communicate problems in handling equipment To ask questions about problems To listen to other students To write legibly To report data accurately To graph data accurately	Ask, analyze, describe, discuss, compose, draw, explain, graph, label, listen, record, sketch, write
Creating	Creating new scientific apparatus for solving problems Designing new scientific devices Inventing different techniques	To create different ways of solving problems To combine different pieces of equipment to form a new science instrument or device To plan ways to solve problems	Analyze, construct, create, design, invent, plan, synthesize

The use of clearly stated objectives in science teaching is significant. Although critics have cited certain pitfalls to be avoided, the overall effect of good objectives appears to be beneficial. Science teachers are more conscious of the performance they expect from their students. Evaluation becomes more precise. Progress toward the attainment of goals is more easily measurable. Science teaching assumes a quality that is more satisfying and defensible.

■ REFERENCES

1. Jay K. Hackett, "Constructivism: Hands On and Minds On," *Science Matters* (Staff Development Series, Macmillan-McGraw Hill, 1992).

2. Ibid.

3. Ibid.

4. Biological Sciences Curriculum Study, "Innovative Science Education" (Colorado College, Colorado Springs, CO, September, 1992).

5. Benjamin Bloom et al., *A Taxonomy of Educational Objectives: Handbook, 1, The Cognitive Domain* (New York: David McKay, 1950).

6. David Krathwohl and others, *Taxonomy of Educational Objectives: Handbook 2, Affective Domain* (New York: David McKay, 1965).

7. R. Kibler and others, *Behavioral Objective and Instruction* (Boston: Allyn and Bacon, 1970).

8. Norman Gronlund, *Stating Behavioral Objectives for Classroom Instruction* (New York: Macmillan, 1970).

-------------------- **INVESTIGATING SCIENCE TEACHING** --------------------

Activity 6–1

OBJECTIVES OF SCIENCE TEACHING

Directions:

1. In the blank provided before each statement of objectives, indicate your evaluation of each. Is it excellent (E), good (G), fair (F), poor (P), or not an objective (NO)? Complete this portion individually.
2. Review your individual responses in a small group of three or four persons. At this stage you should discuss why you evaluated the objectives the way you did.
3. As a class, review the strengths and weaknesses of the objectives as you presently understand them.

Objectives:

_____ 1. Describe the relationship between pressure and volume of an enclosed gas and predict either variable when the other is changed independently.

_____ 2. Demonstrate skill in setting up science laboratory materials.

_____ 3. Know science.

_____ 4. Appreciate the nature of scientific inquiry.

_____ 5. Teach students the concept of density.

_____ 6. Enjoy interacting with friends in science class.

_____ 7. Given a scientific problem, will define variables, formulate hypotheses, and test the hypotheses.

_____ 8. Handle a microscope properly.

_____ 9. Record data appropriately.

_____ 10. At the completion of the lesson, prepare a growth curve showing the relationship of the age of a bacterial culture to the density of organisms and predict the results of continued growth.

_____ 11. Really show curiosity.

_____ 12. Show scientific attitudes, e.g., openness, reality testing, risk-taking, objectivity, precision, perseverance.

_____ 13. Perform skillfully while working in the laboratory.

_____ 14. Judge the logical consistency of a scientific theory.

_____ 15. Display habits of safety.

_____ 16. Know common scientific terms.

_____ 17. To demonstrate to the students different geologic processes.

_____ 18. Having fun in science.

_____ 19. To identify energy chains in a community.

_____ 20. Is able, upon completion of the lesson, to draw, label, and explain it.

_____ 21. Science teaching should make students aware of the relationship between the scientific enterprise and society.

_____ 22. At the completion of this lesson the student should understand the meaning of science as it relates to the good life.

_____ 23. Operational definition of scientific truth.

_____ 24. The student shows the scientific attitude of perseverance by pursuing a problem to its solution.

_____ 25. Understands the basic principle of density.

a. States the principle in his or her own words.

b. Give an example of the principle from life, physical and earth science.

c. Distinguish between correct and incorrect applications of the principle.

UNIT 4

································

CURRICULUM PERSPECTIVES

When you think of the science curriculum, what do you think of? Is it the same as district guidelines, course syllabi, and science textbooks? Is this curriculum made up of the laboratories, computer software, readings, and discussions that science teachers actually present to students? Or is the science curriculum the knowledge, values, and skills that students learn as a result of all the varied experiences in a school science program? Actually, the science curriculum may consist of all of these. Certainly you can find examples of them in any school system or science classroom. The three perspectives just mentioned—the *intended* science curriculum, the *taught* science curriculum, and the *learned* science curriculum—all contribute to an understanding of what we mean by the science curriculum. In particular, these perspectives demonstrate the potential strengths and weaknesses of different efforts to reform the science curriculum.

Think of other questions. What should be emphasized in the students' experiences with science? Should the emphasis be on science principles and concepts? Should the curriculum emphasize scientific inquiry and processes of science? Should science teachers orient the curriculum toward science- and technology-related social issues? How would you justify answers to these questions?

Should you consider a different orientation for science curricula at middle schools and high schools? You can see that an answer to the first question—When you think of the science curriculum, what do you think of?—involves much more than the science textbook. The science curriculum consists of the science content, your expected actions and teaching behaviors, the students' experiences, the educational technologies, the laboratories, and the textbook. As a science teacher you have the responsibility of organizing and orchestrating the curriculum for students.

You have probably also realized that contemporary science education is in a period of reform. The probability is fairly high that you will be involved in improving the science curriculum in your school. The chapters in this section on *Curriculum Perspectives* should provide you with information and understanding about the science curriculum and help you answer some of the questions we posed in this introduction. Beyond background information on middle and high school curriculum, we have included several examples of science curriculum originally supported by the NSF and generally aligned with national standards. You should understand that the programs were developed prior to the national standards; however, the different programs represent many aspects of the standards as they should be translated to curriculum materials.

Chapter 7

....

THE MIDDLE SCHOOL SCIENCE CURRICULUM

This chapter, and the next two, address the science curriculum. By now you probably recognize that curriculum is really more than content. Your curriculum includes science content, manipulative skills, attitudes you wish students to develop, the context or environment of the classroom, various teaching strategies, and the means you use to assess student progress. There will be a difference between the science curriculum represented in your school district syllabus, the national standards, state and local frameworks, science textbooks, and what your students learn. Discussing the curriculum is more complex than it may seem. Rather than resolve all the issues surrounding curriculum, we direct attention in these chapters to the national standards and benchmarks, instructional materials representing different courses of study you may encounter, and a general process for the design and development of curriculum.

■ A BACKGROUND ON CURRICULUM REFORM IN MIDDLE SCHOOL

It is important to first provide background and context for later discussions, beginning with a brief overview of curriculum reform at the middle level of education. We introduce several curriculum frameworks—*Science For All Americans,*[1] *Scope, Sequence, and Coordination,*[3] and the National Center for Improving Science Education (NCISE).[2] These frameworks relate to the chapters on middle school, high school, and interdisciplinary science curriculum. We then briefly review the national standards for grades five through eight and the American Association for the Advancement of Science (AAAS) benchmarks. Finally, we provide examples of middle school science curriculum.

Junior High and Middle Schools

Adolescence is a period of significant physical, intellectual, social, and emotional development. The fact that adolescence generally spans the years of secondary education makes understanding this period generally important, but of particular importance is the period of junior high or middle school. Education during the middle school years, generally from ages 10 to 14, must extend the experiences of elementary school. The goals, curriculum, and instruction for science should be conceptualized and implemented

as unique and congruent with the particular needs of the developing adolescent. In recent years, educators have increasingly realized the crucial and singular role of education during adolescence. In the next section, we review the history of junior high and middle schools.

History of the Junior High

In the latter part of the nineteenth century, most elementary schools included grades 1 through 8 while high schools included grades 9 through 12. By 1920, about 80 percent of students graduating from high school had experienced eight years of elementary school and four years of high school. While the schools were actually structured in this eight-four plan, leading educators continually debated school organization for over three decades beginning in the 1890s. Junior high schools, or school systems with six years of elementary school, three years of junior high school, and three years of high school, emerged in the early 1900s. Not until the 1918 Commission on the Reorganization of Secondary Education (CRSE) did the junior high become firmly established in the American education system. The 1918 CRSE report, *Cardinal Principles of Secondary Education*, stated:

> We, therefore, recommend a reorganization of the school system whereby the first six years shall be devoted to elementary education designed to meet the needs of pupils approximately 6 to 12 years of ages, and the second six years to secondary education designed to meet the needs of pupils approximately 12 to 18 years of age. The six years to be devoted to secondary education may well be divided into two periods which may be designated as the junior and senior periods.[4]

With the Commission on the Reorganization of Secondary Education (CRSE) report, the concept of junior high schools was established. Their numbers grew: in 1920, there were an estimated 800 junior high schools in the United States, while by 1930, there were 1,787. The reasons for the rapid increase of junior high schools were shortages of facilities and economic restraints placed on schools between World War I and World War II. Justifications for junior high programs cited the needs of adolescents, the transition to high school, the elimination of dropouts, and vocational preparation. By 1940, prominent educators had developed a rationale for the junior high school. W.T. Gruhn and N.R. Douglas summarize the essential functions of junior high schools as:

- *Integration.* Basic skills, attitudes, and understanding learned previously should be coordinated into effective behaviors.
- *Exploration.* Individuals should explore special interests, aptitudes, and abilities for educational opportunities, vocational decisions, and recreational choices.
- *Guidance.* Assistance should be provided for students making decisions regarding education, careers, and social adjustment.
- *Differentiation.* Educational opportunities and facilities should provide for varying backgrounds, interests, and needs of the students.
- *Socialization.* Education should prepare early adolescents for participation in a complex democratic society.
- *Articulation.* Orientation of the program should provide a gradual transition from preadolescent (elementary) education to a program suited to the needs of adolescents.[5]

In reality, most teachers were trained for the high school and had little desire to teach in junior high schools. A junior high school teaching job was perceived as a stepping stone to a high school position. Most educators forgot or ignored the important goals of education for early adolescents, and education in grades seven, eight, and nine became scaled-down versions of grades ten, eleven, and twelve. Criticisms of junior high schools began in the 1930s and continued into the 1960s. Some of the criticisms were:

- a shortage of qualified professionals,
- lack of agreement on purpose,
- high dropout rates,
- programs (athletics, music, and social) that were inappropriate for early adolescents,
- ineffective discipline, and
- teachers who did not understand early adolescents.

What of the science curricula in junior high schools? We answer this question in the next section.

Science Curriculum in Junior High Schools

Science in the junior high school has faced perplexing problems. General science was the course offered in the ninth grade of eighty-four schools when the first junior high schools came into existence. Begun in the decade 1910–1920, the course was designed to satisfy the needs and interests of students in early adolescence. The first course was established through research and was designed to fill a perceived need.

Junior high school science encountered several difficulties. For one thing, there was a shortage of well-trained general science teachers. Many teachers at this level were physics, chemistry, and biology teachers whose primary interest was not the problems of junior high school science. Also, teachers in other disciplines, such as English, mathematics, and physical education, were recruited to teach science. For these reasons, the general science texts for these grades were written in an effort to relieve these problems, but the variations in school and grade-level organization such as six-three-three, eight-two-two, and eight-four necessitated much repetition of science topics to produce universally saleable textbooks.

There were also deficiencies in equipment and facilities for teaching science. Many science classes were taught in ordinary classrooms without water or gas outlets and without adequate facilities for demonstrations and experiments. Further, there was no clear knowledge of what junior high school science should actually accomplish. Objectives ranged from "preparation for the rigorous science courses in the senior high school" to "general education for good citizenship." Science educators and teachers gave considerable thought to development of attitudes and interests. Some felt that general science should be exploratory in nature. Courses designed on this premise became rapid surveys of chemistry, physics, astronomy, meteorology, biology, and geology. Others believed that students should study the applications of science in the world around them. Courses of this kind centered on home appliances, transportation, communication, health problems, and natural resources.

Enrollments in general science grew to about 65 percent of the ninth-grade classes by 1956, then declined as new courses began to permeate the ninth grade and as the seventh and eighth grades took over more of the general science offerings.[6]

Revision of junior high school science courses through national curriculum studies of the 1960s was delayed until late in reform, while attention centered on the senior high school courses. Junior high school science is usually organized in one of three patterns: (1) a one-, two-, or three-year program called general science; (2) a three-year program in which life, physical, and earth sciences are taught individually for a year each; (3) a one-, two-, or three-year program of integrated or thematically organized science. One of the first two patterns is found in the majority of schools.[7] The reform movement of the 1960s and 1970s made no effort to improve general science. In fact, many educators hoped that by implementing new life, earth, and physical science programs the traditional general science would eventually be replaced. This did not occur.

Emergence of Middle Schools

During the 1960s, several factors contributed to the emergence of middle schools as an alternative to junior high schools. Some of the factors included general criticisms of the schools and a need to increase the quality of education; an emphasis on curriculum improvement in science, mathematics, and foreign language; renewed interest in preparation for college; recognition of Jean Piaget's work in developmental psychology; the need to eliminate de facto racial segregation; restructuring of schools due to overcrowding; and a general desire to improve education. These and other factors contributed to an increase from 100 middle schools in 1960 to over 5,000 in 1980. In 1988, there were 12,000 separate middle schools with an estimated enrollment of 8,000,000 students. Clearly, middle schools represented more than an educational fad.

We think the middle school is an important conceptual and physical change in the American educational system. Some of the important characteristics of the middle school were described in a 1981 report, *The Status of Middle School and Junior High School Sciences*.[8]

- A program specifically designed for pre-and early adolescents.
- A program that encourages exploration and personal development.
- A positive and active learning environment.
- A schedule that is flexible with respect to time and grouping.
- A staff that recognizes students' needs, motivations, fears, and goals.
- An instructional approach that is varied.
- An emphasis on acquiring essential knowledge, skills, and attitudes in a sequential and individual manner.
- An emphasis on developing decision-making and problem-solving skills.
- Interdisciplinary learning and team teaching.

Middle schools, in structure and function, have many advantages, as follows:

- The middle school has a unique status; the school and program are not junior to another program.
- Specific subjects, like science and mathematics, can be introduced at lower grades by specialists.
- Developing new middle schools provides the impetus for redesigning goals, curriculum, and instruction for the early adolescent learner.
- Development of middle schools can facilitate changes in teacher certification standards, and, subsequently teacher education programs.
- Some discipline problems can be eliminated through different groupings of students, primarily the inclusion of younger students.
- Middle schools can be designed to provide greater guidance and counseling at the time it is needed.

Time will answer questions about the role of middle schools in education. We believe their season has come, and they will be recorded as an important educational advance. The present period of reform should contribute substantially to their implementation and sustained presence in American education.

Science Curriculum in Middle Schools

The 1980s initiated a period of transition and reform for middle/junior high school programs. In 1986, the NSTA published a position statement entitled "Science Education for Middle and Junior High Students." This position statement described the goals and orientation for curriculum and instruction:

> The primary function of science education at the middle and junior high level is to provide students with the opportunity to explore science in their lives and to become comfortable and personally involved with it. Certainly science curriculum at this level should reflect society's goals and scientific and technological literacy and emphasize the role of science for personal, social, and career use, as well as prepare students academically.[9]

This position statement continued with a specific discussion indicating that the science curriculum should fulfill the needs of the early adolescent and address both the personal needs of students and issues of a global society. Experience at this level should be concrete, manipulative, and physical. The position statement recommended the curricula should focus on the relationship of science to:

- content from life, physical, earth sciences, and ecology with frequent interdisciplinary references;
- process skills, such as experimenting, observing, measuring, and inferring;
- personal use in everyday applications and in practical problem solving that allow open-ended exploration;
- social issues that involve individual responsibilities and call for decision making;
- all careers;
- limitations of science and the necessity of respecting differing, well-considered points of view;
- developing written and oral communication skills; and
- positive attitudes and personal success.[10]

The NSTA position statement is important for two reasons. First, the clear emphasis on the student differentiates this curriculum from high school programs. And second, there is a definite trend toward the middle school and away from the junior high school. Figure 7–1 displays some characteristics of science curricula for middle schools and aligns those characteristics with middle school programs.

In 1988, the NSF issued a request for proposals to develop programs for middle school science. The

- Teachers knowledgeable about and committed to the education of early adolescents.
- A balanced curriculum of academic goals and developmental needs of adolescents.
- Different organizational arrangements for instruction, e.g., individual, small group, large group.
- A variety of instructional methods.
- An active learning environment.
- Flexible scheduling.
- Continuous progress.
- Students master skills of decision making and problem solving.
- Cooperative planning and coordinated teaching.
- Exploratory and enrichment studies.
- Interdisciplinary learning.
- Emphasis on all three domains.
- Teacher education programs and staff development for middle school science.
- A balance of knowledge, inquiry, personal needs, social issues, and career awareness goals.
- A mixture of instructional groupings, e.g., individual projects, group activities, and large group presentations.
- Use of traditional and new methods, such as simulations, role modeling, debate, and computers.
- Use of problem solving, laboratory investigations, field studies, and other activities.
- Schedules designed for class presentations, field trips, and individual projects.
- A coordinated science program across the middle school years to provide a smooth transition from elementary to high school.
- Emphasis on scientific processes, information processing, and decision making.
- Science, mathematics, and social studies teachers plan the science curriculum and teach units cooperatively.
- Opportunities to meet individuals in the community whose careers are in science, technology, and mathematics.
- An integrated approach to science.
- Science programs that emphasize knowledge, attitudes, and skills related to science and technology integrated with personal needs and social issues

FIGURE 7–1
Ideal middle schools and science programs: Characteristics of an ideal middle school (Source: The characteristics of an ideal middle school are based on several sources, including *The Exemplary Middle School* by William Alexander and Paul George (1981), *The Essential Middle School* by G. Wiles and H. Bondi (1981), *This We Believe* by the National Middle School Association (1982), *The Middle School We Need* by Thomas Gatewood and Charles Dilg (1975), and a 1973 article entitled, "Do You Have a Middle School?" by Nicholas Georgiady and Louis Romano.)

NSF solicitation contained descriptions of the orientation for middle school programs.

> In *middle school years*, [the students] should begin to develop a more disciplined approach to inquiry and experimentation—improving their ability to organize and articulate knowledge, and to approach problems systematically.[11]

Included in the solicitation were some characteristics of middle school materials. Those characteristics included the following:

- integration of science with other subjects,
- hands-on experiences,
- establishment of a coherent pattern of science topics,
- capitalization on the interests of students,
- use of recent research on teaching and learning, and
- identification of standards of student achievement.

In the early 1990s, the programs developed with these NSF grants became available. You should be familiar with some of the programs. We describe those programs later in the chapter.

■ FRAMEWORKS FOR SCIENCE CURRICULUM

Several frameworks for curriculum have significantly influenced state and local reform of middle school and high school science programs. Those frameworks include the AAAS reports *Science for All Americans* and *Benchmarks for Science Literary*; the NSTA 1989 project *Scope, Sequence, and Coordination*; and the NCISE reports on middle level education[11] and secondary education.[12]

Science for All Americans

Late in the 1980s, F. James Rutherford established Project 2061[13] at AAAS. He designed Project 2061 to take a long-term, large-scale view of education reform in the sciences. This reform is based on the goal of scientific literacy. The core of *Science for All Americans* and in 1993 the subsequent publication *Benchmarks for Science Literacy* consists of recommendations by a distinguished group of scientists and educators about what understandings and habits of mind are essential for all citizens in a scientifically literate society.

Project 2061 staff used the reports of five independent scientific panels. In addition, Project 2061 staff sought the advice of a large and diverse array of consultants and reviewers—scientists, engineers, mathematicians, historians, and educators. The process took more than three years, involved hundreds of individuals, and culminated in the publication of *Science for All Americans* and the characterization of scientific literacy. Thus, its recommendations are presented in the form of basic learning goals for American students. A premise of Project 2061 is that science teachers do not need to teach more, they should teach less so that content can be taught better.

Science for All Americans covers an array of topics. Many already are common in school curricula (for example, the structure of matter, the basic functions of cells, prevention of disease, communications technology, and different uses of numbers). However, the treatment of such topics differs from traditional approaches in two ways. One difference is that boundaries between traditional subject-matter categories are softened and connections are emphasized through the use of important conceptual themes, such as systems, evolution, cycles, and energy. Transformations of energy, for example, occur in physical, biological, and technological systems; and evolutionary change appears in stars, organisms, and societies. A second difference is that the amount of detail that students are expected to learn is less than in traditional science, mathematics, and technology courses. Key concepts and thinking skills are emphasized instead of specialized vocabulary and memorized procedures. The ideas not only make sense at a simple level but also provide a lasting foundation for learning more science. Details are treated as a means of enhancing, not guaranteeing, students' understanding of a general idea.

Recommendations in *Science for All Americans* include topics that are not common in school curricula. Among those topics are the nature of the scientific enterprise and how science, mathematics, and technology relate to one another and to the social system in general. The report also calls for understanding something of the history of science and technology.

Scope, Sequence, and Coordination

A second approach to the reform of middle and high school science has been suggested by William G. Aldridge.[14] In an analysis of school programs, Aldridge found deficiencies related to the scope, sequence, and coordination of programs. These deficiencies were revealed in a comparison with science programs in other countries, specifically the

TABLE 7–1
Example of a revised science curriculum for grades 7 through 12 in the United States

Subject	Grade Level						Total Time Spent
	7	8	9	10	11	12	
Hours Per Week by Subject							
Biology	1	2	2	3	1	1	360
Chemistry	1	1	2	2	3	2	396
Physics	2	2	1	1	2	3	396
Earth/Space Science	3	2	2	1	1	1	360
Total Hours Per Week	7	7	7	7	7	7	
Emphasis	Descriptive Empirical			Theoretical			

Commonwealth of Independent States and the People's Republic of China.

The Project on Scope, Sequence, and Coordination of Secondary School Science is an effort to restructure science teaching primarily at the secondary school level. The project calls for elimination of the tracking of students, recommends that all students study science every year for six years, and advocates the study of science as carefully sequenced, well-coordinated instruction in physics, chemistry, biology, and earth/space science. As opposed to the traditional curriculum in which science is taught in year-long and separate disciplines, the NSTA project provides for *spacing* the study of each of the sciences during several years. Research on the *spacing effect* indicates that students can learn and retain new material better if they study it in spaced intervals rather than all at once. In this way, students can revisit a concept at successively higher levels of abstraction (see Table 7–1).

The scope, sequence, and coordination reform effort also uses appropriate *sequencing* of instruction, taking into account how students learn. In science, understanding develops from concrete experiences with a phenomenon before it is given a name or a symbol. Students need experience with a concept in several different contexts before it becomes part of their mental repertoire. With prior hands-on experience, students can come to understand the main concepts and processes of science. The practical components of this instruction should begin in middle school/seventh grade with issues and phenomena of concern to students at a personal level and then move toward a more encompassing scope in high school. As they mature, students are able to generalize from concrete, direct experiences to more abstract and broader theoretical thinking. With a sequenced approach, students should no longer be expected to memorize facts and information. With practical applications, science should make sense and have meaning.

The third component of the scope, sequence, and coordination project is the *coordination* of science concepts and topics. Earth/space science, biology, chemistry, and physics have significant features and processes in common. Coordination among these disciplines leads to awareness of the interdependence of the sciences and how the disciplines form a body of knowledge. Seeing a concept, law, or principle in the context of two or three different subjects helps to establish it firmly in the student's mind.

At first, students are introduced more intensively to the descriptive and phenomenological aspects of the sciences. The most abstract and theoretical aspects are emphasized in the later years. Empirical and semi-quantitative treatments are emphasized in the middle years. Computers and technology and practical applications are integrated directly into each course. Most important, students are taught science in a way that will enable them to understand and apply it, whether as scientists or citizens.

■ NATIONAL CENTER FOR IMPROVING SCIENCE EDUCATION

Development of local school science programs can be greatly enhanced by frameworks for curriculum, assessment, and staff development: examples include NCISE's framework for both middle school and high school levels.

The curriculum and instruction frameworks for middle school and high school extend the center's proposed framework for the elementary years.[15] Treatments of the recommended organizing concepts, however, are more complex. The organizing concepts detailed in the technical report for middle schools include cause and effect, change and conservation, diversity and variation, energy and matter, evolution and equilibrium, models and theories, probability and prediction, structure and function, systems and interaction, and time and scale. The concepts need not be independent units of study; they should at least, however, link subjects, topics, and disciplines. Curriculum emphases should include scientific habits of mind, such as willingness to modify explanations, cooperation in answering questions, and solving problems, respect for reason, reliance on data, and skepticism. Students also should develop skills for answering scientific questions, solving technological problems, making decisions, and taking action. Content in the program should relate to the life and world of the student and provide a context for presenting new knowledge, skills, and attitudes. The focus of curriculum and instruction should be on depth of study, not breadth of topics.

■ *NATIONAL SCIENCE EDUCATION STANDARDS AND BENCHMARKS FOR SCIENCE LITERACY*

In previous chapters we introduced the *National Science Education Standards.* In this section we direct attention to the *Content Standards,* in particular those for grades 5–8. These standards describe the knowledge, understandings and abilities that students should develop as a result of their educational experiences. They also represent one aspect of a comprehensive vision of science education, which also includes science teaching and assessment. We state this to make the point that as you consider the science curriculum, it is imperative to consider more than content. You also should review teaching and assessment in the consideration of any commercial program or the design of your local science curriculum.

Unifying Concepts and Processes	Science as Inquiry	Physical Science	Life Science	Earth and Space Science	Science and Technology	Science in Personal and Social Perspectives	History and Nature of Science
• Order and Organization • Change and Measurement • Evolution and Equilibrium • Form and Function	• Abilities of Scientific Inquiry • Under-standings of Scientific Inquiry	• Properties and Changes in Properties of matter • Motions and Forces • Transfer of Energy	• Structure and Function in Living Systems • Reproduction and Heredity • Regulation and Behavior • Populations and Ecosystems • Diversity and Adaptations of Organisms	• Structure of the Earth System • Earth's History • Earth in the Solar System	• Abilities of Technological Design • Under-standings about Science and Technology	• Personal Health • Populations, Resources, and Environments • Natural Hazards • Risks and Benefits • Science and Technology in Society	• Science as a Human Endeavor • Nature of Science • History of Science

FIGURE 7–2
Conceptual organizers from *National Science Education Standards* for grades 5-8

The Nature of Science	The Nature of Mathematics	The Nature of Technology	The Physical Setting

• The Scientific World View
• Scientific Inquiry
• The Scientific Enterprise
	• Patterns and Relationships
	• Mathematics
	  Science and Technology
	• Mathematical Inquiry
		• Technology and Science
		• Design and Systems
		• Issues in Technology
			• The Universe
			• The Earth
			• Processes that
			  Shape the Earth
			• Energy Transformations
			• Motion
			• Forces of Nature

The Living Environment	*The Human Organism*	*Human Society*	*The Designed World*

• Diversity of Life
• Heredity
• Cells
• Interdependence of Life
• Flow of Matter
  and Energy
• Evolution of Life
	• Human Identity
	• Human Development
	• Basic Functions
	• Learning
	• Physical Health
	• Mental Health
		• Cultural Effects
		  on Behavior
		• Group Behavior
		• Social Change
		• Political and Economic
		  Systems
		• Social Conflict
		• Group Interdependence
			• Agriculture
			• Materials and
			  Manufacturing
			• Energy Sources and Use
			• Communication
			• Information Processing
			• Health
			• Technology

The Mathematical World	*Historical Perspectives*	*Common Themes*	*Habits of Mind*

• Numbers
• Symbolic Relationships
• Shapes
• Uncertainty
• Reasoning
	• Displacing Earth from
	  the Center of
	  the Universe
	• Uniting the Heavens
	  and Earth
	• Relating Matter and
	  Energy and Time
	  and Space
	• Extending Time
	• Moving the Continents
	• Understanding Fire
	• Splitting the Atom
	· Explaining the Diversity
	  of Life
	· Discovering Germs
	• Harnessing Power
		• Systems
		• Models
		• Constancy and Change
		• Scale
			• Values and Attitudes
			• Computation
			  and Estimation
			• Manipulation
			  and Observation
			• Communication Skills
			• Critical-Response Skills

FIGURE 7-3
Conceptual organizers from *Benchmarks for Science Literacy*

Figure 7–2 presents the conceptual organizers for the *Content Standards.* As you consider curriculum for middle school science, you should try to incorporate opportunities for students to develop the fundamental understandings and abilities associated with these conceptual organizers. (Review the actual document for more details.)

In 1993 Project 2061 also released *Benchmarks for Science Literacy,* based on *Science for All Americans.* The benchmarks consist of specific goals and objectives for science curriculum. Many local school districts and some national organizations began using the benchmarks for different models of science curriculum in 1993. Figure 7–3 presents the major conceptual organizers for benchmarks. The benchmarks used grade levels K–2, 3–5, 6–8, and 9–12.

■ **SCIENCE CURRICULA FOR THE MIDDLE SCHOOL**

In *A Middle School Curriculum,*[16] James Beane identified an insightful question about the middle school movement. Beane had the broad, underlying conception of the middle school in mind when he asked "the curriculum question." Beane was alluding to the fact that many aspects of middle level education had been addressed, but the curriculum continued with an "absent presence" as educators continued improving various aspects of middle schools. Based on the historical transition from junior high to middle schools, it comes as no surprise to learn that many educators have deep loyalties to, and identities with, subject matter disciplines such as science, or even more specifically, life, earth, and physical science. With this view, Beane directly asked: *What should be the curriculum of the middle school?*

Beane argues that "academic disciplines," such as science, do not answer "the curriculum question." He recommends a general education, as opposed to a specialized education approach. General education focuses on the common needs, concerns, and problems of individuals and society. Implementing this position would result in a curriculum that truly recognizes the intellectual, social, emotional, and physical perspectives of early adolescents. In addition, the curriculum would include social perspectives that center on themes such as interdependence, diversity, environment, and technology.

In the examples that follow, we recognize that the needs of science teachers and school districts exist on a continuum from traditional junior high school science to contemporary middle school curricula. Thus, we provide several examples of science curricula that align with the middle school concepts and the curriculum frameworks and policies, such as *National Science Education Standards, Benchmarks for Science Literacy,* and *Scope, Sequence, and Coordination.*

Middle School Science & Technology (Biological Sciences Curriculum Study)

Biological Sciences Curriculum Study, with support from the National Science Foundation, began developing this program in 1989. It is designed to help educators accomplish the following four goals.

1. Develop middle school students' understanding of basic concepts and skills related to science and technology.
2. Increase the participation and success of underrepresented populations in middle school science classes.
3. Improve middle school students' understanding of how science and technology relate to their lives.
4. Promote the development of critical thinking and problem-solving abilities in middle school students.

Seven features make *Middle School Science & Technology* unique. BSCS included the following features because they address the findings of the current research in science education, middle school philosophy, and contemporary learning theory.

The curriculum integrates the sciences. BSCS did not divide the life, earth, and physical sciences into separate books or separate chapters in this curriculum. Instead, they developed each unit using a theme that unifies major ideas from all areas of science and technology. By using a theme such as *Systems and Change,* they incorporated the ideas

from a variety of scientific disciplines into a coherent unit of study (see Figure 7–4).

The program incorporates technology. The students explore many of the concepts of technology—design process, efficiency, costs, benefits, criteria, constraints, and decision making—as part of the program. The *Teacher's Guide and Resources* includes recommendations for integrating educational technology, such as videos, computer programs, telecommunications, and utility software, into each unit.

The program uses a specific instructional model. This instructional model is characterized by the 5 Es: *Engage, Explore, Explain, Elaborate, Evaluate.* This model is explained in detail in Chapter 14 of this book, "Models for Effective Science Teaching." BSCS sequenced and labeled all of the student activities in the program according to the 5 Es instructional model based on a constructivist model of learning. One tenet of the constructivist model is that all students have experiences from which they build (or construct) knowledge. Yet, in a classroom, attempting to help each student construct knowledge based on his or her previous experiences can be an overwhelming task. The task is further complicated by the fact that each student brings a different background to a lesson. The instructional model provides a solution to this dilemma for science teachers.

The program includes cooperative learning strategies. In the classroom, cooperative learning research indicates that collaboration among students increases the level of student success. For this reason, BSCS incorporated cooperative learning strategies into the curriculum. The model used in this program is an adaptation of the work of David Johnson and Roger Johnson at the University of Minnesota.[17] Students must be individually accountable for the work of their team and for their own learning. They also must learn to use a variety of social skills; these skills are assigned to units, with subskills defined for most investigations. The social skills are developed progressively and are based on the students' prior experiences in the program.

The program offers a variety of teaching strategies to meet the diverse needs of your students. The instructional model, cooperative learning theory, and the research on successful middle schools all support using a variety of strategies in the classroom. *Middle School Science & Technology* is more than 60 percent hands-on and minds-on investigations that keep students engaged in the study of science and technology. In addition to these investigations, the curriculum includes strategies, such as simulations, debates, plays, outdoor activities, research projects, and creative writing. Many of these strategies increase the participation and success of underrepresented groups of students in the science classroom. Researchers have noted that certain strategies

Level A: Patterns of Change				
Unit	*1*	*2*	*3*	*4*
Curriculum Emphasis	Personal dimensions of science and technology	The nature of scientific explanations	Technology problem solving	Science and technology in society
Focus Question	How does my world change?	How do we explain patterns of change on the earth?	How do we adjust to patterns of change?	How can we change patterns?

Level B: Diversity and Limits				
Unit	*1*	*2*	*3*	*4*
Curriculum Emphasis	Personal dimensions of science and technology	Technological problem solving	The nature of scientific explanations	Science and technology in society
Focus Question	What is normal?	How does technology account for my limits?	Why are things different?	Why are we different?

Level C: Systems and Change				
Unit	*1*	*2*	*3*	*4*
Sub-theme	Systems in balance	Change through time	Energy in systems	Populations
Curriculum Emphasis	Personal dimensions of science and technology	The nature of scientific explanations	Technological problem solving	Science and technology in society
Focus Question	How much can things change and still stay the same?	How do things change through time?	How can we improve our use of energy?	What are the limits to growth?

FIGURE 7–4
***Middle School Science & Technology* scope and sequence**

and topics help increase the success of minority students; these include cooperative learning, activities that help develop spatial skills, information that helps students prepare for careers, topics that are relevant to the students and that build on their prior experiences, and the reinforcement of basic skills.[18,19] *Middle School Science & Technology* incorporates these suggestions.

The instructional design of the program accommodates different learning styles. Each student has a preferred style of learning. Unfortunately, this method may not match his or her teacher's preferred style of teaching. To help address this discrepancy, BSCS designed four characters to represent the four dominant learning styles as defined by the Gregorc style inventory: concrete random, concrete sequential, abstract random, and abstract sequential. These characters appear in the text periodically and make comments typical of their designated learning styles to give each type of learner someone to whom he or she can relate.

This program broadens the role of assessment so that students become responsible for their own learning. Although tests and grades represent only one aspect of assessment, they are the only component of assessment that most educators practice or consider. In this curriculum BSCS broadened the role of assessment to include an interactive and ongoing process between the teacher and the student that helps determine lesson flow. Broadening the role of assessment allows the teacher to modify lessons to meet the needs of the students. This change also encourages students to be responsible for the results of their education. Ongoing assessment helps the students understand their progress, monitor their growth, and develop specific skills.

Evaluation indicates these BSCS materials represent one of very few science curricula that can actually achieve the program goals. Results from the formative and summative evaluations of the field test provided the following support for achieving the program goals.

Goal 1: Students should understand the basic concepts and skills of science and technology. BSCS administered a test of key concepts from the program to the field-test students after they had completed a year of study. (*Middle School Science & Technology* was field tested with 20,000 students and 200 teachers during the 1990–1991 and 1991–1992 school years.) BSCS administered a pre-test and post-test to both the control and the experimental groups and observed a statistically significant difference in the students' performances. On tests such as the California Achievement Test, students in the program showed gains of one-half to one full grade level over the previous year the test was given. On other standardized tests, such as the Iowa Test of Basic Skills, student groups maintained their scores from years prior to using *Middle School Science & Technology.*

Goal 2: Students from underrepresented populations will increase their participation and success in middle school science class. BSCS monitored the attitude shifts of women, Hispanic Americans, and African Americans as they used the program. Results indicate positive shifts in female students of all ethnic backgrounds. BSCS administered the same attitude survey at the beginning and at the end of the 1991–1992 school year. After using the program for one year, female students indicated that they could not wait for science class to start (a shift from neutral to agree); disagreed that doing science projects at home was dumb (they previously agreed with that statement); and shifted from disagree to agree with the statement that they like discussing science with their friends outside of class.

Goal 3: Students will understand how science and technology relate to their lives. Evidence from the attitude survey and the results of interviews with students after using the program indicated that they thought science and technology were relevant to their lives and that understanding science and technology was very important to them. Baseline interviews with students indicated that science was not important because it was boring or irrelevant. After using *Middle School Science & Technology,* students began to characterize science differently.

Goal 4: Students will develop critical-thinking skills and problem-solving abilities. To assess the development of thinking skills and problem-solving abilities, BSCS documented teachers' perceptions of students' abilities, and students' scores on standardized tests that included skill assessment. Analysis of the teachers'

perceptions of changes in the students showed a direct correlation between the incorporation of cooperative learning strategies and an increase in the students' use of critical thinking skills. On the North Carolina State Science Test, which includes sections on thinking skills as well as on content areas, students' scores improved by a range of three to eight percentage points.

Insights: An Inquiry-based Middle School Curriculum (Education Development Center)

Insights: An Inquiry-based Middle School Curriculum was developed at Education Development Center, Inc. (EDC) and is the result of the *Improving Urban Middle School Science Project,* funded by the NSF.

The curriculum consists of six modules (see Figure 7–5) to be used in either the seventh or eighth grade. The modules can be used as the core for a complete middle school curriculum, which can be extended to meet the needs of a particular school, or used individually as supplements for a curriculum already in place. When combined with *Insights: An Elementary Hands-on Inquiry-based Science Curriculum,* which has seventeen modules across grades K–6, the middle school curriculum completes a coherent and consistent core K–8 science program. Each middle school module is designed to last a minimum of ten weeks.

EDC based the module topic selections on students' interests and provided a context for science classroom experience of inquiry-based investigation, technology, and problem solving. Each module focuses on fundamental scientific concepts and understandings, as well as on conceptual themes in the physical, human and health, life, and earth and space sciences. Although the topics provide a context for the development of deep understanding of science concepts, the themes build within and between the modules, providing connections to other science disciplines and subject areas.

Each of the six modules provides:

- content which is relevant to the students' interests, experiences, and environment;
- inquiry-based investigations which explore science concepts in-depth and allow for connections among sciences;
- opportunities for students to develop science skills, knowledge, and attitudes; and
- investigations of relationships between science concepts and processes, and technology.

Each module is designed to support:

- development of higher-level critical and creative thinking skills within a context of cooperative, collaborative learning;

FIGURE 7–5
Insights: An Inquiry-Based
Middle School Curriculum

Designed for Motion. Students investigate the biological and physical factors involved in human movement. Explorations focus on how the design of the body enables humans to move and function.

Music to My Ears. Students use the musical world for investigating the physics and technology of sound and the physiology of hearing. Learning experiences address common questions about sounds: what they are, how we hear them, and how we shape them in our world.

You Are What You Eat. Students explore the relationship between food and nutrition and the factors that influence what we eat, how our bodies use foods, how we process and package foods, and the role of food in society.

How Do We Know What We Know? This module addresses the question: How do we find out about something? By participating in a long-term inquiry experience focusing on model building and the particulate nature of matter, students explore how they question, investigate, organize, process, and act on information.

Meeting our Needs. Students investigate human needs and how natural resources are used to meet them. They develop an understanding of the environment by exploring the functions of natural resources in their lives and their responsibilities to future generations, and to the earth for sustaining them.

Energy! The Power Source. This module has students examine the role of energy in their lives. As they explore the chemical and physical functions of energy, they develop an understanding of the various forms that energy has, its transferability, and its multifaceted role in their lives.

- students' ability to formulate and investigate meaningful questions which grow out of their own curiosity and interests;
- use of empirical approaches to experimentation; and
- the widely varied interests and needs of diverse student populations.

Each module includes:

- relevant scientific background;
- assessment tools;
- student books and readings; and
- an instructional framework for teaching and management.

The insights program provides student materials, a teachers' guide with overviews of the curriculum, and assessment tools and strategies.

The Human Biology Middle Grades' Curriculum Project (Stanford University)

This *Middle Grades' Life Science Project (HumBio)* is comprised of 22 curriculum units published as individual modules. The modules were developed for use in seventh and eighth grades, although several of the test sites used some of the modules with sixth-grade students. The curriculum is adapted from Stanford's undergraduate program in Human Biology, which interweaves study in the biological and behavioral sciences. The curriculum addresses specific interests and needs of young adolescents in an attempt to capture their interest in studying science. The primary focus throughout the curriculum is on human, rather than animal, biology. Students develop a good grounding in the biological sciences and then extend this knowledge through applications to health and behavior. Physical science is integrated where possible; for example, in units on circulation and the nervous system.

Each unit has resource activities and projects. This feature provides flexibility in the depth of coverage. The basic unit with essential activities takes about three weeks of instructional time. Some test sites, however, taught units for five and six weeks using additional activities and projects. The curriculum project formed an alliance with Dr. Elizabeth Cohen in the School of Education to produce group cooperative learning activities based on *Cohen's Complex Instruction* model for managing heterogeneous classrooms. Most units now contain a series of group work activities, providing an alternative instructional strategy for the teachers (see Figure 7–6 for a list of HumBio units).

From the inception of the Human Biology Project, teachers collaborated in its development. Teachers will continue to modify this curriculum to meet their particular circumstances and to adapt it to their teaching styles and students. It is designed to be flexible and open-ended. The units enable teachers to choose topics appropriate for their classes, and there is no one path through these units. Schools are encouraged to embrace team teaching. Human Biology can serve as the unifying subject through which mathematics, English, reading, physical education, writing, and the arts can be integrated. Human Biology provides an activity/lab driven approach and several instructional strategies.

Unit I	The Changing Body
Unit II	Reproduction
Unit III	Sexuality
Unit IV	Becoming an Adult
Unit V	Your Family
Unit VI	Your Community
Unit VII	Your Place in the History of Life
Unit VIII	Your Place in the Biological World
Unit IX	A Concept of Culture
Unit X	The Transmission of Biological Information
Unit XI	The Relationship Between Biology and Culture
Unit XII	Your Body, an Overview
Unit XIII	The Nervous System
Unit XIV	The Effects of Drugs
Unit XV	The Lives of Cells
Unit XVI	Control of Cell Activities by Chemical Messengers— The Endocrine System
Unit XVII	From Cells to Organisms
Unit XVIII	Circulatory System
Unit XIX	Breathing
Unit XX	Digestion and Nutrition
Unit XXI	Salt, Water, and Nitrogen Balance
Unit XXII	Body Defenses

FIGURE 7–6
Curriculum units for the Human Biology Middle Grades' Curriculum Project

In addition to the NSF and the Carnegie Foundation's, funding for the written materials, the project received a grant from the U.S. Public Health Service in late 1991 to create a multimedia version of the material contained in the units on the nervous system and the effects of drugs and alcohol.

Middle School Life Science (Jefferson County Public Schools)

Middle School Life Science relates science on a personal level that is relevant to a seventh-grade student, rather than presenting it as abstract concepts that are difficult for twelve- to thirteen-year-olds to grasp. Instead of telling students that the ecosystem is made up of many elements, they make their own observations. They look for patterns, ask questions, and discover how ecosystems work.

Middle School Life Science covers fewer topics in more depth so students have more time for investigative activities and to apply what they learn. The program is based on a learning cycle that begins with experience/exploration, then develops a concept, and, finally, applies that concept to the real world. Students learn more from their readings and discus-

Unit 1	Ecosystems and Ecology: producers, consumers, decomposers, abiotic factors, ecosystems, pollution, conservation issues
Unit 2	Body Structure: bones, muscles, skin
Unit 3	Foods and Digestion: fats, sugars starches, proteins
Unit 4	Body Basics: circulatory, urinary, immune, respiratory systems
Unit 5	Body Controls: senses, the nervous system, decision making, drugs
Unit 6	Body Changes: growth, puberty, reproduction, birth
Unit 7	Cells and Genetics: cell structure and function, human inheritance

Middle-level health topics, such as drug, alcohol, and tobacco use prevention, puberty, human reproduction, muscle, fitness and nutrition are integrated throughout the curriculum.

FIGURE 7–7
***Middle School Life Science* curriculum units**

sions when they can relate them to their previous experiences with the subject.

Middle School Life Science is divided into seven units (see Figure 7–7). Six of the units teach life science concepts and science process skills through a focus on the human body, and one places humans in the ecosystem. The units and chapters in the text all follow a parallel structure. They begin with the concrete aspects of the students' world—things they can see, feel, and investigate firsthand. Then they move to more abstract concepts.

The program was developed over four years by the Jefferson County Public Schools (a large district in the Denver, Colorado, metropolitan area) with funding from the NSF. This project involved sixty-six seventh grade teachers in twenty-two schools (including five schools in neighboring districts), content experts, and science education specialists. Virtually every activity had three cycles of trial teaching.

Introductory Physical Science (IPS) for Middle Schools (Science Curriculum, Inc.)[20]

This program is the sixth edition of the IPS developed in the 1960s. IPS has been confined within the boundaries of individual disciplines, primarily chemistry and physics. The central theme of IPS is the study of matter leading to the development of the atomic model. In broad terms, the course divides naturally into three parts. Chapters 1–6 provide the empirical framework without which the atomic model becomes an obstruction. The program progresses from what is around students in the greatest abundance, namely mixtures, to compounds and elements. In the process, students learn about the characteristic properties by which substances are recognized and separated. No distinction is made between physical and chemical properties.

Chapters 7–9 introduce the atomic model. Radioactivity was chosen as the vehicle because the discreteness in radioactive processes is clearly observable, and because the subject, despite its importance, is often neglected.

Chapters 10–12 combined add the electric dimension to the atomic model, reinforcing the material learned earlier. In the process the text lays a valuable foundation for electrochemistry.

The division of the course along these lines provides natural breaking points for those teachers who wish to spread the IPS course over more than one year (see Figure 7–8 for the table of contents).

Some sections of IPS are designated as experiments and serve as guides for students in their laboratory work. The other sections lay the groundwork for new concepts, relate the results of experiments to students' understanding of the nature of matter, or serve as introductions to or summaries of chapters. These sections are often brief, yet they are an integral part of the course. Disregarding the reading sections reduces the course to a succession of unrelated experiments.

The text contains a large selection of problems: some are easy, short, and confidence-building; some are more complex; and, finally, some go beyond the course and serve as an optional extension of the material. The problems and questions found at the end of sections within chapters generally cover single concepts and are designed to reinforce ideas immediately after they are encountered in the text or laboratory.

The set of problems labeled "For Review, Applications, and Extensions" (RAEs), located at the end of each chapter, follows the order of presentation of material within the chapter. The RAEs are designed to extend the students' knowledge to more general applications of the chapter and, in some cases, provide additional practice with important ideas. Many of the RAEs can be assigned to individual students based on their needs and abilities. Thus, it is not necessary to assign the same problems to all students.

This course is designed for students in the eighth and ninth grades. Originally supported by the NSF, the IPS program has been used successfully by thousands of students. Interestingly, many features of this program (teaching less content more thoroughly, engaging students in activities, providing historical perspectives, and working cooperatively) all align with contemporary recommendations for improving science education. At this point you should complete Activity 7–1, "Evaluating Middle/Junior High School Science Programs."

■ SUMMARY

Adolescence is a unique period of life. Throughout our educational history we have seen changes in the science curriculum for this age group. The junior high school was created in the late 1800s. Then in the late 1900s, there emerged the middle school. Junior high schools were junior versions of high school programs, but the middle school curriculum is uniquely designed for the early adolescent.

Although textbooks were significantly changed during the 1960s and 1970s, the 1980s and 1990s have witnessed a return to models similar to those prior to the 1960s. Contemporary reform will have an impact on middle/junior high school programs in the early to mid-1990s. Several new NSF programs serve as models for science education at the middle school level.

Chapter 1	Volume and Mass
Chapter 2	Mass Changes in Closed Systems
Chapter 3	Characteristic Properties
Chapter 4	Solubility
Chapter 5	The Separation of Mixtures
Chapter 6	Compounds and Elements
Chapter 7	Radioactivity
Chapter 8	The Atomic Model of Matter
Chapter 9	The Sizes and Masses of Molecules and Atoms
Chapter 10	Electric Charge
Chapter 11	Atoms and Electric Charge
Chapter 12	Cells and Charge Carrier

FIGURE 7–8
Introductory Physical Science **table of contents**

■ REFERENCES

1. American Association for the Advancement of Science (AAAS), *Science for All Americans* (Washington, DC: Author, 1989).

2. Rodger W. Bybee and others, *Science and Technology Education for the Middle Years: Frameworks for Curriculum and Instruction* (Washington, DC: The National Center for Improving Science Education, 1990).

3. National Science Teachers Association (NSTA), *Scope, Sequence, and Coordination of Secondary School Science. The Content Core: A Guide For Curriculum Designers* (Washington, DC: Author, 1992).

4. Commission on the Reorganization of Secondary Education, *Cardinal Principles of Secondary Education,* Bulletin 1918, no. 35 (Washington, DC: U.S. Bureau of Education, 1918), pp. 12–13.

5. W. T. Gruhn and N. R. Douglas, *The Modern Junior High School,* 3rd ed. (New York: The Ronald Press, 1977), p. 133.

6. A. S. Brown and E. Obourn, *Offerings and Enrollments* (Washington, DC: U.S. Government Printing Office, 1961).

7. Paul DeHart Hurd, James T. Robinson, Mary McConnell, and Norris Ross, *The Status of Middle School and Junior High School Science* (Center for Educational Research and Evaluation. The Biological Sciences Curriculum study, The Colorado College, Colorado Springs, CO, 1981), p. 15.

8. Paul DeHart Hurd and others, *The Status of Middle School and Junior High School Science,* pp. 4–5.

9. Bonnie Brunkhorst and Michael Padilla, "Science Education for Middle and Junior High School Students: An NSTA Position Statement," *Science and Children, 24*(3) (November/December, 1987): 62–63.

10. Brunkhorst and Padilla, "Science Education for Middle and Junior High School Students," pp. 62–63.

11. National Science Foundation, "Program Solicitation: Programs for Middle School Science Instruction" (Washington, DC: National Science Foundation, 1988) p. 2.

12. Audrey B. Champagne and others, *Science and Technology Education for the High School Years* (Washington, DC: The National Center for Improving Science Education, 1990).

13. F. James Rutherford and A. Ahlgren, *Science for All Americans* (New York: Oxford University Press, 1990).

14. W. G. Aldridge, *Essential Changes in Secondary School Science: Scope, Sequence, and Coordination* (Washington, DC: National Science Teachers Association, 1989).

15. Bybee and others, *Science and Technology Education for the Elementary Years: Frameworks for Curriculum and Instruction* (Washington, DC: The National Center for Improving Science Education, 1990).

16. James Beane, *A Middle School Curriculum From Rhetoric to Reality* (Columbus, OH: National Middle School Association, 1990).

17. D. W. Johnson and R. T. Johnson, *Learning Together and Alone: Cooperative, Competitive and Individualistic Learning,* 2nd ed. (Englewood Cliffs, NJ: Prentice-Hall, 1987).

18. Johnson and Johnson, *Learning Together and Alone,* 2nd ed.

19. J. B. Kahle, "SCORES: A Project for Change?" *International Journal of Science Education* 9(3)(1987): 325–333.

20. EDC, *Introductory Physical Science-Physical Science.* (Newton, MA: IPS Group, Education Development Center, 1968), p. 16.

INVESTIGATING SCIENCE TEACHING

Activity 7–1

EVALUATING MIDDLE/JUNIOR HIGH SCHOOL SCIENCE PROGRAMS

At some time in your career, you will select a new science program. This activity introduces you to that process. The form you will complete is adapted from the American Association for the Advancement of Science publication Science Books & Films.

Select three programs from the discipline and grade level you intend to teach. Review the textbooks and complete the following chart. List the textbooks you compare by author(s), title, publisher, and copyright date.

Science Program

1.

2.

3.

GENERAL EVALUATION	N/C	Poor	Fair	Adequate	Good	Excellent
Program						
Content accuracy						
Content currency						
Content scope						
Structure and methods of science						
Organization and coherence						
Comprehensibility						
Labs: in text/ supplementals						
Comprehensibility						
Practicality of required apparatus						
Summary: text supplementals						
Teach the nature of scientific enterprise						
Encourage students to reason to testable conclusions						
Stimulate awareness of science, technology, and society						

1. Were the programs for middle school or junior high school?
2. How were the programs similar? Different?
3. Describe an outstanding feature of each program.
4. Describe the weakest feature of each program.
5. Which program would you select to use? Why?

Chapter 8

THE HIGH SCHOOL SCIENCE CURRICULUM

This chapter focuses on the science curriculum for grades 9–12. In the first section we discuss changes in the high school science curriculum in the 1990s. Aspects of this section, such as the *National Science Education Standards*[1] and *Benchmarks for Science Literacy*[2] have been discussed in previous chapters, so they are not elaborated in detail. The next section discusses contemporary science curricula for grades 9–12. Finally, we provide a discussion on designing your science curriculum.

■ HIGH SCHOOL SCIENCE CURRICULUM IN TRANSITION IN THE 1970s AND 1980s

In chapter three, we reviewed the history and major programs developed during the Golden Age of science education. We now turn attention to the present situation since many of the "new" curricula have been in existence for over twenty-five years and have undergone several revisions.

We should first note that the high school science curriculum is largely determined at a local level by science teachers, administrators, and school boards; in making their decisions they use suggestions and guidelines from national frameworks and policies (such as the national standards) and state departments of education. Even with significant autonomy, recent NSF studies have shown two things to be true: there is considerable uniformity of programs, and the curriculum has not changed significantly in recent history. With emphasis on Goals 2000 and national standards, you can expect significant improvement in the last years of the 20th century.

Typically, the senior high school science curriculum is biology at the tenth grade and chemistry and physics at the eleventh and twelfth grades, respectively. General biology is offered to all students and enrolls three million students each year. In the late 1970s, about 80 percent of graduating seniors took high school biology. Note, however, that *for 50 percent of high school students who graduate each year, biology is their last experience with any science course.*[3] A 1977 NSF survey by Iris Weiss indicated approximately 1.2 million students took a physics course. High school chemistry and physics are generally perceived as college preparatory, as are the majority of other science courses offered in the average high school. As the reform expanded in the 1980s and 1990s, more states increased graduation requirements in science. These new mandates required many students to take a second or third science course in grades 9–12.

The science curriculum is undergoing a major transition in the late 1990s. Some changes include decreasing the number of facts presented in simple and condensed form, and the emphasis on extensive vocabulary; and increasing the focus on a few principles, and conceptual schemes and scientific inquiry. By nature of the emphasis on science facts and vocabulary, there is little attention to the goals of scientific inquiry, investigation, or analytic thinking. Although all the NSF materials developed during the Golden Age acclaimed these aims, recent changes in textbooks have slowly evolved in the direction of neglecting inquiry and analysis. A recent review of the inquiry goal in science teaching found that teachers gave little attention to the aim of inquiry and associated skills.[4]

Although familiarity with and knowledge of science and technology is increasingly important to students' everyday lives, the high school science curriculum gives little recognition of important goals related to personal needs, social concerns, and careers. One study by Faith Hickman suggested that only about 5 percent of the secondary science curriculum was devoted to topics of personal and social significance.[5]

Note that we are pinpointing the status of high school science curricula in the 1970s and 1980s. If confronted with the central question about NSF programs and the Golden Age—Did we accomplish what we set out to do?—the answer would have to be yes. This answer is supported by research.[6] The main point of this discussion is that changes in science, technology, society, and our understanding of student learning all indicate we are improving the high school science curriculum.

In the early 1990s, the NSF funded proposals to develop new programs for high school science. We describe some of these programs in a later section.

■ HIGH SCHOOL SCIENCE CURRICULUM IN THE 1990s

You can look forward to improvements in the science curriculum between now and the year 2000. The formation of *National Science Education Standards* and

Benchmarks for Science Literacy supports this statement.

The Content Standards presented in both the *National Standards* and *Benchmarks* elaborate what students should understand and be able to do in natural science, and the personal and social context that should be considered in the design of science curriculum. These standards emphasize inquiry-oriented activities, connections between science and technology, and the history and nature of science as students develop an understanding of fundamental ideas and abilities in science. The Content Standards of NSES represent one component of a comprehensive vision of the science curriculum, a vision that also includes science teaching and assessment. If you only review and use the Content Standards and ignore other standards on teaching and assessment, or only use a subset of content—such as subject matter for physical, life, and earth science—then the use of the *National Science Education Standards* in the science curriculum is incomplete. Figure 8–1 outlines the major conceptual organizers for science content at grades 9–12. You should also review the *National Science Education Standards* for more specific discussions of the fundamental concepts associated with the conceptual organizers in Figure 8–1.

Many different individuals and groups will use the Content Standards for a variety of purposes. However, there are some groups who will use them immediately and concretely—for example, curriculum developers, science supervisors at state and local levels, and classroom teachers of science. The concepts and understandings described in the Content Standards do not represent a science curriculum. Content is what students should learn. Curriculum includes the way content is organized, what is emphasized, how it is taught, and how it is assessed. The science curriculum includes a structure, organization, balance, and presentation of the content in the classroom and can be organized in many different ways. The national standards indicate what should be learned, not how content should be organized in school science programs.

As you think about your science curricula, teaching, and assessment and begin incorporating the *National Science Education Standards*, you should consider the following criteria:

- Content Standards must be used in coordination with the standards on teaching and assessment. Using the Content Standards with traditional teaching and assessment strategies misrepresents the intentions of the *National Science Education Standards.*
- Science content, at the level of standards, cannot be eliminated. For instance, students should have opportunities to learn *Science in Personal and Social Perspectives* and *History and Nature of Science* in the school science program.
- Science content, at the level of conceptual organizers, cannot be eliminated. For instance, "Evolution of Living Systems" cannot be eliminated from the *Life Science Standards.*
- Science content can be added to elaborate conceptual organizers. In the translation of content to curriculum, the connections, depth, detail, and selection of topics can be varied as appropriate for students and school science programs.

The Content Standards, like the discipline of science itself, will continue to change. The national standards identify important and enduring ideas rather than current topics and contemporary research. The conceptual organizers, fundamental understandings, and abilities outlined in the national standards will provide students with basic concepts, a knowledge base, and skills that will continually improve their scientific literacy.

In considering the science curriculum, you should also review *Benchmarks for Science Literacy* and *Scope, Sequence, and Coordination: The Content Core* (see Figure 8–2 and the discussion of these projects in chapter seven).

The *National Science Education Standards* and other reports on science education have identified important outcomes for all students. Although there are differences among the reports, they represent considerable agreement on the essential outcomes within the domains of science education. The *National Science Education Standards* incorporate many outcomes of the AAAS report. If you are actively involved in science curriculum, you should not view these as mutually exclusive reports. Having said this, we think it is important to understand that the *National Science Education Standards* (and the AAAS report) were developed over extended periods of time, had input from thousands of scientists, engineers, science educators, and science teachers, and used an overall conceptual framework for scientific literacy. Simply selecting topics or themes from the standards and ignoring other components of the standards omits significant, if not essential, aspects of the standards.

■ SCIENCE CURRICULA FOR THE HIGH SCHOOL

In this section we present several examples of contemporary science curricula. These programs were supported by the NSF and published in the 1990s. Although developed prior to the publication of NRC standards and AAAS benchmarks, they represent a

Unifying Concepts and Processes	Science as Inquiry	Physical Science	Life Science	Earth and Space Science	Science in Science and Technology	History and Personal and Social Perspectives	Nature of Science
• Order and Organization • Change and Measurement • Evolution and Equilibrium • Form and Function	• Abilities of Scientific Inquiry • Understandings of Scientific Inquiry	• The Structure of Atoms • Structure and Properties of Matter • Chemical Reactions • Forces and Motion • Conservation of Energy and the Increase in Disorder • Interactions of Energy and Matter	• The Cell • Biological Evolution • The Interdependence of Organisms • The Molecular Basis of Heredity • Matter, Energy, and Organization in Living Systems • The Behavior of Organisms	• Energy in the Earth System • Geochemical Cycles • The Origin and Evolution of the Earth System • The Origin and Evolution of the Universe	• Abilities of Technological Design • Understandings about Science and Technology	• Personal and Community Health • Population Growth • Natural Resources • Environmental Quality • Natural and Human–Induced Hazards • Science and Technology in Local, National, and Global Challenges	• Science as a Human Endeavor • Nature of Scientific Knowledge • Historical Perspectives

FIGURE 8–1
Conceptual organizers for science content—Grades 9–12

The Nature of Science	*The Nature of Mathematics*	*The Nature of Technology*	*The Physical Setting*

• The Scientific World View
• Scientific Inquiry
• The Scientific Enterprise
	• Patterns and Relationships
	• Mathematics
	   Science and Technology
	• Mathematical Inquiry
		• Technology and Science
		• Design and Systems
		• Issues in Technology
			• The Universe
			• The Earth
			• Processes that
			   Shape the Earth
			• Energy Transformations
			• Motion
			• Forces of Nature

The Living Environment	*The Human Organism*	*Human Society*	*The Designed World*

• Diversity of Life
• Heredity
• Cells
• Interdependence of Life
• Flow of Matter
   and Energy
• Evolution of Life
	• Human Identity
	• Human Development
	• Basic Functions
	• Learning
	• Physical Health
	• Mental Health
		• Cultural Effects
		   on Behavior
		• Group Behavior
		• Social Change
		• Political and Economic
		   Systems
		• Social Conflict
		• Group Interdependence
			• Agriculture
			• Materials and
			   Manufacturing
			• Energy Sources and Use
			• Communication
			• Information Processing
			• Health
			• Technology

The Mathematical World	*Historical Perspectives*	*Common Themes*	*Habits of Mind*

• Numbers
• Symbolic Relationships
• Shapes
• Uncertainty
• Reasoning
	• Displacing Earth from
	   the Center of
	   the Universe
	• Uniting the Heavens
	   and Earth
	• Relating Matter and
	   Energy and Time
	   and Space
	• Extending Time
	• Moving the Continents
	• Understanding Fire
	• Splitting the Atom
	· Explaining the Diversity
	   of Life
	· Discovering Germs
	• Harnessing Power
		• Systems
		• Models
		• Constancy and Change
		• Scale
			• Values and Attitudes
			• Computation
			   and Estimation
			• Manipulation
			   and Observation
			• Communication Skills
			• Critical-Response Skills

FIGURE 8-2
Conceptual organizers from *Benchmarks for Science Literacy*

generation of high school science curricula closely aligned with the national standards and benchmarks.

Biological Science: A Human Approach (Biological Sciences Curriculum Study–BSCS)

BSCS has developed an innovative high school biology program that is appropriate for *all* students. The program is designed as a full-year biology curriculum for tenth grade and consists of a student book, an integrated set of technological materials (including videodiscs, educational courseware and microcomputer-based laboratories [MBLs]), a teacher's guide, an assessment package, and an implementation guide.

One of this program's goals is to develop a curriculum that simultaneously empowers both teachers and students. This program provides teachers with alternative activities, points, and ideas, as well as the support a high school biology teacher needs to implement them. At the same time, *Biological Science: A Human Approach* helps students become more responsible for their own learning. Using cooperative learning strategies, hands-on and open-ended activities, and authentic assessment, this program encourages interdependence among students.

Biological Science: A Human Approach achieves a number of specific goals for students and teachers. They are as follows.

Program goals for students:

- understand major biological concepts;
- understand the characteristics that are unique to *Homo sapiens* and those that are shared with other living systems;
- understand the role, place, and interactions of humans in the biosphere;
- understand the personal, social, and ethical implications of biology and biotechnology;
- appreciate the diversity of living systems;
- demonstrate mastery of scientific inquiry;
- understand that science is a way of knowing and that technology is a way of adapting;
- use educational technologies as tools for learning; and
- use such cognitive abilities as critical thinking, problem solving, and ethical analysis.

Program goals for teachers:

- decreased dependence on a central text and increased use of a variety of instructional materials and strategies;
- decreased use of lecture and increased use of activities including laboratory and educational courseware;
- decreased perceptions that science is a body of knowledge and that technology is the application of knowledge, and increased understanding that science is a way of knowing and technology is a way of adapting;
- decreased use of structured materials and increased empowerment through the decision-making process for curriculum and instruction; and
- decreased use of traditional tests and increased use of authentic science assessment, such as portfolios, hands-on performance tests, and checklists for skills.

The program begins with an "Engage" chapter that helps orient students to the program and the inquiry nature of scientific study. The chapter also introduces cooperative learning and the six unifying principles of biology that form the framework of the program (see Figure 8–3 for description of the six units). BSCS will conclude the program by involving the students in a project in which they integrate the major principles, concepts, and processes of biology and, thus, have an opportunity to assess their understandings. Students' projects build on the activities in this first chapter of the program, and also may include investigations of student-initiated questions and involvement in science-related community projects.

Biological Science: A Human Approach can be distinguished by a combination of characteristics. These include unifying themes of biology, inclusion of an instructional model, integration of cooperative learning, authentic assessment strategies, integral use of educational technology, and a student journal.

Unifying themes provide the structure for the biological content. Before the development of *Biological Science: A Human Approach,* BSCS conducted a design study to determine what biological concepts and principles are critical to the study of biology at the high school level. The report *Developing Biological Literacy*[8] listed six unifying principles of biology that form the conceptual organization of *Biological Science: A Human Approach.* Those principles are:

- Evolution: Patterns and Products of Change
- Energy, Matter, and Organization
- Maintenance of a Dynamic Equilibrium
- Genetic Continuity and Reproduction
- Growth, Development, and Differentiation
- Interaction and Interdependence

Two themes are used as threads for making the human approach manifest: Science As Inquiry and Science and Humanity. Science As Inquiry refers both to the discovery process by which data are obtained and evaluated and to the dynamic body of knowledge that makes up current scientific understanding. BSCS uses this theme to take students in progressive steps through the processes of science, including making observations, making inferences, assembling evidence, developing hypotheses, creating experiments, collecting data, analyzing and presenting data, communicating, and evaluating.

The Science and Humanity theme makes the student's study of biology more relevant and approachable by incorporating: the critical elements of human culture; the history of science; the place of ethics, ethical analysis, and decision-making in today's controversial science world; and the importance of human technology as a way of adapting.

The program uses an instructional model based on the constructivist philosophy of learning. BSCS calls the instructional model the *5 Es* because it takes the students through the five phases of learning referred to in Chapter 14: *Engage, Explore, Explain, Elaborate,* and *Evaluate.* This model allows students and teachers to experience common activities, to use and build on prior knowledge and experience, to construct meaning, and to assess continually their understanding of a concept. The 5 Es model is presented in detail later in this textbook (see chapter fourteen).

Cooperative learning is used as a strategy to decrease students' dependence on the teacher and increase students' responsibility for their own learning. In *Biological Science: A Human Approach,* the students use cooperative learning strategies for completing a significant number of the activities. These

---

Unit 1—Evolution: Patterns and Products of Change in Living Systems
What does it mean to be human? That is the central question of Unit 1. Students assess the unique qualities of humans and the diversity of life while trying to place humans in the scheme of living systems. Students consider characteristics that are common to all living systems, as well as those that are unique to humans, and grapple with the definition of life. Unity, diversity, genetic variation, and evolution, including cultural evolution, are conceptual themes in Unit 1.

Unit 2—Homeostasis: Maintaining Dynamic Equilibrium in Living Systems
Unit 2 explores the requirement of a controlled internal environment for optimal functioning of an organism. Beginning with familiar examples, students develop an understanding of the concepts of response, regulation, and feedback. Then they examine the division between internal and external conditions and the processes by which internal conditions are maintained in spite of changes in external conditions. Students expand these concepts to a broader scale, analyzing the way health and disease affect both the individual human and society as a group.

Unit 3—Energy, Matter, and Organization: Relationships in Living Systems
Unit 3 begins with the students trying to explain the requirements of physical performance and considering the effects of fitness, drugs, and alcohol on performance. Students develop an understanding of the relationship between structure and function by using mobility as an example of activity. They proceed to explore the interplay between energy and matter through the organization of metabolic processes such as photosynthesis and cellular respiration, as well as through interactions in a community. Finally, the students consider the role of producers, consumers, and decomposers in the flow of energy and cycling of matter in a community.

Unit 4—Continuity: Reproduction and Inheritance in Living Systems
Unit 4 focuses on reproduction, patterns of inheritance, and the role of genes and DNA in inheritance. The discussion of human sexual reproduction includes reproductive systems and cycles, reproductive behavior, and ethical issues such as contraception, abortion, and sexually transmitted diseases. The students consider continuity and variation in the context of inheritance, and genes as a source of information that is organized as a genetic code stored in DNA. They also study the dynamics of gene expression and replication at a molecular level, which provides a basis for understanding genetic engineering.

Unit 5—Development: Growth and Differentiation in Living Systems
Unit 5 begins with students considering development as a process that involves differentiation and growth and that requires regulation. The students explore patterns of development that appear in stages such as reproductive maturity, aging, and death, are limited by evolutionary constraints, and depend on communication. Finally, the students consider human life stages, looking at biologically programmed events as well as the cultural environment in which they occur.

Unit 6—Ecology: Interaction and Interdependence in Living Systems
Unit 6 centers on issues in the major conceptual area of human ecology, including dilemmas about the interactions among populations, resources, and environments. The students examine the concepts involved in population dynamics, setting the stage for studying the interactions between humans and their environment. Next, they focus on how human actions can modify the environment, especially through the use of technology. The final emphasis is on the ethical issues raised by human actions and technology.

FIGURE 8–3
Biological Science: A Human Approach, **six units of study**

strategies help the students achieve program goals for the following reasons:

- Cooperative learning empowers students, making them responsible for seeking information and achieving a particular task.
- Cooperative learning strategies model one feature of the nature of the scientific enterprise.
- Research has shown that cooperative learning is an effective technique for involving students from groups traditionally underrepresented in science, such as female and minority students.
- Cooperative learning can be a powerful way to interest and motivate students who might not otherwise excel or even be interested in science.

BSCS made every effort to make the cooperative learning experience at the high school level relevant to the students without compromising the elements that are critical to successful cooperative learning.

These elements include the use of roles, the use of working relationship skills, positive interdependence, individual accountability, distributed leadership, group autonomy, heterogeneous grouping, and team self-evaluation.

Assessment strategies, including scoring rubrics, are embedded and varied; they are based on the philosophy that assessment itself should be a learning experience. In tandem with the conceptualization of the content and themes of *Biological Science: A Human Approach*, BSCS conceptualized assessment strategies and materials that promote authentic assessment. The program includes both formal and informal assessments. Formal assessment strategies may be used at the program, unit, or chapter level, and may include the following:

- performance-based assessment,
- written tests with multiple-choice, short-answer, and essay questions,
- working relationships assessment in cooperative learning activities,
- debates,
- presentations, both group and individual,
- written assignments, both group and individual,
- journals that include completed work and long-term projects,
- projects, both ongoing and one-time,
- portfolios, and
- opportunities for self-assessment and peer assessment.

Informal assessment strategies occur within the flow of a chapter and may include the following:

- discussions, both small group and whole class,
- journal entries from activities,
- short written assignments,
- various aspects of performance during experiments.

Educational technology is integral to the program. Educational technology is used as a tool to enhance learning and understanding whenever it provides the best way of learning material. The program includes three major electronic technologies:

- The LEAP-System™ is a computer interfacing system for microcomputer-based laboratories and simulations.
- *Biology Explorer* by LOGAL is an investigative software with modules that investigate genetics, photosynthesis, population ecology, and the cardiovascular system.
- Six videodiscs include interactive activities for the chapters.

A student journal that the students use through the course is a key piece for developing conceptual continuity. The use of a journal is integral to student participation and growth in this program. Students use their journals in the following ways:

- recording data,
- taking notes,
- responding to questions in the activities,
- responding to *Further Challenges* in the activities,
- keeping track of questions they may have,
- keeping track of their responsibilities,
- partaking in assessments, and
- keeping long-term records.

Science teachers can build on the role of the journal by assessing students' work periodically, recommending that students record upcoming assignments or adding reflective exercises.

BSCS has designed a biology program that challenges current perceptions of biology education and provides students opportunities to learn concepts and develop skills aligned with the national standards.

Chemistry in the Community (American Chemical Society)

Chemistry in the Community (ChemCom) is a major attempt to enhance science literacy through a high school curriculum that emphasizes the impact of chemistry on society. Developed by the American Chemical Society (ACS) with financial support from the NSF and several ACS funding sources, *ChemCom* has been written by teams of high school, college, and university teachers, assisted by chemists from industry and government.

This year-long course is designed primarily for the large number of students who plan to pursue nonscience careers. Its purposes are to help students:

- Realize the important role that chemistry will play in their personal and professional lives.
- Use principles of chemistry to think more intelligently about current issues they will encounter that involve science and technology.
- Develop a lifelong awareness of the potential and limitations of science and technology.

Each of *ChemCom's* eight units centers on a chemistry-related technological issue now confronting our society and the world. The topic serves as a basis for introducing the chemistry needed to understand and analyze these issues. The setting for each unit is a community: the school community, the town or region in which the students live, or the world community—Spaceship Earth.

ChemCom consists of eight units (see Figure 8–4). The units include the major concepts, basic vocabulary, and intellectual and laboratory skills

FIGURE 8–4
ChemCom (2nd edition):
units of study

SUPPLYING OUR WATER NEEDS
A. The Quality of Our Water
B. A Look at Water and Its Contaminants
C. Investigating the Cause of the Fish Kill
D. Water Purification and Treatment
E. Putting It All Together: Fish Kill—Who Pays?

CONSERVING CHEMICAL RESOURCES
A. Use of Resources
B. Why We Use What We Do
C. Conservation in Nature and the Community
D. Metals: Sources and Replacements
E. Putting It All Together: How Long Will the Supply Last?

PETROLEUM: TO BUILD? TO BURN?
A. Petroleum in Our Lives
B. Petroleum: What Is It? What Do We Do With It?
C. Petroleum as an Energy Source
D. Useful Materials from Petroleum
E. Alternatives to Petroleum
F. Putting It All Together: Choosing Petroleum Futures

UNDERSTANDING FOOD
A. Foods: To Build or to Burn?
B. Food as Energy
C. Foods: The Building Molecules
D. Other Substances in Foods
E. Putting It All Together: Nutrition Around the World

NUCLEAR CHEMISTRY IN OUR WORLD
A. Energy and Atoms
B. Radioactive Decay
C. Nuclear Energy; Powering the Universe
D. Living with Benefits and Risks
E. Putting It All Together: Separating Fact from Fiction

CHEMISTRY, AIR, AND CLIMATE
A. Living in a Sea of Air
B. Investigating the Atmosphere
C. Atmosphere and Climate
D. Human Impact on the Air We Breathe
E. Putting It All Together: Is Air a Free Resource?

HEALTH: YOUR RISKS AND CHOICES
A. Risk and Personal Decision-Making
B. Your Body's Internal Chemistry
C. Acids, Bases, and Body Chemistry
D. Chemistry at the Body's Surface
E. Chemical Control: Drugs and Toxins in the Human Body
F. Putting It All Together: Assessing Risks

THE CHEMICAL INDUSTRY: PROMISE AND CHALLENGE
A. A New Industry for Riverwood?
B. An Overview of the Chemical Industry
C. The Chemistry of Some Nitrogen-Based Products
D. Chemical Energy-Electrical Energy
E. Putting It All Together: Chemical Industry Past, Present, and Future

expected in any introductory chemistry course. The program contains a greater number and variety of student-oriented activities than is customary. In addition to numerous laboratory exercises, including many developed especially for *ChemCom*, each unit contains three levels of decision-making activities, and several types of problem-solving exercises.

Perhaps the most unique and pervasive feature of *ChemCom* is that chemistry is taught on a need-to-know basis with societal and technological issues/problems and examples serving both as student motivators and as filters to decide the depth and breadth of the concepts taught. For example, you will find that perusing local newspapers, magazines, and TV news for stories related to chemistry will help you and your students understand chemistry in the context of their community's life.

Most of the complex and perplexing issues facing our nation involve individual and social values and group decision-making processes, as well as scientific concepts. Accordingly, *ChemCom* aims to prepare students for informed, effective citizenship by stimulating and engaging the students' hands (manipulative skills), hearts (values and attitudes) and heads (higher cognitive abilities). As such, *ChemCom* places much of the responsibility for learning on students themselves as they explore how chemical concepts apply to their everyday lives. In addition to hands-on laboratory activities (an average of one every four or five days), *ChemCom* includes a variety of student decision-making activities.

The decision-making focus, central to the *ChemCom* approach, will require you to engage in some teaching approaches not used in traditional chemistry courses.

Premises Underlying *ChemCom's* Decision-Making Focus

1. Problem-solving and decision-making challenges are commonly encountered in a variety of personal, social, and work-related settings.
2. Problem solving and decision making require higher level cognitive skills that can be improved with appropriate experience and practice.
3. *Academic* problem solving as presented in traditional school settings has little in common with the kinds of *real-life* decision making students will encounter later as voting citizens and professionals.
4. Science curricula should be designed to include opportunities for students to practice *real-life* decision-making strategies.
5. A science curriculum featuring an issues focus (like *ChemCom*) provides a productive setting to develop students' decision-making skills.

6. Student application and use of chemical knowledge are at least as important as its initial acquisition.
7. Modern society depends on group cooperation as much as on individual competition. Schools should provide opportunities for students to work together on cooperative ventures.
8. Academic preparation for life is at least as important as preparation for a subsequent course of study.

■ ACTIVE PHYSICS CURRICULUM PROJECT *(AAPT, AIP, APS)*

Active Physics is an NSF-supported curriculum development project conducted by the American Association of Physics Teachers (AAPT) and the American Institute of Physics (AIP), with assistance from the American Physical Society (APS). The project will develop an alternative physics course that appeals to high school students who do not currently enroll in physics. Because of its limited prerequisite math and reading skills, this activity-based course can be successfully used with students from ninth to twelfth grades. Figure 8–5 describes units in the *Active Physics* program.

Program Design

There are typically four chapters, each requiring approximately two to three weeks of class time, in each thematic unit. Chapters begin with an engaging scenario or project assignment that challenges the students and sets the stage for the learning activities and chapter assessments to follow. Chapter content and activities are selectively aimed at providing students with the knowledge and skills needed to address the introductory challenge, thus providing a natural content filter in this less-is-more curriculum.

Units are designed to stand alone so that teachers have the flexibility of changing the sequence of unit presentation, omitting an entire unit, or not finishing all of the chapters within a unit. Although intended to serve as a full-year physics course, the units of *Active Physics* can be adapted to spread across a four-year period in an integrated high school curriculum.

The thematic nature of the course requires students to continually revisit fundamental physics principles throughout the year, extending and deepening their understanding of these principles as they apply them in new contexts. This repeated exposure fosters the retention and transferability of learning and promotes the development of flexible thinking skills.

Instead of the traditional structure and sequence of physics curricula, the *Active Physics Curriculum Project* adopts a thematic approach to physics. Students are engaged in learning about physics through hands-on exploration of topics of intrinsic interest in six different units:

SPORTS

Students are immediately immersed in the physics of sports as they try to help their school track team prepare for the Penn Relays. In this unit they audition for a job as a sports commentator, explore the limits of human performance, and design sporting competitions for a colony on the moon.

HEALTH AND MEDICINE

A person is rushed to the emergency room. To diagnose the patient, X-rays, CAT scans, and ultrasound are used as imaging techniques. Students investigate how we are able to image parts of the body not visible to our eyes. In a later unit students explore hearing and whether hearing loss occurs at rock concerts. Students also learn about vision with emphasis on medical technology and our ability to aid individuals who have limited use of this sense.

COMMUNICATIONS AND INFORMATION

Short stories lead students to investigate the generation, propagation, and interpretation of visual and aural signals. Students consider how an object is located, how signals are propagated, and how color provides information. Using concepts developed in the unit, groups of students produce a variety of short imaginative works, such as a science fiction story in which one physical property has an unusual value or one physical law is modified.

HOME

Students are challenged to design a prototype home that can be built in developing countries. They learn about energy, electricity, and scale as they alter the prototype home for specific climates and local resources. Finally, students are required to help the child population of a developing country become more accepting of electricity by playing with a toy that uses a motor and generator.

TRANSPORTATION

In four chapters, students proceeed from exploring the physics knowledge that is an asset to a licensed automobile driver, to assessing automobile and airplane safety features, to investigating a trip to the moon and colonizing Mars. They investigate problems that emerge during such journeys.

PREDICTING THE FUTURE

Why is it that physicists believe in their ability to predict the outcome of certain events but do not believe in the psychic's power to make similar predictions? Science differs from pseudoscience in the criteria by which it determines what is a true result. This unit contrasts legitimate scientific predictions with those of pseudoscience to highlight the characteristics of good science. Among the scientific principles treated are radioactive decay, Newton's first two laws of motion, the Law of Universal Gravitation, and special relativity.

FIGURE 8–5
Active Physics Curriculum Project **units of study**

Instruction and Assessment

Students are continually asked to explore how they think about certain situations. As they investigate new situations, they are challenged to either explain observed phenomena using an existing paradigm or to develop a more consistent one. This approach can be helpful in inducing students to abandon previously held notions in favor of the more powerful ideas and explanations offered by scientists.

At the culmination of each chapter, students are required to demonstrate the usefulness of their newly acquired knowledge by adequately meeting the challenge posed in the chapter's introduction. Students are then assessed on the degree to which they accomplish the performance task. The curriculum includes other methods and instruments for authentic assessment, as well as nontraditional procedures for evaluating and rewarding desirable behaviors and skills.

Use of cooperative groups is integral to the course as students work together in small groups to acquire the knowledge and information needed to address the challenges presented in chapter scenarios. Ample teacher guidance is provided to ensure that effective strategies are used in group formation, function, and evaluation.

Basic Skills

The presentation and use of math in *Active Physics* varies substantially from traditional high school physics courses. Math—primarily algebraic expressions, equations, and graphs—is approached as a way of representing ideas symbolically. Students begin to recognize the usefulness of math as an aid in exploring and understanding the world about them. Since many students are insecure about their math backgrounds, the course encourages and provides instruction for the use of graphic calculators and computer spreadsheets to provide math assistance.

Because it is assumed that the target audience reads only what is absolutely required, the entire course is activity-driven. Reading passages are presented solely within the context of activities and are written at the ninth grade level or below.

Technology

Specially produced videos introduce and explore many of the *Active Physics* topics. There are also opportunities for students to produce their own videos to record and analyze events. Computer software programs make use of various interfacing devices.

For the curriculum to be both meaningful and relevant to the target population, problem solving related to technological applications and related issues is an essential component of the course. Problem solving ranges from simple numerical solutions where one result is expected to more involved decision making where multiple alternatives must be compared.

■ *BIOCOM* (CLEMSON UNIVERSITY)

BioCom, short for Biology in the Community, is a new program supported by the NSF. The course is appropriate for all students and will include key concepts of traditional biology courses in its eight units. The program is laboratory oriented, with activities included in the text.

The content of *BioCom* was based on the following assumptions. First, since covering all biology is impossible, the program introduces students to some fundamentals in-depth so they can learn the material well. Second, students should have significant development of inquiry skills because these skills have practical applications in their personal life. Third, the central conceptual ideas of biology are

in the domains of ecology, evolution, and genetics. Finally, educational research supports an active approach to learning.

The content of *BioCom* has an environmental theme. The biological concepts of all instructional units are related to the students' environment, and the activities touch their lives in community settings. Societal issues in this program include wastes produced by our technological society and effects of that waste on ecosystems and humans; population pressures; biodiversity; ecosystem degradation; human genetics; health issues; the biological basis of behavior; and the global effects of technology.

BioCom recognizes the realities of typical schools and biology teachers. The curriculum is practical in terms of requirements for budgets, facilities, and equipment. Its eight units can be presented within the time frame in Figure 8–6. *BioCom* has a well-designed instructional strategy, with each unit utilizing the same strategy. This consistent pattern allows students to understand how the class is structured, to learn science in a setting which reflects the tentative nature of science knowledge, and to recognize that all such knowledge is constructed within a social context. The role of the teacher is critical and consistent, follows a modified learning-cycle approach, and models the best of inquiry teaching. The goals of *BioCom* are for students to learn biological concepts and skills while developing positive values and attitudes toward science, enhancing their own creativity, and learning how to learn and apply scientific knowledge. In addition, they will come to know the nature of science by participating in scientific endeavors.

The Initial Inquiry (1 day): Used as a whole-class stimulus, this activity includes visuals such as video or pictures. The initial inquiry provides a story and setting which includes a number of inherent problems and issues in a real-world setting. Usually this scenario depicts an event or series of events that really happened. During the discussion the teacher asks open-ended questions focusing on events and possible outcomes in the introductory scenario. During the ensuing classes the teacher tries to get students to generate a number of observations, questions, issues, causes, and consequences.

Structured Inquiries (6–7 days): In this phase the teacher introduces several hands-on investigations. Some will be designed to teach specific skills, while others will provide basic concept information necessary for the ultimate resolution of the issues raised. Other optional activities will also be available as students complete the required core. In each instance students will make choices about variables as they investigate the activity.

The Science Conference (1–2 days): In this phase students communicate their ideas, understandings,

Unit Topic	Required & Sequential	Days	Quarter of the Year
1. Societal Wastes	Yes	20–30	1
2. Ecosystems	Yes	20–30	1
3. Populations	Yes	20–30	2
4. Organismal Maintenance	No	20–30	2–4
5. Inheritance	No	20–30	2–4
6. Behavior	No	20–30	2–4
7. Diversity	No	20–30	2–4
8. The Biosphere	Yes	30	4

FIGURE 8-6
***BioCom* units of instruction**

and questions to the whole class while seeking to answer questions related to the Initial Inquiry and related questions and issues: (1) What do we now know? (2) What do we need to know? (3) How can we find out more? (4) What predictions can we make? Students will make formal and informal presentations, arrange and perform demonstrations and skits, and find other ways to communicate their ideas and concerns. Individual students will then select inquiries to complete on their own.

Individual Inquiries Seeking Further Information (6–7 days): Students, typically working alone or in small cooperative groups where each student has a definite role, will design and complete investigations that will provide data, answers, and more questions. Students will also continue monitoring and collecting data from long-term projects from Structured Inquiries. Some of these individual activities are long term.

The Science Congress (1–2 days): This phase has students compile information and reach consensus on critical points necessary to deal with the issues and questions related to the scenario. The Congress is more formal than the Conference as students, probably in small groups, seek some closure on their issues and questions, devise resolutions to present to the whole class, or reach consensus.

The Town Meeting (1–2 days): In the Town Meeting students determine who are the principal players in the scenario and take on the various roles. Students play these roles and debate the issues, questions, and facts. In doing so, students better understand the issues as well as the questions, data, points of view, and emotions involved. Specific closure will be reached on some resolutions to the problems introduced in the Initial Inquiry. Students will indicate commitments and courses of action and will make entries in their *BioCom Log* indicating "My Best Work" for their personal course of action based upon what they now know about the problem.

The *BioCom Log* is an intrinsic part of the curriculum. Daily log entries are encouraged, and spe-

cific types of entries are required for many activities. Writing about science ideas helps students correct misconceptions and get in touch with their thought processes. Attempting to articulate concepts will also demonstrate to students the extent of their understanding.

Communicating scientific ideas and concepts through discussion and written expression helps all of us to understand basic scientific ideas.

Insights in Biology (Education Development Center, Inc.)

Insights in Biology: An Introductory High School Biology Curriculum is being developed at EDC with funding from the NSF. The curriculum consists of six modules designed for an introductory biology course in either ninth or tenth grade. The modules can be used as the core for a complete biology course or used individually as supplements for the current curriculum.

The curriculum design includes:

- a modular format that provides flexibility for integrating new concepts and information;
- fundamental biological concepts and knowledge presented within the context of major topics that demonstrate the thematic nature of biology and its applications;
- content that addresses current advances in biology and technology;
- pedagogical approaches that are inquiry-based and activity-oriented and that incorporate manipulatives, model building, and quantitative analysis as a bridge between concrete and formal thinking in a cooperative learning environment;
- assessment strategies that measure student understanding of the concepts and students' ability to apply thinking and scientific processes in real-life problem solving and higher order thinking;
- development strategies that involve the collaboration of diverse components of the educational system, including school practitioners, scientists, cur-

riculum and staff development specialists, assessment specialists, publishers, and scientific suppliers.

Each module is designed for a six-week teaching period. Extension activities within the learning experiences provide opportunities for more in-depth exploration of topics of interest. Each module topic has been selected for its scientific and technological significance as well as its relevance to students on personal and societal levels. These topics integrate biology content into a coherent and related set of concepts that can be applied to the students' lives and experiences. Each module will include relevant scientific background, assessment tools, a student book, and an instructional framework for teaching and management (see Figure 8–7 for a summary of units).

Insights in Biology builds on a fundamental belief about science teaching and learning that shaped the conceptual framework and design of its K–8 predecessors. The *Insights* philosophy proposes that students:

- bring a wide variety of experiences, knowledge, understandings, interests, and questions to the classroom;
- construct their knowledge by building on or modifying the understandings they already have; and
- require a variety of learning experiences, each affording opportunities to ask and answer meaningful, thoughtful questions about themselves and their world.

The design of the *Insights in Biology* is based on the belief that biology education must:

- provide an understanding of a core of essential knowledge of biology by exploring specific concepts in depth and in contexts relevant to the student;
- present each concept in several different contexts to demonstrate the unifying themes in biology and to emphasize the connected nature of biology;
- connect the understanding of biological principles with applications to day-to-day living; with social, economic, and ethical issues; and with the responsibility for making decisions about one's own health and environment;
- develop the skills to transfer the knowledge of these concepts to new situations and to apply them appropriately;
- develop critical-thinking and problem-solving skills through direct experience in laboratory experiments, research investigations, inquiry-based activities, and case-study analysis;
- move the student toward formal reasoning and abstract conceptualization through progressions of concrete experiences in appropriate contexts;

- provide support to teachers in developing new instructional strategies and pedagogical approaches that are interactive, inquiry-based, hands-on, and that develop science processing and thinking skills;
- foster in each student the willingness and skills required to engage in inquiry: the ability to address a problem, phenomenon, or issue and to reach an understanding, conclusion, or opinion using knowledge and critical-thinking and problem-solving skills; and
- cultivate in students an appreciation for the aesthetic value of biology as well as for its role in technological advances and in everyday decision making in the home, community, and workplace.

Insights in Biology continues in belief reflected throughout the *Insights* curricula that an understanding and appreciation of science is critical for all students and that the process and content of science—as well as the curiosity, awareness, appreciation, and knowledge of the world around them—must be part of this experience. With this approach to science learning, students will be equipped to make informed decisions about their health, their environment, and their quality of life.

■ DESIGNING YOUR SCIENCE CURRICULUM

Discussion in this chapter has been directed toward national policies and the development of curriculum materials by national projects. In these cases large-scale projects required a team of scientists, science educators, and classroom teachers of science. With the help of major funding, primarily from government agencies such as the NSF, materials were developed, field tested, revised, field tested again, revised, and then published. This is one approach to curriculum development. This model of curricular reform can be characterized as: (1) occurring at a national (or state) level, (2) being heavily funded, and (3) approached from the top down—that is, developed and published first and then implemented by classroom teachers.

A reform movement of the same type and magnitude such as science education experienced in the 1960s and 1970s is not likely in the foreseeable future. Though there is a need for improvement, curriculum development in the near future will also be: (1) at the local or district level; (2) funded within the usual budgets of schools and school districts, perhaps with some assistance from state, federal or private agencies; and (3) approached from the bottom up—that is, initiated and developed by classroom teachers and then implemented within the school district. In some instances the programs may be exported to other districts through groups such as

INFECTIOUS DISEASES

Cell functioning and identity rely on the accurate transfer of information encoded in DNA. This information is expressed as a complement of proteins that determine how the cell carries out both its basic and specialized functions. Throughout scientific research infectious agents such as bacteria, viruses, and parasites are used as models to understand basic processes of the cell and the immune system. This module uses the topic of infectious disease to explore these cellular processes, to illustrate how disruption of basic cellular processes can manifest itself as disease, to investigate the immune system response to infection, and to examine the personal and social ramifications of infectious disease.

PLANTS AS FOOD AND MEDICINE

This module investigates plant structure, plant diversity, photosynthesis as a source of energy for plants and animals, and the plant-produced complex molecules that animals need to survive. Throughout the module students further their understanding of plant biochemistry by exploring the historical and cultural uses of plants as food and medicine.

IN SEARCH OF THE PERFECT ORGANISM

Throughout the ages humans have sought ways to improve the characteristics of their domesticated plants and livestock by manipulating hereditable traits. In this module students investigate how the principles of genetics have been used to breed new animals and develop new crops. Using classical genetics and/or genetic engineering techniques, students then develop a new species of plant or animal, designed with specific characteristics. Students debate the feasibility and ethics of applying this to humans.

WHAT IS LIFE?

What are the characteristics that define life? This module explores the universal characteristics and processes that all living things share. The ways in which organisms carry out the performance of these processes vary, and this variation is reflected in the structural diversity and complexity of the organisms. The performance of these processes is dependent on the availability of required nutrients and substances present in the organism's environment. Students investigate the transformation of biomolecules that occurs when organisms take up nutrients, break them down, and use the resulting building blocks and energy to carry out growth, repair and maintenance, communication, and reproduction. Students transfer their understandings of these processes from the organismal level to the cellular level and explore the benefits of specialization of functions within the cell and within organisms. Students then investigate death as an essential part of life.

ON THE FAST TRACK TO SAVE TROPICAL RAIN FORESTS

In a race against time students are employed as an ecological SWAT team. The students conduct a biological assessment program in order to discover what should and can be saved of the Ecuadorian rain forests. The students investigate biodiversity, components of an ecosystem, carrying capacity and limiting factors, and the impact of human development and technology on rain forests.

PULSES OF EVOLUTIONARY CHANGE

Students explore how changes in climate may be linked to extinctions of certain species and the simultaneous creation of new species. They conceptualize evolution as the interrelationship of the following topics: geological time, natural transition of earth environments and climates, genetics, and the biotic potential of species. With this knowledge students debate the mechanisms of evolution.

FIGURE 8–7
Modules for *Insights in Biology*

the National Diffusion Network (NDN) and the NSTA.

The second approach to curriculum development is a smaller scale approach to change. Here an individual science teacher or team of science teachers is appointed to initiate, develop, and implement a new curriculum. This could encompass anything from a minor revision of an extant course to development of a new K–12 science program for the entire school district.

The new demands for educational improvement—combined with the level of funding at the national level and the implementation of state, urban, and rural systemic initiatives—suggest that in the late 1990s the burden for change will increasingly fall to the local school district and science-teaching personnel.

There is a third approach to curriculum development. Though usually not recognized as such, the adoption of new science textbooks, software, and kit materials represents the selection and implementation of a science curriculum. The curriculum can then be adapted to align with the needs and requirements of local school districts and science teachers. In this approach the emphasis is on adaptation through professional development.

With the preceding paragraphs as background and rationale, direct your attention to a discussion that will be useful to either beginning or experienced teachers confronting the task of designing a science curriculum. We begin by noting several resources that form the basis of our discussion, starting with Ralph Tyler's 1949 classic, *Basic Principles of Curriculum and Instruction.*[9] Approaching 50 years of age, its model has not lost its vitality as an important process for identifying curricular objectives and learning experiences. This model is applicable today because it does not suggest a program, it outlines procedures for developing a curriculum. The utility and simplicity of Tyler's model is found in four basic questions.

- What educational purposes should the school seek to attain?
- How can learning experiences likely to attain these objectives be selected?
- How can learning experiences be effectively organized?
- How can we determine whether these purposes are being attained?[10]

Another resource for our discussion is the *discrepancy model* used in Project Synthesis and reported in the NSTA publication, *What Research Says to the Science Teacher.*[11] The point of this model is to first describe a *desired curriculum* and then your *present curriculum*. By analyzing the discrepancies between such components as goals, materials, facilities, and so on, one can decide what is needed to develop and implement a new program. There is an added strength to this model: a realistic assessment of time, materials, and money is a part of the process.

Although this discussion is about curriculum development by individual teachers and local teams of teachers, the national projects do have some important processes and advice. Joseph McInerney, Director of the BSCS, outlined several criteria for the selection of content in curriculum development. These criteria are paraphrased:

1. How well does the information being considered illustrate the basic, enduring principles of the scientific discipline?
2. Do other teachers, administrators, and parents perceive the proposed materials as useful and important?
3. What is the relationship between the proposed curriculum materials and the prevailing context of general education?[12]

Asking and answering questions such as these will help with the difficult issue of deciding what content should be included and ensure that the program is understandable and acceptable to the scientific and educational communities.

Finally, other valuable sources for individuals developing new programs are *This Year in School Science* (1986),[13] *This Year in School Science* (1989),[14] *The Science Curriculum,* and *Improving Indicators of the Quality of Science and Mathematics Education in Grades K–12.*[15] The discussion that follows is our synthesis of approaches and recommended steps for redesigning and implementing a science curriculum.

Step 1—Review Influences on the Science Curriculum

In the first phase of curriculum improvement, you should spend some time reading, thinking, and discussing three traditional influences on the curriculum—science, society, and students. What are the recent advances in science and technology that are important for students to use in their personal lives and as citizens? Obviously, all scientific knowledge and technology advances cannot be incorporated into school science programs. Science teachers must decide what knowledge is of most worth.

What are the trends, issues, and problems in society that are related to science and technology? Reviewing some of these issues provides another goal component of the science program. An examination of student needs, interests, and characteristics is also essential. Here you can include the unique needs of students in your school or district. After reviewing these three components, you can state a first set of general objectives. This first step is presented graphically in Figure 8–8; Figure 8–9 also provides a list of possible influences.

Step 2—Synthesize Goals into a Proposed Science Curriculum

This phase consists of bringing the objectives identified in the first phase into a proposed curriculum framework. At this point do not make an effort to evaluate or filter the objectives based on various constraints such as time, personnel, or budget. Synthesize your objectives into a program that has a scope and sequence, as well as classroom facilities, materials, equipment, instructional approach, and evaluation components. This can be a very exciting exercise, so use your creativity. Graphically, the development of a curriculum framework now

	Proposed	Present
Goals(e.g., learn science knowledge and processes):		
Grade Levels (e.g., K–6, 10–12:		
Time Requirements (20 Min./Day at K–2; 55 Min./ Day at 10–12:		
Student Population (e.g., all students, at-risk):		
Type of Schools (e.g., urban, rural):		
Academic Subjects (e.g., life science, integrated):		
Description of Program (e.g., STS, fewer topics in greater depth):		
Relationship to Other Subjects (e.g., complements health, supports reading):		
Curriculum Materials (e.g., textbook, student modules):		
Instructional Emphasis (e.g., reading, active learning):		
Instructional Strategies (e.g., hands-on, cooperative learning):		
Instructional Model (e.g., McCarthy, SCIS Learning Cycle):		
Educational Materials (e.g., kits, local equipment):		
Educational Courseware (e.g., MBL, telecommunications):		
Evaluation (e.g., built into instruction, end-of-unit tests):		
Implementation (e.g., concerns-based adoption model, staff development):		

FIGURE 8–8
Characteristics of the proposed and present school science program

appears as shown in Figure 8–10. See also Figure 8–11 for possible categories to consider.

Step 3—Describe the Present Science Curriculum

One mistake often made in local curriculum development is the omission of any consideration of the present curriculum. What are the present goals? What is the textbook? What about the scope and sequence of the present program? What about the role and use of computers in the science program?

Reviewing the present program also includes reviewing any special topics, units, or lessons that you develop. This phase of development is a matter-of-fact approach, outlining what exists in terms of materials, equipment, time, space, budget, and your competencies. Use the categories of goals, curriculum materials, teacher interests and competencies, classroom facilities and equipment, instructional methods, and assessment. Note that the same organizing categories were suggested in the development of the preliminary curriculum. This phase is represented in Figure 8–12.

Priorities	Source of Information
Student Characteristics, Needs, Interests	
Current Practices of Science Teachers	
Current School Program	
Local School Priorities	
State Requirements and Frameworks	
National Trends, Issues, and Standards	
Advances in Science and Technology	
Social Trends and Issues Related to Science and Technology	

FIGURE 8–9
Priorities and information for a school science program

An Analysis of the Proposed and Current Curriculum and Instruction					
	Actual Change	Responsibility	Where	How	Support
Goals					
Grade Levels					
Time Requirements					
Student Population					
Type of Schools					
Academic Subjects					
Description of Program					
Relationship to Other Subjects					
Curriculum Materials					
Instructional Emphasis					
Instructional Strategies					
Instructional Model					
Educational Materials					
Educational Courseware					
Evaluation					
Implementation					

FIGURE 8–10
Changes in the school program

Step 4—Analyze the Discrepancies Between the Proposed and Present Science Curriculum

Using the same categories—i.e., material resources, instructional methods, classroom facilities, and teacher interests and competencies—provides a convenient way to identify the differences between where your science curriculum is and where you want it to be. This phase is represented in Figure

8–13. As a result of this stage you should have a good idea of what is needed in order to develop your science curriculum.

Step 5—Evaluate the Proposed Science Curriculum

This step is critical. Here is a place to reevaluate what you propose doing in terms of what is possible. The phase is infused with reality. Things such as educa-

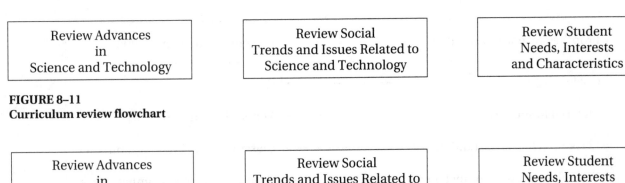

FIGURE 8–11
Curriculum review flowchart

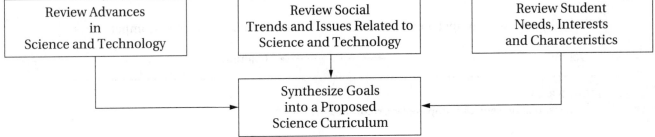

FIGURE 8–12
Curriculum synthesis flowchart

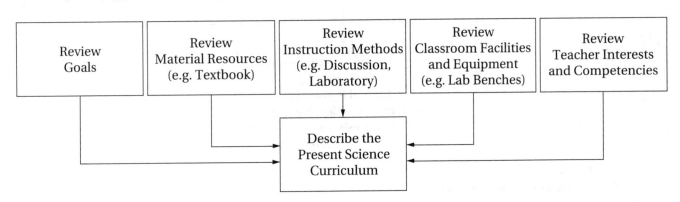

FIGURE 8–13
Curriculum description flowchart

tional philosophy, learning theory, time, budget, and any other real-world items should be factored into the possible science curriculum. Screening everything at this point sets the stage for the review, purchase, development, or synthesis of materials, changes in goals, and suggestions for in-service appropriate to your proposed program. At the end of this phase you should have a realistic picture of what can be done, who is required to do what, and how long it will take, as presented in Figure 8–14. See also Figure 8–15 for possible categories.

Step 6—Development and Implementation of Your Science Curriculum

There are two things to remember at this point. You do not have to develop the program *de nova*. You can select new materials and adapt extant materials. The

second point is that the new science curriculum does not have to be developed in a week, month, or even a year. As a result of your analysis and synthesis to this point, you should have a long-range plan for your: professional development; material acquisition; development of lessons, units, or modules; adoption of new textbooks, and so on. Implementation can occur over a period of time, perhaps a decade.

Step 7—Evaluation of Your Science Curriculum

From time to time it will be necessary to reevaluate the science curriculum. Ideally, you would monitor and change the science curriculum continuously. Doing this would allow you to maintain those curricular components that are appropriate to the present state of science, society, and students, while changing those aspects of the program that have become

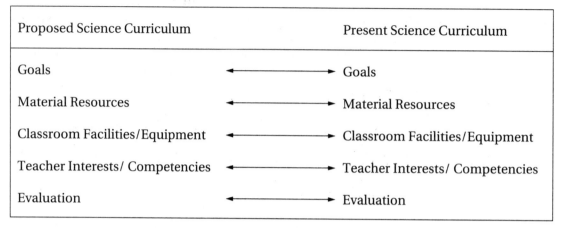

FIGURE 8–14
Comparison of present and proposed curriculum

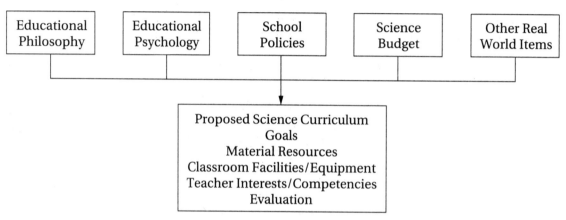

FIGURE 8–15
Curriculum evaluation flowchart

outdated and outmoded. The seven steps we have outlined are summarized in Figure 8–16.

Up to here the process of designing or redesigning the science program has primarily focused on materials. The success of your curriculum development will also depend on the awareness, interactions, and work of the people directly and indirectly involved in the process. The materials of the science curriculum are relatively easy to change, but while changing materials is necessary, it is not sufficient. Efforts to design a new science curriculum must also take into account the beliefs, attitudes, and perceptions that teachers, administrators, and the public have about science and technology education and the particular need to design a new program.

In regard to this we suggest the addition of other components for successful science curriculum development and implementation:

1. Establish the need to change the science education curriculum among the science faculty and with other teachers and administrators.

2. Describe the nature, direction and realities of change to those interested and concerned—especially administrators and the public.
3. Obtain endorsement and support from the principal, school board, and community.
4. Require and develop materials within the budget.
5. Establish a realistic time line for development and implementation.
6. Provide for released time, in-service programs and summertime for personnel directly involved in the project.
7. Monitor and adjust the process of development and implementation.

■ SUMMARY

In the 1980s, a new wave of educational reform was initiated in the United States. Numerous national reports on education in general and also on science education have stimulated new interest in the science curriculum. Aspects of the new emphasis can be summarized as follows:

RALPH TYLER'S APPROACH TO CURRICULUM DEVELOPMENT

  I. Examination of Traditional Factors Influencing the Curriculum to Determine an Initial Set of Instructional Goals
- Examine student interests and characteristics.
- Analyze social trends and issues.
- Synthesize information from disciplines.

  II. Development of Preliminary Curriculum Program
- Synthesize objectives from step I into a cohesive program.

  III. Reconsideration of Objectives in Terms of Philosophy and Psychology
- Review program objectives for congruence with curriculum designer's philosophy.
- Review program objectives for congruence with current learning theories.

  IV. Development of Curriculum Program
- Arrange curriculum objectives into an organized program

PROJECT SYNTHESIS

  I. Identify Primary Goal Clusters of Science Education
- Personal Needs
- Societal Issues
- Academic Preparation
- Career Awareness

  II. Set the Perspective by Developing a *Desired State* (i.e., operational definitions of effective science education) Using the Categories:
- Goals
- Curriculum Programs
- Teacher Characteristics
- Teacher Education
- Facilities and Equipment
- Instructional Practices
- Student Characteristics, and
- Evaluation and Testing.

  III. Determine the Status
- Study and analyze data concerning the actual state in science education.
- Use categories in developing desired state again.

  IV. Analyze Discrepancies
- Compare the desired and actual states of science education for differences.
- Identify aspects of goals, curriculum, instruction and evaluation that need improvement.
- Locate factors that will impede changes and consider alternative means.
- Locate factors that will facilitate change and consider how to utilize them.

FIGURE 8–16
Some models for designing a science curriculum

- Knowledge will be presented in the context of science-and technology-related social issues.
- Inquiry and discovery methods will be expanded to include decision making.
- Laboratory activities will include both holistic and reductive analysis of problems.
- Science curricula will be largely determined by science teachers in local school districts.
- Interrelationships and interdependence of science, technology, and society will be stressed.
- An integration of disciplines to understand contemporary science and technology will be highlighted.
- Science and technology literacy for personal, social, and civic understanding will be the primary emphasis of the secondary science curriculum.

In the 1990s, the initial wave of reforms was sustained by development and implementation of national standards and benchmarks for science education. Legislation for the *Goals 2000: Educate America Act* and the critical role of standards provides support and direction for the improvement of science education in general and the science curriculum in particular.

To design, develop, and implement your own science curriculum we outlined seven steps.

1. Review influences on the science curriculum.
2. Synthesize goals into a proposed science curriculum.
3. Describe the present science curriculum.
4. Analyze discrepancies between proposed and present programs.

FIGURE 8–16
Designing a science curriculum (Continued)

I. Review Influences on the Science Curriculum
- Look at advances in science and technology that have personal and social utility for students.
- Evaluate social trends and issues related to science and technology.
- Consider student needs, interests and characteristics, including national concerns and local issues.
- Outline goals relative to the three areas reviewed.

II. Synthesize Goals into a Proposed Science Curriculum
- Curriculum materials
- Instructional strategies
- Facilities, materials, equipment
- Teacher competencies
- Evaluation

III. Describe the Present Science Curriculum
- Goals
- Curriculum materials
- Instructional strategies
- Facilities, materials, equipment
- Teacher interests and competencies
- Evaluation

IV. Analyze Discrepancies Between Proposed and Present Program
- Compare differences and identify priorities in terms of categories listed above.

V. Reevaluate the Proposed Science Curriculum
- Reevaluate proposed program in terms of priorities and possibilities, e.g., budget.
- Review proposed program in terms of educational philosophy and policies of district, school, and/or science department.
- Revise proposed program incorporating contemporary educational psychology, e.g., development and learning theory.

VI. Development and Implementation of the Science Curriculum
- Review curriculum materials appropriate for the proposed program, e.g., textbooks, teaching modules.
- Consider adaptation of extant materials for proposed program.
- Develop curriculum materials, e.g., lessons, units, modules as necessary.
- Implement new materials in an organized fashion.

VII. Evaluation of the Science Curriculum
- Monitor and adjust curriculum periodically.
- Repeat process of redesign of science curriculum.

5. Evaluate the proposed science curriculum.
6. Develop and implement the science curriculum.
7. Evaluate the science curriculum.

■ REFERENCES

1. National Research Council, *National Standards for Science Education* (Washington, DC: Author, 1995).
2. American Association for the Advancement of Science, *Benchmarks for Science Literacy* (Washington, DC: Author, 1993).
3. Paul Hurd, Rodger Bybee, Jane Kahle, and Robert Yager, "Biology Education in Secondary Schools of the United States," *The American Biology Teacher 42* (7) (1980): 380–410.
4. Wayne Welch, "Inquiry in School Science," in N. Harms and R. Yager, *What Research Says to the Science Teacher, 3* (Washington, DC: National Science Teachers Association, 1981), pp. 53–58.
5. Faith Hickman, "Education for Citizenship: Issues of Science and Society," *The American Biology Teacher, 44* (6) (1982): 358–367.
6. Shymansky, et al., "The Effect of New Science Curricula," pp. 387–404.
7. National Science Teachers Association, *Scope, Sequence, and Coordination. The Content Core: A Guide for Curriculum Designers* (Washington, DC: Author.)

8. Biological Sciences Curriculum Study (BSCS), *Developing Biological Literacy* (Dubuque, IA: Kendall/Hunt Publishing Company, 1993).

9. Ralph W. Tyler, *Basic Principles of Curriculum and Instruction* (Chicago: University of Chicago Press, 1949).

10. Tyler, *Basic Principles of Curriculum and Instruction,* p. 1.

11. Norris Harms and Robert Yager, *What Research Says to the Science Teacher* (Washington, DC: National Science Teachers Association, 1981).

12. Joseph McInerney, "Curriculum Development at the Biological Sciences Curriculum Study," *Educational Leadership* (December 1986/January 1987): 24–28.

13. Audrey Champagne, ed., *This Year in School Science: The Science Curriculum* (Washington, DC: American Association for the Advancement of Science, 1986).

14. Audrey Champagne, ed., *This Year in School Science: The Science Curriculum* (Washington, DC: American Association for the Advancement of Science, 1987).

15. Richard Murnane and Senta Raizen, eds., *Improving Indicators of the Quality of Science and Mathematics Education in Grades K–12* (Washington, DC: National Academy Press, 1988).

Chapter 9

SCIENCE AND OTHER DISCIPLINES: INTERDISCIPLINARY APPROACHES TO CURRICULUM

Many science teachers and school districts are integrating science with other disciplines. Justification for such approaches includes the fact that knowledge growth requires individuals to understand broader concepts that link several disciplines; the observation that schools impose artificial boundaries and constraints on students; the commonsense notion that real world problems do not present themselves in discipline-bound packages; and the understanding that fragmentation of the curriculum reduces relevance and meaning for students.

What do educators mean when they talk about interdisciplinary approaches to curriculum? We can begin with ideas of disciplines and curriculum. Disciplines such as physics, chemistry, and biology represent specific bodies of knowledge with their own history, procedure, and method. From these disciplines educators, curriculum developers, and science teachers select specific knowledge, methods, historical people, and advances to include in school science programs. As Bruner[1,2] points out, students must know the structure of science disciplines to further their development and acquire understandings of how things are related. From a teaching point of view, disciplinary approaches to the curriculum make sense because students can direct attention to specific content and closely related concepts and methods. Focusing on a subject for a period of time—for instance, earth science for a year—allows students time and opportunity to progressively develop the fundamental concepts, methods, and history associated with the earth sciences.

In science the interdisciplinary approach begins with a theme, personal issue, social problem, school event, or science topic and applies the concepts and methods from more than one discipline to the realm of study or investigation. Where the disciplinary approach stresses thorough understanding of the conceptual schemes of a discipline such as biology or physics, interdisciplinary approaches emphasize connections and linkages among disciplines in the pursuit of understanding objects, organisms, and events in the natural and designed world. John Christensen,[3] a science teacher and curriculum developer summarizes the interdisciplinary perspective:

In science, an integrated curriculum is a conceptual framework which weaves together the various concepts, skills and principles of the traditional subject-centered classrooms into a unified whole. This enables the curriculum to focus on the vital question: What from science is important for all students to know? The integrated curriculum is then built around the answer to that question. The relevant issues of our time can now be the primary focus. The concepts and skills of science can be built as these issues are addressed.

Heidi Hays-Jacobs[4] has pointed out some of the problems associated with content selection for interdisciplinary courses. One problem is what she terms the *potpourri problem*. That is, units are a sampling of knowledge from different disciplines without any central focus, scope, or sequence in the curriculum. A second issue emerges as a *polarity problem* where the differences between disciplinary and interdisciplinary approaches become polarized and result in conflicts with departments, schools, or states. To avoid these problems, Dr. Jacobs recommends two criteria for interdisciplinary programs. First, such programs must have carefully articulated designs that include a scope and sequence, a framework for thinking skills, indicators for attitudinal change, and thorough and consistent assessment. Second, the curriculum must include both disciplinary and interdisciplinary approaches.

There are many good reasons to involve students in interdisciplinary studies as part of their science education. One way to encourage the development of understandings and abilities associated with science is to focus on epistemological issues through questions such as, "What do we know?" and "Why do we believe what we know?"

Although many advocate interdisciplinary studies, there are some who urge caution. Kathleen Roth, who teaches science at a middle school and at Michigan State University, has expressed some "Second Thoughts About Interdisciplinary Studies." Her concerns grew out of work on a unit that combined science and history. After designing and teaching an interdisciplinary unit on "1492—Seeds of Change," she realized the theme and teaching approach did not help students connect with the important concepts—especially science—that she had first thought they would. She also found that the interdisciplinary approach did not allow for adequate development of ideas and concepts related to science. It also seemed that the social studies connection constrained some science activities. In conclusion, Dr. Roth suggests, "Before we jump on the interdisciplinary bandwagon, let us engage in debate and study of the kinds of integration that are compelling, meaningful, and powerful for children."[5]

Discussions about interdisciplinary curriculum often point to the use of themes as a central focus. Both the *National Science Education Standards* and *Benchmarks for Science Literacy* identified themes that you might use in the design of science curriculum (see Figures 9–1 and 9–2 for those concepts and processes).

The national standards and benchmarks include conceptual and procedural schemes that cross traditional disciplinary boundaries and provide students with powerful ideas to help them understand the natural and designed world. The content of these unifying and common themes can be introduced at any level in the K–12 science program.

In the following sections we provide examples and approaches to interdisciplinary approaches to science curricula.

■ HISTORY OF SCIENCE AND TECHNOLOGY IN SCIENCE CLASSES

There are several current trends that have relevance for integrating the teaching of the history and nature of science and technology in science classes.[6] There

---

Order and Organization
Evidence, Models, and Explanation
Change and Measurement
Evolution and Equilibrium
Form and Function

FIGURE 9–1
National Science Education Standards **unifying concepts and processes**

Systems
Models
Constancy and Change
Scale

FIGURE 9–2
AAAS *Benchmarks for Science Literacy* **common themes**

is a thrust for developing improved scientific literacy among students and the lay public. There is also renewed interest in instruction in history of science and technology as perceived by policy documents such as the NRC's *National Science Education Standards,*[7] the AAAS's *Science for All Americans,*[8] and *Benchmarks for Science Literacy.*[9] There is an additional trend toward inclusion of Science-Technology-Society themes in science classes in contemporary school programs as noted by the NSTA in its position statement titled, "Science-Technology-Society: A New Effort for Providing Appropriate Science for All."[10]

In the 1990s, an analysis of textbooks for science, U.S. History, World History, and U.S. Government courses reveals very limited attention to the history of science and technology—only about 2 percent of the total pages. An analysis of twenty-seven state curriculum guides in science showed that less than half of them called for the study of history of science and technology. A similar situation was found with local and state social studies curriculum guides.

One science guide (the *Science Framework for California Public Schools* for 1990) includes some emphasis on the nature of science. The *History-Social Science Framework for California Public Schools* for 1988 stresses the importance of intellectual history. These efforts could presage increased attention to these important topics throughout the country.

■ SCIENCE AND MATHEMATICS

> The alliance between science and mathematics has a long history, dating back many centuries. Science provides mathematics with interesting problems to investigate, and mathematics provides science with powerful tools to use in analyzing data. . . . Science and mathematics are both trying to discover general patterns and relationships, and in this sense they are part of the same endeavor.[11]

No scientific discipline has become truly respectable until bolstered by data compiled and analyzed by mathematical methods. The evidence provided by natural phenomena, experimentally tested in the laboratory or in the field, and subjected to intensive scrutiny by mathematics forms the foundation on which science rests. For example, data collected by Tycho Brahe did not contribute substantially to the understanding of astronomy until the mathematical genius of Johannes Kepler put it into order and formulated several laws of planetary motion. A second example is more recent. The hypothesis, developed by Jonas Salk, of polio inoculation by weakened virus did not gain public acceptance until

■■■■■■■■■■■■■■■■■■ **GUEST EDITORIAL** ■■■■■■■■■■■■■■■■■■■■■■■■■■■■■

There's More to Science Teaching Than Facts, Concepts, and Memorizing

Marie Del Toro
Earth Science Teacher
Fountain Valley School
Colorado Springs, Colorado

Whether one has been teaching science for ten years or ten months, in a public or private school, or to a classroom of fifty or five, there is the common belief that teaching is a demanding but very rewarding profession. As a new teacher, I have had my share of good and bad experiences, all of which proved very worthwhile. The purpose of this editorial is to relate some of my experiences and how they have helped me grow as a science teacher.

Fountain Valley is a small college preparatory school located in Colorado Springs, Colorado. Its 220 students come from twenty-eight states and eight foreign countries. As a result, there is a great diversity in student interests, values, and levels of academic performance. Although Fountain Valley encourages individualism, it also strives to further a community spirit. That spirit is exemplified in the following ways: students are assigned advisers to oversee their progress both academically and socially; students and faculty eat family-style dinners twice a week; and finally, faculty live on campus, thus providing personal interaction between students and faculty.

Although the school is small, it offers many science courses. Obviously, every student in science will not choose science as a career. The school is sensitive to that fact. As a result,

Fountain Valley has developed a broad curriculum ranging from traditional one-year courses in biology and chemistry to one- and two-term electives in oceanography, geology, and anthropology. The assumption is that something will appeal to every student through a diversity of offerings.

Teaching in a boarding school requires a great deal of time and effort. It is not enough to teach a student the basics in math or science for, as teachers in a boarding school, we are obligated to a much larger commitment. In effect, we are serving as the student's parents, and so our teaching should encourage growth in all phases of a student's cognitive, affective, and psychomotor learning.

If a student is to develop into a caring, sensitive, and intellectual person, the classroom atmosphere should be conducive to attaining those goals. Like any other subject, science could be five lectures a week. However, it seems that the essence of science, learning through discovery, is lost if this method is used. As a result, the best approach to science I have found is an integration of methods such as experimentation, problem solving, reading and questions, student speeches, and field trips.

Two of my most interesting and rewarding experiences have been associated with field trips. One occurred very early in the fall during interim week. The purpose of this week is to provide students opportunities to expand their intellectual, cultural, social, and vocational horizons. I was fortunate enough to accompany another teacher and thirteen students to the Oregon coast to study marine biology, rain-forest ecology, and coastal geology. Before the trip I knew few of the students but after spending a week living, eating, and talking with them, I developed a very special relation-

it was supported by statistical methods on a large scale.

Science teachers in middle and senior high school have an obligation to convey to students an understanding of the role of mathematics in science. Every opportunity should be used to show the integral nature of mathematics courses in grades seven through twelve, although little crossover between these disciplines is currently afforded. Students are led to believe that science and mathematics are unrelated entities. This attitude is often perpetuated by the teachers of both subjects, perhaps because

they are unfamiliar with possible common objectives and applications. In practice the difficulty of incorporating mathematics into science classes is compounded by extreme variations in mathematical ability among students. At any grade level students in the science classes have mathematics competencies that range several grade levels above and below the average for the particular grade. Some students may have difficulties with simple addition and subtraction operations, while at the same time other students may have an understanding of ratio and proportion, percentage, and use of science notation.

ship with some students which could not have been kindled in any other environment. They have seen me in a situation outside the classroom and they know how I can act. This additional contact with students helps them realize that a teacher is a person too and not just someone whose job it is to give A's and F's.

The other very rewarding experience occurred during a field trip with my geology class. After spending the afternoon driving around Colorado Springs looking at various geologic oddities, two of my students told me that they had become highly motivated about geology due to my influence. They also expressed an interest in pursuing geology in college, which is ironic considering their lack of confidence at the start of the course.

A few days later, one of these students asked me if I would help with her senior independent project which, surprisingly, dealt with geology. Reflecting on the fall term, I must say that those students advanced in their understanding of geology and, more importantly, in their outlook toward science and in their newly acquired confidence.

Experiences such as these certainly make teaching worthwhile. However, it is not always that way. That is where the true challenge begins. The good student will learn regardless of the teacher and the poor student may or may not learn with the most exciting, motivating teacher.

As a first-year teacher, my duties include teaching four courses, coaching two sports, supervising the girls' dorm one night a week and every sixth weekend, co-sponsoring the rock-climbing club, and chaperoning various trips to the school's mountain campus located in the Colorado mountains. With this spectrum of duties, I see many students other than those in my classes and this contact is good. The hard part is in assuming so many roles: teacher, coach, disciplinarian, friend, and surrogate mother, father, brother, or sister. It must be exceedingly frustrating for a student not to know how I will react or, more importantly, how I will act in any given situation. A student rarely sees me perform all of these roles.

Coaching allows me to see students in an environment outside the classroom. It is great to watch students enjoy a sport whether or not they are highly motivated in an academic situation. Sometimes students feel teachers judge them by their level of academic achievement, and so underachievers may tend to shy away from certain teachers. This attitude is rather unfortunate, for there are certain traits, just as important in life as math or science formulas, which can be instilled only in competitive sports. A student who works hard at a sport is learning a great deal about patience, sportsmanship, teamwork, and modesty, all of which are valuable and are not limited to athletics but hopefully will carry over to the classroom.

Teaching is both demanding and rewarding. It is a profession which will take as much as you are willing to give. There are always days when nothing seems to be going right, but then there are days when your students excel. If I had to start again, I would make a concerted effort to listen more intently to various students' needs and excuses; keep my expectations high, for students need to strive for more than they think they can attain; and, finally, I would make it a point to be consistent in my treatment of various classroom activities. At present, teaching is proving to be a very satisfying and exciting experience.

Science teachers confront this great variation and should plan science activities accordingly. The mathematical requirements for any given activity or experiment are also extremely varied. By suitably individualizing the instruction, students can be challenged at their level and in the process gain competence in the particular mathematical skill. See, for example, the "Teaching Science Activities" in the Appendix on pages 396–474.

Mathematics and science have many features in common. These include a belief in understandable order; an interplay of imagination and rigorous logic; ideals of honesty and openness; the critical importance of peer criticism; the value placed on being the first to make a key discovery; the international scope; and even, with the development of powerful electronic computers, the ability to use technology to open up new fields of investigation.

The NCTM, standards,[12] emphasize problem solving, communication, reasoning, connections, estimation, measurement, patterns and relationships, and other areas that are equally important in science and mathematics education. Ronald Good also points out that we are likely to see more efforts

■■■■■■■■■■■■■■■■■■ **GUEST EDITORIAL** ■■■■■■■■■■■■■■■■■■

Astronomy: Exploring Beyond the Earth

Laura P. Bautz, Ph.D.
Division Director
Division of Astronomical Sciences

In late February 1987, the explosion of a star 170,000 light years away became visible in the Southern Hemisphere. It immediately stimulated research all over the world as astronomers raced to observe and analyze this spectacular event. Press coverage of this occurrence attested to the public's interest in the phenomenon by which a star, many times more massive than our own sun, blew itself apart in the last stages of its life.

Events such as the 1987 supernova are not the only ones in astronomy to capture the imagination. Astronomy is the science that leads to understanding conditions found on other planets, how stars form and evolve, what happened to shape the present universe, and other ques-

tions. On an immediate level astronomy assists in measuring time, in explaining tides and seasons, and in enhancing pleasure at viewing the night sky. Professional astronomers gather and analyze information that comes from distant celestial objects. Most of this information comes to earth as light, which we view through telescopes, or radio waves, which we collect through enormous antennae. We then process our data in computers. One does not need sophisticated equipment to view the skies, however. A pair of binoculars is sufficient to reveal craters on the moon, and if there are no city lights to interfere, one can see clouds of stars, bright gas among some stars, and the rich diversity of astronomical objects. These can all be seen in more depth at planetariums, observatories, and science museums.

Astronomy is a physical science and one that requires an initial effort to master the basic principles. Students who want to become astronomers should keep their options open and study mathematics and basic science courses.

---

to coordinate the curriculum and instruction of science mathematics: "The student who sits through math class from 9 A.M. to 10 A.M. is the same student who later sits (or moves around) in science class."[13]

Occasional joint planning between the mathematics and science teachers can bring about improved conditions, in both areas, for relating mathematics and science. If mathematics teachers are aware of the uses of mathematics in the science classes at particular grade levels, they may point out the possible applications to their students. In assigning homework problems they may use currently significant examples from science. Mathematics textbooks can be improved significantly on this point. The scientist is concerned with proper use of units and measurement. Attaching appropriate units to the figures given in word problems in mathematics can develop skills in usage, recognition, and manipulation of units by the students. The problems will take on increased meaning and show the applications of mathematics to science. Team-teaching arrangements between science and mathematics teachers can afford many opportunities for interrelating the two disciplines. Many teachers are trained equally well in both areas and have teaching respon-

sibilities in both. In this case, maximum effectiveness should be achieved.

■ MATHEMATICS AND ITS CONNECTIONS WITH SCIENCE DISCIPLINES

Too often the mathematics learned by secondary school science students seems to have little relevance to the mathematics used in their science courses. There needs to be increased cooperation and planning between mathematics and science teachers to bridge the gap that now exists to make the mathematics relevant to the science being studied. For example, developments in the teaching of biology at all levels reveal the need for students to have a mathematical background and an ability to bring mathematical experience and skills to bear on practical problems of measurement, classification, observation, and recording. It is equally clear that in studying biology meaningful, relevant situations can provide a springboard and motivation for learning and applying mathematics. The authors of biology textbooks assume that students understand the mathematics of measurement. The student may be asked to use a hand

Since students need mathematics knowledge and skills to solve many practical science problems, mathematics and science teachers must work together to ensure that the mathematics curriculum is relevant to the science subject being studied.

lens and to place the object being examined at the focal length of the lens, which is perhaps 6 centimeters (cm). Understanding of the metric system is required here. Reference may be made to the size of a human cell, which may be measured in micrometers and is frequently expressed using exponential notation. This also requires the student to be familiar with the metric system as well as the use of powers-of-ten notation.

Ratio and proportion are other important mathematical concepts frequently used in biology. The ratio of length to width of plant leaves and the proportion of biomass to nutrition provided for plant growth are two concepts that require these mathematical understandings.

Statistical understanding is needed because frequently such things as the mean, median, and mode are expressed when talking about population and growth. When frequency tables are used, students must have the knowledge of collecting a sample in order to make a statistical count. It also is important for students to understand the idea of using discrete and continuous data in graphing notations.

Calculating relationships between two sets of unit measurements such as Fahrenheit and Celsius temperature scales requires mathematical understanding. To be able to make conversions from one temperature scale to another is a skill required not only in biology but in many other sciences.

The concept of very small and very large numbers is another mathematical tool frequently used in biology. For example, giving students a problem involving bacteria growth where the number of bacteria doubles every twenty-five minutes provides a beautiful opportunity for them to calculate exponentially.

Another important concept is the idea of scaling and scaling factors. One exercise is to have students determine the food requirements of a small mammal, such as a mole, and of a very large animal, such as an elephant. Does the food requirement alter with respect to size, volume, mass, or other factors? This concept can also be applied to heat loss and the necessary rate of metabolism to maintain life. All of these are mathematical concepts that are needed in biology and whose application will help students to better understand the use of mathematics in science.

Mathematics concepts used in chemistry at a more sophisticated level are those of ratio and proportion. Concepts of pressure, volume, and temperature change and the use of the general gas laws provide opportunities for students to apply these mathematical operations. Manipulations of equations and formulas also require mathematics. Calculations need to be made in balancing equations. A chemical equation is similar to a mathematical formula in its application. It is evident that mathematics has much to offer chemistry, biology, and other science subjects. Conversely, mathematics can also gain greatly from these subjects if the teachers of mathematics and the sciences make an effort to plan and to standardize the notation systems they use. If the mathematics teachers in their applications will use science examples and if the science teachers will apply the mathematics at every opportunity in working science problems, students will understand that mathematics and science are inseparable entities and highly important to scientific endeavor.

Simple Statistics

An aspect of mathematics in science that needs greater attention is the use of simple statistical techniques. Students should have opportunities to assemble data, construct frequency distributions, and calculate certain measures of central tendency (such as the mode, median, and mean) and certain measures of dispersion (such as the range, average deviation, and standard deviation). Exercises requiring these operations will emphasize the intimate relationships between science and mathematics. Certain experiments lend themselves well to statistical computations, particularly those dealing with biological populations or probability problems.

Science and Reading

A frequently neglected connection is that of reading and science. Because students obtain information

·················· **REFLECTING ON SCIENCE TEACHING** ··················

INTEGRATING SCIENCE AND MATHEMATICS

1. Plan a laboratory assignment in which students are given maximum opportunity to practice mathematics skills with which they are currently familiar from their mathematics classes.
2. Obtain a mathematics textbook of the type usually used in the eighth grade. Select an appropriate chapter and rewrite all the problems at the end of a section or chapter in such a manner as to emphasize the interrelatedness of science and mathematics.
3. Interview a teacher of mathematics to discover the types of mathematics skills students are expected to learn by the time they have completed her/his course.
4. Write a two- or three-paragraph essay on how you would implement the teaching of needed mathematics skills in your science class.
5. Write a one-page position paper expressing your point of view on holistic education in the secondary school.

from science textbooks, their reading skills play an important role, yet too often the level of the reading matter is inappropriate for their grade level. Often students are unaware that reading and understanding science material is quite different from reading novels or short stories. As a consequence they lose effectiveness in their reading.

Larry Yore has noted several points bearing on the beliefs and attitudes school teachers have regarding reading in science.[14] He believes that science teachers place high value on reading as an important strategy to promote learning in science and generally accept responsibility for teaching content reading skills to science students. Many accept the importance of science reading as a component of scientific literacy and as a means of improving science achievement.

Jeffrey Mallow has concluded that students have a great range of misconceptions regarding science reading. Among these students believe: (1) science vocabulary is the same as ordinary vocabulary, (2) science textbook materials are to be memorized, (3) one can read science as rapidly as literature, and (4) all science reading is of the same sort and at the same level. Students commonly think, "If I can't understand a popular account of science, then I must be incapable of grasping science altogether." Some suggestions Mallow makes regarding improving students' ability to read science materials are: (1) use objectives and reviews for orientation toward the material, (2) read slowly and reread, going back and forth between sections, and read any margin notes provided, (3) use questions and exercises interactively with specific chapter sections, and (4) use problems interactively with the whole chapter.[15]

■ AN INTEGRATED APPROACH TO MIDDLE SCHOOL SCIENCE AND TECHNOLOGY

Professional associations, reports, and national standards and benchmarks call for changes in middle level science education that affect the science curriculum.[16,17,18,19,20,21] Some of the key recommendations include:

- emphasizing science as inquiry, especially higher-order thinking skills;
- focusing on personal and social issues and the connections among science, technology, and society;
- integrating science disciplines with one another and other disciplines; and
- organizing the curriculum around unifying themes.

These recommendations provided the foundation for *Middle School Science & Technology*—a curriculum developed by the BSCS. Figures 9–3, 9–4, and 9–5 present the scope and sequence and learning outcomes for this curriculum.

We include here a discussion of this curriculum so you can develop further understanding of an interdisciplinary science curriculum. Pay particular attention to the use of themes to organize experiences and the fact that the curriculum does include traditional science content. The curriculum framework for this program covers three levels (or years) of study and is divided into four units at each level. BSCS chose four units per level to encourage a depth of coverage in one or more unifying themes, rather than a breadth of topics. They also chose this division to coincide with the most common grading periods in school systems.

Level A: Patterns of Change				
Unit	*1*	*2*	*3*	*4*
Curriculum Emphasis	Personal dimensions of science and technology	The nature of scientific explanations	Technological problem solving	Science and technology in society
Focus Question	How does my world change?	How do we explain patterns of change on the earth?	How do we adjust to patterns of change?	How can we change patterns?

Summary of Learning Outcomes			
Unit 1	*Unit 2*	*Unit 3*	*Unit 4*
Recognizing patterns Distinguishing among trends, cycles, and correlations Using patterns to predict Evaluating the quality and quantity of data	Developing explanations for patterns as a way of improving predictive powers Developing if–then statements Reviewing the history of explanations for earthquakes and other features of the earth Identifying patterns that support the theory of plate tectonics	Identifying natural events, disasters, and patterns Building structures to withstand various natural conditions Analyzing the problems of human adaptation Solving problems using a technological approach Analyzing costs and benefits Recognizing probability	Identifying patterns of waste disposal Examining costs and benefits of possible solutions Examining hazardous waste disposal Completing a final action project related to waste disposal

FIGURE 9–3
Middle School Science & Technology (Level A: Patterns of Change)

Level A (fifth or sixth grades) used the unifying theme *Patterns of Change*. Students learn about a variety of patterns in the natural world (including their own patterns of growth) and the relationship between patterns and prediction. Students look at the patterns of natural events and explore the decisions that people make about where to live based on those patterns. The students also look at patterns associated with the increasing size of the human population, such as garbage generation and accumulation.

In Level B (sixth or seventh grades) students examine the themes of *Diversity and Limits*. They learn about the distribution of characteristics in humans and other organisms and the breadth of normal range. They also learn that all people, organisms, and things have limits that define relationships in the living and physical worlds and help inspire humans to develop technologies to overcome these limits. They explore the diversity of materials and products available to people and try to explain that

diversity in terms of particle theory of matter. At the end of the year, students examine genetic diversity and the ethical issues associated with genetic engineering.

The theme of *Systems and Change* unifies Level C (eighth-ninth grades). In Unit 1 the students examine systems that are in and out of balance and develop the basic concept of systems, as well as a vocabulary for describing systems. In Unit 2 they look at change in systems by studying the theory of evolution as an example of an idea that has changed over time, as well as a scientific explanation for changes in living organisms. In Unit 3 students shift their focus to technological systems and examine how these systems can help solve energy problems. By studying population systems in Unit 4, students pull together all of these concepts related to systems and focus on population growth in general, and the human population system specifically, to learn about the interrelationships that influence system-wide changes.

Level B: Diversity and Limits				
Unit	*1*	*2*	*3*	*4*
Curriculum Emphasis	Personal dimensions of science and technology	Technological problem solving	The nature of scientific explanations	Science and technology in society
Focus Question	What is normal?	How does technology account for my limits?	Why are things different?	Why are we different?

Summary of Learning Outcomes			
Unit 1	*Unit 2*	*Unit 3*	*Unit 4*
Identifying human diversity— what is normal? Learning to create operational definitions and control variables Using human diversity to set standards Collecting and graphing data Interpreting normal curves	Understanding diversity in relationship to technology Using a design process Using human factors to design products (ergonomics) Identifying and using criteria and constraints Testing products Designing, building, and testing toys	Developing scientific explanations for the diversity of matter Understanding scientific models and the particle theory of matter Developing if– then statements Testing models	Using the chromosome theory of inheritance to explain the diversity of characteristics Understanding genetic engineering as a science, technology, and society issue Writing a science fiction story Making a book as a final project

FIGURE 9–4
Middle School Science & Technology (Level B: Diversity and Limits)

To vary the approach to unifying themes, each unit has a unique focus question and curriculum emphasis (see Figures 9–3 through 9–5 for Levels A, B, and C). BSCS designed the focus questions to reflect how a student might approach the unit. They also used the focus questions to provide a story line for each unit so that students understand the connection of ideas within and between units. The purpose of a curriculum emphasis is to provide a focus or context for the content presented in a unit. BSCS used four distinct emphases in this curriculum: *Personal Dimensions of Science and Technology, The Nature of Scientific Explanations, The Nature of Technological Problem Solving,* and *Science and Technology in Society.*

The first unit in each level has the same curriculum emphasis, *Personal Dimensions of Science and Technology.* The purpose of the first unit is to engage students in the study of science and technology by increasing the relevance of these areas to their lives. Activities in this unit often have students examine

their own growth, abilities, and lives, but some study of events and phenomena in the natural world are also included.

The second units of Levels A and C and the third unit of Level B have the curriculum emphasis, *The Nature of Scientific Explanations.* The purpose of this emphasis is to help the students understand how science explains events and processes and answers questions about the natural world. In these units the students focus on the characteristics of scientific explanations in the context of a major theory of science, such as the theory of plate tectonics, the particulate theory of matter, or the theory of evolution. The third units of Levels A and C and the second unit of Level B emphasize *The Nature of Technological Problem Solving.* Here students learn about the principles of technology as a discipline. Although many people assume that technology is a set of products, gadgets, or gizmos, this curriculum emphasis presents technological problem solving as a process for adapting to and/or solving problems.

Level C: Systems and Change				
Unit	*1*	*2*	*3*	*4*
Curriculum Emphasis	Personal dimensions of science and technology	The nature of scientific explanations	Technological problem solving	Science and technology in society
Focus Question	How much can things change and still remain the same?	How do things change?	How can we improve our use of energy?	What are the limits to growth?

Summary of Learning Outcomes			
Unit 1	*Unit 2*	*Unit 3*	*Unit 4*
Systems in Balance Understanding dynamic balance in systems Understanding how human body systems maintain balance Learning to graph Recognizing examples of systems that are out of balance Studying how AIDS affects the balance of the immune system	*Evolution* Recognizing change in systems Understanding evolution of scientific explanations Understanding natural selection Differentiating between evidence and inference Developing if–then statements	*Energy Systems* Recognizing when energy is present in a system Identifying types of energy use and energy resources Understanding technological systems for delivering energy Recognizing the input and output of various technological systems Developing strategies to reduce personal energy use	*Population Systems* Identifying dynamics of human and animal populations Understanding exponential growth and limiting factors Conducting a research project Participating in a debate about human population growth

FIGURE 9–5
Middle School Science & Technology (Level C: Systems and Change)

In the units with this emphasis, students use a design process, apply a decision-making model, or analyze systems.

All of the fourth units have the curriculum emphasis *Science and Technology in Society*. This emphasis reflects the gradual transition through the year from a focus on personal issues to a focus on a global issue that is tied to the unifying theme. Science, technology, and society are intertwined, and as a result BSCS used the curriculum emphasis to develop units that have an interdisciplinary approach.

In addition, these final units include a major project that provides the students with a memorable, culminating event for the year. At Level A students choose a project that will in some way change how they or their community deals with garbage. The projects range from interviewing neighbors about

the chemicals they keep in their homes, to beginning a recycling program, to educating others about garbage disposal patterns and associated problems. At Level B students explore the ethical and societal implications of genetic engineering and then create a science fiction story based on these implications. The final project for the students at Level C is a debate about possible solutions to potential population problems. Students conduct research, adopt a role, and examine a variety of viewpoints as they prepare for the final debate.

■ AN INTEGRATED APPROACH TO HIGH SCHOOL SCIENCE AND TECHNOLOGY

Global Science: Energy, Resources, Environment is an environmental science program designed for high

■■■■■■■■■■■■■■■■■■ **GUEST EDITORIAL** ■■■■■■■■■■■■■■■■■■

Earthquakes: Reducing Death and Damage

William A. Anderson, Ph.D.
Program Director
Earthquake Hazard Mitigation Program
Division of Critical Engineering Systems

On September 19, 1985, a large earthquake rocked Mexico City, left thousands of people dead, and caused millions of dollars in property damage. Some years before, on March 27, 1964, an earthquake in Alaska killed over a hundred people and caused millions of dollars in property damage. I studied the social and economic impact of the Alaskan earthquake as a graduate student in sociology. As a result of my work I realized that many parts of the world are threatened by earthquakes such as these—in the United States alone, thirty-nine states are subject to earthquakes.

Because earthquake hazards touch many countries, a global community of researchers study the phenomena. When appropriate, the United States has joined in establishing cooperative international programs for joint research and the sharing of vital information. I have worked with researchers from Japan, China, and Mexico. In particular I have been active in a program, which was established with Mexico following the great 1985 Mexico City earthquake, that has taught us many lessons on how to reduce earthquake hazards.

Many people in different scientific and technical disciplines are required to extend our understanding of earthquakes. Some of the researchers I work with include seismologists, geologists, engineers, and sociologists like myself. Through their investigations, seismologists and geologists are developing a basic understanding of what causes earthquakes. Their goal is to understand seismic events well enough to predict earthquakes, thereby giving the public time to prepare. Engineers are completing equally important work in the design and development of buildings that can withstand the enormous structural strains and stresses caused by earthquakes. More earthquake casualties result from collapsed and damaged buildings than from any other cause, so improved buildings would save many lives.

Sociologists are also contributing to our growing knowledge about the effects of earthquakes. As a sociologist, I study the actions that people and organizations must take to prepare for and respond to earthquakes; some of these actions include finding effective ways to educate the public about the earthquake hazard, reducing the exposure of populations to earthquakes through land-use planning, and organizing such emergency actions as medical response, and search and rescue. The common goal of the researchers who study earthquakes is to reduce the property damage and loss of life that result from these disasters. I find it very satisfying to work with those who are exploring this frontier of science.

school students. This program integrates chemistry, biology, physics, and earth science into a laboratory-oriented curriculum. Labs or classes allow students to analyze social problems and understand how science is relevant to their personal lives. By viewing the world as a dynamic, self-supporting ecosystem, students gain a new appreciation of our planet and the knowledge to manage its resources intelligently. Figure 9–6 provides an annotated table of contents for *Global Science*, which gives an indication of the program's integrated approach. We also include the science disciplines in *Global Science* (see Figure 9–7). This is an example of the second criteria outlined by Hayes-Jacobs; namely, curriculum must include both disciplinary and interdisciplinary approaches.

■ SUMMARY

Justification for interdisciplinary approaches to curriculum vary. Some authors think that fewer students are interested in science courses because of economic reasons; they do not see job possibilities in science, so they pursue other studies. Another proposed explanation for a lack of interest in science is that students often think science is dull, particularly when the only science they encounter is presented in a form that lacks connections to personal and social contexts. Many individuals and reports have proposed that the scientific and technologic understanding and skills that students need should be developed in personally meaningful and socially relevant contexts. These recommendations support an

1. *The Grand Oasis in Space*
   Students build an understanding of ecosystems.
2. *Basic Energy/Resource Concepts*
   Students develop an understanding of the laws governing energy and mineral resource use.
3. *Mineral Resources*
   Students learn how mineral deposits are formed, where they are located, and how they are mined.
4. *Growth and Population*
   Students learn about exponential growth and population issues.
5. *Food, Agriculture, and Population Interactions*
   Students examine nutrition and the fundamentals of food production, modern agricultural practices, and the world food situation.
6. *Energy Today*
   Students build understandings of the energy sources for modern societies.
7. *Nonrenewable Resource Depletion*
   Students examine the depletion pattern for nonrenewable resources and examine resource lifetimes.
8. *Nuclear Energy*
   Students understand the basic principles of nuclear energy and consider its potential as an energy option.
9. *Energy Alternatives*
   This chapter focuses on the energy source alternatives to oil, gas, coal, and nuclear power.
10. *Strategies for Using Energy*
    Students examine energy options and consider options for future planning.
11. *Water: Quantity and Quality*
    This chapter builds an understanding of the importance of having adequate quantities of high-quality water for modern societies.
12. *Resource Management: Air and Land*
    Students examine ways of improving our ability to use air and land.
13. *The Economics of Resources and Environment*
    Students combine scientific information and economic principles related to resource and environmental challenges.
14. *Options for the Future*
    Students develop models of the future.

interdisciplinary approach to the science curriculum—that is, curriculum connections not only between science disciplines but also among other areas of educational and intellectual growth. Increasingly, science teachers recognize the need to integrate science with other disciplines. The ability to synthesize information, to view world problems holistically, and to look at the interrelated dimensions of problems that affect human life are becoming more important. Interdisciplinary programs and unified approaches to studying science appear to be growing. There is a need for greater emphasis on relating mathematics and secondary school sciences. Students of mathematics should have opportunities to apply their mathematical skills to the solution of scientific problems; applications should be called to their attention.

The use of inquiry methods in science teaching provides many opportunities for incorporating mathematics. In this way mathematics is seen as a tool of science for quantifying and testing hypotheses. Students practice, on a realistic and meaningful level, the skills learned in their mathematics classes. In addition to practice in the usual skills of addition, subtraction, scientific notation, logarithms, use of calculators, etc., students in modern science learn to evaluate measurements, express precision of data and results, work with significant figures, and apply

Chapter	Life Science	Earth Science	Chemistry	Physical Science	Physics
1. The Grand Oasis in Space	●	●	●	●	
2. Basic Energy/Resource Concepts	●		●	●	●
3. Mineral Resources		●	●	●	●
4. Growth and Population	●				●
5. Food, Agriculture, and Population Interactions	●	●	●		
6. Energy Today		●		●	●
7. Nonrenewable Resource Depletion		●		●	●
8. Nuclear Energy	●	●	●	●	●
9. Energy Alternatives	●	●	●	●	●
10. Strategies for Using Energy		●	●	●	●
11. Water: Quantity and Quality	●	●	●	●	
12. Resource Management: Air and Land	●	●	●	●	●
13. The Economics of Resources and Environment					●
14. Options for the Future	●	●	●	●	●

FIGURE 9–7
Disciplinary representation in *Global Science*

statistical tests to their data. These skills are practiced at all levels of junior and senior high school.

The *National Science Education Standards* and *Benchmarks for Science Literacy* encourage the inclusion of other areas such as technology, history and nature of science, and personal and social issues in the curriculum. There are examples of interdisciplinary approaches to curriculum that emphasize science concepts and skills as well as other disciplines.

■ REFERENCES

1. Jerome Bruner, *The Process of Education* (Cambridge, MA: Harvard University Press, 1960).
2. Bruner, *Toward a Theory of Instruction* (New York: W.W. Norton & Company, 1968).
3. John Christensen, "Integrated Secondary Science: The Time is Now," *New Directions in Education* (Dubuque, IA: Kendall/Hunt Publishing Company, 1994).
4. Heidi Hayes-Jacobs, *Interdisciplinary Curriculum: Design and Implementation* (Alexandria, VA: Association for Supervisors and Curriculum Development, 1989).
5. Kathleen Roth, "Second Thoughts About Interdisciplinary Studies," *American Educator, 18*(1) (1994): 48.
6. Rodger W. Bybee, et al., "Teaching History and Nature of Science: A Rationale," *Science Education, 75*(1) (1991).
7. National Research Council, *National Science Education Standards* (Washington, DC.: Author, 1995).
8. American Association for the Advancement of Science, *Science for All Americans*, Washington, DC: Author. (1989): X.
9. American Association for the Advancement of Science, *Benchmarks for Science Literacy* (Washington, DC: Author, 1993).
10. National Science Teachers Association, "Science Education for Middle and Junior High Students," *Science and Children, 24*(3) (1986): 62–63.
11. AAAS, *Science for All Americans:* 34.
12. National Council of Teachers of Mathematics, *Curriculum and Evaluation Standards for School Mathematics* (Reston, VA: Author, 1989).
13. Ronald Good, "Editorial: Research on Science-Mathematics Connections," *Journal of Research in Science Teaching* (February 1991): 109.
14. Larry D. Yore, "Secondary Science Teachers' Attitudes Toward and Beliefs About Science Reading and Science Textbooks," *Journal of Research in Science Teaching, 28*(1) (1991): 55-72.
15. Jeffrey V. Mallow, "Reading Science," *Journal of Reading, 34* (1991): 324–328.
16. AAAS, *Science for All Americans.*

17. J. A. Beane, *A Middle School Curriculum: From Rhetoric to Reality* (Columbus, OH: National Middle School Association, 1990).

18. R.W. Bybee, C.E. Buchwald, S. Crissman, D.R. Heil, P.J. Kuerbis, C. Matsumoto, and J.D. McInerney, *Science and Technology Education for the Middle Years: Frameworks for Curriculum and Instruction* (Washington, DC: The National Center for Improving Science Education, 1990).

19. California State Department of Education, *Caught in the Middle* (Sacramento: Author, 1988).

20. Carnegie Council on Adolescent Development, *Turning Points* (New York: Carnegie Corporation of New York, 1989).

21. AAAS, *Benchmarks for Science Literacy*.

UNIT 5

····································

INSTRUCTIONAL STRATEGIES

The fun of teaching science involves figuring out the most interesting strategies and techniques to enhance learning. The most dismal thing that can happen is to get in a rut and keep on teaching in the same old way day after day. Students soon get bored, and you will become jaded in a short while.

The solution to this is to create new, effective, and innovative ways to present material, use games to stimulate interest, and get students personally involved in their learning. For too long science teachers have looked at students as receptacles for knowledge—the fount for which is the teachers themselves, or the science textbook. But things are changing as we employ new ways of teaching and learning. If we look at science classes as a place where students can use their fertile minds to solve problems, gather data, explore new avenues, or create different solutions, we will find that they respond favorably and learn science. There will be some excitement in every class as students look for changes in things they are growing, in results of an experiment, or in some exciting information that relates to the natural or designed world. Students are curious and responsive to new challenges. Our job is to direct these traits so that learning occurs. This is what makes our jobs interesting.

In the process of becoming involved in their own learning, students will develop certain desirable knowledge, skills, and attitudes that will stay with them throughout their lives. Whether they go into science as a career or not, understandings, habits of careful observation, deliberation before drawing conclusions, and healthy skepticism will all be useful characteristics in any field of endeavor. The development of scientific literacy is not merely being able to read science materials with understanding, but to develop full appreciation of where scientific information comes from, the differences between science and technology, and how each of these impinge on society.

Our goal as science teachers should be to produce scientifically literate citizens who can make valid and considered judgments about decisions relating to science and technology. It certainly is true that we live in an increasingly scientific and technologic world that is likely to become even more complex in the future. Citizens of the twenty-first century are in middle and high schools today. What a responsibility we have as science teachers to ensure that these children will be well equipped to cope with the challenges ahead! You have chosen an exciting career in science instruction for secondary school students. With thoughtful preparation, you are destined for success.

Chapter 10

··

INQUIRY AND CONCEPTUAL CHANGE

Inquiry is the process by which scientists pose questions about the natural world and seek answers and deeper understanding, rather than knowing by authority or other processes.[1]

This quote, taken from the draft edition of the *National Science Education Standards* document of 1991, suggests that teaching school science might be more in tune with the practice of science if it were taught in a questioning mode rather than in the traditional expository mode used in most science classes. This chapter posits that teaching in an inquiry manner may result in students learning science in a way that expresses more accurately the true nature of science; this method may also bring about conceptual changes more effectively and more permanently in students' minds.

It is important to begin by saying that inquiry is not solely within the domain of science. Other areas of intellectual endeavor—such as social problems, mathematics, analysis of literature, and history—also use inquiry effectively. For example, suppose that one wishes to study the potential effects of increasing populations (including human, animal species, and plant life) on the environment in a given part of the world. To study this certain questions would need to be asked, certain hypotheses formulated, experiments designed, data gathered and analyzed, and conclusions drawn. These activities represent inquiry and investigation. The information could not be obtained simply by referring to books or authorities because the information may not be available. Inquiry becomes a necessary method of attacking the problem.

When students study science using investigation and inquiry, they employ many different skills. Some of these skills are psychomotor that involve doing something physical, such as gathering and setting up apparatus, making observations and measurements, recording data, and drawing graphs. Other skills students employ are intellectual or academic, such as analyzing data, making comparisons, evaluating results, preparing reports, and communicating results to other students or teachers. Students engage in a full range of performances needed to fully explore a problem, an experience that prepares them for the future when other problems confront them. They are not limited to rote memorization and recitation as is often the case in traditional methods of learning. Instead students have developed certain life-long learning skills that will serve them usefully in the future.

In using investigation and inquiry, students develop their psychomotor skills—such as making measurements—as well as academic skills.

The *National Science Education Standards* suggest several inquiry skills twelfth graders should have mastered.[2] They are as follows.

Students should be able to:

1. Formulate usable questions by:
   a. generating a number of possible questions;
   b. recognizing which questions are in the domain of scientific inquiry;
   c. being aware of the complexity of questions being generated.
2. Plan experiments by:
   a. selecting a question that can be explored through experimental procedures;
   b. designing a procedure for the systematic collection of data; and
   c. choosing appropriate measuring tools.
3. Conduct systematic observations by:
   a. choosing and/or designing and building tools and apparatus;
   b. using tools and apparatus;
   c. collecting and recording data (judging their precision and accuracy);
   d. organizing data; and
   e. representing data.
4. Interpret and analyze data by:
   a. graphing data; and

b. retrieving, using, and comparing data from other investigations.
5. Draw conclusions by:
   a. relating conclusions to data and their analysis;
   b. relating their experiment to other experiments;
   c. relating their experiment to models and theories; and
   d. suggesting further investigations (formulating new questions).
6. Communicate by:
   a. using words, graphs, pictures, charts, and diagrams to describe the results of their experiments;
   b. producing summaries or abstracts of their work;
   c. using technology to improve communications; and
   d. analyzing critically other people's experimental work.
7. Coordinate and implement a full investigation by:
   a. formulating questions;
   b. planning experiments;
   c. conducting systematic observations;
   d. interpreting and analyzing data; and
   e. drawing conclusions and communicating the entire process.

Students should be able to demonstrate each skill in a new experiment. Evidence of individual skills and the ability to conduct a full investigation will be documented in the reports that students write during the communication component.

In addition to the skill development cited above, certain attitudes are fostered that give a realistic picture of how science proceeds in real life. It becomes obvious to students experiencing inquiry and investigation that ready-made answers to problems do not automatically appear. Much hard work and thinking are necessary to solve most problems. Rarely can answers to problems be found by simple reference to authority. Becoming aware of this fact and developing the necessary skills to proceed on one's own gives students a feeling of self-sufficiency that pays dividends in the future.

■ CONCEPTUAL CHANGE

Children entering our science classes at the middle school or high school level already have a vast store of knowledge of science from previous classes and personal experiences. One mistake new teachers make is to assume that their students are somewhat like blank slates and that what one needs to do is start from scratch and build new science concepts in their minds. This would be fine if it were not for the fact that the new concepts have to compete with old information already present. Sometimes these two entities are quite different. They may even be incompatible. In addition, the old information may be preferred. It is often uncomfortable to be told that one's knowledge is incomplete or wrong.

As children construct their world from observations, trial-and-error experiences, instruction from classroom teachers, words of wisdom from their parents, and numerous other sources, they form concepts of how the world works and behaves. Being pragmatists, children use the knowledge they have gained to explain the unfamiliar things they encounter. If the information seems to offer satisfactory explanations and it appears to work for them, it becomes ingrained in their behavior. "What works is true" is a familiar quotation from the famous psychologist, William James. As children process information, many apparent explanations they formulate may not agree with scientists' understandings of the phenomena.

Thus, when these children reach school age and are given formal instruction, the previous concepts retained in their minds may be naive, incomplete, tentative, or incorrect, and may interfere strongly with what the teacher is trying to convey. It has been found that such misconceptions are amazingly tenacious and difficult to change.

Let us consider how children approach their understanding of the world around them. All knowledge comes to us through our senses. All normal human beings have five sense organs that keep on bringing information that is somehow accepted and assimilated into our prior knowledge. This accumulation of knowledge forms the basis on which we respond to the world and to new events. Much of what we learn is based upon common sense. This forms an interpretation of events in which the information provided by our senses forms a strong and convincing argument for what we believe.

Unfortunately, common sense is often uncommonly unreliable. For example, a simple illustration of the unreliability of our sense of touch might be shown by placing each hand in water of different temperatures, one cool and one warm. After a minute or two put both hands in a third container of water in which the temperature is midway between those of the other two. The sensation we get is that one hand tells us that the water is cool and the other tells us the water is warm. In other words, the hands are very unreliable indicators of the temperature of water.

Another sense organ that sometimes fools us is the ears. For example, perhaps a helicopter is approaching our location from a distance. Perhaps we are on a street in which there are several houses

■■■■■■■■■■■■■■■■■■ GUEST EDITORIAL ■■■■■■■■■■■■■■■■■■

Medical Research: Science Lurches On

Carol Wilson
Research Associate
Division of Biological Sciences and the Pritzker School of Medicine
University of Chicago
Chicago, Illinois

Many distributions found in scientific study, in nature, and in the laboratory follow regular, predictable patterns. Examples include the bell-shaped normal curve of probability and the *s*-shaped or sigmoid population-growth curve. In a research laboratory, the actual process of gathering data is much more irregular and unpredictable. Scientific research rarely progresses smoothly; rather, it may vary greatly from day to day, with experimental failures outnumbering successes. This unpredictable quality prompted one research group to adopt the slogan, "Science Lurches On."

The "lurch" effect of research progress is particularly evident in a leukemia research laboratory. Here, most experiments focus on the study of leukemic white blood cells from sick patients. Thus, the workload is largely dependent on when patients become ill or when they schedule clinic appointments. If an experiment on cells from Patient twenty-six flops, the laboratory may have to wait as long as twelve months before she returns to the clinic so that the study can be repeated. In addition, one day could bring seven patient cases to study at once (each case requiring at least two hours of study time) and then there may be no more patients for two weeks! The laboratory must be prepared at all times to accommodate any kind and number of cases.

A research project begins with the definition of a question. This laboratory focuses on the study of hairy-cell leukemia, a rare lymphoproliferative disorder, and related diseases. Questions are asked about the origin and function of the malignant hairy cell. Defining the research problem, the direction of the project, is the easy task. The challenge begins with the development of experimental techniques that will lead to definite answers; in many instances, finding the right methods requires more time than the actual performance of experiments. For example, our laboratory was seeking to identify the different phospholipid components of the hairy-cell membrane using one-dimensional, thin-layer chromatography. First, a literature search revealed thin-layer chromatography methods which appeared to be applicable to our system. Adaptation and expansion of the methods to accommodate our system required nine full months of trial and error experiments before a set of procedures that worked was defined. The actual data collection took only five months before answers to the problem began to fall in place.

Another facet of work in an active medical research laboratory is the coordination of the many projects that are conducted simultaneously. Researchers who work independently on separate problems must be prepared to overlap when an unscheduled case unexpectedly appears from the clinic or the emergency room.

Overall, perhaps the most exciting aspect of working in a medical setting is the interaction with several spheres of the hospital environment. A researcher may work with physicians and patients for part of a day, reviewing the symptoms and development of a disorder. The focus then shifts from patient to laboratory, where the cellular material is isolated, stored, cultured, extracted, and studied in various ways. Through our laboratory, for example, one blood sample may be analyzed by eight to ten different research groups, including the study of surface and cytoplasmic immunologic markers, transmission and scanning electron microscopy, cell-surface hormone receptors, chromosome abnormalities, and biochemical composition (proteins and lipids). Although each laboratory investigation is fascinating in itself, no research would be as interesting or rewarding without putting it all together to study overall patterns and interpret the meaning of the data. It is this interaction, along with development of applications that can improve and expand human life, that makes research so intriguing and worthwhile.

on both sides of the thoroughfare. We may, for example, hear the helicopter approach from the south, and then suddenly, just as clearly, it may seem to be approaching from the north. What the ear has given us is response to sound waves that were echoing from one or more of the buildings on the street, so we have a temporary misconception of the location of the helicopter.

There are hundreds of incidents that occur in the life of a growing child that could be illustrated in simple examples like these. As long as they are temporary misunderstandings and are soon corrected by further experiences or a word from a parent or friend, they do no harm. But a more complex situation, for example the observation of a bright crescent moon, might pose a tougher problem. If children think about why the moon is in a crescent shape, perhaps they might think that the earth's shadow is somehow falling on the portion of the moon that they cannot see. After all, an object produces a shadow when it cuts off the light from the source. Perhaps the earth gets in the way of the light from the sun and casts a shadow on the moon. From this it is easy to extend the idea that sometimes the moon is covered by an even larger shadow, even to the point when it is entirely covered and becomes completely invisible. Maybe this is why we cannot see the moon during certain times of the month.

This misconception is further reinforced by the very correct idea that sometimes, as during a lunar eclipse, the shadow of the earth really does block the light from the sun, thus producing the eclipse. Children in elementary and middle schools are fascinated by eclipses; perhaps this concept assumes an inordinate level of importance in their minds, which they naturally extend to the explanation of the moon's monthly phases. Teachers themselves may be confused on this matter and may even reinforce the incorrect concept.

This leads us to the ultimate problem which concerns teachers at all levels. How can we structure our science classes and other experiences that will help children acquire understandings more in line with those held by scientists or other informed individuals who consider the manner in which the world works?

Most of the time information in science classes is presented in an expository manner by the teacher. Additional information will come from textbooks, films, videotapes, and other sources. A small fraction of class time will be devoted to laboratory work. Some of that time will be oriented toward student inquiry or investigations but probably not more than 2 to 3 percent of the class day. There is not a lot of investigative kinds of teaching going on in most of our science classes.

Is the kind of science teaching described above conducive to overcoming misconceptions that are held rather persistently and stubbornly by most learners? The results seem to show that it is not. We do not appear to be making much progress in increasing science literacy among our students or among members of the lay public. Dismal reports keep pointing to the lack of science knowledge by school children in the United States. During the heyday of science curriculum development projects of the 1960s, we seemed to be making gains as reported by the NAEP. Since then science scores have been on a downhill slide, and our standings as a nation when compared with other industrialized nations usually find our children near the bottom in terms of science knowledge.

We are faced with the problem of devising different and better teaching strategies in science to overcome these deficiencies. Some of the research on generative learning and constructivism may give some clues as to how these problems might be attacked. For example, we might consider:

1. *First the action, then the words.*
   Use of this maxim might help teachers structure their science lessons in such a way that students encounter first hand the phenomena under study, rather than to simply be told about it as a bit of information they must remember and give back on a test. Strictly verbal learning, which tends to foster a false sense of security about one's knowledge, might thereby be minimized. Students would be able to demonstrate the concepts under study, or state principles in their own words, or suggest ways to apply principles in other contexts. As it is now, students concentrate so intensely on memorizing a concept's exact words or wording that they fail to grasp the meaning. The types of factual tests we frequently give them reinforce this manner of study.
2. *Talk through the new concept.*
   On an individual basis, if possible, have students explain their interpretation of the phenomenon. Try to elicit the reasons why students hold the particular point of view they do. Ask questions tactfully to identify the points where clarification is needed. Use the basic premise of science, which is that every cause has an effect and every effect is produced by a cause. During this time use simple demonstrations where possible and examine each phase of the demonstration in detail. Present new information or new points of logical reasoning that are nonthreatening and nonjudgmental. Avoid casting aspersions on previous poor teaching or previous experiences that might elicit resistance from students. Finalize the session by hav-

Active involvement in science investigations gives students a better grasp of the concepts than strictly verbal learning.

ing students explain in their own words their revised understanding of the phenomenon.

3. *Teach the concept to someone else.*

We have all experienced the truth of the maxim that "One really learns a subject when one teaches it." Use this truism to help reinforce the new understanding in the students' minds. On a one-to-one basis to start with, have students explain the phenomenon to each other. Have students ask questions of their pupils to see whether the explanation has been clear and logical. Later, you might have students explain or demonstrate the phenomenon in a classroom environment.

4. *Don't let the concept die.*

Every teacher has probably experienced the situation of memory lapse when explaining a science phenomenon before a class. It is frustrating to suddenly realize that some small point has been forgotten and you get yourself in trouble when explaining the concept. The more frequently you can refresh your memory, through repetitions, the more likely you can avoid this embarrassment. It is exactly analogous to regular practice on a musical instrument. Without such practice things begin to fall apart. This principle applies also in the case of restructuring science concepts. One successful performance does not guarantee success for all time. It has been found that under pressure, such as tests, students have a tendency to revert to former knowledge. Frequent repetitions of the newly learned information are necessary, and use of the information in new contexts helps to reinforce it in the mind.

■ FOSTERING CONCEPTUAL CHANGE THROUGH INQUIRY

Cognitive psychologists have examined our traditional approaches to teaching and have come to the conclusion that American pedagogy has been dominated by a behaviorist model: "In the behaviorist approach, the teacher's task consists of providing a set of stimuli and reinforcements that are likely to get students to emit an appropriate response. If the goal is to get students to replicate a certain behavior, this model works well; but if understanding, synthesis, eventual application, and the ability to use information is our goal in education, a behaviorist approach is not successful. Because there is no place in the model for understanding, it is not surprising that behaviorist training rarely produces it."[3]

The constructivist model of learning, discussed elsewhere in this book, provides greater emphasis on understanding, forming relationships between concepts, relating new learnings to schema already present in the brain, and developing applications of new knowledge to events and problems that the student encounters. It is within this context that inquiry and investigative approaches to problem-solving may be the most efficacious method. To see how this may come about, read the following examples.

To begin, let us identify some of the procedures that characterize learning through a constructivist approach. Among these are encouraging student input of creative ideas, using alternative sources of information, using open-ended questions (questions that may have several possible answers), encouraging students to suggest causes for events, making predictions, testing out one's ideas before acceptance, challenging the ideas of others, collecting evidence to support one's ideas, and restructuring one's concepts on the basis of new evidence.

All of these also characterize investigative activities. Students who engage in inquiry perform all of the listed procedures repeatedly as they study problems. In doing so they develop habits of inquiry in much the same way as do scientists or other investigators. To illustrate, look at the following example.

Suppose an eighth grade science class is faced with the task of measuring the diameter of the sun— a problem found in many earth science textbooks. The class is divided into groups of four persons per group. The first task each group must address is what kind of measurements would give this information? Discussion among the group members might lead to the realization that only inexpensive equipment is available, that measurements could only be made during the daytime when the sun is visible, and certain precautions against direct observation of the sun must be observed. A group prediction of the sun's diameter might be made.

Further discussion, perhaps with teacher assistance, might stimulate the idea that one could use proportions between similar triangles to get the answer. Drawing a diagram of the setup would help here. The task of selecting equipment becomes easier now because it only needs to fit within a classroom or a convenient outdoor area.

Procurement and construction of the equipment comes next. A metric ruler, some three-by five cards, a marking pen, and a paper punch are all that is needed. One bit of necessary information is the distance from the earth to the sun in metric units. This information can usually be obtained from an astronomy textbook.

A convenient circular dot exactly one centimeter in diameter can be drawn on a three-by-five card. This dot should be carefully drawn to increase accuracy of the measurement. The card should be affixed to the end of the metric ruler in a position perpendicular to the ruler. Another card can have a small diameter hole punched in the center of it. The hole should only be about two millimeters in diameter for best results.

To obtain the measurements, point the metric ruler at the sun while holding the punched card at some small distance (perhaps fifty centimeters) from the affixed card at the other end of the ruler. An image of the sun will fall on the affixed card. Move the punched card back and forth until the sun's image exactly covers the dot on the affixed card. Now measure the distance from the punched card to the affixed card.

A proportion may now be written as follows:

Distance between the two cards is to the distance of the earth from the sun as the diameter of the sun's image is to the diameter of the sun. From this proportion the diameter of the sun can be obtained.

What skills and procedures were used by students in this investigation? We can identify discussion, sharing of ideas, seeking information from an authority, construction of apparatus, making a prediction, gathering data, and solving a mathematical relationship, among others. Solution of problems in this manner invariably employs many useable skills practiced by the students. Such procedures should be used frequently enough in science classrooms to give students repeated practice. This is the only way it will become second nature to the students and provide them with a realistic picture of how science advances.

■ SUMMARY

The strategies of inquiry teaching are emphasized in the *National Science Education Standards* as primary methods of conducting science classes to acquaint students with investigative procedures used by scientists and other problem-solvers. Among the inquiry skills needed to conduct investigations are formulating questions, planning experiments, conducting systematic observations, interpreting and analyzing data, drawing conclusions, communicating results, and coordinating an investigation.

In addition to the skill competencies needed, attitudes such as persistence, willingness to do hard work, and developing abilities to proceed on one's own are essential.

Much discussion is now held among science teachers about how children conceptualize subject material. Ideas of constructivism are posited, in which it is theorized that learners "construct" their own world of ideas from the sensory input they receive. In the process of doing this, many misconceptions arise, which must be dealt with by their teachers. The chapter discusses methods of doing this. Also several examples of investigative activities are provided as models.

■ REFERENCES

1. National Committee on Science Education Standards and Assessment, *National Science Education Standards: A Sampler* (Washington, DC: National Research Council, 1992.)
2. *National Science Education Standards: A Sampler.*
3. Robert E. Yager, "The Constructivist Learning Model," *The Science Teacher,* (September 1991), p. 54.

Chapter 11

QUESTIONING AND DISCUSSION

■ THE NATURE OF INQUIRY TEACHING

The essence of inquiry teaching comprises two main elements: arrange the learning environment to facilitate student-centered instruction and give sufficient guidance to ensure direction and success in discovering scientific concepts and principles. One way in which a teacher helps students to obtain a sense of direction and to use their minds is through questioning. The art of being a good conversationalist requires listening and insightful questions. Good inquiry-oriented teachers are excellent conversationalists. They listen well and ask appropriate questions, assisting individuals in organizing their thoughts and gaining insights. Inquiry-oriented teachers seldom tell but often question. A properly given question is a hint. If students are studying a pendulum but have not discovered that its frequency is related to its length, the instructor may notice that the students seem to be having difficulty. The instructors can guide the students by asking a series of questions. Listed below on the left are the questions asked. On the right is an analysis of what the instructor is doing.

Notice that the instructor aided students, through artful questions, to make their own discoveries and to use their minds. The teacher did not steal the thrill of discovery from the students but did facilitate it. Proper questioning is a sophisticated teaching art. To practice it, teachers must know where the students' thoughts are. To do so, instructors must switch from the classical concept of teaching-telling to listening and questioning and being open to the students' ideas. Consequently, the emphasis changes from teaching to student learning. After perceiving students' difficulties, instructors must formulate a question that will be a challenge yet give guidance. To do so, instructors must know what they are trying to teach in a conceptual way and adapt the question so that it is appropriate to the students. Moving about the class, teachers must constantly adapt this procedure from student to student. This process requires unusual awareness and ability. No wonder so many teachers fall back into the classical mode of teaching. To move about a classroom in this manner is to truly individualize instruction, teach for the person and, if done constantly in a positive setting, humanize instruction. Good questioning practices

An Inquiry Discussion

1. What have you found out about the pendulum?	This is a good question because it is divergent. It allows for a number of responses. Students will have found out something, and being able to tell it to the instructor will help clarify any problems.
2. What seems to affect the frequency, i.e., the number of times it swings a second?	This is a more convergent question. It helps students center on frequency. They may not have thought of this before. Students replied that they didn't know.
3. Try some things to find out.	The teacher then leaves and moves on to other students requiring some assistance. Later, the teacher returns.
4. What have you done to find out about the frequency?	Here again the instructor is asking a relatively divergent question since the students may have done many things. The students reply that they have used different weights.
5. How did the use of different weights affect the frequency?	The instructor is asking students to interpret data. Students, however, still have not discovered that the length of the string affects the frequency.
6. What do you think the length of the string would have to do with the frequency?	This question is fairly directive-convergent. The instructor is helping students to center on a particular variable.
7. How would you determine this?	This question asks students to devise an experimental procedure.

By moving about the class, the teacher can question and listen to students individually.

are involved in all areas of science instruction, as indicated in the following list:

Where Is Questioning Involved in Science?

1. Discussion	7. Field trips
2. Laboratory exercises	8. Projects
3. Demonstrations	9. Games
4. Student worksheets	10. Lectures
5. Audio-visual aids	11. Simulations
6. Evaluations	12. Computing

For an example of how questioning can involve several of these aspects simultaneously, see the "Teaching Science Activity: How Can You Use Questions to Solve Problems?" in the Appendix on pages 000–000.

■ TYPES OF QUESTIONS

Questions may be planned before class or may arise spontaneously because of student interaction. It is always wise to prepare a series of questions before entering an inquiry-oriented class. The mere fact that you have done so contributes to your questioning ability. Having thought about the questions gives you

direction and a sense of security, thus enhancing your ability to carry on a discussion.

Inquiry-oriented teachers must remain constantly flexible. Even though they have planned a series of questions, they must be willing to deviate from them and formulate new ones as they interact with students. These unplanned, spontaneous questions may be difficult to create at first, but through developing good questioning techniques, instructors become more sophisticated and more likely to interact appropriately with students.

Before you devise your questions you should decide the following:

1. What talents are you going to try to develop?
2. What critical thinking processes will you try to nurture?
3. What subject-matter objectives do you want to develop?
4. What types of answers will you accept?
5. What skills do you wish to develop?
6. What attitudes and values do you wish to emphasize?

Educational Objectives and Questions

Just as objectives can be classified by this taxonomy, so can questions. Refer back to the preceding questions and classify them, on the left, according to the taxonomy. Then list five of the best questions and decide why you believe they are good. Bloom's abbreviated taxonomy is repeated to help you (see chapter six). An example of how you might use it is shown as a guide.

Bloom's Taxonomy

Cognitive Domain	**Affective Domain**
Evaluation	Generalized Set
Synthesis	Organization
Analysis	Valuing
Application	Responding
Comprehension	Receiving
Knowledge	

Questions requiring responses from the higher levels of the hierarchy are more desirable because answering them involves more critical and creative thinking and indicates a better understanding of concepts.

Using Bloom's Taxonomy to Classify Questions

Classification	**Sample Question**
Knowledge	1. How many legs has an insect?
Synthesis	2. What hypotheses would you make about this problem?

Application	3. Knowing what you do about heat, how would you get a tightly fitted lid off a jar?
Analysis	4. What things do birds and lizards have in common?
Comprehension	5. Operationally define a magnet.
Evaluation	6. If you were going to repeat the experiment, how would you do it better?
Valuing	7. What is your interest in earth science now compared to when you began the course?
Valuing	8. What do you value about this film?
Receiving	9. Do you watch science shows on television?
Responding	10. Do you talk to your friends about science?

■ PROCESSES OF SCIENCE AND QUESTIONS

Another way to classify questions is to use science processes. This approach ensures that the basic structure of science and critical thinking is taught. Shown below is a guide of how you might classify questions using science processes.

Science Processes
1. Hypothesizing
2. Inferring
3. Measuring
4. Designing and experimenting
5. Observing
6. Setting up equipment
7. Graphing
8. Reducing experimental error

Classifying Using Science Processes

Classification	Sample Question
Observing	1. What do you observe about the landscape?
Hypothesizing	2. What do you think will happen to the solution when I heat it?
Designing an Experiment	3. How would you determine the absorption of the different wavelengths of light in water?
Graphing	4. How would you graph these data?
Setting up Equipment	5. Obtain the following equipment and set it up as directed.
Reducing Experimental Error	6. How many measurements should be made to report accurate data?
Inferring	7. What conclusions can you make from the data?

Convergent and Divergent Questions

Another way to classify questions is to determine whether they encourage many answers or just a few. Questions allowing for a limited number of responses and moving toward a conclusion are called convergent. Questions allowing for a number of answers are called divergent; they provide for wider responses plus more creative, critically considered answers. In an inquiry discussion it is generally desirable to start with divergent questions and move toward more convergent ones if students appear to be having difficulties.

Generally speaking, convergent questions, particularly those requiring only a yes or no answer, should be avoided because they allow for fewer responses, thereby giving students little opportunity to think critically. The fundamental purpose in using the inquiry approach is to stimulate and develop critical thinking, creative behavior, and multiple talents. Convergent questions certainly do little to achieve this end. Remember that, in an inquiry investigation, it is important that students have a chance to use their minds. Learning to think rationally and creatively does much to increase a person's self-concept. Many teachers are so concerned with getting the right answer that they prevent students from going through a thought process. Even though students may come up with wrong conclusions, they still have had a mental experience in thinking about the problem. Having this experience is probably more important than a right answer. We as teachers would, of course, like for students to think and obtain the correct answer as well. However, recall for a moment a mathematics teacher who only accepts the correct answer to a problem, ignoring the procedures used in obtaining it. Students may have used very good thinking processes to obtain the answer yet misplaced the decimal point. Is the teacher justified in saying that students have not learned because they don't have the right answer? Students will probably never have that problem again but they undoubtedly will have many situations requiring them to use similar logical strategies. It is the thinking that is most important! Teachers who do not reward thinking may stifle students.

Teleological and Anthropomorphic Questions

Teleological (Greek—*teleos*—an end) questions are those that imply that natural phenomena have an end or purpose. The word *anthropomorphic* comes from two Greek words: *anthropos*, meaning man, and *morphos*, meaning form. An anthropomorphic question implies that some natural phenomenon has the characteristics of humanity. For example, such a question might state that some natural phenomenon has a want or wish—rocks fall because they want to.

Why do you think these questions should be avoided? What do they do as far as developing critical thinking and leading to further investigation? How do they contribute to misconceptions? The answers to these questions should be obvious to you and need no discussion here.

Talent-Oriented Questions

Although the procedures thus far have mainly emphasized the importance of cognitive questions, other types are also important. Teachers should spend a considerable amount of time formulating talent-oriented questions to help them know their students.

We believe that you should not only determine talent but help to manifest it by rewarding students for all types of talent. Some teachers and administrators may argue that the only function of a science teacher is to develop scientific awareness. It is our view that this awareness will occur to a higher degree if students have opportunities to manifest their best talents, thereby building their self-esteem and developing more positive feelings about science. Some examples of talent-oriented questions are listed below.

Questioning to Discover Talent

Talent	Question
Artistic	1. What important ideas should be put on a mural to be hung in our laboratory?
Organizing	2. How should we organize the field trip?
Communicating	3. What should be included in a short article about the science fair for the school paper?
Creative	4. In what ways can we convey to the rest of the school how exciting biology, earth science, chemistry, and physics are?
Social	5. What shall be the social activities for the science picnic?
Planning	6. How shall we plan our investigations of the pond community throughout the year?

Teachers should also ask questions to find out students' interests. What gets them involved? Determining these interests helps the instructor in planning more relevant lessons. Asking students individually about their concerns also conveys to them your interest in them as people and not as sponges to soak up scientific information.

Piaget pointed out that proper questioning gives insights into a student's thought patterns. To do so,

the instructor must hypothesize how the student is thinking, then pose questions to see if the hypothesis was correct. The student's response either confirms the hypothesis or indicates further investigation. The instructor may have to formulate a new hypothesis and construct questions to determine its validity. This type of questioning is particularly necessary when the student seems to be having difficulty in discovering or conceptualizing. Excellent teachers in mathematics, physics, chemistry, and other courses often use this approach to diagnose students' thinking-process difficulties and help them resolve problems.

■ QUESTIONING PROCEDURES

Wait-Time Affects Quality of Responses

Mary Budd Rowe and her coworkers have done an extensive study of the questioning behavior of teachers.[1] In their analysis of taped classroom discussions, they discovered that teachers, on an average, wait less than a second for students to reply to their questions. Further investigations revealed that some instructors waited an average of three seconds for students to answer questions. An analysis of student responses revealed that teachers with longer wait-times (three seconds or more) obtained greater speculation, conversation, and argument than those with shorter wait-times.

Dr. Rowe found further that when teachers were trained to wait five seconds, on the average, before responding, the following occurred:

1. Students gave longer and more complete answers instead of short phrases.
2. There was an increase in speculative, creative thinking.
3. The number of suggested questions and experiments increased.
4. Slower students increased their participation.
5. Teachers became more flexible in their responses to students.
6. Teachers asked fewer questions, but the ones they asked required more reflection.
7. Students gave a greater number of qualified inferences.
8. Teacher expectations for student performance changed; they were less likely to expect only the brighter students to reply.

Dr. Rowe believes that the expectancy levels of students are more likely to change positively if they are given a longer time to respond. She has also found that the typical pattern of discussion: teacher-student-teacher can be altered by training instructors to get student-student-teacher responses. This pattern will occur particularly well when students are involved in some controversy, for example, the best design for an experiment or what conclusion can be drawn from data.

For inquiry teaching to occur, most instructors should increase their wait-time tolerance so that students may have more opportunities to think and create.

Good Discussions Are Student-Centered

Most teachers, when they are involved in a class discussion, dominate it to a considerable extent; an inquiry class should be student-centered, which means that the teacher's talking should be at a minimum. Note the two diagrams of discussion interaction in a class in Figure 11–1.

It is not easy to develop techniques so that the second type of interaction operates. How would you as a teacher get the second pattern to operate in your classes?

■ SOME PRECAUTIONS IN QUESTIONING

It has long been thought that the practice of questioning promotes student thinking and participation, and in most cases it does. However, sometimes certain questioning techniques have the reverse effect, actually shutting off student thinking. Frequently what the teacher actually does is initiate a question-and-answer practice that does not evolve into true classroom discussion and does not promote expressiveness, active participation, or independent thinking. Instead the process may encourage student passivity and dependency.

LOW-LEVEL STUDENT INQUIRY

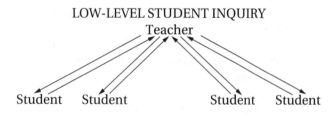

HIGHER-LEVEL STUDENT INQUIRY

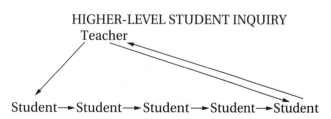

FIGURE 11–1
Discussion interaction diagrams

A few precautions are given here to alert teachers to practices that may hinder discussion. Sometimes using questions simply results in a back-and-forth interchange between teacher and students in which the teacher is the questioner and the student is the respondent. To avoid this you might hold back from asking questions at the start, thus encouraging students to take some responsibility for carrying on the discussion, rather than simply being targets of teacher questions.

Second, questions are sometimes used to make a point in which a particular piece of information or idea is underscored. This practice can be counterproductive because the same information would be more effective as a declarative statement.

Third, questions are often asked to help students who pause or falter in their responses. We sometimes condition students to speak in short bursts in answer to our direct questions, and they don't expect to have to do anything beyond this. True discussion, however, requires thoughtful, sustained reasoning by the students. It requires more time to express complex thoughts or interpretations. If the teacher pushes in with a question too quickly, the effect is to halt student thought processes and substitute the teacher's thoughts.

Fourth, questions are sometimes used to elicit predetermined answers. In this case the teacher has a particular answer in mind and phrases questions so that the student produces the expected answer. This again shuts off speculative responses from students.

Fifth, teachers occasionally ask questions in reply to a student's question. While sometimes recommended as a way of promoting inquiry, the danger is that it may convey the idea that only the teacher gets to ask the questions and that whenever students ask questions all they get is a redirected question.

Sixth, questions are sometimes used to draw out the nonparticipating students. This assumes that every student is in the frame of mind to respond equally with every other student. The practice may instead intimidate some students and cause others to become wary of future questions. They may thus be preparing answers in advance and failing to listen to the argument or the discussion. Such practices may cause students to withdraw even more rather than to draw them out.

Seventh, to use questions to probe the students' personal feelings and experiences in the classroom is risky. This may make the student feel fear and resentment. Such questions ought to be saved for more private contacts in which the teacher and the student can talk together comfortably.

Alternatives to these practices can avoid these pitfalls. For example, the teacher could make a declarative statement rather than asking a question. This can still present the problem or issue to the students and open up avenues for further discussion.

A second alternative to questioning would be to restate the speaker's words. Try to make a statement that interprets what the student has said, thus giving the class an opportunity to reconsider the information.

Third, declare your perplexity when you are confused by what the student has said. Simply state, "I am confused about what you are saying."

Fourth, invite elaboration. Use a statement such as, "I'd like to hear more of your views on that."

Fifth, encourage class questions. In a discussion it should be possible for students to ask other students questions or to direct their questions to the person who is speaking, whether teacher or student.

Sixth, let the speaker pause and ask a question. This promotes discussion, indicates the speculative nature of the statements that are being made, and gives the student an opportunity to obtain feedback.

Seventh, simply maintain silence. Use a longer wait-time to indicate to the student that you are conducting a leisurely practice and you want to provide opportunities for reflection, introspection, and thoughtful answers.[2]

USING QUESTIONING IN A COMPETITIVE LEARNING STRATEGY

A useful technique that employs classroom questioning by the teacher has been described by a group of high school teachers in a Colorado school.[3] This approach is in the form of oral quizzing, which normally takes place once a week, usually during a Wednesday class period.

The rules for the oral quizzing are given in Figure 11–2. The numbers on the seating chart represent the average numerical grade the student currently holds. Each student has an equal opportunity to move upward from the C section to the B section to the A section by successfully answering teacher questions on the day of the oral quiz. The strategy has superior motivating potential as well as serving as an excellent mechanism for classroom control.

Advance planning by the teacher is necessary to ensure that questions give proper attention to higher levels of cognition. Teachers who have used this questioning strategy have reported excellent results and recommend its use to others. It is important to recognize that the competitive spirit is emphasized in this strategy, a fact that may cause some teachers to seek alternatives to its use.

RESEARCH ON QUESTIONING IN THE CLASSROOM

Questioning remains one of the most influential teaching behaviors in the classroom because of its potential in stimulating thinking and learning. The first major systematic research on questioning was conducted by Stevens at Columbia University in 1912. Almost all the research conducted from that time until the 1950s focused primarily on describing teacher questioning behavior. Results uniformly supported the finding that questions stimulating memory and recall were the type being emphasized in classrooms.

WHEN: Any Day

SEATING:
```
76 83 88 94 100
75 82 87 93 99
74 81 86 92 98
73 80 85 91 97
72 79 84 90 96
71 78 83 89 95
```

RULES:
1. Students in A or B seats cannot use notes or text during quizzing.
2. Students in C seats can use notes and text.
3. The student to whom the question is being directed must answer quickly. When the instructor calls for the next person this student's turn is over.
4. By design the questioning must start at the top A with the first question.
5. For missed questions, the first student with the correct answer moves to where the question started. All the students in between move back one seat.
6. Tardy students or those who have been absent *for any reason* must move to the last seat in the last row.
7. Inappropriate behavior will also send a student to the last seat.
8. Each student must keep track of where his or her earned seat is. If there is a dispute or someone forgets where to sit, he or she must move to the last seat in the last row.
9. Questions will *only be asked once.* Some questions may be clarified with the student asking, "What do you mean by _____ ?"

GRADING:
1. Grades for earned seats will be recorded on Wednesday at the end of the period.
2. Oral quizzing grade will be used to replace the lowest test grade each quarter.

FIGURE 11–2
Oral quizzing

Around 1970, a new spurt of activity on teacher questioning began. The emphasis in this research was on identifying specific questioning levels and skills that have an impact on pupil growth.

A major concern today is the impact of teachers' questions on pupil learning as measured by achievement tests. Rosenshine in 1979 found no significant relationship between the frequency of higher level questions and achievement. Although the frequency of such questions appears to be unrelated to achievement, verbalized higher level questions were found to lead to greater achievement than low-level questions in several studies. Using seventh and eighth grade general science teachers and pupils in a study in 1965, Kleinman found the pupils of teachers who asked higher level, critical-thinking questions performed better on a science achievement test than pupils of teachers who asked questions requiring only information recall.

Also using junior high school science teachers and pupils in a ninth grade class, in 1969 Ladd found that teachers who used a greater proportion of higher inquiry questions caused greater change in pupils' achievement as indicated on a post-test composed of high and low inquiry questions.

Other studies conducted more recently have produced mixed conclusions relating to the influence of higher level questioning on achievement. Despite the mixed research findings, questioning is still regarded as an essential and influential instructional behavior. It is the most basic approach teachers use to stimulate thinking and learning in the classroom. Higher level questions produce situations of such complexity that their relative influence has not yet clearly been sorted out.

Fully functioning teachers almost certainly have educational objectives not only at the fact level but also at the concept level and even at the personal meaning and values levels. This necessitates asking higher order questions of students. Teachers then need not determine whether to ask higher level questions but rather how to find an appropriate balance of lower and higher order questions to achieve instructional goals.

There has been much research on the use of questions as a learning strategy. Questions in textual material have been defended on the basis that they provide advance organizers for the material to be learned. The use of questions at the higher levels of cognition (such as application, analysis, synthesis, and evaluation) has been shown to have a significant positive effect on student learning. Questions placed within the text material appear to produce better understanding and retention than text material without questions. And in a study on presentation style, groups of students reading material with questions at the beginnings of paragraphs scored higher on an immediate post-test than did groups reading without questions.

As a result of the research over the past seventy-five years, we can draw several tentative conclusions concerning questioning in the classroom.

1. Teachers appear to persist in asking questions that require students primarily to recall knowledge and information. It is important to consider stressing higher level questions and to devise a variety of instructional objectives that balance low-level memory questions with preplanned higher convergent and divergent questions.
2. Teachers can be effectively trained to raise the cognitive emphasis of their questions.
3. There is a tendency for the cognitive levels of questions asked by teachers and responses from pupils to be positively related.
4. The extent of wait-time teachers use after asking questions dramatically influences the quantity and quality of pupil responses. Teacher educators need to provide training opportunities for teachers to practice increasing their wait-time to a minimum of three seconds.
5. At the primary level there is a tendency for the use of lower cognitive level questions to be related to pupil achievement. Teachers need to stress the importance of balancing low and high cognitive level questions to stimulate productive thinking at all grade levels.[4]

Questioning in the Content Areas

Students in science classes experience general questioning techniques but also encounter questioning in the content of their science classes. The skills of formulating good questions in science and of seeking solutions to questions posed by their teachers, their textbooks, and their laboratory experiments are practiced and developed in the context of the science discipline being studied.

Research on reading and questioning in content areas is reported by Bonnie Armbruster and others.[5] Results showed that most questions were directly related to textbook material that was to have been read by the students in their assignments, and were largely questions on factual information. Only about 15 percent of the questions required students to analyze, predict, or apply information from the text. These questions came from only a small number of the teachers involved in the study, indicating that the use of higher level questions was somehow related to individual teaching styles. There was also a high percentage of rhetorical questions whose purpose was not clear other than to perhaps form a bridge to foster continuity in class discussions.

Gender Differences

Science educators are becoming increasingly concerned about gender differences with respect to expectations, types of experiences, and participation in science classrooms. Roberta Barba and Loretta Cardinale have investigated student questioning interactions in secondary school science classrooms.[6]

Results of the study suggest that female students have fewer interactions with science teachers and receive less attention than males. Questions asked of female students were predominantly low-level questions. Males received more teacher interaction, including more questions of higher levels. All this seems to give females a signal that they have low ability in the sciences. It is also apparent that such behavior occurs before the secondary school level is reached, causing many females to believe that they are incapable of success in science.

Levels of Questions

Studies of teachers' classroom interactions indicate that 60 to 80 percent of teachers' questions require the lowest level of thinking for satisfactory answers.[7]

A practical questioning technique divides teacher questions into soliciting moves and reacting moves. Soliciting moves are categorized as:

- recall questions that draw upon past experience or knowledge;
- data-collecting questions where students react to direct observations;
- data-processing questions, where students hypothesize, analyze, compare, or suggest solutions; and
- verification questions, where students evaluate or judge responses.

Reacting moves by the teacher involve the following:

- accepting or informing the student the response is correct;
- rejecting or informing the student of the incorrectness of the response;
- requesting clarification or further evidence; or
- asking another person.

Employment of the above strategies can raise the level of questions, provide opportunities to practice thinking skills beyond mere factual recall, and foster skills that support inquiry and investigative methods.

Development of effective questioning skills among students is as important as developing better questioning techniques among teachers. As science classes adopt more investigative learning and teaching methods, the ability to ask higher order questions becomes imperative. As with all learning, frequent opportunities to practice the desired skills results in greater improvement.

■ DISCUSSION AS A MEANS OF INQUIRY

An excellent model for leading a discussion is that of a clever talk show host. What is it that such a person does to stimulate the interesting, even exciting discussions that frequently are held on radio and television programs?

A number of clues can be found in the manner in which the host conducts the show—both in preparation and during the show itself. While each host is different, these are certain common elements. A good talk show host:

1. studies the topic before the show,
2. presents an interesting background analysis before eliciting comments from the participants,
3. relaxes the guests,
4. avoids embarrassing anyone,
5. keeps the discussion moving at a good pace,
6. rewords any comments that might be misunderstood,
7. prevents anyone from monopolizing the discussion or going off on a tangent,
8. encourages the participants to speak about their feelings,
9. uses humor to reduce tension,
10. asks good questions of a divergent variety.[8]

With these guidelines a teacher can conduct a similarly interesting discussion that will stimulate students to open up and participate. There is no dearth of interesting topics in science to bring up for discussion, particularly now that the interrelationships of science to technology and society are fair game in science classes.

Advantages of Discussion

Students become more interested when they are involved, thus discussion is a desirable approach for class procedures. Since an objective of modern science instruction is to teach science as a process, with an emphasis on the individual's cognitive development, students must have time and opportunities to think. A student can't think unless given opportunities to do so. The presentation of problems in a discussion requires students to think before they can formulate answers. A teacher who tells students all about a subject offers only boredom. In addition, the students have been robbed of an opportunity to use their minds. All they have to do is soak up information and memorize it.

Discussion is more likely to develop inquiry behavior. A discussion leader interested in developing inquiring behavior seldom gives answers but asks questions instead. In answering, students learn to evaluate, analyze, and synthesize knowledge. They are often thrilled to discover fundamental ideas for themselves.

Another bonus of discussion is that the teacher receives feedback. An astute discussion leader learns quickly from student comments about how much they understand. The leader then guides the discussion, moving it rapidly when students understand the information and slowing it down when they have difficulty. A lecture-oriented teacher seldom knows what students are comprehending. This teacher may concentrate on a point that the class understands or speed through information that confuses students. One of the greatest mistakes a beginning teacher can make is to assume that the lecture method will work well in a secondary school.

How to Lead a Discussion

Leading a discussion is an art that is not easily learned. There is nothing more exciting than to see a master teacher conducting an interesting and exciting discussion. How can you bring students to this point? Excellent class discussions do not just happen. Inexperienced instructors may think they will walk into a class and talk about a subject off the top of their head. After all, don't they know more about the subject than the students? While it's true they may know about the material, they are faced with the problem of helping students discover information and develop their talents. This process requires as much preparation as any other class procedure. The first step in preparing for a discussion is to determine what it is you wish to accomplish—ask yourself what are your objectives? Next, outline questions you think may help students to reach these objectives. Good discussion leaders use the "What do you think?" approach to learning. They ask questions such as were suggested in the section on questioning. For example:

1. Why did you do this experiment?
2. What did the data show?
3. Why did you use this approach?
4. How would you go about finding answers to this problem?
5. How else could you find the answer?
6. What good is this answer for your daily life?
7. What mental steps did you make in solving the problem?
8. How many variables were involved in the experiment?
9. How do you feel about science?

Spend Time Analyzing Thought Processes

Every discussion should stimulate critical and creative thinking. You should spend time analyzing the types of questions you will ask in a discussion to ensure that they require the exercise of these abilities. In this way you will indicate to your students a belief in their *becoming* more exciting persons. You will also contribute positively to their expectancy level of their critical thinking. Showing students that they are performing relatively sophisticated mental operations—inferring, hypothesizing, evaluating data, etc.—will encourage them to accept that they can use their minds to derive answers to relatively complex problems. We come to believe that we are good thinkers only by being successful in thinking and by receiving feedback about our thinking abilities from others. Furthermore, teachers build positive student self-concepts when they involve students in tasks requiring thinking and show them how they are developing their minds. An actual inquiry discussion might follow these steps.

Present a problem such as, "What is the lifetime of a burning candle?" Encourage students to formulate hypotheses or give evidence. For example, say an apparatus is set up as follows: a burning candle is placed upright in a pan in which there is some water, and the candle is then covered with a glass container. Show how the experiment is set up by projecting a transparency of it on a screen. Some types of questions to ask are: What will happen to the candle when it is covered? What else will happen to the apparatus as this is done? What would happen if the candle were lengthened, the size of the jar above it were increased, or the amount of water in the container holding the candle were decreased? How would you find out?

After the students have progressed this far, have some student reflect back on what has been said and summarize the good points of the discussion. As a discussion leader, you might at times have to assist a student in doing this by repeating, "What was the problem?" Review the cognitive processes students used in solving the problem. Ask: "What hypotheses were made?" "What was the best hypothesis and why?" "How were the conclusions reached?" "On what are they based?" and "What is required to make better conclusions?"

Questions Must Be Directed at the Students' Level

A neophyte discussion leader often starts a discussion with too difficult a question. If there is no response to a question, the teacher should rephrase it to make it simpler. This procedure may have to be followed several times before there is a response. A question implies an answer. Similarly, if the question is too vague the students may not respond, and rephrasing it may give them some insight. Leading a discussion by questioning without giving answers is a skill that brings great satisfaction, but to be an astute questioner requires practice and a keen awareness of students' comprehension. By questioning correctly, the experienced discussion leader can guide students toward understanding the concepts and principles involved in the lesson or experiment. The questions must be deep enough to require critical thinking rather than a simple yes or no.

Eye contact is an important aspect in leading a discussion. A teacher's eyes should sweep a class, constantly looking for boredom, a student with an answer or a question, or one with a puzzled look. Eye contact gives the instructor feedback and motivates students to think and participate in the discussion. It also shows that you are more interested in the students than in the information being covered.

A Discussion Started in a Novel Way Gains Attention

A motivational technique useful in beginning a discussion is to start it with an interesting demonstration. A vial of blood placed on a demonstration desk can stimulate questions, leading to a discussion of blood or the circulatory system. Burning a candle can lead to a discussion of several scientific concepts and principles. A good rule to follow is to start a discussion with a percept or observation whenever possible. Not all discussions will lend themselves to this procedure, but those that involve the discovery of a concept almost always do (see, for example, the "Teaching Science Activity—Using a Demonstration to Initiate Discussion: The Rubber Band Wheel" in the Appendix, p. 446).

Use Overhead Projectors When Appropriate

The use of overhead projection with transparencies helps concentrate the class's attention on clarifying a problem. For example, focusing students' attention on some of the approaches to devising a classification scheme can be done easily with an overhead projection. Use different colored acetate cut to various sizes and shapes and ask students how they would group the materials. A discussion can arise from the demonstration of such cognitive processes as analysis, discrimination, and ordering. Another demonstration using the overhead projector might include a discussion of magnetism and magnetic lines of force; using a magnet and iron fillings sprinkled on top of transparent plastic sets the stage for a discussion of the properties of magnetism.

■ GENERAL RULES FOR LEADING A LARGE GROUP DISCUSSION

Some general rules to follow in using discussions are:

1. Create an atmosphere in the class in which questions are not only welcomed but *expected.* Be warm, open, and receptive.
2. As much as possible, include students' interests.
3. When you give reinforcement, do it positively as often as you can. Use very little negative feedback. Say: "That's a good answer." "That's right, you have the idea." "Good, you're thinking; keep it up." "You have something there." "Who would like to react to this answer?" Do not ignore the students; always give some recognition to their answers. No response should be a form of negative feedback. If students have the wrong answer, do not say, "That's wrong" or "No, that answer is no good." Rather say: "Well, that is not quite right." "You may have something there, but I am not sure I understand the point," or "Good, you are thinking; but that is not what I was leading up to."
4. When you encourage a student to think, evaluate the product on the basis of the student's level of comprehension. Even when you, with a more extensive background, are aware that the student's idea is either incomplete or incorrect, accept it or even praise it if it indicates that the student has made effective use of the information required by this stage of the course.
5. Praise a student for being a good listener when the student calls attention to a mistake you have made.
6. When leading a discussion, try to remember previous comments and interrelate them. If at all possible, give recognition by referring to the name of the student who made the comment. For example, a teacher in responding to the idea of a student might say, "Joan believes that there are other factors besides temperature determining the rate of expansion of a metal. George has just suggested that possibly humidity and air pressure may have a minor effect." The teacher has acted as a summarizer for two students' views and has given them recognition by using their names.
7. Maintain a positive and accepting attitude. Your attitude in leading a discussion does much to determine the quality of that discussion. If you walk into a class feeling and looking very glum and with the weight of the discussion on your shoulders, the students' response will be lukewarm. However, if you start a discussion

with the attitude that you and the students are going to have fun wrestling with ideas, their response is more likely to be impressive. In leading a discussion with adolescents, you must be able to laugh at yourself; discreet use of humor captures interest and gains participation.

8. When questions arise for which science does not yet provide an adequate explanation, state that, as yet, there is no answer. This gives students insight into avenues of research which we still need to explore.

9. When necessary, restate a student's answer before going on to your next remarks. Doing so often gives other students time to think about their answers.

10. Call on both students who are willing to answer and those who are not.

11. Do not rush discussions. Remember that the major reason for having them is to give students time to think. When there is silence during a discussion, this may be the period where most of the thinking is going on. Remember that a desirable wait-time averages five seconds.

Breaking the class into smaller groups can also provide variety. A sample design for this type of discussion is found in the "Small Group Problem Solving" in the Appendix, p. 453.

Special Precautions in Leading a Discussion

At times the following suggestions are proper, but the teacher should give serious consideration to their potential disadvantages as well:

1. Toss a question back to a class when it is asked of you. Have another student repeat the question in its entirety. Ask a student to speak up so that the entire class can hear. Ask a student to research an answer to the question.

2. Encourage the entire class to take notes.

3. Avoid the appearance of carrying on a private conversation with the person who asked the question.

4. Deliberately let your eyes roam over the entire class while giving the answer.

5. Use questions requiring hypothesis formation.

6. Avoid sarcasm.

7. Encourage students to seek recognition before answering or have them be courteous of another and wait until that person finishes before they respond.

8. Do not let students make derogatory remarks about another student's question or answer since this is demeaning to the person.

Dividing the class into small groups adds interest and variety to discussions.

9. Suggest an individual conference with the student when:
    a. The degree of difficulty in answering is greater than that expected of the class as a whole.
    b. The subject matter involved bears little relation to the key ideas being stressed.
    c. The answer is both detailed and lengthy.
    d. The time spent in answering the question may destroy the sequence of thought being developed.

■ SPECIAL DISCUSSION TECHNIQUES

Invitations to Inquiry

In its *Biology Teacher's Handbook,* the BSCS gives forty-four class-discussion outlines under the title "Invitations to Inquiry." The main purpose of these outlines is to involve students in the strategies of solving scientific problems—not to teach science subject matter. The invitations engage students in the process of solving problems in the way that scientists are engaged. A typical outline for an invitation is given below.

Format for an Invitation

1. Present a problem to the students.
2. Ask how they would go about solving it.
3. Describe the actual experimental design used by the scientist.
4. Ask the students what they would hypothesize about the experimental results.
5. Give the students the data the scientists collected.

6. Ask: "What conclusions can you make about these data?"
7. Ask: "If you were the scientist, what would be your next problem and why?"

BSCS authors state that "The primary aim [of invitations] is an understanding of enquiry. It is mainly for the sake of this aim that the active participation of the student is invoked. Both practical experience and experimental study indicate that concepts are understood best and retained longest when the student contributes to his own understanding." [9] You can easily make your own invitations. The steps are as follows:

1. Decide what your science processes and subject-matter objectives are.
2. State a problem related to your objectives. The idea for problems can come from actual scientific research reported in journals.
3. Devise questions that give students opportunities to set up experiments, make hypotheses, analyze and synthesize, and record data. Stress the understanding of science as a process and the cognitive skills involved.
4. Write the invitation as a series of steps. In different sections insert additional information to help students progress in depth in the topic or methods of research.
5. Evaluate your invitation, comparing it with the science-process list on page 158 and rewrite it to include more of these processes.

Invitations to inquiry can be written for various levels of learning. As much as possible, they should stress the development of students' cognitive abilities. In addition to the science processes, students should also learn the necessity for having a control, understand cause-and-effect relationships, learn when to use quantitative data and how to interpret it, learn the role of argument and inference in the design of experiments, and so on.

Write an invitation! Your first invitation probably won't be very sophisticated, but in the process of writing it you will gain insight into how to construct invitations, plus a better understanding of how to involve students in understanding science as a process.

Pictorial Riddles

Another technique for developing motivation and interest in a discussion is to use pictorial riddles, that is, pictures or drawings made by the teacher to elicit student response. A riddle is drawn on the chalkboard or on poster board or is projected from a transparency, and the teacher asks a question about the picture.

Pictorial riddles are relatively easy to devise. They can be as simple or as complex as a teacher desires. In devising a riddle, an instructor should go through the following steps:

1. Select some concept or principle he wishes to teach or emphasize.
2. Draw a picture or show an illustration that demonstrates the concept.
3. An alternate procedure is to change something in a picture and ask students to find out what is wrong in the picture. An example might be a picture of a large child being held up on a seesaw by a small child. Ask, "How is this possible?" Or show a farming community in which all of the ecological principles are misapplied and ask what is wrong with what has been done in the community.
4. Devise a series of questions, related to the picture, which will help students gain insights into the principles involved.

There are two general types of pictorial riddles. The first type shows an actual situation. The instructor asks why the situation occurred. Figure 11–3 is of this type.

1. What questions can you ask about this riddle?
2. What is wrong with this diagram?
3. Where do pine trees grow?
4. Why do they grow where they do?
5. If you were going to change the riddle to make it more accurate, what would you do and why?
6. What does the wind have to do with the ecology of the area?
7. Where would you expect to find the most and the least amount of vegetation on the mountain? Why?
8. How could you change this riddle to teach some additional science concepts?

In the second type, the teacher manipulates something in a drawing or a series of drawings and

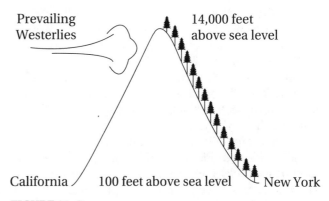

FIGURE 11–3
Pictorial riddle (biology)

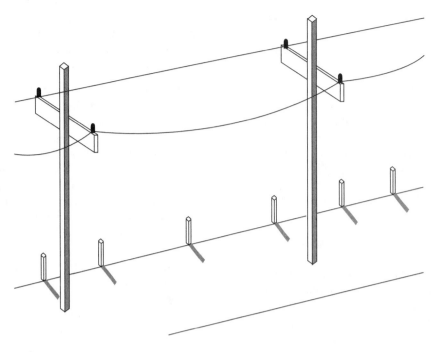

FIGURE 11–4
Pictorial riddle (physical science)

then asks what is wrong with the diagram. Figure 11–4 is an example of this type. Some questions that might be asked about each riddle follow each picture.

1. What do you notice about the things in this picture?
2. What is similar in the picture?
3. Why do the fence and the telephone line appear to be similar?
4. Why would you expect the two telephone lines to be the same?
5. What do you think is the season of the year for each line and why?
6. What does temperature have to do with the appearance of the telephone lines and why?
7. At what time of year would you expect to see the sagging telephone line and why?

A format for a riddle which lends itself particularly well to overhead projection is the before-and-after type of riddle. Students are shown a diagram or picture, some factor is then altered, and the students are shown another picture of the same situation after modification. Students are to hypothesize what happened in the before situation to reach the modification shown in the after diagram. Figure 11–5 shows some examples of before-and-after riddles.

The riddle in Figure 11–6 is constructed like the face of a clock. The arms are turned to different organisms and the class is asked what the ecological relationships are between them.

Riddles may be prepared from many types of materials, such as photographs and Polaroid 35 mm slides, magazine pictures, diagrams, cartoons, greeting cards, and objects.

■ OTHER TECHNIQUES TO MOTIVATE DISCUSSION

Case Histories

Another technique to motivate discussion is to use case histories in science. These histories tell stories about the development of some science concepts. The instructor may tell the students part of what was done and then ask what they think was the next step. Case histories can be constructed from a classic experiment in the history of science.

Covers of Science Magazines

An activity to supplement a science lesson can be constructed around magazine covers depicting various aspects of science. *Science,* the journal of the AAAS, has some very interesting covers that lend themselves well to this approach. The instructor holds up the cover picture and asks questions to give students hints about the topic represented.

The Magic Circle as a Facilitator of Discussion

The magic circle is another means of stimulating discussion in the science classroom. This is simply a

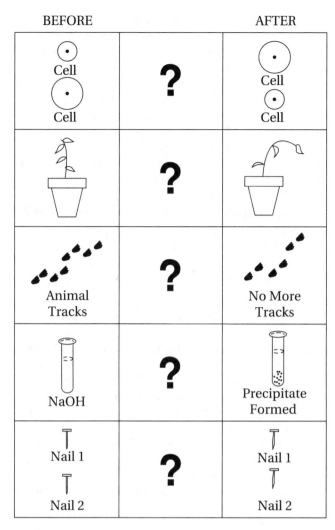

FIGURE 11–5
Sequential pictorial riddles. Can you supple the missing form?

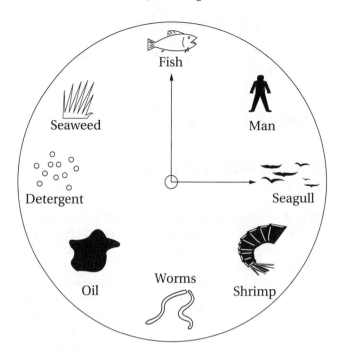

FIGURE 11–6
Riddles to show relationships

teaching technique designed to develop listening and communication skills, an awareness of self-worth, and an interest in and respect for other peoples' ideas.

To promote these objectives it is necessary to:

1. Ask questions that students will react to with personal feelings. For example, ask humanistic questions ("How do you feel about. . . ").
2. Ask divergent questions so that a variety of responses can be made.
3. You, the teacher, must positively reinforce statements made by the students so that they will feel that their contribution is worthwhile and that they, as people, are valuable and able to achieve success.
4. Encourage the other students to listen to the speaker. Students should also reinforce what the speaker has said with their own ideas and experiences so that the entire discussion is a sharing session.

Creativity

Teaching creatively is another means of stimulating discussion. Exactly what teaching creatively means is difficult to say. To get at the meaning and value of creative teaching, consider the following questions:

1. What is creativity?
2. Do you perceive of yourself as a creative individual? Why do you feel this way? How can you use creativity in the classroom?
3. When you have used creative teaching methods, what has been the response of your students?
4. How did they feel about their experience?
5. How did you feel about using creative teaching techniques in the classroom?
6. How might creative teaching be used in the science classroom?
7. How can we help students to be more creative in their thinking?
8. What, if any, are the limitations of creative teaching?
9. What are the advantages and disadvantages of creative teaching?
10. If you had the choice of studying in a creative versus a noncreative classroom, which would you choose? Explain your answer.
11. Select any topic which you traditionally teach in your classroom. How could you make the teaching of that topic more creative?
12. What are some ideas for creative teaching techniques you have used in your classroom?

13. If a student teacher were to ask you about teaching creatively, what would your response be? Would you recommend trying some creative ideas?

14. If you believe creativity is important in education, how might you encourage a traditionalist to give this method a try?

■ DISCUSSION AS A TECHNIQUE OF REVIEW

All of the preceding discussion techniques can be used to good advantage for class review. Discussion may also be used as an excellent review for laboratory work. After you have had a class conduct several experiments in a unit, take time to discuss the conclusions that can be drawn from the laboratory work. Also consider how the information was obtained, what types of problem-solving and cognitive behaviors were involved in determining the answers, and what assurance the students have that their information is correct. A discussion of this type can do much to reinforce learning and divide the trivia from the really important aspects of learning.

The One-Word Type of Review

The one-word approach may be used to involve all students in the review process. After students have read, seen a film, performed a laboratory exercise, or been involved in other types of investigative work, ask them to write their impressions in one word. These words should then be passed to the front of the class, and several of them should be written on the board. The students should then be asked to explain why they wrote their words. After they give their explanations, they should be asked to take any three words and construct a sentence. This technique provides an excellent review of the material and involves all the students.

Persuasion and Discussion

Discussion and formal lecturing are somewhat alike in that both involve elements of persuasion. A useful definition of persuasion is that "Persuasion is the conscious attempt to bring about a jointly developed mental state common to both source and receiver through the use of symbolic cues."[10]

Persuasion and instruction appear to have a great deal in common. Both involve communication that includes giving arguments and evidence for the purpose of getting someone to believe something or to do something. Both are influenced by constructivism. People respond to formal instruction and persuasion in terms of their preexisting perspectives. Both require conscious cognitive activity on the part of the recipient while seeking understanding.

Discussion plays an important role in persuasion because a common objective of discussion in science classes is to develop a new behavior or to modify an existing behavior with respect to learning science. In investigative modes, these behaviors frequently are unfamiliar to the students because of previous repeated exposure to traditional expository methods of teaching. Discussions among students or between students and their teacher provide opportunities for persuasive evidence to be examined and analyzed. These opportunities are particularly necessary when dealing with overcoming misconceptions or with faulty premises in science.

Learning to Lead a Good Discussion Never Ends

Teachers never quite perfect their ability as discussion leaders, but they should never stop trying to improve. Excellence in discussion comes only with wisdom, not only in subject matter but in learning how to develop talents and self-concepts. For dedicated teachers there is probably no greater satisfaction than to walk out of class knowing that they have developed the students' mental abilities to the point where their presence is practically unneeded except as an organizer. To acquire this facility requires preparation and constant self-analysis, but it is one of the intellectual satisfactions that come only with good teaching.

■ SUMMARY

The ability of the teacher to ask questions to stimulate creative and critical thinking and to manifest multiple talents is basic to inquiry teaching. Inquiry types of questions may be involved in all areas of science teaching, such as discussion, laboratory demonstrations, student worksheets, visual aids, and evaluations. Instructors should plan their questions before class but remain flexible and adapt their instruction as dictated by student interaction. Before outlining the question, teachers should decide what talents, critical thinking processes, and subject-matter objectives they hope to develop and the answers they will accept.

Questions may be classified as convergent or divergent according to Bloom's Taxonomy, by the science processes, and/or by the multiple talents they are trying to develop. Divergent types of questions and those requiring more cognitive sophistication should be stressed. Teleological questions, anthropomorphic questions, and those that could be answered by yes or no responses should be avoided.

The time a teacher waits for a response, called "wait-time," is very important. Most teachers wait, on an average, less than one second. A five-second average wait-time results in more responses by slow learners, more creative answers, more complete-sentence answers, more questions, and more suggestions for experiments.

This chapter suggests questioning techniques to involve students in investigations and to stimulate creativity. Research indicates that teachers trained in questioning techniques do change their questioning behavior in the classroom, asking questions requiring greater cognitive ability. Teachers who emphasize higher level types of questions are more likely to have their students do better on national tests, which tend to test for all cognitive levels.

The lecture method should play a relatively minor role in instruction in the secondary schools. Inquiry discussions motivate students and involve them more in cognitive processes than do lectures. There are definite techniques to be used in leading inquiry-oriented discussions. Primarily the instructor should question and give minimal information; the type of question asked by the teacher helps students discover concepts and principles.

To lead a good discussion requires extensive preparation. Discussion leaders should know their objectives, outline a series of relevant questions, and spend time at the end of the discussion analyzing how conclusions were reached. Part of the discussion should be devoted to reflecting on the thought processes used in arriving at these conclusions. This ensures better understanding and development of the cognitive processes.

Discussion leaders should give as much positive reinforcement as possible. They should compliment students on good ideas and suggestions and never deride or make sarcastic remarks about poor suggestions. Regardless of the answers given in a discussion, teachers should try to react positively to the participants; ignoring a response is a poor procedure. Eye contact is important as a motivator and a means of receiving feedback. A good method of starting a discussion is to use a demonstration or overhead projection pertaining to a subject or topic of interest to students. In leading the discussion, attempt to recall previous comments and interrelate the suggestions with the names of the individuals who made them. Remember that students will occasionally test your judgment to determine your competence as a teacher.

Some special techniques used in stimulating discussion are invitations to inquiry, pictorial riddles, case histories in science, questions organized around covers of science magazines, and the magic circle technique. All of these methods can be used to suggest open-ended experiments if students are aware of the factors involved in experimentation. Discussion is also an excellent vehicle for review, both in class and laboratory work. The one-word approach may be used to involve all the students in the review process.

■ REFERENCES

1. Mary Budd Rowe, "Wait-Time and Rewards as Instructional Variables: Influence on Inquiry and Sense of Fate Control," *New Science in the Inner City* (New York: Teachers College, Columbia University, September 1970). Unpublished paper.
2. J. T. Diller, "Do Your Questions Promote or Prevent Thinking?" *Learning, 11* (October 1982): 56–57.
3. Boyce Baker and others, "Oral Quizzes," Conversations with Baker and other teachers at Grand Junction High School, Grand Junction, Colorado, 1988., (conducted by the author.)
4. William Wilen, "Implications of Research on Questioning for the Teacher Educator," *Journal of Research and Development in Education, 2* (1984).
5. Bonnie B. Armbruster and others, "Reading and Questioning in Content Area Lessons," *Journal of Reading Behavior, 23* (1) (1991): 35–39.
6. Roberta Barba and Loretta Cardinale, "Are Females Invisible Students? An Investigation of Teacher-Student Questioning Interactions," *School Science and Mathematics, 91* (7)(November 1991): 306–310.
7. Paul B. Otto, "What Research Says: Finding an Answer in Questioning Strategies," *Science and Children, 28* (April 1991): 44–47.
8. Jeff Passe, "Phil Donahue: An Excellent Model for Leading a Discussion," *Journal of Teacher Education, 35* (43) (January/February, 1984).
9. William V. Mayer, Editor, *Biology Teachers Handbook* (3rd ed.), p. 47. "The Golden Age of Biological Education—1960–1975" (New York: John Wiley & Sons), p. 47.
10. T. R. Kobala, "Persuasion and Attitude Change in Science Education," *Journal of Research in Science Teaching, 29* (January 1992): 63–80.

INVESTIGATING SCIENCE TEACHING

Activity 11–1

RECOGNIZING GOOD QUESTIONS, PART 1

Read the following questions and mark them according to whether they are poor (P), fair (F), good (G), or excellent (E).

_____ 1. Why do roots thirst for water?
_____ 2. Why does water seek its own level?
_____ 3. Are all big trees the same size, shape, and age?
_____ 4. How does a siphon work?
_____ 5. How do seeds sprout?
_____ 6. How does soap clean?
_____ 7. What will happen if clothes are soaked with a bleach before instead of after washing?
_____ 8. How can the bleaching action be accelerated?
_____ 9. If ethylene glycol prevents avalanches, what other chemicals do you suspect might also prevent them?
_____ 10. If you were going to repeat the experiment with yeast, how would you improve it?
_____ 11. How would you design an experiment to _____?
_____ 12. If you have a straight-line graph indicating a relationship between population growth and time but the period ends at two days, what could you say about the population at four days?
_____ 13. How would you define a magnet operationally?
_____ 14. How could you be more certain about the conclusions you made from the data?
_____ 15. What do you think will happen to a potted geranium plant if it is placed near a window?
_____ 16. What evidence does the process of diffusion contribute to the molecular theory?
_____ 17. Look at the culture plates and describe what you see.
_____ 18. Place the organisms into any two groups you wish.
_____ 19. If the distance is doubled between two masses in Newton's gravitational formula, what will happen to the force?

Now provide an explanation for your responses. Why do you think some questions are poor, fair, good, or excellent?

Activity 11–2

RECOGNIZING GOOD QUESTIONS, PART 2

Below are several questions related to the preceding activity. Read each question and attempt to answer it. Record your answers in the space provided and refer to them again after completing this chapter to see how well you did.

_____ 1. Of the preceding questions, which three are the best?
_____ 2. Which are teleological or anthropomorphic questions?
_____ 3. Which questions require the student to analyze?
_____ 4. Which questions require the student to synthesize?
_____ 5. Which questions require the student to evaluate?
_____ 6. Which questions are convergent?
_____ 7. Which questions are divergent?
_____ 8. Which questions require students to demonstrate in their response the processes of science?
_____ 9. Which questions require students to reason quantitatively and what are they required to do?
_____ 10. Which questions require creative responses?
_____ 11. Which questions require students to formulate an operational definition?
_____ 12. Which questions require students mainly to observe?
_____ 13. Which questions require students mainly to classify?

_____ 14. Which questions require students to demonstrate experimental procedure?
_____ 15. Which questions require students to formulate a model?
_____ 16. Which questions require students to hypothesize?
_____ 17. Which question would an authoritarian personality most likely guess at if he or she didn't know the answer?
_____ 18. Which of the following two types of questions suggest a test?
      a. How do seeds sprout?
      b. What is needed for seeds to sprout?
_____ 19. It has been said that "how" questions do not lead to experimentation. Comment on this statement.

After you have answered these questions, compare and discuss your answers with other students in the class.

Activity 11–3

CLASSIFYING QUESTIONS IN NORMAL CONVERSATION

Observe normal conversation and classify the questions asked according to one of the classification systems suggested in this chapter.

Activity 11–4

CLASSIFYING QUESTIONS USING BLOOM'S TAXONOMY

Write some discussion questions to be used in a class discussion and classify them according to Bloom's Taxonomy and science processes.

Activity 11–5

CLASSIFYING QUESTIONS: DIVERGENT OR CONVERGENT?

In the blank in front of each question, place a _D_ if you think the question is divergent, a _C_ if you think it is convergent.

_____ 1. What do you think I am going to do with this apparatus?
_____ 2. What conclusions can you make from the data?
_____ 3. Can anything else be done to improve the growth of the plants?
_____ 4. Is heat an important factor in the experiment?
_____ 5. Do you think the salt precipitated because the solution was cooled?
_____ 6. Which of these three rocks is harder?
_____ 7. What can you tell me about the geology of this area from the picture?
_____ 8. Would you say you have sufficient data?
_____ 9. In what ways can you make the lights burn with the wire, switch, and power supply?
_____ 10. What things can you tell me about the biological make-up of this earthworm from your observations?

Which questions are the most convergent? What answers are possible for these questions? What words start these sentences? How would you change the sentences to make them more divergent?

Activity 11–6

CLASSIFYING QUESTIONS: TELEOGICAL OR ANTHROPOMORPHIC?

In the blank before each question, indicate whether the question is teleological (T) or anthropomorphic (A).

_____ 1. How do you think bacteria feel when ultraviolet light is shined on them?
_____ 2. Why does water seek its own level?
_____ 3. Why do plants seek the light?
_____ 4. Why will a body in motion want to stay in motion?
_____ 5. Why is the end of evolution to become increasingly more complex?

Activity 11–7

LEADING A DISCUSSION

1. Read the booklet *Creative Questioning and Sensitive Listening Techniques, A Self-Concept Approach.* Arthur Carin and Robert B. Sund (Columbus, Ohio: Charles E. Merrill Publishing Co., 1978).
2. Lead a small discussion and have someone check your wait-time and how well you get students to talk to students instead of students to teacher to student.

Activity 11–8

SELF-EVALUATION INSTRUMENT FOR RATING YOUR QUESTIONING ABILITY

Lead a discussion and use a cassette tape recorder to record it. Read through the following questions. Then listen to the tape. Put a check mark in the blank preceding the statement for each time the action described in the statement occurred.

_____ 1. You asked what students knew about the topic before starting the discussion.
_____ 2. You asked a convergent question.
_____ 3. You developed student-student rather than teacher-student interaction.
_____ 4. You asked an effective question.
_____ 5. You reinforced an answer without saying that the response was correct.
_____ 6. You did not stop discussing a point when the right answer was given but asked students if there were other answers or further discussion.
_____ 7. You asked a question requiring science-process thinking (e.g., hypothesizing, designing an experiment, inferring).
_____ 8. You interrupted a student without giving him or her time to complete his or her thought.
_____ 9. You paraphrased a student's statement to clarify or focus for others on the topics.
_____ 10. Measure how many seconds on the average you waited for a response.
_____ 11. Measure how much class time (in seconds) you devoted to routine (e.g., roll taking, announcements), student activity and teacher talk.
_____ Routine:
_____ Student activity:
_____ Teacher talk:
_____ 12. Rate yourself as a listener:
    1 2 3 4 5 6 7 8 9 10
    Poor listener   Average   Good listener
_____ 13. Rate yourself as a questioner:
    1 2 3 4 5 6 7 8 9 10
    Poor listener   Average   Good listener

Evaluate your responses and list those things you most want to change in your teaching. Record and rate yourself again at a later date or have a student or aide do it and note your improvement.

Chapter 12

INVESTIGATION AND PROBLEM SOLVING

For the past three decades, science teachers have read, talked about, and experimented with methods of teaching using investigative, inquiry approaches to learning the content and processes of science. These efforts have met with varying success for many reasons that will be discussed in this chapter. The challenges of inquiry teaching are still very evident, and the shift from traditional, expository methods has been very slow.

Pinchas Tamir states, "The notion of inquiry has been central to science education for the last twenty years."[1] In studying science education literature, Tamir recognized that inquiry has been central to the learning process in secondary school science.

In 1966, Dr. Richard Suchman, of the University of Illinois, did research on inquiry teaching. He said, "Inquiry is the fundamental means of human learning."[2] This is a very important statement when we consider how much of our science teaching is not done by inquiry.

In 1980-81, a large research project was done in the United States that examined science teaching methods being used at that time. The authors of this project stated, "Because the development of inquiry skills is one of the goals for science education, it is a natural focal topic for the study of science education carried out by a group of scholars under the auspices of *Project Synthesis*."[3]

The position statement of NSTA, the largest science teachers' organization in the world, states:

> The major goal of science teaching is the development of scientific literacy for all people. Incorporated within the concept of scientific literacy is both the understanding of key principles in science and the understanding of how scientific ideas are developed.[4]

In a different study Leopold Klopfer stated, "A major emphasis for education for scientific literacy must be placed on the processes of scientific inquiry."[5] These are several authors who have declared inquiry to be an important and fundamental method of learning, and particularly useful in science.

■ DEVELOPMENT OF INQUIRY TEACHING IN THE SCHOOLS

Scientific inquiry and investigation as we presently understand it (much less the practice of science in any important way) did not enter our schools until the mid-nineteenth century.

> Instead, faith was at least as important as empirical data and in many instances it dominated the practice of science. This faith was often a complex mixture of Christian theology, idealism, and entrenched traditions. It also was a condition that had its roots in many centuries of disagreements between the Church and the practices of science.[6]

Changes in the way science was studied—and taught—may be observed more clearly by looking at the innovations of individual scientists and teachers, rather than through any organized curricular movements. Examples include the methods of Louis Agassiz at Harvard's Lawrence Scientific School in which he

> . . . invited students to visit his lab, study specimens firsthand and thereby gain direct knowledge. He directed field trips to the countryside and seashore, encouraged students to make their own collections, and conducted instruction by correspondence with specimen collectors around the country.[7]

During the late 1800s and early 1900s, inquiry teaching was generally a rarity in science classrooms. Pestalozzi's *object method* of the early 1900s may have had the germs of inquiry embedded in it, but it was many decades before firsthand study of objects and phenomena became an accepted practice in science classrooms. Even today many teachers avoid inquiry teaching because of several perceived problems with this method of instruction. These include the necessity for a slower pace, more time consumption, the need for large quantities of materials, a more active and perhaps chaotic classroom, the urgency to cover material to prepare for the next grade level, and high emphasis of most tests on factual memorization instead of focusing on skill development, processes of science, and investigative strategies. This is accompanied by the normal inertia and resistance to changes in methods of instruction. The burdensome problems facing teachers today leave little time for probing new methods of teaching.

■ DEFINING INQUIRY

Welch and others define inquiry as, "a general process by which human beings seek information or understanding. Broadly conceived, inquiry is a way of thought. Scientific inquiry, a subset of general inquiry, is concerned with the natural world and is guided by certain beliefs and assumptions."[8] J. T. Wilson defines inquiry in the following terms:

> Inquiry is a process model of instruction based upon learning theory and behavior. Too often it is confused with open-ended, undirected activity which is assumed to simulate scientific activity. This is not the case. Inquiry results wherever and whenever stimuli challenge the existing expectations of the participant. The situation may occur in a well-equipped laboratory, but it may also occur in a well-planned and produced lecture, a stimulating reading assignment, or a simple novel situation. The emphasis of inquiry is not the mere acquisition of science knowledge or the production of scientists. It is rather an emphasis upon how humans process information in order to make intellectual decisions of all sorts.[9]

Some authors writing on the subject of inquiry make a distinction between general and scientific inquiry. Specifically:

> Scientific inquiry is defined as a systematic and investigative activity with the purpose of uncovering and describing relationships among objects and events. It is characterized by the use of orderly, repeatable processes, reduction of the object of investigation to its most simple scale and form, and the use of logical frameworks for explanation and prediction. The operations of inquiry include observing, questioning, experimenting, comparing, inferring, generalizing, communicating, applying and others.[10]

Scientific inquiry has also been defined as "a systematic investigative performance ability which incorporates unrestrained inductive thinking capabilities after a person has acquired a broad and critical knowledge of particular subject matter through formal learning processes."[11]

Some authors believe that, particularly in secondary schools, inquiry teaching is a way of developing the mental processes of curiosity and investigation so that students learn how information is obtained. Other authors believe teachers should not use scientific inquiry in the classrooms of the secondary school. They believe that it is a mistake to lead students to think that they are acting like scientists when, in fact, they may only be exhibiting general inquiry characteristics. They also believe that true scientific inquiry cannot be done until one has a strong grasp on the subject far in advance, which would limit inquiry to graduate students and laboratory researchers. We believe that it is necessary to introduce children in the secondary schools, and perhaps even earlier, to the ideas of inquiry and investigation, even though they may not know much science before they have this instruction. See

"Teaching Science Activities: Teaching Inquiry Skills" in the Appendix, p. 452, for examples of classroom exercises designed for students with minimal science backgrounds.

■ DISCOVERY AND INQUIRY STRATEGIES DISTINGUISHED

Over the last 35 years, most of the programs funded by the United States government for developing modern instruction in elementary and secondary schools have stressed student involvement in discovery- or inquiry-oriented activities. Millions of dollars have gone into constructing science and mathematics studies and curricula for this purpose.

What is discovery or inquiry? Many educators use these terms interchangeably, whereas others prefer to differentiate their meanings. In our terminology, *discovery occurs when an individual is mainly involved in using his or her mental processes to mediate (or discover) some concept or principle.*

For students to make discoveries they must perform certain mental processes, such as observing, classifying, measuring, predicting, describing, and inferring. Many modern elementary school curriculum-project materials are mainly designed to involve children in discovery activities.

Discovery

Discovery is the mental process of assimilating concepts and principles. Discovery processes include:

- Observing
- Classifying
- Measuring
- Predicting
- Describing
- Inferring

Starting in the middle school and becoming increasingly more sophisticated as students progress through high school, materials are designed to stress inquiry. Inquiry teaching, however, is built on and includes discovery, because students must use their discovery capabilities in addition to other capabilities. *In true inquiry, the individual tends to act more like a maturing adult.* Adults behave in a number of ways to unravel the hidden relationships relative to a problem. They define problems, formulate hypotheses, design experiments, etc. They perform certain relatively sophisticated mental processes, as indicated in the following chart.

Secondary students may be asked to choose and investigate an organism and report their research. If they define their own problems, design experiments, collect data, etc., they are behaving in an inquiry manner. Refer to the paragraphs on discovery and inquiry. How do these processes differ? How would you design a discovery-oriented lesson in your subject field? How would you design an inquiry lesson?

Inquiry

Inquiry is the process of defining and investigating problems, formulating hypotheses, designing experiments, gathering data, and drawing conclusions about problems. Inquiry processes include:

- Originating problems,
- Formulating hypotheses,
- Designing investigative approaches,
- Testing out ideas (e.g., conducting experiments),
- Synthesizing knowledge,
- Developing certain attitudes (e.g., is objective, curious, open-minded, desires and respects theoretical models, responsible; suspends judgment until sufficient data is obtained, checks results).

Because secondary teachers often do not clearly distinguish between discovery and inquiry, they tend to overemphasize discovery activities. Piaget indicated that adolescents are in the process of developing formal thought and should, therefore, have opportunities to use a higher level of thinking. Hypothetical-deductive and reflexive thinking are two characteristics of this stage of development. Formulating hypotheses, designing investigations, evaluating data, and looking over an investigation to determine how it can be improved all require these mental operations. Middle and secondary instruction should, therefore, not only include discovery but an increasing number of inquiry activities.

Clearly, one develops discovery and inquiry thinking abilities only by being involved in activities requiring these mental tasks. Since an individual never really masters any of them completely, there is only a degree to which one becomes proficient in learning how to discover and inquire. Even the most sophisticated Nobel Prize scientist, author, painter, mathematician, or sociologist is still moving forward in developing these skills. The task of the school system is to construct its curriculum so students manifest these human investigative abilities.

■ ADVANTAGES OF DISCOVERY AND INQUIRY TEACHING

You are probably beginning to see some of the reasons that discovery and inquiry teaching are used in the schools. Jerome Bruner has been instrumental in leading the movement toward discovery teaching. He outlined four reasons for using this approach:

1. Intellectual potency
2. Intrinsic rather than extrinsic motives
3. Learning the heuristics of discovery
4. Conservation of memory

By intellectual potency, Bruner means that an individual learns and develops her or his mind only by using it to think. His second point means that, as a consequence of succeeding at discovery, the student receives a satisfying intellectual thrill—an intrinsic reward. Teachers often given extrinsic rewards (As, for example), but if they want students to learn for the fun of it, they must devise instructional systems that enable students to obtain intrinsic satisfaction. In Bruner's third point, he emphasizes that the only way a person learns the techniques of discovery is to have opportunities to discover. Through discovering, a student slowly learns how to organize and conduct investigations. Bruner argues in his fourth point that one of the greatest benefits of the discovery approach is that it aids in better memory retention. Think for a moment of some scientific idea you have thought out yourself and compare it with information you were given in a freshman course. The material you reasoned out and came to some conclusion about is probably still in your mind, even though you may have learned it years ago. On the other hand, concepts you were told often escape recall.

Although these four justifications have been outlined for discovery teaching, they also have relevance for inquiry. The teaching strategies for the two approaches are similar in that they stress the importance of students using their cognitive mental processes to work out the meaning of things they encounter in their environment.

Although Bruner has suggested the salient justifications for modern teaching, there are at least six additional reasons for using student investigative approaches. They are as follows.

Instruction Becomes Student-Centered

One of the basic psychological principles of learning implies that the greater the student involvement, the greater the learning. Usually when teachers think about learning, they picture the student assimilating information. This view of learning is very limited, for learning involves those aspects that contribute to the individual becoming a fully functioning person. For example, in inquiry situations students learn not only concepts and principles, but self-direction, responsibility, and social communication. In teacher-centered instruction, however, many of the opportunities for developing these talents are denied to the student. The instructor provides the self-direction and retains the responsibility. If you look at instruction as enabling a person to improve in all the facets that make up a human being, it is difficult to justify a teacher-centered learning environment.

Inquiry Learning Builds the "Self-Concept" of the Student

Each of us has a self-concept. If it is good, we feel psychologically secure, are open to new experiences, are willing to take chances and explore, tolerate minor failures relatively well, are more creative, generally have good mental health, and eventually become fully functioning individuals. Part of the task of becoming a better person is to build one's self-concept. We can do this only by *being involved in learning* because through involvement we manifest our potential and gain insights into self. Inquiry teaching allows for greater involvement, thereby giving students more chances to gain insights and better develop their self-concepts.

Expectancy Level Increases

Part of a person's self-concept is his or her expectancy level, which means that the student believes or expects that he or she can accomplish a task on his or her own. He or she has learned from previous discovery and inquiry experiences that he or she can think autonomously. In other words, from having had many successful experiences in using investigative talents, this individual has learned, "I can solve a problem on my own without the help of a teacher, parent, or anyone else." As a consequence, there is an I-can-ness.

Inquiry Learning Develops Talent

Humans possess more than 120 talents. Academic talent is related to only a few of them. The more freedom we have to use these academic talents, the more opportunities we have to develop others, such as creative, social, organizing, and planning talents.

Inquiry Methods Avoid Learning Only at the Verbal Level

When you learned the definitions for words such as osmosis, photosynthesis, logarithm, and others, did you play memorization games, or did you work out the meaning in your mind and really understand what you were learning? Could you define these terms operationally, or could you give memorized definitions only? Inquiry teaching, since it involves students working out the meaning of their work, tends to avoid learning only at the verbal level.

Inquiry Learning Permits Time for Students to Mentally Assimilate and Accommodate Information

Teachers often rush learning, which results in students playing recall games. Students need time to think and use their minds to reason out and gain insights into the concepts, principles, and investigative techniques they are involved in. It takes time for such information to become a meaningful part of the mind. Piaget believed that there is no true learning unless the students mentally act on information and, in the process, assimilate or accommodate what they encounter in their environment. Unless this assimilation occurs, teacher and students are involved only in pseudo-learning, which is retained for a short time only.

■ GUIDED VERSUS FREE INQUIRY

How much structure should be provided in inquiry situations? There should be enough to ensure that students are successful in understanding the important implications of their studies.

If students have not had experience in learning through inquiry, initially they should be given considerable structure in their lessons. After they have gained some experience on how to conduct an investigation, the structure should then be lessened. In this text a general term *investigative* is used to include both discovery and inquiry teaching approaches. The term *guided discovery and inquiry* is used where there is considerable structure given, and *free discovery and inquiry* indicates that there is little guidance provided by the instructor. Below is an example of a portion of a guided-inquiry lesson. Note that much of the planning is outlined by the teacher. The students, for example, do not originate the problem, and considerable guidance is provided on how to set up and record the data. In a free-type lesson, the students may originate the problem and determine how to resolve it.

Guided Inquiry

In a guided inquiry approach, the instructor provides the problem and encourages students to work out the procedures to resolve it. Examples of problems teachers might give to involve students in this type of process are:

1. How is algebra used in our community?
2. Given the story up to this point, how would you end it?
3. How would you write a poem to indicate your feeling about seeing the ocean?
4. What do you think about intermarriage?

5. How could you make a better salad dressing?
6. Here are some snails. Find out as much as possible about them.
7. Here is a pond and some apparatus. Find out as much as possible about how this pond changes over a year.
8. How could we make poetry more popular in our school?
9. A new highway is built through the jungles of Brazil and passes by an Indian village that has had little contact with modern civilization. What will happen?
10. Here is some apparatus for studying motion. Set it up in any way you choose to study the movement of an object.
11. How does using a different language change a person's perceptions of other cultures?
12. Here is some apparatus for studying circuits. Use it to find out as much as possible about circuits.
13. Do whatever you wish with this salt to determine its physical and chemical properties.
14. What should be done to improve the environment of our school?
15. Here is some water that is supposed to be polluted. How will you prove that it is?
16. If you were going to produce a piece of art to show contentment, what would you do and why?

In a guided inquiry plan, students are encouraged to resolve problems similar to the preceding, either on their own or in groups. The teacher is available as a resource person, giving only enough aid to ensure that the students do not become too frustrated or experience failure. The assistance the teacher gives, however, should be in the form of questions to help students think about possible investigative procedures. Ask students questions, giving them direction rather than telling them what to do. Good questions, at the right time, may provide just the needed stimulus for students to become more involved in creative investigation. Contrast this method with that of a teacher who says, "Study groups and tell how they are different." In the second instance the teacher has robbed the students of many opportunities for thought and creativity.

Free Inquiry

After students have studied and learned how to attack a problem, gained sufficient knowledge about the subject, and performed modified inquiry, the instructor might invite them to become involved in free inquiry. This method differs from the modified approach in that the students identify what it is they would like to study. The following questions are suggested as a basis for this type of class activity:

1. If you were the teacher of this class and you were going to select the most exciting things to investigate this term, what would they be?
2. What are some problems related to our community that you would like to study?
3. Now that you have studied, for example, salts, algae, light, heat, radiation, animal behaviors, etc., what problems can you come up with that you would like to investigate individually or in teams?
4. Now that you have finished this experiment, for example in population, what other experiments can you think of and which of them would you like to do?
5. When you see problems in the community, such as pollution, or some problem related to science that you would like to discuss, bring it to the class's attention.
6. What types of mathematical investigations would you like to conduct (e.g., determining the acceleration of a skier or a race-car driver)?
7. What authors would you like to read?
8. What biographies would you like to write or read?
9. What kind of play would you like to write, read, or produce?

■ CONDITIONS FOR INQUIRY TEACHING

Suchman lists four conditions for good inquiry teaching.[12] The first one he calls the *condition of freedom*, meaning the freedom of learners to seek out desired information. They must be allowed to try out ideas and invent ways of accounting for what they see. This is the essence of the inquiry approach.

The second condition is the *condition of the responsive environment*. A responsive environment is a classroom, a laboratory, or the outdoors on a field trip—anywhere that provides many opportunities for inquiry. It cannot be a sterile classroom or lecture hall. Teachers must have books, apparatus, experiments, aquaria, and many other things for students to work with. Inquiry can take place only in a responsive environment. The teacher must provide the information the students seek or the sources for that information. The teacher must make available a wide range of materials and facts from which the students can choose to meet their needs of the moment. This is the second important condition for inquiry teaching.

The third condition listed by Suchman is the *condition of focus*. Inquiry is a purposeful activity, a search for greater meaning in some event, object, or condition that raises questions in the inquirer's mind. It is directed toward one goal, toward the solution of a problem. It is not scattered; the energies are not dissipated. This is what is meant by the condition of focus.

Suchman's fourth condition is the *condition of low pressure.* Students will gain their reinforcement directly from the success of their own ideas in adding meaning to the environment or to their understanding of it. The teacher must respond positively to the student but neutrally to the product of the student's thinking. The teacher must recognize that not all students learn at the same rate. The condition of low pressure provides for students with different rates of learning to progress in the same classroom. Contemporary education sometimes defeats that purpose by putting too much emphasis on the class being fifty minutes long. The bell rings and the students must move to another class, which emphasizes educational uniformity. There is very little flexibility for teachers to provide for different rates of learning.

When you teach by inquiry, there are several important elements of an inquiry lesson that need to be followed. The basic elements of such a plan are described below:

- *The Problem:* This is the basic requirement and meets the *condition of focus* described by Suchman. If at all possible, the problem should be real, meaningful, and capable of study. If the problem can be elicited from the class, so much the better. A practical substitute, however, is one identified by the teacher and elaborated for the class.
- *The Background Information:* Some means must be found to provide the necessary information to put the class on a fairly common level of understanding. This may be in the form of a brief class discussion, some common reading matter, a textbook, or a preliminary experiment to give general understanding to all members of the class.
- *The Materials:* This refers to Suchman's *condition of a responsive environment.* Provisions must be made to have adequate quantities of materials at hand, opportunities for individual work with the materials, and a chance for students to choose the materials they will need to solve the problem.
- *The Guiding Questions:* This consists of an anticipated list of questions to be asked by the teacher to direct students' thought processes. Prepare a skeleton outline of these but allow for ample deviation from the basic list in order to provide for student input.
- *The Hypotheses:* These should be formulated as a result of discussions and guiding questions. Permit a *condition of freedom* so as not to inhibit discussion.
- *The Data Gathering and Analysis:* This is the hands-on, experimental part of the inquiry lesson.

Permit a *condition of low pressure* here to allow for mistakes and repeats. Emphasize record-keeping and a systematic approach to the problem.
- *The Conclusion:* This refers to the lesson's closure and should culminate in some final result based on experimentation and discussion. Group conclusions are acceptable.

■ RESEARCH FINDINGS ABOUT USING INVESTIGATIVE TEACHING APPROACHES

Although the research findings still need further investigation, particularly concerning how students vary in feelings about the different approaches (affectivity) and the development of more than just subject-matter achievement differences (i.e., multi-talents, self-concept, etc.), they do indicate that investigative approaches have been successful. Shulman, as a result of a Conference on Learning by Discovery, summarizes the research in discovery as follows: "In the published studies, guided discovery treatments generally have done well both at the level of immediate learning and later transfer."[13]

An early examination of inquiry teaching set up a three-year longitudinal study to determine the differences this type of teaching made on students' learning behavior. Investigators at Carnegie-Mellon University found that an inquiry-oriented social studies curriculum significantly increased students' abilities to inquire about human affairs, compared to those studying noninquiry materials.[14] This study is important because it shows that inquiry teaching over a prolonged period can help individuals become better investigators. When teachers first begin to use this approach, they often become frustrated and think they are not making sufficient progress. These instructors suffer from a covering compulsion; they feel better as teachers if they cover something because they have a mistaken idea of the function of teaching. They are surprised to learn that often students do not assimilate material covered by lecture (see Figure 12–1).

Highly significant research concerning inquiry teaching has been completed using meta-analysis (the analysis of previous analytical studies using a common statistical framework).[15] This meta-research involved a careful study of twenty-five years of research comparing student performance in newer science curricula (i.e., post-Sputnik) to student performance in traditional courses.

Five measures were used in the comparison— achievement, attitudes, process, analytic abilities, and related skills. On a composite basis across all junior high and senior high school curricula in sci-

Noninquiry	Inquiry
Teacher covers more BUT Less is retained	Teacher covers less BUT More is retained
Teacher Orientation	**Teacher Orientation**
Views students as a reservoir of knowledge, subject-centered. Teachers have covering compulsion. The more they cover, the better they think they are.	More holistic view of the learner, student-centered. Teachers more interested in cognitive and creative growth. Teach for the development of multi-talents in helping students develop their self-concepts.

FIGURE 12–1
Differences between inquiry and noninquiry teaching

ence, the average student in the new science curricula exceeded the performance of 64 percent of the students in traditional courses. This consistent pattern of positive effects clearly established the superiority of the new curricula over traditional courses. Students' achievement scores were effectively raised 9–14 percentile points when the students were placed in a classroom using a new program.

Problem Solving

Investigations in the science classroom begin with a problem. Problem solving as a teaching strategy embodies most of the techniques and learning skills science educators consider important when learning science by investigative methods.

Several approaches to problem solving were researched and discussed by Donald Woods.[16] The first approach involves the following:

1. Begin with a task embedded in a familiar setting.
2. Introduce problem-solving techniques that might be applicable.
3. Allow students to create their own paths to a solution.
4. Emphasize collaborative learning and problem solving.
5. Help develop collaborative working skills.
6. Provide different roles for individuals in a group setting.
7. Identify, confront, and discuss misconceptions.

The teacher's role in the problem-solving methods discussed above involve thinking about and presenting everyday situations and experiences that relate to each concept or fundamental law discussed. The teacher should be a facilitator and suppress the urge to tell students what they should try or what they should discover. Encourage sharing of ideas in class and devise a wide range of options for solving the problem.

Teachers using problem-solving approaches to learning science will inevitably find some elements of resistance. There will be a reluctance on the part of students to change their learning styles from what they have been used to in traditional learning. Similarly, they may express concern about assessment and testing methods because emphases on factual memorization will be minimized.

Teachers themselves may have serious reservations about using problem-solving methods because of the additional time required and a deemphasis on coverage of textbook materials. There may also be increased expense because of the wide range of resources needed to fully explore solutions to the problems selected.

The NSTA *Search for Excellence in Science Education* begun in 1981 sought exemplary programs in secondary school science teaching throughout the United States. Many programs were found and reported on in the *Focus on Excellence* published by the NSTA in 1987. At the college level a similar search was conducted by the Society for College Science Teachers (SCST). Results were published in *Innovations in College Science Teaching* by John Dunkhase and John Penick in 1988.[17]

In both of these efforts criteria for exemplary programs in science teaching focused heavily on the use of inquiry and investigative teaching methods. Three main components were deemed necessary to qualify as an exemplary problem-solving type of teaching strategy. The components were identification of a problem, investigation and analysis of the problem, and presentation of the results.

Programs did not qualify as exemplary if the main attention was on presentation of facts and concepts, manipulations of numbers and equations to get a so-called right answer, or verification of scientific phenomena to get a prescribed result in laboratory work.

Students in exemplary programs were introduced to the process of identifying problems, gathering information, organizing and analyzing information, and presenting the best analysis. Active participation in identification and investigation of science-related problems and human endeavors was considered important. Attention was paid to acquisition of new knowledge and the processes by which scientific information is generated and applied to the solution of real problems.

The types of activities in which students engage in classrooms reflect the degree of inquiry practiced in these classes. An analysis of the inquiry level of science activities in junior high school science textbooks was done by Pizzini, and others.[18] They found a significant variation in the frequency of inquiry level activities among science textbooks and activity guides. Four levels of inquiry were identified, ranging from confirmation or verification activities through structured inquiry and guided inquiry to open inquiry in which students formulate hypotheses and design procedures for investigating problems.

The researchers concluded that the first three levels do not produce the mind set nor the skills needed to practice inquiry and investigative problem solving. Only open inquiry provides these experiences. They also concluded that science activities in junior high school science textbooks and commercially published supplementary activity guides are essentially noninquiry approaches to science teaching.

The researchers produced a helpful list of suggestions needed to achieve the goal of science instruction based on open inquiry. To accomplish this, students should:

1. Identify problems and potential solutions, and design plans to test the solutions.
2. Formulate and test hypotheses and test their predictions.
3. Design their own procedures and analyze the processes used.
4. Formulate new questions.
5. Analyze and discuss the underlying assumptions.
6. Share and discuss predictions, procedures, products, and solutions.
7. Consider and develop alternative predictions, procedures, products, and solutions.
8. Develop a questioning base for prior knowledge.
9. Link their own experiences to activities, concepts, and principles.

Although inquiry teaching should receive a major emphasis in science teaching, not everything can or should be taught by inquiry. For example, for students to learn the names of chemical compounds, they must memorize them. If you want students to learn how to handle and use a microscope, you will probably have to show them. If there are safety precautions to be aware of, the instructor must tell the students about them.

You, as a teacher, will have to establish a value system and use it as a guide in determining when you will or will not teach something by inquiry. The preceding section should give you some assistance in evolving your philosophy in this respect.

■ SUMMARY

Many of the modern curriculum materials for the middle and secondary school are discovery- and inquiry-oriented. In discovery teaching, students use their minds to gain insights into some concept or principle. In the process of discovering, an individual performs such mental operations as measuring, predicting, observing, inferring, and classifying. In inquiry, an individual may use all of the discovery mental processes plus those characterizing a mature adult, such as formulating problems, hypothesizing, designing experiments, synthesizing knowledge, and demonstrating such attitudes as objectivity, curiosity, open-mindedness, and respect for theoretical models, values, and attitudes. Discovery and inquiry teaching may vary from a relatively structured approach where considerable guidance is provided by the instructor to free investigation where the students originate problems.

Why use these investigative approaches? The philosophical and psychological advantages appear to be many. These methods increase intellectual potency; cause a shift from extrinsic to intrinsic rewards; help students learn how to investigate; increase memory retention; make instruction student-centered, thereby contributing to a person's self-concept; increase expectancy levels; develop multiple, not just academic talents; avoid learning only on the verbal level; and allow more time for students to assimilate and accommodate information.

Although there is a need to further assess the value of these approaches (particularly relative to attitudes, values, and self-concept attainment), there is much evidence that students taught by these methods perform significantly better on cognitive tasks involving critical thinking than those taught by traditional instruction.

Teachers often suffer from a covering syndrome. If they cover the material, they feel that their responsibility as teachers has been met. But because a teacher covers something is little assurance that students have learned it. Student-centered instruction, because it often requires more time, results in less covering than does traditional teaching. The retention and critical-thinking ability of students in investigative-oriented classes, however, has been found to be greater.

■ REFERENCES

1. Pinchas Tamir, "Inquiry and the Science Teacher," *Science Education, 67* (5) (1983): 657–672.
2. Richard Suchman, *Developing Inquiry* (Chicago: Science Research Associates, 1966).
3. Norris Harms and Robert Yager, "Project Synthesis," *What Research Says to the Science Teacher, 3* (1981): 53–72.
4. *Science Education for the 80s, (1)* (Washington, DC: NSTA, 1979).
5. Leopold Klopfer, "The Teaching of Science and the History of Science," *Journal of Research in Science Teaching,* 6(1) (1969): 87–95.
6. Carlton H. Stedman, "Fortuitous Strategies on Inquiry in the Good Ole Days," *Science Education, 71* (5) (1987): 657–665.
7. Stedman, pp. 657–665.
8. Wayne Welch, Leopold Klopfer, Glen Aikenhead, and J. T. Robinson, "The Role of Inquiry in Science Education: Analysis and Recommendations," *Science Education,* 65 (1) (1981): 33–50.
9. J. T. Wilson, "Processes of Scientific Inquiry: A Model for Teaching and Learning Science," *Science Education, 58* (1) (1974). 127–133.
10. K. D. Peterson, "Scientific Inquiry for High School Students," *Journal of Research in Science Teaching, 15* (2) (1978): 153–159.
11. William Kyle, Jr., "The Distinction Between Inquiry and Scientific Inquiry and Why High School Students Should be Cognizant of the Distinction," *Journal of Research in Science Teaching, 17* (2) (1980): 123–130.
12. J. Richard Suchman, *Developing Inquiry* (Chicago: Science Research Associates), pp. 14–18.
13. Lee S. Shulman, "Psychological Controversies in the Teaching of Science and Mathematics," *Science Teacher* (September 1968), p. 90.
14. John M. Good, John U. Forley, and Edwin Featon, "Developing Inquiry Skills With an Experimental Social Studies Curriculum," *Journal of Educational Research, 63* (1) (1969): p 35.
15. James A. Shymansky, et. al. "The Effects of New Science Curricula on Student Performance."
16. Donald R. Woods, "Three More Approaches to Problem-Solving," *Journal of College Science Teaching* (September/October, 1991).
17. John A. Dunkhase and John E. Penick, "Problem-Solving for the Real World," *Journal of College Science Teaching, 21* (November 1991): 100–105.
18. Edward L. Pizzini and others, "Inquiry Level of Junior High Activity," *Journal of Research in Science Teaching* (February 1991): 111.

Chapter 13

DEMONSTRATION AND LABORATORY WORK

In the first-period general-science class, Mr. O'Brien took a candle out of a box and placed it on the demonstration desk. He told the class he would show them the difference between a physical and chemical change. He struck a match and placed the candle over the flame until the wick burned. Soon some of the wax was melting, dripping, and then solidifying. He said, "This is an example of a physical change. When the candle partially burns, the wax changes to carbon dioxide and water—and then there is a chemical change." The students watched the demonstration and some took notes.

Across the hall, Mr. Jackson was teaching the same unit. He also wanted to have students learn about physical and chemical changes. Uncertain of how he was going to do this, Mr. Jackson asked Mr. O'Brien if he knew a good demonstration to show these changes. Mr. O'Brien suggested he burn a candle. Mr. Jackson, however, taught these concepts differently. After the bell rang and the students were seated, he took a candle and a match box out of his demonstration desk, placed them on top of the desk, and asked, "What am I going to do with the candle and match?" Art answered, "You are going to light it." Mr. Jackson replied, "That's right, but what will happen to the match and candle when I light them? How will they vary? What will happen to the candle when it burns? Will it drip?"

Several students raised their hands and suggested answers to his questions. He lit the candle, and it started to drip. He asked, "Why does the candle drip? What will happen if we try to burn the dripped material? Where did the dripped material come from, and how did it change while the candle was burning?"

George explained that the material merely melted and then solidified. Mr. Jackson asked the rest of the class what they thought of George's explanation, "What evidence was there for his suggestion?" Several members of the class discussed the matter and agreed that this material had only changed form in the process of melting and resolidifying. Mr. Jackson asked, "What is this type of change called?"

Two students raised their hands and suggested that it might be a physical change. Mr. Jackson then asked what was happening to the candle as it burned. What caused it to get shorter, and why would it eventually have to be replaced? The class considered this and eventually realized that the candle was also changing chemically.

■ INQUIRY THROUGH DEMONSTRATION

Which of these teaching methods do you think would be the more effective way to demonstrate physical and chemical changes and why? What did students learn from Mr. Jackson's approach that they might not have learned from Mr. O'Brien's? Which of the methods stressed the inquiry approach and why? Which method do you think took instructors more time to prepare? Which would be more inductive in its approach? Why do you think teachers have traditionally emphasized the deductive method in giving demonstrations? If you were going to teach this lesson, how would you do it better?

A demonstration has been defined as the process of showing something to another person or group. Clearly, there are several ways in which things can be shown. You can hold up an object such as a piece of sulfur and say, "This is sulfur," or you can state, "Sulfur burns; light some sulfur, and show that it burns." Showing things in this way mainly involves observation or verification. Mr. O'Brien's use of demonstration was of this type.

A demonstration can also be given inductively by the instructor asking several questions but seldom giving answers. An inductive demonstration has the advantage of stressing inquiry, which encourages students to analyze and make hypotheses based on their knowledge. Their motivation is high because they like riddles, and in an inductive demonstration they are constantly confronted with riddles. The strength of this motivation becomes apparent if you consider the popularity of puzzles. Inviting students to inquire why something occurs taxes their minds and requires them to think. Thinking is an active mental process. The only way in which students learn to think is by having opportunities to do so. An inductive demonstration provides this opportunity because students' answers to the instructor's questions act as feedback. The teacher has a better understanding of students' comprehension of the demonstration. The feedback acts as a guide for further questioning until the students discover the concepts and principles involved in the demonstration, and the teacher is sure that they know its meaning and purpose.

Demonstrations, in addition to serving as simple observations of material and verification of a process, may also be experimental in nature. A demonstration can become an experiment if it involves a problem for which the solution is not immediately apparent to the class. Students particularly like experimental demonstrations because they usually have more action. Students enjoy action, not words! They love to watch something happening before their eyes.

Demonstration Versus Individual Experimentation

Educators have stressed the importance of self-instruction and less reliance on large-group or class instruction. Education should be preparation for life, and part of that preparation must be to ensure that the individual continues to learn long after formal education ends. It is important that the school reinforce habits and patterns of learning that will prepare students to continue their education many years after they leave organized instruction. Laboratory work, because it involves the individual directly in the learning process, as well as imparting working skills, is thought to be superior to teaching by demonstration. Students working on a laboratory problem have learned far more than just the answer to the problem. They may learn to be efficient, self-reliant, and analytical; to observe, manipulate, measure, and reason; to use apparatus; and, most importantly, to learn on their own. Individual laboratory experimentation helps to attain these goals better than do demonstrations. For this reason demonstrations should play a lesser role in science instruction, with individual student investigation receiving top priority.

Demonstrations can be justified for the following reasons:

1. *Lower cost.* Less equipment and fewer materials are needed by an instructor doing a demonstration. It is, therefore, cheaper than having an entire class conduct experiments. However, cheaper education is not necessarily better education.
2. *Availability of equipment.* Certain demonstrations require equipment not available in sufficient numbers for all students to use. For example, not every student in a physics class needs to have an oscilloscope to study sound waves.
3. *Economy of time.* Often the time required to set up equipment for a laboratory exercise cannot be justified for the educational value received. A teacher can set up the demonstration and use the rest of the time for other instruction.
4. *Less hazard from dangerous materials.* A teacher may more safely handle dangerous chemicals or apparatus requiring sophisticated skills.

5. *Direction of the thinking process.* In a demonstration, a teacher has a better indication of the students' thinking processes and can do much to stimulate the students to be more analytical and synthetic in their reasoning.
6. *Show the use of equipment.* An instructor may want to show the students how to use and prevent damage to a microscope, balance, oscilloscope, etc.

Planning a Demonstration

To plan an efficient and effective demonstration requires extensive organization and consideration of the following points:

1. The first step is to identify the concept and principles you wish to teach. Direct the design of the entire demonstration to their attainment.
2. If the principle you wish to teach is complex, break it down into concepts and give several examples for each concept. For example, photosynthesis involves understanding concepts of radiant energy, chlorophyll, carbon dioxide, glucose, water, temperature, a chemical change, and gases. Students memorizing that green plants can make sugar in light with water results in little understanding if they do not know the meaning of these concepts.
3. Choose an activity that will show the concepts you wish to teach. Consult the sources at the end of this chapter for possible suggestions for activities.
4. Design the activity so that each student becomes as involved as possible.
5. Gather and assemble the necessary equipment.
6. Go through the demonstration at least once before class begins.
7. Outline the questions you will ask during the demonstration. This procedure is especially important in doing an inquiry-oriented demonstration.
8. Consider how you will use visual aids, especially the overhead projector, to supplement the demonstration.
9. Decide on the evaluation technique to use.

   Written Techniques
   a. Essay. Have students take notes and record data during the demonstration, and then have them write a summary of the demonstration.
   b. Quiz. Have students write answers to questions or prepare diagrams to see if they really understood the demonstration. Stress application of principles.

   Verbal Techniques
   a. Ask students to summarize the purpose of the demonstration.

b. Give them problems in which they will have to apply the principles they have learned.

10. Consider the time a demonstration will take. Try to move it rapidly enough to keep students attentive. Prolonged or complicated demonstrations are generally undesirable because they don't hold the students' attention.

11. When you plan a demonstration, do it well, with the intention that you will probably use it for several years. It will then take less time to prepare in the future. Evaluate a demonstration immediately after giving it to determine its weaknesses and strengths. Add any questions that will contribute to the inquiry presentation when you use the demonstration again.

Giving a Demonstration

When giving a demonstration, keep the following guidelines in mind:

1. Make it easily visible. If you are working with small things, can you use an overhead projector to make them more visible?

2. Speak loudly enough to be heard in the back of the room. Do you speak loudly enough and modulate the tone and volume of your voice to avoid monotonous delivery? When a student responds, do you ask him or her to speak up so other students can hear? Do you repeat students' questions and answers for emphasis and audibility?

3. Do you display excitement in giving the demonstration? Do you make it come alive? A good demonstrator is somewhat of a ham. This kind of instructor uses dramatic techniques to excite and involve students. The way in which a teacher makes a demonstration come alive is as much an art as is reading Shakespeare well to an enraptured audience.

4. How do you stage the demonstration? How do you start it to involve everyone immediately? One suggestion is to place unique objects on a demonstration desk. For example, a transfusion container or a Van de Graff generator placed on a desk immediately motivates students' inquisitive minds. Before you even begin, you have the students with you, wondering what you are going to do.

a. Teach inductively. Start your demonstration with a question. If you have interesting equipment, ask your students what they think you are going to do with it. Spend some time just asking questions about the apparatus. In the construction of a transfusion container, for example, there are several scientific principles involved, such as partial vacuum, air pressure, sterile conditions, nutrient for the cells placed in the bottle, and anticoagulants to prevent clotting of the blood.

b. Ask questions constantly about what you are going to do, what's happening, why they think it is happening, and what the demonstration is proving or illustrating.

c. Know the purpose of what you are demonstrating. Use your questions as a guide only. The questions you have anticipated may be excellent, but also be ready to pick up suggestions from the questions students ask while they are observing the demonstration.

When giving a demonstration, ask questions constantly about what you're going to do, what's happening, and why.

d. Give positive reinforcement. Always recognize an answer: "Say, I think you have something there." "Good, you're thinking." "What do the rest of you think of John's remarks?" When a student gives a good explanation, be complimentary. Seldom react negatively to a student's answer. Don't say, "That's wrong." Rather say, "It's good you're thinking, but your answer is not quite right."

5. Allow at least three seconds for students to reply to your questions. This wait-time is important so that the students may think about and reason out the demonstration.

6. Use the blackboard to describe the purpose of the demonstration. Verbal explanations are seldom enough. Any picture or diagram you make on the board immediately attracts the students' attention. Remember that your students have lived in a TV-centered environment; as soon as they see a visual representation on the board, they are drawn to it. A beginning teacher often fails to realize or ever consider how the blackboard can complement the learning activity.

7. At the conclusion of the demonstration have a student summarize what has occurred and its purpose. This summation helps to fix the purpose of the demonstration in the minds of the students.

8. Evaluate your lesson, orally or in a written summary.

Ways to Present a Demonstration

Of the several ways in which a demonstration can be given, a teacher-centered demonstration is seldom the best way because it does not provide enough student involvement. When students participate actively in giving a demonstration, they are more interested and, consequently, learn more. Several types of student-participative demonstrations are shown in the Appendix, for example, "Discovery Demonstration: Bottle and Key," p. 437; "How Long Can You Boil Water in a Paper Cup?" p. 442; "Discovery Demonstration: Inquiring into Falling Bodies," p. 447; "Small Group Problem Solving," p. 453; "Evaluation of Student Understanding of a Basic Physical Principle," p. 443; and "Genetic Engineering: A Splice of Life," p. 397. Here are five ways in which a demonstration can be presented.

1. *Teacher demonstration.* The teacher prepares and gives the demonstration to the class. This approach has the advantage usually of better organization and more sophisticated presentation.

2. *Teacher-student demonstration.* This is a team approach in which the student assists the teacher. This type of demonstration recognizes the student. The class may be more attentive because they like to watch one of their peers perform.

3. *Student-group demonstration.* This method can be used on occasion; it has the advantage of more actively involving students. The group approach can be used to advantage if students are allowed to select their group members. The teacher should evaluate the group as a whole and assign the same grade to each group. The groups will form at first among friends. However, if some of the members are not productive, they will be rejected the next time groups are selected. The peer pressure to produce and become actively involved replaces the necessity for a teacher to encourage students to work. This group arrangement may also be effective in organizing laboratory work. The only problem is that the teacher must be patient until group pressure is brought to bear on the nonproductive students in the class.

4. *Individual student demonstration.* This method can produce very effective demonstrations, especially if the student has peer status. An effective way to have individual student demonstrations is to have upperclassmen, from advanced science classes, demonstrate to the lowerclassmen. A freshman general-science class may become enthralled when a physics or chemistry senior comes into the class to give a demonstration. An upperclassman, excited about giving a demonstration, helps to convey that excitement to the students.

5. *Guest demonstration.* Guest demonstrators can do much to relieve a boring pattern of routine class activities. Other science teachers in the school may be called in to present a demonstration or activity in which they have some special competence. Professional scientists are also often willing to give special demonstrations.

Silent Demonstration

Some authors have stressed the importance and desirability of the silent demonstration. In the passage below a verbal demonstration is compared with a silent one.

> The usual kind of demonstration by which science teachers give their students visual or auditory experiences is the teacher-talking demonstration. In this performance the teacher is actor and commentator. The pupils, who are supposed to be learning from the new experience how to attack a difficulty or develop a concept, are spectators. But they do not necessarily learn scientific facts or principles from a demonstration in which everything is done for them. Pupils really learn when they observe and react to what is presented.

There is a kind of demonstration that is likely to ensure, on the part of the student, careful observation, accurate recording of data, and practical application, later, of the ideas gained from the experience. This procedure is the silent demonstration. The following comparison of the silent demonstration and the teacher-talking demonstration shows how they differ.[1]

The silent demonstration, since it cannot be supplemented or strengthened by explanation, requires more careful planning than does the teacher-talking demonstration (see Table 13–1). In preparing the silent demonstration, the teacher may find this general procedure a good one.

1. Fix clearly in mind the object of the demonstration.
2. Select the apparatus and materials best suited for the demonstration.
3. Determine the beginning point of the demonstration. The beginning is based on what the teacher assumes that pupils know.

4. Consider difficulties as learning steps. Perform the parts of the demonstration to explain these difficulties.
5. Perform the techniques so that they can be observed from all areas of the room. The steps should follow some order in relation to the learning steps.
6. Give pupils an outline of the steps to be used. Outlines may be mimeographed or put on the chalkboard.

Silent demonstrations should not be used frequently because there is no way for the teacher to determine if the students are achieving the objectives while the demonstration is being given. Silent demonstrations can, however, provide a welcome change in the routine activity of the class. They can be used effectively if an instructor's movements are accentuated so that the students can see and have some hints about what is relevant. In a silent demonstration, *visibility* is extremely important and must be ensured; otherwise, the students will quickly become frustrated and discipline problems will ensue.

Storage of Demonstration Equipment

Equipment made by you or your students can lend an added fascination to a science demonstration because students are often more impressed by homemade equipment. Parents, industrial companies, and students will often construct or provide apparatus for the school without cost. Having students build equipment also involves them in improving the science instruction of the school. This personal investment helps to build student morale and to show the community that the science department is an active and dynamic part of their school.

Store equipment after use so that it may be found easily in the future and set up again with little effort. One way to do so is to establish a list of headings under which to store materials. For example, in physics, storage areas might be labeled: electricity, magnetism, heat, light, sound, atomic structure, etc. In biology, storage categories might be: glassware, chemicals, slides, preserved plant and animal specimens, etc. The next time you wish to find the equipment, it is readily available under the proper storage title. Such a system also makes it easy for students to assist you in storing or obtaining equipment for use in demonstrations.

An efficient way to store small demonstration materials is to use several shoe boxes (see Figure 13–1). Place all of the materials you need for a demonstration in the box and label the end. For example, a box might be labeled electrostatic demonstration materials. You might also include in the box a sheet of paper describ-

TABLE 13–1
Comparison of teacher-talking and silent demonstration

Teacher-Talking Demonstration	Silent Demonstration
Teacher states purposes of the demonstration.	Pupil must discover purpose as the demonstration progresses.
Teacher names pieces of apparatus and describes arrangement.	Teacher uses apparatus. Pupils observe equipment and arrangement.
Teacher is manipulator and technician, tells what is being done, points out and usually explains results.	Teacher performs experiment. Pupils observe what is being done and then describe results.
Teacher often points out the things which should have happened and accounts for unexpected results.	Pupils record results as observed. Teacher checks for accuracy and honesty in reporting. Teacher repeats the experiment if necessary.
Teacher summarizes the results and states the conclusion to be drawn. Pupils usually copy the conclusions as stated.	Pupils summarize data and draw their own conclusions based on what they observed. Teacher checks conclusions and repeats experiment if necessary.
Teacher explains the importance of the experiment and tells how it is applied in everyday life.	Pupils attempt to answer application questions related to the demonstration.

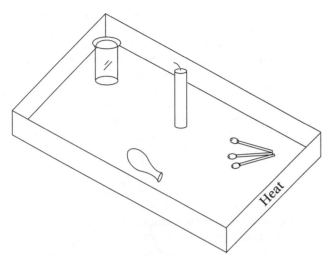

FIGURE 13–1
Storage box for demonstration equipment

ing the demonstration. This helps lessen future preparation time for the same demonstration. A student laboratory assistant can get the box down, read the included sheet, check to see if all of the equipment needed is present, and replenish needed supplies. The box then will be ready for use, and you will require practically no preparation time. This storage procedure works particularly well with general-science and simple physical materials. A drawback is that when many materials and articles of equipment are stored in the boxes, they are not then easily available for other demonstration work during the year.

Special Equipment

Free Sources of Equipment

Science courses often require special science equipment. Some of this specialized equipment may be available to teachers without cost if they go through the proper channels. In some areas of the country there are companies which will donate materials to the schools when they receive a written request from the teacher. Consult with experienced teachers or professional scientists in your community to determine what is available.

Overhead Projector

Every science class should have an overhead projector with suitable transparency supplies. Such a projector can become a valuable teaching aid during a demonstration or discussion. For example, in biology a teacher may want to show how to make a wet-mount slide. This procedure cannot be demonstrated easily except by using an overhead projector. Many of the properties of magnetism can also be demonstrated by the use of such a projector.

Microprojector, Videotape Recorder, and Amplifier

Another special piece of equipment of particular value to biology classes is the microprojector to project slide material. The advantage of this projector is that the teacher and the student view the material simultaneously. These microprojectors cost over $2,000 and are beyond the reach of most schools. An alternative to the use of the microprojector is a closed-circuit television camera adapted for use over a microscope; the students view the material on a television console. Amplifiers can be used to good advantage to study heartbeats of various animals and to let the class hear them. Some teachers have a small tape library that may contain information to be used as an actual part of a demonstration. In the study of sound in general science or physics, tape recorders can be put to good use.

Stressing the Higher Levels of Learning

A demonstration should contribute to the objectives of the course and school. It should be used to stimulate critical thinking and offer opportunities for creativity. A demonstration may further be used to develop understanding of the philosophical basis of science. For example, the instructor may ask:

- How certain are we of our data?
- What evidence is there of certainty in science?
- How do scientists fractionate knowledge to find answers to bigger problems?
- How are the fractional bits of knowledge related to the whole?
- I have just produced a pollutant. What are the social implications of this act?
- How can a scientist be moral, immoral, or amoral?

Questions of this type can be used discriminately throughout a series of demonstrations to build a philosophical awareness of the foundations of modern science. The responsibility to impart knowledge of this sort offers great challenge to the teacher in formulating lessons.

A demonstration technique that embodies higher understanding, more students' individuality, and creative reactions is illustrated in the "Teaching Science Activity: Evaluation of Student Under standing of a Basic Physical Principle" in the Appendix, p. 433.

■ INQUIRY THROUGH LABORATORY WORK

It has often been said that science is not really science unless it is accompanied by experimentation and laboratory work. In the secondary schools there continues to be interest in the laboratory as the focal point for the study of science. It is worth noting that this is not the first time in the history of science education in the United States that the laboratory has come into prominence. The late 1800s saw the construction of laboratories in secondary schools and colleges with a corresponding change in emphasis in the methods of science instruction. The recitation method and the catechetical approach for learning science principles were gradually replaced by experiments in laboratories with the expressed purpose of verifying the laws of physics and chemistry. It was believed that students would learn science best by repeating, in an abbreviated fashion, the classical experiments of Newton, Galileo, Hooke, Priestley, Boyle, and many others. Students would see principles of natural science at work, enabling them to understand the underlying science concepts. Laboratories and apparatus were designed to duplicate as nearly as possible the materials and equipment used in the original experiments, with modern refinements to ensure reasonable accuracy in the hands of science students.

The Inquiry Approach

Beginning in the late 1950s, there was a definite shift in emphasis in high school science. The laboratory became the center of attention at all levels of secondary science, including the junior high school. The particular goals and methods used in the various new curriculum projects of the Physical Science Study Committee, the Biological Sciences Curriculum Study, the Chemical Education Materials Study, the Chemical Bond Approach Project, the Earth Science Curriculum Project, and others are discussed in detail in chapter 3. Without exception, these projects emphasized and provided for inquiry methods in which students themselves were the investigators, and which gave many opportunities for creativity.

The inquiry method in the science laboratory can be promoted by several fairly simple but important changes. Paul Brandwein and Joseph Schwab, in describing the inquiry curriculum had this to say about inquiry methods:

> In general, conversion of the laboratory from the dogmatic to the inquiring mode is achieved by making two changes. First, a substantial part of the laboratory work is made to lead rather than lag the classroom phase of science teaching. . . . Second, the merely demonstrative function of the laboratory (which serves the purpose of the dogmatic curriculum) is subordinated to two other functions.
>
> One of these functions consists in a new service to the classroom phase of instruction. With classroom materials converted from a rhetoric of conclusions to an exhibition of the course of inquiry, conclusions

alone will no longer be the major component. Instead, we will deal with units which consist of the statement of a scientific problem, a view of the data needed for its solution, an account of the interpretation of these data, and a statement of the conclusions forged by the interpretation. Such units as these will convey the wanted meta-lesson about the nature of inquiry. But they will appear exceedingly easy and simple, conveying little of the real flavor of scientific inquiries, unless the verbal statement of the problem situation and of the difficulties involved in the acquisition of data is given meaning by an exhibition of their real physical referents. . . .

> The second function of the inquiring laboratory is to provide occasions for an invitation to the conduct of miniature but exemplary programs of inquiry. The manual for such a laboratory ceases to be a volume that tells students what to do and what to expect.[2]

The inquiry mode of teaching, in addition to requiring a different philosophical approach by the teacher and students, also demands higher levels of proficiency in the use of the tools of inquiry. These tools consist of the skills needed to inquire into natural events and conditions. For example, one could not learn very much about how forces cause masses to accelerate unless one could make careful measurements of distance, time, force, and mass. To learn the interrelationships between all of these factors requires that students refine their measurement skills. It is necessary to know how to use a meter stick or measuring tape, to read the units correctly, to read a stop watch, to operate a beam balance correctly, and to measure force with a spring scale or some other method. In the classroom, students must have opportunities to practice the skills required for a particular inquiry situation; otherwise, the experience will probably be frustrating and the learning minimal.

Traditional laboratory experiments do not provide enough opportunities for students to use their minds to solve problems posed in the laboratory. Frequently, all that is required is to make sure all the detailed instructions found in the laboratory manual are carried out, and that all the blanks are filled in after the experiment is completed. Laboratory manuals have often been compared to a cookbook, which fails to excite students very much and often leaves them unsure about what they were studying, or what they found out in the activity.

Some suggestions for uncookbooking laboratory experiments have been offered by William Leonard.[3] These suggestions are included here for consideration by science teachers in secondary schools because of their relevance to investigative methods of teaching.

1. Give the student a simple task or goal to accomplish. This task can be explained verbally by the

teacher or by brief explanations in written form. The purpose is to focus students' attention on a problem and to encourage creative thinking in solving it.

2. Give the student only essential procedures. Some general suggestions may be made to get the student started but only to spark some creative thinking. Let students tussle with these matters for awhile. If frustration becomes apparent, give some help in the form of possible exploration.

3. Have students work in small, cooperative groups. Ideas for possible procedures can be shared and discussed. Try to see that ideas are not monopolized by one person in the group and that real sharing is taking place.

4. Provide students with ideas and lists of potential resources to use in investigating the problem. When technical procedures are needed, let students recognize the need and call for assistance.

5. Resist telling students how to carry out the investigation. Although this will undoubtedly require more time, it will provide opportunities for reflection and deliberation by the students themselves and help to develop necessary investigative skills.

6. Add some meaningful questions at the end of the investigation. Do not stress obtaining the "right" answer but do emphasize analyzing why certain procedures were used, why certain hypotheses were tested, and why certain conclusions were drawn. The purpose of these questions is to cause students to think about their work, the decisions they made, and even the possible faulty pathways they took in arriving at a result.

The AAAS has argued for an open-ended approach in laboratory work rather than the use of the confirmatory approach that leaves students with an inaccurate view of the practice of science. Instead, it contributes to the notion that the purpose of experimentation is the verification of hypotheses rather than their refutation.

The Advent of Computerized Science Laboratories

Careful thought should be given to replacement of traditional laboratory experiments with computer simulations of the experiments. Certain skills used in traditional laboratory experiments are not capable of being developed or experienced in computer simulations. Such skill development as organizing and recording data, for example, may be taken over by the microcomputer, thereby eliminating that experience for students in the laboratory. When microcomputers are used in the laboratory, their usage should be carefully integrated into the curriculum, thus pro-

viding exposure to important aspects of computer technology while preserving concrete experiences provided by hands-on experiences.

Five skill categories are identified at another place in this chapter (pp. 192–193). Of the five, acquisitive, organizational, creative, manipulative, and communicative, it would seem very difficult to develop the skills of manipulation and communication through computer simulations. An additional skill, use of safe laboratory procedures, would also be nearly impossible to achieve.

A. Winders and B. Yates have commented on the replacement of hands-on laboratory experiments with computer simulations:

> In summary, the time honored hands-on science laboratories have, and will continue to provide essential academic and practical skills for our students. The use of computer technology, chosen carefully and used wisely, will be of great benefit in augmenting traditional laboratories. The challenge before us is to successfully balance the old and the new to gain the best both have to offer.[4]

Research on the Laboratory's Role in Science Teaching

Over the years science educators have examined the influence of the laboratory on achievement and other variables such as reasoning, critical thinking, understanding science, process skills, manipulative skills, interests, retention, and ability to do independent work, among others. Much of this research gave inconclusive results, but science teachers in general feel that the laboratory is a vital part of science teaching.

Joseph Novak described the problems graphically:

> The science laboratory has always been regarded as the place where students should learn the process of doing science. But summaries of research on the value of laboratory for learning science did not favor laboratory over lecture-demonstrations . . . and more recent studies also show an appalling lack of effectiveness of laboratory instruction. . . . Our studies showed that most students in laboratories gained little insight regarding the key science concepts involved or toward the process of knowledge construction.[5]

Some positive findings can be cited. Three studies done between 1969 and 1979 found that laboratory instruction increased student problem-solving abilities. Other researchers reported positive results encouraging cognitive development, introducing scientific ideas, giving concrete examples, and learning how to manipulate materials when working with disadvantaged students in the laboratory.[6]

Data from a national survey in 1978 show that laboratory work and hands-on science activities are not used optimally in science teaching. Many teachers say students are apathetic about laboratory work and that labs are difficult to stock, maintain, and control. However, it is not likely students will experience much of the nature, methods, and spirit of science without this important component of science teaching.

In Texas, the legislature in 1984 mandated that all secondary school science classes must have at least 40 percent of their time devoted to laboratory work. Prior to that date, science classroom teachers had not allocated that much time to laboratory instruction. The first reaction by the teachers was shock and anger. A study by Robert James confirmed that even two years later teachers had difficulty seeing the potential benefits of the mandate, were concerned about the impact of the rule on them, and felt that they have better ideas as to how they should use class time.[7]

Thus, while much lip service is commonly given to the value of laboratory work in science classes, many science teachers appear to discount its value when faced with the realities of organization, materials procurement, time constraints, and lack of familiarity with investigative approaches to laboratory instruction.

Skill Development in the Laboratory

The complaint has frequently been lodged against science teaching that students and teachers alike have difficulty in expressing exactly what the goals of science teaching should be.

In taking up this challenge, we will identify the types of skills that science students ought to be able to do better after having taken junior and senior high school science. We have listed five categories of skills: acquisitive, organizational, creative, manipulative, and communicative. No attempt is made to rank these categories in order of importance, or even to imply that any one category may be more important than any other. Within each of the categories, however, specific skills are listed in order of increasing difficulty. In general, those skills that require only the use of one's own unaided senses are simpler than those that require use of instruments or higher orders of manual and mental dexterity.

Categories of Skills

A. Acquisitive skills
1. Listening—being attentive, alert, questioning
2. Observing—being accurate, alert, systematic
3. Searching—locating sources, using several sources, being self-reliant, acquiring library skills
4. Inquiring—asking, interviewing, corresponding
5. Investigating—reading background information, formulating problems
6. Gathering data—tabulating, organizing, classifying, recording
7. Research—locating a problem, learning background, setting up experiments, analyzing data, drawing conclusions

B. Organizational skills
1. Recording—tabulating, charting, working systematically, working regularly, recording completely
2. Comparing—noticing how things are alike, looking for similarities, noticing identical features
3. Contrasting—noticing how things differ, looking for dissimilarities, noticing unlike features
4. Classifying—putting things into groups and subgroups, identifying categories, deciding between alternatives
5. Organizing—putting items in order, establishing a system, filing, labeling, arranging
6. Outlining—employing major headings and subheadings, using sequential, logical organization
7. Reviewing—picking out important items, memorizing, associating
8. Evaluating—recognizing good and poor features, knowing how to improve grades
9. Analyzing—seeing implications and relationships, picking out causes and effects, locating new problems

C. Creative skills
1. Planning ahead—seeing possible results and probable modes of attack, setting up hypotheses
2. Designing—creating a new problem, a new approach, a new device or system
3. Inventing—creating a method, device, or technique
4. Synthesizing—putting familiar things together in a new arrangement, hybridizing, drawing together

D. Manipulative skills
1. Using an instrument—knowing the instrument's parts, how it works, how to adjust it, its proper use for a given task, its limitations
2. Caring for an instrument—knowing how to store it, using proper settings, keeping it clean, handling it properly, knowing its rate capacity, transporting it safely
3. Demonstrating—setting up apparatus, making it work, describing parts and functions, illustrating scientific principles

4. Experimentation—recognizing a problem, planning a procedure, collecting data, recording data, analyzing data, drawing conclusions
5. Repair—repairing and maintaining equipment, instruments, etc.
6. Construction—making simple equipment for demonstrations and experimentation
7. Calibration—learning the basic information about calibration, calibrating a thermometer, balance, timer, or other instrument

E. Communication skills
1. Asking questions—learning to formulate good questions, to be selective in asking, to resort to own devices for finding answers whenever possible
2. Discussion—learning to contribute own ideas, listening to ideas of others, keeping on the topic, sharing available time equitably, arriving at conclusions
3. Explanation—describing to someone else clearly, clarifying major points, exhibiting patience, being willing to repeat
4. Reporting—orally reporting to a class or teacher in capsule form the significant material on a science topic
5. Writing—writing a report of an experiment or demonstration, not just filling in a blank but starting with a blank sheet of paper, describing the problem, the method of attack, the data collected, the methods of analysis, the conclusions drawn, and the implications for further work
6. Criticism—constructively criticizing or evaluating a piece of work, a scientific procedure or conclusion
7. Graphing—putting in graphical form the results of a study or experiment, being able to interpret the graph for someone else
8. Teaching—after becoming familiar with a topic or semi-expert in it, teaching the material to one's classmates in such a manner that it will not have to be retaught by the teacher

Is there a Need for Science Skill Development?

Courses in elementary and secondary schools should emphasize the processes of science as much as the concepts and generalizations. Understanding a process improves skill competencies, while learning how to learn requires adequate learning tools. In addition, students need confidence in their ability to perform the tasks needed in self-learning. Skill competency strengthens self-reliance.

Can Skill Development Be Guided Through a Graded Sequence of Difficulty—From Simple to Complex?

This progression is possible because of certain characteristics of skills themselves, such as level of difficulty and complexity. For example, skills requiring the use of unaided senses are usually simpler than those requiring the use of instruments. It is easier for students to use their unaided eyes to compare the colors of minerals than to operate a petrographic microscope to do the same thing at a higher level of sophistication. Also, groups of simple skills may be included in more difficult complex skills. Graphing, for example, requires competency in the simpler skills of counting, measuring, and using a ruler (instrument). In the same way, higher levels of learning—such as analysis, synthesis, and evaluation—require higher levels of skill proficiency.

Does Skill Development Enhance or Preclude Concept Development?

Growth in conceptual understanding is enhanced by expertise in skill usage. In teaching skills, concepts form the vehicle by which the skills are learned. One cannot learn a skill in a void—there must be substantive information on which to operate. The skill of comparing, for example, is useless unless there are things to compare. In the same context, a hierarchy of skills forms a framework to which concepts can be attached. As one learns increasingly sophisticated skills, the subject matter (concepts) can be adapted and changed as required.

Can Achievement of Skill Competencies Be Tested?

There is ample evidence that skill achievements can be structured in behavioral terms. Performance can be observed and evaluated. Various performance levels of individual skills can be graded on a continuum from minimum to maximum success. Not only is it possible for teachers to create testing situations using performance objectives, but it is equally possible to provide self-evaluation opportunities for students to gain knowledge of their own progress and levels of performance.

What Are the Implications of the Skill-Development Approach in the Science Classroom?

Conditions necessary for success when emphasizing the skill or process goals are:

1. Time must be provided for practice and experience in the skills being developed. One does not become proficient without practice and drill.

2. Teachers must clearly understand the skill objectives. Planning must revolve around these objectives rather than traditional content goals alone.

3. Ample materials must be available. There must be a responsive environment permitting students to operate with the materials of science.

4. A variety of conceptual materials may be selected to facilitate skill development. Most conceptual themes or topics provide ample opportunities for teaching varied skills. In planning for teaching, however, it is important to concentrate on a few skills in any particular lesson.

5. Evaluation emphasis must be placed on performance or behavioral terms, not mere factual memorization or recitation. The superficial coverage of content must be de-emphasized and performance and depth of understanding brought to the foreground.

Mere identification of skills to be taught is only a first step in the realization of a science objective. To aid in skill development and ultimate mastery of the desired skills, the teacher must devise suitable teaching plans and student activities. In this type of learning, learning by doing is an important maxim. Pupils must be involved in activities that give repeated practice in the desired skills. The laboratory becomes an important facility at this point because most of the skills involve procedures that, to a greater or lesser extent, require materials and apparatus.

A sample lesson, oriented toward skill development, is given in the "Teaching Science Activity: Teaching Inquiry Skills" in the Appendix, p. 452.

Organizing Laboratory Work

Effectiveness of the laboratory experience is directly related to the amount of students' individual participation. Such participation means active involvement in the experiment with definite responsibilities for its progress and success. In theory the ideal arrangement would be to have each student wholly responsible for conducting the experiment from start to finish. In this way the preliminary planning, gathering materials, preparation of apparatus, designing the method, collecting data, analyzing results, and drawing conclusions are unmistakably the work of the individual student, with a maximum level of learning.

In reality, for certain students maximum learning may be achieved by working in pairs or very small groups. With good cooperation and shared duties, the stimulation of pair or small-group activity may be beneficial. In group work, a shy student may be stimulated into action and thought processes not possible when working alone. An extroverted student may assume directive and leadership qualities not

developed in individual work. The science teacher must be aware of these possibilities and plan the methodology of laboratory work accordingly. There should be opportunities in the laboratory to provide experiences using both arrangements. Avoiding stereotyped and inflexible arrangements should be of concern to the teacher of laboratory sciences.

Experiments will vary greatly in complexity. Even in a typical laboratory science, such as chemistry, experiments may be no more than carrying out a preplanned exercise of observation and data-gathering, or they may be as extensive and demanding as research on a problem whose solution is totally unknown. Arrangements for laboratory work must accommodate these extremes. Students of general science in the junior high school may need more of the exercise type of experiment to gain the skills needed for complex experiments. However, they should also be given opportunities to work on true experiments so that they might sense the joy of discovery in the same way as a practicing scientist.

The Use of Laboratory Assistants

Preparations for laboratory work require exorbitant amounts of time on the part of the conscientious science teacher. Ordering materials, providing for their storage, inventorying, repairing equipment, and preparing for laboratory experiments daily are a tremendous drain on the science teacher's time and energy. Some teachers have developed systems where student laboratory assistants are used to perform many of the tasks needed to carry on successful laboratory programs. One teacher has prepared a handbook for laboratory assistants included here to illustrate the organization of such a program.[8] Students are given credit for participation.

Handbook for Laboratory Assistants

Philosophy
Each laboratory assistant should constantly be working to make the Science Department more successful. There are definite responsibilities, duties, and dangers involved in the program for assistants. The department of science depends on you to a great extent. It is expected that each assistant is to be trusted and relied upon to perform his/her duties properly without the necessity of close supervision.

Responsibilities and Duties
It is the purpose of the Laboratory Assistant Program to aid science teachers, help maintain and organize the equipment and supplies of the department, and to improve the science program. Specifically, this includes:

1. the care and organization of the stockroom,
2. the preparation of laboratory exercises and demonstrations for teachers,
3. the preparation of papers, information sheets, class lists and other clerical work for the teachers,
4. the inventorying of supplies,
5. the correction of papers for teachers, and
6. the preparation of charts, posters, signs and labeling of shelves, etc.

Required Individual Project

In all classes, you will have tests and homework but in the Laboratory Assistants Program an individual project is required instead. One project is required each semester, or a partially completed project will be accepted the first semester if the project is extremely complex and permission has been given in advance.

Project Proposal (Plan)

The end of the first quarter a proposal should be submitted. If accepted by the science department, the student will then take data in the experiment.

The Project:

The project should include a substantial report discussing the nature of the project, theories, procedure, data, etc. The report is due the last day of the semester.

Special Short Courses

Classes on special skills will be conducted at the weekly meetings to improve your abilities.

1. Handling glassware I (cleaning)
2. Handling glassware II (cutting, bending, and assembling)
3. Preparation of solutions (molarity, normality)
4. Safety in the laboratory
5. Analytical weighing
6. Setting up a biology lab
7. Setting up a chemistry lab

Grading

Grades will be determined and recorded objectively. A conscientious student should receive A or B in science. However, it is possible to receive a lower grade for unsatisfactory performance. Grades will be based on the following items:

Required Projects: Each laboratory assistant will be required to complete one project each semester. This project may be in any area of science.

Special Projects: Each laboratory assistant should be constantly working to make the science department better. Any ideas that you may have for improving the department will be considered a special pro-

ject when organized and completed by the student. Projects of a student's own initiative must be cleared through a faculty member before starting.

Demonstrations: Teachers will assign demonstrations to the laboratory assistants whose responsibility it will be to find the equipment, set up the demonstration, and run it at least twice to make certain it works properly.

Laboratory Experiments: Teachers will assign experiments to be set up and tried by the laboratory assistants. This will include Physics, Biology, Chemistry, Advanced Biology, Biological Science Laboratory Practicals, and Freshman Science. Students are required to clean up the laboratory after the experiments.

Sections: Each laboratory assistant will have an assigned section in the preparation room and will be responsible for organizing, inventorying and seeing to the cleanliness of the section. The section assignments will be rotated on a regular basis.

Attendance at Meetings: Failure to come to a meeting may drop your grade.

Daily Grades: Teachers will be evaluating the laboratory assistants at all times for cooperation, fulfillment of responsibilities, and adherence to rules and regulations.

Log Book: Keep a notebook to include daily accomplishments, notes of meetings and special classes, to be turned in at the end of each quarter.

Point System	Maximum Points
Section grade =	100 points/week
Preparation of laboratory experiments =	100 points/experiment prepared
Special projects =	200 points/special project
Demonstrations =	100 points/demonstration (if performed for a class)

Semester Grade: Determined from the average of the two quarter grades and the semester special science project.

Meetings

All laboratory assistants are required to attend all meetings since this is a credit course.

Meeting Schedule: Noon meetings every other week on Monday. All students must be present at 12:00 noon. Bring your lunch.

Seventh period meetings on the week when there are no noon meetings (Tuesday, 7th period at 2:10 to 3:05). These meetings are for organizing sections, working on special projects, classes, and individual projects.

Procedure for Preparing a Chemistry Experiment

   I. Obtain experiment number and approximate date it is to be ready

II. Preparation
  a. Read experiment in laboratory manual
  b. Read directions in teacher's manual
    1. Equipment needed
    2. Precautions
    3. Laboratory hints
III. Setup
  a. Check all chemicals, etc.
     (Report anything not available in proper quantities)
  b. Check to see if solutions are old
  c. Make all necessary solutions in proper quantities
  d. Make one set of chemicals per table. Label solutions with formula and concentration. Use correct size bottles.
  e. If experiment has unknown, prepare a key to unknowns to be turned in
IV. Perform Experiment
  a. Make certain experiment is completely set up
  b. Check to see if proper results were obtained
  c. Record data
V. Experiment report ready
VI. Clean up all glassware and put away all materials after experiment is completed.

Procedure for Preparation of Demonstrations

I. Find a demonstration to prepare
  a. Use any source you can find
  b. Consult with a science teacher
  c. Use special demonstration books in science department
II. Read demonstration carefully
III. Organize, collect all material necessary
IV. Try demonstration, perfect it, be certain that it works
V. Find out when teachers could utilize demonstration
VI. Store chemicals in proper place for safekeeping, and clean up work area
VII. Perform demonstration
  a. Give demonstration for proper class, or
  b. Bring in all material for the demonstration (on a cart) for the teacher at the proper time
  c. Don't leave demonstration or experiment equipment lying around if you don't complete it in one period—always put material in proper place even if overnight.

Orienting Students for Laboratory Work

In general, students of the sciences look forward to a laboratory class with pleasant anticipation. Being pragmatic by nature, they sense that this is truly science and that an exciting experience awaits them. This attitude, most prevalent in the junior high school, must be carefully nurtured and guided as the student progresses to more rigorous disciplines. If laboratory work becomes a bore because of excessively rigid formality, unexciting exercises, cookbook techniques, or for whatever reasons, the student will probably have been lost as a potential science participant. An atmosphere of excitement, curiosity, interest, and enthusiasm for science should be encouraged in the laboratory, tempered by care and restraint in use of apparatus and diligence in the tasks assigned. Obviously, a hands-off policy regarding equipment cannot be adopted, nor can a complete laissez-faire attitude be condoned. Respect for the problem, the materials, and the probable results of experimentation must be developed. The laboratory experience is but one vehicle by which the objectives of science teaching are developed. Suitably carried out, it can be one of the most effective methods of teaching and learning.

Orientation for laboratory work may involve creating a suitable frame of mind for investigating a problem. The problem must appear real to students and worthy of study. They must have some knowledge of possible methods of attack. They should know what equipment or apparatus is needed and be familiar with its use.

They must have time to work on the problem. In a given situation, the science teacher may need to give attention to one or more of these factors to begin students on their laboratory investigations.

The Place of Discussion in Laboratory Work

In recent years, there has been a trend toward placing laboratory work at the very beginning of a new unit of study. The laboratory guidebook or manual is designed to identify problems requiring observation and solution. Students perform the assigned tasks or devise procedures to arrive at a solution to the problem. While doing so, they discover the need for further information to explain their observations. They are motivated to read a textbook, search for information in a sourcebook or handbook, read supplementary material, or consult their teacher.

Laboratory work is followed by class discussion or question periods. During these activities, student questions are answered, observed phenomena are clarified, and certain misconceptions may be discussed. Other activities—such as problem assignments, projects, extra reading, reports, tests, and demonstrations—may follow in their proper context as part of the teaching and learning process.

In this method it is likely that more than half of the total class time is spent in laboratory activities. Follow-up sessions become extremely important.

The teacher usually must ascertain the accuracy of the learned concepts, correct misconceptions, and promote maximum learning more than in a conventional course. At the same time, students are more directly involved in the task and may be more highly motivated than they would otherwise be.

Laboratory Work in the Junior High School

Extension of laboratory practices to the junior high school is occurring with greater frequency. Facilities for effective laboratory work are being built into modern junior high schools and students of this age level are beginning to experience laboratory work on a regular, planned basis.

Junior high school students are enthusiastic participants in the laboratory method of teaching. Curiosity and a buoyant approach to learning make this group responsive to the laboratory method, and proper teacher guidance can make this method a fruitful one. Because junior high school science leads to more rigorous and laboratory-oriented sciences in the senior high school, it is worthwhile to consider its contributions to more effective learning when the student reaches biology, chemistry, or physics. It is reasonable to assume that certain attitudes, knowledge, and skills learned in the junior high school contribute to better and perhaps more rapid learning in the senior high school.

Following is a suggested list of basic knowledge and skills that might be developed in fifth- through ninth-grade science and that are considered desirable prerequisites for senior high science:

1. To understand the purposes of the laboratory in the study of science
2. To understand and be familiar with the simple tools of the laboratory
3. To understand and use the metric system in simple measurement and computation
4. To attain the understanding necessary to properly report observations of an experiment
5. To keep neat and accurate records of laboratory experiments
6. To understand the operation of simple ratios and proportions
7. To understand the construction and reading of simple graphs
8. To understand and use the simpler forms of exponential notation
9. To understand the proper use and operation of the Bunsen burner
10. To use the calculator for simple operations
11. To understand and demonstrate the use of a trip balance

12. To work with glass tubing in performing laboratory experiments
13. To keep glassware and equipment clean
14. To put together simple equipment in performing laboratory experiments
15. To measure accurately in linear, cubic, and weight units
16. To use the microcomputer for data gathering, record keeping, word processing, and data storage

Laboratory work in the middle and junior high school can be broadened to include such features as out-of-doors observations, excursions, and certain types of project activities, as well as conventional experimentation in laboratory surroundings. Systematic nighttime observations of planets, constellations, meteors, the moon, and other astronomical objects may properly be considered laboratory work. Similarly, meteorological observations and experiments involving record keeping and correlations of data are included under this heading. Excursions for collecting purposes, observations of topographical features, studies of pond life, and ecological investigations are true laboratory work. The narrow connotation of laboratory work as something that takes place only in a specially designed room called a laboratory must be avoided in the junior high and middle school sciences.

The range and variety of activities performed by students in laboratory work make it necessary to use many evaluation methods. A teacher of science must be aware of these prerequisites and alert to new possibilities as well. Increasing emphasis on laboratory methods is almost certain to broaden, rather than narrow, the range of individual differences among students. Suitable means must be devised for evaluating the progress and achievement of these students in their laboratory experiences.

■ SAFETY PRECAUTIONS IN THE LABORATORY

An inevitable result of greater student participation in laboratory work is increased exposure to potentially dangerous apparatus and materials. Instead of viewing this fact as a deterrent to the laboratory method of teaching, the alert and dedicated science teacher will approach the problem realistically and will take the proper precautions to avoid accidents among students in the laboratory.

Accidents and injuries often occur because students lack knowledge of the proper techniques and procedures. These techniques can be taught in advance if the teacher plans properly. Certain minimum standards of acceptable procedures may be demanded of students before they are allowed to work in the laboratory. The motivation to engage in laboratory work is usually strong enough to overcome students' reluctance to develop the requisite skills, particularly if they are convinced of the inherent dangers and the need for proper safety precautions.

According to the National Safety Council, about 32,000 school-related accidents occur each school year; about 5,000 of these are science-related. Junior high grades 7–9 experience the highest frequency of accidents, while elementary grades report the lowest accident frequency. Another source estimates one major accident per forty students per year in laboratory settings throughout the country.[9]

A 1970 study on high school science safety revealed the following:

- Advanced placement groups have the most accidents.
- Class enrollment and laboratory space have a significant relationship to laboratory accidents; the higher the classroom enrollment and the smaller the laboratory space, the higher the frequency of accidents.
- Fewer accidents occur when individual laboratory stations exist.
- The chemistry class is more prone than other classes to laboratory accidents.[10]

The prevention of accidents can be accomplished through a positive science safety educational program that emphasizes teacher and student awareness of the potential dangers in science-related activities. *SAFETY FIRST* should be the basic motto for the school science program. However, safety considerations should seldom rule out a science lesson. Effective planning can sometimes be used to capitalize on safety problems. Developing and maintaining positive attitudes toward safety require continual efforts in safety education. It is hoped that safety training in the science program will instill in the student the importance of safety in all areas of work and play.[11]

Some general laboratory skills that will prepare the student to work safely are these:

1. Ability to handle glass tubing—cutting, bending, fire-polishing, drawing tubing into capillaries, inserting tubing into rubber stoppers, and removing tubing from rubber stoppers
2. Ability to heat test tubes of chemicals—knowledge of proper rate of heating, direction, use of test tube racks, etc.
3. Ability to handle acids—pouring, proper use of stoppers to avoid contamination, dilution in water, return of acid bottles to designated shelves, etc.

4. Ability to test for presence of noxious gases safely
5. Ability to treat acid spillage or burns from caustic solutions
6. Ability to operate fire extinguishers
7. Ability to set up gas generators properly
8. Ability to use standard carpenter's tools
9. Ability to use dissecting equipment, scalpels, etc.

An excellent publication dealing with safety in the secondary school science classroom is published by the NSTA.[12] In a section entitled "Suggestions for a Safe Science Program," the publication provides many excellent guidelines for teachers and students in science classes.

A survey of accidents in high school chemistry laboratories in California, reported by Robert McComber, showed that accidents were usually caused by poor laboratory techniques. There were more serious accidents in large classes, and accidents were more frequent when horseplay was involved. Forty percent of the accidents occurred among students who were above average in scientific inquisitiveness. The types of accidents that most frequently had serious results were explosions and burns from phosphorus; the easy availability of dangerous chemicals used occasionally in the normal chemistry course seemed to contribute to accidents as well.[13]

The following safety precautions to be observed in the chemistry laboratory may be put into effect in a school by discussing them with the students, supplying copies for students' notebooks, and posting them in a prominent place in the laboratory.

A List of Safety Precautions in the Chemistry Laboratory

The work you do in the chemistry laboratory is a very important part of your chemistry course. Here you will learn to observe experiments and draw your own conclusions about your observations. The following is a list of safety rules to follow in making your laboratory work as safe and efficient as possible:

1. Observe all instructions given by the teacher. Ask for help when you need it.
2. In case of an accident, report to your teacher immediately.
3. Be careful in using flames. Keep clothing away from the flame, and do not use flames near inflammable liquids.
4. Follow the directions carefully when handling all chemicals.
5. If acids or bases are spilled, wash immediately with plenty of water. Be sure you know where the neutralizing solution is located in the laboratory. Ask your teacher how to use it.

6. Read the labels on all reagents very carefully. Make a habit of reading each label twice on any reagent used in an experiment.

7. Dispose of waste materials in the proper receptacles. Solid materials should be placed in special crocks provided for the purpose.

8. Be sure you know the location and proper usage of the fire extinguishers and fire blankets provided in the laboratory.

9. Consider the laboratory a place for serious work. There is no excuse for horseplay or practical jokes in a science laboratory.

■ SAFETY AND THE LAW

The principal is responsible for the overall supervision of the entire school's safety program. The science teacher is similarly responsible for the supervision of safety in the science class.

Individual teachers can be held liable for negligent acts resulting in personal injury to students. Some school boards have liability coverage that might support teachers if legal action is brought against them. Teachers should inquire about the nature of local board coverage and/or their own personal liability coverage. The extent of a teacher's liability is discussed in the NSTA publication, *Safety in the Secondary Science Classroom.*[14]

■ SUMMARY

A demonstration has been defined as showing something to a person or group. The techniques of planning a demonstration involve determining the concepts and principles to be taught, deciding on activities, gathering the materials, practicing the demonstration, outlining the questions to be asked, and deciding on the evaluational methods to be used.

Plan a demonstration with the intention of using it again . A teacher, in giving a demonstration, should be aware of visibility, audibility, and all of the aspects that go with good staging. The teacher should have zest, present the demonstration inductively, ask inquiry-oriented questions, give positive techniques, and summarize and evaluate the demonstration. A demonstration may be conducted by the teacher, by the teacher and students together, by a group of students, by an individual student, or by a guest. More attention should be given to demonstrations other than those presented by the teacher, with accompanying comments. Silent demonstrations offer a different approach and emphasize observational techniques.

Equipment should be stored so that it is easily located for future demonstrations. Special equipment can often be secured from local industries without cost. The overhead projector, microprojector, and TV screen are excellent teaching aids for demonstrations.

Individual experimentation is usually a more desirable teaching technique than are demonstrations, but demonstrations have the advantage of economy of time and money, allow for greater direction by the teacher, and provide certain safety precautions. Demonstrations should contribute to the higher levels of learning—those requiring critical thinking and creativity.

Laboratory work in the junior and senior high school is constantly changing. From the emphasis on verification experiments in the traditional mode, the student is now invited to inquire into or investigate a problem. Laboratory experience becomes the initial introduction to a new topic of subject matter, followed by discussion, reading, and further experimentation. The experiment may lead to new problems that warrant investigation.

The junior high school is becoming increasingly oriented toward a laboratory approach. Not only does this approach give students an early start in learning science methods, but introduces and practices certain skills that will have value in senior high school sciences.

With more of the responsibility for learning in the laboratory being allocated to the student, the matter of safety becomes even more important. The science teacher must carefully train students in the use of laboratory apparatus and materials. This training may precede actual work in the laboratory or be an intrinsic part of the laboratory work early in the students' experience.

The promise of science for the future continues. A breakthrough has been achieved in which students at last have become participants in the search for knowledge, not mere recipients of facts and generalizations dispensed by authoritative teachers and textbooks. The laboratory is the key instrument in science teaching.

■ REFERENCES

1. E. S. Obourn, *Aids for Teaching Science Observation— Basis for Effective Science Learning*, Office of Education Publication No. 29024 (Washington, DC: U.S. Government Printing Office, 1961).

2. Paul F. Brandwein and Joseph J. Schwab, *The Teaching of Science as Enquiry* (Cambridge: Harvard University Press, 1962), pp. 52–53.

3. William H. Leonard, "A Recipe for Uncookbooking Laboratory Investigations," *Journal of College Science Teaching, 21* (November 1991): 84–87.

4. A. Winders and B. Yates, "The Traditional Science Laboratory Versus a Computerized Science Laboratory: Think Carefully Before Supplanting the Old with the

New," *Journal of Computers in Science and Mathematics Teaching*, 9(Spring 1990): 11–15.

5. Joseph D. Novak, "Learning Science and the Science of Learning," *Studies in Science Education*, 15: 77–101.

6. Patricia Blosser, "The Role of the Laboratory in Science Teaching," *School Science and Mathematics*, 83(2) (February 1983).

7. Robert K. James, "The Concerns of Secondary Science Teachers About Required Amounts of Laboratory Instruction," *School Science and Mathematics, 91* (February 1991): 73–76.

8. Clifford Hofwolt, *Laboratory Science Course Handbook for Laboratory Assistants,* (University of Northern Colorado, Greeley: Department of Science Education mimeograph, 1968).

9. George J. O'Neill, Television Series Program #1, *Safety in the Science Laboratory* (Sponsored by the NE Tennessee Section of the American Chemical Society in cooperation with WSJK, Knoxville, TN, 1975).

10. John Wesley Brennan, "An Investigation of Factors Related to Safety in the High School Science Program," Ed.D dissertation, University of Denver, Colorado, 1970 (ED 085 179).

11. *Safety First in Science Teaching*, Division of Science, North Carolina Dept. of Public Instruction, Raleigh, NC (1977).

12. NSTA, *Safety in the Secondary Science Classroom* (Washington, DC: NSTA Subcommittee on Safety, 1978).

13. Robert McComber, "Chemistry Accidents in High School," *Journal of Chemical Education* (July 1961), pp. 367–68.

14. NSTA, *Safety in the Secondary Science Classroom.*

Chapter 14

MODELS FOR EFFECTIVE SCIENCE TEACHING

Over the years, research and curriculum development have shown that effective instruction is much more than the presentation of a concept, process, or skill.[1] In simplest terms, one must think carefully about the objectives; beginning, middle, and end of the lesson; and very important, the use of materials to engage the learners and develop scientific concepts, processes, and skills. Kevin Wise and James Okey summarize the effects of various science teaching strategies on achievement as follows:

> The effective science classroom appears to be one in which students are kept aware of instructional objectives and receive feedback on their progress toward these objectives. Students get opportunities to physically interact with instructional materials and engage in varied kinds of activities. Alteration of instructional material or classroom procedure has occurred where it is thought that the change might be related to increased impact. The teacher bases a portion of the verbal interactions that occur on some plan, such as the cognitive level or positioning of questions asked during a lesson. The effective science classroom reflects considerable planning.[2]

This summary underscores the importance of objectives, feedback, use of materials, and varied activities. We would also have you note that there are both planned and flexible components of instruction. You must know where you are going, and you must be able to detour in the areas of interest, motivation, and relevance for students.

Publication of the *National Science Education Standards*[3] places *Science as Inquiry* very high on science teachers' instructional agenda. The standards on inquiry focus science teachers' attention on developing students' abilities to use observations and knowledge as they construct scientific explanations. The national standards incorporate the traditional processes of science with instructional strategies that require students to use scientific knowledge and evidence from their investigations to formulate scientific explanations. The national standards shift instructional emphasis toward empirical criteria, critical thinking about evidence, and scientific reasoning in the construction of explanations.

Figures 14–1 and 14–2 summarize the inquiry abilities in the national standards. These standards do not represent an instructional model. They do present learning outcomes that should be based in student investigations.

- Identify appropriate questions for scientific investigations.
- Design and conduct a scientific investigation.
- Use appropriate tools and technologies to gather, analyze, and interpret data.
- Construct explanations and models using evidence.
- Think critically and logically about the relationships between evidence and explanations.
- Recognize and analyze alternative explanations and procedures.
- Communicate scientific procedures and explanations.

FIGURE 14–1
Science as Inquiry: Grades 5–8

- Identify questions and concepts that guide scientific investigations.
- Design and conduct a full scientific investigation.
- Use technologies to improve investigations and communications.
- Construct and revise scientific explanations and models using logic and evidence.
- Communicate and defend a scientific argument.
- Analyze a historical or contemporary scientific inquiry.

FIGURE 14–2
Science as Inquiry: Grades 9–12

The next section outlines models that will help you organize for effective instruction. These constitute the planned sequence of instruction. The flexible component is something you will develop with experience in science teaching. The chapter concludes with a general instructional model that incorporates many elements of other models. This model is presented in detail and is recommended as a model that is both usable and effective for science teaching.

■ DESIGNING YOUR INSTRUCTIONAL SEQUENCE

Using the textbook, facilitating learning, grouping students, and sequencing instruction are examples of factors you must consider in designing an instructional sequence. Many talented individuals have considered instructional strategies and sequences that you can use. This section reviews some of the prominent models for science teaching.

Using Textbooks Effectively

You may think it unusual to have a section on using textbooks, but textbooks are central to science teaching. In spite of some common myths, textbooks in and of themselves are not bad; most good teachers use textbooks, and textbooks can enhance learning.

The majority of teachers use textbooks. In a 1985 survey, Iris Weiss found that 93 percent of science teachers in grades 7-12 used a published textbook.[4] Interestingly, the majority of science teachers did not consider textbook quality to be a significant problem in their schools. The most highly rated aspects of science textbooks were their organization, clarity, and reading level. However, a number of individuals and groups do see problems with the quality and usability of textbooks.[5,6,7,8]

Since the 1960s, the prevailing wisdom in science education has been that programs should be activity-based and not textbook dominated. Research shows that the opposite is the case—teachers are using fewer activities and relying more on the textbook.[9] Use of textbooks is necessitated by the need for science teachers to plan for several subjects, the reduction of budgets, and the scheduling of science classes in nonlaboratory rooms.

Our purpose in this section is to assist you in becoming an intelligent user of the textbook—that is, to help you recognize the potentials and limitations of textbooks, and to use them to enhance learning. The section relies on the research and writing of Kathleen Roth and Charles Anderson of Michigan State University.[10]

Science teachers use textbooks in several ways. Textbooks help teachers make decisions about the curriculum. Questions about topics, activities of coverage, depth, sequence, and emphasis are answered by reference to the textbook. Keep in mind that although the textbook helps teachers make efficient decisions, they do not necessarily help them make the best decisions for students.

Textbooks help teachers select teaching strategies. Again, this use of textbooks has both advantages and disadvantages. The clear advantage is efficiency. It takes considerable effort to manage an activity-based program. It is much easier to have students read the textbook. The disadvantage is that reading the textbook may not facilitate student learning. We discuss this in detail later.

Textbooks provide scientific explanations. Descriptions of key concepts and information are usually straightforward and succinct in textbooks. Providing students with good descriptions of scientific ideas is difficult; it is especially difficult when teachers are teaching out of their discipline. So textbooks can be a useful resource for scientific explanations.

You can see that textbooks are quite helpful. Given the function of textbooks, it is easy to see why the majority of teachers rely on them. What do science teachers need to understand in order to use textbooks more effectively? First in importance is to understand how students use textbooks.

We have pointed out that students have prior knowledge about science. Often this knowledge is inadequate or incomplete when compared to true scientific knowledge, thus the label leads to misconceptions. Students' prior knowledge is important to understand when considering students' reading strategies. What happens when students are asked to read a text that has explanations about phenomena that are incompatible with their current explanations? Students seem to use several strategies to accommodate the difference between their conceptions and those presented in textbooks.[11] Here are the different strategies students use.

Reading for Conceptual Change

A few students use the text to change current conceptions to more appropriately scientific conceptions. As students confront concepts that conflict with their own ideas, they give up their concepts and assimilate those presented as formal scientific explanations in the textbook.

Overrelying on Prior Knowledge and Distorting Text to Make It Compatible with Prior Knowledge

Here students use elaborate strategies to link prior knowledge with text knowledge. These students genuinely try to make sense of the text and integrate text ideas with their own knowledge. Still, they just cannot give up their own strongly held ideas. Theirs is the strategy of linking scientific knowledge with their own ideas.

Overrelying on Facts in the Text with an Additional Notion of Learning— Separating Prior Knowledge and Text Knowledge

These students focus on the memorization of vocabulary and facts. They do not relate the facts and

STEPS FOR DESIGNING LESSONS

USING TEXTBOOKS EFFECTIVELY

1. Direct students' attention to important concepts.
2. Challenge students' thinking and misconceptions.
3. Ask students to construct explanations of everyday phenomena.
4. Probe student responses.
5. Provide accurate feedback to students.
6. Construct alternative representations of textbook explanations.
7. Make explicit the connections between textbook explanations and student misconceptions.
8. Select activities that create conceptual conflict and encourage conceptual understanding.

vocabulary to each other or to their prior knowledge. Reading for conceptual change is not possible.

Overrelying on Details in the Text— Separation of Prior Knowledge and Text Knowledge

These students pay great attention to the text. They attend to the details, as opposed to concepts, and fail to attach any meaning to details. The details, most often specialized vocabulary of science, are isolated words that have no relationship to anything. These students think they understand science if they are able to decode the words and identify details in the textbook.

Overrelying on Prior Knowledge and Ignoring Text Knowledge

Some students rely on their own experiential knowledge to interpret the textbook. If asked about text knowledge, they equate textbook explanations with their own explanations, ones that have nothing to do with scientific explanations. To them the text makes sense in terms of their prior knowledge.

What can teachers do? There are a few recommendations for effective use of science textbooks. The principles are based on studies of text-based science teaching[12] and understandings gained from studies of students' reading strategies.[13]

Directing Students' Attention to Important Concepts

Textbooks typically contain numerous ideas and vocabulary words. This situation causes students to memorize facts and lists of words rather than focus on strategies that will result in conceptual change. Focusing students on central issues that are problematic, keeping lessons related to the concepts, and

keeping vocabulary to a minimum will contribute to conceptual change.

Challenging Students' Thinking and Misconceptions

Textbooks are written from a scientist's perspective. Seldom do textbook authors consider students' perspectives as they organize textbooks. Still, students will interpret text material in terms of their prior knowledge. Effective teachers identify the differences between students' concepts and those in the textbook. By asking questions and challenging students' thinking, teachers can initiate the process of conceptual change. The questions should be stated in relation to ideas in the textbooks, or students may not make the connections.

Asking Students to Construct Explanations of Everyday Phenomena

Questions in textbooks seldom have students apply knowledge to everyday experiences. Encouraging students to compare, challenge, and debate each other's explanations are all methods that result in conceptual change.

Probing Student Responses

Listen for students' thinking rather than for right answers. Ask questions that will have students justify and clarify their responses.

Providing Accurate Feedback to Students

Teachers typically respond to student answers by praising correct answers and ignoring incorrect answers. The greatest concern is the latter. Although teachers think this approach helps students, in actuality it does not. Giving positive feedback for any answer encourages students to maintain their current conceptions and to use ineffective strategies to find correct answers. You should give clear and accurate feedback about the strengths and limitations of student responses.

Constructing Alternative Representations of Textbook Explanations That Make Explicit the Relationships Between Scientific Explanations and Student Misconceptions

Give the students time to struggle with explanations in the textbook. Most textbooks are packed with explanations that are presented in one way only, and then the text moves to the next explanation. There is little time and variation to help students consider alternative explanations and construct new concepts. After students have time to grapple with concepts, you should provide different representations of the ideas. The representations will be most effective if they clearly contrast the students' and the text's explanations.

Selecting Activities That Create Conceptual Conflict and Encourage Conceptual Understanding

Selection of activities is based on criteria such as student interest, a sense of important science concepts, and the need to do inquiry-oriented activities. Discrepant events are good examples of the types of activities that create conceptual change. In the end, doing activities is not as important as helping students make sense of their experiences.

In the Exploration phase of the learning cycle, students are actively involved in exploring new materials and ideas.

■ THE LEARNING CYCLE

The learning cycle originated in the 1960s with the work of Robert Karplus and his colleagues during the development of the Science Curriculum Improvement Study (SCIS). Originally, the learning cycle was based on the theoretical insights of Piaget, but it is consistent with other theories of learning, such as those developed by Ausubel.[14]

There are three phases to the learning cycle. *Exploration*, *Invention*, and *Discovery* were first used in the SCIS program. Later, these terms were modified to *Exploration*, *Concept Introduction*, and *Concept Application*. Although other terms have been used for the three original phases, the goals and pedagogy of the phases have remained similar.

During the first, or *Exploration*, phase of the learning cycle, students learn through their involvement and actions. New materials, ideas and relationships are introduced with minimal teacher guidance.

The goal is to allow students to apply previous knowledge, develop interests, and initiate and maintain a curiosity toward the materials. The materials should be carefully structured so involvement with them cannot help but engage concepts and ideas fundamental to the lesson's objectives. During the exploration, teachers can also assess students' understanding and background relative to the lesson's objectives.

Introduction of the concept is the next phase. Various teaching strategies can be used to introduce the concept. For example, a demonstration, film, textbook, or lecture can be used. This phase should relate directly to the initial Exploration and clarify concepts central to the lesson. Although the Exploration was minimally teacher-directed, this phase tends to be more teacher-guided.

In the next phase, *Application*, students apply the newly learned concepts to other examples. The teaching goal is to have students generalize or trans-

STEPS FOR DESIGNING LESSONS

APPLYING THE LEARNING CYCLE

Concept Exploration

1. Identify interesting objects, events, or situations that students can observe. Student experiences can occur in the classroom, laboratory, or field. Many instructional methods can be used to explore a concept.
2. Allow students time to explore the objects, events, or situations. During this experience, students may establish relationships, observe patterns, identify variables, and question events. In this phase, the unexpected can be used to your advantage. Students may have questions or experiences that motivate them to study what they have observed.
3. The primary aim of the exploration is to have students think about concepts associated with the lessons.

Concept Introduction

4. The teacher directs student attention to specific aspects of the exploration experience. Initially, the lesson should be clearly based on student explorations. In this phase, the key is to present the concepts in a simple, clear, and direct manner.

Concept Application

5. Identify different activities in which students extend the concepts in new and different situations. Several different activities will facilitate generalization of the concept by the students. Encourage students to identify patterns, discover relationships among variables, and reason through new problems.

---

fer ideas to other examples used as illustrations of the central concept. For some students, the period of psychological self-regulation, equilibration, and mental reorganization of concepts may take time. Having several activities where a concept is applied can provide the valuable time needed for learning. An excellent introduction to and science teaching examples of the learning cycle have been developed by Howard Birnie,[15] and Karplus and colleagues.[16]

John Renner and his colleagues examined the effectiveness of altering the sequence of the learning cycle. They found that the normal sequence (described above) is the optimum sequence for achievement of content knowledge.[17]

Anton Lawson has made important connections between research on student misconceptions and use of the learning cycle. Lawson suggests that use of the learning cycle provides opportunities for students to reveal prior knowledge (particularly, their misconceptions) and opportunities to argue and debate their ideas. This process can result in cognitive disequilibrium and the possibility of developing higher levels of reasoning.[18]

Lawson proposes three types of learning cycles: descriptive, empirical-inductive, and hypothetical-deductive. Although the sequence is similar to that described above, the difference among the types of learning cycles is the degree to which students gather data in a descriptive manner, or in a manner that empirically tests alternative explanations. In descriptive learning cycles, students observe natural phenomena, identify patterns, and seek similar patterns elsewhere. According to Lawson, little or no disequilibrium occurs in descriptive learning cycles.

Empirical-inductive learning cycles require students to explain phenomena, thus expressing any misconceptions and providing opportunities for dialogue and debate. Hypothetical-deductive learning cycles require students to make explicit statements of alternative explanations of phenomena. Higher order reasoning patterns are required to test alternative explanations.[19]

Cooperative Learning

As a science teacher, you will be in a position to structure lessons in several different ways. Most commonly, lessons are structured so students compete with one another for recognition and grades. You also might design your lessons so students can follow an individual approach, or learn on their own. There is a third option that lends itself to science teaching, especially when the laboratory is a central part of instruction. This is a cooperative approach where students are arranged in pairs or small groups to help each other learn the assigned material. David Johnson, Roger Johnson, and their colleagues have

■■■■■■■■■■■■■■■■■ **GUEST EDITORIAL** ■■■■■■■■■■■■■■■■■■■■■■

A Message to Teachers on Structuring Student Interactions in the Classroom

Roger Johnson
Professor of Science Education
University of Minnesota, Minneapolis
David Johnson
Professor of Social Psychology
University of Minnesota, Minneapolis

There are instances where traditional practice in schools has gone one way, while empirical research indicated that another course was more productive and desirable. Such is the case with the use of cooperative, competitive, and individualistic student-student interaction patterns for instruction. In the past forty years, competition among students has been emphasized in most American schools. In the past fifteen years, individualistic efforts toward achieving learning goals have been increasingly emphasized. The research indicates, however, that cooperative interaction among students would be more productive on a wide range of cognitive and affective instructional outcomes than either competitive or individualistic interaction patterns.

Perhaps the major reason for this discrepancy between educational practice and research is the fact that how students interact with one another has not been emphasized in the development of curriculum and in teacher preparation. The spotlight has been on the ways that students interact with materials and the role of the teacher; however, how students interact with each other during instruction has powerful and important effects on their learning and socialization.

There are three basic choices for student-student interaction patterns: competitive, individualistic, or cooperative. A competitive interaction pattern exists when students see that they can obtain their goals if and only if the other students with whom they are linked fail to obtain their goals. An example would be a spelling bee where students spell against each other to find the best speller in the class. Norm-referenced evaluation systems, such as rank-ordering students from best to worst or grading on a curve, set up competitive interaction between students. An individualistic interaction pattern exists when the achievement of students' learning goals are unrelated to the goal achievement of other students. An example of this we're-all-in-this-alone situation would be a spelling class where each student has his or her own set of words to learn and a criterion for measuring individual success, so that the achievement of one student has no effect on the achievement of another.

A cooperative interaction pattern exists when the students perceive that they can obtain their goal if and only if the other students with whom they are linked obtain their goals. An example of this sink-or-swim-together situation is a group of students working together as a spelling group, preparing each other to take the spelling test individually on Friday. Each student's score is the number of words his or her group spells correctly. In competition there is a negative interdependence in terms of goal attainment, in the individualistic situation there is independence between goal attainment, and in cooperation there is a positive interdependence in terms of goal attainment.

There are many research studies which have compared cognitive and affective results for students working cooperatively, competitively, and individualistically. The results indicate that, in comparison to competition and working individually, cooperation produces:

developed a substantial research base for the use of a cooperative learning model.[20] Over the years, the Johnsons also have developed the practical instructional approach based on their model. We base this discussion on their book *Circles of Learning: Cooperation in the Classroom.*[21] (We recommend that you read the guest editorial by David and Roger Johnson, "A Message to Teachers on Structuring Student Interactions in the Classroom.")

There are four basic elements in cooperative learning models. To be truly cooperative, small groups must be structured for *positive interdependence, face-to-face interactions, individual accountability,* and *use of interpersonal and small group skills.*

Positive interdependence is established when students perceive that they are in affirming and cooperative relationships with other members of their group. There are several ways of achieving positive interdependence. You can establish mutual goals for the group; establish a division of labor for a mutual task; divide materials, resources, or information to ensure cooperation among group members; assign

1. Higher achievement and longer retention of the material learned;
2. More positive attitudes about the subject matter and the teacher;
3. Higher self-esteem;
4. More effective use of social skills; and
5. More positive feelings about each other. (This *positive cathexis* works regardless of differences between students and has implications for the integration of different ethnic groups, main-streaming of handicapped students into regular classroom settings, and managing the heterogeneity present in every classroom.)

These results represent only a few of the many which have been researched, but they emphasize the powerful nature of cooperative learning. Furthermore, the importance of cooperative learning experiences goes beyond improving instruction and making teaching more satisfying and productive for teachers, although these are worthwhile goals. The ability of all students to cooperate with others is the keystone to building and maintaining friendships, stable families, career success, neighborhood and community membership, and contributions to a society. Knowledge and skills are of no use if the students cannot apply them in cooperative interaction with other people.

With strong empirical support for cooperative learning and the fact that it makes sense for students growing up in society, we must be careful not to overgeneralize. The research into cooperative learning does not say that having students work together cooperatively is a magic wand that will solve all classroom problems. It does say that those problems probably have a better chance of being solved in a cooperative than in a competitive or an individualistic setting, but it is not reasonable to expect hyperactive students to suddenly become calm or low mathematics students to suddenly master all the material. It does give the teacher a powerful edge to go to work on the problems of orchestrating effective instruction for students.

We recommend that all three interaction patterns be used in a classroom setting. Students must learn how to compete appropriately and enjoy the competition, win or lose; they must learn how to work independently and take responsibility for following through on a task; and they must learn how to work with one another effectively in cooperative relationships. Each of these interaction patterns must be used appropriately and integrated effectively within instruction, realizing that cooperation is the most powerful of the three.

There is little doubt that teachers who master the strategies needed to set up appropriate interaction patterns, maximizing the use of cooperation, will have a powerful and positive effect on their classroom learning environment. This addition to the teacher's repertoire does not mean a new curriculum. It takes only a few minutes to make clear to students the kind of student-student interaction that is expected, with some additional time needed at first to teach the appropriate interaction skills to the students.

The initial effort on the teacher's part and the time needed to carefully structure student-student interaction are effort and time well spent. It would be exciting to see the gap between the research findings and traditional classroom practice disappear so the students would say, "School is a place where we work together to learn and share our ideas, argue our point of view, and help each other find the most appropriate answers and understand the materials. Sometimes we have a fun competition and sometimes we work individually, but most of the time we learn together."

students different roles, such as recorder, researcher, organizer; or create joint rewards for the group.

Face-to-face interactions among students is a central aspect of cooperative learning. Cooperative work and verbal exchanges among students form the learning experience. Though they work in groups, students must still be individually accountable for learning the assigned materials. Cooperative learning is not having one person do a report for two or three others. The aim is for all students to learn the material. To accomplish this, it is necessary to determine the level of mastery among students and then assign groups to maximize achievement.

Finally, students have to learn to use interpersonal and small group skills. Students are not naturally skilled at cooperative learning. They must learn the social skills of collaboration; they must be given time and experience in collaboration; and they must be taught to analyze the group process to see if effective working relationships have been maintained.

Science teachers will have to teach students the skills of cooperation. This statement leads to the obvious questions, "What skills need to be taught?" and "How does one teach these skills?" We refer again to *Circles of Learning: Cooperation in the Classroom.* In answer to the first question, there are four levels of cooperative skills. First, there are *forming skills*: that is, the basic skills needed to organize a group and establish norms of behavior for cooperative interaction. Here are some suggestions to help the initial formation of cooperative groups.

• Students should move into groups without undue noise and unnecessary interaction with other students.
• Students should stay in their group.
• Students should speak softly.
• Students should encourage each other to participate.
• Students should use names and look at each other during discussions.
• Students should avoid sarcastic remarks toward other people.

Group functioning is the second skill level that you will need to develop. Here the lessons involve those skills that will maintain the group and facilitate effective working relationships. Some important skills of group maintenance are:

• Students should understand the purpose, time allotment, and most effective procedures to complete their work.
• Students should support each other's ideas and work.
• Students should feel free to ask for help, information, or clarification from other group members or the science teacher.
• Students might learn how to paraphrase and summarize another student's ideas.
• As appropriate, students should learn how to express their feelings about the assignment and group process.

The next phase is *formulating understanding* of the concepts, processes, and skills of the assigned lesson. The skills are designed to maximize each student's learning. Here are some suggestions:

• Each student should summarize—aloud—important ideas contained in the material.
• Other students should correct and clarify summaries.
• Students should elaborate on each other's summary.
• Students can give hints about ways to remember ideas.
• All group members should participate in the discussion.

The last stage is *fermenting ideas and understandings*. Students should develop skills that will help reconceptualize and extend ideas. At this level, there is already a firmly developed group structure, so it is possible to introduce challenges, conflicts, and controversies. Because of already developed skills, challenging situations can bring about deeper thinking, further synthesis of ideas, gathering of more information, and constructive arguments about conclusions, decisions, and solutions. In this case, the science teacher may be the person who encourages the extension of ideas. It is possible, even desirable, for students to function at this level. The teacher will have to decide about the degree of group development and level of interaction as this level is reached. Skills that facilitate this stage include:

• Criticize ideas, not other students.
• Clarify disagreements within the group.
• Synthesize different ideas into a single statement.
• Ask other students to justify their conclusions.
• Ask probing, clarifying questions.
• Generate several answers or conclusions, and select the best for the given situation.

We now turn to the second question, "How does one teach these skills?" As a science teacher interested in cooperative learning, it will be critical to identify students who have not developed the group skills discussed earlier. There are several ways that you can teach the skills required for cooperative learning:

• Be sure that students understand the need for group skills.
• Be sure that students understand the skill and when to use it.
• Be sure that students have time and situations where they can practice the skills.
• Be sure that students have the opportunity and procedures for discussing their use of group skills.
• Be sure that students continue using the skills until they are a natural part of group work.

Since much work in science classes, and later life, is dependent on group work, we think your time and effort required to implement cooperative skills will be well spent. There is still a time and place for individual and competitive learning. The cooperative learning model provides an excellent complement to other models used in science teaching.

■ THE MADELINE HUNTER MODEL

Over the years, Dr. Madeline Hunter endeavored to develop materials and a teaching model designed to increase instructional effectiveness. Her model is based on psychological theory, primarily behaviorism, and educational research. The model is quite practical. It seems a simple and complete way to

STEPS FOR DESIGNING LESSONS

APPLYING THE COOPERATIVE LEARNING MODEL

Objectives
1. **Objectives for the lesson should be clearly specified.** You should make clear the two types of objectives: academic and collaborative skills. The former objective is used in most science lessons. The latter provides students with the specific skills used for cooperative learning.

Decisions
2. **Deciding on group size.** This decision may be influenced by time, materials, equipment, and facilities. A general recommendation is to use pairs or groups of three.
3. **Deciding on who is in the group.** Generally, it is best to have heterogeneous groups randomly assigned. Other alternatives include homogeneous grouping and having students select their own group.
4. **Deciding on the room arrangement.** Again, this decision may be influenced by facilities and equipment. For optimum cooperative learning, group members should sit in a circle and be close enough for effective communication.
5. **Deciding on the instructional materials to promote interdependence.** In early stages of developing cooperative learning groups, pay attention to the ways materials are used to facilitate interdependence. Three ways are suggested: materials interdependence (e.g., one set of materials for the group); information interdependence (e.g., each group member has a resource needed by the group); and interdependence with other groups (e.g., intergroup competition).
6. **Deciding on roles to ensure interdependence.** You can assign roles—such as summarizer, researcher, recorder, and observer—that will encourage cooperation among group members.

Explaining
7. **Explain the assignment.** Be sure students are clear about the academic task. Make connections to past experience, concepts, and lessons. Define any relevant concepts and explain procedures and safety precautions. Check on students' understanding of the assignment.
8. **Explain the collaborative goal.** Students must understand that they are responsible for doing the assignment and learning the material, and that *all* group members learn the material and successfully complete the assignment.
9. **Explain individual accountability.** Each individual should understand that he/she is responsible for learning, and that you will assess learning at the individual level.
10. **Explain intergroup cooperation.** Sometimes you may want to extend the cooperative group idea to include the entire class. If so, the method and criteria of access should be clear.
11. **Explain the criteria for success.** In the cooperative learning model, evaluation is based on successful completion of the assignment. It is therefore important to explain the criteria by which work will be evaluated.
12. **Explain the specific cooperative behaviors.** Since students may not understand what is meant by cooperative work, you should give specific examples of your expectations of their behaviors. For instance: "stay as a group," "talk quietly," "each person should explain how he/she got the answer," "listen to other group members," and "criticize ideas, not people."

Monitoring and Intervening
13. **Monitor student work.** Once the students begin work, your task is to observe the various groups and help solve any problems that emerge.
14. **Provide task assistance.** As needed, you may wish to clarify the assignment, introduce concepts, review material, model a skill, answer questions, and redirect discussions.
15. **Teaching collaborative skills.** Because collaboration is new, it may be important to intervene in groups and help them learn the skills of collaboration.
16. **Provide closure for the lesson.** At the end of the lesson, it may be important for you to intervene and bring closure. Summarize what has been presented, review concepts and skills, and reinforce their work.

Evaluation
17. **Evaluate the quality and quantity of student learning.** Evaluate the previously decided-upon product (e.g., a report).

Processing
18. **Assess how well the groups functioned.** If group collaboration is truly a goal, then some time should be spent on assessment. Point out how the groups could improve next time.

integrate many essential aspects of instruction into a teachable plan. This discussion is based on two of Dr. Hunter's books.[22]

The first step is a prelesson evaluation. The aim of the evaluation is to place your objectives at the correct level and best sequence for your students. Although this seems simple enough, it is often not done. As a part of this process, you also may consider analyzing the task of achieving your objectives and designing an activity to diagnose student understanding before and enroute to your final objective.

Next, design the beginning of your lesson. There are three components to be considered. A readiness activity, in which the present lesson relates to the learner's past, involves the learner and establishes relevance of the instructional objectives. Another aspect of the readiness activity is to inform the students of your objective—that is, what they will learn and how you will know if they have learned it.

After the readiness section of the lesson, consider the actual input of information, processes, or skills. For instance, you might review the catalogues of instructional strategies outlined in chapter 2 and consider which methods will best deliver the material. Teaching efficiency, learning effectiveness, and availability of facilities, materials, and equipment should be the criteria of evaluation and choice.

Next comes a consideration of assessment. How can you check for student understanding and comprehension? You may wish to sample the class, give a quiz, have a discussion, or ask questions of individual students. This assessment need not be formal, but there should be some type of feedback, for you and the students, concerning the lesson's effectiveness.

Finally, there should be closure: the lesson should not just stop. There should be an ending in which you and/or the students summarize what has been learned.

This discussion has been on planning the lesson; the obvious next step is teaching it. What is it that will make the lesson effective? Once you have formulated instructional objectives, be sure you teach to the objective. Include actions and strategies that relate to the objective. Are your questions, concepts, processes, skills, and activities clearly related?

As you teach the lesson, you will want to monitor student progress and adjust instruction accordingly. Monitoring student progress can be done overtly by asking students to do something indicating the degree to which they have learned the material. Or, monitoring can be done covertly by observing student work and listening to student discussions of the assignment. Based on this feedback, you will have to make one of several decisions: continue the lesson as planned, alter the lesson, reteach the lesson, or end the lesson and prepare a new one.

■ THE 4MAT SYSTEM

The 4MAT System is based on the premise that individuals perceive and process experiences and information in different ways. These ways are referred to as learning styles. There are four identifiable learning styles, and each is an equally valid way of learning. Here is a brief summary of learning styles according to Bernice McCarthy, who developed the 4MAT System.

1. Type-one learners are primarily interested in personal meaning.
2. Type-two learners are primarily interested in facts that lead to conceptual understanding.
3. Type-three learners are primarily interested in how things work.
4. Type-four learners are primarily interested in self-discovery.

You can probably already see the different aspects of the 4MAT learning cycle. McCarthy claims that all students should be taught in all four styles. That way, students will experience the comfort and success of learning in their preferred mode about one quarter of the time and be stretched to develop their learning capacities in other modes the rest of the time.

The 4MAT System moves through a four-step learning cycle in sequence. An additional style that McCarthy incorporates is students' preference for right-or left-hemisphere (brain) functioning. The right/left modes are embedded in each of the four steps in the learning cycle.

The first portion of a 4MAT lesson should have the learner move from concrete experience to reflective observation. Begin with a concrete experience and allow students time to discover the meaning that experience has for them. This approach creates a reason for learning. The first phase of the 4MAT System is displayed graphically in Figure 14–3.

The second phase is the formulation of the concept. The student moves from reflective observation to abstract conceptualization. Teachers teach in the traditional sense. The second phase is represented in Figure 14–4. This approach gives the big idea.

In the third phase, students move from abstract conceptualization to active experimentation. Students who are common-sense learners do best in this phase. This is the hands-on approach to science. You can tell the students who have this learning style because they need to try it. They are concerned with finding out how things work. The teacher's role is to provide the materials and opportunity. The graphic representation of this phase of the 4MAT System is displayed in Figure 14–5.

The final phase is the progression from active experimentation to concrete experience. The stu-

STEPS FOR DESIGNING LESSONS

APPLYING THE HUNTER MODEL

Before designing a daily lesson, you should complete the following evaluation:

Prelesson Assessment

- Determine the continuing strand or theme of science concepts and processes.
- Identify a major objective based on science concepts and processes. Then, locate the students' understanding relative to the major objective.
- Select specific objectives for daily lessons.

Lesson Planning and Lesson Sequencing

For each teaching sequence, you should use the following steps to determine if and how they are appropriate for your objectives and students' mastery of past and present concepts and processes.

Anticipatory Set. Early in the lesson, you should include an activity that will elicit students' attention to the content and processes. The anticipatory set will:

- focus the students' attention during the period of transition;
- elicit attending behavior and mental readiness for the day's lesson;
- provide a connection between past lessons and the lesson to be taught;
- last long enough to orient students to the immediate objectives and lesson.

Objective and Purpose. This step is one of communicating to the students the day's objectives. The objective and purpose statement will:

- inform the students of the day's objectives, and outline what they will be able to do at the end of the lesson;
- clarify how and why the lesson is important and useful.

Instructional Input. Here, the teacher actually teaches. Instructional input will:

- require the teacher to determine the content and processes that relate directly to the objectives;
- select the best means available to facilitate students' learning of the desired objectives.

Modeling. Where appropriate, you should try to provide examples of the science content and processes included in your objectives. Modeling will:

- provide examples of expected learning outcomes;
- give the students visual and auditory input.

Monitoring Student Understanding. Monitoring is assessment that occurs during the lesson. You should check for students' understanding of essential information and concepts by sampling, signaling, and explaining. Monitoring will:

- identify students' understanding;
- provide ways and means to adjust the instructional sequence.

Practice. Lessons should include opportunities for students to practice the content and processes they have learned. Initial attempts should be teacher guided; later practice can be done on an individual basis. Practice will:

- provide opportunities to apply concepts and processes with your supervision;
- extend student understanding to new situations.

Postlesson Assessment. Sometime after the lesson, you will assess students' understanding of the concepts and processes. Base the assessment on the major objectives identified in the prelesson assessment and the specific objectives of the lessons.

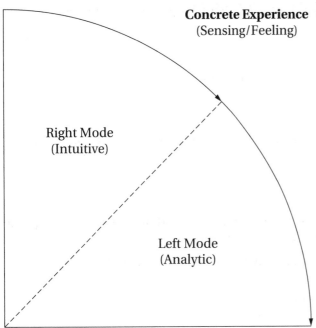

FIGURE 14–3
First phase of the 4MAT system, refective observation

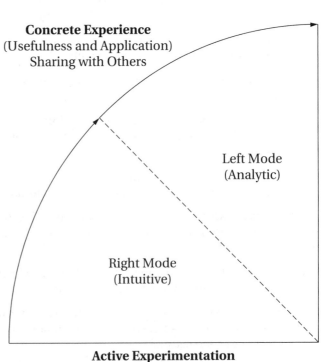

FIGURE 14–4
Second phase of the 4MAT system, abstract conceptu-alization

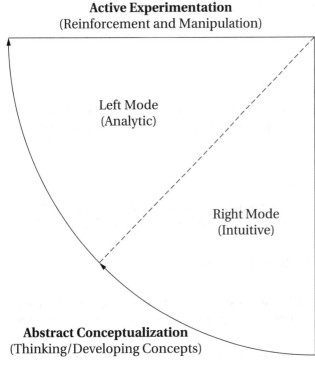

FIGURE 14–5
Third phase of the 4MAT system, active experimenta-tion

FIGURE 14–6
Final 4MAT system phase, concrete experience

STEPS FOR DESIGNING LESSONS

THE 4MAT SYSTEM

Quadrant One

1. Express the value of the learning experience.
2. The lesson should have personal meaning for the student.
3. Create a learning environment where students can explore ideas without being evaluated.

Quadrant Two

1. Provide information to the students.
2. Present concepts in an organized way.
3. Encourage students to analyze data and form concepts.

Quadrant Three

1. Provide activities for students.
2. Coach the students as they progress in the activities.

Quadrant Four

1. Allow students to discover meaning and concepts by doing.
2. Challenge students to review what has happened.
3. Analyze experiences for relevance and originality.

---

dents combine knowledge from personal experience and experimentation. They extend the original concepts by asking, "What can this become?" They apply the ideas in new and different forms. The quadrant is represented in Figure 14–6.

The entire 4MAT System is represented in "Steps for Designing Lessons, The 4MAT System." This diagram is from McCarthy's book *The 4MAT System.*[23]

■ THE 5E INSTRUCTIONAL MODEL: AN INTRODUCTION

In the early 1960s, J. Myron Atkin and Robert Karplus first proposed a learning cycle.[24] Karplus, Herb Thier, and their colleagues later used the learning cycle in the SCIS, and based the learning cycle for SCIS on the psychological theories of Piaget. We have extended and elaborated the original design for a teaching model by Atkin and Karplus and have based the 5E model proposed in this chapter on that work.

Over the years, many curriculum designers have elaborated, modified, and applied teaching models in different educational programs.[25] The approach in this chapter is first to describe the form and function of a teaching model, then to discuss the psychological basis for the proposed model, and finally to describe the model.

Form and Function

The 5E instructional model has five phases: engagement, exploration, explanation, elaboration, and evaluation. Each phase has a specific function and is intended to contribute to the learning process. We have described the phases in terms of: (1) assumptions about the mental activity of students, (2) activities that students would be involved in, and (3) strategies used by the teacher. Later in this section we shall discuss the five phases in detail.

An instructional model has two functions. A model provides guidance for curriculum developers as they design a program. Depending on the instructional model, curriculum developers can use the model at different levels. One level is equivalent to a year-long sequence; another is equivalent to a unit; and another is equivalent to an activity or series of daily lessons. The second function of an instructional model is to help the classroom teacher improve instructional effectiveness through a systematic approach to and use of strategies closely aligned with educational outcomes.

A Constructivist Orientation

Historically, educators have explained learning by classifying it into one of three broad categories. In simple terms, these are transmission, maturation, and construction (see Figure 14–7). In recent years, cognitive scientists and science educators have

Perspective	View of Students	View of Knowledge	Approach to Teaching
TRANSMISSION	They must be filled with information and concepts.	Core concepts are a copy of reality.	External to Internal
MATURATION	They must be allowed to mature and develop.	Emergence of core concepts.	Internal to External
CONSTRUCTION	They are actively involved in learning.	Construction of core concepts.	Interaction Between Internal and External

FIGURE 14–7
Perspectives on education

focused on the constructivist model in their work on the misconceptions of students, differences between novice and expert explanations of phenomena, and naive versus canonical theories individuals hold.[26,27]

In the constructivist model of learning, students reconstruct core concepts, or intellectual structures, through continuous interactions between themselves and their environment (which includes other people). Applying the constructivist approach to teaching requires the teacher to understand that students have some conceptions or prior knowledge of the world. Such conceptions may be inadequate (i.e., misconceptions) and need further development (i.e., conceptual change).[28,89,30,31] In teaching for conceptual change, teachers should be sure that students are focusing on objects or events that engage concepts of interest to the science teacher. That is, they are related to science or technology. Then, students can encounter problematic situations that are slightly beyond the current level of understanding. In so doing, the student will experience a form of cognitive disequilibrium. Teachers then structure learning experiences that assist the reconstruction of core concepts. New constructions can then be applied to different situations and tested against other conceptions of the world.

Science teachers are beginning to implement the constructivist view.[32,33] Doing so requires: (1) teaching in a manner that recognizes the students' level of conceptual understanding, and (2) an understanding that the students' construction of knowledge occurs through the confrontation and resolution of problem situations. The key here is that confrontation should be challenging but within students' parameters of intellectual accommodation. Challenges that are actually included as instructional strategies are described by terms such as moderate novelty, appropriate dissonance, optimal discord, tolerable mismatch, and reasonable disequilibrium.

Research by Peter Hewson and his colleagues suggests that conceptual change may occur in several different ways. There may be the addition of new con-

ceptions, a reorganization of current conceptions, and a rejection of conceptions. An important instructional aspect of the model proposed by Hewson and others is that students must be *dissatisfied* with the current conception, the new conception must be *intelligible*, the new conception must be *plausible*, and the new conception must be *fruitful*. You can imagine this from a teacher-students interaction point of view. A science teacher introduces a new concept, and students are unable to reconcile the new concept with current knowledge and experience. The teacher then provides experiences and information that helps students make sense of the new conception. As students consider and try to incorporate the new conception, they must see that a world in which the conception is true is generally reconcilable with their world view. Finally, students must see that there are instances where there is good reason to supply the new conception—namely, it works and it helps explain things. Regardless of the specific instructional model, helping students to develop more adequate scientific concepts is an important goal of science teaching. It is also a difficult task.

An assumption of this model is that using sequences of lessons designed to facilitate the process described above will assist in students' construction of knowledge. Another is that concrete experiences and computer-assisted activities will assist in the process of constructing knowledge. The following are general strategies based on the constructivist view of learning.

1. Recognize students' current concepts of objects, events, or phenomena.
2. Present situations slightly beyond the students' current conceptual understanding. One could also present the student with problems, situation conflicts, paradoxes, and puzzles.
3. Choose problems and situations that are challenging but achievable.
4. Have students present their explanations (concepts) to other students.

5. When students are struggling with inadequate explanations (misconceptions), first help them by accepting their explanations; second, by suggesting other explanations of the same phenomena or activities designed to provide insights; and third, by allowing them time to construct their explanations.

The 5E instructional model is based on a constructivist view. Constructivism is a dynamic and interactive conception of human learning. Students redefine, reorganize, elaborate, and change their initial concepts through interaction between the individual and the environment and other individuals. Individual learners interpret objects and phenomena and internalize the interpretation in terms of current concepts similar to the experiences being presented or encountered. In other words, changing and improving conceptions often requires challenging the current conceptions and showing them to be inadequate. The instructional and psychological problem is to avoid leaving students with an overall sense of inadequacy. If this occurs, educators have encouraged psychological problems. If a current conception is challenged, there must be opportunity, in the form of time and expenses, to reconstruct a more adequate conception than the original. In short, the students' construction of knowledge can be assisted by using sequences of lessons designed to challenge current concepts and provide opportunities for reconstruction to occur.

There is one other factor worth noting. Though not the primary orientation of the instructional model, learning styles are a contributing factor to the learning process. The approaches used in the different phases of the instructional model accommodate varied learning styles as recommended by Paul Kuerbis.[34] You will note that many of the ideas presented earlier—for example, use of textbooks, cooperative learning, and the 4MAT System—are applicable to the instructional model presented here.

The 5E Instructional Model: The Phases

Again, the model's five phases are engagement, exploration, explanation, elaboration, and evaluation.

Engagement

In the first phase, you engage the student in the learning task. The student mentally focuses on a problem, situation, or event. The activities of this phase make connections to past and future activities. The connections depend on the learning task and may be conceptual, procedural, or behavioral.

Asking a question, defining a problem, and showing a discrepant event are all ways to engage students and focus them on the instructional task.

Orientation

This phase of the teaching model initiates the instructional task. The activity should (1) make connections between past and present learning experiences, and (2) anticipate activities and organize students' thinking toward the learning outcomes of current activities.

Students

- Establish an interest in, and develop an approach to, the instructional task.

Teachers

- Identify the instructional task.

Activities

- May vary, but should be interesting, motivational, and meaningful to students.

Learning

- Initiated by, exposure to, and experience with concepts, processes, and skills.

FIGURE 14–8
Engagement

The teacher's role is to present the situation and identify the instructional task. The teacher also sets the rules and procedures for establishing the task.

Successful engagement results in students being puzzled and actively motivated in the learning activity. Here we are using activity in the constructivist and behavioral sense—that is, students are mentally active. If we combine the external events with the basic needs and interests of the students, instruction contributes to successful learning. Figure 14–8 summarizes the engagement phase.

Exploration

Once you have engaged the students' interest in ideas, students need to have time to explore these ideas. You can specifically design exploration activities so that students in the class have common, concrete experiences that begin building concepts, processes, and skills. To use Piagetian terms, engagement brings about disequilibrium, while exploration initiates the process of equilibration. Some of the key words used to describe the type of activities used in this phase are concrete and hands-on. Courseware can be used in the phase, but it should be carefully designed to assist the initial process of conceptual reconstruction.

The aim of exploration activities is to establish experiences that a teacher can use later to formally introduce a concept, process, or skill. During the activity, the students have time in which they explore objects, events, or situations.

Orientation
This phase of the teaching model provides the students with a common base of experiences within which current concepts, processes, and skills may be identified and developed.

Students
- Complete activities directed toward learning outcomes.

Teachers
- Facilitate and monitor interaction between students and instructional situations, materials, and/or courseware.

Activities
- Provide mental and physical experiences relative to the learning outcomes. These activities provide an initial context for students' explanations as they have unanswered questions based on the exploration.

Learning
- Directed by objects, events, or situations.

FIGURE 14–9
Exploration

Orientation
This phase of the teaching model focuses students' attention on a particular aspect of their engagement and exploration experiences and provides opportunities to demonstrate their conceptual understanding, process skills, or behaviors. This phase also provides specific opportunities for teachers to introduce concepts or skills.

Students
- Describe their understanding, use their skills, express their attitudes.

Teachers
- Direct student learning by clarifying misconceptions, providing vocabulary for concepts, giving examples of skills, modifying behaviors, and suggesting further learning experiences.

Activities
- Provide opportunities to identify student knowledge, skills and values, and to introduce language and/or behaviors related to learning outcomes.

Learning
- Directed by teacher and instructional courseware.

FIGURE 14–10
Explanation

As a result of their mental and physical involvement in the exploration activity, students establish relationships, observe patterns, identify variables, and question events.

The teacher's role in the exploration phase is that of facilitator or coach. The teacher initiates the activity and allows students the time and opportunity to investigate objects, materials, and situations based on each student's own concepts about phenomena. If called upon, the teacher may coach or guide students. Use of concrete materials and experiences is essential. Figure 14–9 summarizes the exploration phase.

Explanation
The word *explanation* means the act or process in which concepts, processes, or skills are made plain, comprehensible, and clear. The process of explanation provides the students and teacher with a common use of terms relative to the learning task. In this phase, the teacher directs student attention to specific aspects of the engagement and exploration experiences. First, students are asked to give their explanations. Second, the teacher introduces scientific or technological explanations in a direct and informal manner. Explanations are ways of ordering the exploratory experiences. The teacher should base the initial part of this phase on students' explana-

tions and clearly connect the explanations to experiences in the engagement and exploration phases of the instructional model. The key to this phase is to present concepts, processes, or skills in a simple, clear, and direct manner, and move on to the next phase. You should not equate telling with learning. The explanation phase can be relatively short because the next phase allows time for restructuring and extends this formal introduction to concepts, processes, and skills.

The explanation phase is teacher (or technology) directed. Teachers have a variety of techniques and strategies at their disposal. Educators commonly use oral explanations, but there are other strategies, such as video, film, and educational courseware. This phase continues the process of cognitive construction and provides words for explanations. In the end, students should be able to explain exploratory experiences using common terms. Students will not immediately express and apply the explanations— learning takes time. Students need time and experience to establish and expand concepts, processes, and skills. For a summary of the explanation phase, see Figure 14–10.

Elaboration

Once students have an explanation of their learning tasks, it is important to involve students in further experiences that extend or elaborate the concepts, processes, or skills. In some cases, students may still have misconceptions, or they may only understand a concept in terms of the exploratory experience. Elaboration activities provide further time and experiences that contribute to learning. According to Audrey Champagne:

> During the elaboration phase, students engage in discussions and information-seeking activities. The groups' goal is to identify and execute a small number of promising approaches to the task. During the group discussion, students present and defend their approaches to the instructional task. This discussion results in better definition and gathering of information that is necessary for successful completion of the task. The teaching cycle is not closed to information from the outside. Students get information from each other, the teacher, printed materials, experts, electronic databases, and experiments they conduct. This is called the information base. As a result of participation in the group's discussion, individual students are able to elaborate upon the conception of the tasks, information bases, and possible strategies for its completion.[35]

Interactions within student groups is an application of Vygotsky's psychology to the teaching model. Group discussions and cooperative learning situations provide opportunities for students to express their understanding of the subject and receive feedback from others who are close to their own level of understanding.

The phase is also an opportunity to involve students in new situations and problems that require the application of identical or similar explanations. Figure 14–11 is a summary of the elaboration phase of the teaching model.

Evaluation

At some point, students should receive feedback on the adequacy of their explorations. Informal assessment can occur from the beginning of the teaching sequence. The teacher can complete a formal assessment after the elaboration phase. As a practical educational matter, teachers must assess educational outcomes. This is the phase in which teachers administer tests or performance activities to determine each student's understanding. This is also the important opportunity for students to use the skills they have acquired and evaluate their own understanding. The 5E instructional model is aligned with many processes involved in scientific inquiry. In science, the methods of scientific inquiry are an excellent means for students to test their explanations. This is, after all, congruent with science. How well do student explanations stand up to review by peers and teachers? Is there need to reform ideas based on experience?

Figure 14-12 summarizes the evaluation phase.

Orientation

This phase of the teaching model challenges and extends students' conceptual understanding and skills. Through new experiences students develop deeper and broader understanding, more information, and adequate skills.

Students

- Present and defend their explanations and identify and complete several experiences related to the learning task.

Teachers

- Provide an occasion for students to cooperate on activities, discuss their current understanding, and demonstrate their skills.

Activities

- Provide experiences through challenges, repetition, new activities, practice, and time.

Learning

- Encouraged through challenges, repetition, new experiences, practices, and time.

FIGURE 14–11
Elaboration

Orientation

This phase of the teaching model encourages students to assess their understandings and abilities and provides opportunities for teachers to evaluate student progress toward achieving the educational objectives.

Students

- Examine the adequacy of their explanations, behaviors, and attitudes in new situations.

Teachers

- Use a variety of formal and informal procedures for assessing student understanding.

Activities

- Evaluate the concepts, attitudes, and skills of the students.

Learning

- Repeat different phases of the teaching model to improve conceptual understanding and/or skills.

FIGURE 14–12
Evaluation

Stage of the Instructional Model	What the Teacher Does	
	That is Consistent With This Model	*That is Inconsistent With This Model*
Engage	• Creates interest • Generates curiosity • Raises questions • Elicits responses that uncover what the students know or think about the concept/topic	• Explains concepts • Provides definitions and answers • States conclusions • Provides closure • Lectures
Explore	• Encourages students to work together without direct instruction from the teacher • Observes and listens to students as they interact • Asks probing questions to redirect students' investigations when necessary • Provides time for students to puzzle through problems • Acts as a consultant for students	• Provides answers • Tells or explains how to work through the problem • Provides closure • Tells students that they are wrong • Gives information or facts that solve the problem • Leads students step-by-step to a solution
Explain	• Encourages students to explain concepts and definitions in their own words • Asks for justification (evidence) and clarification from students • Formally provides definitions, explanations, and new labels • Uses students' previous experiences as the basis for explaining concepts	• Accepts explanations that have no justification • Neglects to solicit students' explanations • Introduces unrelated concepts or skills
Elaborate	• Expects students to use formal labels, definitions, and explanations provided previously • Encourages students to apply or extend the concepts and skills in new situations • Reminds students of alternative explanations • Refers students to existing data and evidence and asks: What do you already know? Why do you think. . . ? (Strategies from Explore apply here also.)	• Provides definitive answers • Tells students that they are wrong • Lectures • Leads students step-by-step to a solution • Explains how to work through the problem
Evaluate	• Observes students as they apply new concepts and skills • Assesses students' knowledge and/or skills • Looks for evidence that students have changed their thinking or behaviors • Allows students to assess their own learning and group-process skills • Asks open-ended question, such as: Why do you think. . . ? What evidence do you have? What do you know about x? How would you explain x?	• Tests vocabulary words, terms, and isolated facts • Introduces new ideas or concepts • Creates ambiguity • Promotes open-ended discussion unrelated to the concept or skill

FIGURE 14–13
Applying the 5E instructional model

Figure 14–13 provides additional details about what the teacher does and what the student does at different stages in the instructional model. We have provided descriptions of methods and activities that are both consistent and inconsistent with this model.

In conclusion, the basis of the 5E instructional model is the original learning cycle used in the SCIS program. We have modified and extended this learn-ing cycle and drawn on research in the cognitive sci-ences—research that deals primarily with student misconception and conceptual change. Three factors support the use of this instructional model: (1) research from the cognitive sciences, (2) concor-dance of the model with the scientific process, and (3) utility to curriculum developers and classroom teachers.

Stage of the Instructional Model	What the Student Does	
	That is Consistent With This Model	*That is Inconsistent With This Model*
Engage	• Asks questions, such as: Why did this happen? What do I already know about this? What can I find out about this? • Shows interest in the topic	• Asks for the "right" answer • Offers the "right" answer • Insists on answers or explanations • Seeks one solution
Explore	• Thinks freely, but within the limits of the activity • Tests predictions and hypotheses • Forms new predictions and hypotheses • Tries alternatives and discusses them with others • Records observations and ideas • Suspends judgment	• Lets others do the thinking and exploring (passive involvement) • Works quietly with little or no interaction with others (only appropriate when exploring ideas or feelings) • Plays around indiscriminately with no goal in mind • Stops with one solution
Explain	• Explains possible solutions or answers to others • Listens critically to one another's explanations • Questions one another's explanations • Listens to and tries to comprehend explanations offered by the teacher • Refers to previous activities • Uses recorded observations in explanations	• Proposes explanations from thin air with no relationship to previous experiences • Brings up irrelevant experiences and examples • Accepts explanations without justification • Does not attend to other plausible explanations
Elaborate	• Applies new labels, definitions, explanations, and skills in new, but similar, situations • Uses previous information to ask questions, propose solutions, make decisions, design experiments • Draws reasonable conclusions from evidence • Records observations and explanations • Checks for understanding among peers	• Plays around with no goal in mind • Ignores previous information or evidence • Draws conclusions from thin air • Uses in discussions only those labels that the teacher provided
Evaluate	• Answers open-ended questions by using observations, evidence, and previously accepted explanations • Demonstrates an understanding or knowledge of the concept or skill • Evaluates his or her own progress and knowledge • Asks related questions that would encourage future investigations	• Draws conclusions, not using evidence or previously accepted explanations • Offers only yes-or-no answers, memorized definitions or explanations as answers • Fails to express satisfactory explanations in his or her own words • Introduces new, irrelevant topics

FIGURE 14–13
Continued

■ SUMMARY

This chapter describes several instructional models. Although textbooks are used by the majority of science teachers, there has been little effort to use them effectively. Science teachers should recognize that students' use of textbooks is influenced by their prior knowledge (i.e., misconceptions) and that this prior knowledge can dominate or distort text material.

Some recommendations for using a textbook include the following:

• Direct students' attention to important concepts.
• Challenge students' misconceptions.
• Ask students to construct explanations of everyday phenomena.
• Probe student responses.
• Provide accurate feedback to students.

- Construct alternative representations of textbook explanations.
- Select activities that create conceptual conflict.

Another instructional model is the learning cycle. This cycle is a three-step instructional sequence that includes:

- concept exploration,
- concept introduction, and
- concept application.

Cooperative learning is an effective strategy in the science classroom. Students learn a number of strategies that help them develop and function as a group. Formation of a group, group functioning, formulating understanding of the task, and time to discuss and reform concepts are all important aspects of cooperative groups.

Hunter's model is described in this chapter. The teaching sequence in this model includes:

- anticipating set,
- objectives and purpose,
- instructional input,
- modeling,
- monitoring student understanding, and
- practice.

■ REFERENCES

1. See the entire issue on major questions related to curriculum and instruction in science education. *Journal of Research in Science Teaching*, *20* (5) (May 1983).
2. Kevin Wise and James Okey, "A Meta-Analysis of the Effects of Various Science Teaching Strategies on Achievement," *Journal of Research in Science Teaching*, *20* (5) (May 1983): 434.
3. National Research Council, *National Science Education Standards* (Washington, DC: Author, 1995).
4. Iris Weiss, *Report of the 1985–86 National Survey of Science and Mathematics Education* (Research Triangle Park, NC: Research Triangle Institute, November 1987).
5. Jean Osbourn, Beau Jones, and Marcy Stein, "The Case for Improving Textbooks," *Educational Leadership*, April 1985.
6. Stephen Jay Gould, "The Case of the Creeping Fox Terrier Clone," *Natural History*, January 1988.
7. Joseph D. McInerney, "Biology Textbooks—Whose Business?" *The American Biology Teacher*, *48* (7) (October 1986).
8. Audrey Champagne et al., "Middle School Science Texts: What's Wrong That Could Be Made Right?" *American Association for the Advancement of Science Books & Films*, May/June 1987.
9. Weiss.
10. Kathleen Roth and Charles Anderson, "Promoting Conceptual Change Learning from Science Textbooks," in *Improving Learning: New Perspectives*, P. Ramsden, ed. (New York: Kogan Page Publishers, 1988).
11. Kathleen Roth, *Conceptual Learning and Student Processing of Science Texts* (Research Series No. 167) (East Lansing, MI: Institute for Research on Teaching, Michigan State University, 1985).
12. Charles Anderson and Edward Smith, *Teacher Behavior Associated with Conceptual Learning in Science*, paper presented at the annual meeting of the American Educational Research Association, Montreal, Canada, 1983.
13. Roth, *Conceptual Learning and Student Processing of Science Texts*.
14. Robert Karplus, "Teaching for the Development of Reasoning," in 1980 Association for the Education of Teachers of Science Yearbook, *The Psychology of Teaching for Thinking and Creativity*, Anton E. Lawson, ed. (Columbus, OH: ERIC Clearinghouse for Science, Mathematics, and Environmental Education, 1979).
15. Howard Birnie, *An Introduction to the Learning Cycle* (Saskatoon, Canada: University of Kastachewan Press, 1982).
16. Robert Karplus, et al., *Teaching and the Development of Reasoning* (Berkeley: University of California Press, 1977).
17. John Renner, Michael Abraham, and Howard Birnie, "The Importance of the FORM of Student Acquisition of Data in Physics Learning Cycles," *The Journal of Research in Science Teaching*, *22* (4) (1985): 303–326.
18. Anton Lawson, "A Better Way to Teach Biology," *The American Biology Teacher*, *50* (5) (May 1988): 266–278.
19. Lawson.
20. See for example, David Johnson, et al., "Effects of Cooperative, Competitive and Individualistic Goal Structures on Achievement: A Meta-Analysis," *Psychological Bulletin*, *89*, (1981): 47–62 and Roger Johnson and David Johnson, "What Research Says About Student Interaction in Science Classrooms," in *Education in the 80s: Science*, Mary Budd Rowe, ed. (Washington, DC: National Education Association, 1984), pp. 25–37.
21. David Johnson, Roger Johnson, Edith Johnson Holubec, and Patricia Roy, *Circles of Learning: Cooperation in the Classroom* (Alexandria, VA: Association for Supervision and Curriculum Development, 1986).
22. Madeline Hunter, *Mastery Teaching* (El Segundo, CA: TIP Publications, 1982) and *Improved Instruction* (El Segundo, CA: TIP Publications, 1976).
23. Bernice McCarthy, *The 4MAT System: Teaching to Learning Styles with Right/Left Mode Techniques* (Barrington, IL: Excel, Inc. 1987).
24. J. Myron Atkin and Robert Karplus, "Discovery or Invention?" *The Science Teacher*, *29* (1986): 45–51.
25. John W. Renner and Michael Abraham, "The Sequence of Learning Cycle Activities in High School Chemistry," *Journal of Research in Science Teaching*, *23* (2) (1986): 121–143.
26. Charles W. Anderson, *Incorporating Recent Research on Learning into the Process of Science Curriculum Development*, commissioned paper for IBM-supported design project (Colorado Springs: CO: Biological Sciences Curriculum Study, 1987).

27. Audrey Champagne, *The Psychological Basis for a Model of Science Instruction,* commissioned paper for IBM-supported design project (Colorado Springs, CO: Biological Sciences Curriculum Study, 1987).

28. Peter Hewson, "A Conceptual Change Approach to Learning Science," *European Journal of Science Education, 3* (4) (1981): 383–396.

29. Peter Hewson, and N. Richard Thorley, "The Conditions of Conceptual Change in the Classroom," *International Journal of Science Education, 11* (Special Issue) (1989): 541–653.

30. Peter Hewson and Mariana Hewson, "An Appropriate Conception of Teaching Science: A View from Studies of Science Learning," *Science Education, 72* (5) (1988): 597–614.

31. G. J. Posner, K. A. Strike, P. W. Hewson, and W. A. Gerzog, "Accommodation of a Scientific Conception: Toward a Theory of Conceptual Change," *Science Education, 66* (2) (1982): 211–227.

32. W. Kyle and J. Shymansky, "Enhancing Learning through Conceptual Change in Teaching," in *Research Matters. . . to the Science Teacher, 21,* (1989), National Association for Research in Science Teaching.

33. C. W. Anderson, "Strategic Teaching in Science," in *Strategic Teaching and Learning: Cognitive Instruction in the Content Areas,* Joens, ed. (Alexandria, VA: Association for Supervision and Curriculum Development, 1987).

34. Paul J. Kuerbis, *Learning Styles and Elementary Science,* commissioned paper for IBM-supported design project (Colorado Springs, CO: Biological Sciences Curriculum Study, 1987).

35. Audrey Champagne, *The Psychological Basis for a Model of Science Instruction,* p. 82.

Chapter 15

PLANNING FOR EFFECTIVE SCIENCE TEACHING

Science teachers are especially fortunate because of the many interesting and motivational things connected with science that they can use in their teaching. Examples of natural and scientific phenomena abound. The daily cycle of news events, the endless variety of clouds and weather, the growth of plants and animals, the passage of the seasons—all contribute to an endless store of materials for scientific and technologic discussions. There are rocks and minerals to be collected, flora and fauna to be investigated, and many examples of scientific ideas and technological devices to be used as teaching aids in science classes.

Alert and enthusiastic science teachers do not miss the opportunity to incorporate these in their teaching plans. Clever use of appropriate items and examples will inject a degree of interest and spontaneity into science classes that are unmatched in other disciplines. How does the science teacher put the things of science to use? Are there meaningful ways to plan for effective teaching? Can the teacher maintain sequence and organization and at the same time stimulate interest? Can the objectives of science teaching be realized while permitting the objects of science to dominate the scene? These are questions teachers must face when planning their yearly and daily work.

At this point, we recommend that you complete at least one of the following activities—"Planning a Simple Lesson" and "Evaluating a Lesson"—located at the end of this chapter. Doing these activities will provide some initial thought and experience for the following sections of this chapter. In the next sections, we introduce some elements and strategies of effective teaching. These are the "pieces" that science teachers use in designing individual lessons or teaching units. The chapter is structured so that you develop an idea of different types of planning for effective science teaching. This chapter presents the practical, how–to of science teaching—the actual planning of a science program, a teaching unit, and daily lesson plans.

■ DEVELOPING SCIENTIFIC LITERACY IN THE CLASSROOM

A primary emphasis in this edition of our book is that of increasing scientific literacy among students and ultimately among the citizens who occupy positions of authority in the nation. The NSTA in 1982 developed a position paper entitled "Science-Technology-Society: Science Education for the 1980's," which dealt with matters of improving scientific literacy.[1] This position of NSTA is extremely relevant today as we struggle with problems of the interrelationships between science, technology, and society. We need to know what is meant by scientific literacy and what are the attributes of a scientifically literate person. The NSTA position paper helps us with this. According to NSTA, a scientifically literate person is one who:

1. uses science concepts, process skills, and values in making responsible everyday decisions;
2. understands how society influences science and technology as well as how science and technology influence society;
3. understands that society controls science and technology through the allocation of resources;
4. recognizes the limitations, as well as the usefulness, of science and technology in advancing human welfare;
5. knows the major concepts, hypotheses, and theories of science and is able to use them;
6. appreciates science and technology for the intellectual stimulus they provide;
7. understands that the generation of scientific knowledge depends upon the inquiry process and upon conceptual theories;
8. distinguishes between scientific evidence and personal opinion;
9. recognizes the origins of science and understands that scientific knowledge is tentative and subject to change as evidence accumulates;
10. understands the applications of technology and the decisions entailed in the use of technology;
11. has sufficient knowledge and experience to appreciate the worthiness of research and technological development;
12. has a richer and more exciting view of the world as a result of science education;
13. knows reliable sources of scientific and technological information and uses these sources in the process of decision making.

The above list is important, but it is not useful for the science teacher unless it goes on to contain specific examples. It is necessary to show how planning science lessons can result in student experiences that illustrate the development of scientific literacy. We propose to provide an example for this.

Example: Locating a New Airport

A junior high school science class was presented this problem: Shall Larimer County, State of Colorado, construct a new airport in Rocky Mountain National Park to serve the needs of tourists, visitors, and commuters from the Estes Park area?

The teacher raised several issues that students might consider in coming to a decision. They included the following:

1. What will be the benefits to the economy of Larimer County if an airport is built?
2. What will be the environmental impact of such action—on wildlife, mountain terrain, drainage patterns, and aesthetics?
3. What input must be obtained from residents of the area?

Students were encouraged to think of other issues and to discuss them with one another, with their parents, and with persons in authority. Students were permitted to form two groups: those tentatively in favor of the plan and those opposing it. Each group was assigned tasks of gathering information about the area and about the issues raised in class.

Over a period of two weeks, students interviewed residents of the area, talked to county officials, and obtained information on air traffic control, construction costs, environmental impact, and other relevant matters. At the end of two weeks, a general meeting was held jointly by the two groups at which information was presented, resource persons were invited to speak, and a vote was taken. The vote was narrowly in favor of building the airport. The opponents, however, were able to place certain constraints on the activity to better insure compliance with national and state environmental legislation.

Where is there evidence that scientific literacy was enhanced in this exercise? Some experiences provide such evidence. For one thing, students learned that there are usually no simple answers to a complex problem such as building an airport. They also learned that decisions are usually made on the basis of certain trade-offs, such as giving up certain environmental points while gaining certain economic factors. In the process, students learned multitudes of factual information in an interesting manner. Such information was learned in the context of a real problem instead of merely as isolated facts.

In addition, students learned that there are many connecting bridges between science, technology, and society. They also learned that problem solutions are obtained by inquiry and investigation, rather than merely by submission to some authority, such as the teacher or textbook. The overall influence of this activity is unknown, but one can reasonably expect that the students will be able to remember some of the issues discussed and the diverse elements that needed to be considered. This will undoubtedly influence their approach to solving other problems of a similar nature later on in their lives as citizens and taxpayers.

■ PLANNING A UNIT OR COURSE OF STUDY

The prospects of designing a course, unit, or even a daily lesson plan may be quite daunting for a new teacher. Fortunately, the textbook you will use will have done much of the preplanning of the organization and content of your prospective unit. Your particular goals and objectives, however, will certainly dictate the specific manner in which the accomplishment of these goals and objectives will be met.

In your planning there are several components to consider. First, you should have a clear idea of the rationale for the course or unit. Why is this material being included? How does the new information fit into the overall course or unit? You will need to think about the intended learning outcomes. What specific student objectives are to be accomplished? Which of these are conceptual, which are skill objectives, and which are expected values outcomes?

It is helpful to construct some type of conceptual map showing the relationships among the ideas of the unit or course. Which are major ideas? Which are minor or subordinate ideas? In what order should they be presented? Concept mapping is discussed more fully in chapter eighteen.

A very important component is the instructional plan, which will consume much of your planning time. How can you best accomplish your objectives? What materials lend themselves best to the task? How can you make it interesting? How will students become actively involved? How can you avoid a traditional didactic approach and employ inquiry methods? These are all important questions you will need to think about.

Finally, you need to think about your evaluation plan. There are many forms of evaluation, each of which can serve a specific purpose in your teaching. Begin to think about evaluation as you plan your unit or course, not as you approach the end of it. For further help on this aspect, read chapters seventeen and eighteen in this book.

■ SOME ELEMENTS AND STRATEGIES OF EFFECTIVE SCIENCE TEACHING

Teaching is more than telling. Often individuals approach teaching as the relatively simple task of telling about a scientific fact or concept. As you will see, it is much more. Teaching is not necessarily more difficult. As it turns out, telling is sometimes a difficult way to teach an idea. Effective teaching requires a great deal of thought, preparation, and design. In the following paragraphs we introduce some ideas that you might keep in mind while designing a lesson, teaching unit, or entire science curriculum.

Before a Lesson or Unit

Several times in this book we have indicated the importance of goals and objectives. They emerge here as the fundamental consideration of the planning process.

Goals and objectives are like maps. They indicate the journey and the day's destination, respectively. Goals and objectives indicate where you are going and tell you when you have arrived. In teaching, it is often well to remember that, like travel, the destination defines the trip, and the means of travel accommodates other aspects of the trip (for example, budget, time, and access). We recommend careful thought and identification of goals and objectives at an appropriate level for the individual or class. Once you actually have designed the lesson and begun teaching, it is important to continually direct and redirect teaching to your goals and objectives. To use the trip analogy again, one can have educational side trips, but it is essential to continue in the general direction of your daily objectives and your unit or yearly goals.

After you have identified goals and objectives, you will have to decide on such things as *content, time, pacing, grouping,* and *activities.* These decisions were described in chapter two.

Beginning a Lesson or Unit

How you begin sets the stage for the lesson and unit. The beginning of a lesson should achieve several things. First, it should connect what has been learned in the past with what is going to be learned in the present lesson. While the connections may seem obvious to you as the teacher, it is not always as clear to the students. Second, a good beginning can provide a focus or context for the present lesson. Effective beginnings answer the why and what questions that students may have. Third, the beginning should be exciting and engaging. Students should be enthusiastic about what they are going to study.

There are many effective ways to begin a unit of study or a daily lesson. Demonstrations, current events, confrontation with problems, pictorial riddles, discrepant events, counter-intuitive situations, and challenging questions are but some of the ways to begin a teaching sequence.

The Middle of a Lesson or Unit

Once the lesson or unit is underway, there is a lot to do. With experience, you can incorporate more elements and strategies into science teaching. Here are a few initial ideas to consider as you design lessons. Active participation with materials, equipment, and audiovisual aids is a good way to engage the learner's attention and develop the concepts, skills, and values of your objectives. You want to optimize the amount of time students are *engaged* in learning tasks.

There are different means of capturing, maintaining, and enhancing students' attention. These motivational strategies include showing the personal meaning of the lesson in the students' lives. Personal meaning can be provided through a rationale, or by connecting an idea or concept to the students' lives, or answering a personal question. Success is another motivator. New objects and experiences can improve student interest and attention as much as success.

Once you are into the lesson, remember to apply the principles of learning and development. At a minimum, use reinforcement to discourage non productive behaviors. When introducing skills it is often essential to model what you want the students to do. For example, demonstrate how you want them to set up and dismantle laboratory equipment or use the probes of a microcomputer-based laboratory.

Practice is another element of learning. Some ideas, skills, and values are learned because they have great personal meaning. In others, proficiency is achieved through repetition of a task. Don't hesitate to schedule time to practice the skills that you perceive to be important. Sometimes practice can be done with the entire class, usually at the initial stages of learning; other times practice can be individualized and either distributed throughout or clustered at the end of the learning sequence.

As you teach the lesson, it is valuable to monitor student progress. How are they doing? Do they understand what has been taught? If students are not progressing as you had anticipated, it is well worth adapting the sequence or method to better enhance student learning. The assessment can be as simple as spotchecking papers, asking questions, or giving a quiz. The crucial point is to change instruction based on the assessment.

There is another, sometimes illusive, set of factors that are important for planning and teaching.

These factors can be thought of as the classroom climate. What plans should be made to establish a classroom environment that enhances student learning? Planning your lesson or unit should include *communicating expectations of achievement—your goals, procedures for a safe and orderly work environment, anticipation and sensible management of disruptive behavior, and establishment of cooperative learning.*[2]

Yes, there is a lot that goes into teaching. Some of the factors described above can actually be a part of your planning, while others are part of your instructional theory.

Ending a Lesson or Unit

Too often lessons and units just stop. Plan an ending to your lesson. There should be closure, an opportunity for you or your students to summarize what has been taught. At the lesson's end, you should be able to indicate how well the objectives were met. Students ought to leave the room with a feeling of accomplishment and closure for the day's lesson or the unit.

After a Lesson or Unit

When a lesson or unit is over, you should have some measure of the lesson and student achievement. The measure can be an informal assessment of how things went and what they learned, or a formal evaluation of the lesson through a quiz or test of student achievement. These procedures are feedback for you and the students. They indicate what might be changed in the instructional sequence and the problems students may be having with the material. The next section is a more complete description of planning for effective science teaching.

■ DESIGNING PROGRAMS, UNITS, AND LESSONS

This section is designed to have you take steps toward the practical, everyday matter of science teaching. You have just read about some general strategies of effective teaching. Here many of the elements and methods are combined into a sequence of instruction. While there are many models and methods for teaching science, the purpose of this section is to have you begin thinking generally about your science program and specifically about planning science lessons. We take the approach of beginning with the science program, the year-long plan. Although this is probably not your most immediate concern, having the big picture of your science program provides the framework for consistent and coherent units and lessons. The sequence is the science program, unit plans, and lesson plans.

■ THE LONG-RANGE PLAN: A SCIENCE PROGRAM

Our goal for this brief section is to have you begin thinking about a full year's science program. The essential elements for this section are discussed in length in the chapters on curriculum. We recommend review of chapters 7 and 8. To accomplish our goal of conceptualizing a total science program—seeing the forest before looking at trees—you should complete the activity "Designing a Full-Year Program," at the end of this chapter.

Designing your science program will be a major challenge. You will have to synthesize many diverse ideas and recommendations into your program. Objectives, topics, and activities come from a variety of issues. These sources may include the following:

- science department requirements,
- district syllabi,
- state guidelines,
- textbook organization, and
- national organizations.

Sorting all of these recommendations is not easy. Fortunately, many of the recommendations are more consistent than not. In the end, you will decide on your science program. That is why we encourage you to begin thinking about how to organize your program. There are many ways to organize programs. We briefly describe some of those ways in the next section.

Structure of the Discipline

Science disciplines are organized by major conceptual structure. Themes such as thermodynamics in physics, bonding in chemistry, and diversity in biology are examples of conceptual schemes that organize disciplines. Curriculum projects of the 1960s and 1970s were organized by the structure of disciplines.

Nature of Scientific Inquiry

Inquiry refers to the ways scientists within disciplines determine the truth or falsehood, validity or invalidity of knowledge claims. The inquiry includes the processes scientists use—observation, classification, controlling variables, forming hypotheses, and designing experiments. But organizing on the basis of inquiry includes more—the study of how and why scientific propositions are accepted or rejected. If scientists have competing theories, how does one know which is acceptable?

TABLE 15–1
Yearly calendar for a course orgaized by concepts and issues

Unit	Issue	Concepts	Days Alloted
I	Science and technology in society	The nature of science and technology	10
II	Air quality	Cycles	20
III	Land use	Scale	20
IV	Water quality	Equilibrium	20
V	Hazardous substances	Gradient	25
VI	Space exploration	Systems	40
VII	Population, resources, environment	Interactions	45
			(Total 180 days)

Topics of Science Disciplines

Topics can be used to organize science courses. Electricity, magnets, rocks and minerals, cell division, and photosynthesis are examples of topics.

Issues Related to Science

In recent years, there has been a trend toward using issues to organize courses. In many cases, the issues cut across the science disciplines. If carefully and properly done, organizing a program by issues can be exciting for students and will include many important science concepts and processes. Some issues are: air quality and atmosphere, water resources, land use, population growth, food resources, mineral resources, and environmental quality.

Organizing a science program can take the form of a yearly calendar. The calendar indicates the order of units and time allotted to them. Table 15–1 is a calendar for a course organized by both integrating concepts and social issues. Examination of textbooks and state syllabi will provide other examples of yearly calendars.

In preparing this calendar, the order of issues and concepts generally moves from simple to complex. The more complex problems come later in the year, and more time is allotted for study of these issues. There are 180 days, the average number of classes a science teacher has in a school year.

■ THE MIDDLE-RANGE PLAN: A SCIENCE UNIT

Ms. Henderson was a new teacher of tenth-grade physical science at Warren High School. The head of the science department, Mr. Longwell, who had taught the course the previous year, had talked briefly with Ms. Henderson about the objectives and general nature of the course.

No textbook was being used. Mr. Longwell believed that most physical science textbooks tried to cover too many topics in a one-year course. To permit time for greater depth of study, only five major areas were taught in physical science at Warren High: the nature of the atom, the nature of the molecule, nuclear energy, radiant energy, and human applications of physical science. Materials for the course were provided by the purchase of small paperback books on appropriate science topics and the development and photocopying of activities.

When they discussed the objectives of the physical science course, Ms. Henderson and Mr. Longwell agreed that it should serve a dual role: to introduce students to the more rigorous specialized chemistry and physics courses in the eleventh and twelfth grades of Warren High School, and to function as a terminal science course for those students who were planning to go into nonscience areas of study. As much as possible, chosen topics were approached from an activity and laboratory point of view.

With this background for the course, Ms. Henderson decided to outline the year's work. Her first task was to plan the sequence of topics. She decided that the sequence used by Mr. Longwell—atom, molecule, nucleus, radiations, applications—had stood the test of experience and seemed to be a logical sequence; therefore, she would use this sequence the first year and modify it in the future if necessary. With only five areas to study, it seemed feasible to plan about six weeks on each of the first three topics and eight weeks on each of the last two. This schedule would enable the class to finish the third topic at the end of the first semester. Ms. Henderson realized that this schedule might have to be modified, but she was prepared to make the necessary adjustments when needed.

Over the next few days, other parts of the long-range plan were finalized. Films were ordered to arrive as near proper times as could be estimated so early in the year. Dates of holidays and examination periods were considered. Some thought was given to a possible excursion or two during classes on applications, but the dates were left tentative. The storage room was checked for apparatus and laboratory supplies and seemed adequate, but Ms. Henderson knew that certain unavailable materials might be needed on short notice. She checked with Mr. Longwell and found that expendable items could be obtained within a week from a laboratory-supply house.

Ms. Henderson kept a loose-leaf planning notebook for each of her classes. The long-range plan and schedule were placed in the front of this notebook, and space was allotted for notes and modifications.

A beginning teacher is assisted by a teaching-unit plan designed in moderate detail for a period of a month or six weeks. The unit topic is usually a cohesive area of study that fits into long-range plans and objectives. The teaching unit frequently contains the following sections and characteristics:

1. Title
2. Purpose statement
3. Objectives
4. Content
5. Methods
6. Materials
7. Evaluation
8. Teaching sequence

The *title* is simply an identifying name for the unit. It need not be anything complicated; for example, "An Introduction To Physics," "Human Ecology," or "Earth Processes: Folds and Faults."

A *purpose statement* is a synopsis of *why* this unit is important and generally *what* will be accomplished by the teaching unit.

The *objectives* should be specific, brief statements of purpose for the unit. They should serve as constant reminders to the teacher of the things to be accomplished in the time allotted. They should be practical, timely, and carefully suited to the capabilities of the class. Objectives should be clearly written and testable.

Content refers to the actual material to be taught in the unit. Because this material may be extensive, the teaching-unit plan cannot list all of it in minute detail; however, the plan may list major principles, pertinent facts of major importance, examples and illustrations, and references to specific knowledge in text material deemed important for the unit. An outline form may be used in this part of the unit plan. Because of the chronological nature of the teaching unit, specific content and references to subject matter can be distributed sequentially throughout the unit.

Methods to be used in teaching should be planned as carefully as possible. This is where the use of one (or a combination) of instructional models is highly recommended. Plan through the sequence of lessons using a model. Based on the model and your objectives, certain parts of the teaching sequence may be taught more suitably by one method than by another. For example, a film may be the most effective teaching agent for an introduction (e.g. engagement, anticipatory set) and a simulation game may be most appropriate as an elaboration of the lesson's concepts. At another time you may deem a discussion or individual project to be the best teaching method.

Materials must be planned with care to ensure their availability when they are needed. In some cases, ordering a few weeks in advance is necessary. Apparatus should be checked to see if it is in working order. Development of the teaching unit will undoubtedly involve hours of library work, getting ideas for reading materials and activities. Consideration should be given to the needs of slow and gifted learners and suitable materials should be arranged for them.

Evaluation should be thought of as a continuing process throughout the unit. One of the major functions of evaluation is to keep students informed of their progress and to give them realistic assessments of their own abilities. Assigned work, short quizzes, conferences, and unit tests must be planned in the teaching unit. Not all of the evaluative devices and techniques can be planned in detail in advance, but provision for them can be made. Evaluation should be based on the objectives of the unit.

The *teaching sequence* may be outlined for the period of time involved, but flexibility for change must be provided. This can be done by arranging for alternative procedures, omitting or adding certain subject matter, and providing for unplanned periods that can occasionally be interspersed to take up slack or give needed time for completing a topic.

The teaching unit should be thought of as a guide for action rather than a calendar of events. Slavish attention to the preplanned schedule can result in ineffective rigidity. On the other hand, reasonable attention to the sequence, objectives, and procedures of the teaching unit can promote better learning, satisfaction, and accomplishment. A general outline for a unit is presented here.

Outline for a Science Teaching Unit

- Title
- Purpose Statement
- Outline for a Year Program (Use "Designing a Full-Year Program" and indicate where your unit is located in the total program.)
- Objectives for the Unit
- Weekly Schedule for the Unit (See Table 15–2 for an example.)
- Pretest
- Daily Lesson Plans (Use a specific model or combination of models.)
- Unit Test

TABLE 15–2
Example of a weekly schedule for a middle school science class studying environmental change

Content Outline	Class Period	Phase of Teaching Model	Class Activity
Environmental problems in paper	Homework	Engagement	Students collect examples of the newspaper articles dealing with environmental problems, e.g., hazardous substances, or pollution.
Evidence of environmental change • change is common • There are good, bad, and neutral changes	1	Exploration	Class goes outside and gathers evidence of change in local environment. They should find good, bad, and neutral changes.
Factors related to environmental change • Immediate • Delayed • Cycles • Growth	2	Explanation	Film "The Saga of DDT." Use film to focus discussion on key concepts. End class with short lecturing, defining and giving examples of immediate change, delayed change, cyclical change, and change through growth.
Changing environmental systems	3	Elaboration	Do silent demonstrations of changes in aquatic and terrestrial ecosystems. Have students identify potential immediate, delayed, cyclical, and growth changes.
Limits to change in environmental systems	4	Elaboration	Do Invitation to Inquiry on "Tragedy of the Commons." Use cooperative groups.
End of section	5	Evaluation	Quiz on concepts. Students will define concept and give one local and one global example.

■ CHECKLIST OF REQUIREMENTS FOR THE SCIENCE UNIT

Your teacher will indicate those things he/she requires for your unit. You can use this checklist to organize your science unit.

1. *Title Page.* Give the title of the unit, grade level, and whether it is based on a new curriculum. If it uses a modern curriculum, state its name. List your name, the title and number of the course, and leave a space for the unit evaluation.
2. *Purpose Statement.* Give the reason for the scope and sequence of the unit. Indicate the broad goals to be achieved through the unit.
3. *Objectives.* Preferably, these should be stated in behavioral terms.
4. *Weekly Schedule of the Unit.* A brief, one-page survey of what will take place each day as shown in Table 15–2.
   a. Include reading assignments.
   b. Include homework activities.
5. *Laboratory Exercises.* These should be some of your own laboratory activities, including the following:
   a. The subject-matter objectives (concepts) the laboratory will teach.

   b. Critical thinking and problem-solving processes the lesson will develop, indicated in the margin of the activity.
   c. A discussion section preceding the lesson and open-ended possibilities following the lesson.
   d. Other (assigned by your instructor).
6. *Invitations to Inquiry.* (You are to prepare these invitations.)
7. *Discussion Questions During or at the End of the Unit.*
   a. List the questions you will ask to determine if the students understood the material studied and if they can apply what they have learned.
   b. When possible, the questions should develop critical thinking and problem-solving processes. The type of mental process the student must use—for example, predicting or inferring—should be placed in the margin to indicate what is required.
8. *Pictorial Riddles.* The pictures or diagrams for these riddles should be included. Place under them the questions you will ask.
9. *Demonstrations.* Include only if they are required because of a shortage of equipment or examples of safety reasons.

10. *Bulletin Board Display.* Prepare a diagram for at least one bulletin board display, indicating how it will appear.
11. *Supplemental Materials.*
    a. Laboratories or investigations
    b. Reading materials
12. *Audiovisual Materials.*
    a. Films
    b. Film loops and filmstrips
    c. Audiotapes
    d. Transparencies
    e. Models, charts
13. *Consideration of Safety Precautions.* What, if any, special considerations should be made about safety?
14. *Consideration of Special Students.* You might wish to include the variations on the lesson you would implement if you have special students—for example, deaf or gifted.
15. *Reference or Resource Materials.* Include magazine materials and books you might want to use to improve your knowledge about the topic; may include teacher's manuals.
16. *Tests and Evaluation.* All tests should evaluate your objectives.
    a. Quizzes—Include at least one quiz.
    b. Practicals—These are tests using actual laboratory materials.
    c. Unit tests—Include higher-order questions and indicate the course objectives.
17. *Self-Evaluation of the Unit.*
    a. After compiling this unit outline, go back over it and write what problems you think you might have in teaching.
    b. After teaching this unit, evaluate how you think it could be improved. (Leave this space for your information so you may record your evaluation later.)

■ THE RESOURCE UNIT

Many science teachers prepare a resource unit for the different topics they teach. A resource unit is, as the title indicates, a collection of resource materials that can be used for a specified topic (e.g., acids and bases, the laws of thermodynamics, the rock cycle, or photosynthesis) or various issues (e.g., population growth, air quality, world hunger, or health and disease). Rather than assemble the resources in a teaching sequence such as we have discussed above, a resource unit is usually arranged by teaching strategies or methods. If you begin organizing resource units now, it will only be a few years before you have an extensive collection of ideas and methods. While you will have to determine the topics or issues for your science program, we can provide some general

organizational categories for resource units. You would probably want to develop resource units for each of the major topics you plan to teach.

Organization Categories for Resource Units
- Aims and Goals
- Objectives
- Bulletin Boards
- Computer Software
- Demonstrations
- Discussion Topics
- Field Trips
- Films
- Filmstrips
- Games
- Homework
- Invitations to Inquiry
- Lecture Notes
- Overhead Transparencies
- Projects
- Supplementary Readings
- Tests and Quizzes
- Videos
- Worksheets
- Miscellaneous

You will probably not use all of these categories, and will perhaps add some of your own, but this list should help you begin organizing your resource units. Use of a personal computer and a database or Hypercard program will greatly enhance your organization, filing, and search capacity. Table 15–3 is a more complete description of the categories and examples of materials for a resource unit.

■ THE SHORT-RANGE PLAN: THE SCIENCE LESSON

The sequence of topics in this chapter may have seemed unusual to the science teacher facing a first lesson. We think there is added advantage for all teachers who have thought through their year's program and a unit before writing a daily lesson plan. Planning gives direction. A yearly plan guards against disconnected units, and unit plans protect against disconnected lessons. For all teachers, planning is an essential component of effective instruction. Approaching a science class with a well-organized plan gives the teacher personal assurance and leaves the students with confidence in the teacher's abilities.

Thought planning should precede any written plans. Ask yourself questions such as:

- What are my goals?
- How can I best achieve my goals?
- What will motivate the students to learn the concepts? Processes? Skills?

TABLE 15–3
Resource unit: Examples of categories and contents

Categories	Contents
Aims and goals	Lists of aims and goals from your local district, state education agency, national organizations, and textbooks.
Objectives	Lists of objectives from your local district, state education agency, national organizations, and textbooks.
Bulletin boards	Sketches and designs, newspaper and magazine articles, pictures, and maps.
Computer software	CAI programs, microcomputer-based laboratory, tutorial, simulation, HyperCard, models.
Demonstrations	Collections of good demonstrations from journals such as *Science Scope, The Science Teacher, The American Biology Teacher, The Physics Teacher;* ideas from workshops and college courses.
Discussion topics	Questions and issues that are successful with students.
Field trips	Description of where to go, what to do, and who to contact.
Films, filmstrips, filmloops	Lists of films from school, local media center, state education agency, good films previewed at conventions, and college courses.
Games	List of games in science department, local media center.
Homework	Unique and interesting homework assignments for the topic.
Invitations to inquiry	Lists of appropriate invitations from *Biology Teachers Handbook,* invitations you have developed, ideas for invitations.
Lecture notes	Revised notes from past courses.
Overhead transparencies	List (by title or content) of transparencies on file.
Projects	Problems and ideas for projects.
Supplementary readings	Books and articles in media center, your file, or public library.
Tests and quizzes	Copies of quizzes, tests, and questions.
Videos	List of videos from NOVA, DISCOVERY, etc. for VCR replay.
Worksheets	Masters for worksheets.
Miscellaneous	Other items that will help in the unit.

- How can the concepts, processes, or skills be presented most effectively?
- What can be done for an effective beginning, middle, and end of the lesson?
- How can I evaluate the lesson's effectiveness?

Since students vary in abilities and interests, plans must provide for these variations. Some method of motivating each student must be found. Only by knowing something of the background of each student can the teacher be effective. This fact argues strongly for taking a personal interest in the students in one's classes. The small human contacts in a friendly classroom, an interested question here and there, can motivate students better than any other method.

Planning for effective science teaching is more than just making sure that there is something to do for the entire class period. For example, unless it is the very first lesson of the year, it is probable that assignments have been made and that the nature of the subject matter is understood. Thus, the basis for planning has already been established.

To conduct an interesting class period, the teacher must vary the methods from day to day and even within the class period itself. It is eventually ineffective to use the same pattern of teaching every day. Even an excellent method can suffer from overuse. With the great variety of methods from which to choose and with the potential excitement of inventing a new technique or of modifying one, the science teacher is in an excellent position to plan a highly effective lesson.

The teaching model described in chapter fourteen can be used to organize lessons. Recall that the model is designed to promote conceptual change and skill development. You should review Table 15–4, which is a summary of the teaching model.

The written plan should be concise and functional. The format may vary with the situation and individual teacher, but most importantly it should be a practical, usable plan. In general, there should be provision for listing *objectives* and the related *concepts.* The learning *activities* and required procedures should be listed. The procedures ought to be in adequate detail—for example, write out questions and directions to ensure a smooth class. All *materials* needed for the class period should be listed and checked. Two last essentials are *assignments* and *evaluation.* A skeletal form for a daily lesson would include the topics listed below.

1. Objectives
2. Concepts
3. Activities/Procedures
4. Materials
5. Assignments
6. Evaluation

TABLE 15–4
An instructional sequence for planning lessons

Engagement

This phase of the instructional sequence initiates the learning task. The activity should (1) make connections between past and present learning experiences, and (2) anticipate activities and focus students' thinking on the learning outcomes of current activities. The student should become mentally engaged in the concept, process, or skill to be explored.

Exploration

This phase of the teaching sequence provides students with a common base of experiences within which they identify and develop current concepts, processes, and skills. During this phase, students actively explore their environment or manipulate materials.

Explanation

This phase of the instructional sequence focuses students' attention on a particular aspect of their engagement and exploration experiences and provides opportunities for them to verbalize their conceptual understanding, or demonstrate their skills or behaviors. This phase also provides opportunities for teachers to introduce a formal label or definition for a concept, process, skill, or behavior.

Elaboration

This phase of the teaching sequence challenges and extends students' conceptual understanding and allows further opportunity for students to practice desired skills and behaviors. Through new experiences, the students develop deeper and broader understanding, more information, and adequate skills.

Evaluation

This phase of the teaching sequence encourages students to assess their understanding and abilities and provides opportunities for teachers to evaluate student progress toward achieving the educational objectives.

More general formats appear outlined here. We recommend you use one of these for your first lesson. With experience, science teachers often use less detailed plans, but if they are effective, they have thoroughly thought through their plan, no doubt in the detail suggested by these formats.

If you examine the "Teaching Science Activity: An Introduction to Population, Resources, and Environment" in the Appendix, pp. 402–403, you will see a thorough lesson plan. In this plan we have combined many instructional strategies, methods, and the instructional model to show how these can be pulled together for a teaching lesson. We suggest that you plan at least one lesson in this detail as a portion of your methods course experience. To this end, we recommend completing "A Complete Lesson Plan" at the end of this chapter.

During the class hour, a teaching plan should be as unobtrusive as possible, yet referred to when needed. Main ideas, questions, and procedures may be memorized. Be sure the plan is handy if you need it for reference. As we mentioned above, a plan gives direction. You should also plan for flexibility: Realize that you will have to make some decisions about the direction of a particular lesson based on circumstances that arise in class.

After each lesson, we recommend evaluating the lesson plan. The experience gained in teaching a lesson should be recorded with brief notations on the written plan, either during the class period or immediately after class. Suggestions for timing, organization, student involvement, or modification of a technique can be noted for future use. (See "Evaluation of Instructional Skills" at the end of this chapter.)

We will conclude this section with some helpful hints for contemporary lesson planning. Planning lessons that include goals such as problem solving, inquiry, study of controversial science-related social issues, and decision making present certain unique problems. To help organize your planning in advance, we here list some features of lessons for contemporary science teaching.

Students are involved in broad, open-ended questions related to science, technology, and/or social issues related to science and technology. Generally, students do not know the answer to the question.

Students are required to understand the problem before designing an experiment.

Students design their own investigations and make their own observations and conclusions.

Students write their results using the standard protocol of science papers. Students extend their findings in several ways: to new problems, methods and experiments; to decisions relative to the issues; and to practical applications for life and living.

Students in contemporary science classes are given much more responsibility in planning experiments and carrying them to completion than has traditionally been the case. Effective handling of this responsibility will depend largely on how well the science teacher can provide experiences that will develop students capable of designing experiments, gathering data, and drawing conclusions from them.

Planning for such experiences should be done with the following points in mind:

1. Students probably have not had many previous opportunities of this type. Some may feel the need for explicit directions. The initial progress made by these students may be disappointing and frustrating, both to student and teacher.

2. Accepting responsibility for one's own learning is a challenge that some students may tend to resist. Passive learning in which the teacher has been the key person for initiating a course of action has probably been ingrained in the students' backgrounds.

3. First attempts should be on a small scale, with opportunities for greater choice and greater responsibility increasing as the student gains experience.

4. Rather than acting as a dispenser of information, the teacher should provide situations in which questions are asked. Students should be encouraged to formulate and ask questions of themselves, of the experiment, of resource persons, and of library resource materials.

5. Means must be provided for students to gain experience in analyzing the results of an experiment. The ability to see relationships, to organize data so that meaningful patterns emerge, to draw inferences, and to visualize ways of improving the experiment is a necessary skill which must be developed for effective learning by the inquiry method.

■ SUMMARY

Planning is one of the critical aspects of effective science teaching. When designing a lesson, teaching unit, or total course, you should keep in mind some ideas that are fundamental to effective instruction: use objectives, focus teaching on the objective, be sure students actively participate, apply principles of learning and motivation, and develop lessons with a beginning, middle, and end that are educationally productive.

A variety of methods are used in contemporary science teaching. Some of the key methods are lecturing, questioning, discussing, demonstrating, reading, role playing, presenting reports, doing projects, working in the laboratory, solving problems, taking field trips, showing films and filmstrips, conducting simulations, and debating.

Science teachers can use models of teaching that combine strategies and methods into an instructional sequence. Using teaching models contributes to more efficient design of science lessons, and the synthesis of many elements of instruction into a workable and effective form.

The long-range plan of science teaching is the full-year program. This idea has been introduced briefly. There are at least two kinds of middle-range

unit lesson plans. The teaching unit is planned with a time sequence in mind and usually provides for statements of objectives, outlines of content, methods, materials, and evaluation techniques. The resource unit is not usually concerned with chronology but a reservoir that the teacher uses for daily lesson planning. It may contain lists of aims, important knowledge objectives, lists of activities and projects, computer software, suitable demonstrations and experiments, references, films, bibliographies, sample tests, assignments, and other teaching aids.

The lesson plan is a guide for action, not a rigid blueprint to be followed unswervingly. It should be flexible and should be modified when necessary. Much thought precedes the writing of a lesson plan. Consider such questions as, "What is the purpose of the lesson?" "What major generalizations are to be taught?" "How is the material best presented?" and "What kinds of individuals are in the class?" before planning the sequence on paper.

The format of the lesson plan should be functional and comfortable to the teacher. Individual teachers select the format most useful to them. Lesson plans should be as concise as possible within the limitations of effective teaching. While teaching, the lesson plan should be unobtrusive but available for reference.

Planning for contemporary science teaching usually requires a somewhat different approach than more traditional methods. The role of the teacher becomes one of guidance and direction, with students accepting greater responsibility for learning. Plans must provide more time, more questioning, greater variety of materials, and willingness on the part of the teacher to allow individual variations in progress by students.

Thorough lesson planning is a necessary facet of effective science teaching. Good teaching does not happen by accident. It is particularly important that a prospective teacher of science recognizes the values and benefits to be derived from careful, inspired planning in the art of science teaching.

■ REFERENCES

1. NSTA, "Science-Technology-Society: Science Education for the 1980's," position paper (Washington, DC: Author, 1982), pp. 1–2.

2. David Berliner, "The Half-full Glass: A Review of Research in Teaching," in *Using What We Know About Teaching*, Philip Hosford, ed. (Alexandria, VA: Association for Supervision and Curriculum Development (1984), pp. 51–77.

INVESTIGATING SCIENCE TEACHING

Activity 15–1

PLANNING A SIMPLE LESSON

1. Select a simple and specific short-range objective for a science class, such as "to develop skill in correct use of the microscope," or "to learn how to use a balance," or "to operate a microcomputer." Plan a lesson to achieve this objective, incorporating the features of a good lesson plan.
2. Using the lesson plan prepared above, or a similar one, teach your classmates the lesson. Invite them to play the role of secondary science class, with appropriate questions and activities. Solicit their constructive criticisms and comments on your lesson and the effectiveness of your teaching.

Activity 15–2

EVALUATING A LESSON

A lesson plan for an eighth-grade science class is described below. Read through the description of the teacher's preparation and topic and study the teacher's written lesson plan. Then respond to the questions at the end of the section.

Mr. Foster looked forward to planning the eighth-grade science class on Monday morning. The topic for consideration was the simple Mendelian ratio of 1:2:1 for the offspring in the first generation produced by crossing of two pure strains. As he thought of the students in his class, it seemed that he might involve them in class participation and generate enthusiasm by doing a demonstration experiment. He would use the crossing of pure white and pure black guinea pigs as a simple case to illustrate this phenomenon.

In pure strains the genes for coat color in the parents could be represented by BB and ww. The only possible combinations in the first generation offspring would be Bw. These animals would be black but each would carry the gene for white. If animals of this genetic makeup were crossed, the possible combinations in their offspring (second generation) would by BB, Bw, wB, and ww.

To demonstrate the purely statistical nature of the results obtained in this cross and of the effect of dominant over recessive genes, Mr. Foster decided to make a simple arrow spinner that would be attached to the blackboard with a suction cup. Then a circle could be drawn on the blackboard, around the spinner, and labeled as shown in the figure. With this device, he could engage the class in a "game of chance," give them practice in keeping a record of the data, and put across the point of the lesson in an interesting manner.

After constructing the spinner, Mr. Foster decided to give it a trial run to see if it would perform satisfactorily and if the demonstration could be accommodated in the fifty-minute class period. Out of forty trials, the results he obtained in his trial run were

	BB	BW	WB	WW
Trials:	11	8	11	10

It took ten minutes and the results appeared to be close enough to the expected values to illustrate the point. He decided to plan his class period around this demonstration experiment.

On paper, Mr. Foster's lesson plan looked like this:

Life Science 8

Topic: Simple Mendelian ratio
Purpose: To show the statistical nature of the Mendelian ratio
Objective: At the completion of this lesson the student should be able to predict the approximate proportions of each gene combination obtained with 100 trials of the spinner.

Introductory remarks and questions (10 min.):

1. What is meant by *dominant gene?* By *recessive gene?*
2. Suppose a pure-bred black and a pure-bred white guinea pig (BB, ww) were mated. What genes have they for color? What would be the color of their offspring?
3. What are the possible combinations of dominant and recessive genes for color of coat? (BB, Bw, wB, ww)
4. What might be the proportions of each of these combinations in the offspring? (1:1:1:1—since Bw and wB are the same, the ratios appear as 1:2:1)
5. How would we show that this is the result of statistical probability?

Activity: Set up the blackboard spinner. Select a volunteer to spin it. Select another volunteer to keep a record on the blackboard under the headings BB, Bw, wB, and ww. Continue for 10-15 minutes.

Discussion (20 min.):

1. What are the actual colors of offspring which have each of the possible gene combinations? (three black and one white)
2. Why aren't the results in an exact ratio of 1:2:1? (change variations when few trials are used)
3. Could we improve the results? (more trials)
4. Student questions (anticipated)

Assignment (a volunteer assignment): Two boys or girls might run this experiment for more trials to see what the results would be.

Evaluation:

Time OK?___Interest?___Understanding?___Student Learning?___

_____

1. How would you improve Mr. Foster's lesson?

2. What pitfalls and precautions would you advise Mr. Foster about?

3. What features would you identify as a well-planned lesson?

Activity 15–3
PLANNING A UNIT: PRELIMINARY QUESTIONS

Suppose you are faced with the task of planning and carrying out a unit of work (e.g. 4-5 weeks) in your teaching area. What questions might you ask yourself? How will you organize your thoughts and plans? Consider each of the following questions:

1. What will be some important factors to take into consideration?

2. How might you involve students in the planning? How much student involvement is desirable?

3. What different levels of planning will probably be necessary?

4. What parts of your plans will you, of necessity, put down in written form?

5. What parts of your plans might you prefer to note mentally but not necessarily write down?

6. How much importance will you grant to a time budget?

7. How will you provide for the anticipated procedure questions and activities of the class? For the unanticipated questions and activities?

8. How will you provide for flexibility so that unexpected events can be handled adequately?

9. What purpose will evaluation serve in subsequent planning?
   a. From the standpoint of knowledge acquired by the students?

   b. From the standpoint of modification of the plans for the next teaching session?

Activity 15–4

DESIGNING A FULL-YEAR PROGRAM

As best you can, design a year's science program. We have found it best to complete the preliminary items as a way of thinking through your ideas. Then, complete the weekly schedule. You may wish to indicate major units within the weekly outline. Finally, complete the questions at the end of the investigation.

Title of Program: Preliminary Textbook:
Discipline: Supplemental Textbook(s):
Grade Level:
Purpose Statement:

Weekly Schedule for an Academic Year: Unit Topics for an Academic Year:
  1.
  2.
  3.
  4.
  5.
  6.
  7.
  8.
  9.
 10.
 11.
 12.
 13.
 14.
 15.
 16.
 17.
 18.
 19.
 20.
 21.
 22.
 23.

24.
25.
26.
27.
28.
29.
30.
31.
32.
33.
34.
35.
36.

Questions:

What was your rationale for the sequence, or order, of topics outlined?

Activity 15–5
A COMPLETE LESSON PLAN

Think through all aspects of a lesson plan. The experience will contribute to your doing this on a less formal basis for future lessons.

Use the general format in "Teaching Science Activity: An Introduction to Population, Resources, and Environment," pages 402–403.

- Topic
- Aims
- Objectives
- Materials
- Instructional Plan
- Evaluation

Activity 15–6

EVALUATION OF INSTRUCTIONAL SKILLS

This form is provided for a self-evaluation of a lesson you teach. The evaluation is directed toward the use of strategies, methods, and models discussed in this chapter.

	Highly skilled, superior application and integration	Very skilled, instruction is integrated, evenly consistent, and smooth	Good use of skill but does not apply consistently	Poor application of skill	Unable to observe
Selects appropriate objectives	1	2	3	4	5
Makes objectives and purposes of lesson clear to students	1	2	3	4	5
Teaches to the objective	1	2	3	4	5
1. Asks questions relevant to objective	1	2	3	4	5
2. Provides information relative to objective	1	2	3	4	5
3. Responds to learned questions/ problems related to objectives	1	2	3	4	5
Demonstrates continuity in lesson	1	2	3	4	5
1. Beginning	1	2	3	4	5
2. Middle	1	2	3	4	5
3. End	1	2	3	4	5
Uses different methods	1	2	3	4	5
Applies a model of teaching	1	2	3	4	5
1. Concept Mapping	1	2	3	4	5
2. The Learning Cycle	1	2	3	4	5
3. Cooperative Learning	1	2	3	4	5
4. Madeline Hunter	1	2	3	4	5
5. Textbook	1	2	3	4	5
6. 4MAT	1	2	3	4	5
Shows continuity of plans	1	2	3	4	5
1. Long Range (year)	1	2	3	4	5
2. Middle Range (unit)	1	2	3	4	5
3. Short Range (daily)	1	2	3	4	5

Activity 15–7

STUDENT ATTENTION

The following technique can be used to analyze student attention in class. Enlist the aid of another teacher or friend to observe your teaching for a full class period. Provide him with a form similar to the following:

OBSERVATION SHEET

Name_____Class_____

Date_____Time_____

Instructions: (a) At intervals of three minutes, count the class and determine the number of students who are actively paying attention to the lesson or activity. Use your best judgment as to whether a student is paying attention. (b) Keep a record of the types of activities engaged in by the teacher and/or class (e.g., lecture, discussion, demonstration, experiment, film, student report). Note the time of transition from one type of activity to another. Note any major occurrences, such as disciplinary action, public address system coming on, entrance of a visitor, or any unusually distracting event. Plot a graph of percent attention versus time for each class observed.

Total attendance_____

Time	Class Count	Percent	Comments
0	_____	_____	_____
3	_____	_____	_____
6	_____	_____	_____
·			
·			
·			
·			
·			

Activity 15–8

EFFECTIVENESS OF METHODS

The effectiveness of different teaching methods can often be judged by student attention. In this investigation you are provided with a class attention record for a middle school physical science class. The record is for a week and the different activities are noted. You are to review the high and low points of the week and draw conclusions about the different methods used and pupil attentiveness.

- How many methods did the teacher use?
- Which methods seemed most effective?
- What can you tell about transitions between activities?
- If you were to redesign the lessons for this what would you change?

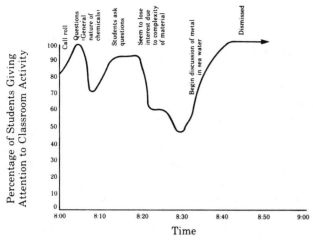

Type of class — Physical Science
Activity — Lecture discussion
(Nature of chemicals)

# of Students — 12
Monday

Class attention on Monday

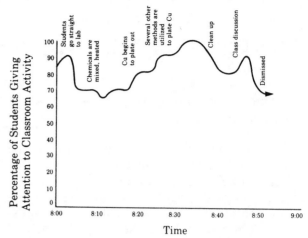

Type of Class — Physical Science
Activity — Lab (reactions)

# of Students — 11
Thursday

Class attention on Thursday

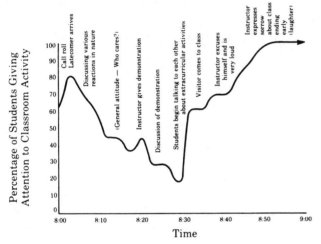

Type of class — Physical Science
Activity — Discussion (Various types
of reactions)

# of Students — 11
Tuesday

Class attention on Tuesday

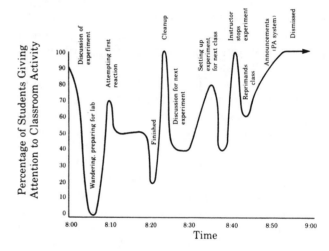

Type of Class — Physical Science
Activity — Laboratory experiments on
chemical activity of various metals

# of Students — 10
Friday

Class attention on Friday

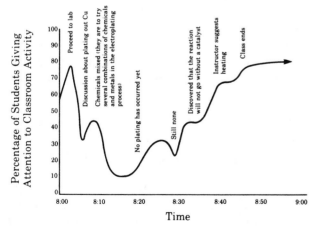

Type of class — Physical Science
Activity — Lab (electroplating)

# of Students — 9
Wednesday

Class attention on Wednesday

Chapter 16

CONTROVERSY IN THE CLASSROOM

A problem certain to face every science teacher is how to deal with controversial issues that come up in discussions in the science classroom. These may crop up unexpectedly, or they may be anticipated many months in advance. If they are anticipated, the teacher will have the advantage of preplanning, thinking through strategies, and arranging for necessary materials and information. If they occur unexpectedly, it behooves the teacher to have a general plan of action that has been considered and prepared in advance. It is wise to take the point of view that students have mind-sets, opinions, or even biases (which may reflect opinions learned at home), that they have a right to those opinions, and that the teacher's role is not one of promoting a particular point of view, but rather one of fostering orderly discussion of the issues.

Controversial issues may cover a wide range of topics and will often reflect national issues, local or parochial issues, or issues of a regional or statewide nature. The latter may occur frequently on the occasion of state or local elections, at which time the electorate will consider a variety of referendums. Some recent issues that have recently gained notoriety in the media are doctor-assisted suicide, environmental concerns regarding protection of endangered species, research on human embryos, use of human fetuses in medical research, teaching of creationism vs. evolution, controlling population growth, controlling growth of cities, use of water resources, and restrictions on smoking in public places. There is no foreseeable end to these issues, nor to the inevitable controversies that develop among the public.

Part of science education for developing children in our schools is to learn how to deal with opinions of persons whose views differ from their own. Avoiding discussion of the issues will not bring about necessary learning, changes in attitudes, understanding of others' opinions, or interaction skills with people with differing ideas. Science teachers, particularly, have a responsibility to develop skillful strategies for handling discussion and resolution of differing points of view.

Areas of biology teaching are fraught with issues that are controversial in today's world. One is the issue of genetic engineering. This is a topic that deals with genetic screening/eugenics, cloning, gene therapy (modification of human genes that cause disease), and gene alteration (of plants and animals including humans). A teaching strategy that shows promise in dealing with this and similar issues in the classroom is a debate format. An experimental procedure carried out by two teachers in Rosemount, Minnesota, has taught us much about what makes debate an effective strategy for teaching. [1]

Certain objectives were established for the unit, including: understanding of topics of genetic engineering and biotechnology; identification of different issues within the field, such as cloning; gene therapy and gene alteration; and production of a final essay summarizing the students' learning in genetic engineering.

The formal debate format worked well after thorough planning and adherence to the rules of debate. A selected judge monitored the debate procedures, and a jury of peers rendered a decision at the end of the debate. The total time required to carry out the sequence of preparation, debate time, and final discussions required seven days of class time, which was considered reasonable, considering the benefits achieved.

Some of the obvious benefits were that many students indicated they had formed their own opinions on the issues, rather than just following the crowd. Pre and posttest results showed a decrease in the number of unsure responses concerning resolution of the issues. Each student was accountable for some part of the exercise, and students maintained a high interest level throughout the period.

For teachers faced with the perplexing problem of how to approach discussion of controversial issues in class, the debate format described above offers a positive strategy. Part of the fun of using this approach is the opportunity for creative modifications and diversions of the method.

■ SCIENCE, TECHNOLOGY, AND SOCIETY (STS) AND CONTROVERSIES

Incorporation of Science, Technology, and Society topics within science classes, by their very nature, brings forth many situations subject to differing interpretations, differing values, and differing points of view. Frequently, environmental concerns come to the foreground. Matters of resource allocation and conservation generate intense interest and strong opinions among students. Pitting the economic benefits of cutting forests against the endangerment of flora and fauna living in these areas is often personalized by students, who take strong positions. Students often reflect the opinions of their parents on these matters.

In addition to the problems of providing opportunities for fair and objective discussions of the conflicting points of view found in one's classes, the teacher must also be concerned about student achievement and anxiety while sensitive topics are being discussed. Such concerns take one beyond the realms of simple evaluation and grading into areas of concern for feelings, attitude development, and values formation.

The effects of controversy relating to an STS issue on achievement and anxiety among secondary school science students were studied by Jon Pedersen, who found that "A controversy can exist when one student's ideas, information, conclusions, theories, or opinions are incompatible with those of another student or when incompatible activities occur and the students involved try to reach an agreement."[2]

A group of students studying the CHEM-COM chemistry program was divided into two sub groups. One group used a method called *cooperative controversy,* and the other group used *individualistic study.* In the cooperative controversy model, student groups of four each were formed and divided into pairs—one pair to present a pro position, and the other pair to present a con position of the issue being studied. Each pair, after sufficient preparation, presented its position, and the positions were debated by the group, which then reached a consensus and wrote a collaborative report.

In the individualistic model, students worked on their own and were told to read, study, and research the assigned issue using any resources available.

The period of time involved was twenty days (four weeks). At the end of the period, two measures were used for evaluation. Anxiety levels were measured using a State-Trait Anxiety Inventory. Class achievement was measured by a teacher-made achievement test.

The research concluded that the cooperative controversy treatment had a positive effect on the dependent variable, anxiety, but no effect on the dependent variable, achievement. Anxiety was reduced, possibly because of the opportunities for sharing information and tasks, which may have minimized difficulties of understanding among individuals. Working independently on an issue did not provide this kind of help and reinforcement.

The results shown above appear to substantiate what has been learned previously about cooperative learning and group work.

■ ETHICAL DILEMMAS

Many of the issues that pose controversial problems for discussion in science classrooms are of an ethical nature. This creates the need to consider the development and maturity of students with respect to their innate abilities to deal with complex ethical problems. Matters of moral development of children were studied by Lawrence Kohlberg in the early 1970s.[3] Kohlberg used Piaget's research on moral development as the foundation for advancing further investigation into this area. He carried out numerous studies in the United States and other countries striving to better define moral development.

One of his main works, started in 1958, involved a longitudinal study of boys at ages ten and sixteen, and followed their development past the ages of twenty-four and thirty. Kohlberg also made several cross-cultural investigations. His research has substantiated Piaget's belief that moral development is hierarchical in character. Kohlberg believed it consists of three levels, each containing identifiable stages. The three levels are: preconventional, or premoral; conventional, or conforming; and postconventional, or self-accepting moral principles.

At the preconventional level, children are responsive to such rules and labels as good and bad, right and wrong. They interpret these labels in purely physical or hedonistic terms—if they are bad, they are punished; if they are good, they are rewarded. They also interpret labels in terms of the physical power of those who enumerate them. Two stages in this level consist of punishment avoidance and reward seeking.

At the conventional level, expectations of the individual's family, group, or nation are perceived as valuable in their own right, regardless of immediate and obvious consequences. The attitude is one not only of conformity to the social order but of loyalty to it; of actively maintaining, supporting, and justifying the order; and of identifying with the persons or group involved in it. There are two stages recognized in this level: socially approved orientation and law and order orientation.

At the postconventional level there is a clear effort to teach to others a personal definition of moral values—to define principles that have validity and application apart from the authority of groups or persons and apart from the individual's own identification with these groups. Two stages in this level consist of a social-contract legalistic orientation and an orientation toward universal ethical principles. In the first of these stages, there is a clear awareness of the importance of personal values and opinions, and a corresponding emphasis on procedural rules for resolving conflicts. In the latter stage, rights are defined by the conscience in accordance with self-chosen principles, which are based on logical comprehensiveness, universality, and consistency. These principles are abstract and ethical (for example, the golden rule).

■ DESIGNING ETHICAL DILEMMAS FOR THE SCIENCE CLASSROOM

For the teacher, consideration of the moral development and maturity of students provides clues for structuring discussions of ethical dilemmas and controversial issues. Some suggestions follow:

1. Identify the conflict and theme for the dilemma (e.g., life, liberty, justice, truth, etc.).
2. Introduce the scientific or technological problem.
3. Clarify the conflict.
4. Be sure there is a dilemma (i.e., a choice between two equally unfavorable alternatives). Should the person be maintained on life-support systems or be allowed to die? Should justice be done for the individual or the group, concerning air quality that affects everyone?
5. Describe the situation and dilemma to the student in understandable terms.
6. Delineate the decision made by the main characters in the dilemma.
7. Review the moral dilemma and describe what you perceive to be the pro/con positions for each stage.
8. Ask for a definitive decision with reference to the dilemma (e.g., what should Mary do—stand up for her rights or allow the person to die?).
9. Remember that a good dilemma is simple, straightforward, and relevant to students.
10. Ask for a justification for the response.

After introducing the dilemma, the science teacher should guide the discussion, making sure the students stay on the topic. The teacher can point out inconsistencies in reasoning and more adequate resolutions to the dilemma. Be sure to let the students answer the dilemma and justify their positions.

■ OTHER STRATEGIES FOR TEACHING ABOUT CONTROVERSIAL ISSUES

Useful methods to use in science classrooms when exploring and discussing current issues of concern are role playing, the learning cycle, morphological analysis, instructional games, small-large group discussions, pictorial riddles, creativity-synectics, and others. Several of these will be described in the following pages.

Role playing is a particularly useful technique because it allows students to place themselves in someone else's shoes. One example used by the author in a teaching situation dealt with the problem of the proposed construction of a superhighway through valuable agricultural land. The issue revolved around the selection of an appropriate route that would minimize the agricultural damage. Obviously, there are more than two sides to such an issue.

To set up the situation, describe the following: There is the federal transportation department, a cabinet-level position, that has jurisdiction over interstate highways. There is the truckers' union that is concerned with economy of delivering goods. The agricultural community, represented by several state and federal agencies, is intimately concerned and affected by any decisions. In addition, a number of organizations are concerned with environmental issues; business groups from small cities and towns that might be bypassed by such a superhighway express their concerns; and other groups interested in aesthetics and general quality of life are also vocal in their expressions of concern.

To get the teaching activities started, the instructor suggested a number or roles that might properly be included in the exercise. Such roles might include the representative of the highway department, chair of one or more agricultural agencies, president of a local environmental club, a number of farmers along the proposed route who would be directly affected by the construction, a lawyer for the highway department, as well as a lawyer for the agricultural agencies, and others. Students were encouraged to suggest other roles that might enhance the discussion of the issues.

A short prospectus was written by the instructor for each of the proposed roles. The prospectus in each case was general and suggested general points of view that the player might take. Ample opportunity was provided for role-players to create, amplify, or embellish their points of view. This generated superb interest on the part of class members and led to much humor and good feeling. Roles were chosen or assigned, and the portion of the class not involved in the role-playing function were assigned the task of evaluating the effectiveness of each presentation and deciding on the outcome.

After one or two days of preparation to gather facts and figures, prepare statements, discuss pros and cons, and research data, a day was chosen for the meeting of the various representatives. This hearing was open to the public, i.e., other members of the class. The meeting was chaired by an impartial moderator and was carried on during a normal fifty minute class period.

An obvious benefit of this teaching strategy was the evidence of high interest generated by the discussion. No students were apathetic or bored, even those with a peripheral role to play. Preparation for the event was excellent as students sought out supporting data for their arguments. An extension of the role-playing strategy could be made by inviting other classes to sit in as observers. The author's experience led him to believe the method could be used frequently, with variations on other issues and topics covered in the science class.

Morphological analysis has potential as a method for exploring and explicating solutions for problems arising in controversial situations. This is a creative problem-solving strategy that helps to identify and relate various independent variables or factors. The approach involves several steps:

1. A problem is stated in as general terms as possible.
2. Students are invited to identify as many independent variables as possible.
3. Students state these variables or factors in as many ways as possible.
4. Each of the factors becomes an axis on a grid of a two-dimensional or three-dimensional model.
5. Students then combine the axes or locate intersections within the grid that provide multiple ways of viewing and resolving the problem. To illustrate: suppose the issue was how to rationalize the problem of replacing all of the vehicles dependent on burning fossil fuels in the United States with vehicles that use some other nonpolluting source of energy, such as electricity, solar power, or wind power.

The first step would be to have the class identify independent variables associated with each form of energy (presently in use or proposed). Two axes of a grid might be type of energy versus efficacy of use in a national transportation system. In the first category might be listed fossil fuels, solar energy, nuclear energy, wind energy, water power for electricity, or others. The second axis might contain cost per mile, average highway speed, maintenance of vehicles, convenience of use, conversion costs, and other factors.

A grid might be set up as shown in Table 16–1.

Studying the grid by placing intersecting points at desired places and by inserting estimated but realistic values for each factor would enable students to decide what traits of the new transportation system to consider as viable alternatives to the present system. The exercise could be done in a group format or individual format as desired. A general discussion could be held after the exercise to consider the advantages or flaws of each system suggested. The level of interest in this exercise would probably be higher than traditional methods of lecture, recitation, or discussion.

We include a final example to illustrate how an unusual strategy may become useful in dealing with controversial problems. The technique, creativity-synectics, was developed by William J. J. Gordon and colleagues in the 1960s and was suggested primarily for stimulating creative talents.[4]

Synectics centers around students being invited to form three types of metaphors to gain different perceptions of a problem. These are used to break mental *structural fixedness* or *psychological set* in looking at a problem, thereby contributing to the stimulation of creative thought. The three metaphors are: *direct analogy, personal analogy,* and *compressed conflict.*

In *direct analogy,* students are asked to compare and contrast two objects or concepts and state how

TABLE 16–1
Model grid

		Type of Energy				
		Fossil	*Solar*	*Nuclear*	*Water Power*	*Wind Power*
EFFICACY	Cost	____/____	____/____	____/____	____/____	
OF	Speed	____/____	____/____	____/____	____/____	
USE	Upkeep	____/____	____/____	____/____	____/____	
	Convenience	____/____	____/____	____/____	____/____	
	Conversion	____/____	____/____	____/____	____/____	
	Other	____/____	____/____	____/____	____/____	

they are similar or different. For example, in a controversy about cutting down the rain forest, they might be asked to compare and contrast birds with airplanes, or tropical woods with corn, or pharmacists with medicine men.

In *personal analogies*, students might be asked to state how they would feel if they were an endangered species of animal. They might be encouraged to identify with an object or concept such as a river or an evaporating water molecule. They might express their feelings about their potential future or fate in the rain forest.

The two steps above can then lead to a situation of *compressed conflict*. Students are asked to identify contradictions in the analogies. Work to bring the contradictions closer together by making certain concessions or accommodations.

The above strategy will help students perceive problems in a more diverse and creative manner. They will have motivation to explore something unfamiliar and create something new or different. One desirable outcome may be the ability to see a problem from another person's point of view and avoid responding to problems in sterotypical ways.

Small group discussions around an identified topic, followed by an all-class discussion, with small group leaders presenting the consensus of their groups will become an effective method of dealing with controversial issues in the classroom. The creativity-synectics strategy will set the stage for more fruitful class discussion.

■ SUMMARY

Facing the prospect of dealing with controversial issues in science classes is almost a certainty for teachers today. A well-prepared teacher will not wait until a serious issue suddenly makes its appearance in the classroom. Instead, the instructor will think through many possibilities and potential strategies for dealing with the issues.

Many issues develop out of various referendums that appear on the ballot during elections. Rather than to be feared, these should be looked upon as golden opportunities to get students thinking beyond the closed confines of their school activities. These are real-life problems that students will themselves face when they finish their formal education.

Other sources of controversy come from the increased emphasis in science classes on relationships among science, technology, and society. These issues are usually of global nature, frequently have an environmental context, and are invariably extremely complex, affecting many segments of society in diverse ways. In addition, there are often highly vocal groups that express their points of view through the media, committees, and political agendas. Fortunately, many of these groups provide free literature explaining their concerns, and students may obtain information for discussions and actions.

Strategies for teaching about controversies suggested in this chapter include class debates, role playing, morphological analysis, creativity-synectics, small and large group discussions, and other techniques.

An overriding principle when dealing with controversial issues is that the teacher's job is to provide suitable opportunities for discussion and explication of the issues, while at the same time avoiding injecting personal views. To do otherwise is to invite repercussions from parents, school authorities, and community groups.

■ REFERENCES

1. Kerri Armstrong and and Kurt Weber, "Genetic Engineering—A Lesson on Bioethics for the Classroom," *The American Biology Teacher, 53* (May 1991): 294–297.
2. Jon E. Pedersen, "The Effects of a Cooperative Controversy, Presented as an STS Issue, on Achievement and Anxiety in Secondary Science," *School Science And Mathematics, 92* (7) (November 1992): 374–380.
3. Lawrence Kohlberg, "The Cognitive-Developmental Approach to Moral Education," *Phi Delta Kappan* (June 1977), pp. 670–677.
4. William J. J. Gordon, *Creativity-Synectics*, Synectics Educational Systems, 121 Brattle Street, Cambridge, MA 02138.

UNIT 6

ASSESSMENT

As a teacher of science, you have incredible power. Power for learning. Power for teaching. Where do you get this power? From assessment! Do you know that you can influence the motivation of students to learn science? That you can modify the study habits of students in your classes? That you have the power to change attitudes and develop new interests and directions for learning?

Most science teachers look at assessment as an unpleasant task—one that unfortunately has to be done and the quicker the better! Because of this assessment is frequently left until the end of a unit or lesson. Then some kind of test is hastily developed and given to the student: sometimes the test fits what was taught, sometimes it is far removed. However absurd, this happens frequently. These test results are then often put into the form of grades and given to the students, mainly for ranking students and providing reports to parents. The teacher relaxes in the knowledge that the students have been tested, at least for another month or so.

Happily, there is much more to assessment that this. With careful planning and sufficient time to prepare the form of assessment, evaluation can be an integral part of the teaching and learning process. This is what it should be. There is diagnostic evaluation that helps you understand your students' background, knowledge, and skills as you begin teaching. There is formative evaluation in which the assessment helps you learn about student difficulties as you go through class instruction. The kind of assessment you do at the end of your instruction is called summative evaluation and is generally used for giving grades, ranking students, or placing them in groups.

Throughout this book we have been talking about innovative and effective teaching and learning strategies, such as investigative learning and inquiry. This requires different kinds of assessment than is found in traditional, expository teaching. Especially with the greater emphasis on developing life-long learning skills, new tests have to be devised that assess those skills. Chapter eighteen, on "New Models for Assessment," will deal with some testing techniques for these skills.

When you finish this unit on assessment, we hope you will look upon evaluation with anticipation because it will give you many ideas for performing this necessary task. In fact, it is often fun to develop some creative techniques and see how well they work and how well students like them. Students realize that evaluation is in the cards for them. They know much of their success depends on it. What they want is interesting, fair, and comprehensive evaluations that test what they really know and how they perform. You may be surprised at how interesting this can be. This unit should contribute to a successful testing adventure in your science classroom.

Chapter 17

ASSESSING STUDENT LEARNING

A common perception among teachers is that evaluation is limited to giving tests. The broader aspects of evaluation—including self-evaluation by students, evaluation of laboratory work, diagnostic, formative, and summative evaluation, and other aspects of the total evaluation process—are sometimes misunderstood by teachers. Most teachers have received little formal training in evaluation, and so their evaluation methods have traditionally tended to be formal, concentrating on quizzes and end-of-term tests.

As a result, instruction and evaluation are thought of as separate entities. In addition, an adversarial relationship seems to exist between the evaluator and those being evaluated. This minimizes the evaluation's effectiveness and destroys one of the very reasons for doing it—the valid assessment of achievement, attitudes, skill development, and progress. Evaluation should be considered a vital part of instruction and inseparable from it. In this chapter, many illustrations will show the connections between instruction and evaluation.

■ ASSESSMENT STANDARDS

Science Assessment Standards prepared by NCSESA serve as criteria against which to judge the quality of assessment practices used to determine student attainment in science and to determine the opportunity provided students to learn science. These standards serve as guides and statements of principles identifying essential characteristics of exemplary assessment practices.

The standards include focusing on what is most important for students to learn in science and providing data that may lead to valid inferences about student science attainment. The data collected should be consistent with the particular aspect of science attainment being assessed and should be equally fair for all students. Science teachers should be involved in the design and implementation of the assessment materials and procedures and should consider the intended use of the resulting information. Finally, equal attention should be given to the assessment of the opportunities to learn as well as student attainment.

■ ORIENTATION OF INSTRUCTION AND EVALUATION TOWARD SUCCESS

All instruction and evaluation in science classes should be oriented toward success rather than failure. Students respond favorably toward successful experiences, whereas they are quickly turned off by repeated failures. This does not require a teacher to sacrifice standards or water down coursework to a meaningless level. It simply recognizes that pupils function better when they have positive concepts about their own worth and class performance. Therefore, tasks should provide potential for successful accomplishment at some level for all students regardless of their academic abilities. In most cases, final achievement is more closely related to one's rate of learning than it is to some questionable I.Q. level.

A dramatic example of the use of success-oriented instruction and evaluation is given in an article entitled "Dear Class, I Love You" by Harry Wong. Excerpts from this article are used here to illustrate the main point:

> No lesson lasts more than two or three days. The time factor is important because the students have a short attention span. More important, I recognize that the students need frequent successes, because successes are the basis for an improved self-concept. Thus, the first lesson is finished by the second day of school and returned on the third. And when it is, every student dies. They all look at me with shock and suspicion. You can read the "you've-made-a-mistake; we're-a-class-of-dummies" look. They not only all have A's on their papers, they are praised for their work. They sit there dumbfounded by my praise; a kind word is a rarity in school. But they're happy, and while they're smiling, I slip them the next four pages. An inscrutable Oriental trick!
>
> We live in a society that guarantees everything. The Bill of Rights guarantees us freedom of speech and the right to trial by jury. If we are dissatisfied with a purchase, we take it back to the store and get a refund or replacement. And with the replacement we may get a 90-day guarantee, a one-year guarantee or even a five-year warranty. In other words, we guarantee everything in our society—except for success in school. Not only do we not guarantee success in school, we believe in the failure system, because it is supposed to maintain some nebulous set of standards.
>
> To a baker, the only relevant standard is a perfect loaf of bread. A mechanic only desires to repair each

car perfectly. A secretary's goal is to type nothing but perfect letters. But the concept of designing a curriculum in which everyone succeeds is foreign, and even repugnant, in education. Contrary to popular belief, none of my administrators have ever questioned the high percentage of successful students in my classes. Rather, these questions have come from colleagues who suspect that my methods are designed to disgrace their techniques.

If I have succeeded with my students, it is because I believe that a person's self-concept is related to his school achievement. For this reason my entire curriculum is success oriented. There is a continuum of success, reinforced every two or three days. As early as the end of the first week, I have every student hooked on success. In fact, success is guaranteed.

As the successes reinforce each other, I see a definite change in my class. For instance, by the third week of school I no longer see despair and frustration, yet neither do I face a sea of bright smiles. Instead, I see faces that are deliberately holding back. Some thirty students are trying to act like cool cats. They know I will return the papers and follow it with words of praise. They have come to enjoy hearing these words, but they're not going to let on. I hold up my grade book and say, "Look, you've all been great. Everyone's not only turned in the assignments, you have gotten mostly A's and B's. You're a fantastic class and I love you all."[1]

■ THE NATURE OF EVALUATION

Evaluation involves the total assessment of students' learning. It includes evaluating their understanding of the process of science, subject matter competence and achievement, multiple talents, scientific attitudes, laboratory skills, and willingness to work. The progress of the students toward the objectives of the course and goals of the school, as well as the effectiveness of instruction, are considered. Good evaluation indicates the strengths and weaknesses of instruction. Once a teacher has made a thorough assessment, she or he has an indication of how to improve her or his teaching. Evaluation acts as feedback in the experimental process of teaching. A teacher must experiment in order to progress and become more skilled. There must be a willingness to try new methods and new techniques, and by so doing evolve toward teaching mastery.

Science teachers should be experiment-oriented, not only in the laboratory but in their daily approaches to teaching. An experimental approach assumes collection of data to verify the success of the methods used. The data must come from the evaluation techniques. The better the evaluation instruments, the greater the information available to the teacher for improving her or his teaching. There are three types of evaluation usually considered in the teaching area—*diagnostic*, *formative*, and *summative*. These three primary types differ mainly by their chronological position in the instruction sequence.

Diagnostic evaluation normally precedes instruction but may be used under special circumstances to discover student learning problems. Diagnostic evaluation can provide information to teachers about the knowledge, attitudes, and skills of the students entering a course and can be used as a basis for individual remediation or special instruction.

Formative evaluation is carried on during the instructional period to provide feedback to students and teachers on how well the material is being taught and learned. Since teaching is a dynamic process, formative evaluation can provide useful information that teachers can use to modify instruction and can improve teaching effectiveness for individuals and groups.

The third kind of evaluation, *summative*, is the kind that is used most often by teachers and is primarily aimed toward providing student grades and reports of achievement. It is most frequently based upon cognitive gains and rarely takes into consideration other areas of the intellect.

Recent decades have given educators much information concerning areas of intellectual development, including the *cognitive, psychomotor*, and *affective domains*. The *cognitive domain* has been traditionally the main area of concern by most teachers. Achievement in the form of memorized information, concepts, problem-solving skills, and other aspects of information acquisition has been tested thoroughly and in many forms. The *psychomotor and affective domains*, however, have not been given the same thorough study. In later sections of this chapter, we will provide recommended procedures in each of the areas that broaden the concept of evaluation and provide increased total assessment information for teacher and student.

Evaluation is an ongoing process and shows evidence of change over the years. Rodney Doran has listed several predicted trends in measurement and evaluation of science instruction. These are given in Table 17–1.

■ THE USE OF OBJECTIVES IN EVALUATION

Well-stated behavioral objectives include within them statements of the performance expected and the level of achievement to be realized by the students.

TABLE 17–1
Predicted trends in measurement and evaluation of science instruction

From	To
1. Primarily group-administered tests	A variety of administrative formats including large groups, small groups, and individuals.
2. Primarily paper-and-pencil tests	A variety of test formats including pictorial and laboratory performance tests.
3. Primarily end-of-course summative assessment	A variety of pretest, diagnostic and formative types of measurements.
4. Primarily measurement of low-level cognitive outcomes	The inclusion of higher level cognitive outcomes (analysis, evaluation, critical thinking), as well as the measurement of affective (attitudes, interests, and values) and psychomotor outcomes.
5. Primarily norm-referenced achievement testing	The inclusion of more criterion-referenced assessment, mastery testing, and self and peer evaluation.
6. Primarily measurement of facts and principles of science	The inclusion of objectives related to the processes of science, the nature of science and the interrelationship of science, technology, and society.
7. Primarily measurement of student achievement	The inclusion of measuring the effects of programs, curricula, and teaching techniques.
8. Primarily teacher-made tests	The combined use of teacher-made tests, standardized tests, research instruments, and items from collections assembled by teachers, projects, and other sources.
9. Primarily concern with total test scores	Interest in sub-test performance, item difficulty and discrimination, all aided by mechanical and computerized facilities.
10. Primarily a one-dimensional format of evaluation (e.g., a numerical or letter grade)	A multidimensional system of reporting student progress with respect to such variables as concepts, processes, laboratory procedures, classroom discussion, and problem-solving skills.

Source: Rodney L. Doran, *Basic Measurement and Evaluation of Science Instruction.* Washington, D.C., National Science Teachers Association, 1980. p. 13. Used with permission.

Cognitive Domain

As an example of how to use behavioral objectives in the cognitive domain suitable for testing and evaluation purposes, consider the following statement: "The student should be able to state the Third Law of Motion in written or oral form when called upon to do so."

The Third Law of Motion states, "For every action there is an equal and opposite reaction." The evidence for the student's achievement of this objective would be to have the student verbally state in your presence or write for later inspection a correct statement of the Third Law of Motion.

Another example of a cognitive objective is, "The student should be able to describe how a cloud is formed." The evidence of achievement of this objective is either a verbal or written description of the processes involved in formation of a cloud, one which meets satisfactorily all the conditions expected by the teacher.

Cognitive behavioral objectives may be simple or complex but should be stated in such a way that certain desired knowledge, thought processes, or thinking skills are demanded that meet the general objectives of the instruction. The evaluation of student achievement is simplified when such objectives are carefully formulated.

Psychomotor Domain

Psychomotor objectives are no less important than cognitive ones in science, although less attention has traditionally been paid to them. These objectives refer to certain manipulative skills that are vital to learning in science. Such skills as measuring, calibrating, constructing apparatus, using refined instruments, and many others are important, and as such they deserve the attention of teachers and students.

Psychomotor objectives may be stated similarly to cognitive ones, as in the following example: "The student should be able, using a meter stick, to measure accurately the length, height and width of a prescribed object." Evidence for the achievement of this objective is a written record of the measurements obtained with the proper units associated. The degree of success in meeting this objective is an evaluative measure of the student's achievement of this psychomotor skill. Another example would be, "The student should be able, following written reactions, to focus a laboratory microscope clearly on an object placed upon the microscope stage." Evidence of achieving this objective might be either a direct confirmation of the student's success by the teacher actually looking through the microscope or by having the student draw what is seen and presenting the product to the teacher. In either case, evaluation of the student's progress is provided directly. This represents the important role of behavioral objectives in the evaluation of instruction—progress can be directly observed.

Affective Domain

Affective objectives present a somewhat more difficult problem. These objectives represent legitimate expectations of students in secondary school science classes but until recently have received minimal attention in the overall consideration of teaching outcomes.

One can classify affective objectives in two forms—overt and covert. A sample statement of an overt behavioral objective is, "The student should be able to give evidence of supporting the argument of another student concerning a particular topic under discussion." Overt actions are those that are observable to the teacher or another person. A valid assessment of whether a given overt affective objective is achieved by the student depends upon some voluntary expression. Without this, it is uncertain whether the student is registering an actual behavioral change or is merely attempting to please the teacher for other reasons, such as obtaining a better grade.

The second type of affective objective, the covert, is even more difficult to assess. Covert objectives depend upon some form of voluntary self-expression by the student; for example, "The student will be able to give evidence of behavioral change by voluntarily self-reporting that he or she enjoys working with live animals in the laboratory." Evidence of the achievement of this objective would be obtained by an informal accounting of voluntary, self-reported statements by the student of this, or similar, supporting evidence. As in the previous type, the validity of the assessment depends upon registering expressions through noncoercive means. One may go even further and state that any indication that the student is responding to some teacher directive or implied assignment may render the responses suspect.

Evaluating Objectives

Just as there are levels of objectives, there are also levels of testing. Much evaluation does not test for all of the important objectives in science. Teachers attempting to evaluate the quality of their instruction from a purely cognitive test may not discover how well they are teaching. The psychomotor and affective areas need to be considered to give complete feedback to teachers so they can effectively modify their instructional techniques.

The first rule of test construction is to use your objectives and scientific principles as guides in devising your test. Students tend to learn in the way in which they are tested. If the emphasis is on memorization of facts, they will memorize facts to the satisfaction of the teacher. If the emphasis, however, is on the understanding of principles, development of process skills, creativity, other aspects of inquiry, or investigative types of teaching, these tests will bring forth those types of student response. It is important for the teacher to consider whether the test emphasizes all of the important course goals. When tests are given, they should evaluate how well the students have attained these objectives, irrespective of whether they are student- or teacher-defined.

It is relatively easy to write objectives, but to evaluate their achievement is often difficult. Bloom identified six levels of cognitive objectives: knowledge, comprehension, application, analysis, synthesis, and evaluation.[2] It follows, therefore, that questions should be devised to evaluate each of these levels. If you write good behavioral objectives and use them as guides for constructing your tests, they probably will provide better examinations than those prepared by teachers who do not.

One way to ensure that your test follows your objectives and gives adequate attention to each of the areas desired is to devise a Table of Specifications, such as is shown in Table 17–2, a blueprint of a ninth-grade science examination. It indicates on the left-hand side the six levels of Bloom's taxonomy and across the top the various content or topic areas covered in the course. By using this table of specifications during instruction and noting the amount of time devoted to each of the respective areas and objective levels, and by following the table carefully when making a test (particularly of the summative variety), you will create a test that has better content validity than one that is put together hastily from memory or based upon the teacher's recollection of time spent on each area.

Although the Table of Specifications shown in Table 17–2 is designed to analyze the cognitive domain, it can be easily modified to include the affective domain by adding another category on the left, entitled *Affective Domain*. Constructing and analyzing tests using this grid helps to ensure your growth in writing tests that evaluate the higher levels of learning. Teachers who do not evaluate all their objectives or classify their test questions in some way similar to the preceding grid tend to evaluate for the lowest levels of Bloom's taxonomy. Research reported

TABLE 17-2
Blueprint of grade nine science examination, 1965

		Topic or Content Area							
	Matter and Energy Force, Work & Power	*Mechanics*		*Chemical Reactions*	*Heat*	*Light*	*Trans-portation*	*Measure-ment*	*Science as Inquiry**	*Emphasis %*
Objectives		*Machines*	*Fluids*							
1. Knowledge										
2. Comprehension										
3. Application										
4, 5, and 6—Analysis, Synthesis and Evaluation										
Emphasis %										

*Note: The topics "Measurement" and "Science as Inquiry" cut across Content Areas. The latter category will be used for items that involve more than one content area or that involve inquiry as, for example, Items 6 to 10 under Analysis.

Source: "Summary Description of Grade Nine Science Objectives and Test Items. Revised Edition," The High School Entrance Examination Board, Department of Education. Edmonton, Alberta. March, 1965. Reprinted with permission.

in 1960 found that the major emphasis in chemistry tests produced by teachers in four-year high schools was on factual knowledge.[3] Application, analysis, and synthesis were virtually neglected.

■ EFFECTS OF TESTING ON LEARNING

Science educators are becoming more concerned about the effects of standardized and textbook tests in science classes. A recent study by NSTA[4] has shown that the majority of science teachers use textbook tests, or develop their own closely modelled after tests accompanying the class textbook. This practice, in itself, is not a bad one for the busy science teacher, but the problem lies in the poor quality of the textbook tests. The study showed that only about 25 percent of the questions in these tests require higher level types of thinking, involving generating examples of concepts, using models, applying concepts or properties, synthesizing ideas, evaluating ideas and the like. Three quarters of the questions were of low level type involving simple recall, labeling, concept identification, memorization, applying a definition, etc.

The study made the point that this practice is hindering the progress of the reform movement in science education because of the significant effect tests have on instruction and learning. Teachers frequently teach to the test in order to produce higher scores for college entrance or for other purposes of grouping students. Research indicates that minority students are most affected in a negative fashion by these practices.

■ EVALUATING LEARNING ON SCIENCE, TECHNOLOGY, AND SOCIETY

In middle level and high school science, new curriculum emphases that give attention to scientific, technological, and societal issues require evaluation methods more closely attuned to the special nature of these topics. Many of the techniques described earlier in this chapter can be adapted or modified for this purpose.

The multidisciplinary and integrative nature of STS studies demands the use of a variety of evaluative techniques in the classroom. To illustrate, the familiar multiple choice tests can be adapted to STS topics by using suitable care in selection of items and format. For example, in one item used in the Program Evaluation Test in Social Studies for sixth graders in New York State,[5] the student is presented with a drawing of three sequential photographs showing technological progression in the baking industry and a decreasing number of bakers making products.

The student is asked, "Which idea is best illustrated in the drawing?" and is given the following choices:

A. Changes in technology affect employment.
B. Industrialization results in higher costs of goods.
C. The use of machines requires a skilled labor force.
D. The growth of technology caused the beginning of labor unions.

Similarly, a sample item from a 1990 Regents Competency Test in Science for ninth graders throughout New York State shows how a similar item might look in a science area:

"What does the paragraph in the box below show most clearly about the relationship between science and technology?"

Engineers build a new type of spacecraft and land it on Mars. The spacecraft sends information about Mars back to Earth and scientists learn more about Mars.

(1) Science and technology solve society's problems.
(2) Science and technology give people more choices in their lives.
(3) Science and technology create new jobs.
(4) Science and technology help advance one another.

Another type of question useful for STS items is an open-ended assessment item exemplified in the following taken from the 1989 STS examination from the Joint Matriculation Board in the United Kingdom:

After reading about Ethiopia's soil-reclamation program, students are tested on the following items:

(a) Name two natural features which may make soil erosion likely (2 points)
(b) What is "food for work" aid? (2 points)
(c) Explain, in your own words, the two valid criticisms of this kind of aid program which are mentioned in the article (4 points)
(d) What does the writer mean by trees which can "fix" nitrogen? (not explained in the article) (2 points)
(e) Terrace building in Kenya during colonial times was responsible for much political resentment. Can you suggest any way in which this resentment might have been avoided? (no additional ways are mentioned in the article) (5 points)

Another type of test item is the essay examination. This requires carefully made guides for marking answers to the questions and takes more teacher time for grading. An example from the 1989 Program Evaluation Test in the Social Studies for sixth graders in New York State illustrates this:

People use technological developments to improve the quality of their lives. Technological development might have both positive and negative effects on society. Some of these technological developments are a dam, an interstate highway, a factory, a nuclear power plant, an airport, a housing development.

Write an essay of about 150 words explaining a positive and a negative effect that three of these technological developments could have on society.

Levels of Testing

The lowest rung on the ladder in the hierarchy of Bloom's taxonomy is the *knowledge* level. This emphasizes simple recall or recognition and represents the lowest level of learning, requiring only memorization. Teaching mainly for recall is the lowest level of instruction, but teachers have often devoted excessive amounts of time to this because recall questions are simple to write. A rule of thumb is that no more than 20 percent of any test should consist of simple recall questions.

The next level is the level of *comprehension*. It is sometimes considered the first level of understanding. Students may know something about a topic, be able to follow a process, or know how to write an equation without understanding it fully. Comprehension questions require the student to: (1) interpret a statement; (2) translate or describe a process or idea in their own words; (3) extrapolate, i.e., go beyond the data; or (4) interpolate, i.e., supply intermediate information. Comprehension questions are not difficult to write but require some thought on the part of the teacher to be worded in a form that demands a higher level of thinking than simple memorization.

The third level is *application*, which can best be described by comparing it with comprehension. A comprehension problem requires that the student know an abstraction well enough to correctly demonstrate its use when specifically asked to do so. Application, on the other hand, requires a step beyond this. Given a new problem, students can apply the appropriate abstraction without having to be shown how to use it in that situation. In comprehension, students show that they can use the abstraction when its use is specified. In application, students show that they can spontaneously use the abstraction correctly.

The fourth level of Bloom's taxonomy is *analysis*. It is related to both comprehension and evaluation. Analysis emphasizes breaking down the material into its constituent parts and detecting the relationships of these parts in the organization. It is also sometimes directed at the techniques or devices used to convey a meaning or establish a conclusion.

The fifth level, *synthesis*, involves putting together elements and parts to elucidate a previously poorly defined pattern or structure. This procedure usually involves combining previous experience with new material, constructing a more or less well-integrated whole. It is a creative act. This category is in the cognitive domain and may not always involve free creative expression since the student is usually expected to work within the limits set by the particular problem, materials, or methodological framework.

The highest level of the taxonomy is *evaluation*. This is the process of judging the extent to which ideas, solutions, methods, and materials satisfy criteria. It also involves using criteria as standards for appraising the extent to which particular items are accurate, effective, economical, or satisfying. Such judgments may be either quantitative or qualitative, and the criteria may be determined by the student or may be provided.

■ QUANTITATIVE TERMS IN TESTS

All sciences use mathematics to ensure more accurate communication. Mathematics brings exactness to science where vagueness once flourished. When we describe phenomena, we may do so by use of dichotomous or metrical terms. A dichotomous explanation is of the either-or type: Something is tall (or short), small (or large), heavy (or light). Science strives to escape from such explanations because they are ambiguous; what may be tall to one person may be short to another. Scientific explanations are usually given in metric terms. Instead of saying a person is tall, a scientist says he or she is 1.8 meters tall. Instead of stating, "Place some glucose in water," the scientist is more likely to say, "Place 10 grams of glucose in 100 cm^3 of water." The use of quantitative, metric terms ensures exactness.

Exactness in science is important for ensuring better communication and for replicating research. It is the nature of the scientific enterprise to have one scientist check the results of another, which would be impossible without the use of exact metric terms. The following examples underline the obviousness of this statement.

A nonquantitative explanation: "A small amount of penicillin was injected into a human organism suffering from a bacterial infection. The infection was cured in a short time."

A quantitative explanation: "Sixty subjects and ten control patients infected with streptococcus were administered 500,000 units of penicillin. On the third day, forty of the patients no longer evidenced the infection in the nasalpharyngeal passages."

The importance of quantitative terms can be easily pointed out to a class by holding up an eraser and having them describe it so completely that it could be produced by someone who had never seen one. Students will often write a description without giving exact dimensions. An instructor can then discuss the necessity of giving the dimensions, thereby emphasizing the place of mathematics in science. There are other uses of mathematics in science aside from those discussed here, but the important points are that mathematics become a part of each examination and that students gain insight into association with science.

■ USING GRAPHS IN TESTING

One quantitative tool used to a considerable extent in science is graphing. Graphing has the following advantages: (1) it gives a tremendous amount of information in a small space (try to describe verbally all the information depicted by a curved line on a graph, and this point immediately becomes apparent); (2) it helps the viewer to quickly see relationships that are not as apparent when one looks at a set of numbers; and (3) a pictorial representation of data is more easily retained by students than are other forms of data. Below are examples of graphing exercises used in secondary science.

Graph Interpretation

Exercise 1.

The following graph represents data collected on *E. coli* bacteria in the laboratory. *E. coli* is found internally in a symbiotic relationship with the human body.

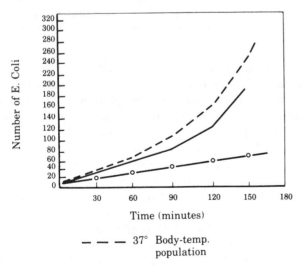

— — — 37° Body-temp. population

1. From the data given in the graph, what are your conclusions about the effect of temperature on *E. coli* population?
2. At 375°C, approximately how long does it take for *E. coli* to double its population? at 10°C?
3. Why do you think *E. coli* is successful in its relationship with the human body?

4. What would be the approximate population of *E. coli* in four hours at 37°C? at 26°C?
5. Each population is in 100 ml of nutrient. What could you predict about the eventual curve of bacteria populations at 37°C? at 10°C?
6. Which of the three populations will reach its maximum growth development first? Why?

Exercise 2.

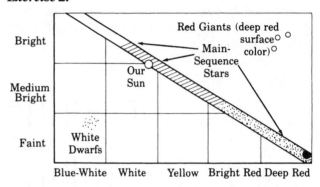

1. The graph preceding indicates that which of the following is not true?
   a. The sun is an exceptional star.
   b. The sun is a medium bright star.
   c. The sun is between yellow and white in color.
   d. The sun will some day become a red giant star.
2. Which of the following is true of the information found in the graph?
   a. Red giant stars are faint.
   b. The sun is a main sequence star.
   c. White dwarf stars are brighter than red giants.
   d. Deep red stars and red giant stars have the same weight.

Exercise 3.

A flask of sterile beef broth was inoculated with a single species of bacteria. The flask was not sealed; thus, mold spores were able to enter. The growth patterns for the bacteria and mold are shown here in a graph. Using the graph, answer the following questions:

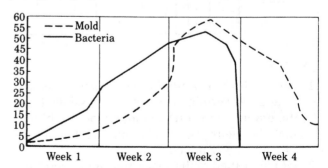

1. Why do you think the bacteria flourished at first and then all died by the end of the third week?
2. Why do you think the mold population decreased so rapidly during the fourth week?

3. Notice the shape of the growth curve for the mold during the first two and one-half weeks. What important concept of growth rate does this illustrate?

Exercise 4.

Answer the following questions in relation to conclusions that can be drawn from the graphs. Before being tested for germination, corn seeds represented in Graph A were soaked 0 hours, in Graph B, 24 hours, and in Graph C, 72 hours.

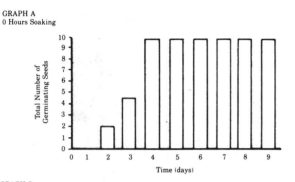

GRAPH A
0 Hours Soaking

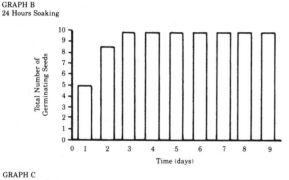

GRAPH B
24 Hours Soaking

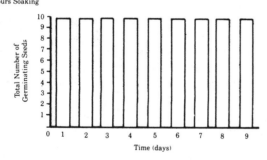

GRAPH C
72 Hours Soaking

1. Farmer Brown wants to plant corn seeds and have them germinate as soon as possible. From the graphs, how long would you advise him to soak the seeds prior to planting? (a) 0 hours, (b) 24 hours, (c) 72 hours.
2. Which of the graphs shows maximum germination after three days? (a) Graph A, (b) Graph B, (c) Graph C.
3. How many days does it take for 50 percent germination of seeds soaked for 24 hours? (a) 1 day, (b) 2 days, (c) 4 days, (d) 10 days.

4. Moisture applied to seeds for 24 hours before planting has a greater effect on seed germination than soaking them: (a) 0 hours, (b) 36 hours, (c) 72 hours, (d) 100 hours.
5. In the graphs, which group of seeds would be considered the control? (a) That in Graph A, (b) That in Graph B, (c) That in Graph C.

Graphing Data

Another way to determine students' understanding of graphing is to have them complete a graph. Exercises such as the ones here can be used for regular assignments or homework.

Exercise 1.

The following graph applies to the red-fox population on an island that is ten miles long and twenty miles wide. It is located in the center of a very large lake in Canada. This island supports several species of animals; however, detailed population studies have been conducted only on the fox population. These population studies began in 1958 and continued for six full years.

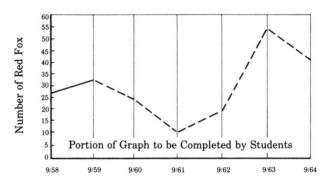

During part of the year, October to May, the lake is frozen, allowing a fluctuation in the fox population because of immigration and emigration across the ice. The breeding population for each year was determined in late May, as soon as the lake thawed. The young are born early in June and are counted in early July.

Total population counts were continued for six full years. These counts were always made in late September by elaborate trapping methods. Immigration and emigration counts were determined by tagging the foxes as they were trapped and counted.

In September of 1958, the total population of foxes was twenty-seven. In September of 1959, it was thirty-one. Data compiled for each one-year period from September 1959 to September 1964 appear in the Table in Exercise 2.

Exercise 2.

From the data below, compute the total population for each year and complete the following questions:

	9/59– 9/60	9/60– 9/61	9/61– 9/62	9/62– 9/63	9/63– 9/64
Breeding population	20	14	8	22	41
Natality	24	17	16	26	59
Mortality	11	16	4	6	43
Immigration	1	0	7	16	3
Emigration	9	5	3	6	15
TOTALS	25	10	24	52	45

1. Plot your computed populations on the graph for each year and then complete the graph by drawing the line from point to point.
2. What was the density of foxes in September of 1960?
3. From September 1961 to September 1963, there is an increase in population; however, you will notice that there is a very high rate of mortality during the same period of time. Can you offer a valid conclusion about this high mortality rate? What would the graph probably look like if the population studies had been continued for ten more years?

Drawing Graphs

Another way to test for understanding of graphs is to require the students to devise a graph. For example, students could be given these instructions: "Graph the rate of expansion of copper for temperatures 10°C to 100°C" or "Draw a graph showing the rate of absorption of the red wavelengths of light in water."

■ GENERAL CONSIDERATIONS IN TEST CONSTRUCTION

This section contains some suggestions for constructing tests. They are not exhaustive, but they are fundamental.

True-False Tests

If the examination is limited to true or false questions, statistics show that seventy-five or more items are necessary to overcome the guessing factor. On a 100-question true-or-false test, students should be able to answer about fifty questions correctly merely by guessing. Some instructions eliminate this problem by subtracting the number of wrong answers from the number of right ones to determine the score; they penalize for guessing. This procedure is not recommended because students usually think the instructor is using this technique maliciously. It is also undesirable because the student is penalized for guessing; in science we wish to have students make hypotheses—that is, good guesses.

Avoid overbalancing the test with too many true or too many false questions. Try to make them fairly even in number so that a student who knows a little about the material cannot get a high score simply by assuming that more questions are true (or false). Here are some other suggestions:

- Avoid using statements that might trick students.
- Do not use the same language as in the text, or students will tend to memorize.
- Do not use double negatives in a statement.
- Avoid ambiguous statements. For example, do not write, "Erosion is prevented by seeding."
- Avoid using complex sentences in your statements.
- Do not use qualitative language if you can possibly avoid it. Do not write, for example, "Good corn grows at a slower rate than hybird corn," or "The better metals conduct electricity faster."
- Arrange your statements in groups of ten to twenty. This procedure relieves excessive tension for students.
- Put answer blocks on one margin so that they can be easily checked using a key.

Multiple-Choice Tests

A multiple-choice test is composed of items having more than three responses. If there are not at least four possible responses to each question, a correction formula should be used. A multiple-choice test differs from a multiple-response test in that only one answer is correct for each question in the first type of test. We suggest the following approaches:

- In a multiple-choice test, make all responses plausible.
- All answers should be grammatically consistent.
- Try to keep all responses about the same length.
- Randomize the correct answers so that there is no pattern in the examination. Students often look for a pattern.
- Remember that the correct response often can be determined by a process of elimination as well as by knowing the correct answer. Try to prevent this in phrasing the answers.
- Present first the term or concept you wish to test for.
- Test for the higher levels of understanding as much as possible.
- Require a simple method for the response. Provide short lines for the answers along one margin of a page so they can be easily keyed.
- Group your items in sections. This system makes it easy to refer to various sections of the test and helps break the monotony in taking the test.
- Group together all questions with the same number of choices.

Completion and Matching Tests

Since completion and matching tests usually emphasize recall and are often verbally tricky, they should be minimized. If matching questions are used, they should be grouped. When there are more than fifteen matching items in a group, the test becomes cumbersome. Number your questions and use letters for your answers, or the reverse, but be consistent. Have more matching choices than questions to minimize obtaining answers by elimination.

Although matching tests have traditionally stressed simple recall, they can be used to test for recognition or application principles. Three sample matching questions follow:

1. A machine that would require the least amount of friction to move it twenty feet.
2. A machine that could best be used to pry open a box.
3. Which of the listed devices is made up of the greatest number of simple machines?
   A. Pliers
   B. Wheelbarrow
   C. Ice tongs
   D. Seesaw
   E. Doorknob
   F. Pencil sharpener
   G. Saw

Self-Tests

A self-test is similar to any other test in its construction but is taken by students mainly as a learning device. It usually has questions on one side of a page and the answers on the other. Students take the test, then turn the page and check their answers. The instructor can use the completed tests as a means of stimulating discussion.

Teachers usually set up self-tests on ditto masters and run off enough copies for their students. A suggested format is shown in Figure 17–1. The back page should contain a detailed explanation for each answer so that students learn from the test. Students fold under the answers on the right side of the page. Their answers are then next to the correct answers and explanations on the left margin of the back page, making it easy to correct the test.

Student Correction of Tests

Student correction of tests can be done in several ways. A student can act as an aide using a key prepared by the instructor. An instructor can pass the tests to students at random, read the answers to the class, and have them correct and compute scores. Students may be given a key after they have taken the test; they then correct their own tests. For wrong answers, they should write on the back of the test or on a separate paper an explanation for their incorrect responses. These explanations can be analyzed to determine the questions that should be modified or eliminated in future testing.

■ EVALUATION AND THE LEARNING CYCLE

In chapter two, you read about a modification of the learning cycle that includes a fourth phase, that of evaluation. At some point in the learning cycle, it is important to provide feedback to students concerning their understanding of concepts and process skills. The results of the evaluation should provide the teacher with information about the students' understandings and competencies in the processes of gathering information in investigative lessons.

Among the techniques of evaluation that can be used in the fourth phase of the learning cycle are self-evaluation, peer evaluation, quizzes, tests, and other formal methods. In addition, simple techniques of asking questions, initiating discussions, and observing classroom and laboratory behaviors are also effective means of evaluation in this phase. Evaluation using all of these techniques should focus on giving students feedback on their conceptual understandings and abilities to use science skills and processes. Formal evaluations for the purpose of giving grades should be given late in the learning cycle after ample opportunities for exploring, developing concepts, applying information, formulating new problems, and evaluating one's own progress.

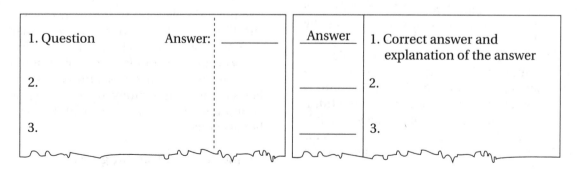

FIGURE 17–1
Format for self-test

Some specific suggestions for the evaluation phase of the learning cycle are:

1. Test for reasoning as well as content memorization.
2. Ask students to justify their answers.
3. Help students who are reasoning at lower levels to employ higher level reasoning skills, such as analysis, synthesis, and evaluation.
4. Devise ways of evaluating skill and process development as well as cognitive accomplishments.

In general science the teacher might arrange for a laboratory period for plotting graphs of volume vs. mass. In this period the students could use rulers, calipers, graduated cylinders, and balances to determine the volumes and masses of objects of widely differing shapes and various materials. Using a Science Activity Evaluation Checklist such as is described in chapter eighteen would enable the teacher to evaluate the skill and process achievement level of the students.

In earth science, the teacher might arrange for the class members to operate a small weather station with which they are able to gather data on temperature, pressure, humidity, and wind information for a period of time. Skills of graphing could be developed and evaluated during this time, as well as informal assessments of concept understandings achieved by the students.

In biology, a museum trip might be arranged where students are able to observe fossils, study geologic history, and look for relationships between climatic changes and changes in populations of organisms. Another evaluative activity could involve providing students with chalk and meter sticks, along with a list of important events in geologic and archeological time, to construct a time line indicating the relative occurrence of various historical events. Observation of student performance, accomplishment of specific tasks or process skills, and informal assessments of concept understanding could take place at this time. The basic plan is to give students an opportunity to perform rather than simply to regurgitate information on a paper and pencil test.

In physics, students could engage in a laboratory experiment in which they used air tracks, springs, weights, timing tapes, flexible ramps, Polaroid cameras, strobe lights, and stop watches to observe accelerated motion under various conditions. These activities provide perfect opportunities to evaluate both skill development and understanding of concepts in an informal setting.

As you can see, the evaluation phase of the learning cycle is an important aspect of this learning and teaching strategy. Not only is it important for student assessment: it also provides guidance and feedback to the students while they are learning new concepts and developing new skills. An additional bonus in this type of evaluation is that it largely removes the threat and intimidation students often feel when faced with the prospect of being evaluated, especially if such evaluations culminate in a grade with all its usual connotations.

■ EVALUATION OF LABORATORY WORK

Broad concepts of evaluation include giving attention to all of the activities in which students are engaged during their secondary-school years. With increasing time and emphasis devoted to laboratory work, it becomes necessary to devise suitable methods for evaluating this activity. As with all evaluation, the goals of the activity or teaching method must be identified before determining the actual procedures to be used in evaluation. For laboratory work, a suggested list of goals follows:

1. To develop skills in problem solving through identification of problems, collection and interpretation of data, and drawing conclusions.
2. To develop skills in manipulating laboratory apparatus.
3. To establish systematic habits of record keeping.
4. To develop scientific attitudes.
5. To learn scientific methods for solving problems.
6. To develop self-reliance and dependability.
7. To discover unexplored avenues of interest and investigation.
8. To promote enthusiasm for the subject of science.

Specific activities in which students are usually involved in laboratory work include the following:

1. Planning an experiment and forming hypotheses.
2. Planning an excursion for collecting purposes.
3. Setting up apparatus.
4. Constructing materials and apparatus.
5. Observing natural phenomena.
6. Observing a process in an indoor laboratory.
7. Searching for authoritative documentary information on the topic.
8. Gathering and recording data.
9. Collecting specimens.
10. Classifying and organizing materials.
11. Modifying equipment.
12. Reading instruments.
13. Calibrating apparatus.
14. Drawing charts and graphs.
15. Analyzing data.
16. Drawing conclusions from the data.
17. Writing a report of the experiment.
18. Describing and explaining an experiment to someone else.

19. Identifying further problems for study.
20. Dismantling, cleaning, storing, and repairing apparatus.

These activities and the general results of laboratory work may be evaluated in several ways, such as practical tests, use of unknowns, achievement tests, direct observation of laboratory techniques, written reports, individual conferences, and group conferences. (For an example of such evaluation, see the "Teaching Science Activity: Evaluating Laboratory Work" in the Appendix, p. 428.)

Practical Laboratory Tests

In a practical test a student may be directed to perform a certain laboratory task. The teacher may observe the techniques used, the correctness of procedures, and the results obtained. Procedures such as identification of unknown chemicals, a common practice in qualitative analysis in chemistry, might be extended to earth sciences, biology, and physics. Achievement tests, designed to assess understanding of course content, are an important evaluative technique for laboratory work because of the concern that correct knowledge be obtained through laboratory methods. Pure recognition and recall tests are not usually suitable forms for achievement tests of laboratory experience. Tests that depend on accurate observation, recognition of pertinent data, and ability to reason logically are more suitable for measuring results of laboratory work.

Laboratory work involving the testing of materials, determining unknowns, recognizing and classifying organisms, and outlining experimental procedures is valuable. The problem with practical laboratory examinations is that they take a great deal of time to set up. Student laboratory assistants or one or two of the students with grades of A can be very helpful in setting up the examination before or after school.

Laboratory Reports

The written report, a frequently used method of evaluating progress and understanding in the laboratory, must be scrutinized. Too often the written report becomes a stereotyped form that loses its value as an instrument of evaluation. Each student is required to use a standard form that leaves little opportunity for creativity and flexibility.

The following characteristics of a good experiment report point out the essential required items yet leave room for student initiative and creativity. In this type of report, students begin with a blank sheet of paper. As they write, they keep the following criteria in mind:

1. The reader can tell exactly what the students are trying to determine.
2. The reader can see the procedure the student is using to arrive at an answer to the problem. The description is clear, concise, and complete.
3. The data collected are well-organized and easily understood.
4. All measurements are shown with their proper units.
5. Diagrams, if used, are clear and carefully labeled. Diagrams are useful only for making the experiment clearer to the reader.
6. Graphs, if used, are titled, labeled, and neatly drawn. The purpose of a graph is to show relationships between data obtained so that conclusions may be drawn.
7. Conclusions should answer the problem, using the data obtained in the experiment.
8. The report should help students, in reviewing the course, to recall exactly what the experiment was about and what conclusions they reached.
9. The main criterion for evaluation of this experiment report is: Is this report written clearly enough that an uninformed person could read it, know exactly what was being attempted, how it was done, and what conclusions were reached, and if necessary, could this person duplicate the experiment, using this report alone as a guide?

Recording Student Performance

A convenient form for recording student performance of activities associated with laboratory work is shown in chapter 18, pages 268–269. It should be used as a sampling technique rather than as a daily record form, which would be too time-consuming for large classes. Students' names are written in on the diagonal lines above the chart. In the cells of the chart, evaluations are recorded (0 = low; 5 = high).

Occasionally, the laboratory work might be scrutinized carefully. At other times it might be skimmed. The form could be referred to at the end of the quarter or semester as an aid in determining grades for the laboratory aspect of science classes.

■ EVALUATION OF MASTERY LEARNING

Mastery learning is an area of instructional strategy that relates to the processes of evaluation. It refers to the student's mastery of certain prescribed objectives at identified levels.

In the 1950s, a series of studies indicated that in the United States, the difference between the highest and lowest achievement means obtained by students in schools across the nation was approximately one standard deviation. This implies that in some states it required twelve years of schooling to attain the same level and achievement scores as required only eight years in other states. The implications of this led a number of researchers to consider the ideas of mastery learning. The first of these was John B. Carroll of Harvard University, who in 1960 developed a model using the element of time as the central instructional variable in the learning process. It was his premise that, given sufficient time and perseverance to complete the task, students should be able to reach a desired criterion level of achievement. While rates of learning would vary from student to student, the final outcome would be the same. Carroll identified five factors that influence learning: (1) aptitude, (2) ability to understand instruction, (3) quality of instruction, (4) time allowed for learning, and (5) perseverance.

In 1974, Bloom developed a plan for mastery learning based on Carroll's findings. He theorized that under favorable conditions 95 percent of the students in our schools should be capable of attaining the level of achievement now reached by only the top 20 percent. Bloom criticized present educational evaluation methods when he warned that one of the most destructive effects of modern education is basing students' performance standards on the traditional distribution of grades based upon the normal curve. The result, he stated, is that only a small proportion of students are provided with a successful educational experience. He also stated that efforts in education can be judged unsuccessful to the extent that student achievement is distributed normally. This tells us that practically all students have the ability to learn what we propose to teach them in the secondary schools. The difference lies in the amount of time it takes and in the difficulty in accommodating these varied rates of learning within the traditional time structure of our school day.

Bloom has observed that the initial work done on mastery learning was in subjects in which there are few prerequisites, such as algebra and science. When subjects rely heavily on previous course learning, it is unlikely that many students will attain mastery within a normal course-time schedule. Science is one of those areas in which the mastery learning concept can be used favorably. Science content areas meet the requirements of being both closed and sequential. This means that they require a minimum of prior learning, are sequentially learned, emphasize convergent thinking, and are closed insofar as they possess a finite set of ideas and cognitive behaviors upon which teachers can usually agree.

Bloom has defined five provisions that the instructor in a mastery learning class must fulfill successfully to be effective:

1. The students must be informed of the course expectations, usually through the use of learning objectives.
2. Standards for mastery are set in advance, and grades are assigned in terms of performance.
3. Short diagnostic tests, called formative tests, are used for each unit.
4. Additional learning to help students reach the criterion level is prescribed at appropriate points.
5. Additional learning time is provided for students needing it.[6]

Bloom is critical of ideas of competition that are sometimes used as justification for the traditional evaluation system and preparation for life. He cautions that much learning and development may be destroyed if competition is the primary basis for motivation. Instead students should be given a performance standard, and grades denoting success should be awarded to all who attain the criterion level. In the past we have usually based the mastery level standard upon what has historically been A and B achievement levels in our classes. Typically, this refers to mastery of 75-85 percent of the tasks required in a particular series of objectives.

The most important elements in Bloom's mastery learning strategies are the feedback/correction procedures, which are a product of formative testing. Formative tests are given periodically throughout the instruction and are used to provide feedback to students as well as to teachers. They are not graded, and students may repeat the tests enough times to reach the mastery level. The rationale for this is that patterns for learning should be structured as part of a cyclic process whereby students can test their knowledge and then be given feedback necessary to direct their learning efforts.

Traditional methods of giving a summative test at the end of the chapter do not serve the needs of students for learning because they are not apprised of the results, and no attempt is made to relearn any missed material. Summative tests measure only achievement and fail to identify weaknesses. We are forced to give grades in most school systems, and summative tests should be limited to that purpose, as quantitative adjuncts to a more holistic student evaluation.

One way to look at mastery teaching is to consider that a course consists of two types of concepts: one type outlines the subject's core objectives and represents the minimal expectations required of all; the other outlines noncore objectives that go beyond the minimal requirements. Bloom maintains that spending extra time within the same calendar period to reach the same level of achievement as classmates gives students the feeling that they are doing well. This is a reasonable expectation, as long as the time required is not inordinately long so that students begin to experience frustration and decreased motivation for school.

In summary, it has been found that mastery learning can be implemented with practically any course content. The major constraint is the time and the dedication necessary to specify the learning outcomes and to develop the criterion-referenced measures to assess achievement. The teacher is faced with the task of refining test items and objectives, and developing new materials as situations change.

Mastery-based learning is not an educational panacea. It demands an equal and perhaps greater amount of time than traditional classwork on the part of the teacher and the learner. However, studies show that attitudes remain generally positive, achievement levels increase, and enthusiasm for the learning process does not diminish. These are substantial and notable gains to experience in a learning process in our school systems.

■ USING SCIENCE TESTS WITH DIFFERENT CULTURE GROUPS

Problems in interpreting and using tests frequently occur in classes in which pupils of different cultural backgrounds are present. The results of such tests are usually suspect when there are wide differences in home environments, which may not provide opportunities to learn the types of tasks included on the tests. These differences may include children from disadvantaged homes, those who are not highly motivated by school work, those children with weak reading skills, those children in families in which English is a second language, and those children with emotional problems.

In addition, there are differences in motivation, attitude toward testing, competitiveness, rates of reading, writing, and thinking, practice in test taking, and variations in opportunities to learn the skills and knowledges being tested.

Some of the techniques a science teacher can use to minimize the differences in test results because of the cultural or psychological differences mentioned above are as follows:

1. Nonverbal tests can be prepared, using diagrams and pictures familiar to the various culture groups being tested. In the case of language difficulties, use of translations might be considered.
2. Attempts can be made to use items that are intrinsically interesting to the students to encourage motivation. Selection of items that have relevance to the experiences of the test takers will increase the likelihood of success.
3. Time is made less of a factor, to provide less emphasis on speed as an important condition for success on the test.
4. Test procedures are kept simple, and clear instructions are given.
5. The content of the test is based on intellectual skills and knowledge that is familiar to the group being tested. Of course, this is good advice in the preparation of tests for students at any time.

Some examples of types of test items that minimize verbal responses are those that require understanding of a series (that is, selection of the item that comes next in a series); those of classification where it is necessary to select the item that does not belong with the others; those which use matrices where the pupil is required to select the item that completes a matrix; and those with conditions where one is to match the conditions in a sample design with those of several alternative designs.[7]

■ GENERAL GUIDELINES FOR USING TESTS

When you are confronted with the prospect of preparing a test, there are several methods that will contribute to appropriate, effective evaluation. Some guidelines for testing are listed here.

1. Use tests humanely as learning and diagnostic devices. Give students opportunities to demonstrate that they have learned what they missed on a test; adjust the grade.
2. Never use a test as a punishment.
3. Minimize the use of completion and matching questions.
4. Use tests or self-evaluational inventories to evaluate all of your behavioral objectives, including science processes and attitudes.
5. Spend time with each student going over missed questions. This may be done while the class is involved in laboratory work.
6. Remember that tests are only a sample of what has been learned, and probably not a very good one. Therefore, they should not be used as the only means of evaluation. Take into consideration all the things students have done in class to develop their multitalents.
7. Test for all levels of Bloom's Taxonomy and use a test analysis grid to see that this is done.
8. Ask questions to determine how students feel about the material being used.
9. Place the easier questions at the beginning of the test so students gain confidence and minimize their frustration and nervousness.
10. Consider the time factor. How long will it take students to complete the test? Some students will finish much sooner than others. What will

you do with them? If you do not have some work outlined, they are likely to present discipline problems.

11. Design the test to be easily scored. Leave a space for all the answers on one margin.

12. Rather than having the students write on the test, have them place their responses on an answer sheet. This procedure ensures ease of recording and saves paper since the test may be used for more than one class.

Encourage honesty. Remove the temptation to copy by spreading students out or by making two versions of the same test and alternating them when you pass out the tests. You may wish to try the honor system; some instructors in high school have used this with success. Caution students as soon as you see anyone cheating. It is usually better not to mention the name of the culprit at the first infraction. You might just say, "I see cheating" or "Some people are looking at other students' papers." If you really stress honesty in the first tests your task of trying to prevent dishonesty will be lessened during the rest of the term. Set a pattern of honesty immediately in your classes. Be present while students take tests, and discipline a pupil guilty of continued dishonesty.

■ ALTERNATIVES TO TRADITIONAL GRADING

The evaluating process in itself is neither negative nor positive. Its function depends on how the instructor uses it. He or she can use it to diagnose his or her teaching and student achievement or to compare one student with another.

Unfortunately, most teachers use testing to obtain a class range in which some students are identified as high and others as low as determined by achievement scores. These scores are then used to grade students. Increasingly, educators are questioning the desirability of using tests for this purpose and even if grading should be used. They argue that grading establishes a competition system that is bound to depreciate and demean the self-concepts of many students. It is true that competition may be a motivating force for some people; however, an individual will compete only if he or she knows he or she has a chance of winning. The hierarchy game, placing one person above another, is bound to contribute to the beliefs of some students that they are trapped in a system in which they have few opportunities for success. If this is true, it is no wonder that the newspapers frequently carry stories about young vandals breaking into schools and destroying thousands of dollars worth of equipment. The general reaction of the public is that these children are bad and must be punished. But what made them bad? Why do they

hate and strike out at the school? Certainly it is human nature to avoid harming the things you love. The facts are that the American school system has a high percentage of dropouts. The individuals who drop out often leave because they do not have feelings of success and thereby opportunities to enhance their self-concepts in the school environment.

Teachers aware of the problems in using evaluation to establish student achievement hierarchies have devised various approaches to deemphasize the importance of testing and grading. Some of these methods are:

1. Self-motivation, where the student evaluates her or himself and then decides, in cooperation with the instructor, where she or he needs to improve.

2. Performance criteria, where the teacher outlines what materials must be completed for a certain grade. The teacher may also use certain performance criteria to see if the student has achieved a certain level.

3. Written evaluations, where the instructor writes a summary of the student's achievements and weaknesses, preferably with the student.

4. Pass-fail, where students are given pass or fail as a grade. This system reduces competition but does not recognize excellence.

5. Giving all students the same grade. This system eliminates competition but usually is not well received by all students, particularly if a grade less than an A is given.

6. Grading secretly, where the teacher gives grades but doesn't tell the student what the grade is, only that the student is doing above or below average work. A disadvantage of this approach is that a student may experience anxiety over how the instructor feels about the student.

7. Student-teacher contract, where the teacher, in cooperation with the students, establishes the amount of work that must be done to receive a grade of A, B, C, etc.

Many years ago, Combs became concerned about the negative aspects of grading. As a result, he devised a contract system that he has continually modified and tested with students over the past fifteen years. A brief summary of his system is outlined below.[8] Although his system has been tested mainly with university students, it has many components that could be modified for use in the secondary school.

A desirable grading system should:

1. Meet college and university standards of effort, performance, and excellence.

2. Evaluate the student with his/her personal performance rather than in competition with his/her fellow students.

3. Permit students to work toward their personal goals.
4. Provide the broadest possible field of choice for the student.
5. Challenge students to stretch themselves to their utmost.
6. Eliminate, as much as possible, all sources of externally imposed threat.
7. Actively involve the student in planning for his/her own learning, placing the responsibility for this learning directly and unequivocally on the student's shoulders.
8. Free the student as much as possible from the necessity of pleasing the instructor.
9. Provide maximum flexibility to meet changing conditions.

Combs states:

> To meet these criteria my current practice is to enter into a contract with each student for the grade he would like to achieve. Each student writes a contract with his instructor indicating in great detail: (a) the grade he would like to have, (b) what he proposes to do to achieve it, and (c) how he proposes to demonstrate that he has done it. Once this contract has been signed by the student and instructor, the student is free to move in any way he desires to the completion of his contract. When the contract has been completed "in the letter and in the spirit" the student's grade is automatic.

■ SUMMARY

Evaluation means that the teacher makes a total assessment of a student's learning. Traditionally, teachers have evaluated students mainly by tests and laboratory reports. Just as there are different varieties and levels of instruction, so are there various levels and methods of testing.

Modern teacher-made tests should stress the higher cognitive levels of Bloom's Taxonomy more than just recall questions. Affective and psychomotor areas should also be evaluated. Tests should be constructed from an instructor's list of behavioral objectives so that he or she evaluates what is considered most important in the learning process. A test only samples a portion of what is taught and should be valid in terms of the content being tested.

Because mathematics and graphing are so much a part of science, tests should incorporate many graphs and mathematical data. A good technique for determining if students understand graphing is to have them complete or devise a graph.

Tests should contain questions or exercises that will enable the teacher to evaluate students' under-standing of scientific methods. Students should know how to recognize a problem, make hypotheses, interpret data, draw valid conclusions, and devise experiments.

Certain features of each type of test must be considered before tests are constructed. Completion and matching tests, because of their emphasis on recall, are to be discouraged. A teacher should consider how long a test will take and should provide assignments for those who finish before the class ends, to avoid discipline problems. Cheating must be strongly discouraged early in the term and throughout the year.

Mastery learning provides an additional challenge in evaluation. Criterion-referenced tests must be devised that provide clear levels of performance. Satisfactory grades are given for successful performance.

Increasing use of the learning cycle poses new dimensions for assessment. The evaluation phase of the learning cycle, with its emphasis on constructivism, means that testing must somehow get at the thought processes and analytical skills of students as they construct new relationships between information and internalize new meanings in their understandings of science.

Good evaluation requires considerable sophistication if sole dependence on memorization is to be discouraged; therefore, teachers are urged to acquire further training in this very important part of their professional competence.

■ REFERENCES

1. Harry K. Wong, "Dear Class, I Love You," *Learning* (December 1972), pp. 20–22.
2. Benjamin S. Bloom, *Taxonomy of Educational Objectives* (New York: David McKay Company, Inc., 1956).
3. Dale P. Scannel and Walter R. Stillwagen, "Teaching and Testing for Degrees of Understanding," *California Journal of Instructional Improvement* (March 1960), pp. 88–94.
4. NSTA, "Standardized and Textbook Tests Hinder Reform", *NSTA Reports*, December 1992/January 1993.
5. Dennis W. Cheek, "Evaluating Learning in STS Education," *Theory into Practice*, *31*(1) (Winter 1992).
6. Benjamin S. Bloom, "The 1955 Normative Study of the Tests of General Education Development," *School Review*, *64* (3) (1956): 110–124.
7. Norman E. Gronlund, *Measurement and Evaluation in Teaching*, 5th ed. (New York: Macmillan and Company, 1985), pp. 308–309.
8. Arthur W. Combs, *A Contract Method of Evaluation* (Gainesville, FL: University of Florida, no date).

Chapter 18

....

NEW MODELS FOR ASSESSMENT

■ ALTERNATIVE MODELS FOR ASSESSMENT

With the realization that teaching methods in science are expanding to include more inquiry and investigative techniques, there has come an equally important realization that assessment methods must be adjusted to match the newer teaching methods. No longer can teachers rely on traditional paper-and-pencil tests as the sole means of assessing student progress and achievement. Students are aware that for fairness in evaluation of their work in science classes, efforts must be made to develop authentic assessment techniques that get to the heart of the tasks they are expected to perform. Teachers sensitive to this need are developing a host of alternative assessment techniques to deal with the enlarged variety of activities students engage in during their studies in science.

Among these techniques are concept mapping, creative assessments, journals, oral interviews, essay tests, portfolios, observations, projects, extended tasks, open-ended labs, and others. Some of these will be elaborated on in this chapter. Each technique is planned to fit a particular kind of activity or instruction in which students are engaged. While many alert and sensitive teachers may have used some of these in their teaching for years, recent emphases in nontraditional teaching methods have brought them to the forefront of our attention.

■ PERFORMANCE-BASED ASSESSMENT

Several of those techniques listed above may be categorized as *performance assessments*. Any that emphasize evaluating what students do in an activity or that allow teachers to observe students engaged in a problem-solving learning experience might be designated as performance assessments.

Paper-and-pencil tests have severe limitations in evaluating student performance in activity-based science classes. How does a teacher make a valid assessment of how well a student can perform an investigation of how the sun's altitude changes from hour to hour during different seasons? Or how the location of the sun at sunrise changes from season to season? Such an assessment requires actual performance of the task by the student over a period of time. Results of angular measurements alone are not sufficient evidence in themselves that the student can perform the task independently in an investigation. Some method must be devised to witness the performance of the task, and certain criteria of acceptability met, by the student. This usually requires more time than is normally available for assessment in science classes.

Oral contributions in class and laboratory are also a part of performance-based assessment. Some items to consider in oral contributions to group or class work are the following:

1. Makes occasional contributions.
2. Makes occasional significant contributions and usually listens carefully and responds to the points made by others.
3. Usually effective, occasionally shows the ability to analyze previous contributions and take the discussion forward.
4. Makes pertinent contributions on a wide variety of issues in both large and small groups without overdominance, but is able to lead a discussion when necessary. Is a good listener as well as a good talker.[1]

There are many other types of performance assessments. One type has been in use in NAEP in recent science assessments. These are short items that use a multiple-choice format and require students to do projects, design experiments, or evaluate situations; these necessitate students' using higher levels of Bloom's taxonomy—application, analysis, synthesis and evaluation.[2] An example follows:

> "The hardness of a mineral can be determined by comparing the sample to a standard hardness scale. A softer mineral cannot scratch a harder mineral." Use the hardness scale below to answer the following question:

Least hard							Most hard
1	2	3	4	5	6	7	8
Talc	Gypsum	Calcite	Fluorite	Quartz	Topaz	Corundum	Diamond

Quartz will not scratch which of the following materials?
(A) Gypsum (B) Calcite (C) Talc (D) Corundum

Another type is an *event task*, such as the following example:

> "You will be given an Alka-Seltzer tablet, container of water, gram weights, and balance. Place the container of water and the Alka-Seltzer in the left pan of the balance (do not put the Alka-Seltzer in the water). Add gram weights to the right pan of the balance until the right pan and the left pan are balanced. Now predict what will happen to the balance if the Alka-Seltzer is placed in the water. After you have written your prediction down, add the Alka-Seltzer to the water. Explain what has happened in terms of the Law of Conservation."

Performance criteria:

- degree of accuracy of data collection
- extent to which the Laws of Conservation are adequately explained and related to the experiment
- accuracy and completeness of initial prediction

A third type is an *extended task*. A chemistry class is given a small sample of river water late in the semester, after significant introductory chemistry has been taught.

> "Here is a sample of raw river water. It is quite polluted. Your task is to devise procedures to clean up this water so that you feel it is safe to drink. (How will you determine this safely?) You may use any methods you can think of, but check with your teacher before you proceed with the procedure. Also, register (or patent) your procedure with time and date so that you may receive credit for the innovation."

Performance criteria:

- care in identifying the problem or problems inherent in the task
- care in recording data with dates, procedures used, and results obtained
- clarity of experiment report
- discussion of results and implications

■ VALIDITY OF PERFORMANCE-ASSESSMENT MEASURES

As with any testing procedure, one needs to be confident that the procedure gives valid results (content validity), and reliability (consistency of results). Performance-assessment measures, perhaps because of their relative newness in school usage, may be more vulnerable to validity and reliability errors than traditional procedures used in testing. A study by the Center for Research on Evaluation, Standards, and Student Testing (CRESST) at the University of California, Los Angeles, "found that measurement error in performance assessments was largely due to task sampling variability. Student performance varied significantly from one task sample to another."[3] It was estimated that one needs somewhere near "ten tasks in science in order to get a reasonably reliable estimate of a child's understanding of the domain." This may pose a serious difficulty in science classrooms because of the cost and time burden of performing many similar tasks to obtain good reliability in performance assessment.

■ CONCEPT MAPPING

Concept mapping is a means of organizing ideas. It is used in instruction and can be used in assessment as well. The student begins by identifying the major and minor concepts of a topic under study, then organizing these concepts in hierarchical relationships. When used as assessment tools, concept maps provide the teacher with information on how the student relates the concepts he or she has learned. In this way, a better picture of the student's understanding of the topic can be ascertained.

When analyzing the concept maps produced by students, the teacher should look for concepts that are definitely related to the topic at hand, show a hierarchical relationship from simple to more complex, are informative as to scientific accuracy, and are replete with examples showing how the concepts are or can be applied in real situations. Assessments of this type are of necessity quite subjective and should be used to glean clues as to the student's misunderstandings or misconceptions.

■ CREATIVE ASSESSMENT

In creative assessment, students are given the opportunity to show what they have learned in a nontraditional manner. Some students might use scrap books, home videos, or cartoons to show information and relationships that illustrate what they have learned in the unit. Instead of simply recalling facts, they can use higher level thinking skills, such as application, analysis, synthesis, or evaluation.

To implement creative assessment in the classroom, the teacher might spend a short time suggesting the kinds of things students could do to show their knowledge. This should not in any way limit their creativity, but many students need guidance to avoid frustration, especially if this is the first time they have been exposed to nontraditional ways of assessing their progress. By its very nature, this form of assessment is quite subjective and should be used as motivation or formative evaluation during instruction in a unit.

■ JOURNALS AND ORAL INTERVIEWS

The first of these provides a teacher with information of a sequential nature showing how the student has progressed in his or her study of the science material. Some teacher guidance is needed to help students focus on the topics at hand and avoid irrelevancies. Some questions of the type, "How might this information help you plan a traveling vacation?" or "What new facts did you learn that could make your life more interesting?" might help guide the students' responses. Journal entries should be regular and need not be voluminous. They should promote reflective thinking and may generate further questions for study.

Some students are more adept at speaking than writing. Oral interviews in a relaxed atmosphere may supply information to the teacher and student alike that will benefit future work. The teacher has an opportunity to give verbal support to students as well as to obtain clues about their study habits, difficulties of understanding certain topics, misconceptions, and gaps in knowledge. The student, at the same time, may gain a better understanding of what is expected, the location of resources, and a realistic measure of his or her own strengths and weaknesses.

This type of assessment is most useful when coordinated with instruction in the formative stages of development of the unit or chapter.

■ PORTFOLIOS

A portfolio is put together by a teacher for individual students, using materials produced by the student. These materials can include a large variety of products, such as worksheets, pictures, assignments completed, data sheets, written conclusions, experiment reports, maps, stories, plans, and any other written materials related to the work completed for a unit or course. It is usually long range—perhaps up to a year, or longer—and can form the basis for other types of assessments, such as interviews and conferences.

An advantage of a portfolio is that it is highly individualized and avoids to some extent the syndrome all teachers have—that of comparing students with other students in a competitive atmosphere. Another advantage is that the students can use the enclosed materials to evaluate themselves and gain a more realistic picture of their own accomplishments.

■ PRACTICAL ASSESSMENT

This method of assessment provides information on students' skill and problem-solving abilities through the use of apparatus set-ups, experiments, and open-ended situations that can reveal certain thinking processes. Students who have become familiar with investigative learning will be able to display their abilities to best advantage. Students who have been taught in highly traditional, expository classes will find this method of assessment distasteful and possibly unfair. One should not expect students to perform satisfactorily in an assessment procedure strange or different from the instructional methods they have experienced.

■ PROBLEM TESTS

This kind of test presents a problem and asks the students to work on it. It is similar to an invitation to inquiry except that it is done by an individual student. The test usually contains a series of questions which the students must answer to solve the problem. A problem test can be constructed with relative ease if it is based on a problem that has actually confronted a scientist. These problems can be easily obtained from a scientific journal. Give the students information about the problem and have them devise their own hypotheses, research designs, or methods of collecting and recording data. A problem test can best be used to acquaint students with scientific processes. The test may have an answer sheet similar to that for a self-test, or it may be used to stimulate discussion. Open-ended scientific problems are preferable for this kind of test. Some examples of problems that might be used in constructing a test of this nature are:

1. How would you reduce the amount of pollution from a smoke stack?
2. A citizen thought the local river was polluted; how could he find out? What experiments could he do?
3. A scientist thought fungus might produce a chemical that inhibits the growth of bacteria. What kind of experiments must he conduct to verify his hypothesis?
4. What are some general considerations to be kept in mind when making a true-false, a multiple-choice, and a completion test?
5. Prepare a picture or problem test.

■ DIAGRAMS OR PICTURE TYPES OF TESTS

Most science tests evaluate more for reading than they do for science. Many students understand the science principles, but because they have verbal difficulties (such as reading and interpreting what they have read), they do poorly on tests. Studies indicate that many students do significantly better on tests consisting mainly of pictures and requiring them only to check the correct responses.[4] The BSCS, in preparing a special course in biology for the mentally retarded, found when evaluating achievement by using 35-mm slides that both the teachers and specialists were amazed at how well the students did.[5]

■ SELF-EVALUATION

One of the important values of instructional evaluation is that it provides feedback to students. Included in this aspect should be the component of student self-evaluation with respect not only to her or his feelings and concerns regarding the class but also concerning her or his understanding of her or his own progress in the course. One of the objectives for which we strive in education is to teach students to establish aims and objectives for themselves and then carry out the necessary procedures to achieve these aims or objectives. Self-evaluation is a natural and necessary part of this process, and students should be encouraged to acquire the habit early. All individuals from time to time look introspectively upon their own progress and achievement; it is natural that such opportunities ought to be provided in the classroom with respect to students' instruction as well.

Research by Clifford Hofwolt, Bill Tillery, James Duel, and others, during the 1950s and 1960s, has established that students can do a reliable and valid job of evaluating themselves.[6,7,8] However, student self-evaluation and the importance of giving students opportunities to self-judge their gains during the course of instruction have only recently been emphasized.

To be effective in providing self-evaluation opportunities for students in the classroom, teachers must be aware of certain guidelines to promote best results:

1. Students must know what the class objectives are and how they are to be met.
2. Students must be able to relate to specific tasks, e.g., discussions, class projects, tests, attendance, book reports, etc.
3. Students should have repeated practice in evaluating themselves.
4. A Likert scale (in which categories of Strongly Agree, Agree, Neutral, Disagree, and Strongly Disagree are used) or some other form of continuum should be used instead of a letter grade.

5. Ratings on the continuum should be explained and clarified.
6. Students should know the purpose for which the evaluation is to be used.
7. The teacher has the final responsibility for evaluation. Student self-evaluation can assist in this task.
8. There must be good rapport and a trusting atmosphere.
9. The teacher should be knowledgeable about the students' attitudes toward the class.
10. Self-evaluation should not be used in conjunction with other traditional evaluations.
11. Substantive, not trivial, questions should be assessed.
12. A variety of self-evaluation methods should be used, e.g., checklists, semantic differential scales, interviews, picture symbols, etc.
13. A low pressure, nonthreatening situation should prevail.
14. Results on the self-evaluation should be kept confidential.
15. The teacher should provide for administration of the self-evaluation procedure on suitable days, e.g., avoiding Mondays and Fridays.
16. The teacher should consider the individuals and class temperament on the day of self-evaluation.
17. The student should be able to see some value in the self-evaluation for his/her own benefit or improvement.
18. Skills in self-evaluation should be developed over a period of time, not in a one-time effort.
19. Self-evaluation ratings should not be used directly for grading.
20. Research shows a satisfactorily high correlation between self-evaluation ratings and teacher grading scores.

■ SUMMARY

New instructional methods demand new methods of assessment. As teachers conduct their science classes more frequently in an inquiry or investigative mode, the skills and other outcomes expected of students change from those of traditional objectives. To assess the achievement of these outcomes fairly, evaluation methods must be designed to be in tune with the new instructional techniques and objectives.

Performance-based assessment requires that students be given the opportunity to perform an activity, laboratory experiment, or other learning mode and be evaluated on how well they function in accomplishing the task set before them. Certain assessment tasks, such as concept mapping, creative assessment, journals, oral interviews, portfolios, picture tests, problem tests, and others, are used for this purpose.

Design of new type assessment instruments and methods requires creative thought by the teacher and a recognition that not all evaluation necessarily should culminate in a letter grade or percentage of achievement. Much evaluation should be informal and used to give feedback to students as to their success or to give the teacher information about the success of his or her instructional methods.

Evaluation should provide many opportunities for students to be successful in order to build positive self-concepts and attitudes favorable for learning. Opportunities for self-evaluation promote this. To use self evaluation effectively, students should know what the class and individual objectives are, and have some knowledge of how their performance can be improved. Generally, self-evaluation should not be used for grading but for developing realistic understandings of expectations and class objectives.

■ REFERENCES

1. Dennis W. Cheek, "Evaluating Learning in STS Education," *Theory Into Practice, 31* (1) (Winter 1992).
2. Shirley Lauterbach and V. Daniel Ochs, "Performance Assessment: Everyone Talks About It, But What Is It?", *NSTA Reports* (December 1991/January 1992).
3. Richard Shavelson, "Challenging Technical News for Performance Assessment," *CRESTLINE*, National Center for Research on Evaluation, Standards, and Student Testing, Spring 1993.
4. Leonard B. Finkelstein and Donald D. Hammill, "A Reading-Free Science Test," *The Elementary School Journal* (October 1969), pp. 34–37.
5. Richard R. Tolman and James T. Robinson, "Formative Evaluation of Unit 1, Digestion and Circulation," *BSCS Newsletter 9* (43) (1971): 7.
6. This self-evaluational section is based on material prepared by Dr. Clifford A. Hofwolt of Vanderbilt University, Nashville, TN.
7. James H. Duel, *A Study of Validity and Reliability of Student Evaluation of Training* (Ed. D. dissertation, University of Washington, Seattle, 1956).
8. Bill W. Tillery, *Improvement of Science Education Methods Courses Through Student Self-Evaluation* (Ed. D. dissertation, Colorado State College, 1967).

INVESTIGATING SCIENCE TEACHING

Activity 18–1

SCIENCE ACTIVITY EVALUATION CHECKLIST

Class_____Unit_____Date_____File_____

Objectives: Student should be able to:

a.

b.

c.

(student's name)

Affective												
Values												
Cooperation, sharing												
Respect for materials												
Respect for peers, acceptance of ideas												
Neatness and organization												
Efficiency in using time												
Interest												
Curiosity												
Active participation												
Enthusiasm												
Attitudes												
Scientific												
Scholarly												
Psychomotor												
Manipulation and Articulation												
Setting up apparatus												
Dismantling and storing apparatus												
Using measuring instruments properly												
Drawing illustrations												
Naturalization												
Dexterity, hand-eye coordination												
Expression, dramatization												
Cognitive												
Knowledge												
Use of correct terminology												
Evidence of recall and recognition												
Understanding symbols												
Understanding purpose												
Comprehension												
Understanding symbols												
Understanding diagrams												

(student's name)

Application Predicting results																
Comparing and contrasting properties																
Graphing																
Analysis Interpreting graphs																
Problem-solving																
Synthesis and evaluation Forming judgments																
Drawing conclusions																
Laboratory reports (e.g., neatness, organization)																
Verbal reports (e.g., post-laboratory discussions)																
Process Skills Organizes work																
Initiates actions																
Records data properly																

Comments:

UNIT 7

....

UNDERSTANDING AND WORKING WITH STUDENTS

In our attempt to find and describe excellent teaching, we identified a veteran science teacher named Pat Hasagawa. She is an earth science teacher with 25 years' experience and many awards, including the Presidential Award for exemplary science teaching.

When we went to observe Pat Hasagawa, we found her teaching a lesson on the water cycle. We saw that she had a well-planned lesson and knew science concepts such as the states of matter and phase transition. Some students worked on a simple experiment on evaporation, others worked on a computer simulation of the water cycle, and others read short passages from their textbook and then discussed what they had read. Although students were engaged in a variety of activities, the classroom was well managed, and Hasagawa continually moved about the classroom. Her interactions changed as she encountered students individually and in groups. She organized questions, framed problems, gave directions, and suggested different procedures—sometimes directly, other times indirectly. With each student or group, she responded differently.

When we commented on what we observed, Hasagawa acknowledged that over the years she had come to believe that the single most important aspect of science teaching was the relationship she established with each student. Certainly, a science teacher had to know science, use different instructional strategies, and arrive in class with lessons planned. She acknowledged all this as necessary, but there was another dimension that some science teachers missed: the interpersonal, the basis of which is understanding students.

Hasagawa shared her ideas with us. She maintains a mental index (and an actual file) of each student while she moves about the science classroom. Remembering what students know and can do, she uses different strategies with different students. Her flexible teaching style is adapted to students' characteristics and needs. When students have serious misconceptions, she gently and consistently prods them, or she places them in a group that would challenge their view. She carefully monitors their cognitive and emotional response: if a student gets too frustrated, for example, she helps with a hint to facilitate the process of reconstructing a more scientific explanation. She gives feedback to students about their science comprehension, their use of inquiry strategies, their work in groups, and their ability to conduct themselves in a manner conducive to maintaining a community of learners.

Is Pat Hasagawa a gifted science teacher? Probably so, but her gifts developed over years of experience, with conscious attempts to understand students. In the following chapters, we present the psychological basis for teaching science and introduce some techniques for effective classroom management and conflict resolution.

Chapter 19

THE PSYCHOLOGICAL BASIS FOR EFFECTIVE SCIENCE TEACHING

Students' behaviors result from the interaction of many psychological factors. You will have to understand the complex and interacting factors that affect your students and their capacity to learn science. Although you have experience with psychology courses, in this chapter we review the general areas of *motivation, learning, development,* and *group behavior.* We place this review in the context of science teaching, which will provide you with a slightly different perspective on psychology. We begin this chapter with a set of *Learner-Centered Psychological Principles* adapted from a report from the American Psychological Association (APA) and the Mid-continent Regional Educational Laboratory (McREL). This chapter also includes several activities that you can use to investigate various aspects of psychology and science teaching (see the "Investigating Science Teaching" activities at the end of the chapter). We include activities on motivation, reinforcements, cognitive development, and group structure.

■ LEARNER-CENTERED PSYCHOLOGICAL PRINCIPLES

In 1990 Charles D. Spielberger initiated a Presidential Task Force on Psychology in Education with the goal of synthesizing the knowledge base from psychology and education on learners and learning. That project resulted in the aforementioned "Learner-Centered Psychological Principles." In this section we present the principles as they were reproduced in a January 1993 report from the APA and McREL. You should recognize that the principles are designed to present a holistic understanding of students. The first ten principles refer to metacognitive and cognitive, affective, developmental, and social factors. The remaining two principles address individual differences. In the discussion following these principles, we have adapted the original discussions for science teaching. The Learner-Centered Psychological Principles provide you with a holistic perspective of students. The following discussion includes many ideas and theories that have direct application to your work as a science teacher. You will recognize the ideas of theorists you have probably heard about, such as David Ausubel, Albert Bandura, and Abraham Maslow,[1,2,3] Jean Piaget,[4,5]

and Carl Rogers,[6] as well as contemporary ideas such as constructivism,[7] conceptual change,[8,9,10] and cooperative learning.[11,12,13]

Metacognitive and Cognitive Factors

Principle 1: The Nature of the Learning Process
The process of learning occurs naturally, through pursuit of personally meaningful goals. It is an active, volitional, and internally mediated, process of discovering and constructing meaning from information and experience, filtered through the learner's unique perceptions, thoughts, and feelings.

You should assume that science students want to pursue personally relevant learning goals. They are capable of assuming personal responsibility for learning: for example, monitoring their progress, checking for understanding, and engaging in self-directed learning. The science classroom should be an environment that takes past learning into account, ties new learning to personal goals, and actively engages students in the learning process. During this process, individuals create their own meanings and interpretations on the basis of current knowledge, understandings, and beliefs. Support for this principle comes from a constructivist/cognitive learning perspective.[14–26]

Principle 2: Goals of the Learning Process
Learners seek to create meaningful, coherent representations of knowledge regardless of the quantity and quality of data available.

As students learn science, they generate integrated mental representations and subsequent verbal explanations for their experiences. Sometimes those explanations may demonstrate poorly understood or inadequately communicated facts, concepts, principles, or theories of science. Learning processes operate holistically in the sense that students develop internally consistent understandings that are often inconsistent with an objective, externally oriented perspective of scientific knowledge and comprehension. As learners internalize values and meanings within science, however, they can refine their conceptions by incorporating missing ideas, resolving inconsistencies, and revising current conceptions so they are more consistent with accepted scientific explanations. The second principle is supported by research on human learning, memory, and cognition.[27]

Principle 3: The Construction of Knowledge

The learner links new information with extant and future-oriented knowledge in uniquely meaningful ways.

All science teachers soon realize that learners organize information in individually important ways. The unique knowledge construction of students is the result of their backgrounds and experiences and the learning model that proposes constructions of knowledge through linkages of experience with mental concepts and scientific knowledge.

Given that backgrounds and experiences of individuals can differ dramatically, and that the mind works to link information, science education aims to have all learners create shared understandings and conceptions regarding fundamental knowledge and skills that define and lead to valued outcomes relative to the sciences—for example, the *National Science Education Standards*[28] and *Benchmarks For Science Literacy*.[29]

Science teachers can assist learners in acquiring and integrating knowledge by teaching them strategies for constructing meaning, organizing content, accessing prior knowledge, relating new knowledge to general themes or principles, storing or practicing what they have learned, and visualizing future uses for the science knowledge. Research supporting principle number three is from developmental and cognitive psychology.[30,31,32]

Principle 4: Higher-Order Thinking

Higher-order strategies for *thinking about thinking*—for overseeing and monitoring mental operations—facilitate creative and critical thinking and the development of expertise.

By the time science students enter middle school, they are generally capable of thinking about their own thinking. Such metacognitive strategies include self-awareness, self-inquiry or dialogue, self-monitoring, and self-regulation of the processes and contents of thoughts, knowledge structures, and memories. As science students become aware and use metacognitive strategies, they also develop higher levels of commitment, persistence, and involvement in learning. From a science teacher's perspective, you should understand that learners require settings where their personal interests, values, and goals are respected and accommodated. Research in the areas of metacognition, cognitive learning strategies, and novice/expert development form the research base for this principle.[33]

Affective Factors

Principle 5: Motivational Influences on Learning

The depth and breadth of information processed, and what and how much is learned and remembered, are influenced by (1) self-awareness and beliefs about personal control, competence, and ability; (2) clarity and saliency of personal values, interests, and goals; (3) personal expectations for success or failure; (4) affect, emotion, and general states of mind; and (5) the resulting motivation to learn.

Students' constellation of beliefs, goals, expectations, and feelings can enhance or interfere with their quality of thinking and information processing. The relationship among thoughts, mood, and behavior underlies individuals' mental health and ability to learn. As a science teacher, you should recognize that learners' cognitive constructions of reality affect motivation, learning, and performance. Positive learning experiences in science can change any negative thoughts and feelings and enhance student motivation to learn science. Research on intrinsic motivation, attribution theory, emotion, and self-esteem (as it relates to motivation) support this principle.[34,35,36]

Principle 6: Intrinsic Motivation to Learn

Individuals are naturally curious and enjoy learning, but intense negative cognitions and emotions (e.g., feeling insecure, worrying about failure, being self-conscious or shy, and fearing corporal punishment, ridicule, or stigmatizing labels) thwart this enthusiasm.

Science teachers who support and develop students' natural curiosity and intrinsic motivation to learn, rather than using fear of corporal punishment or excessive punishments of any kind, will experience greater interest and learning in the classroom. Both positive interpersonal support and instruction in self-control strategies can enhance learning by offsetting factors that interfere with optimal learning—factors such as low self-awareness, negative beliefs, lack of learning goals, negative expectations for success, anxiety, insecurity, or pressure. Research supporting this principle was synthesized from the areas of intrinsic motivation, anxiety, and curiosity.[37,38]

Principle 7: Characteristics of Motivation-Enhancing Learning Tasks

Curiosity, creativity, and higher-order thinking are stimulated by relevant, authentic learning tasks of optimal difficulty and novelty for each student.

As science teachers create classrooms that learners perceive as personally relevant and meaningful, they will also witness positive affect, creativity, and insight. For example, science students need opportunities to make choices in line with their interests and to have the freedom to change the course of learning in light of self-awareness, discovery, or insights. Science investigations similar to real-world situations in complexity and duration will develop students' higher-order thinking skills and creativity. In addition, curiosity is enhanced when students work on personally significant tasks of optimal difficulty and novelty. Motivation, learning goals, and higher-order thinking provide the research foundation for this principle.[39,40,41,42]

Developmental Factors

Principle 8: Developmental Constraints and Opportunities

Individuals progress through stages of physical, intellectual, emotional, and social development that are a function of unique genetic and environmental factors.

Students learn best when instructional material is both appropriate to their developmental level and is presented in an enjoyable and interesting way. Investigations and activities in the science classroom should challenge students' intellectual, emotional, physical, and social development. Unique environmental factors—such as the quality of language interactions between teachers and students, and parental involvement in students' schooling—can significantly influence development. An overemphasis on developmental readiness, however, may preclude learners from demonstrating that they are more capable intellectually than schools, teachers, or parents understand. Awareness and understanding of developmental differences of students with special emotional, physical, or intellectual disabilities, as well as special abilities, can greatly affect efforts to create optimal contexts for learning. This principle is based on research from developmental psychology.[43]

Personal and Social Factors

Principle 9: Social and Cultural Diversity

Learning is facilitated by social interactions and communication with others in flexible, diverse (i.e., in age, culture, family background, etc.), and adaptive instructional settings.

Learning science is facilitated when students have an opportunity to interact with students of different cultural and family backgrounds, interests, and values. Classroom situations and student groups that allow for and respect diversity encourage flexible thinking as well as social competence and moral development. Individual students should have opportunities for perspective taking and reflective thinking, thereby developing insights and formulat-

ing new levels of science comprehension. Research in social constructivism, adaptive instruction, and cultural diversity supports this principle.[44]

Principle 10: Social Acceptance, Self-Esteem, and Learning

Learning and self-esteem are heightened when individuals are in respectful and caring relationships with others who see their potential, genuinely appreciate their unique talents, and accept them as individuals.

Students need personal relationships that give them access to higher-order, healthier levels of thinking, feeling, and behaving. Teachers' states of mind, stability, trust, and caring are preconditions to help students establish a sense of belonging, self-respect, and self-acceptance. Self-esteem and learning can be mutually reinforcing in the science classroom. Research from social psychology, personality theory, and self-esteem support this principle.[45,46,47]

Individual Differences

Principle 11: Individual Differences in Learning

Although basic principles of learning, motivation, and effective instruction apply to all learners (regardless of ethnicity, race, gender, physical ability, religion, or socioeconomic status), learners have different capabilities and preferences for learning mode and strategies. These differences are a function of environment (what is learned and communicated in different cultures or other social groups) and heredity (what occurs naturally as a function of genes).

Although the basic principles of learning, motivation, and development apply to all learners, individuals are born with and develop their own capabilities and talents. They acquire different preferences for the style and rate of learning science through learning and social acculturation. Curricular and environmental conditions are important factors that also affect learning outcomes. A part of your task as a science teacher is to understand and value cultural differences and the cultural contexts in which learners develop. Such an understanding enhances the possibilities for designing and implementing the learning environment of a science classroom that encourages science literacy for all students. Principle 11 is based on research from social and developmental psychology, and individual differences.[48]

Principle 12: Cognitive Filters

Personal beliefs, thoughts, and understandings resulting from prior learning and interpretations become the individual's basis for constructing reality and interpreting life experiences.

Science students have unique cognitive constructions that form a basis for beliefs and attitudes about others. Individuals use these *separate realities* as if they were true for everyone. Such behaviors can lead to misconceptions and conflict. Awareness of these phenomena allows greater choice in what students believe. It also offers more control over the degree to which students' beliefs influence their actions and enable them to see and take into account other points of view. The cognitive, emotional, and social development of a student and the way that student interprets life experiences result from prior schooling, home, culture, and community factors. Research on belief systems, thinking, and self-system variables support this principle.[49,50,51,52]

■ IMPLICATIONS FOR SCIENCE TEACHING

As a science teacher you recognize the importance of research and its role in the formulation of knowledge about the natural world. Research from psychology in areas such as cognition, motivation, development, and social interactions, provides the science teacher with valuable insights about his or her students. The only trouble is, you have to apply this knowledge into action. In this section we outline some implications of the discussion on learner-centered psychological principles. Our theme is applying psychology for effective science teaching, science curriculum, and science assessment.

Effective Science Teaching

Learner-centered principles have many numerous implications for science teachers and teaching. Here we have limited the discussion to those implications that are based on the APA and McREL report and that are consistent with recommendations of the *National Science Education Standards*:

- Effective science teaching involves students in inquiry-oriented activities that engage their curiosity.
- Effective science teaching provides opportunities for students to explore ideas and make connections among extant scientific knowledge, new information, and their current conceptions.
- Effective science teaching provides opportunities for student-teacher and student-student interactions.
- Effective science teaching includes a concern for extant scientific knowledge and the incorporation of that knowledge into students' formulation of new ideas and understandings.

- Effective science teaching encourages students to elaborate and generalize their understandings through new inquiries, problem solving, debate, group projects, and personal actions that require higher-order thinking.
- Effective science teaching employs policies and strategies that assure fairness, a regard for students, and a safe learning atmosphere.

Effective Science Curriculum

Although you will probably inherit a school district's curriculum and textbooks, you will have opportunities to improve the science curriculum through your modifications and additions and through the adoptions of new science programs. An important consideration of curriculum improvement would certainly be the aforementioned psychological principles:

- Effective science curricula include activities and investigations that engage the whole student in the development of scientific knowledge and abilities.
- Effective science curricula provide a variety of opportunities for students to actively engage in the construction of scientific explanations, the testing of those explanations against scientific knowledge, and the opportunity to communicate scientific explanations.
- Effective science curricula are developmentally appropriate for the unique aspects of students—intellectual, emotional, social, and physical.
- Effective science curricula include authentic tasks and performance assessments.
- Effective science curricula incorporate activities and strategies that encourage all students to interact and develop positive perceptions of other students regardless of race, gender, culture, physical abilities, or other individual differences.
- Effective science curricula recognize the importance of psychological factors, such as affective and emotional development, higher-order thinking, metacognitive strategies, reflective self-awareness, and personal goal setting.

Effective Science Assessments

Science teachers continually assess student progress. Some assessments are informal and rely on your qualitative judgment about student work. Other assessments are formal in the sense that they are included in the curriculum and instruction and provide explicit feedback about student learning. We provide some ideas about effective science assessments:

- Effective science assessments are embedded in the instructional activities and consistent with the goals of the science program.

- Effective science assessments focus on personal achievement more than group comparisons.
- Effective science assessments provide teachers, students, and parents with information about student growth and performance relative to developmentally appropriate standards.
- Effective science assessments provide opportunities for students to identify examples of successful work and progress.
- Effective science assessments strive to avoid bias and provide a fair evaluation of student learning.
- Effective science assessments incorporate opportunities for students' reflection on their progress and on feedback from others.

■ SUMMARY

This chapter presented Learner-Centered Psychological Principles based on a synthesis of research from psychology. Those twelve principles included:

1. The nature of the learning process
2. Goals of the learning process
3. The construction of knowledge
4. Higher-order thinking
5. Motivational influences on learning
6. Intrinsic motivation to learn
7. Characteristics of motivation-enhancing learning tasks
8. Developmental constraints and opportunities
9. Social and cultural diversity
10. Social acceptance, self-esteem, and learning
11. Individual difference in learning
12. Cognitive filters

Science teachers should consider these principles as they are consistent with decades of psychological research from a variety of areas, such as clinical, developmental, social, cognitive, and personality. Very importantly, these principles offer science teachers a holistic view of students and the various factors that affect learning.

The chapter also included implications of these psychological principles for teaching, curriculum, and assessment.

■ REFERENCES

1. Abraham Maslow, *Motivation and Personality* (New York: Harper & Row, 1970).
2. Abraham Maslow, *The Farther Reaches of Human Nature* (New York: Viking Press, 1971).
3. Abraham Maslow, *Toward a Psychology of Being* (New York: Van Nostrand Reinhold, 1968).
4. Jean Piaget, *The Development of Thought: Equilibration of Cognitive Structures* (New York: Viking Press, 1977).
5. Jean Piaget and Barbel Inhelder, *The Psychology of the Child* (New York: Basic Books, 1969).
6. Carl R. Rogers, *Freedom to Learn* (Columbus, OH: Charles E. Merrill, 1969). See also Rogers, *Freedom to Learn for the '80s* (Columbus, OH: Charles E. Merrill, 1983).
7. Ken Tobin, W. Capie, and A. Bettencourt, "Active Teaching for Higher Cognitive Learning in Science," *International Journal of Science Education*, 10(1) (1988): 17–27.
8. B. Watson and R. Konicek, "Teaching for Conceptual Change: Confronting Children's Experience," *Phi Delta Kappan*, 71(9) (1990): 680–685.
9. Peter Hewson, "A Conceptual Change Approach to Learning Science," *European Journal of Science Education*, 3(4) (1981): 383–396.
10. P. Hewson and M. Hewson, "An Appropriate Conception of Teaching Science: A View From Studies in Learning," *Science Education*, 72(5) (1988): 597–614.
11. David Johnson and Roger Johnson, "The Socialization and Achievement Crisis: Are Cooperative Learning Experiences the Solution?" in L. Bickman, ed. *Applied Social Psychology Annual 4* (Beverly Hills, CA: Sage Publications, 1983).
12. David Johnson, et al., "Effects of Cooperative, Competitive, and Individualistic Goal Structures on Achievement: A Meta-Analysis," *Psychological Bulletin*, 89(1) (1981): 47–62.
13. R. E. Slavin, "Cooperative Learning and Student Achievement," *Educational Leadership*, 45(2) (1988): 31–33.
14. A. Bandura, "Human Agency in Social Cognitive Theory," *American Psychologist*, 44(9) (1989): 1175–1184.
15. J. G. Brooks and M. G. Brooks, *The Case for Constructivist Classrooms* (Alexandria, VA: Association for Supervision and Curriculum Development, 1993).
16. H. Gardner and W. Boix-Mansilla, "Teaching for Understanding—Within and Across the Disciplines," *Educational Leadership*, 51 (1994): 14–18.
17. R. Glaser, "Education and Thinking: The Role of Knowledge." *American Psychologist*, 39 (1984): 93–104.
18. J. W. Getzels and P. W. Jackson, *Creativity and Intelligence* (New York: John Wiley and Sons, Inc., 1962).
19. Abraham Maslow, *The Farther Reaches of Human Nature* (London: Penguin, 1983). (Original work published 1971.)
20. B. L. McCombs, "Learner-Centered Psychological Principles for Enhancing Education: Applications in School Settings," in L. A. Penner, G. M. Batsche, H. M. Knoff, and D. L. Nelson, eds., *The Challenge in Mathematics and Science Education: Psychology's Response* (Washington, DC: American Psychological Association, 1993.)
21. B. L. McCombs and R. J. Marzano, "Putting the Self in Self-Regulated Learning," *Educational Psychologist*, 25(1) (1990): 51–69.
22. Jean Piaget, "Development and Learning, Part I of Cognitive Development in Children," *Journal of Research in Science Teaching*, 2(3) (1964).

23. Jean Piaget, *The Construction of Reality in the Child*, trans. M. Cook (New York: Basic Books, 1954).

24. D. Kuhn, "Thinking as Argument," *Harvard Educational Review*, 62(2) (1992): 155–178.

25. N. Burbules and M. Linn, "Response to Contradiction: Scientific Reasoning During Adolescence," *Journal of Educational Psychology*, 80(1) (1988): 67–75.

26. B. Eylon and M. Linn, "Learning and Instruction: An Examination of Four Research Perspectives in Science Education," *Review of Educational Research*, 58(3) (1988): 251–301.

27. David P. Ausubel, *Educational Psychology: A Cognitive View* (New York: Academic Press, 1968).

28. National Research Council, *National Science Education Standards* (Washington, DC: Author, 1995).

29. American Association for the Advancement of Science, *Benchmarks for Science Literacy* (Washington, DC: Author, 1994).

30. J. Anderson, *The Architecture of Cognition* (Cambridge, MA: Harvard University Press, 1983).

31. S. Carey, "Cognitive Science and Science Education," *American Psychologist*, 41(10) (1986): 1123–1130.

32. M. Linn, C. Clement, S. Pulos, and S. Sullivan, "Scientific Reasoning During Adolescence: The Influence of Instruction in Science Knowledge and Reasoning Strategies," *Journal of Research in Science Teaching*, 26(2) (1989): 171–187.

33. F. Barron, "The Needs for Order and For Disorder as Motives in Creative Activity," in C. W. Taylor, and F. Barron, eds., *Scientific Creativity: Its Recognition and Development* (New York: John Wiley and Sons, Inc., 1963): 153–162.

34. C. Ames, "Achievement Goals and the Classroom Climate," in D. H. Schunk and J. L. Meece, eds., *Student Perceptions in the Classroom* (Hillsdale, NJ: Lawrence Erlbaum Associates, Inc., 1992): 327–348.

35. R. Ames and C. Ames, "Motivation and Effective Teaching," in M. L. Maehr and C. Ames, eds., *Advances in Motivation and Achievement: Motivation Enhancing Environments*, 6 (1989): 247–271.

36. A. Bandura, "Self-Efficacy Mechanism in Human Agency," *American Psychologist*, 37 (1982): 122–147.

37. E. L. Deci and R. M. Ryan, "A Motivational Approach to Self: Integration in Personality," in R. Dienstbier, ed., *Nebraska Symposium on Motivation. Vol. 38. Perspectives on Motivation* (Lincoln, NE: University of Nebraska Press, 1991).

38. J. P. Connell and R. M. Ryan, "A Developmental Theory of Motivation in the Classroom," *Teacher Education Quality*, 11 (1984): 64–77.

39. Maslow, *Motivation and Personality*.

40. Maslow, *The Farther Reaches of Human Nature*.

41. Barron, The Needs for Order and for Disorder as Motives in Creative Activity.

42. Connell and Ryan, A Developmental Theory of Motivation in the Classroom.

43. S. Harter, "Affective and Motivational Correlates of Self-Esteem," in R. Dienstbier, ed., *Nebraska Symposium on Motivation: Vol. 40. Developmental Perspectives on Motivation* (Lincoln, NE: University of Nebraska Press, 1992).

44. D. W. Johnson and R. T. Johnson, *Cooperation and Competition: Theory and Research* (Edina, MN: Interaction Book Company, 1989).

45. Bandura, Human Agency in Social Cognitive Theory.

46. Brooks and Brooks, *The Case for Constructivist Classrooms*.

47. Harter, Affective and Motivational Correlates of Self-Esteem.

48. M. Almy, *Young Children's Thinking* (New York: Teachers College Press, 1966).

49. Ames, Achievement Goals and the Classroom Climate.

50. Brooks and Brooks, *The Case for Constructivist Classrooms*.

51. McCombs and Marzano, Putting the Self in Self-Regulated Learning.

52. Rogers, *Freedom to Learn*.

INVESTIGATING SCIENCE TEACHING

Activity 19–1

STUDENT MOTIVATION

This activity is to be completed during an observation period in a science classroom. First, identify three students of differing motivation levels—one highly motivated, the second about average, and the third unmotivated. You may have to ask the science teacher for recommendations. Second, observe these students for fifteen minutes each. During this time note the behaviors that you think reveal their level of motivation. Finally, indicate what you would recommend to increase their motivation.

	Observations	Recommendations
Highly Motivated Student		
Student of Average Motivation		
Unmotivated Student		

1. How would you modify the science class to increase student motivation?

2. What role do the curriculum materials play in student motivation?

3. What role do instructional methods play in student motivation?

Activity 19–2

"HOW CAN I MOTIVATE STUDENTS TO LEARN?"

This activity is based on the discussion of external motivation. You are to spend a period of time (at least one class period and preferably two or three) observing a science teacher. During this observation period you are to note examples of the factors Madeline Hunter suggests will increase student motivation. (See the text of her book. *Mastery Teaching.*)

Factors	Examples	Effect on Students
Level of Concern		
Feeling Tone		
Success		
Interest		
Knowledge of Results		

How do these factors interact?

Provide your own examples of the way you would implement these factors.

1.

2.

3.

Activity 19–3

MOTIVATIONAL NEEDS

Imagine that you observed these behaviors in a tenth-grade biology class.

Mary was restless and fidgeting during the lesson; something seemed to be competing for her attention. The science teacher ignored her. Two desks away Robert sat quietly, head on his desk, sleeping. The teacher awakened Robert and firmly suggested that he pay attention. Karen paid close attention to the teacher. she was careful to record the important points of the lesson and then started her assignment. After completing her work and handing it to the teacher, she was given recognition that was earned and deserved. Martin came into the class and immediately started clowning around, climbing on desks and causing a commotion. He was also given recognition—it was also earned and deserved: however, the teacher had to make a great effort to get him to behave in an appropriate manner.

1. What do you think might be motivating these behaviors?

2. How could you find out more about the motivations of these students?

3. How would you respond to the students in a different way?

Activity 19–4

REWARDS AND PUNISHMENTS

In connection with learning about psychology as it is applied in education, you should plan to spend several hours in observation of a science class. Your task is to determine the reinforcements and punishments that are given. Use the following guide to help systematize your observations. Review the definitions involved and then make a check each time you observe a reinforcement or punishment.

	Present Stimulus	Remove Stimulus
Pleasant Stimulus		
Aversive Stimulus		

1. Which did the teacher use most—reinforcement or punishment?

2. What types of reinforcers and punishments were used?

3. Did any particular method seem effective? Ineffective?

4. What did you learn about the use of reinforcement and punishment in the science classroom?

Activity 19–5

ASSESSING COGNITIVE DEVELOPMENT: CONCRETE OPERATIONS

The administration of tasks outlined in this section should provide you with insights into the cognitive abilities of middle school students. You should have little trouble administering the tasks. It will require making arrangements for the interview session and preparing the required materials. Interpreting the results may present problems. For this reason, some discussion is provided on how tasks can be interpreted. The experiences of questioning students about their reasoning will provide valuable insights into the stages of cognitive development.

Here are some specific suggestions for administering the tasks. Also, a suggested interview form is provided.

Each of the tasks to be administered outlines a basic structure for the interview. Certain specific suggestions for giving the tasks should be followed:

1. *Establish rapport.* It is important that the person giving the interview establish good rapport with the child before administering the tasks (i.e., ask her/his name, age, etc., as suggested on the interview form which follows). Tell her/him you have some games to play, and all answers are acceptable. Try to make the tasks fun to do, smile while the child does them, and do what you can to lessen the child's feeling that the interview is a threatening experience.
2. *Do not give answers.* Do not tell the child she/he is wrong or right, just accept her/his answer and either you or an assistant record them on the interview form.
3. *Ask for justification.* Always ask for the justification of an answer. In the interview we are interested in determining how the child thinks (i.e., Is she/he really conserving or is she/he just giving a correct answer?)
4. *Hypothesize about the child's thinking.* Formulate in your mind certain hypotheses about how the child is thinking. Ask the child questions to test your hypotheses to determine whether or not they are correct.
5 *Use the "another child told me" approach.* In asking the child to justify an answer, you may ask her/him why she/he thinks it is correct. Experience shows that some children will not respond to why questions. Generally, however, if you restructure your questions giving an episode like the following, they will respond: "The other day a boy told me that the rolled out clay in the form of a hot dog weighed just as much as the clay before it was changed. What would you say to him?"
6. *Allow for wait-time.* Remember that most tasks require some form of logical-mathematical reasoning. Thinking takes time. Therefore, do not rush the child in your interview. Allow her/him time to think: five or more seconds time allowance is not too much.
7. *Have fun.* Most of all, have fun giving the tasks and try to see that children have similar experiences.

Outlined below is an interview form to be used to note the task achievement of the student. It will probably be best for you to record the responses while you interview. The interview form needs some clarification. In each session you should plan on *giving six or seven tasks.* The time for administering these will vary from twenty to forty minutes, depending on the age and cognitive level of the child. Place a description of each task in the left-hand column. Check in the appropriate column whether the child achieved or did not achieve the task. In the column provided for the level of cognition, write the period the student demonstrated. With many students you will not get a clear demarcation of stage. They might perform preoperationally on three tasks and concrete operationally on four. You probably would indicate the transitional stage on the basis of your limited interviewing measures.

Piagetian Interview Form: Concrete Operational Period

Name of Child_____Interviewer's Name_____Location_____

Age_____Grade_____Gender_____

Activity description (e.g., conservation of substance, class inclusion)	Achievement: -Task achieved -Not achieved	Indication of cognitive level (e.g., operational). Note: If child doesn't achieve level of task, it is assumed she/he is at a lower level.	Other comments about the student's behavior or statements	Justification (child's reason for responding as she/he did)
1.				
2.				
3.				
4.				
5.				
6.				
7.				
8.				
9.				
10.				

How many tasks were achieved?

How would you classify this student's level of development? Transitional? Concrete operational?

How would you justify this classification?

How could you confirm this level?

What are the educational implications of your interview?

Piagetian Interview Activities

Time and distance. Tell the child two persons are walking the same speed and distance, except one is walking on a straight path and one is walking on a crooked path. Ask, "Which one reaches his house first? Why?" Use two strings of equal length to represent the paths.

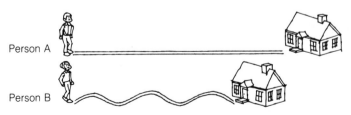

Discussion: Up to age nine, children usually have difficulty comparing the time taken and distance covered of two moving persons or objects. They believe going farther (in direction) takes more time. They do not compensate by increasing or decreasing the speed. For this reason, preoperational and early concrete operational children believe Person A will take more time.

Seriation. Prepare ten cards of stick people, dolls, flowers, or some animal so that they progressively increase in size. Place the first and last of the series on a table and tell the child to place the rest of them in order.

Discussion: During the concrete operational period, a child develops her/his ordering ability. This ability usually occurs during ages seven and eight. Many children, however, even in the third grade, cannot do the task. If they cannot do it, they probably also have difficulty with number because ordering is basic to understanding mathematics.

Ordering. Show children, ages six through eight, stages of a developing moth, including the egg, larva, pupa, and adult. Discuss how the moth develops through these stages. Let the children look at the various stages of the organism and have them draw the stages in order of development.

Next, show them a picture of one of the stages and ask, "What would be the next stage? What was the stage before this? Why do you think so?"

Discussion: If the children can do this and give reasons for their placement of the stages, they probably are able to order. Many young children will not be able to do this. The activity is still valuable because it helps children grasp some concepts of development although they may not be able yet to interrelate them. If they do not order correctly, they probably do not see the stages as a continuum of an organism slowly progressing to maturity. Children unable to do this probably reason by transduction.

Speed. Obtain two toy cars of different colors. Draw on a piece of paper a line to indicate the end of a race. Place one of the cars behind the other at the start. Move both of these cars with each of your hands so that they come to the finish line at the same time. Ask, "Which of the cars was going faster, or did they both move the same? How do you know? How about the distance traveled? Did one cover a greater distance? When was one car ahead of the other? Why? Which one moved faster?"

Discussion: Young children believe if the cars finish the race together, they must be moving at the same speed. This is because they believe order, being in front or together, indicates speed. Usually at age nine or ten children take into consideration where an object started and stopped, distance traveled, and the time it took. If the child does not grasp this realization, she/he will have difficulty doing mathematical speed problems. This may occur even into the fifth and sixth grades. If a child cannot do such problems, use toy cars and other objects to help her/him discover the relationships of speed to time and distance so that he/she eventually will understand that speed = distance/time.

Conservation of substance. Show a child a diagram of a kernel of popcorn and then draw a picture of it after it has popped. Ask, "Is there more corn after it is popped than before it is popped? Why has the volume changed?"

Discussion: Preoperational children, being perception bound, believe there is more corn to eat after it is popped. Concrete children know that altering the corn's state does not change its amount.

Reversibility. Have children grow bean seeds or show them plants in various stages of development. After they have raised some plants, have them draw how they grew. Their drawings should be similar to the ones shown here. Give the children a diagram of a young plant and ask them to draw how it would look in stages before and after this picture. Next, have the children draw several pictures showing the stages of development of plants in reverse order. Ask, "Why do you think your pictures are true?"

Discussion: If the children can reverse properly and give you reasons why they are drawing the plants in this order, they have probably achieved reversibility in their thinking. Checking for reversibility can be easily done whenever the children have prepared and learned something in one order and are then asked to reverse the order.

Reverse seriation. Obtain twenty straws. The straws should be cut so that you have two series of ten straws each that progress in length. Set up one series from short to long and then ask the children to take the other set and place them in reverse order.

Discussion: This task identifies whether or not children can reverse the order of a series of objects. Children of seven can usually seriate, but many children ages eight through nine have difficulty in reversing the order.

Classification—Ascending and descending hierarchy. Prepare a number of cards, some labeled *birds* with pictures of birds on them, some labeled *ducks* with pictures of ducks on them, and some labeled *animals* with pictures of various animals on them. Show these to a group of eight- to ten-year-old children. Ask them to arrange the cards in groups according to each of the three labels. Next, place the bird pile on the duck pile and ask, "Is the bird label, now on top, still appropriate? Why?" Now place the animal pile on the others. Ask, "Is this appropriate? Why? Do all the cards belong in this pile? Are birds animals? Are ducks animals? If all the animals in the world died, would there be any ducks? Why or why not?"

Discussion: This activity determines whether a child understands class inclusion: that is, ducks are not only ducks but also birds (an ascending hierarchy). Ducks are a subgroup belonging to birds, a higher major group. Asking if ducks would remain if all the animals are killed determines whether the child can also descend a hierarchy (go from animals, a major group, to ducks, a subgroup).

Conservation of area. Obtain eight cubes of sugar. Stack four together so that they appear as shown in diagram A below. Then, arrange the other four so they appear as in diagram B. Or prepare and show the child diagrams of the two situations. Ask, "Is the distance around (perimeter) A the same as that around B? Why?" Tell the child, "The other day a girl told me they were not the same perimeter, or distance around. What would you tell her? How would you prove it?"

Discussion: By this age, children will usually conserve area. But they think that if the area is the same, the perimeter must be the same too. If each square were two centimeters wide, the perimeter of A would be sixteen centimeters and of B, twenty centimeters. If the child does not come up with correct responses, have her/him count the sides of each of the diagrams and then ask, "What do you think about the perimeters?"

Conservation. Rip a newspaper in half. Ask, "Do I have more, less, or the same amount of newspaper as I had before?" (conservation of substance). Ask, "Do the combined pieces of newspaper weigh more, less, or the same as the paper did before it was torn? Why?" (conservation of weight). Ask, "If I put these torn pieces of newspaper in a large tank of water, would they occupy more, less, or the same amount of space as when the paper was whole? Why?" (conservation of volume).

Discussion: Children do not develop conservation usually until after age six. In other words, they do not realize that physically altering one property of matter does not necessarily change its amount, weight, or the volume it will occupy. Conservation of substance and weight usually develop by age eight, while conservation of volume occurs later.

Number. Obtain ten straws. If the child can count, have her/him count them one through ten. Point to a middle straw and ask, "If the last straw is ten, what is the number of this straw?" Place the straws together and have the child count them. Move the straws apart. Ask, "Do I have more, less, or the same number of straws now as before?"

Discussion: Preoperational children often can count but do not know number. To fully comprehend number children must understand the following:

1. *Classification*—realize that the straws, although they may not look alike, are still straws.
2. *Cardination*—realize that no matter how you arrange objects in a set, you still have the same number.
3. *Ordination*—place the straws in order and realize that where the object is in the order determines its number.

Class Inclusion. Show the children some fruit (e.g., ten raisins and two pears). Ask, "In what ways are these alike? What do you call them? Are there more raisins than fruit? It I took the fruit and you took the raisins, would I have more, or would you have more? How would you be able to prove who had more?"

Discussion: This activity tests again for class inclusion. Does the child realize that the subclass *raisins* is included in the major class *fruit?* Is the child overcome by the perception of a large number of raisins?

Activity 19–6

ASSESSING COGNITIVE DEVELOPMENT: FORMAL OPERATIONS

Valuable insights concerning patterns of reasoning can be gained from interviewing students and asking them to respond to simple tasks. The tasks in this activity are designed for assessment of formal operations. You may wish to include some tasks from Activity 19–5, "Assessing Cognitive Development: Concrete Operations." You should also review the suggestions for interviewing in that activity.

Piagetian Interview Tasks: Formal Operational Period

Name_____   School_____

Class or Subject_____   Teacher_____

Gender_____   Level_____

Age_____(yrs.)_____(months)   Gender Demeanor_____

Date_____   Other_____

Proportional Reasoning

This task assesses the student's ability to apply the concept of ratio and proportion. The student is given an 8½x11-inch card. Stickpeople are drawn on each side of the card, one being two-thirds the height of the other. The small and large stickpeople should be constructed to measure four and six jumbo paper clips respectively. Ask the student to measure the height of each of the stickpeople with a set of eight connected jumbo paper clips. After the student has measured and recorded the heights of the two stickpeople, the jumbo clips are replaced with a set of small paper clips. Ask the student to measure only the short stickperson with the new set of clips. Remove the stickperson. Then ask, "How tall is the large stickperson in terms of the small paper clips?"

Task 1—Proportional Reasoning Responses

1. Predicted height of tall stickperson:_____

2. Justification for prediction:_____

_____

3. Key statements indicating cognitive level:_____

_____

4. Classification of performance:_____

5. Suggestions for teaching:_____

Discussion: The measurement of the tall stickperson should be six jumbo clips and nine small clips in length, and the small stickperson should measure four jumbo clips and six small clips. The criterion for success on this task is the ability of the student to accurately predict the height of the tall stickperson in terms of small clips (i.e., nine clips). The student's justification must include a reference to direct ratio or proportion. The student may just guess and give you a number. If the child does, she/he is not demonstrating the use of formal thought. If, however, she/he tries to figure it on paper or reasons in a rational way, indicating that the situation is a simple proportion, she/he is demonstrating formal thought:

Small Stickperson		Large Stickperson
4 clips	=	6 clips
6 clips	=	x clips

Separation and Control of Variables

This task utilizes a simple pendulum consisting of a length of string about eighty cm long and a set of varying weights. Ask the student to determine which variable or variables affect the frequency of oscillation of the pendulum (the number of swings per unit of time, e.g., second). (Note: Since the length of the string is the only relevant variable, the problem is to isolate it from the others. Only in this way can the student solve the problem and explain the frequency of oscillations.)

Task 2—Separation and Control of Variables Responses

1. Question: Which variable or variables affect the frequency of oscillation of this pendulum?

   Response:_____

   _____

2. Question: Can you design an experiment to prove that your choice is correct?

   Response:_____

   _____

3. Key statements indicating cognitive level:_____

   _____

4. Classification of cognitive level:_____

   _____

5. Suggestions for teaching:_____

   _____

Discussion: The criterion for success on this task is the student's ability to identify the one variable (length of string) that affects the oscillation of the pendulum. The student's justification must indicate that she/he held *all variables constant while manipulating only one variable* in reaching her/his conclusion. The student should initially indicate that variables involved in the problem could be weight, length of string, or height at which the pendulum is dropped. She/he may initially think a combination of these may affect the frequency. She/he may then describe a set of hypotheses and test these. However, before finishing she/he should *design an experiment controlling one variable at a time,* such as length of string, to find out whether her/his hypothesis is correct. In this way she/he should systematically eliminate the irrelevant variables. The ability to plan experiments to separate and control, or manipulate, *one variable at a time,* observe it accurately, and make proper conclusions characterizes formal thought.

Proportional Reasoning

The student is presented with a balance scale consisting of a wooden rod with equally spaced numbered positions. Weights are attached as indicated in the diagram. Begin by using equal weights (ten grams) equidistant from the fulcrum (pivoting point). Remove one. Maintain equilibrium of the balance by holding the force arm. Ask, "Using any of the weights in front of you, how could you get the scale to balance?" After the student responds ask, "What other ways are there to balance the scale besides the one you chose?" Remove the weight from the scale. Place another weight nearer the fulcrum and maintain equilibrium by holding the force arm. Ask, "How may the scale be balanced by using the weights? How do you justify your responses?"

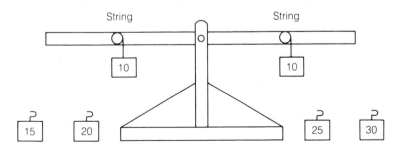

Task 3—Proportional Reasoning Responses

1. Question: Using any of the weights presented here, how could you get the scale to balance?

   Response:_____

2. Question (Justification): How did you arrive at this answer?

   Response:_____

   _____

3. Key statements indicating cognitive level:_____

   _____

4. Classification of cognitive level:_____

   _____

5. Suggestions for teaching:_____

   _____

Discussion: The criterion for success on this task is the student's ability to equate length times weight on one arm of the fulcrum with length times weight on the other arm or to figure out the problem by using proportions. In order for the student to balance the scale, she/he must apply the principle of levers.

Combinatorial Logic

Obtain five medicine droppers, baby food or other jars, and ten clear plastic cups. Prepare stock solutions of the following:

1. Dilute sulfuric acid (H_2SO_4)—10 ml concentrated H_2SO_4 to 100 ml H_2O
2. Distilled H_2O
3. Hydrogen Peroxide—3 parts of H_2O_2 added to 97 parts H_2O
4. Sodium Thiosulfate—10 grams sodium thiosulfate to 1 liter of H_2O
5. Potassium Iodide—5 g to 1 liter H_2O

Pour the stock solutions into the baby jars as follows: jar one, dilute sulfuric acid; jar two, water; jar three, hydrogen peroxide; jar four, sodium thiosulfate; and jar five, potassium iodide, labeled g. The student is then given the four jars containing colorless, odorless liquids which are perceptually identical. Then present her/him with two glasses, one containing solutions one-three, the other containing solution two. The contents of the glasses are not revealed to the student. Several drops from jar g are poured into each of the two glasses. The student is asked to notice the reactions. (The container containing one + three turns yellow, the other remains unchanged.) The student is told that the two samples were prepared from the jars and that each contains g.

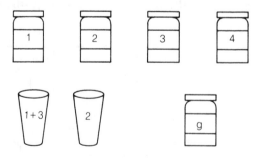

Ask, "Can you reproduce the color?" Ten plastic cups are made available, and the student is allowed to attempt to reproduce the color. Record the student's procedure. If the color is successfully reproduced, ask questions to determine if she/he can identify the functions of each liquid. (The child should indicate that jar two does not alter the reaction one way or the other and jar four eliminates the color.)

Task 4—Combinatorial Logical Responses

Record the procedure the student takes in solving the problem.

_____

_____

_____

_____

1. Analysis of procedure. Check which one(s) of the following the student was able to do.
   a. Made the color in one way._____
   b. Made the color in two ways._____
   c. Knew that all of one, three, and g were necessary._____
   d. Knew that two had no effect, or did not help or produce the color._____
   e. Knew that four removed or prevented the color._____
2. Key statements indicating cognitive level:_____

   _____

3. Classification of cognitive level:_____

   _____

4. Suggestions for teaching:_____

   _____

Discussion: The main criterion for determining whether the student is a formal operational thinker is whether she/he establishes a *systematic procedure* for the role played by each of the solutions. Does she/he use, for example, a process of elimination? Does she/he realize that by combining one, three, and g the yellow solution occurs? If she/he cannot state these facts, but just goes about the activity by trial and error and does not indicate she/he understands the role of all the combinations, she/he is not a formal operational thinker.

Task 5—Hypothetical Reasoning

Show a student the following diagram of the top of a pool table. Ask her/him to trace how she/he would hit ball *y* so that it would collide with ball *x*, in each of the positions shown, to make *x* go into one of the corner pockets. After she/he has drawn several ways she/he could hit the *y* ball, ask her/him to describe any rule that could be used in the future. You might have to help the student construct a rule. Ask, "If you hit the ball straight on, how will it move? If you hit it on a 45° angle, how will it move?" (You have to diagram a 45° angle to ensure that she/he understands what you mean.) Ask, "Can you compare the reaction of a ball bouncing off a wall with *y*'s reaction to *x*?"

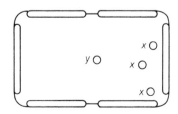

Task 5—Hypothetical Reasoning Response

1. Student's description of rule:_____

2. Justification for the rule:_____

3. Key statements indicating cognitive level:_____

_____

4. Classification of cognitive level:_____

_____

5. Suggestions for teaching:_____

_____

Discussion: The student should, in her/his own words, state that the angle of incidence equals the angle of reflection. If the student does state this rule, she/he should explain the meaning to be sure she/he has not memorized it. She/he need not use the above words, as long as she/he can explain the law or state some rule.

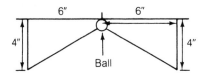

Activity 19–7

GROUP STRUCTURE

You will need to spend at least one class period observing a secondary science class. During the class, try to direct your attention to the students as a group.

To gain insights into group structure in a science class, you should answer the following questions. Use the one to seven continuum to indicate the degree to which the group characteristic is present. These questions are based on the earlier discussion of the defining characteristics of groups.

	Low		Medium		High	
1. To what degree do the students have a *solidarity* of opinion, purpose, and interests when they work in this class?	1	2	3	4	5	6	7
2. To what degree are the students *satisfied* with the class?	1	2	3	4	5	6	7
3. To what degree are members of other classes *attracted* to this class?	1	2	3	4	5	6	7
4. To what degree do students in the class group feel they are *wanted* and *belong* in the class?	1	2	3	4	5	6	7
5. To what degree (both quality and quantity) do students *interact* through various types of communication?	1	2	3	4	5	6	7
6. To what degree is the group *structure* beneficial to achieving goals?	1	2	3	4	5	6	7
7. To what degree are the *norms* of behavior adhered to by group members?	1	2	3	4	5	6	7

What behaviors did you observe that allowed you to make these decisions? How can you identify these properties of groups? After each of the words listed below place two or three behaviors that you think support your judgment.

Solidarity of group:

Satisfaction with group:

Attraction of group:

Interaction of group:

Structure of group:

Norms of group:

Chapter 20

....

INDIVIDUAL AND CULTURAL DIFFERENCES IN SCIENCE CLASSROOMS

A great diversity of students come to science classes. They come from urban, suburban, and rural environments; they come from poor, middle class, and affluent homes. Some can read, others cannot; some are interested in science, others are not. Some are gifted, some are slow, and most are average. The list could go on. In fact, if we started a classification system, it could continue until we described each individual in each school. Saying that each student is a unique individual is to state the obvious. And few teachers disagree, in principle, with the logical educational implication of such a statement: namely, all students require individual attention and opportunities to learn.

■ EXCEPTIONAL STUDENTS IN EDUCATION: A RATIONALE

Of the many issues that educators face during the 1990s, perhaps one of the most encompassing is that of a right to education for *all* students. In the late 1970s, attention was focused on the educational rights of students who were traditionally placed in restricted, special-education programs. One result of this movement is the recognition of individual differences and the conclusion that has been clear to many teachers for a long time—*all students are exceptional.*

All educators stand to gain from having exceptional students in science classrooms. Although it is only natural to expect some initial hesitation, frustration, or fear on the part of students and teachers alike, once these feelings pass the gains are clear: Exceptional students encounter a whole new range of educational opportunities; regular students learn that in terms of basic human needs and wants, exceptional students are not very different from themselves; and teachers become more sensitive to the realities of different learning styles, subtleties of instruction, and of modifying curricula to meet students' personal needs. In the end, we all find out more about what it means to be human.

The points made in the preceding paragraph are important reasons for having exceptional students in science classrooms. There is another reason; it is the just thing for science teachers to do. We have a responsibility to provide the best science program for all our students. Science teachers know that students have unique needs that are not fulfilled by curriculum materials alone. An essential task for science teachers is accommodating our programs and teaching to the needs of students, not to making students adapt to our science programs and teaching strategies.

■ EXCEPTIONAL STUDENTS IN SCIENCE PROGRAMS: THE LAW

Appeals to personal and professional benefit and to justice do not completely convince teachers of the need to include exceptional students in the science classroom. The most immediate and forceful argument seems to be the law. We have a legal responsibility to include exceptional students in the mainstream of school programs.

One of the first laws that included protection of the rights of exceptional students was the Rehabilitation Act of 1973, Public Law 93-112, Section 504 of which states:

> No otherwise qualified handicapped individual in the United States . . . shall, solely by reason of his handicap, be excluded from participation in, be denied the benefits of, or be subjected to discrimination under any program or activity receiving federal financial assistance.

Since most, if not all, school systems receive federal financial assistance under this law, exceptional students must be allowed to participate in, receive the benefits of, and have open access to educational programs.

Other federal legislation that included safeguards concerning the rights of exceptional students was Public Law 93-380, the Education Amendments of 1974. This law mandated due process procedures at the state and local levels for the placement of exceptional students, assured placement of exceptional students in the least restrictive environment, and set a goal of providing full educational opportunities for all handicapped students within each state. Public Law 94-142, the Education for all Handicapped Children Act of 1975—the regulation with which most United States school personnel are probably familiar—requires that exceptional students be integrated into regular classrooms whenever possible:

> It is the purpose of this Act to assure that all handicapped children have available to them . . . a free

appropriate public education which emphasizes special attention and related services designed to meet their unique needs, to assure that the rights of handicapped children and their parents or guardians are protected, to assist states and localities to provide for the education of all handicapped children, and to assess and assure the effectiveness of efforts to educate handicapped children.

Specifically, Public Law 94-142 requires the following of school personnel:

1. *Zero Rejection.* No student may be rejected from a free public education and related services. Court cases, such as *Pennsylvania Association for Retarded Children v. Commonwealth of Pennsylvania*, 334 F. Supp. 1257 (E. D. PA 1971) and *Mills v. Board of Education of the District of Columbia*, 348 F. Supp. 886 (D. D. C., 1972) have resulted in a legal commitment to the public schools for the education of all school-age students. That all students have a "right to education, regardless of their present level of functioning" results in a principle of zero rejection. You also should note that education is defined as the development of students from their present level to the next appropriate level. In brief, the assumption is all students are educable.

2. *Classification and Placement.* Evaluation of students shall be nondiscriminatory. Diagnostic and assessment procedures are to be established by each state to ensure that cultural and racial bias are not evident in the system used for identifying exceptional students. Tests shall be a fair evaluation of the student's strengths and weaknesses.

3. *Appropriate Education.* This stipulation is a requirement for an Individualized Education Program (IEP). An IEP should have statements concerning the student's present level of performance, how he or she will participate in the regular educational program, the type of special services needed, the date special services were initiated, and the expected length of services. In addition, the IEP should set short- and long-term minimum standards, measures of achievement, and an evaluation of educational progress that includes a conference between school personnel, parents, and the exceptional students.

4. *Least Restrictive Placement.* To the maximum extent possible, exceptional students will be educated with all other students. "Least Restrictive Placement" means that exceptional students should be educated in the "mainstream," the regular educational environment. They can be educated in special programs when the nature or severity of their handicap requires such treatment.

5. *Due Process.* The exceptional student (usually through parents or a guardian) has a right to question testing and placement. That is, exceptional students are guaranteed procedural safeguards in the placement and provision of special services.

6. *Parental Participation.* Parents of the handicapped student have the right to be present for their child's evaluation, placement, and development of the IEP.

Public Laws 93-112, 93-380, and 94-142 stand on fundamental principles guaranteed in the Constitution. Exceptional students have been systematically excluded from many educational programs, which, in essence, has been a violation of the Constitutional rights of approximately thirty-five million Americans. The Fourteenth Amendment guarantees equal protection under the law for all Americans. Recall that the *Brown v. Board of Education of Topeka*, 347 U. S. 483 (1954) overturned the earlier "separate but equal" ruling of *Plessy v. Ferguson*, 163, U. S. 537 (1896). It is instructive to read the *Brown v. Board* decision and make appropriate changes in the wording, such as *disabled* or *challenged* for *Negro* or *race*, and *classroom* for *school*. Separate educational facilities for some students are, by definition, unequal; thus, exceptional students have been deprived of the equal protection of the laws guaranteed by the Fourteenth Amendment of our Constitution.

Of the three laws, Public Law 94-142 was probably the most significant piece of educational legislation of the 1970s, and its effect will be felt throughout the 1990s. There are several reasons for this fact. First, Public Law 94-142 incorporates parts of the other laws and clarifies the fundamental right of all students to an education. Second, because it is a federal law, it establishes the right to education as a national priority. Third, Public Law 94-142 commits us to recognize individual differences and to appropriate educational programs for all students because it is permanent legislation with no expiration date. This fact demonstrates the importance Congress placed on this legislation.

■ EXCEPTIONAL STUDENTS IN SCIENCE CLASS: SOME GUIDELINES

Teachers' concerns are not in understanding why exceptional students *ought to be* in science classrooms but rather in dealing with the fact that they *are* in our classrooms. And, so the problems may be stated: What can be done to provide the best science education program possible? What are the first steps? What should I do now? The next sections are addressed to these questions. The ideas about teaching exceptional students have been synthesized from many sources and should give you some information, some confidence, and some direction in working with exceptional students.

There are some simple, straightforward things that you can do that will help most students. Certainly, there are unique problems in integrating any exceptional student into the science classroom. You can anticipate some personal tension and educational problems during the period of adjustment. And, understandably, we cannot provide suggestions that will cover all situations. Nevertheless, there are some approaches that have proved helpful with most exceptional students.

General Guidelines for Helping Exceptional Students

1. Obtain and read all the background information available on the student.
2. Spend time educating yourself on the physical and/or psychological nature of the student's exceptionality and how it affects the student's potential for learning.
3. Determine whether or not special help is available to you through the resources of experts within and outside the school system.
4. Determine any special equipment needed by the student.
5. Talk with the student about limitations and about particular needs in the science class.
6. Use resource teachers and aides to assist you.
7. Establish a team of fellow teachers (including resource teachers and aides) to share information and ideas about the school's exceptional students. A team approach is helpful in overcoming initial fears and the sense of isolation in dealing with the student. You may need to take responsibility for contacting appropriate school personnel and establishing the team; if so, have courage and do it.
8. Other students are often willing to help exceptional students. Encourage them to do so.
9. Be aware of barriers, both physical and psychological, to the fullest possible functioning of each student.
10. Consider how to modify or adapt curriculum materials and teaching strategies for exceptional students without sacrificing content, processes, or activities.
11. Do not underestimate the capabilities of exceptional students. Teachers' perceptions of students' abilities have a way of becoming self-fulfilling prophecies. If these perceptions are negative, they may detrimentally affect students and your ability to create new options for them.
12. Use the same standards of grading and discipline for exceptional students as you do for the rest of the class.
13. Develop a trusting relationship with all students.
14. Educate the other students about exceptionality in general, as well as specific handicaps of students in their class.

Auditorially Challenged Students

From an early age, most children learn through listening—and there is every indication that most teaching is through telling. So, it becomes quite difficult for students with hearing problems; science teachers have to adjust. Hearing impairment is defined as an auditory problem that may adversely affect the student's educational performance. Students with hearing impairments often have developmental delays in speech and language. These delays have obvious effects on the ability to communicate. Students with hearing impairments will not necessarily have problems acquiring science concepts, although they may have difficulty learning the written or oral language to communicate their understanding.

Helping Auditorially Challenged Students Learn Science

1. Individuals with hearing impairments depend heavily on visual perception. Therefore, seat the student for optimal viewing.
2. Determine whether an interpreter will be needed and the nature of the student's speech/language problems.
3. Learn the student's most effective way of communicating.
4. Find the student a listening helper.

Visually Challenged Students

Like students with hearing impairments, students with visual impairments are those whose vision is limited enough to require adaptations in materials and strategies. Students who can read material with the use of magnifying devices and/or enlarged print are classified as partially seeing. Students who require braille or taped materials are classified as educationally blind.

Helping Students with Visual Impairments Learn Science

1. Students with visual impairments learn through sensory channels other than vision, primarily hearing. Therefore, seat students for optimal listening.

2. Determine from the student what constitutes the best lighting.
3. Change the room arrangement whenever necessary but always make a special effort to reorient the student.
4. Allow the student to manipulate tangible materials, models, and when possible, real objects. Do not unduly protect students from materials.
5. Speak aloud what you have written on the board and charts.
6. Use the student's name; otherwise, the student may not know when he or she is being addressed.
7. Since smiles and facial gestures might not be seen, touching is the most effective means of reinforcing the student's work.
8. Be aware of eye fatigue. This fatigue can be overcome by varying activities, using good lighting, and providing close visual work.
9. Have the student use his/her visual capacity when possible (unless otherwise directed).

Physically Challenged Students

Students with physical and health impairments represent a diverse group of special needs, for this category includes students with allergies, asthma, arthritis, amputations, diabetes, epilepsy, cerebral palsy, spina bifida, and muscular dystrophy. Some are mobile and others are confined to wheelchairs; some have good use of their limbs and others do not. Some have a single condition and some have multiple disabilities. The range of needs is such that some can work in the regular science classroom with little or no problem, whereas others require full-time care.

Helping Physically Challenged Students Learn Science

1. Eliminate architectural barriers.
2. Become familiar with the basic mechanics and maintenance of braces, prostheses, and wheelchairs.
3. Understand the effects of medication on students and know the prescribed dosage.
4. Obtain special devices, such as pencil holders or reading aids, for students who need them.
5. Learn about the symptoms of special health problems and appropriate responses.

Speech- and Language-Challenged Students

Until recently, classroom teachers had more contact with students with speech and language impairments than with any others with disabling conditions. This situation may still be true in most schools,

but learning disabilities programs are growing rapidly. Speech and language disabilities that you might encounter are articulation (the most common problem), dyslexia, delayed speech, voice problems, and stuttering. In addition, students with other disabilities, such as cleft palate, cerebral palsy, and hearing loss, may have speech and language problems.

Helping Students with Speech and Language Disabilities Learn Science

1. Help the student become aware of his or her problem; students must be able to hear their own errors.
2. Incorporate and draw attention to newly learned sounds in familiar words.
3. Know what to listen for and match appropriate remedial exercises with the student's problem.
4. Be sure your speech is articulate; students often develop speech and language patterns through modeling.

Students with Learning Disabilities and Mild Mental Disabilities

There is a distinction between learning disabilities and mild mental disabilities. The difference is much too long and technical to summarize. Students with mild mental disabilities should be identified only through the use of multiple criteria. Classroom teachers may observe indications of mental disabilities in a student's social interaction, general intelligence, emotional maturity, and academic achievement. In contrast, students with learning disabilities show a significant discrepancy between their achievements and the apparent ability to achieve. The problem is manifest as a disorder of learning and not mental ability. Science teachers may observe learning disabilities in the areas of arithmetic, listening, reading, spelling, logical thinking, speaking, and writing.

Helping Learning Disabled and Mentally Challenged Students Learn Science

1. Listen closely so you can understand the student's perception and understanding of concepts and procedures.
2. Use an individualized approach based on the student's learning style, level of understanding, and readiness.
3. Use multisensory approaches to learning: visual, auditory, kinesthetic, and tactile.
4. Find and use the student's most refined sensory mode to aid in development of mental capacities.
5. Make use of the student's strengths and work on diminishing his or her deficiencies.

6. Reduce or control interruptions since many exceptional students have short attention spans.
7. Stay within the student's limits of frustration. Rely on your judgment, not the level of curriculum materials.
8. Begin conceptual development at a sensory-motor or concrete level and work toward more abstract levels.
9. Work on speech and language development.
10. Help students to develop self-esteem; a good, firmly grounded self-concept is essential to their continued development.

Emotionally Challenged Students

These students probably cause the greatest concern and frustration for science teachers. As it turns out, they also are the ones who have been in science classrooms all along! Emotionally challenged and disruptive students show behavior that ranges from mild, attention-getting pranks to violent assault. They also may demonstrate withdrawn behavior ranging from mildly withdrawn to clinically depressed and suicidal. Other examples of behavior that teachers might identify as disturbed or disruptive include regression, fears and phobias, chronic complaints of pains and illness, aggressiveness, overdependence, social isolation, perfectionism, excessive dieting, obesity, chemical dependency, defiance, and vandalism.

The student's behavior may be a result of forces within or from the environment. The first may be either physiological or psychological in origin. Environmental factors might include violence in the home, school pressures, and/or social problems. In some cases, schools and teachers may contribute to the development of disruptive behaviors. How so? Extreme emphasis on grades, teacher comments, harsh and punitive treatment, unwarranted social comparison, unrealistic physical and academic requirements, and teacher conversations about student behavior that in turn become fulfilled prophecies when other teachers have the same student, are but a few things that can contribute to the development of disruptive behavior.

Helping Emotionally Challenged Students Learn Science

1. Spend time with the student when he or she is not being disruptive.
2. Make rules reasonable and clear.
3. Provide realistic, reasonable, and appropriate consequences if rules are broken.
4. Disruptive behavior ranges from low levels at which a student may merely be looking for attention or recognition through a spectrum that ends

in rages, tantrums, or complete withdrawal. Try always to be alert to behaviors that, though minimally disruptive, could become more serious problems.
5. Avoid personal confrontations or situations that provoke troubled students.
6. Make directions for assignments, classwork, and laboratory procedures direct, clear, and complete.
7. Be aware of and prepare for transitional times in the classroom.
8. Provide troubled students with success experiences.
9. Resolve conflicts by talking about specific behaviors, reasoning, and involving the student in the problem-solving process. Once a course toward aggressive or uncontrolled behavior begins, it is hard to stop.
10. Convey your intention to help resolve the problem mutually: "We have a problem here, and we are going to resolve it."
11. If behavior problems escalate, try to talk about the process while providing solutions to the problem. For example, "We are both getting angry; can't we settle this calmly?" or "I see you are upset; let's try to solve the problem."
12. Avoid using comparison, embarrassment, ridicule, and unwarranted threats to change behavior.
13. Avoid using physical punishment for rule violation.

Academically Unsuccessful Students

These students have normal abilities and do not have any significant physical or psychological disabilities, yet they are below their expected level of achievement. Their challenges may be caused by such things as extreme poverty, a home environment that does not encourage learning, poor reading abilities, diminished self-concept, negative attitudes toward school, and language problems due to a first language other than English. In the past, these students were labeled culturally deprived, slow learners, economically disadvantaged, and underachievers. We have used the words *academically unsuccessful* to suggest that the science teacher's attention should be directed toward the educational problems and their remediation or resolution, not to the student's culture, home, or economic condition. The role of the science teacher is to help these students overcome their educational problems and continue their development. It is neither to identify a cause for the problem nor to excuse one's self from important educational goals, such as developing scientific literacy.

Helping Unsuccessful Students Learn Science

1. Identify the *educational* problem—for example, reading—and concentrate on resolving this problem.
2. Convey your expectations for achievement within a realm of reasonable possibilities for the student.
3. See that physiological, physical, and psychological needs are fulfilled.
4. Use concrete learning experiences, such as the laboratory.
5. Provide experiences where the student will succeed.
6. Eliminate educational approaches that have not worked and try something new.
7. Give recognition to talents the student does have.
8. Approach the educational impairment with an attitude of, "When you are in science, we are going to work on this."
9. Provide time, materials, and experiences within the learning capabilities of the student.
10. Adapt instruction and the curriculum to the student, not the reverse.

■ GIFTED AND TALENTED STUDENTS IN SCIENCE CLASS: PERSPECTIVE AND RESOURCES

If you had a serious illness, you would want the best physician. If you had economic problems, you would want the best financial advisor. Everybody recognizes the need for unusual gifts and talents, yet this is a much neglected area in education. In the late 1990s, this problem will gain increasing recognition, attention, and solutions.

Definitions of giftedness vary. Most, however, are paraphrased from the congressional report submitted by past Commissioner of Education Sidney Marland in *Education of the Gifted and Talented*.[1] Gifted and talented students are those identified by professionals who, by virtue of their abilities, are capable of high achievement. These students require educational programs beyond those normally provided to fulfill their personal potentials and encourage their contribution to society. In a less cumbersome definition: gifted students have superior academic abilities. Talented students have special aptitudes in specific areas. The difference between giftedness and talents is not distinct, since most gifted students have talents and most talented students are gifted in some areas. Gifted and talented students may have demonstrated abilities in any of the following areas: academics (general or specific), leadership, visual and performing arts, music, creativity, mechanics, and athletics.

As a science teacher you should be interested in the characteristics of giftedness that you may encounter in the classroom.

Characteristics of the Gifted and Talented Student in Science Class

1. Enjoys asking scientific questions
2. Solves problems easily and logically
3. Demonstrates advanced ethical, cognitive, and aesthetic development
4. Learns science faster than other students
5. Understands scientific concepts quickly
6. Asks many questions about science
7. Shows an awareness of science far beyond that of other students
8. Is motivated to read and study science
9. Demonstrates unique abilities in designing laboratory equipment to solve problems
10. Is highly creative
11. Shows normal social adjustment

In addition, there are a few negative behaviors—such as boredom, frustration, and complaints—that you may observe. This list gives a subjective and preliminary means of identifying gifted and talented students. If you think you have such a student, it is best to consult the school counselor so she or he can administer appropriate tests to confirm your initial impressions.

Adapting school programs for gifted and talented students can be achieved in many ways. Businesses, industries, colleges, and universities often have programs for students showing special abilities. There are special honors classes, programs, and schools. Gifted students can work on advanced placement courses and accelerated schedules, take extra classes, enter college early, and work part-time and/or summers in projects where they can develop their talents. You can easily find many options for the gifted students in your school.

Although resources are available, probably the crucial question is, "What can I do to help the gifted and talented student in science class?"

Helping Gifted and Talented Students Learn Science

1. Use questions, problems, and projects that will facilitate higher levels of cognitive, affective, and psychomotor development.
2. Develop independent study programs.
3. Have special honors seminars.
4. Initiate extracurricular science activities, such as having science fairs or helping teach an elementary science club.

■■■■■■■■■■■■■■■■■ GUEST EDITORIAL ■■■■■■■■■■■■■■■■■■■■■■■

Science for Exceptional Students

Elizabeth Karplus
Special Education
Campolindo High School
Moraga, California

Every science teacher is familiar with the case of Albert Einstein who failed mathematics as a young student because he could not memorize and had a nonverbal style of thinking. Or, they have heard of Thomas Edison who was declared mentally retarded and whose mother taught him at home because she did not believe he was stupid.

Einstein and Edison are not just special isolated cases. I remember Alan, a very tall, skinny, slightly stooped, dark-haired student. In high school, he carried all of his books and papers in total disarray in a large backpack. As a child, he had been diagnosed as dyslexic, dysgraphia, and dyscalculic at the California State Diagnostic School for the Neurologically Handicapped. This diagnosis was based on his profound problems with orientation in time and space and mild cerebral palsy evidenced in shaking hands, poor coordination, and poor throat-muscle control (and, therefore, poor speech). He was very distracted by the sensory stimuli around him and unable to attend selectively because he could not decide which signal of many was the important one for the current task.

After diagnosis, he was placed in a self-contained class for the learning disabled, where remedial mathematics and reading were begun by a large, loving woman. He ran away from school. The drill on symbols and phonics frustrated him because he was unable to get meaning from them in isolation. What he needed was an awareness that the events in the world, including symbols, were consistent and made sense and that the symbols were only useful in helping to describe that sense. He needed hands-on experiences where he could observe what happened. He needed contact with ideas and with other bright students who could discuss those ideas, since reading about them was so difficult. Alan needed to learn to sequence his symbols (writing 73, not 37, when he meant seven tens and three units) and sequence directions according to the meaning or the expected result rather than trying to remember them in detail step-by-step since his memory was so poor. He needed taped textbooks so that he could listen to them to get information. He needed to ask "why" and "what." He needed the encouragement of accepting teachers who weren't dismayed by his poor writing or his unusual approaches to problems. Those teachers, in turn, often needed to reword their explanations as class work became increasingly abstract, because words never carried quite the same meaning for him that they did for most of the class.

It was in the science classes that he had the greatest triumphs, and it was the activities in these classes that provided the best environment for him to learn from his mistakes and to monitor his own learning, developing a style of learning he could apply to other subject areas. He is currently majoring in physics at a California State University—a modern success story.

Learning-disabled students, such as Alan, need science or other activity courses (shop, home economics, arts, crafts) as much or more than the normal students. In science classes the students

---

5. Assign special projects.
6. Use inquiry and problem solving.
7. Emphasize scientific inquiry.
8. Individualize a program based on the student's interests.

■ TEACHING SCIENCE FOR INDIVIDUAL DIFFERENCES

After reading the previous sections, it should be clear that, as a science teacher, you will encounter a broad range of students. All students have individual differences that should be recognized in the science classroom. With increased recognition of the science-for-all orientation and because of the laws cited earlier, more and more school systems are modifying their instructional programs to give greater attention to individual differences. Psychological research indicates that there are human differences that have implications for teaching. This research indicates that:

1. Individuals come to the classroom with different conceptions of natural phenomena.

themselves can control variables, change conditions, observe results, and learn to discriminate between variables that affect the outcome of the experiment and those that do not.

The science classes can provide exposure to new equipment and ideas in a hands-on setting. New learning can be firmly embedded in a situational context so that it is easier to remember and reapply. Old learning can be applied in new situations so that concepts are refined. Language usage itself can be refined and vocabulary increased. Science activities are filled with opportunities to measure along, around, through, diagonally, up, and down. The student can easily distinguish among thin, narrow, short, light, and weak, and learn when each is an appropriate replacement for "little." Position and direction are encoded in the prepositions in, out, among, under, over, between, by, and up, as well as in adjectives such as contiguous or nouns such as circuit, test tube, or breaker.

In science classes, instructions make sense and are usually monitored by the progress of the experiment, not by remembering an *a priori* order. You cannot filter a precipitate before the two interacting solutions have been mixed. If you haven't connected the battery, the bulb will not light. Most important, the student learns that failures do not represent disaster but are useful as sources of new information. The creative teacher can use each failure of an experiment, each mismeasurement to help the student to a new understanding of the phenomenon.

However, there are two cautions the science teacher of the learning-disabled student must observe. You must take special pains to recognize the learning-disabled student's preferred sensory channels (visual-reading; auditory-listening; kinesthetic-demonstration) for information input and his or her preferred channels for output or reporting his or her understandings to you (visual-writing or diagrams; auditory-oral speech; kinesthetic-demonstration). You also may need to change your preferred methods of presentation to match the student's methods; otherwise, he or she may not be able to understand the lesson or you may not be able to discover how much he or she has actually learned. In my classes, we often read test questions or put laboratory instructions and text on cassette tapes so that the student may listen and understand rather than read and misunderstand.

Sometimes, it is necessary to change laboratory setups to make them more usable for students, particularly the physically handicapped whose movements may be jerky or ill-defined. Equipment can be clamped tightly to the desk or otherwise anchored. Special laboratory measuring devices are available for the blind or deaf, and they are often useful to the learning-disabled student, who can then use more than one sense and thus monitor his or her own collecting of accurate information.

Science classes are for everyone, including the learning-handicapped student. Learning science involves attention, reasoning, and questioning skills that are of constant value throughout life. Learning science can bring great satisfaction to the learning-disabled high school student because it is an important academic discipline and because he or she can develop skills so necessary for self-esteem in these classes. We owe these students their chance to learn how to learn—a skill most easily taught through well-designed science experiments.

2. Individuals vary in the rate at which they learn concepts.
3. Individuals have different levels of motivation toward learning.
4. Individuals have different levels of psychomotor skills.
5. Individuals have different attitudes, values, and concepts in regard to science.

There are many more such statements that could be made concerning individual differences among students in the science classroom. Common sense and observation confirm the statements as much as research evidence. Yet, there has been reluctance on the part of teachers to modify instruction. In this section, we describe several ways you can individualize instruction in your science classroom.

Individualized instruction is a process of adapting curriculum materials and instructional procedures to the student's needs. The aim of individualization is to maximize student learning. Many schools have used grouping as a way of reducing instructional differences in a classroom or grade level. However, grouping alone cannot meet the needs of all students. Other approaches are important.

There are some variations on individualized instruction in science. The entire science program may be individualized for all students, or only for students with exceptional needs. Individualized instruction may be based on any or all of the following: rate of learning (e.g., accelerated, extra time); direction of learning (e.g., independent study, student-selected projects); different methods (e.g., alone, small-group, teacher-directed); different materials (e.g., reading, laboratory activities); and levels of achievement (e.g., assessments, projects completed). So you see that there are many variations available to science teachers. These approaches only describe things you can do in the classroom and do not include approaches requiring administrative or school-wide reorganization. The following sections are brief descriptions of different approaches to teaching science for individual differences.

Grouping

In one plan the students are grouped according to ability. They are assigned units of work to complete and, when they finish these units, they may be moved at the end of the semester to another group of higher ability and achievement. Sometimes teachers group within a classroom so that there might be high, middle, and low groups in a class of thirty. This system allows the teacher to adjust instruction to the different levels. It is usually not a good idea to maintain these groups on a permanent basis because that defines a class structure whose disadvantages outweigh the advantages.

Continuous Progress

A second approach is the continuous-progress plan. It allows students to progress from subject to subject with no time restriction. If a student finishes biology in six weeks and passes an examination, he or she then moves into chemistry. This approach is linear—that is, it progresses through the regular sequence of science courses.

Enrichment Programs

Enrichment programs provide extra opportunities for students who complete the regular program and the extra time needed for others to complete the chapter or unit. Here the faster students have the opportunity to work in depth and breadth within the science course. Using an enrichment program may require extra materials and a resource center.

Team Teaching

Another attempt to give greater attention to individual differences is to use some large-group instruction in a team-teaching situation on certain days, with small-group and individualized instruction on other days. This method is a compromise between having traditional group instruction and completely individualized instruction. This approach has the advantage of releasing teachers during the large-group instruction so that they may prepare and organize materials. When this method is used, there is no reason why the students cannot be taught on an individualized basis when the group is divided into smaller sections.

■ HONORS CLASSES, SPECIAL SEMINARS, AND SECOND-LEVEL COURSES

Some schools have honors classes for science-talented students. Students in these classes are encouraged to work in laboratories on their own. They usually consult with the science teacher on a special problem or topic of study. The students are assigned laboratory space and have access to the materials needed for their work. Monthly reports of their progress are often required, as are seminars where they report on their research. In addition, the students may visit local scientific industries and/or have scientists visit and discuss the students' work and research.

Science teachers may have special seminars on selected topics. These seminars are similar to regular classes in that students may meet daily, weekly, or monthly to discuss a book or movie or interact with a visiting scientist. Students and/or teachers can select topics of study. All students are studying the same topic, but the seminar gives them an opportunity to work beyond the regular science curriculum.

Second-level science courses are another alternative for meeting individual differences. The courses can be in physics, chemistry, biology, or earth sciences. These courses vary widely. Some simply use college-level texts and laboratory manuals. Some biology teachers use materials of the BSCS, such as the laboratory blocks, or *Biological Science: A Molecular Approach* for second-level courses.

Special Science Courses

Some schools have instituted courses for those students who, for whatever reason, do not do well in the regular science program. They can be designed as special courses, which are taught like a seminar and use different materials designed for students with lower reading levels. Although there are clear advantages to these courses, it also is possible that they may become known as science for slow students or referred to by some other derogatory phrase. One way to avoid this problem is to let the students select the courses they wish, look over the texts, and discuss their career plans, motivation, and past achievement in science with you or their advisors. Nothing need be said about students for whom the course is designed; it is simply an option within the science sequence.

Small schools are seldom able to offer special classes. They have, however, encouraged students to do coursework on their own. The procedure is usually to have one or two students study a science film series or read the text and do laboratory experiments. The students may not have direct supervision, although a science instructor meets with them from time to time to discuss their progress and assignments. This plan has the advantage of developing more self-direction and responsibility on the part of the students. Gifted students usually respond well to this type of arrangement; others may need more attention and help. Still, with a little thought and planning, you should be able to use some of these ideas in setting up special science courses for individual students.

The approaches discussed thus far require varying degrees of administrative reorganization and support. The next section outlines an approach that requires only time and effort on your part.

Mastery Learning

Learning for mastery was first formally described by John Carroll.[2] In recent years, the idea has been researched and developed by the late Benjamin Bloom.[3,4] The assumption underlying traditional science teaching is that if students are normally distributed with respect to aptitude for science and they are all taught the same material in the same amount of time, then the expected result with respect to achievement will be a normal distribution. The assumption underlying mastery learning in science is that all students are normally distributed with respect to aptitude for science but the quality of instruction, and particularly the amount of time available for learning science, is designed to meet the characteristics and needs of each individual student. When this is the approach to teaching, the majority (about 80 percent) of students can be expected to master the material. The primary variable is time to master the learning task.

The approach used by Bloom and his colleagues has been to supplement regular classroom instruction by using diagnostic evaluations and prescribing alternative materials and teaching methods. There are three main components to Bloom's strategy: *preconditions*, *operating procedures*, and *outcomes*. Below, we have listed some operational elements of these components:

Preconditions—Defining the Goals
• Specification of Objectives
• Specification of Content

Operating Procedures—Use of Formative Evaluation
• Divide Unit of Study into Smaller Units of Learning
• Use Mastery Test for Each Unit of Learning
• Use of Alternative Learning Resources on a Prescribed Basis

Outcomes—Use of Summative Evaluation
• Final Examination of Material
• Consideration of Outcomes—for example, Cognitive, Affective, Psychomotor, Self-esteem

To summarize, mastery learning provides for individual differences within the regular classroom. Mastery learning includes testing and feedback processes plus extra time for students who need it. Supplementing regular instruction with feedback and time allows for all (or almost all) students to master the material for a particular unit. Mastery learning assumes that if students have time they can learn, especially if they have corrective feedback on what to learn and how they are progressing. Many teachers like the mastery learning approach because it is an adaptation of regular classroom instruction. Listed below are steps in the mastery learning strategy. We slightly modified the strategies for science.

Steps in the Mastery Learning Approach

1. Divide the science course into units of one or two weeks. These units may be chapters in your text or combinations of chapters and other learning activities.
2. Specify objectives for each unit. The objectives should represent a wide range of cognitive, affective, and psychomotor results for the unit.
3. The science units are taught using regular group instruction, laboratory activities, demonstration, films, and so on.
4. Progress assessments are administered at the end of a science unit.
5. Assessment results are used to diagnose learning errors of those who failed to master the material at a predetermined level, usually 85 percent. The assessments provide positive reinforcement for those who master the unit.

6. The science teacher uses the assessment results to prescribe procedures for those students who did not master the unit. Based on the assessment results, the teacher may suggest rereading the text, redoing laboratory work, using computer-based programs, having private tutorials, or reviewing audiovisual aids. Additional time is provided for the student to master the material.

7. A test is administered at the end of the course. The test score is used to determine the student's grade. Grades should be predetermined levels of mastery; for example, 90 percent is an A, 80 percent is a B, and so on. These tests are criterion-, not norm-referenced. They should represent absolute levels of mastery.

8. Results from the final examination, unit assessments, student responses, and effectiveness of materials and instruction are used by the science teacher to improve units for the next term or year.

Mastery learning emphasizes the achievement of all students for a given science unit and eventually the science program. Assessment is used to identify learning difficulties and correct them through specific recommendations. Additional time is provided for students to learn material they missed or did not learn the first time through the unit. Student achievement is determined by an absolute level of mastery on each unit, not a performance relative to all other students in the class. The mastery learning approach makes a great deal of educational sense. As science teachers we want all students to understand science. This goal is accomplished through varying the learning time and designing the program for uniform mastery of science concepts, skills, and processes. In contrast, we usually hold time constant and accept a wide range of achievement from students.

■ TEACHING SCIENCE FOR CULTURAL DIFFERENCES

For several decades, the issue of equity in science classes has received attention but little action. Beginning in the 1990s, science educators rallied to the slogan "science for *all* students" as this was a prominent theme in *Science for All Americans*,[5] *Benchmarks for Science Literacy*,[6] and the *National Science Education Standards*.[7] Embracing science for *all* students means that science teachers will have to translate general ideas such as "all students can learn" and "all students can participate in science activities" into actual classroom practices.

Whether the discussion centers on helping girls succeed in science,[8] multicultural education,[9,10,11] or disabilities,[12] the unifying value that science teachers should recognize is equity. Equity in this case means that all students, regardless of gender, race, ethnicity, or disability, will have access to high-quality science education programs and fair opportunities and treatment in science classrooms. Equity in science classrooms also means that students develop an understanding of views and perspectives of groups and cultures other than their own. It is certainly the case that science teachers must maintain a balance among the unique perspectives of individuals, common values and ideals of society, and the defining characteristics of science.

Science, mathematics, and engineering have been predominately spheres dominated by white males. The issue now is not a recitation of past sins but a remedy of future practices. As a beginning teacher, what do you need to know and do to implement the goal of science for *all* students in your classroom?

Following are some things you should know. This discussion is adapted from a summary by Ana Maria Villegas.[13]

Respect for Cultural Differences

Develop a perspective of cultural *differences* rather than cultural deficits. The former will help you see that cultural groups have different views and learning styles, the accommodation of which will greatly enhance learning science. The latter perspective perpetuates the myth that differences equal deficits and that girls, minorities, and exceptional students have problems learning science.

Respect for cultural differences means that you understand there is not one best way to learn science and that every student has a unique perspective and approach to learning.

Cultural Resources of Your Students

Although diverse groups may be in your science class, it is difficult to know exactly which groups (and how many individuals) will predominate. The point here is your openness to understanding the groups represented in your classes. You might consider home visits, involvement in community activities, talking with parents, observing students in nonclassroom and nonschool settings, and reading about different cultures.

Using Understanding to Enhance Learning

In numerous places we have discussed the model of learning that begins with students' current conceptions of science and constructs more adequate conceptions aligned with science. So it is that some students will have prior knowledge influenced by their culture-bound experiences. You should not avoid using this as a foundation for teaching and learning.

Just as you may have a variety of groups and individual learning styles, so you may have to use many different methods and strategies to teach science.

Making Decisions that Enhance Learning

From the moment you begin teaching a lesson, you will receive feedback from students about their interest, attention, and understanding. You will have to decide what to do—how to adjust your plans—in order to enhance learning. In classrooms with culturally different groups, you will have to be more sensitive to student signals because some may vary from what you have previously experienced. Although the subtleties of culturally influenced responses may take some time to understand, it is not too early to be aware of their influences and to carefully evaluate each lesson, asking where students had difficulty, if all students were involved, which students seemed interested, and what evidence you have that learning occurred.

By this point is should be clear that effective science teaching for individual and cultural differences is probably effective science for *all* students. In the next sections we discuss some things you can do that will help all students learn science.

Provide Positive Role Models

Students should learn from individuals who represent different cultural groups. Students have to recognize that women, minorities, and individuals with handicaps can all do science and make contributions to society.

As part of fulfilling the national standards on the History and Nature of Science, you should introduce students to the diversity of individuals who have contributed to advances in science, engineering, medicine, and other related professions.

Use Cooperative Groups

Research shows that cooperative groups, when adequately implemented, help all students become involved and learn science. Cooperative groups shift responsibilities among members and thus subtly confront stereotypes and prejudices while allowing for individual and cultural differences.

Use Hands-On Investigations

In general, all students are motivated through active involvement. The physical manipulation of materials, the intellectual encounter, and cooperation with peers that occurs while doing investigations contribute to all students learning more science.

Provide Equal Opportunities and Expectations

All students should have experiences with science equipment, computers, field trips, and materials. Again, we point out the advantage of cooperative group work in achieving the goal of equal opportunity for student involvement. You also should make it clear that you expect all students to become involved and develop the abilities associated with inquiry and the use of facilities, materials, and equipment.

Use Appropriate Language

When teaching science you will often use analogies and metaphors. Try to balance male and female metaphors and use examples that incorporate other cultures.

Be Sensitive in Questioning

Science teachers ask a lot of questions. When you ask a question—WAIT—so all students have time to ponder and reflect on the answer. You also should be aware of who responds and who you ask to respond. Teachers often have different reactions to different students, and the differences too often reveal the teacher's perceptions of student abilities.

Maintain High Expectations

Regardless of the diversity in your science class, you should make it clear that you expect all students to achieve higher levels of achievement. You expect all students to participate, and you will do everything you can to help all students succeed in science class.

■ TEACHING SCIENCE FOR INDIVIDUAL AND CULTURAL DIFFERENCES: ADVANTAGES AND DISADVANTAGES

Now that you have some information about what is possible, it is appropriate to review some of the advantages and disadvantages in teaching science for individual and cultural differences. The aforementioned approaches endeavor to respond to the overwhelming evidence on individual variation. They are efforts to respect the person. Science teachers who have gone from group-centered to more individualized instruction often state that they didn't realize how futile it was in the traditional approach to try to have all students learn particularly difficult material at the same rate. The fact that the slower

■■■■■■■■■■■■■■■■■■ GUEST EDITORIAL ■■■■■■■■■■■■■■■■■■

Women in Science

Jane Bowyer
Professor of Education
Mills College
Oakland, California

My interest in the question of female participation in school science began five years ago when I realized, quite by accident, that there were interesting implications on this topic in some of my research data from the study of a particular elementary science curriculum (SCIS). The unique feature of the SCIS was that students had no textbooks but rather learned about science concepts from their own experiments. I found that children who had used this curriculum from first through sixth grade were better able to understand and think logically about science problems. The unexpected finding was that the girls did as well as the boys. This was a surprise because reports from a nationwide assessment of school children's knowledge during the last decade have repeatedly shown that girls all over the United States are less knowledgeable than boys in science. If particular curriculum experiences can significantly modify girls' knowledge of science in elementary school, then taking high school science courses becomes a more realistic possibility for women.

Studies show that girls of all ages are consistently less positive than boys in their attitudes and feelings toward science. But my studies showed that girls' attitudes regarding science and the scientists can, in fact, be positively affected by special curriculum experiences. Interestingly, the boys' attitudes in the study were also positively changed so that the differences between the girls' and boys' attitudes were identical to those of the control group. Innovative curricula might be able to modify attitudes, but male-female differences still persist. Appropriate curriculum experiences appear to be necessary but insufficient for changing deeply held societal values toward science and women.

Teacher behavior appears to have a positive effect on female participation in science at both the elementary and secondary levels. Whether a teacher is male or female, if the following cluster of behaviors exists, girls participate more fully and positively in school science: (1) a responsive, flexible teaching style; (2) a positive attitude toward science; (3) an interest in science; and (4) a belief in the ability of all students to learn from their own science experiments.

In addition to particular curriculum and teacher effects, another approach that has been successful for increasing girls' performance in science is relying on older girls to counsel, encourage, and tutor younger ones. Modifying sexually stereotypical textbook materials is also extremely useful in counteracting prevailing popular attitudes toward science and the scientist.

Schools are socializing agencies that have the potential for modifying student attitudes and knowledge when it is important to do so. However, schools cannot accomplish important changes, such as the democratization of opportunity, unless social reforms accompany the educational effort. When cultural values mediate against boys' and girls' achievements, as they do in science, disproportionate amounts of academic support are necessary to overcome their effects.

Science teachers are in a unique position to provide professional support for the 50 percent of our population who are conspicuously in need of more attention if women are to contribute fully to the scientific and technological achievements in our society.

---

academic students are not demeaned and frustrated because they don't learn rapidly or gifted students are not held back until their classmates catch up is perhaps the major advantage of recognizing individual differences.

There is, furthermore, a shift in emphasis from extrinsic to intrinsic rewards. A student doing an assignment at his or her own rate gains self-confidence and a sense of competence that may not manifest themselves so easily in group instruc-tion. The real joy of learning in this manner comes in students completing the task on their own initiative, not simply because of grades given by the teacher.

Although an individualized approach ideally has many practical advantages, there also are several disadvantages. A science teacher considering taking a position in a school or seriously thinking about the implementation of such a system should be aware of these disadvantages before he or she makes the pertinent decisions. Generally, the problems involve facilities, scheduling, materials, and cost.

Facilities

Schools implementing learner-centered instruction seldom completely individualize their courses, for to do so means that there must be facilities available for large and small groups, as well as for individualized learning. To design and provide facilities to accommodate these various modes of teaching, architects must know in advance how many of each type are required to ensure maximum utilization of the school facility.

Scheduling

Because of the diversity of the program and this type of instruction, scheduling can become a problem. For example, if there is one large group-instructional room, it must be scheduled and used by several departments to ensure maximum utilization. Obviously, this use by various departments limits the flexibility for any one program because the instructors will be able to use the room only when they are scheduled to do so.

Staff

Individualizing a science program means that the faculty must operate as teams. Instructors must be well prepared in several subjects because they may be supervising a large laboratory containing students working on units spread over several areas in different subjects. Because students are often working on different units within each of these subjects, a teacher cannot read a chapter ahead of the students the night before and be prepared. Individualized teachers must know the subjects and curriculum well to interact appropriately with each student's needs.

Acting as a member of a fully functioning team is often difficult because of the differences in how members view their functions as teachers and what they think are appropriate requirements for the learners. For example, if some teachers believe that students should be directed to cover a lot of material and others think they should be given considerable freedom to become autonomous investigators, there are bound to be conflicts among the faculty team members.

Materials

Individualized science instruction demands more reading matter and audiovisual aids than does conventional teaching, since multilevel learning aids must be available to adjust materials to students' academic abilities. For example, some students may read college-level books or use computers and videodiscs while others work on laboratory investigations.

Cost

Because of the need for multilevel, multilearning aids for varied student abilities, individualized instruction is more costly than traditional approaches, particularly because students use more equipment (such as computers and educational software and tapes). The problems of maintenance of these materials and equipment require that a resource center be staffed by technically competent people, thus increasing the need for financial support.

■ SUMMARY

Because of legal mandates, science teaching in the late 1990s and beyond will include greater recognition of the unique disabilities, gifts, and talents of students. Exceptional students will be mainstreamed in regular classrooms, and the gifted also will receive special attention. Although each exceptional student, whether disabled or gifted, presents a distinctive case, there are some guides and suggestions that can help the science teacher meet the specific needs of students.

Science teachers have recognized the needs of students at either end of a continuum, disabled to gifted. The process has clarified individual differences in general, and it emphasizes the theme of this chapter—all students can learn science.

Students come to the science classroom from varied cultures and with different experiences. They vary in their perceptions of school and science and in their cognitive, affective, and psychomotor development. Schools ordinarily have not taught for individual differences because of traditional philosophy and practices, problems of scheduling, poor teacher preparation, instructional costs, poor facilities, and poor equipment. In spite of these problems, many schools are now endeavoring to change the traditional pattern of instruction. This change also has been encouraged by laws requiring individualized programs for exceptional students who are being taught in the regular classroom. Individualized grouping, continuous progress, enrichment programs, team teaching, honors classes, seminars, second-level science courses, and special science classes have been successful.

There are predesigned approaches to individualizing, such as individually prescribed instruction or mastery learning. In general, however, most science teachers like to design their own individualized program.

Science teachers also recognize the unique influences of culture on students' perceptions and learning styles. Teaching guidelines include having respect for cultural differences, recognizing the cultural resources of students, using your understanding to enhance learning, providing positive role models, using cooperative groups, actively involving students in inquiry, using appropriate language, and maintaining high expectations for all students.

Although there are advantages and disadvantages to teaching science for individual differences, on balance, the advantages outweigh the disadvantages. To achieve the goals of teaching science for individual and cultural differences, all students must develop their understanding of science and abilities of inquiry. You can embody these aspirations in a vision that includes expectations that all students will achieve national standards in science, provision for rich and varied experiences with science content, instruction that accommodates different needs and learning styles, direct action on equity issues, and appropriate assessment strategies.

■ REFERENCES

1. Sidney Marland, *Education of the Gifted and Talented* (Washington, DC: U. S. Government Printing Office, 1972).

2. John Carroll, "A Model of School Learning," *Teachers College Record, 63* (1963): 723–733.

3. Benjamin Bloom, *Human Characteristics and School Learning* (New York: McGraw-Hill Book Company, 1976).

4. Benjamin Bloom, *All Our Children Learning* (New York: McGraw-Hill Book Company, 1981).

5. F. James Rutherford and A. Ahlgren, *Science for All Americans* (Washington, DC: American Association for the Advancement of Science, 1989).

6. American Association for the Advancement of Science, *Benchmarks for Science Literacy* (Washington, DC: Author, 1993).

7. National Research Council, *National Science Education Standards* (Washington, DC: Author, 1995).

8. Meg Milne and Whitney Ransome, "Helping Girls Succeed," *Education Week, 13*(8) (October 1993): 23.

9. Mary M. Atwater, "The Multicultural Science Classroom," *The Science Teacher, 62*(2) (1994): 20–23.

10. James A. Banks, "Multicultural Education: Development, Dimensions, and Challenges," *Phi Delta Kappan* (1993), pp. 22–28.

11. Gerry Madrazo and Paul B. Hounshell, "Multicultural Education: Implications for Science Education and Supervision," *Science Educator, 2*(1) (1993): 17–20.

12. Renee Roberts and Judith Bazler, "Adapting for Disabilities," *The Science Teacher, 60*(1) (1993): 21–25.

13. Ana Maria Villegas, "Culturally Responsive Teaching," in *Foundations for Tomorrow's Teachers #1*, (Princeton, NJ: Educational Testing Service, 1991).

Chapter 21

CLASSROOM MANAGEMENT AND CONFLICT RESOLUTION

Two major concerns for beginning science teachers are student discipline and classroom management. You have probably asked yourself, "How will the students behave?" "Will they do what I tell them to do?" "What can I do if a student is disruptive in science class?" In this chapter we provide some answers to such questions.

Many individuals share your concern about discipline. The American public consistently indicates that lack of discipline is one of the most important problems facing public schools. What about science teachers? Do they perceive discipline as an important problem? Actually, very few science teachers believe that discipline is a serious problem. In a 1986 survey, Weiss found that only 9 percent of teachers in grades 7–9 and 6 percent of teachers in grades 10–12 reported "difficulty in maintaining discipline" as a serious problem in their school. If you include "lack of student interest in science," those percentages are increased by an additional 14 percent and 16 percent respectively.[1]

What do science teachers consider "lack of interest" and what is meant by "maintaining discipline"? There are many answers to these questions. Our discussion is primarily directed to conflicts between teachers and students and to the constructive resolution of conflicts.

Before proceeding, you should complete the first two "Investigating Science Teaching" activities at the end of this chapter, "Conflicts: What Would You Have Done?" and "Resolving Conflicts." Doing these will give you some information about the ways you resolve conflicts and so will serve as a useful preparation for this chapter.

■ CLASSROOM CONFLICTS

Classroom conflicts occur when the activities of one or more individuals are incompatible; such conflicts can be interpersonal or intergroup. An action that is incompatible with another action interferes, obstructs, or reduces the effectiveness of the action.[2] For the most part, we can discuss conflicts between teachers and students since a teacher must often take some action, even when two students are in conflict. In most classrooms the difference between compatible and incompatible activities is defined by rules, policies, or expectations of behavior. A classroom conflict usually results in disruption of normal activities and educational objectives.

The preceding definition is neutral. We have not defined rules or passed judgment on whether certain rules or expectations of behavior are good or bad. Science teachers have a wide range of rules and expectations for students. Similarly, students have a remarkable ability to adapt to different teachers and classroom situations. Rather than trying to define rules, we think it better to focus on the inevitable conflicts within the classroom and suggest ways that science teachers can either prevent conflicts or resolve them constructively.

We begin by presenting two views of the same conflict. First is the report of a student teacher who had eight weeks of experience; the second is the report of the student teacher's supervisor, a science teacher with ten years of experience.

The Student Teacher's Perceptions

A new seating chart was set up for the class. In the shuffle, a student (the most openly aggressive and hostile student I've seen) started to swing at a student sitting behind him. I'm not sure of the reason, but I suspect that the boy behind him had his feet sticking out under the desk and the student either kicked him or tripped over him or slid his chair into his feet, and words were exchanged. I was close enough to verbally stop him and then collar him and send him up to the front of the class. My words were something like, "Alright, you're moved, right now, up to the front; turn forward and don't turn back around or away from the chalkboard or you'll be out of here immediately. If you can't get along with the people around you, then you can sit by yourself with no privileges until you're ready to be part of the class." I thought for a minute he was going to explode (both mentally and physically), but he moved, sat and did nothing, very belligerently withdrawn, incredibly strong, and negative.

The Teacher's Perceptions

A new seating chart was established in the class. As one student took his newly assigned seat he appeared to be belligerent but not verbally so. Another student immediately behind made a comment, and he responded by turning around and pushing the table,

■■■■■■■■■■■■■■■■■ **GUEST EDITORIAL** ■■■■■■■■■■■■■■■■■■■■■■■■■

Reflections on Student Teaching

Mark Helpenstell
Student Teacher
Northfield Middle School
Northfield, Minnesota

When I first thought about being a science teacher, the question I most often asked myself was, "How can I possibly create enough material to keep students interested for an hour, every day, all week?" I was sure that my greatest problem would be finding enough things to do to fill an hour-long class and still keep all of the focus on one concept or topic. I knew that I could use film-strips, overheads, group discussions, movies, laboratory exercises, worksheets, textbooks, and so on, but the problem was how to create an ordered and cohesive exercise without losing the interest of most of the students.

As I approached student teaching, the focus of my apprehensions changed. I found myself worrying less about gathering together enough materials and thinking more about my personal capabilities, strengths, and weaknesses. Could I do it? Did I really have the ability to teach (whatever that meant)? This was, for me, probably the hardest part of preparing to be a science teacher. I experi-enced some days of strong confidence and other days of dread and foreboding, when I was quite sure that I could never be an adequate teacher.

When I actually found myself in a classroom, the problems changed perspective drastically. Suddenly, I was out of time and overloaded with resources. Out of the milieu of possible subjects, aids, references, and texts, I had to narrow down the usable material to fit it into a one-hour class. The problem was not filling the hour but picking the very best methods and an interesting means of conveying the material available. I was faced with several possible ways of presenting a topic, trying always to make the class as interesting as possible for the students.

I found that I had the capability to teach but that I was very unsure of myself. The knowledge was there, and the ability to teach, it was there too—it just needed to be brought out, trained, and refined.

Once I realized that I had the capability to be a science teacher, I found that it was much easier to be objective about what was happening in my classroom. I began to be more critical of my own teaching methods, and when things didn't go as I had expected them to, I could usually figure out for myself several possible factors which could have affected these "failures." I began asking myself, "How well am I doing? How well can I do? How well

and made a comment which I did not hear. The action was bad enough to get the attention of the majority of the class. The instructor (student teacher) responded by giving the student a seat at a lone table in the front corner of the room. He took the seat but refused to do any work in class for the next three days. Whenever he attempted to turn or communicate with others, he was told to turn around. The student remained belligerent during this entire three-day period. After the teacher made corrections or comments he, usually, unknown to the instructor, had some obscene comment or verbal reaction to the correction.

Teachers' perceptions of the same situation can vary. Teachers' perceptions of students can also influence the way they interact with the student to resolve the conflict. This conflict was not unique as classroom conflicts go—it was short, resolved by the teacher, and ended with little difficulty.

We can continue by looking at another typical classroom conflict. What is unique about this conflict is that it has been described by *both* the student and the teacher.

The Student's View

I was sitting at a table in the science laboratory with a few friends. We had finished our work and were engaged in normal conversation. The teacher approached our table and told us to get some work out, "You can't just sit there and talk."

I ignored her, and after she left our presence, we resumed our conversation. She came back soon after that, a bit more perturbed, and repeated her previous order. This time I spoke and told her I must be responsible enough to know when and how to do my school-work since I had an A average in school. "So," I said, "I don't need you to supervise my study habits." I reminded her we weren't being noisy, just talking among ourselves; that we weren't bothering anyone.

She became angry. She told us we were bothering others and stated that there was a rule of no talking in can these particular kids do? What things can I change to help increase their understanding? How effectively am I able to 'get to' these kids?"

Perhaps the biggest challenges I faced as a student teacher were those problems related to discipline. Sure, I'd been in some education classes and spent some time thinking about, and discussing, discipline problems and in some cases even reacting to specific classroom situations. Somehow, though, being in the actual classroom created a totally different atmosphere. Dealing with disciplinary problems in class added new aspects of tension and challenge. Suddenly the student was challenging me before the other students, and although I knew that my response should be cool, carefully thought out and rational, more often than not many other factors intervened: defending my own ego before the class, cooling an initially very angry reaction (either mine or the student's), responding to an irrational student action, dealing with intense emotional tensions—all of these facts created a completely different atmosphere than any preparatory discussions or readings were able to develop. Responding to the situation, while trying to maintain an effective learning atmosphere was the greatest challenge I faced as a student teacher.

What did I learn from student teaching? A few things that I now find very important in teaching are: (1) Don't look for an ego trip—although teaching can be very gratifying at times, it also contains more than its share of disillusion, frustration, and disappointments. (2) Always try to show off the students' knowledge, not your own—they know that *you* know it—what they need is the gratification of finding out that they know it. (3) Don't set your expectations and goals too high, either for yourself or the students—better to be pleasantly surprised than to be disappointed. (4) LET GO!!! This is probably the most difficult part of teaching, but if you can really drop your own inhibitions in front of your students, they will respond by doing the same thing. Although this may at times cause problems, I found that the benefits more than outweighed the disadvantages in the long run.

In summary, I found myself dealing with two major issues in the classroom: (1) How do I create a positive atmosphere in which topics are presented in a way that will keep the students' interest, and (2) How do I minimize the effect of disciplinary problems on the classroom experience. Although student teaching has not fully answered these questions, it has helped me to develop some personal means and methods of meeting these challenges, and it has given me new insights into some aspects of their resolution.

---

the science laboratory. In general, she tried to control the situation with power and authority instead of tact and reason. I, in turn, got a little indignant, lost my temper, and smarted off. She then kicked me out of science for the remainder of that day.

The Teacher's View

It was about halfway through the period when I noticed three boys sitting at a table talking. I went over to the table and told them that this is a science class and they should finish their science laboratory. I said they should do something besides talk.

I went about my business until, a few minutes later, I noticed that the boys were still talking. So I went to the table again and explained that they should be working. I hadn't even finished what I was saying when one of the boys said he was "smart enough to take care of himself so you can just leave me alone."

At this, I told the boy that a few students do not have the right to talk and disturb other students who wanted to work. The boy got angry and said, "The hell with you and the other students." At this, I asked the boy to leave the room and he did.

This situation is a typical classroom conflict in several respects. The context was related to undefined time in class, apparently the conflict lasted only four to five minutes, and there apparently was a rule governing conduct for the situation.

The reports described above reveal several other factors common to school conflicts. The perceptions of the individuals in conflict were very different, as is clear in the descriptions of the confrontation. Communication was somewhat accurate at the beginning but deteriorated as the situation continued to the point of threats, name-calling, and assertion of power. Characteristics of a trusting attitude were lacking. Finally, each party to the conflict thought he or she was correct; thus, the problem belonged to the other person. Note also that the conflict ended but was not

FIGURE 21–1
Levels of school conflicts

Level I: Normal conflicts for individuals of this age and stage. Although the behavior may have violated general rules or norms of peers or society, the conduct is not a typical pattern for the individual.

Active	*Passive*
Mischievous	Aloof
Temperamental	Sulky
Overeager	Slow to Warm Up

Level II: Occasional conflicts for the individual. The conflicts are violations of minor school policies, classroom rules, and age-appropriate societal norms. There may be an emerging pattern that is subtle but should not be overlooked.

Active	*Passive*
Clowning	Dawdler
Impulsive	Shy
Acting Out	Dreamer
Seeks Affirmation	Alienated

Level III: A pattern of behaviors that consistently conflict with minor school policies, classroom rules, and age-appropriate societal norms. The pattern is clear, but the major rules and basic rights of others are seldom violated.

Active	*Passive*
Disobedient	Avoidant
Oppositional	Shut Down
Negativistic	Withdrawn
Provocative	Alienated

Level IV: A pattern of behaviors that persistently violate major school policies, classroom rules, and the basic rights of others. The pattern is clear to school personnel and peers.

Active	*Passive*
Aggressive	Depressive
Destructive	Self-destructive
Angry	Substance Abuse

Level V: Episodes of behaviors directed toward the physical harm of self, others, or property.

Active	*Passive*
Violent	Substance Addiction
Vandalism	Suicidal

resolved. Left the way it was, there is every reason to suspect that future problems would occur between the student and the teacher, and in fact they did.

All conflicts are different. Figure 21–1 outlines different levels of student behavior that may result in classroom conflicts. Understanding different student (and teacher) behaviors that lead to conflict situations can help prevent some conflicts and give direction and guidelines on the intervention and resolution of others. Also, such understanding clarifies how conflicts escalate; that is, each party moves to a higher level, hoping the other party will back down. In some unfortunate cases, simple conflicts can escalate to violent and destructive episodes within the school.

■ CAUSES OF CONFLICTS

Understanding the origins and causes of disruptive behavior can provide you with responses that prevent many conflicts. The causes discussed below are arranged from origins common to almost all adolescents to the beginnings of unique disorders of only a few adolescents.

The Middle School Student

The fifth through ninth grade student is going through the period of early adolescence. Students at this period are sometimes mature and reflective; they are also sometimes immature and impulsive. They sometimes want to separate themselves from adult authorities, such as science teachers, and they sometimes want to be directed by adults. They sometimes want to be treated as individuals who can make decisions and act responsibly, and they sometimes want to be told what to do and when to do it. You can probably see from this discussion that it is difficult to know the appropriate way to respond to early adolescents.

The middle school teacher should take into account the developmental needs of early adolescents.

The classroom can be a place where there is a certain amount of testing of adult roles and learning to be responsible. The result can be real bursts of energy for learning science and, also, great energy lulls. Frustrating? Yes. What can you do? First and foremost, you must understand that these behaviors are part of the developmental process and more often than not you should not internalize as something directed at you, your teaching, or science. Second, you must establish the limits of tolerable activity for your class. The limits vary from teacher to teacher, and so we cannot define your limits. But you must have limits, and it is in your interest to identify them early, be sure they are clear, and make them known to your students.

Discipline for this age level is largely a matter of instilling controlled self-discipline. Thus, limited freedom must be permitted so that self-discipline can be exercised. Students will not develop self-discipline and reliability if they are never given the opportunity to practice them. Overly rigid, authoritarian control, in which the primary motivation for good behavior is fear of the teacher's reprisal, will not develop the kind of student who is capable of self-discipline. At the same time, you cannot permit chaos by allowing uncontrolled behavior. A productive environment allows students to show initiative and be responsible for their actions within a framework of supervisory control by the teacher.

Early adolescents are usually quite responsive and sensitive to their peers. You can provide a positive approach to discipline by showing them that their actions influence the actions of other class members. Where students misbehave and take up valuable class time, they are infringing on the study time of classmates. As a result, they are likely to lose the favor of peers and be seen as troublemakers; their status will correspondingly change.

The middle school science teacher can use peer pressure to bring about improved classroom behavior. You should constantly refer to the need for cooperation, the value of class time, the real purposes of the study of science, and mutual obligations to one's classmates.

The Senior High School Student

Sharp character differences between middle school students and senior high students do not exist. You can easily find younger students who are as mature as those in the senior high school. The reverse is also true. In general, however, as students mature, one finds more inhibition and less boisterous behavior in the classroom. This change is a natural result of the student's nearing adulthood. More thought is given to future plans, career choices, or decisions about advanced education.

From the standpoint of discipline, this increased maturity is salutary. The frequency of classroom incidents requiring disciplinary measures usually decreases. The student is more likely to respond to treatment normally accorded adults. Because of the student's sensitivity in this regard, the most effective measures you can use in disciplinary matters are those that treat the student as an adult, with responsibilities for adult behavior.

Some students cause discipline problems because they are bored with the activities. Although you may think that science is interesting and exciting, many students do not. Many students may not understand the concept being discussed or demonstrated, but some may. These difficulties can cause boredom and subsequent behaviors that lead to conflicts. Gearing class activities to the needs and interests of a wide range of students is certainly desirable. We also recommend having interesting and relevant lessons.

"Negative attention is better than no attention at all" is the motto for some students. Often students who are not successful academically, athletically, musically, and so on, become the class clowns or enact other behaviors that result in minor conflicts with the science teacher's activities. Attention-seeking behavior is often hard for teachers to change because the responses that teachers think reduce or eliminate the disruptive behavior are the very responses that reinforce the students' behavior.

The best way to reduce this behavior is to give the student attention in educationally constructive ways. Give recognition for the types of behavior you desire and try to ignore the attention-seeking behaviors you do not wish to have reoccur.

We can refer to Maslow's hierarchy of basic needs—food, water, sleep, safety and security, love and belongingness, and self-esteem—for another source of discipline problems. Sometimes students' basic needs have not been fulfilled, and the result is inappropriate behavior. The teacher's response is to try and fulfill those needs in the best way possible.

In other cases students can be frustrated with the amount of effort required in science versus the amount of learning and the rewards they receive. Other problems can be students' resistance to required subjects; that is, they feel forced to do activities they are not interested in or do not like, and they occasionally must comply with rules that conflict with personal preferences (for example, wearing safety goggles).

We are not suggesting that you can provide a frustration-free environment. If frustrations are mounting, you can change the pace, switch activities, take a break, let the students have a discussion day, and so on. Forcing a tense situation can result in a conflict that could have been avoided.

We turn to the origin of one of the more persistent and difficult discipline problems, alienation. Simply defined, alienation is a feeling of being separated or removed from one's group or from society. There is also a weakening of the social bond between the individual and society or the school system as a subsystem of society. The latter results in the student's rejection of school and the appropriate behaviors for those in school. Melvin Seeman, a sociologist, has written a classic paper in which he suggests five components which influence alienation.[3] We present this discussion as background for many school-related problems, such as assaults, gangs, guns, and general alienation of youth in schools. We will discuss the components of alienation in terms of the science classroom.

First, there is *powerlessness*. This is the individual's belief that he or she is unable to influence his or her life under the present rules. This feeling was described by Rowe as fate control.[4] Control over one's life is directed by something besides the individual. Here, science teachers can show individuals that they can achieve and that there are positive results for appropriate behavior.

Second, there is *meaninglessness*. This is the absence of a clear set of values and connections between the individual and society. We have heard this problem discussed as relevance of instruction and the curriculum. Trying to present the concepts and processes of science in a context that is meaningful to the student helps reduce this problem.

Third, *normlessness* is a reduction in the regulatory power of social rules and laws over individual behavior. To overcome this problem, the science teacher should make classroom rules clear and enforce them consistently and fairly. Let the students know that there are rules, that you intend that rules are obeyed, and that all students are subject to the same rules and consequences for rule violation.

Fourth is the feeling of *isolation*. Here the individual feels left out of the group, class, or school. This problem occurs most frequently in large and impersonal schools and science classes. Be sure students know that you care for them and want them in your classroom and that you show some personal attention to their work.

Finally, there is *self-estrangement*. The individual comes to rely on external rewards and is easily frustrated when they are not received. The individual lacks self-confidence. This problem suggests a need for experiences where the student's confidence in completing a task is supported and he or she learns that there are some internal rewards for learning science.

Our discussion of the origin of students' discipline has been general. There are more specific descriptions and recommendations concerning behavior problems of adolescents. Too often science teachers construct their own explanations for adolescent behavior, and they do not consult individuals or resources who are knowledgeable. Science teachers provide explanations of adolescent behavior with theories such as, "He only wanted attention," "She comes from a broken home," or "They associate with the wrong group." Although these are explanations, they are also incomplete and hold every possibility of having misconceptions about the causes of adolescent behavior. If you do not think you have an adequate understanding of a particular student, or if you think something is seriously wrong, please consult a counselor, school psychologist, or a book on behavior problems of adolescents. If you are wondering about a student's behavior, ask yourself these questions:

- Is there a *pattern* of behaviors? Does the student behave the same way in other classes?
- Does the student continually demonstrate inappropriate behaviors for his/her age?
- Are the basic rights of others (including you) consistently violated?
- Is there the possibility of personal harm, either to the student in question, or to others?

If you find yourself answering yes to these and similar questions, you should consult other resources because the behaviors are probably not in the acceptable range for your classroom and school. There is no need to try and solve the problem yourself. Many of your colleagues in the school system—special educators and school psychologists—are immediate and valuable resources.

■ DISCIPLINE PROBLEMS AND THE SCIENCE CLASSROOM

Science has numerous applications to the daily lives of students. Every student has had contacts with the environment that reveal scientific relationships. This gives you many opportunities to engage students in the study of science and avoid discipline problems.

Science classes also have the advantage of many demonstration devices and laboratory equipment that stimulate interest. Students may find themselves drawn away from unruly influences and toward scientific interests. Furthermore, for students whose poor behavior may stem from lack of recognition, science classes may offer opportunities to gain prestige in the eyes of their peers.

On the negative side, certain unique problems exist in science classes. The laboratory by its very nature offers freedom of movement that may lead to discipline problems. Students without self-discipline will find many opportunities to cause trouble. The teacher's control must be completely effective, although not rigid, or the learning opportunities of the laboratory will be sacrificed. Learning requires considerable self-direction and attention to the task, and the laboratory, under skillful guidance of the teacher, can help develop self-discipline. We recommend completing "Classroom Discipline" at the end of this chapter.

■ CONFLICT RESOLUTION AND REGULATION

In recent decades social psychologists have learned a great deal about the resolution and regulation of conflicts. *The Resolution of Conflict* by Morton Deutsch is probably the singly most important accumulation of these research findings.[5] For this reason, we rely on Deutsch's ideas in this discussion.

We assume that conflicts will occur in the science classroom. We also assume that you are interested in their *constructive* resolution. Further, we assume that in those rare situations of intense conflict, you are interested in regulating the conflict so that the results are not destructive to you or others.

David and Roger Johnson and their colleagues have used the cooperative learning model to help students learn how to mediate conflicts in the classroom. Science teachers will find such strategies helpful.[6]

Avoiding Destructive Conflicts

Destructive conflicts tend to escalate from minor encounters to major events in the classroom. Involved persons increasingly rely on power and authority to resolve, regulate, and finally control the situation. As the conflict takes a destructive course, threats, coercion, and demonstrations of power steadily displace open discussion and the processes of peaceful resolution. The destructive course is set once: (1) the conflict becomes a win-lose situation, (2) communication decreases and, thus, misperceptions increase, and (3) commitments for personal and social consistency decrease. We can look to the opposite of these three ideas for some means to avoid destructive classroom conflicts. We suggest that you consider the following to avoid destructive conflicts:

1. Encourage cooperation.
2. Communicate clearly.
3. Commit yourself personally and socially to resolve the conflicts peacefully.

Encouraging Constructive Resolutions

Conflicts will take a constructive course when science teachers use a creative problem-solving model for intervention. This model would include: (1) motivation to resolve the problem, (2) finding conditions to redefine the problem, and (3) suggesting ideas that might solve the problem. Here are some suggestions that will contribute to constructive resolutions of conflicts:

- Define the conflict as small.
- Resolve the conflict as soon as possible.
- Focus on the problem, not the person.
- Reduce the conflict to several smaller problems and resolve them.
- Emphasize similarities and common goals.
- Be sure all parties agree on the problem.
- Acknowledge that a conflict exists.
- Use a third party to resolve the conflict.

What should one do when conflicts cannot be resolved? On some occasions, problems persist and for many reasons cannot be easily resolved. When a situation such as this exists, try to regulate the conflict so it does not take a destructive course.

Regulating Classroom Conflicts

In regulating conflicts, you attempt to set limits or boundaries on the interaction between conflicting parties. Regulating conflicts is obviously harder than resolving them. Both parties are often on a thin edge leading to destruction. There is little doubt about teachers fearing for their safety and having intense emotional responses. The same is true of students who find themselves in these situations. Although we must accept the legitimacy of these human responses, we must also guard against the detrimental consequences of a destructive conflict. What can a science teacher do? The following recommendations will help you regulate conflicts:

1. Wait until parties are calm, rational, and organized and then begin talking about the conflict.
2. Demonstrate the legitimacy of all parties to the conflict.
3. Reach agreement on the limits of interaction.
4. Use new and different approaches when other ones have failed.
5. Develop a sense of community for all parties.
6. Make sure rules are known, clear, and unbiased.
7. Remedy rule violations as soon as possible.
8. Use counselors for third-party regulation when necessary.

This is an excellent time to complete the activity "Resolution and Regulation of Conflicts" at the end of this chapter.

■ SOME RECOMMENDATIONS FOR SCIENCE TEACHERS

Developing Self-Discipline

The goal of all discipline training should be the development of responsible self-discipline. Students should reach a point of inner motivation to complete learning tasks. Discipline of this type is positive and self-rewarding.

To reach this goal, students should have numerous opportunities to practice self-discipline or peer-group discipline. As with the development of any skill, there must be time to practice.

Teaching science by inquiry methods provides a setting for developing self-discipline. Individual work in the laboratory or on projects carried out in the classroom or at home gives many opportunities to develop good work habits and qualities of self-reliance, persistence, and reliability.

The following suggestions may assist the science teacher in providing an environment in which student self-discipline can be developed.

- Capture interest through activities, experiments, projects, and other student-oriented learning methods.
- Allow a degree of unstructured work commensurate with the maturity and experience level of the students.
- Give suitable guidance to students who require direction and external control, until it is no longer needed.
- Treat students as adults from whom you expect mature behavior and evidence of self-discipline.

Developing Techniques to Influence Behavior

Science teachers have techniques they use to influence student behavior. In light of earlier discussions of conflicts, many of these techniques are early warning signals for the student. In this respect, the actual conflict is prevented, usually because the student responds to the signal.

Here are some suggestions you may consider:

- Use nonverbal signals, such as staring, clearing your throat, shaking your head, or stopping discussion and waiting.
- Use physical closeness or proximity control. While continuing the discussion, move near the disruptive student.
- Use humor to let the student know that enough is enough. Humor should not be sarcastic or personally demeaning.

- Ask the disruptive student a simple and direct question that will bring him or her into the discussion.
- Provide help for particularly difficult problems, laboratories, or assignments.
- Help the students through transitional periods in class, such as shifting from a laboratory to seat work. Provide the time and be sure not to expect immediate responses.
- Establish patterns for laboratory work, cleanup, and other routine or common activities in the classroom.
- Modify routines such as attendance and distributing papers.
- Remove particularly tempting laboratory equipment.
- Have well-prepared lessons, use a variety of instructional methods, and show a personal interest in students.

Developing Means in Resolving Classroom Conflicts

The following recommendations may help avoid serious conflicts and bring about constructive, as opposed to destructive, consequences.

- Try to recognize the consistent patterns of behavior that can result in conflicts (see Figure 21–1).
- Clarify classroom rules. This may require mentioning particular rules relating to daily activities.
- Clarify each person's perceptions of the conflict situation. "How does this situation seem to you?"
- Maintain communication. You should be able to keep the lines of communication open for several minutes by avoiding personal insults, threats, or the use of power.
- Define the conflict as a mutual problem. "Look, you would like to visit, and I would like it quiet so the students can work. How can we resolve this?"
- Avoid using power to resolve the conflict. This can escalate the conflict and/or end it without resolution.

Developing a Discipline Policy

One of the strongest recommendations we can make to science teachers is to develop a discipline policy. Having a policy will result in consistency and clear expectations for both you and your students. Once you have developed a set of rules (and we suggest you do this with the students), the following suggestions should be considered when there are rule violations or conflicts.

- Request that the student stop the behavior and remind the student of the rule he/she is violating.

FIGURE 21-2
Steps in assessment of a discipline problem

Understand the Problem
- What happened in the last forty-eight hours of the adolescent's life?
- What were the circumstances of the problem?
- What patterns of behavior are identifiable?

Clarification of Current Difficulties
- What is the nature of present school-related problems?
- What is the duration of all problems, i.e., academic, behavioral, with peers?
- Have there been any recent changes in behavior? Achievement? Friendships?

Review of Background
- What is the relevant family background?
- What is the student's relation to peers?
- How has the student related to other teachers? Administrators? Counselors?

Identification of Coping Style
- How does the student handle stress?
- What triggers a discipline event?
- How does the student think he/she could avoid problems?
- What resources are available to help the student avoid difficult situations?

Assessment of Psychological and Developmental Status
- What is the student's mood?
- What are the student's cognitive, moral, social, and emotional levels of development?

List All Current Problems
- What are the present problems as perceived by (1) the student, (2) school personnel, and, if appropriate, (3) parents?
- Which problems have highest/lowest priority?

Establish Help That Is Required
- What does the student want (or agree) to do?
- What do school personnel recommend?
- What will all parties agree to?
- Should anyone else be involved?

Develop a Contract
- What terms are acceptable to student, school personnel, and parents?
- Who is responsible for doing what? When? How?

- If the behavior continues, inform the student that the behavior must stop and that "we will have to resolve the problem."
- Establish what the problem is and what can be done to resolve it.
- Help establish the new rules and procedures of the student's behavior and make clear the consequences for any further rule violations. Avoid using personally or physically harsh or abusive measures. Be consistent with the rules and consequences you have both agreed to. Be kind and firm. Being kind shows respect for the student, being firm shows respect for yourself as a person and as a science teacher.

Meeting Parents to Solve a Discipline Problem

Occasionally, you will find it necessary to meet with parents concerning their child's behavior in school. As a first step we recommend that you do a thorough assessment of the student's discipline problems; the steps are outlined in Figure 21-2. Scheduling a meeting with parents indicates a high level of concern about the student, which suggests the need for information, documentation, and understanding of the problems and their potential resolution.

As you approach the meeting, keep several things in mind. First, have the information (and examples) concerning the student's problems with you. Second, realize that you have two goals: to gain further understanding of the student's background and role in the family, and to join with the family in a cooperative approach to intervene and improve the student's behavior.

Outside of the natural nervousness about meeting with parents, you have other challenges to bear in mind. The family will usually be very concerned and often quite defensive about being called to school. To work effectively, you must have the cooperation of other school personnel. Finally, to develop a plan of action to be implemented, you will have to identify and work with the central decision makers in the family.

Here we list some suggestions for a meeting with parents to solve a discipline problem. We also would point out that some of the ideas in this section are applicable to any meeting with parents concerning school-related problems, whether academic, social, or behavioral.

- *Be sure the meeting is scheduled.* Do not plan to just see the parents after school or stop by their house unannounced.
- *Have data, documentation, and examples.* The more specific you can be, the more the parents will realize the seriousness of the problem.
- *Try to recognize and overcome the parents' anxiety and defensiveness.* Some simple statements such as, "I'm sure you are concerned about your child's problems" will help. Also acknowledge that the parents know about their child and can contribute to the problem's resolution.
- *Define and clarify the current problem.* Present the problem in a clear and concise manner. Direct the discussion toward actual behaviors and avoid derogatory comments relative to the student.
- *Allow the parents to respond.* If the parents do not respond, then review the problems to impress on them the serious nature of the issues. If the parents seem confrontive, then direct their attention to the problem and not other issues, such as the personalities of school personnel. If the parents are cooperative, then develop a list of means that might be used to help them resolve the problems.
- *Develop a Plan of Action.*
  a) Identify the behaviors to be increased/decreased.
  b) Are there other problems that should be attended to—for example, reading difficulties or learning disabilities?
  c) Identify the consequences of inappropriate behaviors. A logical-consequence approach often works very well.
  d) Decide on who, what, when, where, and how the plan will be implemented.
  e) Clarify the responsibilities of school personnel, parents, and others.
  f) Determine what all parties would see as improvement.
  g) Schedule other meetings to review progress.

■ SUMMARY

The matter of class control and management is of primary concern to science teachers. The multiple problems of preparing for class, devising suitable teaching methods, and keeping the class orderly are frequently overwhelming.

The actual statistics indicate that most science teachers do not perceive maintaining discipline as a problem. Nor do they think that they need assistance with discipline and class management. Although statistics indicate that discipline problems are not a major concern, it is nonetheless true that there will inevitably be conflicts in the science classroom. Conflicts occur when the activities of one individual or group are incompatible with the activities of another individual or group.

The causes of conflicts vary, but some of the more prevalent origins of conflict are: adolescent need for separation and individuation; the need for attention; boredom; frustration; tension; and alienation. It is also true that the very nature of the science classroom can cause some problems.

Conflicts can be resolved using a few simple procedures: define the conflict as small, work to resolve the conflict immediately, focus on the problem, reduce the problem to smaller parts, be sure there is agreement on the problem, and use a third party if necessary. If conflicts are headed in a destructive direction, you should: wait until all parties are calm; recognize legitimacy; reach limits on interactions; use new approaches if old ones do not work; make rules clear, known, and unbiased; and, again, use a third party if necessary.

There are many possible ways to resolve conflicts in the classroom. For students an important first step is to develop self-discipline. A second step is developing a set of techniques that can prevent or resolve a conflict before it develops. Next, it is recommended that the teacher use the various means of resolving conflicts. Finally, each teacher must develop a discipline policy. Such a policy will result in a fair and consistent pattern of conflict resolution in the science classroom. All of these methods converge in the recommendation to be firm, friendly, fair, and consistent in your interactions with disruptive students.

■ REFERENCES

1. Iris Weiss, *Report of the 1985–86 National Survey of Science and Mathematics Education* (Research Triangle Park, NC: Research Triangle Institute, November, 1987).
2. Morton Deutsch, *The Resolution of Conflict* (New Haven: Yale University Press, 1973).
3. Melvin Seeman, "The Meaning of Alienation," *American Sociological Review, 24* (December 1959): 783–791.
4. Mary Budd Rowe, *Teaching Science by Continuous Inquiry* (New York: McGraw Hill, 1979).
5. Morton Deutsch, "Typical Responses to Conflict," *Educational Leadership* (1992): 16.
6. David Johnson, Roger Johnson, B. Dudley, and R. Burnett, "Teaching Students to be Peer Mediators," *Educational Leadership* (1992): 10–13.

INVESTIGATING SCIENCE TEACHING

Activity 21–1

CONFLICTS: WHAT WOULD YOU HAVE DONE?

The following three incidents were recorded by student teachers. The incidents occurred in science classrooms and represent discipline situations you might encounter. Read each incident and decide what you would have done had you been in the situation. After this you might share your response with other students in class to see what they would have done.

Incident 1

I was tutoring seven students who had fallen behind in their ninth-grade general-chemistry class. As I proceeded, two male students made sly remarks which related to my subject material. I laughed at first, but then said, "OK, fun is fun, but let's get down to business." Since they did not take this as a warning, I told them that if they did not keep quiet and listen, they would have to return to the classroom. At this point I realized that I had "threatened" them in the form of a warning—the old "do or die" situation.

The two students continued this behavior, so I asked them to leave and just stand and wait. It was tough for me since I really did not want them to leave. They needed the help I was there to provide but they infringed on the learning opportunity of the five other students. Class went well after the two boys left.

What would you have done in this situation?

Incident 2

This was a conflict between two students during a laboratory period. I stepped in to try to resolve it before it grew out of control.

The laboratory required a perch made of books. One student borrowed a book from a laboratory partner that was large enough to meet his needs. However, the partner decided he wanted to have the book available for reading during the period and asked for his book back. The first student didn't want to move his setup since it was all prepared and checked, so he refused the other's demands. The partner was slowly losing patience when I stepped in. Since the problem wasn't very grave to me, I told the two that we could easily solve the conflict and asked for the student's help in exchanging the book and rechecking the setup while the partner cooled off. The tension subsided, and they were able to work together during the period.

What would you have done in this situation?

Incident 3

I passed out a test. An A+ student forgot to do one section of the test. I graded all the tests. This student received a B+. She is a talkative student, always making some jokes or puns in class to gain attention. After I returned the test, she said nothing in class for two days.

On the second day, I approached the student to help her on some problems in balancing equations. She had some trouble, so I was able to help her. After class she came up to me and insisted that I change her grade. I listened to her explain her mistake. Then I asked her what she thought should be done. She said I should change her grade. She decided that it would be fair to give her a better grade.

What would you have done in this situation?

Activity 21–2

RESOLVING CONFLICTS

There are many factors that influence the direction and resolution of a conflict. In this activity we are going to have you examine your preferred methods for resolving problems. In other words, how do you typically try to resolve conflicts with other people? The insights you gain from the exercise will be beneficial when you have to resolve conflicts with students in your science class.*

The following sayings can be thought of as descriptions of different ways individuals resolve conflicts. Read each of the statements carefully. Using a scale of 1 through 5, indicate how typical each saying is of your actions in a conflict situation.

5—Very typical of the way I act in a conflict
4—Frequently typical of the way I act in a conflict
3—Sometimes typical of the way I act in a conflict
2—Seldom typical of the way I act in a conflict
1—Never typical of the way I act in a conflict

_____ 1. Soft words win hard hearts.
_____ 2. Come now and let us reason together.
_____ 3. Arguments of the strongest have the most weight.
_____ 4. You scratch my back, I'll scratch yours.
_____ 5. The best way of handling conflicts is to avoid them.
_____ 6. If someone hits you with a stone, hit the person with a piece of cotton.
_____ 7. A question must be decided by knowledge and not by numbers if it is to have a right decision.
_____ 8. If you cannot make a person think as you do, make the person do as you think.
_____ 9. Better half a loaf than no bread at all.
_____10. If someone is ready to quarrel with you, the person isn't worth knowing.
_____11. Smooth words make smooth ways.
_____12. By digging and digging, the truth is discovered.
_____13. One who fights and runs away lives to run another day.
_____14. A fair exchange brings no quarrel.
_____15. There is nothing so important that you have to fight for it.
_____16. Kill your enemies with kindness.
_____17. Seek till you find, and you'll not lose you labor.
_____18. Might overcomes right.
_____19. Tit for tat is fair play.
_____20. Avoid quarrelsome people—they will only make you unhappy.

Some insights about your typical style of resolving conflicts can be gained by adding the responses to different sayings. Add your typical responses to the sayings as indicated.

Sayings	Total	Response Style
1, 6, 11, 16	_____	Smoothing
2, 7, 12, 17	_____	Negotiating
3, 8, 13, 18	_____	Forcing
4, 9, 14, 19	_____	Compromising
5, 10, 15, 20	_____	Withdrawing

Science teachers are concerned with two goals as they resolve conflicts. One goal is personal and involves achieving, gaining, or maintaining something; for example, achieving an educational goal, gaining personal recognition, or maintaining one's sense of security in the science classroom. The second goal has to do with preserving or changing the relationship with the conflicting party. In the science classroom this usually means preserving the relationship with a student, while changing the patterns of behavior.

*This activity is based on ideas from P. Lawrence and J. Torsch, *Organization and Environment: Managing Differentiation and Integration* (Cambridge, MA: Division of Research, Graduate School of Business Administration, Harvard University, 1967), and from David Johnson, *Human Relations and Your Career: A Guide to Interpersonal Skills* (Englewood Cliffs, NJ: Prentice-Hall, 1978).

The five different response styles to conflicts have direct bearing on the personal and relational goals of science teachers. We describe briefly the results of typical conflict responses relative to personal and relational goals of teachers.

Withdrawing

Withdrawing from a conflict fulfills neither the personal nor the relational goals. Essentially it is a lose/lose approach to conflict resolution since the educator gives up whatever educational goals he or she had and does not try to maintain the relationship with the student. In brief it is:

PERSONAL—LOSE
RELATIONAL—LOSE

Smoothing

Smoothing over the conflict gives highest priority to maintaining the relationship, often at all costs, including giving up personal goals. This is a resolution that usually results in:

PERSONAL—LOSE
RELATIONAL—WIN

Forcing

Here, personal goals are achieved at any cost. The cost is often to give up a personal relationship with the students. We have a situation of:

PERSONAL—WIN
RELATIONAL—LOSE

Compromising

The educator gives up some personal goals, and some relational goals are modified in order to resolve the conflict. All parties to the conflict give up something and are often dissatisfied with the results. The grounds for resentment by both educators and students have been established. The amount of resentment will depend on the perceived amount of compromise by each party to the conflict. In essence, this is a resolution of:

PERSONAL—TIE
RELATIONAL—TIE

Negotiating

Educators and students resolve conflicts through cooperative problem solving. Though some changes occur, essentially the goals of both educators and students are achieved and relationships are maintained. This approach is one of:

PERSONAL—WIN
RELATIONAL—WIN

There are times when each of the different means of resolving conflicts is an appropriate course of action. Science teachers should understand this and make judgments concerning the situation, the student, and their personal and relational goals.

Think of a classroom situation where each of the response styles would be appropriate.

Withdrawing:

Smoothing:

Forcing:

Compromising:

Negotiating:

You might observe some actual classroom or school conflicts and examine the teachers' response style. Go back and review your responses to the conflicts presented in "Conflicts: What Would You Have Done?" Would you try to use a different response style?

Activity 21–3
CLASSROOM DISCIPLINE

One of the best ways for you to gain an understanding of conflicts in the science classroom is to analyze a situation that you perceive to be a serious discipline problem. You will have to spend some time observing in a science classroom or recall a situation from earlier experience.

Incident. Describe the actual behaviors and statements between the science teacher and the student during a conflict incident. This should be an objective statement. What did the teachers say and do? What did the student say and do?

After describing the incident complete the following:

Grade Level_____   The conflict was between: Teacher   Student

School_____   Male_____   Male_____

Class_____   Female_____   Female_____

Other(specify)_____

How long did the conflict last?

_____Less than one minute   _____7–10 minutes

_____1–3 minutes   _____Longer than 10 minutes

_____4–6 minutes   _____Indicate how long_____

Level. Most classroom conflicts involving individuals can be categorized at one of the levels described in Figure 21–1. Indicate the individual student's behaviors in terms of the categories outlined:

1. Affirmation_____   Alienation_____

2. Assertion_____   Withdrawal_____

3. Aggression_____   Depression_____

4. Violence toward others_____   Violence toward self_____

Was this incident part of a recurring or consistent pattern of behavior for the student?

Yes_____   No_____   Don't know_____

Context. Describe the classroom setting, circumstances, and origin of the conflict. What preceded the conflict?

Complete the following questions concerning the context of the conflict.

1. Was the situation during: Comments

_____Teacher presentation, e.g., lecturing

_____Class discussion, e.g., teacher leading

_____Class presentation, e.g., film

_____Group work, e.g., laboratory

_____Individual work, e.g., reading

_____Student presentation, e.g., discussion of project

_____In-between time, e.g., between a laboratory activity and class discussion

_____Free time in class, e.g., after a test before bell

_____Free time in school, e.g., hall, cafeteria

_____Free time outside of building, e.g., after school

_____Other (specify)

2. Were there any unusual circumstances that should be noted?

3. What was the rule, policy, or expectation of behavior?

4. Was the rule, policy, or expectation presented or enforced as:

_____Prohibitive (e.g., You should not . . .)

_____Prescriptive (e.g., You should . . .)

_____Benefit to group (e.g., You must, so we can . . .)

_____Benefit to individual (e.g., We must, so you can . . .)

_____Other (specify)

5. To your knowledge was the rule, policy, or expectation:

Stated_____Unstated_____by either party to the conflict?
Written_____Unwritten_____prior to the conflict?
Known_____Unknown_____to the accused?
Comments:

Resolution: Describe how the conflict was ended or resolved. Would you say the resolution was:

_____Mutual, e.g., agreed on by both parties

_____Coercive, e.g., one party got the other to stop through warnings

_____Assertive, e.g., one party threatened the other

_____Aggressive, e.g., one party physically did something to the other

What happened in the brief period (three–five minutes) after the conflict ended or was resolved?

Did the behaviors change for the persons directly involved in the conflict?

How did behaviors change for those indirectly involved (i.e., the other students)?

Were there any other consequences of the conflict/resolution?

Interpretation
How would you interpret the conflict you have described?

What general statements can be made concerning the conflict?

Recommendations

What could be done to avoid further conflicts such as the one you described?

What would you do if you had to resolve a similar conflict?

If the entire methods class completed this investigation, it may be interesting to compile the observations and discuss your findings.

Activity 21–4

RESOLUTION AND REGULATION OF CONFLICTS

In this exercise we present some conflicts that may occur in science classrooms. Based on the earlier discussions of conflict resolution and regulation you are to suggest what should be done: First, list what you would do. Then join with other members of your class and share ideas about the resolution or regulation of the conflicts.

Incident 1

At the beginning of class, the last period of a Friday afternoon, the students came in talking and laughing. They didn't settle down when the bell rang. The teacher didn't say anything for a while, just watched the students with an amused half-smile on her face. After about a minute she said something like, "How much time are you going to waste? You've already wasted 45 seconds, and you're going to have to stay after class for 45 seconds to make up for it."

What would you do?

Incident 2

Mary Beth was extremely withdrawn in science class. When I talked to her she would say, "Leave me alone and go away." Yet she was failing class, mostly due to not completing her assignments.

What would you do?

Incident 3

Gil was always causing a disturbance. He would continually clown around in class. His antics would disrupt the other students and my teaching. I must admit that he was occasionally funny.

What would you do?

Incident 4

Glen had a chip on his shoulder from the first day he entered earth science. This one day we were cleaning up and he dropped a beaker of sand. I told him to clean it up and he responded, "I don't feel like it." I then said he had spilled it and he had to clean it. He replied, "Make me."

What would you do?

Incident 5

This wasn't the first time Jane had been in trouble. She just could not follow the rules. It didn't ever seem serious, at least until this incident. Well, she came into class and was chewing gum. I told her to get rid of the gum. Then she started talking to her neighbor. I told her to pay attention. Then she started making remarks about my discussion. I was at my wit's end.

What would you do?

UNIT 8

....

TEACHER RESOURCES

Common concerns of new science teachers are, "What materials will I use?" "How will I choose them?" and "What materials work best with middle and high school students?" Many science teachers worry about whether they will have enough materials to keep students busy for an hour a day, five days a week. This turns out to be a minor problem. In fact, the reverse is usually true—the problem of having enough time to accomplish everything the teacher sets out for students to do.

The first resource a new teacher turns to is the textbook. This is understandable and acceptable since textbooks represent organization of content and the presentation of up-to-date information, plus they supply many techniques for teaching the material effectively. Innovative ideas and appropriate textbooks, with precautions against over-reliance on the textbook, are given in this unit.

With newer methods of teaching involving inquiry and investigation and with increased reliance on data-gathering and problem-solving, other materials and facilities become at least as important as the textbook. Among these resources is the microcomputer with its marvelous potential for tutoring, data gathering, data analysis, graphing, record-keeping, and simulating science experiments. It behooves the new science teacher to become familiar with the microcomputer and to use it in as many ways as possible to maximize its potential to enhance student learning. You will find that students take to the microcomputer quickly and will challenge you to keep up with them. What better way to develop good rapport with students as you all figure out new things to do with the microcomputer to make the classroom interesting and exciting! Many suggestions are given in this unit to help you to use the new technologies available to the science teacher today.

Chapter 22

COMPUTERS IN SCIENCE CLASSES

The authors of *Benchmarks for Science Literacy* present science teachers with the dual challenge "to build technology education into the curriculum, as well as to use technology to promote learning, so that all students become well informed about the nature, power, and limitations of technology."[1] Although many different tools, instruments, and machines should be encountered in science classes, nowhere is there a better opportunity to "build technology into the curriculum" and "use technology to promote learning" than through the use of computers.

This chapter on computers in science teaching has four main purposes. The first is to portray educational technology as an example of technology in general. Many educators have equated computers with technology. But, in science education it is important to consider the term *technology* much more broadly. Learning *about, with,* and *through* computers can help students to better understand how science, technology, and society interact.

The second purpose is to attempt to set educational technology within a broader context of theories of learning, instruction, and curriculum design. Modern educational technologies are very often developed by teams of software designers, science educators, subject matter specialists, and psychologists working together from fairly well-defined theoretical perspectives. New materials are more likely to be effective and to fit within the flow of instruction in the science classroom if the teacher understands the theory from which they are developed.

The third purpose is to describe various examples of computer-assisted instruction (CAI) software, simulations, data probes, computer-based laboratory (CBL) systems, CD-ROM, videodiscs, multimedia packages and authoring systems, and telecommunications applications available to science teachers today. The foundations in educational theory of each of these technologies and how and where they might be used in the science classroom will also be explored.

The fourth purpose is to suggest some ways that teachers can develop their own expertise in computer technology.

This text chapter, at best, is introductory. You will need to expend considerable effort throughout your career in learning about and keeping up with the latest advances in educational technology. How successfully the new educational technologies will be integrated into the science classroom to develop technological understanding and to promote science learning among future generations of students will depend on you, the science teacher.

■ COMPUTERS AS TECHNOLOGY

Modern science and modern technology are highly interactive, with science influencing technological developments, and, technology, in turn, contributing to advances in science.[2] The impetus for technology is the problems of human adaptation to natural, constructed, and social environments. Through technological advances people are provided with new ways of adapting to and even shaping their surroundings. New technologies can make even more powerful technological innovations possible. Further, new instruments and techniques enable new observations of and scientific explanations about the world.

The story of the development of computers provides many excellent examples of the interactions among technology, science, and society. The world's first electronic, digital computer was dedicated in 1946.[3] By the 1980s, computer technology had advanced from the 30–ton ENIAC computer to the microprocessor, a computer on a silicon chip made possible through progress in solid state physics. Chips were thousands of times cheaper than the ENIAC, operated on the power of a night-light rather than that of 100 lighthouses, and could perform a million calculations a second, more than 200 times as many as ENIAC. Continued research has led to the almost unimaginable miniaturization and astounding memory capabilities of today's chips. Through the interplay of scientific and technological advances, the computer has become pervasive in modern society in less than fifty years.

Modern science and modern technology are different enterprises, but they are inextricably bound to one another. It is often difficult to determine where one begins and the other leaves off. For example, the transistor was invented in 1948 by John Bardeen, Walter H. Brattain and William B. Shockley.[4] Bardeen, Brattain, and Shockley won a Nobel prize in physics for these efforts. Within a short time, transistors made from silicon had become a main component in

---

This chapter was written by Joel E. Bass, Ph. D., Professor of Education and Physics, Sam Houston State University.

the construction of computers and many other electronic devices. The need for materials that could conduct electrons at greater speeds and switch off and on more quickly than silicon, led to additional basic research in solid state physics and eventually to the development of gallium arsenide technology. Gallium arsenide, which does not occur naturally, was first formulated in the laboratory in the 1950s. It has been extensively investigated in university and industrial laboratories since that time. Although it is not likely to replace silicon, scientists and engineers are finding important roles for gallium arsenide in satellite-receiving dishes, the transmission of data through optical fibers, visual display technologies, audio-disc players, and many other technologies.

The development of computer capabilities has contributed to enormous changes in society. For example, computers have been critical components of America's space program. The availability of high-speed computation helped to turn the human dream of exploring realms beyond earth into reality. The real-time calculations and moment-by-moment course corrections that are required in space missions, but are much too large and complex for human memory and information processing capabilities, are made possible through high-speed computers. Bold journeys to outer space, in turn, have given society many new products and procedures and a new view of the fragility of life on our own tiny, blue planet.

Technology can greatly affect the job market, as well as the type of education that workers need. The multiple uses of computers in business and industry—such as in data processing, communications, robotics, and inventory and quality control—have resulted in the reduction or elimination of many jobs, particularly at the lower level. At the same time, a broad array of new occupations, demanding higher levels of cognitive functioning, have opened up. Because of the rapid pace of technological developments, workers need continual up-dating, as well as retraining every few years. It is more important than ever that education, particularly in science, mathematics, and technology, focus on real understanding of conceptual and principled knowledge and on the development of higher order thinking, decision-making and problem-solving processes and strategies, and learning skills and attitudes that support lifelong learning.

■ COMPUTERS AND LEARNING

Alan McKay, a researcher with Apple Corporation who has extensively explored the use of computers by children, has identified a number of potential benefits of using computers in education.[5] First, computers have the potential of providing instant access to any and all existing media. Texts, images, sounds, and movies can be readily accessed, manipulated, and placed in appropriate form to support learning through the use of word processors, desktop publishing, and multimedia systems. Second, and more importantly, computers can provide for great interactivity. For example, students can mold presentations to fit their own tastes, and ideas can be explored from many different perspectives. Third, computers can go beyond static representations to present dynamic simulations of attributes, processes, and relationships that can be used to test conflicting theories. Fourth, pervasively networked computers are fast becoming a universal library, offering resources now beyond individual means (e.g., supercomputers for complex simulations, information being gleaned by satellites, and large compilations of data). In science classes the use of computers can demonstrate the course of technological progress, enrich instructional presentations, encourage students to become more active explorers of their environment, and significantly enhance curiosity and motivation—all of which leads to deeper understandings and improved thinking and problem-solving capabilities.

The uses of computers and associated technologies in science education might be placed into three categories:

- Learning about computers;
- Learning through computers; and
- Learning with computers.

The use of computers in classrooms enriches instruction and encourages students to become actively involved in the learning process.

In *learning about computers,* students develop technological literacy. In the process of *learning through computers,* computers either take over or assist the teacher with various functions of instruction. In *learning with computers,* students use computers as a tool in: data acquisition, analysis, and display; communicating with other people; information retrieval; and the myriad other ways computers are used by research scientists, medical professionals, technicians, managers, and others in the workplace.

■ LEARNING ABOUT COMPUTERS

Activities in this category have generally been treated in relation to computer literacy—that is, to acquiring computer-related terminology, learning about the history and development of computers, understanding uses of the computer as a tool, learning to communicate instructions to the computer through simple programming, and learning about problems and issues related to the use of computers in society. In science classes computer literacy should be considered to be merely one aspect of the more comprehensive goal of understanding technology and its relationships to science and society.

Examine the sample computer literacy objectives given below and consider how they relate to Science-Technology-Society (S/T/S) themes. The objectives are extracted from the "Essential Elements" for Computer Literacy for secondary students in Texas schools.[6]

1. *Computer-Related Terminology and Use.*
   Identify computer terms.
   List uses of computers in a variety of situations.
   Understand the uses and limitations of computers.
   List computer attributes.
   Classify types of computers.
   List advantages and disadvantages of using specific types of computers for various applications.
2. *History and Development of Computers.*
   Identify generations of computers.
   Investigate the development of various computing devices.
3. *Use of the Computer as a Tool.*
   Load software from an external storage medium.
   Use software packages in a variety of applications.
   Learn editing procedures in the context of data entry or other applications.
   Review and evaluate software.
   Determine which software is most appropriate for various applications.
   Practice data entry and error checking.

Learn editing procedures in the context of data entry, or other applications.
4. *Communicating Instructions to the Computer.*
   Use and develop flowcharts.
   Develop problem-solving skills.
   Learn the syntax of a higher-level computer language.
   Apply the syntax of a computer language to problem-solving situations.
   Write reasonable, structured programs.
   Find, interpret, and correct program errors.
   Predict output of given programs.
5. *Problems and Issues of Computer Use in Society.*
   Identify computer-related careers, including training requirements and the impact of automation on the job market.
   Identify the importance of ethics in accessing and manipulating automated information.
   Identify issues and potential solutions regarding computer-related law, copyright privacy, and computer crime.

Students often take a separate computer literacy course at the middle school or high school level. Also, computer programming courses, such as in Pascal programming, are often available to students as electives in grades 9–12. But the goal of computer literacy is also important in secondary school science. Learning with and through computers in science classes can furnish an authentic context for developing improved understanding of computers as technology.

■ LEARNING WITH AND THROUGH COMPUTERS

Judah Schwartz—noted software designer and Professor of Engineering Science and Education at the Massachusetts Institute of Technology, as well as Co-Director of Harvard's Educational Technology Center—has suggested that educational technology be viewed in terms of four choices about content to be learned and methods of instruction:

· Use computers to teach traditional content with traditional approaches;
· Use computers to teach new content with traditional approaches;
· Use computers to teach traditional content with new approaches; and
· Use computers to teach new content with new approaches.

For the most part, Schwartz concludes, CAI uses traditional approaches to teach traditional content. What is to be learned in science has traditionally been facts, concepts, principles, and procedures. CAI does not depart far from the direct instruction or expository mode in teaching this traditional content. The material to be learned is broken into small bits and presented in clear ways, augmented by questioning and problem solving to check for student understanding. Instructional approaches are adjusted as needed—for example, through branching of the CAI program at various levels of complexity. Students are provided with considerable opportunities for drill and practice, with appropriate reinforcements in the form of various bells, whistles, and flashing lights being given for correct responses.

Although much has been written about the new curriculum that computers are supposed to enable, a curriculum in which students are free to explore and learn from cyber-environments (such as the Internet, and thesauruses, atlases and dictionaries on CD-ROMs), Schwartz expresses skepticism about its appropriateness for students today. Thus, he is not particularly interested in using the computer to teach new content in either traditional or new ways. Rather, he comes down firmly in favor of using the computer to teach traditional content in new ways. In particular, the computer furnishes a new and powerful tool for enhancing conceptual understanding. Schwartz has taken a lead in the development of a new generation of computer simulations based in constructivist approaches to learning.

The two main types of instruction alluded to by Schwartz, traditional direct instruction and new constructivist approaches, are reviewed below in order to provide a better perspective on uses of computers and associated educational technologies in science classes.

Direct Instruction

The approach to teaching called *direct instruction* has generally been associated with behavioral learning theories. Behaviorism developed beginning in the early years of the twentieth century through the experimental and theoretical work of behavioral scientists such as John Watson, Ivan Pavlov, Edward L. Thorndike, and B. F. Skinner. Behavioral theories are concerned primarily with the learning of narrow behaviors, but they have been extended to describe the learning of the type of knowledge about the world that is already known by others and can be passed more or less intact from the teacher or instructional materials to students. Bodies of knowledge—including facts, definitions, concepts, principles, and theories—are often presented through direct instruction. Facts about astronomy—such as the names of the planets, the distance from the earth to the sun, and the size of the moon—are examples of information known by the teacher that can be

directly imparted to students. Definitions for concepts, such as weight and magnetic field, might also be learned through direct instruction. Similarly, statements of principles, such as Newton's First Law of Motion, might also be passed along from the teacher to the student through direct instruction. Although direct instruction plays an important role in learning, research indicates that real comprehension of the meaning and the many applications of concepts and principles must be worked out by the student through constructive learning processes.

From the classical behaviorist's perspective, learning—at least the learning of preset *behavioral* objectives—was considered to be a matter of *associating* a particular response with a given stimulus. In newer cognitive-behavioral approaches, learning is more likely to be described in terms of the *association* of the new material to cognitive *schemata*. In classical as well as modern cognitive behaviorism, associations are not constructed by the learner but are imparted through external forces.

Behavioral theories of learning have often been translated into specific strategies of instruction and classroom management. Behavioral learning, whether of new information, skills, or classroom behaviors of students, can be shaped by the teacher (or by the computer) through presenting stimulus materials clearly, encouraging active responding, reinforcing desired responses, providing corrective feedback when needed, and providing for ample practice of correct responses.

Hunter set the various instructional functions involved in behavioral learning into a teaching strategy called Lesson Design.[7] In Hunter's approach, preliminary to beginning a lesson, the teacher should determine major learning goals and specify behavioral objectives to be attained by the students. The instructional steps in Hunter's Lesson Design include:

- *Anticipatory Set.* In this phase, the students are prepared for the day's lesson. Attending behaviors and mental readiness are elicited through some activity or presentation. Connections between prior knowledge, such as from previous lessons, and the knowledge to be acquired in this lesson are made.
- *Objectives and Purpose.* Here, students are informed of the objectives for the day—that is, of what they will be expected to be able to do by the end of the day's lesson. The instructor also clarifies how and why the lesson is important and useful.
- *Instructional Input.* In this phase the teacher uses a wide variety of instructional means—including lecture, media presentations, role playing, simulations, and even laboratory and other hands-on activities—to help the students achieve objectives.

The specific content and processes that relate directly to the objectives to be learned are contained explicitly within the instructional input.

- *Modeling.* Through modeling the teacher provides examples of the content knowledge and procedures expected from the students when they are demonstrating learning of the lesson's objectives.
- *Monitoring Understanding and Adjusting Instruction.* The teacher elicits active, observable responses from each student and assesses the response for evidence of understanding. The teacher adjusts the instructional sequence as necessary to improve understanding.
- *Independent and Guided Practice.* Because practice is essential in behavioral learning, ample opportunities are provided for students to practice the content and processes they have learned. Practice involves both maintenance rehearsal (i.e., repeating the learned material often) and elaborative rehearsal (i.e., relating the new material to previously learned material and using it in new contexts).

There are many possible roles for educational technology in carrying out the various instructional functions in direct instruction. For example, multimedia presentations might be used to develop anticipatory set or in instructional input. CAI is useful in instructional input, in checking for understanding, and in practice. CBL and simulations might be used in instructional input and in modeling. Such applications of computer-based technologies in direct instruction will be discussed in more detail later in this chapter when the various technologies are described.

Constructivism

According to the constructivist perspective, which draws on the work of Piaget and other theorists, useful knowledge is not passed along intact from one person to another, nor is it *discovered* in the external world. Rather, knowledge is *constructed* by the learner. Through their own constructive processes, individuals impose order and predictability on the phenomena and events of the world. Unlike the behavioral approach, constructivists contend that we cannot directly teach a student the principles of science. Newton's First Law of Motion, for example, cannot be passed directly from the teacher to the student. Even though the student may learn to repeat the law, it is not likely to be tied to the phenomena from which it is derived; it does not initially support inferences and predictions about moving objects seen in novel contexts; and it is likely to mask a host of misconceptions about motion. When understanding does come, it comes through a great deal of reflective interaction with the real world and with other people. And it is always a personal construction. This construction is based largely on the individual's prior knowledge, i.e., on his or her own active and developing structuring of facts, concepts, principles, and models derived from previous, thoughtful encounters with the world.

Cultural constructivist approaches to learning assume not only an active learner—as did Piaget— but an equally active culture and a usually more powerful cultural agent.[8] The cultural agent, which might be an adult, a peer, or even a computer, serves to mediate the learning process. Through relevant presentations, questions, hints, diagnoses of faulty processes and misconceptions, appropriate prescriptions, and so on, the agent assists in the constructive learning process. All of us—scientist and non-scientist alike—are strongly influenced by other people through social interactions.

Constructivism and Teaching

A constructivist approach to science teaching called the *learning cycle* was developed by Robert Karplus and the SCIS group at the University of California, Berkeley. Research on the learning cycle shows that students understand science better and are more likely to apply what they learn if they are given opportunity and time to explore natural phenomena directly, but also have opportunity to interact with a knowledgeable teacher who can provide relevant instruction and feedback related to their questions. In this approach to learning, teachers act as facilitators, guides, and informers. The learning cycle has three instructional phases:

- *Exploration,* in which students are allowed to explore materials freely, leading to questions and tentative ideas;
- *Invention,* in which the teacher, generally through inquiry and expository methods, guides students to invent concepts and principles that help them answer their questions and reorganize their conceptions; and
- *Application,* in which students try out their newly learned ideas by transferring them to new situations.

At the exploration phase, prior knowledge relevant to the problem is accessed and used in initial organization of new ideas. At the invention phase in the learning cycle, students are guided in forming new, powerful ideas and linking them with prior knowledge. In this phase, students' incorrect notions should be squarely confronted. Students need repeated opportunities to realize that there may be problems with their spontaneous ideas and to modify those ideas under the guidance of a tutor. In the application phase, the newly formed ideas are elaborated and strengthened through their use in new situations.

The learning cycle is a first generation constructivist model of instruction. This model has been expanded by the BSCS group to include five functions: engaging, exploring, explaining, elaborating, and evaluating.[9] The engaging function in the BSCS model, sometimes referred to as the 5-E model, is very similar to Hunter's anticipatory set. Exploring plays the same role in the 5-E model that it does in the learning cycle. Invention and explaining play similar functions, as do application and elaboration. The addition of the evaluation function represents the current understanding of the importance of continued assessment in the service of learning. The evaluation phase in the 5-E model is quite similar to monitoring understanding and adjusting instruction in the Hunter model.

■ CONSTRUCTIVISM AND COMPUTERS

One of the most difficult tasks in science teaching is to help students develop real conceptual understanding. Joseph Snir, Carol Smith, and Lorraine Grosslight, researchers with Harvard University's Educational Technology Center, have proposed the use of "conceptually enhanced computer simulations" to address the problem of teaching for conceptual understanding.[10] The Educational Technology Center group has identified three levels of students' understanding of natural phenomena:

- Level 1: Knowledge of facts and simple generalizations
- Level 2: Conceptual and theoretical understanding
- Level 3: Meta-conceptual understanding.

At the first level are directly observable facts and simple generalizations based on these facts. At the second level, students learn theories that enable the facts and simple generalizations learned at this level to be conceptualized and explained. These first two levels of understanding in Snir, Smith, and Grosslight's model are similar to the levels of understanding addressed by the exploring and inventing phases in Karplus' learning cycle and the exploring and explaining phases in the 5-E instructional model. The third level of understanding is a metacognitive, or *meta-conceptual*, level in which students reflect about the basis of the level two conceptual relationships. At the third level of understanding, students must learn what a model is and how scientists develop and test models to help them understand phenomena.

In terms of the Harvard model, the problem in teaching for understanding is to help students make the transition from the concrete facts and empirical generalizations of Level 1 to the conceptual and theoretical understandings of Level 2. This transition is difficult for three main reasons. First, concepts and theories are *abstract;* they cannot be directly observed by the learner. Second, conceptual and theoretical understandings are *complex,* consisting of many aspects that must be held in mind simultaneously. Third, students already have their own *misconceptions* about the phenomena, which can be almost impervious to change. In teaching for understanding, each of these three factors—the abstractness and complexity of concepts and theories and the misconceptions of students—must be addressed.

At the core of Smith, Snir, and Grosslight's conceptually enhanced simulations are computer-generated visual representations of the abstract, unobservable concepts and complex relationships used in explaining a specific phenomenon. Students manipulate the visual analogue in the computer simulation in learning to think about the phenomenon conceptually. Thus, the visual representation serves as a bridge from the concrete to the conceptual level. Further, the visual representation is a kind of model, which helps students to think about the general problem of models in a more concrete way.

Examples of various applications of educational technology in science teaching are described and discussed in terms of learning and instruction models in the following sections.

■ COMPUTER-ASSISTED INSTRUCTION

Computer-assisted instruction (CAI) is the use of a computer to provide course content and interactive instruction in a variety of forms. Main methods of CAI include drill and practice, simulations, and tutorials.

Drill and Practice

Drill and practice, a repetitive approach emphasizing rote memory, was one of the earliest forms of CAI. An example of a drill and practice program in mathematics is *Space Mouse*, which is aimed at middle school and high school students.[11] In the program the computer randomly generates problems related to the multiplication and division of fractions. If the student solves the problems correctly, he or she is rewarded by being allowed to fly a rare space mouse through a maze in a video-game type setting. Through enhanced motivation and ample practice afforded by the CAI program, learners improve their abilities to solve the type problems presented.

Computer-aided instruction provides students with enhanced motivation and ample practice in science subjects through drill and practice, simulations, and tutorials.

Software design has now gone well beyond the drill and practice stage; this form of CAI is rarely emphasized today.

Simulations and Tutorials

Many CAI programs developed in the last few years combine tutorials and simulations. Tutorials use the computer in a traditional question-and-answer, dialogue-type format. Industry has long been using computers to simulate and explore complex phenomena and processes. Simulations provide a computer model of the attributes, concepts, and relationships in the real world.

In CAI simulations, the student plays an active role in manipulating various factors in the computer simulation to better understand real world phenomena. Through the variation of various factors, the computer generates creative, perhaps even impossible environments. The computer may, for example, permit time compression by condensing a great amount of data into a very short time frame, or it may expand the time base to allow longer looks at changes that take place within a short time span. It can produce graphic displays of processes at work and the effects of different variable factors on the processes. Simulations allow the effects of changes to be seen in a model before irrevocable changes are made in the real system. In this sense, minor or hypothetical risks can be taken without the cost or danger of carrying out the experiment in real life. Students using simulations are often forced to make decisions on the basis of incomplete data, and the results of these decisions can be seen quickly. This is

excellent practice for the real world, in which important decisions frequently need to be made on the basis of meager information.

Simulating Motion

One example of a computer simulation relates to the physics of motion. Students have notorious difficulties in understanding motion. A commercially available simulation called *Interactive Physics II* allows students to explore the relationships among such variables as force, mass, acceleration, initial velocity, and instantaneous velocity.[12] The paths of a projectile (such as a soccer ball) launched at different angles and with different initial velocities might be presented graphically. Through the graphic presentation, students might explore, for example, what initial velocities are needed to make the projectile move a specified distance horizontally when it is launched at different angles. The instantaneous velocity, position in space, and acceleration of a ball thrown upward in the air might also be studied. Contrary to expectations, students can see graphically that the acceleration is not zero when the ball reaches its highest point and has a momentary zero velocity. Such simulations can be invaluable in enhancing student motivation, correcting misconceptions, and building understanding of complex concepts and relationships.

Another motion simulation, *Newton,* was developed by Alfred Bork and his colleagues at the Educational Technology Center at the University of California, Irvine.[13] This simulation is directed toward building up a student's insight or intuition about motion and forces, particularly those involved in planetary orbits about the sun. The force in planetary motion is the gravitational force holding the planet in orbit. The gravitational force varies with the distance, following an inverse-square relationship. Students pick slightly different initial velocities for a planet and explore its resulting orbit about the sun. Bork points out that no one has ever seen a planet move around the sun. Direct experience is not available to understand the planet's motion. Through the use of the *Newton* simulation students experience orbiting as an actual fact, not simply as an abstract idea. The student observes phenomena not ordinarily seen.

Planetarium Simulations

Planetarium simulations display the sun, stars, planets, moon, and other celestial bodies in their correct spatial positions. *Voyager: The Interactive Desktop Planetarium,* is one of several such simulations available commercially.[14] Voyager allows the user to set the sky display for the present, the future, or any day in the past to 2500 B.C. The latitude and longitude of the viewing position on earth and the magnitude limits of the celestial objects to be viewed can be set. Users also have control of the horizon profile.

Computer sky simulations can be used in many ways in understanding sky relationships. For example, the rise and set times and azimuths (i.e., angular displacements toward the east from true north) of stars over the course of a year might be studied. Although the rise positions of stars are fixed over the short term of a few years, explorations with the planetarium simulator reveal that they vary systematically over the centuries, a consequence of the phenomenon known as precession, the slow wobbling of the earth's polar axis.

The ability of planetarium simulations to access and display arrangements of celestial bodies in the distant past has been useful in the interdisciplinary field of archaeo-astronomy. Heliacal rise refers to the first predawn appearance of a star or planet after conjunction with the sun. Heliacal rise times and positions of major stars were known by Native Americans far in the past. Astronomer John Eddy has investigated the stellar alignments of the spokes in an ancient structure near Saskatchewan, Canada, called the Moose Mountain Medicine Wheel.[15] Medicine wheels were constructed by Native American people, probably for ritual reasons, by laying out long, straight lines of rocks in spoke-like fashion from a fixed central position. Archaeologists have dated the Moose Mountain Medicine Wheel to about the time of Christ. Eddy measured the azimuths of the rock spokes of the Moose Mountain Medicine Wheel. He found that at the time the structure was built, some 2,000 years ago, its spokes were directed toward the rise positions of three bright stars— Aldebaran, Rigel in Orion, and Sirius in Canis Major. Specific data and conclusions from Eddy's research at Moose Mountain are available (see reference 15.) His conclusions can be readily checked by students using a planetarium simulation program.

Conceptually Enhanced Computer Simulations

The Harvard Educational Technology Center has developed a computer simulation on flotation called *The Sink or Float Lab,* intended for students in grades 6, 7, and 8.[16] This conceptually enhanced simulation follows the software design principle of building the attributes, concepts, and relationships in some natural phenomenon into a visual computer model that responds to the learner's manipulations of real-world factors. By seeing what happens in the visual model, the learner is aided in constructing a bridge from the concrete to the abstract theoretical concepts and relationships that explain the phenomenon. In the computer simulation of flotation students move objects in and out of a container of liquid and observe whether the objects float or sink.

Objects of different densities, each shown in a different color, are available to put into the computer water. Data on the mass and the volume of the objects are made available to the students.

According to physical theory, an object floats or sinks according to its density and the density of the liquid it is placed in. For an object that floats the greater its density, the greater the proportion of the object's volume that will be submerged. When the density of the object surpasses the density of the liquid it is placed in, the object sinks.

The flotation simulation allows students to observe the mass-volume relationships and determine them visually. The mass of an object to be placed in liquid is depicted visually on the computer screen as the number of small black boxes corresponding to its measured mass in Mass Units (Mu). Similarly, the volume of the object is depicted visually as the number of small, open rectangles corresponding to its measured volume in Volume Units (Vu). The density is then depicted visually by placing the available black Mass Unit squares into the available open Volume Unit rectangles so that the Mass Units are equally distributed. For example, if there are 60 Mass Units and 20 Volume Units, three Mus will be available for each Vu, and the density of the object can be seen to be 3 Mu/Vu. Through manipulating the densities of the objects and of the liquids in the simulation, students are led to construct more powerful understandings of the theory of floating and sinking.

Regardless of the density of the object or of the liquid chosen by the student, the computer knows whether the object will float or sink, and if it floats, how deeply it will be submerged. Two physical laws embedded in the programming code—the first concerning conservation of matter and the second involving hydrostatic pressure—enable the computer to respond correctly. The computer screens are created by the student's investigative search processes, rather than being predesignated by the programmer. According to Snir, Smith, and Grosslight, it is this condition that allows the creation of a software environment in which the student can explore the phenomenon of flotation in a rich and open way.

The flotation simulation is an outstanding example of how to use the computer to teach old content in new ways. Simulations such as this one can easily be integrated into science courses, greatly enhancing students' conceptual understanding.

Teacher-Made Simulations

David Saiz, a high school chemistry teacher from Illinois, has provided an interesting example of a teacher-made computer simulation, along with helpful suggestions on programming simulations for personal computers.[17] The sample simulation is of

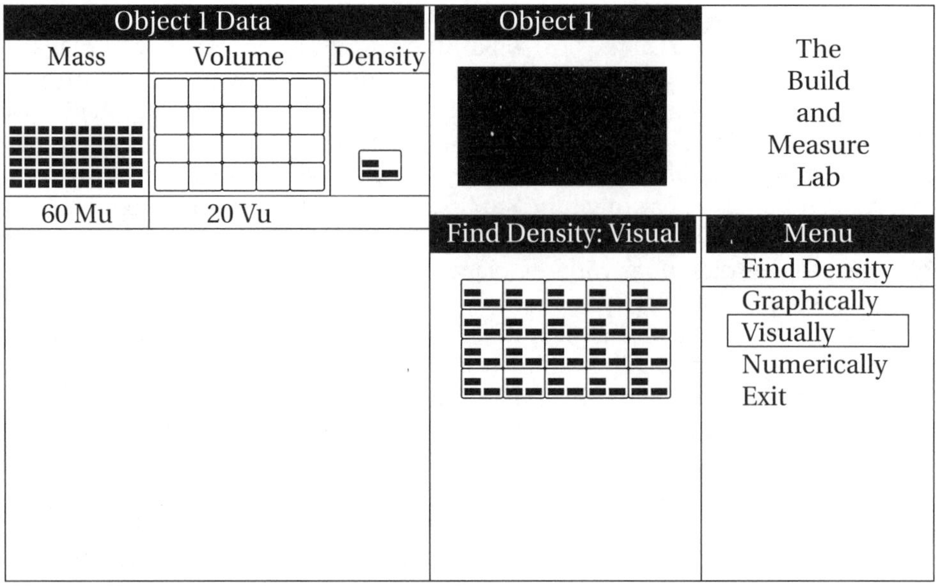

FIGURE 22–1

The object weighs 60 Mass Units (Mu) and has a volume of 20 Volume Units (Vu). The density, shown visually, is 3 Vu/Mu.

Source: Joseph Snir, Carol Smith, and Lorraine Grosslight, "Conceptually Enhanced Simulations: A Computer Tool for Science Teaching." In David N. Perkins, Judah L. Schwartz, Mary Maxwell West, and Martha Stone Wiske (Eds.), *Software Goes to School: Teaching for Understanding with New Technologies* (New York: Oxford University Press, 1995), p. 119.

the motion of a pendulum. At the heart of the computer program controlling the simulation, hidden from the view of the student, is the equation for the period T of a pendulum,

$$T = 2\pi \sqrt{L/g}$$

where L is the length of the pendulum and g is the acceleration due to gravity. The simulation program prompts the student to enter a value for the length of the pendulum and a value for the acceleration due to gravity. Students might initially vary L, setting g at the acceleration due to gravity on the earth (approximately 10 m/s^2), to see what happens to T. The output data can be printed out or displayed through a graphic simulation. Plots of T versus L can be made to show the relationship between the two variables. Students might also explore the effects of different values of g on the period of a pendulum of fixed length. The value of g on the moon and on other planets might be used here.

Sometimes students have difficulty in comprehending the concepts of the frequency and wavelength of a wave. Saiz suggests that the personal computer's graphic capabilities might be used to create waves of different frequencies and wavelengths for students to study. The computer's speaker might also be made to sound a tone of the same frequency as the wave while the wave is displayed. The wave simulation can help students to better see (and hear) the meanings of and relationships between frequency and wavelength.

Students might be challenged to produce their own simulations to explore questions such as:

- How is the moon's journey around the earth affected by the sun?

- How does the speed of a rocket change as it exhausts its fuel and reduces its mass?
- How does a population of rabbits and foxes change over time given seasonal changes in vegetation?

By developing simulations to explore such questions, students can develop richer conceptual knowledge, enhanced problem-solving skills, and experience-based knowledge of the capabilities and limitations of computers.

■ COMPUTER-BASED LABORATORIES

A computer-based laboratory (CBL), or microcomputer-based laboratory (MBL), is a microcomputer equipped with a *sensing probe* for collecting data on physical phenomena in real time, and special software for recording and displaying the results.[18] For instance, temperature data might be collected with a temperature-sensing probe over a fixed time sequence, such as every five minutes, and the data converted into line graphs and data tables.

The powerful CBL tools for investigation have been available to students at the secondary level only since the mid 1980s. The Technical Education Research Center (TERC) in Cambridge, Massachusetts, has played a pivotal role in their development. Probes on the market currently include the following sensors: temperature, sound, light intensity, motion, atmospheric pressure, pH, EKG, EMG, heart rate, brain waves, humidity, wind speed, and wind direction. Commercial packages for computer-based laboratories are marketed by a variety of companies.

A goal of CBL instruction should be to increase students' intuitive feel for events and to build causal links between external events and the graphs.[19] Time for exploring the probes and finding out what they can tell us about the world is necessary in developing physical intuitions. Writing about all aspects of an experiment and telling the story of the graph is a good way to help students build correlations between the world and the graph and to reveal what students are seeing and thinking. Used in this way, computer-based laboratories represent another way to help bridge between the concrete physical world and abstract conceptualizations.

Computer-based laboratories provide for an almost unlimited range of traditional and new investigations by students. TERC researchers have emphasized the importance of using the probes in student science projects.[20] For example, a student might use a temperature probe to investigate the effects of adding ice cubes to drinks.[21] In the investigation an ice cube of a given mass might be added to a given volume of water at room termperature and the temperature of the water measured over an extended period of time. Using the graphing option of the CBL software, a line graph of the temperature versus time might be drawn and printed out. The investigation might focus on a number of questions with consequences in daily life, such as:

- How quickly does the water temperature begin to change after an ice cube is added?
- How low can the temperature of water be brought with ice cubes?
- How many ice cubes (or what mass of ice) are needed to lower the water to $0°C$? How does this depend on the volume of the water?
- What factors affect the rate at which the water is cooled by the ice? Do more ice cubes increase the rate? Does stirring the water help?
- What kind of container can keep water (without ice) at cold temperatures longer?

A project in environmental science might use a pH probe to explore the effect of acid rain on seed germination and plant growth. Water at different levels of acidity might be prepared and the pH measured with the sensor probe. The effect of water at different pH levels on the rate of germination of seeds and the growth rate and health of plants could then be explored. Additionally, the pH of soil that has been soaked with water at different pH levels might also be investigated.

■ MULTIMEDIA PRESENTATIONS

Interactive multimedia is a collection of computer centered technologies that give a user the capability to access and manipulate text, sounds, and images.[22] Multimedia authoring software, such as Apple's *HyperCard,* enable the user to control computer text, graphics, and sound, as well as external multimedia devices, including videodisc, audiodisc, and CD-ROM players.

Student-Developed Multimedia Presentations

In Frank Hinerman's high school biology class in Pennsylvania, as part of a course assignment students develop multimedia lessons on the DNA and RNA molecules using a special authoring system.[23] Working in cooperative groups of four, students develop a concept map on the topic, then break into groups of two to construct a flowchart. When the flowchart is completed, students go to the computer lab to complete their final project. Each of the student programs contains drawings, questions, and videodisc references. The DNA and RNA video images are taken from commercially available videodiscs in biology. Hinerman uses IBM's *Link Way Live* as an authoring system but comments that other authoring systems would also be appropriate. According to Hinerman, the use of a multimedia application in instruction creates an active atmosphere in the classroom and fosters student enthusiasm and communication, as well as creativity and learning. Student presentations enable the elaborative linking of ideas that otherwise might remain isolated and separate.

Commercial Interactive Media Presentations

Interactive media presentations, combining the interactivity of the computer with images, sound, and music presented on videodisc, are available from various commercial sources. An example is the National Geographic Society's *Planetary Manager.*[24] This production provides for an examination of the state of the earth, with students cast in the roles of planetary managers. Overviews of major environmental issues are featured on one side of the disc. Nine shows illustrate broad concepts such as the complexity of environmental issues and human impact on the environment. Eight shows on the other side of the disc focus on specific environmental topics, such as the complexity of environmental issues and human impact on the environment. The presentations feature the stunning photography and folksy communication style that characterize *National Geographic.*

As an example, a show on water pollution, "Shall We Gather at the River?" shifts the normal water pollution discussion away from faceless factories and industry out of control to the pollution that arises out of our own personal worlds. The narrator in oratorical tones, framed by the faint background strains of the religious song from which the title is taken, emphasizes that all of the world's rivers come together (a watershed), and he traces the ills of the oceans, rivers, and aquifers to bad practices that arise out of everyday actions (water pollution). In dramatic fashion, still and moving pictures play out the story line simultaneously with the narration.

Along with the narration, captions and additional information about who, what, when, where, and why of each scene are available on the computer screen. Also, the interactivity of the computer allows the teacher or students to write their own captions or provide their own relevant information. Search features in the computer software enable the user to locate images on a variety of environmental topics, e.g., fossil fuels. Still and moving pictures on the topic can be selected in any combination to create customs presentations to fit individual curriculums.

Many other outstanding media presentations in science designed to compete with the television shows, ads, and music videos that grab young people's attention, are available. Interactive media presentations would appear to be most useful in the anticipatory set, instructional input, and modeling phases of Hunter's model of direct instruction, or in the engagement, exploration, and elaboration phases of BSCS's 5-E model.

A Science Course Taught Through Interactive Video

The Texas Learning Technology Group (TLTG) has developed a two-semester 160-hour course in physical science that utilizes interactive video-disc technology, along with computer-aided lesson presentations, simulations, and tutorials.[25] The course package includes videodiscs, software, and supporting print materials. The program is designed to be used in large group, small group, and individualized instruction.

In one TLTG physical science lesson, for example, a motion picture sequence on the videodisc shows a student on a high step-ladder dropping a large watermelon and a small ball simultaneously. Students working in small groups around the computer and TV screen view the scene, then discuss and answer questions about the fall of the two objects presented by the computer in tutorial fashion. Problem-solving partnerships of students working at the computer are intended to mirror relationships that are valued in business and industry today. The teacher, who has been taken off the stage and placed out among the students, is available as a guide for the constructive processes required in bringing about conceptual understanding in physical science.

Assessment results provided by the course developers indicate that in the chemistry portion of the course, TLTG students outperformed their control group peers in all categories tested. Low verbal ability students showed the greatest performance increases. Teachers rated the course more effective than the methods they ordinarily used.

■ TELECOMMUNICATIONS AND THE LEARNING OF SCIENCE

Ruopp and Pfister define telecommunications as computer-to-computer communication via phone lines.[26] A modem is used to convert the digital data output of a computer to audio signals that are transmitted across telephone lines. At the other end a modem converts the audio signal back to digital so that it can be read by the receiving computer. Telecommunication has many applications in science teaching.

One interesting example is *National Geographic Kids Network*, designed for upper elementary and middle school students.[27] Most of the units in this curriculum involve local investigations in which students collect data and then share their data on a computer network. Conversations are encouraged among classes using the network. In one investigation entitled "Too Much Trash!" students study the trash generated in their own school, homes, and city. To begin, students discuss problems of waste and waste management. Researchable questions are then formulated, such as "How much food waste is generated in your lunchroom daily?" Students design their own data collection procedures with guidance from the teacher. Appropriate controls are considered and applied, such as monitoring the food waste containers in the lunchroom regularly throughout the lunch periods. Food wastes are weighed at the end of each day's lunch periods. The weight of the food and the number of students who ate in the lunchroom that day are recorded. Students determine such things as the average waste per student and the average waste each day during a five-day period. Students enter their data on the network and hold conversations with other schools about the waste problem.

The *Kids Network* programs are highly informative and motivational, with students becoming sensitive to the problems of waste in general and to the importance of the systematic application of a waste management hierarchy—use less, reuse, or recycle—to reduce the burden on landfills. Students also tune into the global problems of pollution through communicating with far distant schools.

Additional NGS *Kids Network* units focus on weather, water pollution, acid rain, and other topics. Although current units are intended for grade 6 and below, units for higher levels are being produced.

Remote Access Astronomy

Both national and local area networks, such as the Texas Education Agency's TENET, increase the opportunities for students to communicate with students in other schools about projects. There is also the possibility of accessing useful scientific data being produced in real time.

The Remote Access Astronomy Project (RAAP) is a computerized 14-inch optical telescope and dial-in data distribution system that places high quality images and image processing techniques into computer workstations in high school and junior high school classrooms.[28] The telescope is remotely controlled and is equipped with a very sensitive digital camera for direct electronic imaging. The telescope accepts observation requests for a given night via a central computerized bulletin board system from participating RAAP schools. Remote access to the telescope enables high school students to design their own research projects.

In addition to immediate, real time views of the sky, images from Voyager, IRAS, COBE, Hubble Space Telescope, and many other sources are available through RAAP for secondary school students to use. The combination of high quality data and low-cost technology allows the classroom teacher to present the traditional science curriculum in the context of recent developments in astronomy. The RAAP system is a very strong means for motivating students and promoting learning in science.

■ CONTINUING TECHNOLOGICAL EDUCATION FOR SCIENCE TEACHERS

It is important for teachers for the 21st century to feel at ease with technological equipment, software, and information resources and be able to effectively integrate technology in instruction to improve student motivation and learning. One way of learning about available new technologies is to attend the annual national and area conventions of the NSTA and spend considerable time in the exhibit area. Virtually every supplier of educational technology for science will have a booth and a helpful staff to demonstrate products and to help you feel comfortable in working with them. Workshops, summer institutes, and college courses are also often available to help you learn to use new technologies. Nothing, however, can substitute for extended hands-on, trial-and-error exploration of computer-based materials individually or in a small group.

A set of technology-related objectives for teachers has been developed by the BSCS technology education project, ENLIST-MICROS, directed by Dr. James Ellis. These objectives provide new and experienced science teachers with an excellent framework for establishing personal and professional development goals related to educational technology. The ENLIST-MICROS objectives, which are divided into three categories—General Technological Literacy, Technology in Education, and Integrating Technology in Instruction—are given below.

I. *General Technological Literacy*
   1. Demonstrate an awareness of the major types and applications of technology, such as information storage and retrieval, simulation and modeling, and process control and decision making.
   2. Communicate effectively about technological equipment.
   3. Recognize that one aspect of problem solving involves a series of logical steps and that programming is translating those steps into instructions.
   4. Understand thoroughly that computers only do what they are instructed to do.
   5. Respond appropriately to common error messages when using software.
   6. Load and run a variety of software packages.

II. *Technology in Education*
   7. Demonstrate an awareness of technology usage and assistance in the field of education.
   8. Describe the ways technology can be used to learn about computers, to learn through computers, and to learn with computers.
   9. Describe appropriate uses for technology in education, including:
      • computer-assisted instruction (simulation, tutorial, drill and practice)
      • computer-managed instruction
      • microcomputer-based laboratory
      • problem solving
      • word processing
      • equipment management
      • record keeping
   10. Value the benefits of technology in education.

III. *Integrating Technology in Instruction*
   11. Use technology to individualize instruction and increase student learning.
   12. Demonstrate appropriate uses of technology for basic skills instruction.
   13. Demonstrate ways to integrate the use of technology-related materials with other educational materials, including textbooks.
   14. Respond appropriately to changes in curriculum and teaching methodology caused by new technological developments.

15. Plan for effective technology interaction activities for students (for example debriefing after a simulation).
16. Locate commercial and public domain software for a specific topic and application.
17. Use an evaluative process to appraise and determine the instructional worth of a variety of computer software.
18. Voluntarily choose to integrate technology in instructional plans and activities.

■ SUMMARY

Computers in the classroom do not represent a cure-all for science education problems but should be seen as complementary to other traditional and new approaches to teaching science. Educational technologies are placed in a clearer perspective when they are viewed in terms of the traditional goals and the two main instructional strategies for science teaching: direct instruction and constructivist approaches. Some types of learning are clearly associative and can be acquired through direct instruction. Early uses of the computer in instruction were aimed primarily at associational learning and used variations of direct instruction. But complex and abstract conceptual knowledge can neither be adequately described through the principles of associationism nor acquired through direct instruction. The true power of the computer in developing conceptual understandings in students is only just now being realized.

■ REFERENCES

1. American Association for the Advancement of Science, *Benchmarks for Science Literacy* (New York: Oxford University Press, 1993).
2. Rodger W. Bybee, C. Edward Buchwald, Sally Crissman, David R. Heil, Paul J. Kuerbis, Carolee Matsumoto, and Joseph D. McInerey, *Science and Technology Education for the Elementary Years: Frameworks for Curriculum and Instruction* (Washington, DC: The National Center for Improving Science Education, 1989).
3. Allen A. Boraiko, "The Chip," *National Geographic, 162* (4) (1982): 420–457.
4. Mark H. Brodsky, "Gallium Arsenide: A Dynamic Technology Comes of Age," *Scientific American,* 262 (20) (1990): 68–75.
5. Allen Kay, "Computers, Networks and Education," *Scientific American,* Special Issue, *The Computer in the 21st Century,* (1995), pp. 148–155.
6. Texas Education Agency, *State Board of Education Rules for Curriculum* (Austin: Texas Education Agency, 1984).
7. Madeline Hunter, "Knowing, Teaching, and Supervising," in *Using What We Know About Teaching,*

8. Philip L. Hosford, ed., (Alexandria, VA: Association for Supervision and Curriculum Development, 1984), pp. 169–192.
8. Tom Scott, Michael Cole, and Martin Engel, "Computers and Education: A Cultural Constructivist Perspective," in *Reviews of Research in Education,* Volume 18, Gerald Grant, ed., (Washington, DC: American Educational Research Association, 1992).
9. Biological Sciences Curriculum Study, *Science for Life and Living: Integrating Science, Technology, and Health: Sneak Preview* (Colorado Springs, CO: BSCS, 1990).
10. Joseph Snir, Carol Smith, and Lorraine Grosslight, "Conceptually Enhanced Simulations: A Computer Tool for Science Teaching," in *Software Goes to School: Teaching for Understanding with New Technologies,* David N. Perkins, et al., eds. (New York: Oxford University Press, 1995), pp. 106–129.
11. Jack A. Chambers and Jerry W. Sprecher, *Computer-Assisted Instruction* (Englewood Cliffs, NJ: Prentice Hall, 1983).
12. *Interactive Physics II* is marketed by Knowledge Revolution, 15 Brush Place, San Francisco, CA 94103.
13. Alfred Bork, "Computer-Based Instruction in Physics," in *Learning with Personal Computers* (New York: Harper and Row, 1987), pp. 87–100.
14. *Voyager* is sold by Carina Software, 830 Williams Street, San Leandro, CA 94577.
15. John A. Eddy, "Probing the Mystery of the Medicine Wheels," *National Geographic, 151* (1) (1977): 140–146.
16. Snir, Smith, and Grosslight (1995).
17. David Saiz, "PC Possibilities," *The Science Teacher, 61* (3) (1994): 28–31.
18. Richard Ruopp and Meghan Pfister, "An Introduction to LabNet," in *LabNet: Toward A Community of Practice,* Richard Ruopp, Shahaf Gal, Brian Drayton, and Meghan Pfister, eds.(Hillsdale, NJ: Lawrence Erlbaum Associates, 1993), pp. 1–20.
19. Nathan Kimball, "Essential Elements of MBLs," in *LabNet,* pp. 257–262.
20. Richard Ruopp and Sarah Haavind, "From Current Practices to Projects," in *LabNet,* pp. 21–57.
21. Peter Dublin, Harvey Pressman, and Thomas Vaughn, *Integrating Computers in Your Classroom: Middle and Secondary Science* (New York: HarperCollins, 1994).
22. Sueann Ambron and Kristina Hooper, "Introduction," in *Learning with Interactive Multimedia: Developing and Using Multimedia Tools in Education,* Sueann Ambron and Kristina Hooper, eds., (Redmond, WA: Microsoft Press, 1990), pp. xi–xii.
23. Frank Hinerman, "Multimedia Labs," *The Science Teacher, 61*(3) (1994): 38–41.
24. National Geographic Society, *Planetary Manager Teachers Guide* (Washington, DC: National Geographic Society, 1993).
25. Videotape, Texas Learning Technology Group, *TLTG Physical Science Curriculum* (Austin, TX: Texas Association of School Boards, 1989).
26. Ruopp et al., *LabNet.*
27. Candace Julyan, "Conversations: Their Importance in Project Science," in *LabNet,* pp. 250–257.
28. Erin O'Connor, "Remote Access Astronomy," *The Science Teacher, 61*(3) (1994): 49–52.

-------------------------------- **INVESTIGATING SCIENCE TEACHING** --------------------------------

Activity 22–1

REVIEWING EDUCATIONAL TECHNOLOGY MATERIALS AND SYSTEMS

Examine and evaluate several CAI programs or multimedia presentation systems available to you. Using a computer, perhaps with a partner, study the teacher's guide accompanying the materials, load the software, and work your way through the instructional phases of the materials. Evaluate the programs or systems in terms of the following questions:

1. What are the instructional goals of the program or package?
2. What is the quality of the graphics and text in the program or package?
3. How easy is the program or package to work with?
4. Which phases of Hunter's direct instructional strategy are provided for or utilized in the program or package?
5. Which phases of BSCS's 5-E constructivist model of instruction are provided for or utilized in the program or package?
6. How would you integrate the program or system into your science classes?

Activity 22–2

Develop a multimedia presentation on a topic in science. Refer to the article by Frank Hinerman (see reference 23 at the end of this chapter) in the March 1994 *Science Teacher* for ideas and procedures.

Chapter 23

MATERIALS FOR SCIENCE TEACHING

Science teachers are fortunate in having an abundance of teaching materials to draw on. Their problem is selecting the proper materials and techniques to accomplish this task. Recent years have seen a proliferation of teaching materials of every description; the display areas of any large convention of science teachers present an overwhelming variety of these materials.

With so many teaching aids available, it helps to consider their purposes in the process of educating science students:

1. More of the students' senses are stimulated by teaching aids. They frequently activate the avenues of learning involving sight, sound, touch, smell, and taste. Combinations of senses are appealed to more often.
2. Teaching aids maintain interest. Students are likely to be in a receptive frame of mind for maximum learning.
3. Teaching becomes less fatiguing when a variety of methods and materials is used and the teacher's enthusiasm is maintained.
4. Individual differences are most adequately served by a variety of teaching aids. Students frequently learn better by one method than by another.
5. Teaching aids provide opportunities for frequent changes of pace, which is particularly useful in middle school teaching.
6. Specific materials designed for specific teaching tasks are more effective because of their refined nature. For example, a well-designed model of certain geological features may illustrate a point better than a photograph—or in some cases better than an actual field trip.

■ USING SCIENCE-LEARNING MATERIALS

Printed materials will continue to be important in science teaching. Textbooks are still a basic source of information in science classes, and when they are used judiciously and with recognition of their limitations, textbooks contribute substantially to the teaching-learning situation.

A publication by the NSTA provides some guidelines concerning science-learning materials.[1] Their recommendations are intended to offer guidance in determining kind and quantity.

1. When needed for learning, individual textbooks and laboratory manuals should be available without cost to every student.
2. The science textbooks used by students at any time should be no more than four years past the date of the last major revision.
3. For each science course there should be an ample supply of diverse printed materials to supplement the textbook and laboratory manual.
4. The school science library should contain an adequate selection of books, periodicals, and pamphlets on the sciences, the applications of science, and the history, philosophy, and sociology of science.
5. An adequate supply of modern science equipment should be available for individual and small-group activities and experiments.
6. A diverse supply of audiovisual learning materials must be readily available for each science course.
7. Certain items of audiovisual equipment should be provided as permanent equipment for individual courses.

■ USE OF TEXTBOOKS

The teaching of science in general and of physics in particular has been textbook-centered in the English-speaking world since the 1820s. Countless teachers of science have learned their basic information from textbooks. They have transferred this information to their students and may have considered that doing this successfully has satisfied their objectives of teaching science to the best of their ability.

Arthur Stinner maintains that rigid adherence to the textbook formulations of scientific information, with their inherent mathematical emphasis, frequently leaves a large vacuum in students' understanding of science concepts. Because of the apparent efficiency of this method, learning science really becomes a matter of memorizing facts, principles, and mathematical formulas, and using these to solve textbook problems that may or may not have relevance to the real world.[2] The physicist and science writer Hans Christian von Baeyer (quoted in Stinner) has said:

Having students memorize formulas and problems on paper is easier and cheaper than staging experiments and demonstrations. But it avoids the confrontation

A wealth of instructional materials is available to science teachers, who must play an active role in their selection and use.

between the real and the abstract, so it misses the essence of physics. A student learns a mechanical sequence of mathematical manipulations—an algorithm—and executes it adeptly, with wide variety of input data. Instead of a set of ideas to be matched against the real world, physics becomes a sequence to be carried out swiftly and accurately.[3]

What does this tell the new teacher about the use of textbooks in science teaching? While much of the information of science in the classroom will continue to come from textbooks, the teacher is advised to be duly forewarned of their possible deleterious effects; the teacher must also constantly guard against their misuse as the sole source of information, their highly abbreviated nature, and their emphasis on results rather than on the ways in which the information has been obtained. Frequent use of investigative methods to ferret out the solutions to real problems may help to minimize the inherent dangers of overuse of textbooks alone.

There is much evidence that the single textbook is still the source of most science information taught in science classes at the secondary level. Research by R. E. Stake and J. A. Easley produced the following conclusion:

> The source of knowledge authority was not so much the teacher—it was the textbook. Teachers were prepared to intercede, to explain, but the direct confrontation with knowledge for most students was with printed information statements. Teachers did it differently from classroom to classroom, but regularly there was deference to the textbook, or lab manual, or encyclopedia, map or chart. Knowing was not so much a matter of experiencing, even vicariously (self-knowledge perhaps was not to be trusted), but of being

familiar with certain information or knowing how to produce the answers to questions that would be asked.[4]

Because of the wide range of reading abilities, problems arise with respect to providing suitable reading materials for all students. David Memory and Kenneth Uhlhorn suggest one response to the dilemma by the use of multiple textbooks at different readability levels.[5] Several benefits of the use of multilevel textbooks are suggested:

1. The approach enables teachers to hold each student responsible for assigned reading because suitable reading levels are available to all.
2. Using more advanced reading materials can better challenge the able readers and challenge them to higher achievement.
3. The approach allows students to practice the comprehension, vocabulary, and study skills taught to them in English and reading classes.
4. It increases the likelihood of success for mainstreamed handicapped students.
5. The approach provides exposure to different viewpoints of authors and instills appropriate scientific skepticism.
6. It reinforces the idea of *fluid inquiry*—the idea that the overall concept of an area of science can change over time (for example, plate tectonics, genetics, particle physics, etc.).
7. It reduces the need to simply repeat the content of single texts in class discussions and fosters better individual comprehension by students.
8. The approach results in improved student attitudes because of generally higher levels of achieved success.

Selecting Textbooks

The selection of science textbooks frequently reflects concerns for readability, topical content, recency or currency of information, and other factors that emphasize the practical and pragmatic matters associated with textbook choice. Decisions based on what is best for particular students sometimes lack perspective. An example of an attempt to use a sociological perspective in selecting science textbooks was reported by Lynn M. Mulkey at Hunter College in New York City.[6] The main research question was, "Does selection of science textbooks deprive younger children in working-class school districts the benefits of perspectives that will help make them 'participants' in science while simultaneously enriching the scientific preparation of older children in middle-class school districts?"

The findings indicated that the availability of (textbook) knowledge important for the development of a scientific role (career) was, on the average, the same for both middle- and working-class districts. However, social class had a distinctive effect on orientation to cognitive flexibility. The middle-class child is more likely to receive encouragement in developing cognitive flexibility (the privilege to be nonconforming). Textbooks appear to be written and selected for children who are perceived as prepared for cognitive flexibility and may have "an accumulated advantage which may or may not be attributable to differences in capacity."[7] Science teachers must place the textbook in its proper perspective in their classes. Students generally feel more comfortable with a textbook than without one. It serves to organize information, stress important concepts, direct activity, and set goals for the study of a particular science. All of these contributions are important. It must be remembered, however, that a textbook alone cannot achieve even a majority of the objectives of science teaching. It cannot provide laboratory experiences, develop true inquiry skills, or teach self-reliance in solving problems. These are objectives that are achieved best by other methods and materials. In *collaboration* with a variety of other materials, the textbook is an important contributor to these objectives.

Selecting a textbook for a given science class is frequently a haphazard affair. Textbooks are often chosen after superficial inspection. Color may influence one's choice more than content; photographs may carry more weight than organization of subject matter; advertising appeal may be more of a deciding factor than usefulness.

In selecting a textbook in science, establish criteria against which competing books can be rated. These criteria include:

A. Factors that deal with the subject-matter content and organization.
   1. Logical organization, sequence of difficulty, grouping of topics.
   2. Emphasis on principles and concepts.
   3. Accuracy of information.
   4. Usefulness of information, applications, and functional nature of the material.
   5. Recent information, modern concepts, theories, and applications.
B. Factors that deal with development of noncontent objectives.
   1. Attention given to development of interests, appreciations, and attitudes.
   2. Attention given to problem-solving approach.
   3. Attention given to skills of science learning.
   4. Attention given to the role of science in society and to scientific literacy.

C. Factors that deal with experiments, demonstrations, and activities.
   1. Inquiry or verification approach.
   2. Student participation, activity, and investigation.
   3. Use of simple materials, degree of structure in laboratories.
   4. Emphasis on drawing conclusions on the basis of observation and experimentation.
D. Factors that deal with mechanical features of the textbook.
   1. Binding, size, durability, attractiveness.
   2. Size of type, level of reading difficulty, summaries, glossaries, index.
   3. Illustrations, maps, charts, graphs, captions.
   4. General ease in using the book.
E. Factors that deal with authors of the textbook.
   1. Qualifications (experience, level of preparation).
   2. Quality of writing, interest, and readability.
   3. References to purposes of the book and intended use.
F. Factors that deal with prospective useful life of the textbook.
   1. Copyright date, revisions, and reprintings.
   2. Nature of material, rate of obsolescence, years of usability.

It is suggested that these criteria be used with a rating scale for comparison with competing textbooks. A number scale like the one that follows might be used:

0____ Book totally lacking in the characteristic
1____ Occasional evidence of the characteristic
2____ Greater evidence of the characteristic but below average
3____ Reasonably frequent evidence of the characteristic
4____ Excellent evidence of the characteristic
5____ Superior in all aspects of the characteristic

Readability Analysis

Probably the most important consideration when analyzing textbooks for a science class is their readability. The reading level of students in any given class varies by several grade levels. To meet individual differences, to avoid discouraging students with low reading levels, and to avoid frustration, it is necessary to select a book that will meet the needs of a variety of students. Usually, these criteria result in the selection of books with reading levels at or slightly below the grade level for the class.

Just what is readability? Readability refers to reading difficulty of a book, paragraph, or prose passage. Many factors enter into readability, such as types of sentence construction, length of sentences, vocabulary, number of syllables in words, type of print, and concept density. At the present time there are several readability formulas that are frequently used in analyzing textbooks. Unfortunately, the results obtained by the various formulas do not agree. (See Activity 23–1, p. 360.)

■ AUDIOVISUAL MATERIALS

Recent years have seen the development of many audiovisual aids for the science teacher. These materials have not always enjoyed the best possible usage because of certain limiting conditions. It is important for the science teacher to have a good working knowledge of several audiovisual devices and to be aware of their teaching possibilities.

In using an audiovisual aid, the teacher's most important consideration is, "Is this the most effective method at my disposal for teaching these concepts?" If the answer is yes, every effort should be made to incorporate the aid into classroom planning. Mental inertia or unwillingness to try a new device should not remain a deterrent to good teaching in science.

Films

Motion-picture films have been used with varying effectiveness for many years. Their limitations are:

1. Poor scheduling or inability to secure the film at the optimum time or place in the course.
2. Poor showing techniques, such as unfamiliarity with the equipment, inadequate room darkening, or general ineptness, all resulting in wasted time.
3. Poor choice of film. Films thirty minutes long may have only five minutes of appropriate learning material in them. The intellectual level of the film may not be appropriate for the class.
4. Indiscriminate use of films that do not contribute to attainment of the course objectives.
5. Cost of rental or purchase, which may be prohibitive for some school systems.

On the other hand, the advantages of motion-picture films are numerous. They include:

1. Close-up sequences, which may be superior to a live demonstration.
2. Organization of content in succinct and capsulized form.
3. Showing of experiments not feasible in the average laboratory because of time and expense.
4. Slow-motion or time-lapse photography, which demonstrates phenomena too rapid or too slow for first-hand observation.
5. Showing of natural scientific phenomena from places not accessible for class visitation.
6. Animated sequences that help to clarify difficult concepts.
7. Creative sound and visual effects for dramatic learning reinforcement.

Variations on the standard film techniques are becoming more common. Single-concept films are produced by several companies. These films are brief and develop a single important idea that can be further pursued in class discussion.

Teacher's guides for films are often provided. They give a resume of the major film ideas, suggestions for use, questions raised in the film with possible answers, and a list of supplementary reading materials.

Eight-millimeter film loops are now available in a number of areas in biology, chemistry, physics, and general science. Fitted into a small cartridge with a specially designed silent-film projector, these film loops can be operated by individual students when necessary. Since they are usually less than ten minutes long, they can be run repetitively until the concepts are thoroughly understood.

Filmstrips and Slides

Filmstrips have several advantages for science teaching:

1. Relatively inexpensive and can be purchased by a library or science department for a permanent collection. The projectors are correspondingly less expensive than motion-picture projectors.
2. Can be stopped at a given frame for whatever time is needed to discuss the ideas presented.
3. Students may study these films individually with minimum disruption of other class work. They are noiseless and require only a moderately darkened area.
4. Frequently available at no cost from industry and government sources. They are usually accompanied by a printed narrative guide or lecture for use when showing the film.

There is no single rule for the best usage of films. The science teacher must be free to use films creatively and flexibly, as they can be fitted into the teaching objectives.

Slides present innumerable opportunities for good teaching. Their relatively low cost and flexibility in use are points in their favor. A science teacher may acquire a highly effective teaching aid by making a collection of his or her own photographs on colored slides. The purchase of a tripod and inexpensive close-up lens enables a teacher to make pictures of plant and animal life for use in the classroom. The slide collection acquired in this way becomes more valuable each year. Students frequently can produce their own slides for reports, projects, or classroom research activities.

Overhead Projection

Most science teachers are using overhead projection as an aid to teaching. The versatility of this instrument makes it an extremely handy tool for everyday classroom use. Some teachers consider it indispensable. An overhead projector costs relatively little—much less than a motion-picture projector, for example. The cost of transparencies, or the materials for making them, is likewise low. Only moderate darkening of the room is needed for satisfactory visibility. The instrument is as convenient to use as the chalkboard and is frequently used as a replacement for it.

Materials that can be used with the overhead projector in science teaching are contained in the Tested Overhead Projection Series (TOPS) produced by a project of the NSF.[8] In this series, several chemistry demonstrations were designed to be conducted on the overhead projector in full view of the entire chemistry class. There are other adaptations for physics and biology.[9] In many cases, demonstration apparatus is designed to be used with standard overhead projectors.

Television

Radio and television have not yet fulfilled their promise as teaching aids for the science teacher in the average classroom. Ordinary AM radio has occasional use, as special programs in science or science-related areas are broadcast, but at best they are of a general nature for lay consumption. A few educational FM stations have produced science programs, but the average science student has not benefited perceptibly from them. Probably the most direct benefit has been derived from on-the-spot news reports of scientific events, such as space exploration, natural disasters, or scientific breakthroughs.

The dream of television as an effective teaching tool has still to be realized. However, news coverage of scientific events has become immeasurably more dramatic since the advent of television and probably has contributed to vastly improved understanding of these events. The opportunity to witness a space shuttle launch or a television program about planetary exploration is tremendously stimulating. It undoubtedly molds public opinion in regard to scientific problems and progress. In this respect, one of the objectives of science teaching—development of

scientific attitudes—is being met by forces outside the control of the science teacher. It remains to be seen whether this will be beneficial. A false impression of science as a gimmick-filled world of spectacular technological advancements may be created at the expense of a sound understanding of the role of science in society.

As a direct teaching tool television has yet to come into common use. The technical problems and expense of installation and upkeep are formidable. Closed-circuit television may become the tool of the future, but it has not yet received wide acceptance; too few science teachers are trained to use it and explore its many possibilities. Furthermore, very few schools are equipped to make use of it on a planned and regular basis. For an example of television's educational use, see "Weather: Air Masses and Fronts" in the Appendix, pp. 429–431.

A more feasible use of television results from the development of inexpensive portable videotape recorders. Many schools and teacher-training institutions are using this tool for instruction and microteaching experience. In many cases one-half-inch tape units are completely satisfactory and introduce an element of versatility into the teacher's instructional plans. It is important that units be designed for compatibility so that tapes can be interchanged and recorded or played on several different models.

Some of the advantages that may be realized from television are:

1. Direct teaching to large numbers of students by a well-prepared master teacher with access to adequate demonstration equipment.
2. Opportunity for close-up viewing by the television camera, giving optimum visibility to all students.
3. Opportunity for on-the-spot viewing of scientific events.
4. Opportunity for training science students in television techniques and familiarizing them with its teaching and learning possibilities.

Desirable as these results are, it is important to realize that television has limitations as well. It cannot replace the science teacher. It cannot develop laboratory skills or substitute for the difficult, repetitive problem-solving practice necessary for mastery of certain science concepts and skills.

Tape Recorders

Tape recorders have become popular as teaching aids in science as well as in other subjects. In biology, for example, they might be used to record sounds of nature, such as bird calls and other forest sounds.

Classroom use of the tape recorder might include taping student reports, interviews with community resource people, or scientific programs on radio or television. The tape recorder is an instrument most science students take to readily. Their resourcefulness in its use may surprise the science teacher at times.

The advent of reliable cassette tape recorders has placed this teaching aid in the nearly indispensable class. Inexpensive units with almost maintenance-free care for years of satisfactory use, even when subjected to rough handling, make the cassette tape recorder an innovative teaching tool.

Materials for the Laboratory

Science deals with the phenomena of nature. These phenomena cannot be studied effectively through abstract or theoretical discussion alone, although this may be necessary at times. Most science students find that actual objects, models, or living specimens make a phenomenon concrete enough to be understood. Science materials and apparatus—demonstration equipment, as well as materials for experimentation—are designed to fulfill this function.

One of the major problems for the junior and senior high school science teacher is the procurement and maintenance of laboratory equipment. Questions of what and how much to order, how to use the apparatus most effectively, and how to store it conveniently for future use are difficult ones, especially for a beginning science teacher. Frequently, it is the teacher moving into a new position who faces these problems in their most acute form. If the pre-

Laboratory equipment such as microscopes can make a concept easily understandable to students.

ceding teacher has not kept careful records of apparatus and equipment and maintained them in good working order, the job of inventorying can be overwhelming.

If possible, it is wise for a teacher beginning a new science position to plan on spending several days in advance of the regular opening of school to work on inventorying equipment, checking its condition, and preparing orders for needed supplies for the year. This preparation will contribute to more effective teaching. Teaching plans may be built around certain materials that are available in sufficient quantities for classroom demonstrations and experiments. It is highly recommended that schools and science departments use their microcomputers to inventory their materials and equipment.

Ordering and Inventorying

Factors to be considered in purchasing equipment and laboratory materials are:

1. Is this the best available item for the teaching purpose intended? Because of the importance of the teaching task and the limitations of time, it is essential to have the best possible tools at hand. The equipment must be basically simple, be capable of illustrating the intended principles, and be engineered to work well.
2. Will the materials serve their intended purpose for a reasonable length of time? Classroom equipment and other materials receive hard use as successive classes work with them. They must be designed to withstand rough handling for several years. A poorly engineered and constructed apparatus, though possibly less expensive to purchase, is rarely economical in the long run.
3. Are the materials functional? Can they be stored easily without excessive disassembly? Do they lend themselves to student use? It is generally a mistake to purchase overly delicate apparatus or equipment with unnecessary precision capabilities for the secondary science class.
4. Is the cost reasonable for the quality of equipment purchased? Comparing catalog prices from several companies can result in savings. It is essential to check the specifications carefully on all apparatus ordered, to ensure that they meet the requirements of the situation.

New equipment and materials of the nonexpendable variety should be inventoried on receipt. A three-by-five card file system is a useful method to keep a record of new purchases and current stock of materials and apparatus. A suggested form for an inventory card is shown in Figure 23–1.

FIGURE 23–1
Inventory card

(Subject)

Inventory for_____

Item_____Catalog No._____

Company_____Cost_____

Storage Code_____

_____

Date No. Condition Reorder Date Cost_____

FIGURE 23–2
Inventory checklist

Inventory of Expendables, Chemistry

Date	Item	Condition	On Hand	Needed	Cost
4 81	Tubing glass (4 mm.)	Ex.	10 lbs.	0	
4 81	Tubing glass (5 mm.)	Ex.	10 lbs.	0	
4 81	Tubing glass (10 mm.)	Ex.	0	5 lbs.	$.75/lb.
4 81	Tubing rubber (4 mm.)	Good	50 ft.	0	
4 81	Tubing rubber (5 mm.)	Good	10 ft.	40 ft.	$3.50/ 100 ft.

Each nonexpendable item in stock should be inventoried on a card of this type. Expendable items should be inventoried on a longer form of the checklist variety. With a well-kept inventory checklist it should be possible to ascertain the amount and condition of expendable items at a glance. Since the preparation of such a list and the effort required to keep it current is quite time-consuming, this task should be assigned to student laboratory assistants if possible. An inventory checklist might look like the one shown in Figure 23–2.

■ SUPPLEMENTARY TEACHING AIDS

The sources of supplementary teaching materials are multiplying year by year. For the science teacher a major problem in using them is proper selection. Educational departments of industrial companies have created or made available to teachers innumerable aids for science teaching. Many of these materials are free or can be obtained at minimal expense. Many kits and project materials for the use of junior and senior high school students are now available. Some of them are free if ordered in small quantities.

A very useful type of supplementary teaching aid is student science periodicals such as *Science News,*

Student science periodicals offer current information on science topics in an interesting and attractive format.

Current Science, Science World, and *Science and Math Weekly.* Subscription rates for students are nominal. In addition to highly informative articles on current science topics, these publications frequently contain suggested student activities and experiments. A teacher's edition, containing suggestions on how to use the activities and other materials, is sometimes provided. The science teacher of today would be remiss in failing to use these very teachable science materials.

Some activities require minimal materials, often very simple items the students can make themselves. For an example, see the "Teaching Science Activity: The Evolution Simulation Game," in the Appendix, pp. 405–409.

As with the standard equipment and materials discussed earlier, storage and availability for effective use are problems in the classroom. A storage file for printed materials, indexed by subject, is a necessary item, and periodic updating is required.

■ THE ROLE OF THE SCIENCE STAFF IN PLANNING FACILITIES

Assisting in the planning of modern science complexes and the remodeling of old facilities to meet the demands of new instructional methods is the responsibility of the science teacher. It is a rare

REFLECTING ON SCIENCE TEACHING

DESIGNING FACILITIES

1. Discuss what Winston Churchill meant by the statement, "We shape our facilities; thereafter they shape us."
2. What relevance does the statement "form follows function" have for science teachers?
3. Who should be involved in the planning of science facilities and why?
4. Many schools are built with little or no consultation with school personnel. Why is this an undesirable practice?
5. What does a teacher's philosophy of education have to do with facilities?

---

teacher who will not be involved in this type of activity during a professional career.

Planning a facility that will be educationally effective and efficient for thirty to forty years requires the best minds available. Several well-qualified persons should be involved in the planning, including science teachers with vast experience, science educators, and local, state, and national science supervisors. Building a structure that may cost millions certainly warrants expenditures for planning. It is desirable that some science teachers be hired during the summer so that they can devote their full time to this task.

A teacher's philosophy of education defines activities that suggest facilities. It is important that teachers consider what they wish to accomplish educationally and then what type of facilities will enable them to reach these objectives. Teachers must remember, however, that they will not be the only instructors to use the plan. It will undoubtedly be in use long after they have retired. It is paramount that teachers think to the future, to science teaching in the 2000s, and ask, "What can I help design today that will not hinder other teachers two or three decades from now?"

It is the responsibility of science teachers to outline the educational specifications for the architect, but the science teacher does not design the room. Designing the area for optimum fulfillment of the educational specifications is the responsibility of the architect. The design of the science area obviously must fit into the total scheme for the school.

The science staff has a role to play in site selection. Before the site is selected they should urge the administration to consider how the site can add to the school's instructional program. Such a consideration is of particular importance in biology, where field work complements class instruction. The final decision in this matter is the responsibility of the Board of Education and must be based on cost and other factors. For example, a site desirable because it offers a good natural area for science work may present a problem in transporting students to and from school.

■ INFLUENCES ON SCIENCE FACILITIES

Trends in Science Instruction

To ensure that facilities will not be outdated, the science staff must be aware of instruction trends. Science education has undergone a dynamic revolution in curriculum and in teaching methods and techniques. Modern technology and research in learning theory alter the present methods of instruction. To guard against facilities restricting new methods of instruction, they should be designed to be flexible, easily modifiable, and able to take into account the trends in science education.

Teaching Methods

Two instructional approaches that are receiving attention are team teaching and individualized instruction. Team teaching involves some large-group instruction for eighty to 100 students, with smaller laboratory sections. Instruction for large lecture-demonstration classes is afforded by lecture complexes or by rooms divided by operable walls that open for large groups. Individualized instruction is designed to allow each student to progress at his or her own rate. This approach requires many individual work areas. Both group and individualized instruction require diverse facilities far removed from those of the traditional classroom.

A variation on this concept is that of differentiated staffing. In this concept, various groups of teachers serve different functions. There may be one or more master teachers in each subject-matter discipline. Other teachers serve in supporting roles, along with noncertified teacher aides, specialists, and other individuals. The differentiated concept is

■■■■■■■■■■■■■■■■■■ **GUEST EDITORIAL** ■■■■■■■■■■■■■■■■■■■■■■■■■■■

Preparing for the First Year

Susan Stewart
Physical Science Teacher
Kenny C. Guinn Junior High
Las Vegas, Nevada

Are there really slot machines in the classrooms? Do cacti grow on the playground? Do most of the teachers lose their paychecks in the local casino once a week? These and similar questions were asked by the folks back home when I left my conservative Midwestern hometown to start an adventure as an eighth-grade science teacher in Las Vegas. Regardless of the different images people have of this city, I am certain that my experiences as a first-year teacher here are very much like those of my fellow graduates in other parts of the country. Adolescents are adolescents no matter where they live. The first year of teaching junior high is frustrating and exhausting. But as my colleagues assure me, it gets easier with experience, and I believe them.

Las Vegas is growing by leaps and bounds and consequently is one of the few places in this country crying for teachers. Kenny C. Guinn Junior High just opened this fall with 1,150 students drawn mainly from a rapidly expanding part of town. Most of the parents in this area are employed by the hotels on the Strip. Because of the growth of this town and the fact that in most cases both parents work, Clark County is a fairly wealthy district. Comprehensive special education programs, vocational-technical education, and career exploration are emphasized at all levels. Strong emphasis is placed on basics, and comprehensive programs are offered in all schools for youngsters who need special help in reading and mathematics. The Clark County School

District reflects all ethnic backgrounds in its student population, staff, and approach to learning. The ethnic distribution of students is 78 percent Caucasian, 15 percent Black, 5 percent Spanish-American, 0.4 percent American Indian, and 1.6 percent others.

With three new schools opening in September 1979, the district had 110 schools. It is a privilege to be a member of the staff that opened one of these new schools. It is exciting and challenging to participate in setting precedents and in creating new curricula for over 1,100 students. Other "thrills of opening a new school" (as my principal loves to say) include dealing with unfinished rooms and laboratory facilities, as well as undelivered supplies and equipment; waiting for defective doors and pencil sharpeners to be repaired; and running a program that has never been tried before. These are times that call for the highest virtues a teacher can possess: flexibility, creativity, and patience.

This first year as a junior high science teacher is an eye-opening experience. There are so many things I am facing now for which no college course or textbook ever prepared me. Who could have taught me how to handle the politics within an administration or of a district school board? What course trained me to deal with the parents of different students? Was there a textbook recipe on how to deal with the normal day-to-day stress that confronts anyone who works with teenagers up to eight hours a day?

I am very thankful for the preparation I did have in my undergraduate years. There I developed very important organization skills. I learned how to express my creativity and my love for science through writing curricula. I was challenged to develop an educational philosophy and to learn how to apply it to practical and realistic objectives for the classroom.

considered more efficient in the use of the school's time and allows more teacher-student interaction. It also provides a basis for differentiation of pay scales and the application of merit-pay concepts.

In recent years, a different concept of education has been tried, namely, that of the open school (sometimes called free school). There are several examples of this type in the United States and in Europe. The open school may be completely ungraded, yet it may extend from ages four or five up through ages seventeen and eighteen, corresponding to the

twelfth grade. Some of the innovations in the open school are the use of noncompulsory attendance, freedom of choice by the students for the classes they wish, and the use of teacher aides, parents, specialists, and individuals who can work through a broad spectrum of problems. To be effective, the open school must have a responsive and rich environment with ample materials available for students to work with. At the present time, most open schools are at the elementary level, but there are several exceptions that continue to ages seventeen and eighteen.

My strength as a teacher lies in my enthusiasm for my subject and in my wholehearted conviction that it is valuable for every youngster. I also have a certain empathy for junior high students and a genuine concern for guiding them through "those difficult years." Supposedly, those qualities are enough to start the young teacher off with a smooth-running classroom. Well, if you do not discover it in student teaching, you soon find out on your first job how fragile all those idealistic goals and perceptions of education are; they shatter before your eyes within the first three months. It takes persistence and faith to piece together again a modified educational philosophy consistent with the classroom realities.

One of the major areas for which college courses have failed to prepare teachers in the past is discipline. As a first-year teacher, I did not anticipate spending 70 percent of the class time in teaching students that there are logical consequences to their actions. Genuine concern, conscientious hard work, and creative lesson plans are not enough. The prospective teacher needs to be *trained* in effective classroom control. I, like many other teachers, have learned classroom management by trial-and-error and have ended up using methods that just seem to work. For certain periods of time, my actions became mechanical and/or inconsistent; they were designed to eliminate my stress and they did not always consider the best interests of the child. To create a workable and consistent philosophy of discipline, the young teacher needs more background in adolescent psychology and more practical experience in the classroom with time to apply, evaluate, and revise this philosophy.

Teaching is not an eight-hour-a-day job; you are a teacher around the clock. The demands by the public for what a good teacher should be are increasing. The trend to make teachers accountable for cranking out reading, writing, and calculating students is on the uprise. More and more guidelines and restrictions are being established as to what you can teach. College is the place to learn some self-preservation and sanity-saver techniques. Gather ideas for your future curricula. Learn how to express your creativity in concrete objectives. Spend as much time as you can in the classroom—observing, experimenting, and evaluating. Solidify what you believe about children, the role of the teacher, and the role of the school and start to observe how it works in practice.

There are still several things for which no text or course can prepare you. At times, as a first-year teacher, there will appear to be few rewards, and even those few will not be immediately visible. You need to be aware of the potential morale problems you will face among your faculty. Although you confront disillusionment, you must resist being drawn into a negative attitude. Keep hold of those ideals; you may have to reconstruct them, but do not ever abandon them. Budget cuts, crowded classrooms, and apathetic parents are other challenges which await you. It is part of the occupation, however, and your decision to stick with it boils down to your own conviction that you possess a potential power to make a dent in it all.

My personal conviction is strong enough that I know I want to make teaching my career. I plan to finish coursework for a Master's degree in geology or biology. With that, I would like to try teaching overseas for a few years. Environmental education also appeals to me, and I may want to move into the position of consultant. This first year is just the beginning, of course, and there are many possibilities ahead.

It appears that a developing trend throughout science education is the application of more humane methods of teaching. There is more concern about student attitudes and interests and other aspects of the affective domain. Teachers are beginning to make an effort to develop feelings of mutual trust between the students and themselves. They consider that each student has individual worth. Increasingly, teachers attempt to develop and maintain positive attitudes for education and schooling.

There is an increased use of audiovisual aids by small groups and individuals engaged in special work. Tape recorders are being used more often to enrich class instruction. Some of the new schools have multiple tape-recording outlets and a series of tapes so that individual students can listen to various tapes at the same time. This arrangement is similar, on a limited basis, to the type of activity that goes on in language laboratories. Provision must be made to ensure widened use of audiovisual material on both individual and group bases.

REFLECTING ON SCIENCE TEACHING

TRENDS AND FACILITIES

1. What trends of science education have implications for facilities?
2. Can you think of other trends that have implications for science facilities?

Another development is emphasis on more varied instruction. Not all students necessarily perform the same experiment in the same class period. In one class students may be engaged in several different activities.

More space for both equipment and storage is being provided in many schools. This change includes the provision of more preparation areas.

Curriculum

Certain curriculum changes have become more and more evident in the past twenty years. Among them are the use of new curricula at the middle school, junior high, and senior high levels. Frequently the sequence in the junior high is *living sciences* in the seventh grade, *physical science* in the eighth grade, and *earth science* in the ninth grade. Some schools have developed minicourses, which are one-semester courses on rather specialized topics offered on an elective basis so that students may choose them to satisfy individual needs. In recent years, various courses in environmental sciences have been developed as part of the minicourse offerings.

A discernible change in the interpretation of the word *laboratory* seems to be evident in recent years. Rather than thinking of the laboratory as merely a room equipped with gas, water, and electricity, it now is thought of as a place where experiments can be conducted. This conception might include the outdoors as well as the indoors, and it might include observational experiments, particularly with respect to the life and earth sciences. Modern curricula emphasize laboratory approaches, which require more laboratory space and supporting facilities, such as preparation rooms, live rooms, greenhouses, and student research and project areas.

Most of the modern curriculum developments emphasize inquiry. Facilities must be provided to allow for inquiring in several ways, such as reading, observation, experimentation, study of models, films (sixteen- and eight-millimeter), charts, preserved specimens, field work, slides, overhead projection, and film-strip projection. Information from a variety of sources is becoming more available to students, requiring greater flexibility in space utilization.

Some curriculum developers discern a recent trend in science classrooms toward a return to teacher demonstrations and seatwork.[10] This trend may reflect higher costs of laboratory equipment.

Some schools use the block approach to learning science. This method is most advanced in the BSCS biology course, in which students concentrate on laboratory work in depth for four to six weeks. This arrangement requires greater storage space, as do some other modern developments in science instruction. Advanced science courses, such as science seminars or advanced placement, are frequently used and require more work areas.

Trends in Science Facilities

Flexibility of design is an important feature of science facilities. This means that the facilities must be designed so that they can be changed or defined by the people who use them. In other words: (1) the equipment used should have optimal functionality and mobility, and (2) the degree of flexibility is determined by the number of usable changes; that is, the more usable changes, the greater the degree of flexibility. There should be the capacity for immediate change (changes that require only minutes to make) and long-range changeability (something that might take place over a weekend or during a vacation period).

The adaptation gaining popularity is the *service sandwich*, a 36-inch space between floors in which are contained wiring, lighting fixtures, TV conduits, air ducts, plumbing, and other utilities. Access to these utilities may be through the ceiling at designated points, spaced so that rooms may be changed at will but utilities will be easily accessible. There is not much point in being able to change partitions around if one cannot also change the lighting arrangements, plumbing, air conditioning controls, and other services. Grid troughs containing electrical conduits, ducts for hot and cold air and return ducts, fluorescent light tubes, telephone lines, electrical wiring conduits, switches, outlets, radio and TV circuitry, and intercom systems are designed into the service sandwich.

Between 1970 and 1972, exemplary science facilities were studied by the NSTA.[11] Six task force members visited more than 140 schools in the United

FIGURE 23–3
Contrasting modes of science instruction

States. These schools had been nominated by individuals, state science groups, and the National Science Supervisors Association (NSSA). The purpose of the study was to assess the status of science teaching facilities in the middle, junior high, senior high, and junior college levels.

Two characteristics of science facilities were considered necessary to earn the judgment of *exemplary.* They were *flexibility* and provision for *individualization.* Early in the study it was found that facilities themselves could not be studied separately or isolated from other characteristics of science teaching, including programs, curriculum materials, and instructional staff. Two modes of science instruction, showing the trend toward greater emphasis on student-centered learning through the use of materials and facilities, are shown in Figure 23–3. In the first mode, the traditional teaching situation involves a teacher, resource materials, books, and other sources of information impinging on the student from many directions. The student has little control over what he or she receives. In the second emerging pattern of school instruction, the student finds him or herself at the center of learning, with freedom and opportunities to select from a variety of teaching modes—including resource rooms, carrels, laboratories, resource persons, lectures, textbooks, and other materials. The difference between these two modes is based on the place at which the student is put in the learning pattern.

The evolving patterns in facilities and programs are shown in Figure 23–4. The arrows indicate the transition from rigid, traditional patterns near the bottom to flexible and optional modes at the top of each ladder.

Trends in School Buildings

One of these trends is that of the *open-concept* school. Schools designed along this line frequently do not have interior walls—or if they do, walls are minimal and frequently not load-bearing. Movable partitions are often used, and bookcases and room dividers replace cinderblock walls. The environment in such schools is usually pleasant, particularly if the interior of the building has been acoustically treated. This treatment includes carpeting of the floors and walls, if possible, and the use of acoustical tile or varied ceilings to break up sound patterns.

The open-concept schools give considerable freedom of movement and, when combined with flexible scheduling patterns, provide a casual and aesthetically pleasing atmosphere. Students move from area to area in small groups or individually, and the typical clatter of the traditional classroom (with its bell at the end of a class period) is usually absent. Freedom of movement requires flexible furniture and ample work areas for small groups. Laboratories are often placed along the perimeter or are designed in some kind of movable fashion, leading to innovation in laboratory furniture. One trend is the use of *power islands,* which include electricity, gas, and water, as well as waste disposal units. For maximum flexibility there is access through the floor for connections to all the necessary utilities. Using such connections enables one to cover the floor access port completely, move the power island out of the way, and redesign the room as much as one wishes. Movable laboratory tables, which can be used to form work areas, are usually associated with the power island; these extend from the power center.

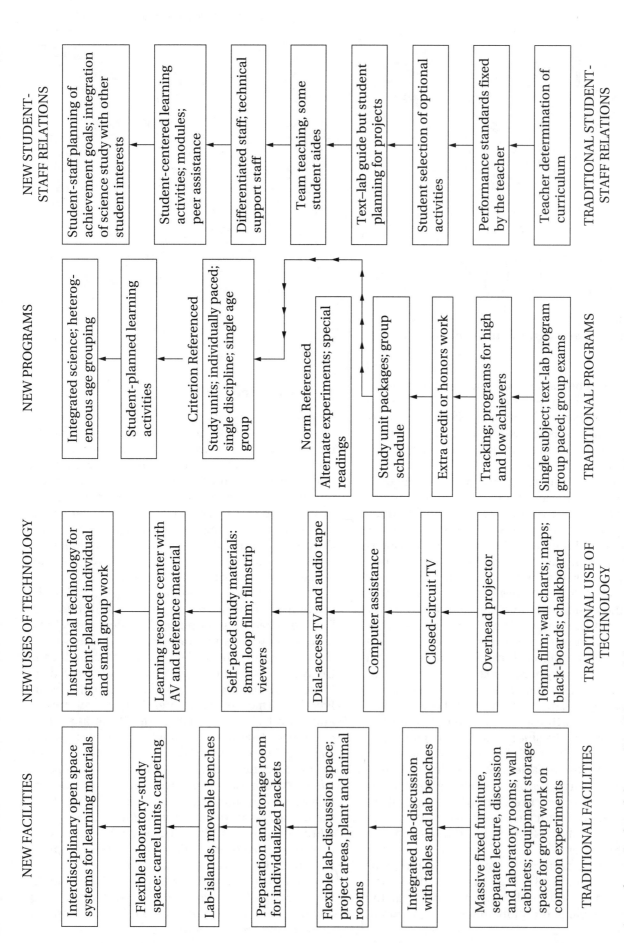

FIGURE 23–4
Evolving patterns in facilities, technology, programs, and student-staff relations in science teaching

Arrows show general trends from traditional (bottom of chart) to emerging characteristics (top), with descriptions ordered in approximately the sequence of development observed by the study team.

A new innovation in laboratory furniture is a portable carrel. Such a carrel stands about six feet high and is about three feet wide and folds into a compact unit that may be locked. When a student wishes to use his or her carrel, he or she unlocks the combination, pulls out a door, and a seat appears with bookshelves and writing surfaces immediately available.

Another innovation, which is appearing in new schools and is conducive to better science teaching, is computer terminals for using computer-assisted instruction facilities. A second innovation is the provision of a combined teacher-office work area to facilitate team planning. This area is particularly useful when curriculum planning is done by the individual teachers in the district or in team-teaching situations.

The use of ramps to accommodate wheelchairs is another important change. The use of color and of aesthetically pleasing work areas is also a welcome change. Another innovation is the use of adjoining outdoor-environment centers to which students in the earth science and biology classes may have immediate access.

As teachers remove themselves more and more from the position of being the primary information source, their role changes to that of director of learning or diagnostician. Consequently, students have more control over the rate at which they proceed and the sequence of information with which they interact. Information from a wide variety of sources is becoming more available to the students, thus there is a demand for greater flexibility in space utilization.

Large, open laboratories are becoming more common, as is the growth of technologically assisted study. Calculators and computer terminals are sometimes installed for individualized instruction. The open laboratories must be large enough for sufficient separation between groups. This space acts as a sound barrier and works adequately as long as the total number of students is not excessive. Other methods of breaking up the large, open areas while retaining flexibility include using book shelves as room dividers, varied furniture arrangements to give visual and aesthetic satisfaction, or movable self-supporting partitions.

■ GUIDELINES FOR PLANNING A SCIENCE COMPLEX

It is clear that the science complex must contain more of everything and must be designed with an emphasis on flexibility. In planning science facilities, attention should be given to the following principles.[12]

Planning Facilities

1. Those who select the school site should consider the potential contributions of the surroundings to the teaching of science. The location of science rooms within the science complex in relation to supply, outdoor areas, and sunlight exposure needs consideration. For example, a biology classroom is best located on a ground floor with access to growing areas.
2. Planning of science rooms should incorporate the ideas of many qualified individuals who have had experience in planning science facilities, not just the architect's ideas.
3. The needs of science should be considered in floor planning, illumination, ventilation, plumbing, and placement of sinks and water taps. Electric plugs for each student should be provided if necessary.
4. Consideration should be given to windowless classrooms since they do have some advantages for storage, thermal control, and audiovisual programs.

Area and Space Resources

1. The amount of floor space provided should be thirty-five to forty-five square feet, or more, per student (fifty square feet if storage area is included).
2. The number of rooms and how much they will be used throughout the day should be carefully determined. If a room will not be filled with science students all day, what other classes will be in it?
3. There should be enough space for projects to remain assembled for varying periods of time.
4. Enough space should be provided for proper storage of all materials.
5. Space should be provided for displaying student-constructed projects and other products and devices.
6. Space should be provided for the science teacher to work in.
7. More aisle space must be provided in multipurpose laboratories because of greater student movement.

Different Learning Activities

1. The science rooms should provide for a wide range of learning activities for individuals, small groups, and the entire class.
2. Facilities should permit students to experiment with many materials.
3. Areas should be provided where experiments and projects may be conducted for others to observe.

REFLECTING ON SCIENCE TEACHING

INSTRUCTIONAL FACILITIES

1. What five considerations do you think most important in facility design for science teaching?
2. Design a modern floor plan for a science complex. Justify your design.
3. How do the facility requirements for individualized instruction vary from those of group instruction?

---

4. Facilities should be available for individual experimental work.
5. There should be provision for small-group or individual conferences with the science teacher.

Furniture and Decor

1. Rooms should be pleasant and attractive. Using several colors in cabinets and display cabinets helps to give the room a pleasant appearance.
2. Rooms should be flexible, to accommodate a variety of uses. Furniture that is not permanently installed ensures greater flexibility since it can be easily moved as conditions warrant.
3. Adaptable furniture should be provided.

Auxiliary Facilities

1. Planning science facilities should include consideration of the community resources that can be used to supplement the program (i.e., libraries, museums, parks, etc.).
2. There should be a facility for construction and repair of equipment.
3. Provisions should be made for published materials to be available.
4. Facilities should be provided for effective use of audiovisual aids.

In planning a science complex, careful consideration must be given to the study of space relationships. Where should the biology rooms be located in relation to the physics, chemistry, and other science rooms? What relationship should they have to the storage areas? Should there be a central storage area with access to all classrooms, or should each classroom have a storage facility? The advantage of the former arrangement is that it requires less space and makes equipment available for multiple use. For example, a vacuum pump may be easily available to physics, chemistry, physical science, and general science classes. A central storage area, however, requires greater organization and agreement among the faculty involved on how the equipment will be used and returned to the storage area.

The NSTA, through its Commission on Professional Standards and Practices, has prepared a document entitled "Conditions for Good Science Teaching."[13] In its recommendations, it has dealt with resources for learning, among which are science rooms and laboratories. A list of its recommendations follows:

Conditions for Good Science Teaching

1. There should be at least one separate laboratory for each kind of science course offered.
2. There must be enough laboratory rooms provided for each science course to accommodate all students who can profit from the course and wish to take it.
3. Each laboratory must be large enough to accommodate real experimentation.
4. Each laboratory should have ceilings that are at least 10 feet (3 meters) high.
5. Each laboratory should be appropriately furnished for each science.
6. Each laboratory should have conveniently located electric, gas, and water outlets.
7. Waste-disposal facilities must be provided in all laboratories.
8. For work efficiency and safety, laboratories should have lighting that takes into account the variations in working conditions common to science laboratories.
9. Reasonable considerations of comfort and health require that each laboratory have the capability of renewing the room air at a rate compatible with normal student occupancy and the potential uses of science laboratories, such as maintenance of animals, noxious gases, etc.
10. Fire blankets and fully operable fire extinguishers must be located where they are quickly accessible. Every laboratory should be protected by automatic overhead sprinklers.
11. Chemistry laboratories must contain an emergency shower, an eye-wash fountain, and safety goggles for all students.
12. Every science laboratory must have two unobstructed exits.

13. There should be an annual, verified safety check of each laboratory.
14. No more than twenty-four students should be assigned to a space intended for group discussion and activity (as distinct from large-group lecture).
15. A science classroom should have full audiovisual capability and facilities for conducting scientific demonstrations.
16. Specialized facilities are needed (plant growth facilities, animal room, darkroom, and science shop).
17. Individual project areas are needed for students working on special experiments.
18. Ample science-library space must be available.
19. Conference rooms are needed for teacher-student conferences.
20. Ample space is needed for the storage of supplies and equipment.
21. Every science teacher requires access to a preparation area free from students.
22. Every science teacher should have private office space.
23. The science department budget should appear as a separate account within the whole school budget, and it should be subdivided functionally.
24. Supplies should be budgeted on a per capita basis with the amount varying according to the nature of the course and the consumables involved.
25. Budgets should provide leeway for items to be ordered during the school year for new projects, perishable materials, and unforeseen contingencies.

■ SCIENCE FACILITIES AND STUDENTS WITH DISABILITIES

In 1977, Joseph A. Califano, then Secretary of Health, Education, and Welfare, signed the regulations implementing Section 504 of the Rehabilitation Act of 1973. Section 504 provides that "No otherwise qualified handicapped individual . . . shall solely by reason of his handicap be excluded from the participation in, be denied the benefits of, or be subjected to discrimination under any program or activity receiving federal financial assistance."

In many cases there have been dramatic changes in the actions and attitudes of institutions and individuals receiving federal funds. Some of the implications of the regulation are as follows:

1. All new facilities must be barrier-free.
2. Programs or activities must be made accessible to persons with disabilities, and/or structural changes must be made within a given time period.
3. Qualified persons with disabilities may not, on the basis of a disability, be denied admission or employment even if facilities have not been made barrier-free.
4. Colleges and universities must make reasonable modifications in academic requirements, where necessary, to ensure full educational opportunity for students with disabilities.
5. Educational institutions must provide auxiliary aids, such as readers for the blind or interpreters for the deaf.

It is evident that the educational systems and the design professions, as well as material and product manufacturers, must determine the needs of persons with disabilities. In turn, this understanding must be translated into practical, economical ways of providing opportunities for these individuals so that they may achieve educational accomplishment.

In the past, architects and educators have been content to function with respect to the so-called average person. They have often been unaware of the many individuals with physical disabilities who are striving to function as productive citizens. This has been true not only in the design of buildings but also in the design of the science curricula.

Since, as much as possible, persons with disabilities should participate equally in campus activities with those who are nondisabled, it is imperative that the entire educational facility be considered. This consideration not only benefits the participant who has a disability but also aids staff members and visitors who may have disabilities.

Various institutions have been modified so that they are accessible to persons with disabilities. Stairways are being supplemented with ramps and elevators. Braille letters and symbols are used for signs. The problem is not easily solved in laboratories, however. In many cases, spacing work areas in the laboratories requires complete remodeling. Since the standard laboratory table does not accommodate a person using a wheelchair, many facilities are totally inadequate for compliance with the new laws.

Furthermore, a laboratory that has been modified to accommodate a person using a wheelchair does not necessarily meet the needs of every individual with a disability. Problems involving manual dexterity require additional modifications that have an impact on not only the station but also the specific items of equipment associated with that station.

Physical barriers present just one phase of the problem of accessibility for persons with disabilities. Another aspect relates to the affective approach to the problem. For this reason, the overall environment for the student must be looked at.

The new regulations may encourage more students with disabilities to study science. One of the reasons that individuals with disabilities may have avoided the science field, or any other program requiring science courses, could be their inability to find appropriate means of completing laboratory requirements. For the first time, these students may have the opportunity to satisfy the requirements for a particular major.

■ SUMMARY

Science teachers in today's schools have almost unlimited choices of materials with which to enhance their teaching. Wise selection of appropriate materials is a major problem. In making these choices, it is important to recognize the basic reasons for using a variety of materials in science teaching. Individual differences among students demand variations in methods and materials. The psychology of learning supports the thesis that variety of materials promotes better learning. More of the senses are stimulated, and more avenues of learning are activated. Availability of many materials gives opportunity for individual work and experimentation.

Published materials form a large segment of today's science-teaching arsenal. Textbooks continue to be essential tools, although their limitations are better recognized. It is still important to select textbooks in science carefully and with an understanding of their contribution to learning. Many supplementary monographs and pamphlets are now available. These materials are usually written at a level suitable for junior and senior high school students. Authors of these publications have done an excellent job of communicating difficult concepts from the research frontiers as understandable science for the nontechnical reader. At the same time, they have demonstrated the processes of science admirably and conveyed realistic ideas of the role of science in society. Audiovisual equipment and materials continue to gain in sophistication. Although radio and television have not yet realized their potential as teaching aids in the average classroom, increasing strides are being made in their use. New techniques with overhead projectors, film-loop projectors, and single-concept films are finding increased popularity. Individual differences are being better served by these materials, and individualized instruction is enhanced by more flexible audiovisual aids.

Science teaching depends greatly on laboratory work. Materials for the laboratory are increasing, both in variety and in abundance in science classrooms. The science teacher must become familiar with sources of laboratory apparatus and supplies. In choosing equipment, educational value is paramount. In addition, durability and usefulness are important considerations. Once purchased, equipment must be maintained in usable condition. An up-to-date inventory is necessary, and an adequate budget for purchase of new materials must be available.

In this chapter we have not attempted to give an exhaustive treatment of the problems of facilities design. We have tried to show teachers' responsibilities in ensuring that new facilities are an improvement over the old ones; we have also pointed out some considerations in providing modern facilities. Science teachers are the people most competent to know what facilities are needed for efficient and effective teaching. It is their responsibility to work toward getting these facilities.

In writing educational specifications, teachers must take care that the facilities will not be outdated in twenty or thirty years. This problem can be avoided if facilities are made flexible and if teachers understand trends in teaching that have implications for science instruction.

New federal requirements mandate that students with disabilities be provided with suitable facilities, materials, and services to ensure full educational opportunities for this group. Substantial modification of laboratory space and facilities is required.

■ REFERENCES

1. National Science Teachers Association, *Conditions for Good Science Teaching in Secondary Schools* (Washington, DC: Author, 1970), p. 6.
2. Arthur Stinner, "Science Textbooks and Science Teaching: From Logic to Evidence," *Science Education*, *76* (1) (1992): 1–16.
3. Hans Christian von Baeyer, quoted in Stinner, pp. 13–15.
4. R. E. Stake and J. A. Easley, *Case Studies in Science Education*, (Urbana, IL: Center for Instructional Research and Curriculum Evaluation, University of Illinois, 1978).
5. David M. Memory and Kenneth W. Uhlhorn, "Multiple Textbooks at Different Readability Levels in the Science Classroom," *School Science and Mathematics*, *91* (February 1991): 64-72.
6. Lynn M. Mulkey, "The Use of a Sociological Perspective in the Development of a Science Textbook Evaluation Instrument," *Science Education*, *71* (4) (1987): 511–522.
7. Mulkey, pp. 511–522.
8. Hubert N. Alyea, "Tested Overhead Projection Series," *The Science Teacher*, *29* (March, April, September, October, November, December, 1962).
9. Walter Eppenstein, *The Overhead Projector in the Physics Lecture* (Troy, NY: Rensselaer Polytechnic Institute, 1962).

10. Marjorie Gardner, "Ten Trends in Science Education," *The Science Teacher* (January 1979): 30–32.

11. J. D. Novak, *Facilities for Secondary School Science Teaching: Evolving Patterns in Facilities and Programs* (Washington, DC: National Science Teachers Association, 1972).

12. This list has been modified from *Science Facilities for our Schools*, Publication K–12 (Washington, DC: National Science Teachers Association, 1963).

13. *Conditions for Good Science Teaching in Secondary Schools* (Washington, DC: National Science Teachers Association, 1984).

INVESTIGATING SCIENCE TEACHING

Activity 23–1

READABILITY ANALYSIS

For the busy teacher or review committee selecting textbooks, a primary consideration is ease of use. Fortunately, one of the readability formulas, the Fry Readability Graph, is a simple tool which can be used by the average classroom teacher in selecting textbooks. It is a good exercise to try your hand at determining the readability of a textbook that you might use for your particular subject, to familiarize yourself with the difficulty and usefulness of such a formula. Remember, however, that the results are only approximate and largely dependent on the technical nature of the material being analyzed. Many of the readability formulas do not take into adequate consideration the technical nature of many science subjects.

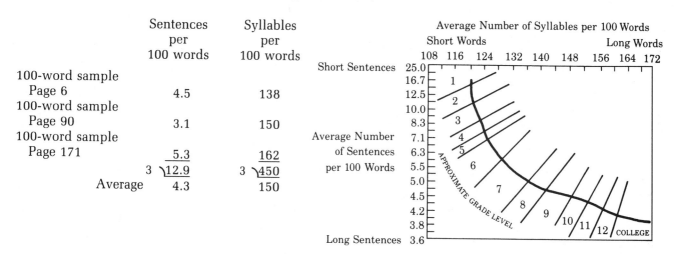

	Sentences per 100 words	Syllables per 100 words
100-word sample Page 6	4.5	138
100-word sample Page 90	3.1	150
100-word sample Page 171	5.3	162
	3 ⟌12.9	3 ⟌450
Average	4.3	150

FIGURE 23–5
Graph for estimating readability (Edward Fry, "A Readability Formula That Saves Time," *Journal of Reading* (November, 1968), pp. 513–516; 575–578.

Fry's Readability Graph. The Fry graph is used for narrative and expository writing only; do not use it for poetry, dialog, drama, or unusual styles of writing. The Fry graph assesses technical difficulty, not interest, style, or content.

Directions for Using the Readability Graph

1. Select three 100-word passages from near the beginning, middle, and end of the book. For anthologies, average nine samples (three samples from each of three stories or essays).
2. Avoid samples from the beginnings and ends of chapters.
3. Include proper nouns (except for common names like Dick or Sue) in your word count.
4. Count the total number of sentences in each 100-word passage (estimating to nearest tenth of a sentence). Average these three numbers.
5. Count the total number of syllables in each 100-word sample. There is a syllable for each vowel sound; for example: cat (1), blackbird (2), continental (4). Don't be fooled by word size; for example: polio (3), through (1). Endings such as -y, -ed, -el, or -le usually make a syllable; for example: ready (2), bottle (2). Average the total number of syllables for the three samples.
6. Count numbers in figures (1973) as one syllable. If the number is written out, count it in full syllables.
7. Plot on the graph the average number of sentences per hundred words and the average number of syllables per hundred words. The point where these plots coincide designates the grade level. If your computation places the estimated reading level in the shaded area on the graph, start over again with different samples. (Plot these two points on the Fry Graph in Figure 23–5. What is the approximate grade difficulty level of this material?) Most plot points fall near the heavy curved line. Perpendicular lines mark off approximately grade level areas.
8. Add one year to the estimated reading level if the material has been translated from another language.
9. Add one year to the estimated reading level if the material was written before1900.
10. If great variability is encountered either in sentence length or in the syllable count for the three selections, randomly select several more passages and compute their average before plotting.

Activity 23–2

EVALUATING TEXTBOOKS

Select three textbooks for secondary science teaching in your field of preparation or interest. Evaluate them using the criteria in this chapter. What are the major strengths and weaknesses of the books you have chosen?

Science Textbook Evaluation Form

Guidelines for Evaluation of Science Texts Scoring:
10 = Outstanding, 8 = Excellent, 5 = Good, 3 = Fair, 1 = Poor

Text A:_____

Publisher:_____Copyright date:_____Cost_____

Text B:_____

Publisher:_____Copyright date:_____Cost_____

Text C:_____

Publisher:_____Copyright date:_____Cost_____

Grade level:_____

	Textbook					Textbook		
	A	B	C			A	B	C

I. Content: (sample all units/chapters)
   A. Most of the necessary topics/units for this level
   B. Historical development of science/scientists
   C. Present-day environment/energy/social/scientific issues
   D. Balance of life/physical/earth topics/units
   E. Appropriate level of mathematics/science content (i.e., Piaget)

II. Presentation: (sample all units/chapters)
   A. Balance of content vs. inductive laboratory skills/methods/inquiry
   B. Development of ideas prior to use of scientific vocabulary
   C. Interesting informal writing style
   D. Unfamiliar/important terms/principles in italics/boldface
   E. Problem solving and scientific methods are integrated

III. Accuracy: (sample 5-10 of each item)
   A. Indexed topics were scientifically correct
   B. Measures are only SI metric and technically correct

C. Glossary is scientifically correct and understandable
   D. Directions for structured activities are precise and they work
   E. Appropriate safety is stressed at all times

IV. Organization: (sample 2-3 units)
   A. Unit introduction/abstract sets the stage for student involvement
   B. Sequential development of ideas/concepts/skills
   C. Investigations are integral, not just add on
   D. End of unit questions require thinking/application
   E. Well-indexed cross references

V. Readability
   A. Words per sentence =_____(for grades 5-6, below 21 = outstanding)
   B. 60% of sentences are simple or compound (not complex)
   C. Reading level is .5 to 1.5 grade levels below text level
   D. 3-4 personal references per 100 words
   E. 1-2 examples/applications of abstract principles (low concept density)

Textbook

	A	B	C

VI. Adaptability
 A. Provisions for wide range of student skills/interests/learning styles
 B. Useable as a reference book
 C. Provides for a wide range of learning activities (not just verbal)
 D. Chapters/units can be omitted
 E. Includes appropriate controversial topics (i.e., evolution)

VII. Teaching Aids
 A. Annotated references for teachers
 B. Annotated references for students (books, periodicals, films, etc.)
 C. Publisher provides appropriate in-service
 D. Teacher's Guide includes wide variety of activities, methods, etc., besides answers
 E. Complete lists of permanent/consumable kit materials and sources

VIII. Illustrations
 A. Boy/girl and white/minority balance sex/minority stereotype
 B. Photos/art: large, clear, and appropriate (not too "arty")

Textbook

	A	B	C

 C. Illustrations integrated as direct references
 D. Adequate labels for all art/photos
 E. Modern art/photos, except for historical settings

IX. Activities
 A. At least 1/3 of activities are laboratory-oriented
 B. Balance of large/small muscle, in/out seat activities
 C. Wide range of difficulty = success for all levels
 D. Balance of structured/inquiry activities
 E. Activities stress understanding/application, not just memorization

X. Appearance
 A. Size/style/layout of print makes for easy reading
 B. Appropriate pleasing page balance/placement of art/copy
 C. Size/shape of book is appropriate for grade level
 D. Durable, non-glare, opaque paper
 E. Attractive/durable binding and cover

Total

Activity 23–3

LEARNING MATERIALS

1. Begin a file of free and inexpensive materials related to your teaching area. Arrange an indexing system for easy access and location of items when needed.
2. Survey the current research in science education for information on the effectiveness of teaching by television. On the basis of your findings, what conclusions can you draw concerning the future of educational television in the field of science?

Activity 23–4

DESIGNING THE SCIENCE FACILITIES FOR A SMALL MIDDLE-SENIOR HIGH SCHOOL

At some point in your teaching career, you may be called upon to participate on a committee to design or contribute plans for a science room, science wing of an existing building, or perhaps to help plan an entirely new structure, including science classrooms and laboratories. For practice in this, use the following information to design a science wing for a school of 600 pupils, grades 7–12. Assume there are 350 students in the sciences in a given year. The classes include 2–7th grade life science, 2–8th grade physical science, 2-9th grade earth science, three 10th grade biology classes (required), 2 classes of 11th grade chemistry (optional) and one 12th grade physics class, also optional.

After discussing this with your classmates and considering all the possibilities, draw the plans for the science wing giving attention to the following points:

1. Number and size of science classrooms required
2. Number of laboratories—either combined with classrooms or separate
3. Required storage space for equipment, chemicals, and projects
4. Plant growing room and animal facilities
5. Safety factors, traffic flow for students, gas, water and electrical services
6. Site selection, facilities for science outdoors
7. Any other factors of importance

Remember as you plan, you are building for at least 25 years into the future. Consider possible changes in enrollment patterns of growth or decline. Be able to justify your choices in class discussions. Remember a science facility should be built to accommodate a variety of teaching methods and should be planned with flexibility in mind.

UNIT 9

PROFESSIONAL DEVELOPMENT

You are about to embark on the most exciting and important part of your professional education as a science teacher: your student teaching experience will begin soon. As a student teacher you will learn more useful information and strategies and more of the experiences of teaching science than you have learned thus far.

Now you will face students and see their enthusiasm or apathy, their smiles and frowns, their understanding and perplexities. You will also have the chance to interact with them. You will probably practice under an understanding and sensitive professional teacher who will give you freedom (but not too much), help when you need it, and the opportunity to grow into a confident teacher of science.

Most prospective science teachers look forward to these opportunities with pleasant anticipation. At last they are nearing the end of a long and arduous professional program and are about to encounter the classroom with a good mentor. A wise apprentice will make the maximum effort to learn the tricks of the trade. He or she will realize that much hard work is in store, and many perplexing problems may come up. Here the test of one's commitment to science teaching will be met.

There will be some experienced teachers whom you may want to emulate. Get to know them and see what makes them successful. Beware of the jaded and cynical teachers who will try to discourage you because they are unhappy in their jobs. You will find both kinds. Retain your idealism but be a realist too. Recognize that you are choosing a noble profession but one in which there will be many difficult challenges to overcome. Good teachers are those who keep children foremost in their thinking and persist in their efforts, regardless of the difficulties. Statistics show that only about half of the new entering teachers these days stay in the profession more than five years. Staying the course can be tough sometimes. Plan on being one of those who stays the course.

The best way to grow into the profession of science teaching and to remain there is to associate with other professional teachers at meetings, conventions, workshops, and special courses. Keeping up-to-date is critical. Reading science and teaching journals for ideas is important. You should invest a little money to do these things—you will find the rewards much greater than the cost. Put your time and energy in committee work, writing for publication, and serving in the community. You will gain recognition and other possibilities in the future.

We are all aware of the many challenges facing science education today and of the dismal showing of American children when compared to many other cultures. In *Science for All Americans* (AAAS, 1989), the statement is made that "To turn this situation around will take determination, resources, leadership, and time. The world has changed in such a way that scientific literacy has become necessary for everyone, not just a privileged few; science education will have to change to make that possible" (p. 14). Be a part of this challenge and help to solve the problems that face us!

Chapter 24

STUDENT TEACHING AND PROFESSIONAL GROWTH

Students nearing the end of their teacher training grow increasingly anxious to get on the job. They may look forward with anticipation to trying their wings as full-fledged teachers in charge of a class. At the same time, they are apt to feel apprehensive at the prospect of facing a roomful of students. Will they be able to hide their nervousness? Will their knowledge of the subject be adequate for the task? Will they be able to handle discipline problems? These questions and many others may cause concern as they face the future—a future that will see them transformed from science students to teachers of science.

■ WHY STUDENT TEACH?

The student-teaching experience is designed to smooth the transition from the role of student to that of teacher. It is the students' opportunity to test their liking for the teaching task. They will discover whether they really enjoy teaching the subject for which they have prepared themselves. They will learn through their close contacts with children whether they are really interested in teaching children of the particular age level for which they are assigned. Most important of all, they will, it is hoped, find a genuine enthusiasm in the teaching task, an enthusiasm sufficient to convince them that this should be their chosen vocation. At the same time, the student-teaching assignment will give the training institution an opportunity to evaluate students' teaching capabilities. Successful student-teaching experiences, under the supervision of qualified classroom teachers, will enable the training institution to place its stamp of approval on the student teachers' work, with reasonable assurance of their future success.

The prospective science teacher can confidently expect to gain the following values from the student-teaching experience. These values will not accrue automatically. Much of the responsibility rests with the student teachers as they attempt to profit from this culminating experience in their teacher training.

1. *Improvement in Confidence.* Actual experience with a science class will take away the fear of the unknown that everyone experiences when faced with a new situation. Many of these fears may turn out to be groundless. The experience will actually prove to be fun and exhilarating once the initial uneasiness is overcome. Psychologists have learned that the way to overcome the butterflies of fear of the unexpected is to become deeply involved in the experience. The immediacy of the routine problems then supersedes the anticipated difficulties.

2. *Putting Theories into Practice.* Here new teachers will be able to test what they have learned in methods classes (and in other classes) about ways of handling various problems. Handling individual differences among students, discipline cases, techniques of presenting science material, laboratory methods, working with small groups, etc., will provide situations in which student teachers can apply educational theories to classroom reality.

3. *Learning About Student Behavior.* Firsthand, responsible relationships with students will give student teachers the chance to study them, observe their behavior under a variety of conditions, and learn about motivation, competition, enthusiasm, boredom, and many other factors which make up the climate of a typical classroom.

4. *Testing Knowledge of Subject Matter.* Regardless of the student teachers' self-assurance and confidence in their own knowledge of the subject they are planning to teach, there is likely to be a certain amount of apprehension about their ability to transmit this knowledge to others. The responsibility of teaching enthusiastic and sometimes critical students can be unnerving and is certain to convince student teachers of the necessity of knowing their subject thoroughly and of preparing for their contacts with the class. One frequently hears the comment, even among experienced teachers, "I really learned my subject when I had to teach it."

5. *Receiving Constructive Criticism.* At no other time in their long-term teaching experiences will student teachers have the benefit of prolonged, intensive observation of their teaching by an experienced teacher who can be constructive in criticism and advice. This value is not to be taken lightly. If the criticism and suggestions are taken receptively, with the intention of putting them into practice, this experience can be the most valuable part of the student teacher's assignment. It is important, therefore, to select one's supervising teacher wisely. The chance to

Student teaching offers an opportunity to study students' behavior and what motivates them.

observe and be observed by a master teacher in an atmosphere of mutual respect and helpfulness is immeasurably worthwhile.

6. *Discovering Teaching Strengths and Weaknesses.* Student teachers will have the opportunity to discover their own strong and weak points in the handling of science classes. They may find that performing demonstrations results in the most successful teaching and gives them the most pleasure. It may be that organizing classes into effective discussion groups brings about maximum learning under their direction. The questioning technique and the Socratic method of carrying on teacher-pupil discussions may be most successful under their guidance. On the other hand, these same activities may be the least effective for them. Knowing these facts early in their career will enable them to improve their weaknesses and capitalize on their strengths. It is certainly to the advantage of a science teacher to be highly competent in many methods of teaching, but it is equally important to recognize that individual teachers have certain innate teaching strengths and should use techniques that capitalize on these strengths.

7. *Gaining Poise and Finesse.* Because teaching is as much an art as a technique, experience should improve ways of handling classes (such as, anticipating student questions and problems, timing, exploiting enthusiastic and dramatic classroom events, sensing the proper time for introducing a new activity, and commending good work). These factors will contribute to smoother functioning of class activities and generally more

effective learning. It is important to recognize, of course, that this kind of improvement will continue as long as a teacher teaches and that rarely, if ever, does a teacher reach complete perfection in the art.

Selecting Your Supervising Teacher

Frequently, a certain amount of latitude is allowed the prospective student teachers in their choice of school, subject, and teacher under whom they wish to work. The extent of this freedom will vary with the institution and circumstances in which the student-teaching program is operated, and it is entirely possible that assignments may be made quite arbitrarily. However, it is more likely that, within certain limitations, the wishes of the student will be taken into consideration.

Therefore, it is to the advantage of the student teacher to make a careful selection of school, subject, and supervising teacher. Often, new teachers feel that their student-teaching assignment was the most valuable experience in their training program. This can be true if the selection is well made and the experience fulfills its potential.

Prospective student teachers should obtain the maximum advantage by teaching in their major field. It is this area for which they are best prepared and in which they will probably feel the greatest confidence. If the situation permits, teaching in their minor field also, under a different supervising teacher, may be advantageous; they will benefit from constructive help from two experienced teachers. This experience may be analogous to an actual

A new student teacher tries out his skills while the supervising teacher looks on.

situation as a full-time teacher in a small or medium-sized school system.

It would be wise to visit several classes in a number of schools in the quarter or semester before your student-teaching assignment. Arrangements can be made through the principal of the school, and advance notice can be given to the teachers involved. If the purpose of the visits is explained, the prospective student teacher will probably be favorably received, particularly if it is a school in which student teachers have customarily been supervised.

The advantages of the visit can be manifold. Students will be able to refresh their memory of the atmosphere and activities of a high school classroom. They will be able to observe an experienced teacher in action. They will mentally attempt to project themselves into an equivalent situation as a teacher in charge of a class, a desirable step in preparation for their actual student-teaching assignment. They may be able to talk briefly with the teacher at the close of class to gain further insights. After several such visits to a variety of classes (including several outside the field of science), prospective student teachers will be able to choose more intelligently the kind of teaching situation they wish to select for their student-teaching experience.

Some suggestions of criteria to look for in the teaching situation are:

1. Is the teacher well prepared, and is she/he teaching in her/his major field?
2. Does the teacher have good control of the class?
3. Do the students appear to be alert and interested in the activities?

4. Is there a genuine atmosphere of learning?
5. Do the facilities and materials appear to be adequate for the kind of science being taught?
6. Does it appear that the teacher is a person from whom one can learn valuable teaching techniques?
7. Is there opportunity for a certain degree of flexibility in carrying out one's teaching plans?
8. Does the teacher have a moderate work load, thus affording time for constructive help for a student teacher?
9. Does the teacher appear to be interested in serving as a supervisor for a student teacher in her or his charge?

Meeting Your Supervising Teacher

Once the assignment is made for a particular school, class, and teacher, it is imperative that the student teacher arrange for a short interview before attendance at the first class. This interview can be brief but should be a day or two in advance and by appointment. You will then avoid incurring the displeasure of the supervising teacher by intruding on her or his last-minute preparation for class and will provide for an interchange of questions and answers.

At the interview the student teacher should be punctual, interested, enthusiastic, and suitably dressed. The purpose of the interview is to become acquainted and to exchange ideas and information. The supervising teacher is interested in knowing the background and preparation of the student teacher. She or he is also interested in any special qualifications the student teacher may have, such as the ability to handle audiovisual equipment, take charge of a science club, or talk on travel experiences. The student teacher is interested in learning what her or his role is to be in the classroom, what meetings she or he should attend, what text materials are in use, etc.

The supervising teacher will probably suggest a period of class observation, perhaps a week or two, at the outset. There may be certain room duties to perform, such as roll-taking, reading announcements, and distributing materials. Each of these tasks will enable the student teacher to learn the names of pupils quickly, a necessary step in establishing rapport with members of the class. The student teacher will probably be encouraged to prepare a seating chart immediately. Text materials may be discussed and the teacher's long-range objectives clarified. The student teacher will probably be asked to read certain assignments so that she or he will be acquainted with the students' present studies. She or he will find it imperative to do this regularly in order to best assist students who need help.

Facilities and apparatus available for teaching the science class may be shown to the student teacher during the interview. Location of the library and special preparation rooms may be pointed out. The place in the classroom where the student teacher may observe the activities of the class may be designated. (In one school, it was customary for the student teacher to sit next to the demonstration desk, facing the class. In this way, she learned to recognize pupils more quickly; but, more importantly, this arrangement enabled the student teacher to see the expressions on the faces of the pupils as they responded to questions or watched a demonstration, as they showed perplexity or registered insight into problems under discussion.)

Students who intend to teach in urban-area schools are advised to seek out student-teaching experiences that will give them the best possible preparation for such an assignment. Such an experience might involve student teaching in a school similar to the type they wish to be teaching in ultimately.

■ BEING A STUDENT TEACHER

Your First Days in the Class

Observing pupils in the science class can be a profitable experience the first few days or weeks. Student teachers have an advantage in this situation because they are not preoccupied with teaching plans and conducting the class, as is the regular teacher. The alert student teacher can, in fact, be of assistance to the regular teacher in recognizing incipient discipline problems, lack of interest, or special conditions that might lead to better teaching if recognized early.

Student teachers may wish to follow a systematic observation program to become familiar with all class members. For this purpose, a checklist of individual differences is suggested. Place a check mark in the column opposite the observed characteristic. The numbers represent individual pupils observed.

Recognizing Individual Differences in a New Class During the First Few Weeks[1]
Things to observe and consider:

Pupils 1 2 3 4

1. Health
2. Physical defects and differences
3. Personality
4. Basic skills
5. Relationships with fellow pupils
6. Relationship with teacher
7. Class participation
8. Class attitude and cooperation
9. Dependability
10. Probable ability combined with effort

The first days in the student-teaching class should afford opportunities to give individual help to pupils who need it. Do not answer questions directly but use inquiry methods—that is, ask guiding questions. It is wise to confer with the supervising teacher about the extent of such help. There may be some reason to withhold assistance on certain assignments. At the same time, contact with students on an individual basis is an excellent way to gain confidence in your ability to explain, teach, or convey information. The student teacher should capitalize on every possible opportunity to develop this skill.

If the science class is one in which laboratory work plays a large part (i.e., chemistry, physics, biology, or earth science), there will be many opportunities to give individual help. The student teacher can also be of significant help to the regular teacher in preparing laboratory apparatus and supplies. In this situation the student teacher will realize that teaching a laboratory science requires extensive planning and attention to detail.

Because the initial period of observation may be rather brief, perhaps only a few days or a week, student teachers will do well to begin thinking about the choice of a teaching area or unit. Such a choice may have already been made in conference with the supervising teacher. It will certainly depend on the subject-matter goals of the course during the semester or quarter of the assignment. In anticipation of their student teaching, students will wish to gather

■■■■■■■■■■■■■■■■ **GUEST EDITORIAL** ■■■■■■■■■■■■■■■■■■■■■■■

Student Teaching in Science

Melinda Bell
Student Teacher
Northfield Senior High School
Northfield, Minnesota

"We never learn as much with a student teacher."

"The student teachers are always nervous, lack confidence, and can't keep the classes under control."

"The student teachers expect us to be like college students because that is what they are most familiar with."

These comments were generated by high school students in the school where I am doing my student teaching. I think it is important to take them seriously, although I will rapidly deny that they characterize each and every student teacher. Sure, we're all bound to be a little nervous and to be somewhat unsure of how to discipline or how to present material so it is clear, understandable, and interesting to the students. But that doesn't mean we have to be bogged down by those things!

There is so much else that we, as student teachers, have going for us. We are well-armed with a knowledge of our subject and a delightful artillery of methods in which we can present our material. We are bright and enthusiastic and willing to try things in new, innovative ways. We have taken a science teaching methods course that has hopefully prepared us in some other ways. We even have students who will see advantages in our being there!

"Student teachers are young and don't seem as fuddy-duddy as the regular teacher."

"Student teachers are more on our level so they are easier to approach."

"Sometimes the student teacher can explain things in a different way than the regular teacher so more students understand it."

All of these things don't make student teaching easy; rather, they make it an exciting challenge and an opportunity for you to practice your skills—accepting the lesson plans that don't work, as well as feeling accomplishment and pride when your lesson goes over well, and the students get excited about something that you taught them! Not all of your students are going to enjoy you as a teacher, but some will welcome you openly, along with the fresh change and enthusiasm you bring to the classroom.

Some of my friends are amazed by the amount of enjoyment I get out of student teaching.

"Don't you get bored teaching the same material over and over?" is a question commonly asked.

---

appropriate materials and to prepare general plans. Some of the details of the preliminary planning are considered in the next section.

Preparing to Teach a Lesson

Some of the problems involved in lesson planning are detailed in chapter fifteen. However, a brief review of the salient factors may be worthwhile.

A teacher facing a class for the first time may expect to accomplish far too much in a given amount of time. Although it is not necessarily wasteful to overplan a lesson, it is a mistake to try to teach everything on the lesson plan just because it is there. Sometimes the learning pace of the pupils does not allow the entire lesson plan to be completed. You must constantly be in tune with your class, sensing the proper pace and modifying your presentation as the situation demands.

A second common fault of the beginning teacher is the tendency to teach beyond the students' comprehension. This fault may be a result of recent contact with college courses, in which the level is very high, or the inability to place abstract ideas into concrete terms for comprehension by secondary school students. The problem is important enough that beginning teachers make certain that their presentation is at the appropriate level for the class involved. Perhaps they could try a few test trials with individual students to acquire a realistic sense of the proper difficulty level before they teach the entire class.

Construction of unit and daily lesson plans is an important task at this stage (see chapter fifteen for suggested formats). It is important to have a clear idea of what you wish to accomplish in the allotted time and what specific objectives are to be met. Student teachers should attempt to place themselves in the position of a science pupil who is learning

■■

Once I've recovered from the shock of picturing myself bored, I reply that I can teach the same or similar materials in such a variety of ways that it remains interesting to me. In fact, the personalities of each class are generally so varied that the best way of presenting the material to one class might be the worst method for another. Gauging the class correctly and presenting the material in a suitable manner for that class is the challenge in making the lesson a successful one.

My friends also worry that teaching will not be intellectually satisfying enough for me. After all, it is only high school material! That is the *least* of my worries! I really learned about DNA when I had to understand it thoroughly enough to answer the students' questions on it, and when I had to be able to explain what newspaper articles meant when they talked about genetic engineering. To make DNA relevant, I had to ensure that it touched something that they are conscious of as happening in the world today. That holds for whether we are talking about DNA and test-tube babies or about photosynthesis and the greenhouse effect. If it doesn't make sense to them and if they don't find it relevant, it will be rapidly forgotten.

The intellectual challenge for me is to keep up on the recent advances in different areas of science and understand how these advances are applicable to the students' world today.

Some people are curious as to why I am going into education when I could go on into research or a medical profession. Selfishly, it is because I hope that I will be an influence through teaching and other aspects of my life in helping people to understand that every decision they make is a reflection on how they look at the world. And science to me has an important message for everyone. Science is a way of looking at the world and dealing with the world on a physical level. Science gives us a method we can use for finding solutions to problems that come up in everyday life. It is unfortunate that science, for many people, is an object to be feared or held in mystified awe. Science is not magic. It is merely a way of putting curiosity and creativity together to come up with reasonable explanations for unanswered questions.

Not everyone has the capacity to become a nuclear physicist, but everyone can learn what processes a scientist goes through in his or her thinking and can apply these same methods to areas of his or her own life. If I can get that across to my students, I will feel that I have accomplished something.

Because I believe in science and because I am excited about the things we can learn from it, I want to share that with others. My own interest in it causes me to be enthusiastic and to remain involved myself.

about the material for the first time. They should consider factors of interest, motivation, individual differences, time limitations, facilities, and equipment; they should try to anticipate the kinds of problems that may occur and prepare possible solutions. When they have considered these elements, they will feel more secure and will have fewer discipline problems.

Beginning teachers should also anticipate questions from the class. First attempts at planning tend to neglect preparation for handling these questions and fail to provide enough time for dealing with them in the class period. Yet the frank interchange of ideas between teacher and students, which is provoked by questions, can be an effective teaching technique and should not be ignored. In planning, try to anticipate the kinds of questions students may ask. If you remember that the students may be encountering the subject matter for the first time, it

is not too difficult to foretell what questions may come to their minds. Jot down these probable questions on your lesson plan, along with suitable answers or with suggested procedures for finding the answers. Time spent in this manner is not wasted, even if the specific anticipated questions do not arise. Beginning teachers will gain confidence in their own understanding of the subject matter and in their ability to provide suitable answers.

A final point to consider is that of proper pacing and timing of the class period. The written lesson plans may have suggested time allotments for various activities, but the actual class is certain to deviate to some extent. The important thing is to be flexible enough to accommodate minor variations within the class period. However, to avoid gross miscalculations of time requirements for certain activities, rehearse them in advance. A short lecture, for example, can be tried out on one's roommate, who will be able to give critical comments on clarity and organization, as well as timing. In the case of student activities or laboratory work, it is usually advisable to allot about 50 percent more time than appears adequate for the teacher to do the work. This leeway is also recommended in giving written tests.

At all stages of planning for the first day of teaching, it is imperative that student teachers keep the supervising teacher informed of their plans, solicit advice and assistance, and, in general, plan in such a way as to make the transition from regular teacher to student teacher as smooth as possible.

The First Day of Teaching

If student teachers have had frequent opportunities to work with individuals and small groups before their first day of actual teaching, they will find the new experience a natural extension of these tasks and a challenging opportunity for growth in the art of teaching.

A good introduction will get the class off to an interesting start. A brief explanation of the purpose of the lesson and the work at hand, followed immediately by plunging into the class activities, will convey to the students an appreciation of the tasks to be accomplished. A forthright and businesslike manner by the student teacher will elicit class cooperation and leave no doubt about who is in charge.

Attention should be given to proper speech and voice modulation. A good pace should be maintained, and, above all, genuine enthusiasm must be displayed. This enthusiasm will normally be infectious and will secure an enthusiastic response from the class. If possible, students should be encouraged to participate. Questions from students should be encouraged and a relaxed atmosphere maintained for free interchange of ideas.

It is usually advisable, especially with junior high school classes, to vary the activity once or twice during the class period. Perhaps a short lecture can be followed by a brief film and the period concluded with a summarizing discussion. Or a demonstration by the teacher might be followed by a period of individual experimentation. It is true that planning and execution of a varied class period requires more work on the part of the teacher, but the dividends appear in the form of enthusiasm, alert attention, and better learning.

The last five or ten minutes of a class period are often used to summarize the major points of the lesson and to make appropriate assignments. It is important to recognize that students need to have a feeling of accomplishment and progress to keep their motivation high. A final clarification of what is expected of them in preparation for succeeding

lessons is worth a few minutes at the close of a class period.

Completion of the first day of teaching by the student teacher should be followed as soon as possible by reflection on the successes and failures of the class period and an effort to diagnose any problems that may have arisen. This evaluation can usually be done profitably in conference with the supervising teacher and can be a useful follow-up to the day. Any required adjustments in future plans can be made at this time, necessary additional materials can be gathered, and the stage can be set for a new day of teaching to follow.

Your Responsibilities

The opportunity to student teach in a given school system under a competent supervising teacher should be considered a privilege. Contrary to an apprentice in a typical trade situation, the apprentice teacher is not working with inanimate materials, such as wood and metal, but with live human beings of infinite worth. Student teachers must never forget their responsibility to provide the best possible education for the students and to avoid possible harmful measures.

It is, therefore, extremely important to make lesson plans with care, to consider individual differences in interest and ability, and to conduct the class in an atmosphere of friendly helpfulness. Each student should be considered a potential learning being with capabilities for infinite growth. The teacher's responsibility is to develop this potential to the maximum extent.

The student teacher's responsibility to the supervising teacher rests in the area of recognition of authority and respect for experience. Certainly, there may be disagreements about teaching methods, but the final authority is the supervising teacher, who is officially responsible for the class. At the same time, an alert student teacher can be of great help by anticipating the needs of the class, suggesting materials, preparing materials, and in general earning the title of assistant teacher, which is used in some school systems. The varied backgrounds of student teachers and their willingness to share experiences and special talents can make the science classroom more interesting and educationally effective.

The responsibility of student teachers toward themselves and their potential as science teachers is also important. It would be relatively easy to sit casually by, waiting for things to happen in the student-teaching assignment. The student teachers who gain the most, however, from the standpoint of personal growth, will be those who enter into the experience with a dynamic approach, intent on learning everything they can in the time allotted. They will participate, when permitted, in meetings of the school faculty, in attendance and assistance at school athletic events, in dramatic and musical productions of the school, and other functions relating to school life. In this way they will see their pupils in many roles outside of the science classroom and will gain insight into the total school program. They will be able to achieve a balanced perspective of their own role as teachers of science among the other academic disciplines and curricular activities. Such experience will enable them to become mature teachers of science and will complete the metamorphosis from the role of college science student.

Concerns of the Student Teacher

A questionnaire listing nine areas of preparation was distributed to forty student teachers of secondary science at the University of Northern Colorado. They were asked to indicate those areas in which they felt the need of greater preparation.

Four areas receiving the greatest number of responses were: evaluating students and grading, handling discipline problems, answering students' questions, and stronger preparation in subject matter, in that order. Other areas of consideration were: lesson planning, record keeping, extracurricular activities, demonstrations, and handling laboratory work.

In the same survey, when asked to suggest improvements in the methods courses in physical and biological sciences, the following suggestions were made:

1. Put more emphasis on discipline, problems, and on answering students' questions.
2. Have more discussion on techniques for handling slow and fast learners.
3. Do more demonstrations and experiments.
4. Emphasize methods of evaluation.
5. Provide opportunities to hear the experiences of recent student teachers.
6. Evaluate the texts and materials of the new secondary curriculum projects.
7. Provide more opportunities to speak in front of a group and do demonstration teaching.
8. Cover a greater variety of topics, including test construction, extra-credit work, interest development, grouping of students, policies regarding student failures, science fairs and exhibits, etc.
9. Provide opportunities to observe several teachers in one's field.
10. Acquire more information on specific source-books of activities, demonstrations, and experiments.

■ PROFESSIONAL DEVELOPMENT STANDARDS

The *National Science Education Standards* provide criteria for judging the opportunities and activities available for prospective and practicing teachers of science. Among these criteria is a recurring reference to the requirement of learning a breadth and depth of science content through the perspectives and methods of inquiry. Teachers must be actively involved in investigating scientific phenomena, interpreting results, and making sense of the findings. Problems should be organized around significant issues and events and should give opportunities to practice inquiry skills. There must also be opportunities to integrate science knowledge, pedagogy, and understanding of students.

A further interesting standard is that schools must become *Centers of Inquiry* that support the professional growth of science teachers. This includes involving teachers in leadership roles and providing an environment for support of new science teachers in their classroom responsibilities.

■ LICENSURE OPTIONS

Some states require prospective teachers to take certain mandated tests before securing approval to teach in the state's schools. One example is the state of Colorado, which requires, as a result of the recent passage of the Educator Licensing Act, four assessments in the field of preservice education. Licensure requires four tests. An entry test in basic skills is followed by three exit tests in: (1) liberal arts and sciences (general education), (2) professional knowledge, and (3) content knowledge. The tests are called the Program of Licensing Assessments for Colorado Educators (PLACE) Exams. The tests are designed by the National Evaluation Systems of Amherst, MA in contract with the state of Colorado.

Other states have implemented or are considering implementation of similar preservice licensing procedures.

Becoming a Professional

The science teacher today is a member of a dedicated group of professional educators that includes classroom teachers, supervisors, coordinators, administrators, and other educational specialists. This group has the responsibility for developing curriculum plans and effectively teaching the nation's youth.

Science teachers greatly influence our country's young people. Science courses are regarded as respectable academic subjects in any secondary curriculum, along with such courses as mathematics, English, foreign languages, and social sciences. The science teacher, by virtue of subject choice, is viewed with respect by other teachers and by laypeople of the community.

The young science teacher cannot help but feel pride in being a part of the science teaching profession. Science holds the spotlight in many of our country's schools. It is an exciting time to be a science teacher, and the rewards are abundant. Along with a favorable focus of attention comes responsibility for dedication to the task and for self-improvement as a teacher. It is for this reason that in this chapter attention is directed to the preparation of the professional science educator.

Prospective science teachers in an undergraduate program at a college or university are nearing their goal of becoming qualified specialists in their subject. In most cases their decision to prepare themselves as teachers of a particular science subject was made early in their college career on the basis of interest, environmental background, previous training, and prospective rewards in the teaching field. As they approach the end of their training, prospective teachers look forward to an interesting and productive career as professional educators in a demanding field. They are concerned that their training has been adequate for the task and that they will be successful in meeting the challenges ahead.

Even if you obtain the best undergraduate preparation available to the prospective science teacher, it is a mistake to assume that your goal has been reached when you are granted your bachelor's degree. Because of the rapid and continuing pace of science achievements and the ever-changing pattern of teaching methods and curriculum organization, the science teacher must constantly be alert to new knowledge and new techniques. For this reason, conscientious science teachers will consider that their education is never finished as long as they wish to remain effective contributors to their profession.

■ SECURING A TEACHING POSITION

Recent years have shown a fluctuating job market for teachers. Prospective teachers must work diligently at finding a suitable position. Competition is high, and they must use all available avenues to secure a satisfactory teaching job.

Getting Ready to Look for a Job

As preparation to enter the job market, there are several necessary steps. Prospective employees of a school system will wish to secure several recommendations from their college instructors in their major and minor fields, their methods instructors, and perhaps others of their own choosing. Be sure to obtain permission to use an instructor's name for a reference and request the recommendation personally, either by letter or by personal conversation. Remember that instructors are asked to write many recommendations and that a thoughtful instructor will put in a reasonable amount of time in writing a good one. To make the job as easy as possible, supply your instructor with specific information about yourself. For example, provide information on your hobbies and on your experiences in working with children, such as coaching, camp counseling, summer recreation programs, Sunday school teaching, etc. Relate any special competencies that you have, such as the ability to handle a photography club, or special knowledge of rocks and minerals, or model airplane building, or any other relevant experiences. Give specific evidence of the kinds of experiences that would qualify you to be a good science teacher. This kind of information will pay off and will secure for you the immediate attention of a thoughtful school administrator.

When requesting a recommendation, if the contact with the instructor is several months old, it is a good idea to supply a snapshot of yourself to refresh your instructor's memory. A sample recommendation request form is shown in Figure 24–1.

Using Placement Services

You will probably wish to use one or more teacher placement services to secure a satisfactory position. Most teacher-training institutions have placement offices. There may be an enrollment fee for this service. You would be well advised to get all of your required materials in early, usually by January 1, because the placement offices begin to make appointments with school administrators early in the new year to interview applicants for positions. If you are conscientious about submitting all of your requirements, you will be eligible to meet with prospective employers.

Second, many state departments of education have placement bureaus. It is wise to contact them and give them the necessary information so that they can assist you in locating vacancies within the state where you plan to teach.

Letters of Application

Once you have been notified of a suitable vacancy for which you wish to apply, you must prepare a letter of application that will be considered favorably by the recipient. If you plan to type your own application letter, it is a good idea to check with someone to

FIGURE 24–1
Sample recommendation request form

Personal Recommendation

Name_____

Classes from me _____

_____

Grades_____

Because many of you will be applying for teaching jobs (or other jobs in the near future), you will be required to obtain letters of recommendation for your files at the Office of Appointments. If requested to write such a recommendation, I shall be happy to oblige but I should like to have some further information about you to include in the recommendation. It is my belief that the following types of information can be very meaningful to a prospective employer and may make the difference between being hired and not being hired.

Please give information on the following points.

1. Any experience you have had working with young people in any capacity other than practice teaching, such as scout leader, Sunday school teacher, swimming instructor, camp counselor, or other. Give specific information.
2. Any scientific hobbies or specialties you may have (past or present), such as specimen collecting, lapidary, ham radio, model airplane building, amateur telescope making, special reading in a topic, expertise with computers, etc.
3. Any travel you have done which may have been scientifically broadening or educational, such as Carlsbad Caverns, Grand Canyon, Yellowstone Park, or any others.
4. Any other experiential information which may be important for a prospective employer to know.

refresh your memory on style and form. In many cases, your letter of application will merely elicit a standard application form from the school to which you apply. In this case, give the complete information required by the school.

If possible, have your letter of application typed by a professional. This adds quality and dignity to the correspondence, and you will impress the recipient. A poorly constructed letter with typographical errors, erasures, and other evidence of carelessness will certainly get tossed into the reject file.

In your letter of application, be sure to include all of the necessary information to give a clear picture of your qualifications for the job for which you are applying. Include your major and minor teaching areas, information on special competencies (such as ability to handle specific types of clubs), and information on your familiarity with new teaching trends (such as inquiry teaching, team teaching, individualized instruction, new curriculum projects, open-school concepts, and other current trends).

You might conclude the letter by volunteering your willingness to meet the superintendent for an interview at a mutually convenient time. A sample letter of application you might use as a guide is shown in Figure 24–2.

The Job Interview

If you are interviewed by the principal or superintendent of schools, you will wish to present yourself in the best possible manner. Be sure to arrive on time, dress appropriately, and be well-groomed. Allow the employer to conduct the interview at his or her own pace and in his or her own manner. Supply information about yourself as requested. If asked, discuss your philosophy of teaching briefly, tell about your training and special competencies, and mention your professional memberships (such as the NSTA, Academies of Science, National Association of Biology Teachers (NABT), and other organizations to which you belong.)

You will have the opportunity to ask questions. You will want to know some of the details of the position, such as the level of the class, its probable size, the text materials that are used, and the availability of supplies. Perhaps you will want to ask questions about the community, such as the availability of

FIGURE 24–2
Sample letter of application

January 12, 1986
123 Hope Avenue
Caton, MO

Dr. Harold Oglesby
Superintendent of Schools
Wichita Falls, Missouri

Dear Dr. Oglesby:

I wish to apply for the position as teacher of junior high school science announced as a vacancy in your school system. The placement office at Webster State College, Webster, Kansas, will send my complete credentials.

My major teaching area is junior high school science and my minor is mathematics. In addition, I have secured a teacher's permit for driver education and am qualified to give the driver education course for the state of Missouri.

Photography has been a hobby and a vocation of mine for many years, and I would be interested in supervising a junior high school photography club.

I shall be happy to come for a personal interview at your convenience.

Sincerely yours,

John Tryst

housing, churches, and recreation facilities. Let the interviewer supply you with information on the prospective salary and other fringe benefits associated with the job.

After Obtaining the Job

Securing a position as a new teacher is a major accomplishment and may give you the feeling that your teaching career is set for all time. However, this would be a short-sighted view. Of course it should be your intention to remain on the job with the expectation of doing excellent work, but you should also recognize that you may want to move upward professionally. Therefore, it is a good idea to keep your placement file up to date. Keep in contact with the placement office by informing them of any new coursework you have taken, such as institutes or summer school attendance. Have updated transcripts supplied to the placement office, which may include the completion of a new degree or additional coursework. When you are ready to apply for a new position, be sure to get recommendations from your principal and supervisor.

■ SCIENCE-TEACHING STANDARDS

The current teaching standards of the *National Science Education Standards* provide criteria to be used in making judgments about the quality of teaching in science classrooms. They set forth a vision of good science teaching to be used as a model for prospective and practicing teachers of science. Several roles and responsibilities are outlined in the following areas:

1. Teachers of science should plan inquiry-based programs for their students. This means selecting science content and curriculum directions to meet student interests, knowledge, skills, and experiences. It also means using teaching strategies that develop understanding and skills for doing inquiry science.

2. Teachers should interact with students to focus and support their inquiries, recognize diversity and provide opportunities for all children to participate fully in science learning, and challenge students to take responsibility for individual as well as collaborative learning.

3. Teachers should engage in ongoing assessment of their teaching and of resulting student learning. There should be formal assessment activities, as well as guidance, for students to do meaningful self-assessment.

4. Conditions for learning should provide students with time, space, and resources needed for successful science learning. This includes adequate tools and materials, as well as a safe working environment.

5. Teachers should foster habits of mind, attitudes, and values of science by being good role models for these attributes.

6. It is important for teachers to become active participants in on-going planning and development of the school science program. This includes taking leadership roles and developing their own professional growth potential.

■ CHARACTERISTICS OF A GOOD SCIENCE TEACHER

Administrators and supervisors constantly evaluate teachers for salary increments, promotions to department chair, differentiated staffing, and other reasons. Unfortunately, many evaluations are made on the basis of superficial characteristics or personal qualities that happen to please or displease the evaluator, rather than on more basic characteristics that exemplify good teaching. Following is a question checklist that can be used by an administrator, supervisor, or by the science teacher for self-evaluation.[2]

Question Checklist

1. Is the teacher enthusiastic about what she/he is doing and does she/he show it?

2. Is the teacher dynamic and does she/he use her/his voice and facial expression for emphasis and to hold attention?

3. Does the teacher use gadgets or other illustrative devices extensively to make each new learning experience as concrete as possible?

4. Does the teacher show originality in making teaching materials from simple or found objects?

5. Does the teacher have a functional knowledge of her/his subject so that she/he can apply what she/he knows to everyday living?

6. Does the teacher possess the ability to explain ideas in simple terms regardless of the extent of her/his knowledge?

7. Does the teacher stimulate actual thought on the part of her/his students, or does she/he make parrots out of them?

8. Is the teacher a have-to-finish-the-book type of teacher, or does she/he teach thoroughly?

9. Does the teacher maintain calm and poise in the most trying of classroom circumstances?

10. Does the teacher use a variety of teaching techniques, or is it the same thing day after day?

11. Does the teacher exhibit confidence, and are the students confident about her/his ability?

12. Does the teacher encourage class participation and questions, and does she/he conscientiously plan for them?

13. Does the teacher maintain a good instructional tempo so that the period does not drag?

14. Does the teacher use techniques to stimulate interest at the beginning of new material, or does she/he treat it merely as something new to be learned?

15. Does the teacher concentrate on key ideas and use facts as means to an end?

Of a more formal nature is the *Stanford Teacher Competence Appraisal Guide.*[3] It may be used to assist the individual teacher in assessing her/his strengths and weaknesses, or it may be used for formal evaluation purposes. For rating, each item may be evaluated on the basis of eight points and totaled for a cumulative score. The ratings are:

0	Unable to observe
4	Strong
1	Weak
5	Superior
2	Below average
6	Outstanding
3	Average
7	Truly exceptional

Stanford Teacher Competence Appraisal Guide

Aims

1. *Clarity of aims.* The purposes of the lesson are clear.

2. *Appropriateness of aims.* The aims are neither too easy nor too difficult for the pupils. They are appropriate and are accepted by the pupils.

Planning

3. *Organization of the lesson.* The individual parts of the lesson are clearly related to each other in an appropriate way. The total organization facilitates what is to be learned.

4. *Selection of content.* The content is appropriate for the aims of the lesson, the level of the class, and the teaching method.

5. *Selection of materials.* The specific instructional materials and human resources used are clearly related to the content of the lesson and complement the selected method of instruction.

Performance

6. *Beginning the lesson.* Students come quickly to attention. They direct themselves to the tasks to be accomplished.

7. *Clarity of presentation.* The content of the lesson is presented so that it is understandable to the pupils. Different points of view and specific illustrations are used when appropriate.

8. *Pacing of the lesson.* The movement from one part of the lesson to the next is governed by the

students' achievement. In pacing, the teacher stays with the class and adjusts the tempo accordingly.

9. *Pupil participation and attention.* The class is attentive. When appropriate, students actively participate in the lesson.
10. *Ending the lesson.* The lesson is ended when the students have achieved the aims of instruction. The teacher ties together chance and planned events and relates them to long-range aim of instruction.
11. *Teacher-student rapport.* The personal relationships between students and teacher are harmonious.

Evaluation

12. *Variety of evaluative procedures.* The teacher devises and uses an adequate variety of procedures, both formal and informal, to evaluate progress in all of the aims of instruction.
13. *Use of evaluation to provide improvement of teaching and learning.* The results of evaluation are carefully reviewed by teacher and students to improve teaching and learning.

Professional

14. *Concern for professional standards and growth.* The teacher helps, particularly in her/his specialty, to define and enforce standards for: (1) selecting, training, and licensing teachers; and (2) working conditions.
15. *Effectiveness in school staff relationships.* The teacher is respectful and considerate of colleagues, and demonstrates awareness of their personal concerns and professional development.
16. *Concern for the total school program.* The teacher's concern is not simply for her/his courses and her/his students. She/he works with other teachers, students, and administrators to bring about the program's success.
17. *Constructive participation in community affairs.* The teacher understands the particular community context in which she/he works and helps to translate the purposes of the school's program to the community.

■ RESEARCH ON SCIENCE TEACHER CHARACTERISTICS

In 1980, Cynthia Druva and Ronald Anderson carried out a research project, using the principles of meta-analysis of research, that focused on science teacher characteristics.[4] The results were reported by displaying correlations between these identified teacher characteristics, teacher behavior, and student outcomes. The meta-analysis was conducted of research

studies that used characteristics of gender, course work, I.Q., and so forth, as independent variables; and as dependent variables: (1) teaching behavior in the classroom, such as questioning behavior and teaching orientation; and (2) student outcome characteristics, such as achievement and attitudes toward science. The subject population was chosen from teachers and students in science classes throughout the United States from kindergarten through 12th grade.

With respect to the relationships between teacher characteristics and teacher behavior, the following outcomes were reported:

1. Teaching effectiveness is positively related to training and experience as evidenced by the number of education courses, student-teaching grade, and teaching experience.
2. Teachers with a more positive attitude toward the curriculum that they are teaching tend to be those with a higher grade-point average and more teaching experience.
3. Better classroom discipline is associated with the teacher characteristics of restraint and reflectivity.
4. Higher level, more complex questions were employed more often by teachers with greater knowledge and less experience in teaching.

With respect to the relationships between teacher characteristics and student outcomes, several relationships were discovered:

1. Student achievement is positively related to teacher characteristics of self-actualization, heterosexuality, and masculinity. It is also related positively to the number of science courses taken and attendance at academic institutes.
2. The process-skill outcomes of students are positively related to the number of science courses taken by teachers.
3. The outcome of a positive attitude toward science was positively associated with the number of science courses taken by teachers and the number of years of teaching experience.

One of the implications of the study is that there is a relationship between teacher preparation programs and what their graduates do as teachers. Science courses, education courses, and overall academic performance are positively associated with successful teaching.

For student teachers the research reported above is significant because it gives direction and guidance to their career and goal preparation. While the results may seem to be natural, common-sense results, it is significant that data now show that teachers with better preparation in science, as well as in the pedagogical areas, do a better job of teaching. Also significant is the finding that a positive attitude toward their task relates to better results for the students in their charge.

One of the difficulties brought about by the daily routine of hard, laborious work in teaching—the incessant planning, paper grading, and all such work—is that this often has a debilitating effect on young teachers. It may cause them to become cynical and skeptical of the results they are achieving. Many times they will tend to blame the students or the system, when in fact it may be the negative attitude they themselves bring to the teaching task that is at least partially responsible for their poor results.

It is very important to maintain zest for teaching. In no other profession is it as important to exhibit a positive and enthusiastic relationship with individuals. Young minds in your charge are vulnerable to your attitudes and enthusiasm as well as your obvious background of preparation and experience. A caring teacher is able to overcome many shortcomings in background and preparation, but an uncaring teacher cannot be successful, though he or she may have excellent preparation in terms of subject matter and teaching techniques.

■ OPPORTUNITIES FOR PROFESSIONAL GROWTH

Among the opportunities for professional growth while on the job are graduate work during the summer or at night, depending on the available opportunities; inservice workshops and institutes; government- or industry-sponsored summer institutes; committee activity on curriculum revision or evaluation; membership in professional organizations, with accompanying attendance at regular meetings and participation in committee work; reading professional journals, scientific publications, and current books in science and teaching; writing for professional publications; and keeping up to date on new materials, teaching resources, and education aids.

Graduate Work

The NSF reported that 39 percent of science and mathematics teachers in the United States have master's degrees and that over 75 percent hold credits for at least ten semester hours of graduate work.[5] Twenty percent had completed at least one NSF summer institute.

There are many opportunities for graduate work. The usual requirement for completion of a master's degree in education is one year or four summers of coursework. Theses are generally not required, but comprehensive examinations in a major and minor

field usually are. The monetary rewards for science teachers with master's degrees are well worth the time and expense involved in obtaining the degree. Most school systems have a salary differential of several hundred dollars for holders of master's degrees; furthermore, opportunities for higher-paying jobs are greater, and a better selection of teaching positions is available for the applicant who holds a master's degree.

Inservice Training and Institutes

Inservice workshops and institutes are usually sponsored by public school systems for improvement of the teachers within that system. Degree credit may or may not be offered, depending on the arrangements with the colleges or universities from which consultant services are obtained. Such workshops and institutes often have objectives designed to stimulate curriculum improvement or to improve teacher competencies in subject-matter understanding and teaching techniques. New teachers are encouraged to avail themselves of these opportunities to familiarize themselves with broad problems of curriculum improvements and to benefit from the experience of older teachers in the system.

Government- or industry-sponsored summer and inservice institutes provide excellent opportunities to grow professionally. Although fewer of these institutes are available now than before, the usual requirement is three years of teaching experience; however, this rule is frequently relaxed for one reason or another.

Dedicated teachers invest time and energy in inservice training to improve their skills and keep their knowledge up to date.

Committee Work

Committee activity is an excellent way to develop a professional attitude and become aware of the many problems facing the science teacher. Active school systems frequently have a curriculum committee, a professional committee, a salary and grievance committee, a textbook-selection committee, or other committees of temporary nature as needed. Participation on one or more of these committees can be enlightening and can contribute to the professional growth of the new teacher; however, committee responsibilities mean extra work, and the new science teacher should consider the total work load and weigh carefully the ultimate benefits of participation.

Professional Organizations

There are many professional organizations serving the science teacher. They are listed here along with their respective journals.

1. American Association of Physics Teachers—the *American Journal of Physics* and *The Physics Teacher*
2. The American Chemical Society—the *Journal of Chemical Education*
3. The National Association of Biology Teachers—*The American Biology Teacher*
4. The National Science Teachers Association—*The Science Teacher, Science and Children, Science Scope,* and *The Journal of College Science Teaching*

Exchanging ideas with other teachers while participating in committee work stimulates professional growth.

5. The School Science and Mathematics Association—*School Science and Mathematics*
6. The National Association for Research in Science Teaching—*Journal of Research in Science Teaching*
7. The American Association for the Advancement of Science—*Science*
8. Council for Elementary Science, International—*Science Education*

Membership in a professional organization carries benefits proportional to the member's active participation in the organization. Attendance at periodic meetings contributes to a sense of cohesiveness and shared objectives, the stimulation of meeting professional coworkers, and the absorption of new ideas. Voluntary participation as a panel member or speaker at a discussion session is a highly beneficial experience. It is not necessarily true that a teacher must have many years of experience before she or he can be considered worthy of a presentation at a professional meeting. A young, enthusiastic science teacher with a fresh approach to a problem can make a definite contribution to a meeting of this type.

Professional journals provide another source of teaching ideas. A science teacher should personally subscribe to one or two and make it a habit to regularly read others that may be purchased by the school library. Occasional contribution of teaching ideas for publication in a professional journal is highly motivating and is to be encouraged. The professional benefits of such a practice are unlimited because it helps one to become known in science teaching circles and to make valuable contacts.

Professional journals usually contain feature articles on subject-matter topics of current interest; ideas for improvement of classroom teaching techniques; information on professional meetings; book reviews; information on teaching materials, apparatus, and resource books; information on career opportunities for secondary school students in science; and information on scholarships and contests for students and teachers.

■ SELF-INVENTORY FOR SCIENCE TEACHERS

The NSTA Commission on Professional Standards and Practices has published a Self-Inventory for Science Teachers.[6] The NSTA has summarized its beliefs concerning the professionalism of science teachers in this way:

The professional science teacher: (a) is well educated in science and the liberal arts, (b) possesses a functional philosophy of education and the technical skills, (c) continues to grow in knowledge and skill throughout his career, (d) insists on a sound educational environment in which to work, (e) maintains his professional status, (f) contributes to the improvement of science teaching, (g) takes a vital interest in the quality of future science teachers.

This is the first time that a science teachers' organization has developed a set of standards against which science teachers can measure themselves and which provides stimulation and motivation for improving their professional practices.

■ EVALUATION OF TEACHERS

Increasingly, teachers are faced with periodic evaluations by their principals, peers, and students. Such evaluations are for the purpose of comparisons, retention, merit pay, salary increments, promotion, and/or tenure. Teacher evaluation is defined as "the process of an external observer (administrator or supervisor) gathering information regarding a teacher's instructional performance to determine the value and worth of that teacher."[7]

In 1987, a study of a teacher evaluation was reported by two researchers at McGill University, William Searles and Naile Kudeki. From the results of their study it was possible to develop a profile of an outstanding science teacher as follows:

The profile of an outstanding science teacher obtained from this study describes a person who is able to maintain a classroom with a pleasant atmosphere where learning can occur, one who is sure of the subject matter being taught, and presents the material to be learned in a clear and effective manner. This person is concerned about the students and ensures that they understand the concepts of science they are being taught by relating new knowledge to that which they already know. This instructor's teaching shows evidence of creativity and resourcefulness by utilizing various materials and methods of teaching as deemed necessary. The teaching is definitely "pupil-centered" for an outstanding science teacher is able to perceive then make provisions for the needs and abilities of the individual student. The teacher is a person who is available after school for those students who need extra help. As an interested, enthusiastic science teacher, the instructor tries to develop the students' interest in science by varying instructional methods to keep up-to-date with contemporary developments in the teaching of science. An outstanding science teacher presents thought-provoking laboratory activities and encourages the students to develop hypotheses and theories. As a self-confident person, the science teacher attempts to develop the attributes of self confidence and motivation in the students. Such an individual is consistently fair and emotionally calm when enforcing the rules of the school, has a good sense of humor, and is respected by the students.

Outside of the classroom, the outstanding science teacher cooperates with colleagues, consults with them in case of difficulties, is interested in academic self-improvement, and keeps up-to-date with scientific developments by reading journals and taking refresher courses.[8]

■ SUMMARY

Student teaching is the most important phase of the prospective teacher's training. Entered into with enthusiasm and a willingness to learn, the experience will be a valuable culmination of college preparation for teaching.

The selection of subject, school, and supervising teacher is enhanced by visits to schools before the semester or quarter of student teaching. It is advisable to do one's student teaching in the major field of preparation to capitalize on one's strength of subject-matter competency.

The usual pattern of preparation is to spend several days or a week observing the class one is going to teach. Such observation can be done on a systematic basis and promotes real insight into the individual differences present in the class. Student teachers can be assistant teachers in the truest sense if they are alert to developing problems, anticipate future activities of the class, and prepare themselves accordingly.

Taking over the class to teach a lesson or a unit will be completely successful if student teachers plan adequately in consultation with their supervising teachers and make their preparations carefully. Advance rehearsal for the first day of teaching is an advisable procedure, particularly if the time budget is questionable or if class questions are anticipated. An immediate followup of a day of teaching with a brief conference with the supervising teacher is advisable. Necessary changes in lesson plans can be made at this time.

A desirable arrangement is to follow the student-teaching quarter with a final quarter on the college campus before graduation. At this time, seminars in special problems of teaching can be most profitable, and the student teacher can reflect on the teaching experience. This affords the opportunity to give maximum attention to the important choice of a first teaching position in the light of the recent experience in student teaching.

Today's science teacher is in a position of respect and responsibility. The demand for well-prepared science teachers has never been greater, and the rewards are exceptional.

Proper education of the science teacher in this fast-moving scientific age is a matter of increasing concern. A suitable balance of general education, subject-matter preparation, and professional training must be achieved. The current trend is toward strengthening all of these areas, particularly subject-matter preparation. Attainment of a bachelor's degree does not end the science teacher's education. More and more, graduate work, up to and beyond the master's level, is being demanded. From a financial standpoint, it is generally to the teacher's advantage to obtain this advanced training as soon as possible. Better-paying jobs with other attractive features frequently await the applicant who has additional training.

The science teacher can grow professionally in many ways. Graduate coursework, inservice institutes and workshops, summer institutes, committee involvement, membership in professional organizations, a program of reading, participation in meetings, and writing for professional journals are but a few possibilities. It is important to realize that continual growth and experience are necessary if one is to be an enthusiastic, productive science teacher.

The professional educator of today faces a challenging future. Investment in superior preparation and recognition of the need for continual professional growth can provide rich rewards: a citizenry better educated in the area of science.

■ REFERENCES

1. Checklist from Lawrence A. Conrey, University School, University of Michigan, Ann Arbor, 1960.
2. Prepared by Conrey.
3. *Stanford Teacher Competence Appraisal Guide* (Stanford, CA: Stanford Center for Development in Teaching).
4. Cynthia Ann Druva and Ronald D. Anderson, "Science Teachers' Characteristics by Teacher Behavior and by Student Outcome: A Meta-Analysis of Research," *Journal of Research in Science Teaching, 20* (5) (1983): 467–479.
5. National Science Teachers Association, "Secondary School Science and Mathematics Teachers," *NSF Bulletin* 63–10 (Washington, DC: U.S. Government Printing Office, 1963), p. 4.
6. National Science Teachers Association, "Annual Self-Inventory for Science Teachers in Secondary Schools," *The Science Teacher, 37* (9) (December 1970): 37.
7. G.D. Bailey, "Teacher Self-Assessment: In Search of a Philosophical Foundation," *National Association of Secondary School Principals Bulletin, 62* (422) (1978): 64–70.
8. William E. Searles and Naile Kudeki, "A Comparison of Teacher and Principal Perception of an Outstanding Science Teacher," *Journal of Research in Science Teaching, 24* (1) (1987): 1–13.

INVESTIGATING SCIENCE TEACHING

Activity 24–1

INDIVIDUAL DIFFERENCES

1. In your observation of a science class use the checklist like the one on page 000 to discover the individual differences present in the class. At the end of a week, discuss your observations with the teacher. How does the student's achievement appear to correlate with your observations of study habits and classroom behavior?
2. List the traits you would like to see in the supervising teacher with whom you wish to do your practice teaching. Using this list as a guide, objectively analyze your own traits and compare them. Do you think similar or opposite traits are preferable or that a judicious blend of both is preferable?

Activity 24–2

APPLYING FOR A JOB

1. Write a letter of application for a teaching position.
2. Briefly describe your qualifications, special areas of interest, and teaching field.
3. Volunteer to make an appointment for an interview at a mutually convenient time.
4. Write a short description of your philosophy of education. This need not be included in the letter of application but should be held in reserve for an appropriate time when called for.

Activity 24–3

BEING A PROFESSIONAL SCIENCE TEACHER

1. Write to the department of education in your state and obtain a summary of the current salary schedule in the major cities. Compare the starting salaries for teachers with bachelor's degrees and master's degrees. Compare the annual salary increase and the number of years required to reach maximum salary.
2. Obtain a copy of *Guidelines for Preparation Programs of Teachers of Secondary School Science and Mathematics* from the American Association for the Advancement of Science, Washington, DC. Compare the training you have received with that recommended by this group.
3. Prepare a critical analysis of two professional journals, such as *The Science Teacher, School Science and Mathematics, The American Biology Teacher,* and *The Physics Teacher.* Examine the feature articles, the classroom teaching tips, the articles contributed by teachers in the field, the book reviews, and other parts of the publications.
4. Prepare a critical review of two research-oriented professional science teaching journals, such as *Science Education* and *Journal of Research for Science Teaching.* Report on the results of one research study published in each of the journals reviewed.

Chapter 25

BEING A SCIENCE TEACHER

■ MAKING THE TRANSITION TO A PRACTICING TEACHER

Up to this point, you have been a student preparing to meet the challenges of teaching science. You have studied your chosen subject(s) carefully, taking in volumes of factual knowledge with the expectation of using it at some time in the near future as a science teacher. You have been regaled with information about teaching methods and strategies and have observed other science teachers perform in the classroom. You have studied the psychology of adolescents and young adults to learn what makes them tick, what motivates them in and out of school. And you have gotten your feet wet in the science classroom by doing your student teaching under the supervision of an experienced science teacher.

Now, you are approaching the end of this long process and are looking forward to being a science teacher in a classroom of your own. Perhaps you are a bit apprehensive at this point. Perhaps you have seen enough of the reality of teaching to feel intimidated by the thought of taking full charge of a class. On the other hand, perhaps you have gained confidence, through your student-teaching experience and with the guidance of sensitive science teachers, so that you are enthusiastically anticipating the real world of science teaching. The authors hope this is the case. To put this situation in a more concrete setting, we shall present four examples of prospective teachers as they move toward this final stage of their preparation.

Josh

Josh is a student teacher in earth sciences at a medium-sized high school. He teaches five classes of ninth-grade earth science under the tutelage of two different science teachers. His assignment of teaching was gradually increased from observing to teaching one class to ultimately taking over five classes. Although all classes were ninth-grade level, there were perceptible differences in the nature and character of the five classes. The vagaries of grouping children and the dynamics that prevailed in different classes promoted a distinctive character obvious even to an outside observer. Josh found it necessary to make adjustments in his planning, teaching style, and handling of each of the classes.

As is common with new teachers, who have most recently sat through dozens of college classes

in which lectures were the prevalent form of presenting material, Josh tended to emphasize lectures in his classes too. While the topics under study were potentially interesting, the lecture format didn't capture the interest of the ninth graders. They were restless, somewhat noisy, and carried out Josh's assigned tasks rather perfunctorily. The main emphasis for them seemed to be to memorize the factual information presented by Josh to be ready to give it back on a factual test. While some of the students did all right with this teaching method, the majority of the class looked upon it as a rather onerous way to learn science. In fact, they did not clearly understand what the purpose of learning the facts was and did not perceive how the information would benefit them.

The experienced teachers under whom Josh was working talked with Josh and suggested he try an activity approach to teaching the topics. They gave him some concrete suggestions of materials he could use and procedures to follow. Josh tried out some of the suggestions in his next class periods and found the students enjoyed them. To his surprise, Josh found that he had fun using activity labs and was actually less exhausted at the end of the day. The students did as well on the tests as they had in the former lecture approach. In addition, they seemed to have a better attitude toward their learning. There were no discipline problems.

Barbara

Barbara is a student teacher in a junior high school in a medium-sized city. She teaches earth science to seventh graders three class periods a day and physical science to eighth graders two periods a day. She feels most comfortable with the seventh-grade classes, mainly because they are less disruptive and easier to manage.

Barbara's supervising teacher has not had a student teacher before. He feels a bit intimidated by the new responsibility and has turned over much of the class management to her. While this is a challenge to Barbara, it is also a good experience because she is given considerable freedom to operate the classes as she wishes. Her teacher has operated his classes in a rather perfunctory manner and has not given much help to his student teacher other than to suggest Barbara follow the standard format prevalent in the class.

Barbara has tried to provide a modicum of activity labs (at least once a week) in which the students participate in some type of investigation. These are followed by short postlab discussions. Students usually have some type of short write-up to turn in at the conclusion of the class period.

The discipline in the seventh-grade classes is average. Most students are serious learners, but one or two give way to their adolescent urges to show off or distract their classmates. Barbara has learned infinite patience in dealing with these children and has good results without having to resort to authoritarian measures of discipline control. This is perhaps the best indicator of Barbara's potential success as a teacher of junior high school children in the future.

Sam

Student teaching for Sam took place in a modern high school under the tutelage of an experienced science teacher with a reputation for good teaching and control of his classes. Sam has two tenth-grade physical science classes and one called global science which is a class of students who have not taken a regular science sequence in high school but need at least one science to graduate.

Although physical science was not Sam's major field in college, he had several courses in physics and chemistry that prepared him adequately for this assignment. He seemed to prefer teaching the physical science classes over the global science, mainly because of the quality and motivation of the physical science students. He has some very bright students in these classes, which lends challenge and satisfaction to his teaching. It is not uncommon for beginning teachers to face two or three different subject assignments in their first year of teaching. A student-teaching assignment that gives varied experiences and responsibilities in different kinds of classes is an excellent preparation for this eventuality.

Sam has a relaxed approach to his teaching and develops good rapport with the students. He is firm about tasks and requirements but is willing to listen to the students and is helpful in working with them. These traits carried over to his first job will smooth the transition and raise considerably his chances of having a satisfying and productive teaching career in the sciences.

Erica

Erica teaches biology and chemistry as her student-teaching assignment. She has three biology classes and two of chemistry. She is fortunate to have two highly qualified experienced teachers as her supervisors in the classroom. They feel that she is doing an excellent job and are lavish in their praise of her teaching.

Two of Erica's classes are college-prep classes, with more than 80 percent of the students planning to go on to college. Consequently, Erica instructs them largely in a typical college manner, with much lecture, note taking, and factual emphasis on terminology, taxonomy, and high-level concepts in biology. The students seem to eat it up. They realize, it seems, that Erica knows what she is talking about when she informs them that they are getting excellent preparation for their coming experience in college. The small fraction of students in the classes who are not college bound are not sure how the information they are getting will help them in their careers but are sure that somehow it represents science, which seems to be in the news quite often these days.

The examples described here represent four different sets of experiences by prospective teachers of science. A common thread is that each experience is unique and is the result of many factors coming together—individual natures of the students, varying traits and expertise of the supervising teachers, class makeup and objectives, and the subject matter of the class, among others. So it will be in your first employment opportunity as well. Perhaps the lesson to be learned is to be prepared for anything. A teacher needs to be flexible and adaptable. Of course this is what makes teaching exciting and rewarding as well!

Throughout this book we have used the theme *Becoming a Science Teacher* to bring unity and clarity to the organization and presentation of chapters. Here, we are switching to the theme *Being a Science Teacher.*

Becoming is the process of developing suitable or appropriate qualities needed for science teaching. Becoming, then, represents a change from that which you were to that which you are now. It is your coming to be all that you potentially can be as a science teacher, given the time and constraints of this textbook, your life, the methods course, etc.

Being is the existence of a particular state or condition—in this case, that of a secondary school science teacher. The title of this chapter signifies that you are one step closer to actually being a science teacher. In many ways you have probably already developed many qualities and attitudes of science teachers. Paradoxically, you will always be at some degree of both becoming and being a science teacher. For example, during the science-methods course you have been involved with a variety of experiences, all contributing toward your becoming a science teacher. Simultaneously, you have developed a set of interests and attitudes similar to those of science teachers. Perhaps you imagined yourself as a science teacher and, on occasion, actually experienced this position through teaching a class and

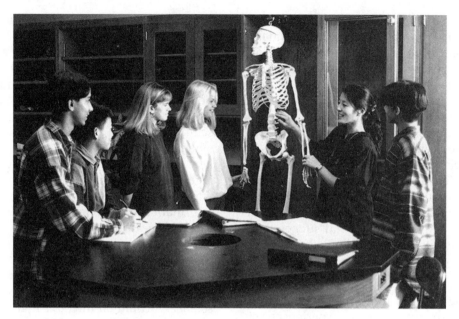

Science teaching is both personally and professionally fulfilling.

working with students. We are referring to your own attitudes and values and your own interest and desire to be a science teacher. These are the most significant variables in the becoming-being equation.

If we had to identify one symbolic point at which the percentage of becoming and being shifted in favor of being, it would be the first day of your first job. Throughout the practice-teaching experience, becoming and being will probably be about equal. However, there has been some degree of being a science teacher from the moment of your career decision, and there will be some degree of continually becoming a better science teacher throughout your career.

These two situations summarized in "Fulfillments and Frustrations" at the end of this chapter are two ends of an emotional continuum for science teachers. There are indeed frustrations and fulfillment, and both are a part of becoming and being a science teacher. For some reason, more time is devoted to the frustrating aspects of science teaching than to the fulfillments; yet, without a doubt, the latter occur each day and in many ways. Science teaching is a source of personal fulfillment because it contributes to the development of students and ultimately to society. Occasionally, we lose sight of this simple fact because of the daily frustrations, dissatisfactions, and challenges.

■ PERSONAL FULFILLMENT

In chapter 21, we discussed Maslow's hierarchy of motivational needs. The context of that presentation

was the fulfillment of student needs. Here the emphasis is on teachers' needs. The fulfillment of your needs can lead to your personal growth as a science teacher.

Safety and Security

Some teachers have a very real need for safety. Recent occurrences in which middle school and high school students have been found carrying weapons such as knives and guns to school, have increased this perceived need. Fortunately, the numbers are still small. However, the numbers of incidents are growing and school systems are working hard to change this situation. In chapter 21, we offered suggestions for alleviating concerns about safety and control in the science classroom.

Science teaching is generally a secure career. From time to time, however, budget cuts and other economic problems make it difficult; there are also occasional reductions in the teaching force. These are short-term problems; our society always needs good teachers. Moreover, science teachers will be important as long as science and technology have a central role in society.

Love and Belongingness

The need for love and belonging can also be fulfilled through science teaching. At the secondary level, however, students do not express their closeness as clearly and unabashedly as at the elementary level. Adolescents are in their quest for separation from authorities and for development of their own identity, which makes their closeness and expression of appreciation toward an authority figure, such as a science teacher, particularly difficult. Often the students who like you the most will demonstrate it the least. Still, the picture is not all gray. Science teachers can and do earn the respect and affection of their students. It is often subtle, oblique, and obtuse. But it is there. You can contribute to the feelings of belonging by establishing a climate of caring in your science classroom, thus fulfilling both your needs and those of the students.

Self-Esteem

What about the self-esteem of the science teacher? If self-esteem is equated with having material possessions, which in turn relates to a high salary, then the prospects for fulfilling this need are not very encouraging. There is, however, prestige within the educational community for science teachers, and there is a long tradition of respect for teachers in our society. Although education is frequently criticized, it is also looked to as a source of remedy for many problems. There is deserved, earned esteem in knowing you have helped young people understand more about the world in which they live, thus helping their personal development and improving society.

It would be nice if we could simply state that all of your needs would be met through science teaching and you would experience continued growth as a professional and as a person. Such is not the case. We can say that this is possible, in fact even probable, but part of the task will be your own contribution. For everything that Maslow did say about motivation and personal growth, he *never* said that it was easy.

Fulfilling Needs

How does an individual know which needs are important? Knowing this, how does one proceed to fulfill personal needs in the context of a science classroom? The first question is most directly answered by you. Our contribution to the answer has been to provide activities that direct you to reflect on various aspects of science teaching. Self-awareness is essential if you wish to know more about your needs and possible ways to fulfill them.

Once you have some insights concerning your personal needs as a science teacher, there are many ways to fulfill them. Here are a few suggestions listed under Maslow's categories.

Safety
1. Establish rules for the science classroom.
2. Clarify consequences of rule violation.

Security
1. Talk to your principal or personnel director about future goals, budgets, etc.

2. Work to develop a strong science program.

Belongingness
1. Have personal conferences with students.
2. Evaluate the class to see how it might be improved.
3. Have the students work on cooperative projects.
4. Spend more time talking to the students on a personal level during class.

Esteem
1. Conduct a workshop on a topic of interest to the rest of your school staff, e.g., energy, pollution, nutrition.
2. Attend a local or national meeting of science teachers.
3. Present a talk on science to a community group.
4. Join a local committee that is working on a science-related problem.

These are a few simple suggestions that can stimulate your thoughts about change and growth as a science teacher. The list is not unique; most of the ideas are simply a part of being a science teacher.

■ PROFESSIONAL CHALLENGES

It is hard to identify all of the trends and issues that will affect science teaching in the years to come. We can assure you there will be new challenges. Here we discuss a few challenges that will face science teachers in the last half of the 1990s.

Enrollments

Enrollments in secondary schools increased during the 1950s, 1960s, and 1970s. However, in the 1980s, they declined. Principals surveyed in the NSF studies confirm the importance of declining enrollments by ranking it fourth among all problems in science and mathematics education. However, science teachers did not rank low enrollment in courses as one of their most important problems. In light of the recent decline in student enrollment it should be noted that there is not a shortage of secondary school science teachers, and there will not be until the late 1990s.

Equality of Educational Opportunity

The issue of equality of educational opportunity has resulted in a conflict between current educational practices used in mass education and democratic principles. To date, it seems that the confrontation has been subtle and beneficial to neither teachers nor students. The confrontation centers on the Fourteenth Amendment rights of students and the pedagogic practices of teachers. Since *Brown vs. Board of Education* (1954) there have been increasing legislation and regulation requiring that the handicapped, minorities, children from low-income families, and women be allowed an education.

The impact of these requirements on science education is not clear. Science teachers encounter a dichotomy between their belief in the principle of human rights as guaranteed in the Constitution and the concrete facts of the need to modify their teaching style and adapt their curricula to the individual needs of students.

Facilities and Equipment

Science equipment and supplies, or the lack of them, greatly influence science teaching. Funds for the purchase of science supplies is, obviously, a major factor in science programs. In light of these statements, 26 percent of science teachers rate inadequacy of facilities as a serious problem and 42 percent as somewhat of a problem. To some degree, facilities are a problem for 68 percent of science teachers.

Curriculum

In the early 1980s a number of reports on education recommended increasing graduation requirements by adding another year of science. While most applaud such requirements, there are implications not generally recognized by those making the recommendations. Who will take the extra courses? What are the curricular implications? Who will teach the courses? To answer the first question, students who have decided *not* to take any more science will now be required to take at least another course. The curricular implication is related to the inappropriateness of existing courses for the group of students now required to take another year of science. The result will be a need for new curriculum materials. Finally, increasing the requirements will increase the need for science teachers. There is the possibility of unqualified teachers teaching the newly required courses, and the need for inservice programs to better qualify these science teachers.

Instruction

In 1978, 13 percent of secondary science teachers were teaching at least one class for which they did not feel qualified. Most of these teachers were referring to courses within science and not a course such as mathematics or history.

Disruptive Students

Student discipline and classroom management are concerns of science teachers. Junior high science teachers think their students are not well behaved. An estimated 5 percent of science teachers indicated that maintaining discipline was a serious problem

and 24 percent indicated that it was somewhat of a problem. These data are consistent with a National Institute of Education (NIE) report, *Violent Schools—Safe Schools*.[1] There are higher levels of violence (in intensity and numbers) at the junior high level than at elementary levels. Approximately 8 to 10 percent of schools see violence and disruption as a serious problem. Interestingly, one study showed that less than 10 percent of teachers, principals, and district program respondents indicated that maintaining discipline was a serious problem.

Careers

Although it is seen in various forms, the recent emphasis on career education is being felt in science education. In the 1970s, a concern for vocational or career skills and knowledge became increasingly important. This change is, in part, a response to public opinion. When teachers, parents, and science coordinators were asked about vocational goals of science courses, they agreed that science courses should be more vocationally oriented; yet, the majority would select a good general education over a vocational program if they had to select between them.

Science teachers should be aware of the continuing need for scientists and engineers. They should also be aware that career choices are often made based on experiences in science classes. We think most science teachers understand these two points. A more difficult issue is the fact that science teachers contribute to a filtering process that eliminates significant numbers of individuals from the talent pool of scientists and engineers. The imbalance is one of historical record and one that eliminates not on the basis of intelligence and ability, but in large measure on the basis of gender, race, handicap, and cultural advantage.

Preparation

In the early 1980s, an estimated 30 percent of all teachers currently teaching science and math in secondary schools were either completely unqualified or severely underqualified to teach those subjects.[2,3]

When asked about the areas of greatest need, science teachers listed several items directly related to instruction. Approximately 66 percent of all teachers surveyed (science, mathematics, and social studies) indicated that they needed information about instructional media. Sixty-one percent indicated a need for assistance in learning new teaching methods. Fewer than 50 percent of teachers surveyed felt they are not competent enough to implement the discovery/inquiry approach. They felt they needed the assistance of a coordinator or other resource person. Forty-eight percent of all science, mathematics, and social studies teachers indicated they would like assistance in the use of manipulative materials. This need may relate to the fact that manipulative materials are generally used less than once a week in most science, mathematics, and social studies classes.

Funding

Funding is perceived to be a major problem facing science teachers. An estimated 66 percent of science teachers indicated that funding is, to some degree, a problem. It is evident that there is a need for improving the financing of science education and addressing this problem.

These are some of the challenges that lie ahead. They are not insurmountable, but they do cause frustration. One thing is certain; they will not be reduced without the cooperation of all school personnel and others working within the science education community.

■ DECISION MAKING

During any single class period, a science teacher makes many decisions about students and the lesson. Often science teachers are unaware of these decisions. "Shall I tell John to be quiet?" "What is Pat doing?" "Do the students understand density?" "Should I use a different example of convection currents?" "Would it be best for the students to work in groups of two or three on this laboratory project?" The decisions may not seem that important, but they all add up to effective instruction and classroom management.

Teaching science is simultaneously directed and flexible. Decision making in science teaching is the process of synthesizing your planned direction with the instantaneous and spontaneous factors in the classroom.

Direction in teaching science is provided in two ways: first, through the organization of textbooks, curriculum guides, lesson plans, and objectives; and, second, from the science teacher's own instructional theory. When a situation emerges in the classroom, the teacher evaluates the situation, goals, curriculum, and consequences of choices and then decides on a course of action. One important, though seldom considered, variable in the decision-making process is the direction suggested by the science teacher's own instructional theory.

An instructional theory helps establish a frame of reference for decisions, gives consistency of responses, and provides a general direction as science teachers encounter different classroom situations. With the aid of an instructional theory, science teachers are in a better position to make instruction effective and fulfilling. In the final analysis, the individual science teacher is the one who can best relate the possible solutions to the actual situations when it comes to different students, classrooms, and schools. An instructional theory provides an underlying direction that transcends immediate classroom problems. Being able to go beyond the immediate situation affirms one's ability as a science teacher. Clarifying one's long-term goals and intentions helps provide

In making decisions, the effective teacher takes into account spontaneous happenings in the classroom as well as instructional theory.

■■■■■■■■■■■■■■■■■■ **GUEST EDITORIAL** ■■■■■■■■■■■■■■■■■■■■■■■■■

Empathy, Understanding, and Science Teaching

Eric Johnson
Science Teacher
Northfield Middle School
Northfield, Minnesota

The best teachers are those who aren't boring. They challenge us with the quality of classwork, encourage extra work, and are available out of class to provide help. This type of teacher cares that we learn, listens actively, and is open-minded.

Having summarized the feelings of four of my high school science students on what makes an excellent teacher, I would like to suggest two key traits that we, as science teachers, need to strive constantly to develop: the first is empathy for students and the second is an understanding of science based on experience rather than books.

Webster defines empathy as "intellectual or emotional identification with another," and science as "systematized knowledge derived from observation, study, etc." Since neither empathy nor scientific involvement is fully attained by completing an undergraduate program culminating in earning a teaching certificate, how can the beginning teacher actively pursue these two important goals? Moreover, how can these goals be pursued while handling several laboratory preparations, five classes, and 150 students?

I shall begin with the question of understanding and experiencing science since increased empathy can follow from it. One type of active encounter with science can be found in the many summer programs run by colleges and universities. Those courses specifically designed for teachers may not necessarily involve problem identification and data collection, but the best combine factual updating with experience in scientific process. Those courses established as summer programs for graduate students in research, such as the university biological field stations, are geared entirely to "systematized knowledge derived from observation." A teacher returning to class in the fall after engaging in this type of scientific challenge will approach classwork and students differently. There will be a closer "intellectual or emotional identification" with the role of students and with the processes of science. Empathy can be a side benefit.

Another major area of teacher experience that can enhance the quality of student learning is in applying lessons from the summer programs to the biology, chemistry, or physics class. In biology the connection might be a natural area near the school.

an organizational pattern that slowly becomes a personal style of teaching. The power of an instructional theory is in the direction it provides. There must be another component: the freedom to deviate from the direct path in response to different classroom scenarios. This is the spontaneity and flexibility required in science teaching. Look at "Developing an Instructional Theory" at the end of this chapter.

Effective science teachers are able to deviate from the lesson. The degree of flexibility varies with the teacher's goals, students' needs, and environmental contingencies. The problems described in "What Would You Do—Now?" at the end of this chapter are similar to those presented earlier. This time, however, no solutions, directions, or ideas are suggested—you must resolve the incident on your own.

When confronted with problem situations such as those described in "What Would You Do—Now?" science teachers usually respond: "I would have to know more," "I would have to be in the situation," or "It depends; every teacher would probably do some-thing different." This is precisely the point. The individual science teacher must decide the course of action in response to the classroom situation. Science teachers intuitively know that they are the primary source for effective education when they ask such questions as, "When should I answer the student's question if I am teaching by inquiry?" There is usually an implicit tone of voice that says, "There is no direct answer except as the individual teacher responds to the situation."

Science teachers enter the classroom with knowledge, techniques, plans, textbooks, and curriculum materials. It is also the teacher who combines all of these and builds a helping relationship with the students. In the classroom the helping relationship is characterized by situations requiring the teacher to react spontaneously. Science teachers must think critically, diagnose, decide, and respond to conditions in the teaching environment. The creative, insightful, and perceptive science teacher does react effectively to the instanta-

Annual studies by students of soil or water conditions, of phenology with wildflowers, of growth rates in trees, or of chemical changes downstream from a sewage-treatment plant provide immediate application of concepts, a respect for the comparative value of data, and an opportunity to contribute to an understanding of local habitats.

In chemistry class, students in farming communities might analyze drinking water from various local sources, looking for nitrate levels. Urban schools might collect rain or snow samples for pH studies of combustion-related acid precipitation.

A physics class could measure the solar constant throughout the year and relate its change to the distance of the sun, angle of incident light, or recent volcanic activity. Application of solar-energy studies in home heating could be conducted by comparing energy use in a gas- or electric-metered home on a sunny versus a cloudy day in winter. The difference in the quantity of energy used each day is a measure of the effectiveness of solar gain through windows. Whose home is most effective? Is every home a solar home to some extent? These and other questions can make the process of learning science pertinent, memorable, and exciting for teacher and students.

Knowing that investigations can be conducted by students on local subjects sets a tone early in each school year that suggests that science involves practicing, not just reading and memorizing, and that contributions are needed to sustain the momentum of past work. Students experiencing science in this way will continue to look for ways to apply what they've learned. The rate of technological change will intimidate them less. Critical-thinking skills will more often be applied to problems beyond the classroom.

To succeed with this process of actively becoming involved in science, the teacher must include the scientific process in each aspect of the class—including laboratories, field trips, and discussions—must be committed to taking risks in the process of learning, and must be convinced that the course is relevant. Beyond the content benefits, a teacher following the active-participant role will necessarily show increased empathy for students by being more closely attuned to what is challenging and exciting. In addition, the teacher organizing the class in this way will not become bored teaching the same course time and again: discovery of new patterns and problems will continue to present fresh challenges for investigation. Most important, we who use this approach can view each new year with the expectation that we will acquire further insights into our subject, our students, and ourselves.

neous needs and demands of the children, classroom, or school.

Developing a consistent direction through an instructional theory and flexibility in classroom situations will evolve into a personal teaching style that can help overcome frustrations and contribute to your fulfillment as a science teacher.

■ BECOMING A BETTER SCIENCE TEACHER

As discussed in the Introduction to this text, part of being a science teacher is engaging in the process of becoming a better science teacher. In this chapter, we will use a self-evaluation inventory to examine some of the immediate concerns of science teachers. (See "Improving My Science Teaching" at the end of this chapter.) Although this activity concentrates on improving various aspects of science teaching, the feedback will also contribute to your becoming a better educator and a more fulfilled person.

Remember, you do not have to be a bad science teacher to become a better one. Science teachers want to improve, as is shown by their continued involvement in workshops, college courses, attendance at conventions, etc. The responsibility for improving is yours; moreover, the means of developing as a science teacher are unique to your preferences, problems, and potential. Based on the categories in the self-evaluation inventory, several possible means are suggested.

Scientific Knowledge

There are a number of relatively easy ways to update and/or keep abreast of scientific developments:

1. Read an introductory textbook in the area you feel needs improvement.
2. Enroll in science courses at a local college or university.
3. Contact the district or state science supervisor and see if a workshop can be organized.

4. Join the American Association for the Advancement of Science and read their journals, *Science* or *Science '90* (the figure changes with year of publication). The editorials will keep you up-to-date on social concerns and scientific developments.
5. Read *Scientific American* or purchase offprints of articles or the monographs of accumulated articles on important topics.
6. Join the National Science Teachers Association and read one of their journals: *Science and Children, The Science Teacher, Science Scope,* or *Journal of College Science Teaching.*
7. Subscribe to and read *Science News* or *Science World.*
8. Attend local, state, regional, and national conventions of scientific societies, and academies of science, science teachers, and teachers.
9. Make a point of watching television programs on scientific issues. *Nova* is a science program sponsored by the National Science Foundation and is shown on the Public Broadcasting System.
10. Read the science sections of weekly magazines, such as *Time* or *Newsweek.*
11. Go to local museums and planetariums.

Planning and Organization

If this is a concern, part of the problem can be improved through personal effort toward better lesson planning and classroom organization. We suggest that you:

1. Read the chapters on planning in any teaching-methods textbook.
2. Find a colleague who is well-organized and ask if the two of you could spend some time planning classes together.
3. Ask the science supervisor to look over your science program and suggest ways to improve the organization.
4. Have a colleague observe your teaching and make suggestions concerning your lesson plans and class management.

Teaching Methods

Teachers often find it difficult to break old teaching habits and try new methods of teaching, but you can do it. Here are some suggestions:

1. Read chapters on different methods in any science methods textbook and then imagine how the different approaches could work in your classroom.
2. Look over journals—such as *Science and Children, The Science Teacher, The American Biology Teacher, The Physics Teacher,* and *Journal*

of Geological Education—for new approaches to science teaching.
3. Take a *professional day* and observe several science teachers who use methods that you are interested in adopting.
4. Read *Models of Teaching* by Bruce Joyce and Marsha Weil. This is an excellent book that presents many teaching methods.
5. Team-teach with another science teacher who uses different methods.
6. Request a student teacher; they often have new and different approaches to science teaching.

Interpersonal Relations

This is an area that is essential to effective science teaching, yet often neglected in the education of science teachers. Some suggestions that may help include the following:

1. Practice active listening when students talk.
2. Use questions that encourage students to express their ideas on certain issues.
3. Read and apply ideas from *Questioning and Listening* by Robert Sund and Arthur Carin.
4. Attend a workshop or course on human relations.
5. Read and apply ideas from *Teacher Effectiveness Training* by Thomas Gordon.
6. Read and apply ideas from *Human Relations and Your Career: A Guide to Interpersonal Skills* by David Johnson.

Personal Enthusiasm

If you lack enthusiasm for teaching science, the problem is difficult, but not impossible, to resolve. The reason for the difficulty is that the problem involves a very personal dimension of your teaching. We can recommend an introspective route to improvement:

1. Think about your original interest and excitement in science and teaching. What made you choose science teaching? Now, think about what you know about yourself and teaching science. What is lacking? Where did the spark of enthusiasm go?
2. List your frustrations with teaching. What are the problems you have encountered as a science teacher? What caused a burnout or your change of interest in science teaching?
3. Attend meetings of science teachers such as NSTA or NABT. This often can inspire enthusiasm through new ideas and new colleagues.
4. Form a group to improve teaching in your school. You will probably find others who share your problem, and the discussion and support

can certainly assist you in developing your enthusiasm for teaching.

5. Take a professional day and visit other science teachers who are dynamic and enthusiastic.
6. Request a sabbatical.

■ BEING A PERSON, EDUCATOR, AND SCIENCE TEACHER

Young children are often surprised to find that their teacher does not live at school. Older students think it is funny to meet their teacher shopping or on a picnic. Students often perceive the science teacher and not the person. We are all, however, first and foremost persons. What does this mean? Being a person means we share qualities with all other people: we struggle with decisions; we are sad and happy; we succeed and fail; we make mistakes and get things right; we are frustrated and fulfilled. Too often students do not see us as people. Students should understand that we belong to the community and have hobbies, interests, and ideas that go beyond science teaching.

As an educator, science teachers are in the helping professions. Their identity is with people more than objects. Their goal is to help people improve their health, education, and welfare. There are aspects of science teaching that are shared with other helping professionals, such as doctors, counselors, social workers, nurses, and psychologists. The shared qualities have to do primarily with the interpersonal relations—the personal dimension of science teaching, those qualities that contribute to effective interactions between people, and eventually contribute to someone facilitating another's personal development.

The science teacher has elected to help others through a better understanding of the physical and biological world, the methods of gaining knowledge about this world, and the role of science in society. Here the qualities of the person, the educator, and the science teacher should unite to achieve the dual goal of furthering the personal development of students and society through science education.

Much time, money, and effort have been expended on improving the science curriculum. Most science curricula have carefully structured texts and materials so the science teacher will have the maximum opportunity for a good teaching experience. The contribution of new programs and textbooks has been invaluable. But although curriculum materials are necessary and can account for some success in the classroom, they are not sufficient; they cannot account for effective and successful science teaching. The science teacher is still the crucial variable and the one person who must pull all the pieces together for effective teaching.

A review of the research literature on good, ideal, effective, or successful teaching reveals that it is impossible to identify any particular set of variables that amounts to being a good teacher. Yet, we all have had good science teachers, we know good science teachers, and, most importantly, we want to be good science teachers. Rather than looking at the research and concluding that we can't identify the characteristics of good science teaching, perhaps we can take a different view and thus form a different conclusion. Perhaps good science teachers have developed their potential, their talents, and their attributes, all of which give them an identifying teaching style. It is understandable then that our research efforts cannot find common characteristics, for the answer is to be found in uniqueness, not commonality.

Being a science teacher means improving. Science teachers want to improve, and can improve. Even an especially good science teacher can become a better one. Often science teachers complain, "I just didn't seem to be effective today; the students seemed confused and frustrated. I didn't get the concept across." However, they never finish the statement with, "and if you think I was bad today—wait until tomorrow. I'll really be much worse!" Unfortunately, just the desire to improve is not enough; there must be a commitment to becoming a better science teacher through changing or altering your personal teaching style.

Critics of education have done much to point out the wrongs of education and little to give direction. One result of this critical confrontation has been defensiveness by many teachers and administrators. Displacing blame is one manifestation of this defensiveness, the "let's blame somebody or something else" syndrome: "We would if we had money." "I have thirty-five children in my class." "Well, what do you expect?" and "The home has more influence than the short time students are in my classroom." The "let's try something new" syndrome is another manifestation. Teaching machines, contract performance, accountability, competency-based programs, and the open classroom are examples of this approach. The ideas presented in this chapter center on the science teacher developing as a person and as an educator. Our theme might be, "Let's get with it as people and perform as professionals." You can be in any classroom, with any children, and with any curriculum to develop your competency as a science teacher. The ideas presented are not easy; they deal, for the most part, with personal improvement and fulfillment.

Start being a science teacher by looking at your potential and not your limitations. Becoming aware of the importance of the suggestions for improvement and translating them into actual practice can result in your development as a science teacher. The process of becoming a better science teacher is long, and it takes courage to overcome the many small barriers to personal and professional growth. It is not something that can occur through the purchase of a new set of science materials, a single workshop, or reading one methods textbook. Being a science teacher requires continuous personal development aimed toward the ideal of being a great educator, and for those who say, "I can't be a great science teacher," we reply, "If not you—then who?" We all have much more potential than we are now using. It is the actualization of this potential that will help you become a better science teacher, educator, and person.

■ SUMMARY

In this chapter we changed from the theme of *becoming* to a theme of *being*. Becoming is changing and moving toward a goal, which was the orientation of most of this book. Being is a state or a condition: in this instance, that of a science teacher. The title of this chapter tells you that student teaching and your first job are very near. Subsequently, it is time to think in terms of being a science teacher.

Being a science teacher has its professional frustrations and motivational needs; safety, security, love and belongingness, and self-esteem are ways of thinking about levels of fulfillment in your job. Some of the professional challenges of the 1990s are competency and accountability, facilities and equipment, curriculum and instruction, funding, disruptive students, and career education.

Decision making is a crucial aspect of being a science teacher. The particular focus of decision making is on two seemingly paradoxical aspects of teaching—that one must maintain a direction and that one must demonstrate flexibility. The balance between these variables is set by the science teacher's decisions. A personal theory of instruction will help guide the science teacher's decisions and develop a consistent pattern of responses to the instantaneous demands of the classroom.

Being a science teacher is more than signing your first contract or teaching your first class. It is more than your knowledge of science, capacity to plan, ability to use different methods, and your enthusiasm for teaching. Although these attributes are included, being a science teacher means:

1. *Courage* to continue your professional growth
2. *Commitment* to doing a better job tomorrow
3. *Competence* to fulfill your professional duties
4. *Compassion* toward your students
5. *Caring* for your own dignity, integrity, and worth *and* for the dignity, integrity, and worth of those in your care

■ REFERENCES

1. David Boesel, *Violent Schools—Safe Schools*, Vol. 1 (Washington, DC: National Institute of Education, 1978).
2. Bill G. Aldridge and Karen L. Johnston, "Trends and Issues in Science Education," in *Redesigning Science and Technology Education*, 1984 NSTA Yearbook, R. Bybee, J. Carlson, and A. McCormack, eds. (Washington DC: National Science Teachers Association, 1984).
3. James A. Shymansky and Bill G. Aldridge, "The Teacher Crisis in Secondary School Science and Mathematics," *Educational Leadership, 40* (November 1982).
4. Don Cosgrove, "Diagnostic Rating of Teacher Performance," *Journal of Educational Psychology, 50* (5) (1959): 200–204.
5. Rodger Bybee, "The Teacher I Like Best: Perceptions of Advantaged, Average and Disadvantaged Science Students," *School Science and Mathematics, 62* (5) (May 1973): 384–390.
6. Rodger Bybee, "Science Educators' Perceptions of the Ideal Science Teacher," *School Science and Mathematics, 78* (1) (January 1978): 13–22.

INVESTIGATING SCIENCE TEACHING

Activity 25–1

FULFILLMENTS AND FRUSTRATIONS

Joan is approaching your desk, "Look, I solved the chemistry problem. It was easy after you explained the difference between ionic and covalent bonding." Then, with a warm smile, she said, "I really appreciate the extra time you spend helping me; you are a good teacher and I'm glad I decided to take chemistry." What would you do?

1. Ask her if she solved the other chemistry problems.
2. Say nothing, smile, and go on with your work.
3. Tell her that it is just part of your job.
4. Smile and thank her for the compliment.
5. Tell her you are glad she asked you about the problem.

You have just sat through one more insufferable faculty meeting. The results of the meeting: your clerical work will increase due to a new grading system; your budget has been reduced by 50 percent (and the price of science materials, equipment, and textbooks has gone up 25 percent); your new duty is to supervise the cafeteria; your new class will be a "difficult, but small" group of students; your salary increase for next year will be 3 percent below the present rate of inflation. What would you do?

1. Quit.
2. Go to the next NEA or AFT meeting and demand a change in contracts.
3. Ignore the situation because one-fourth of the problems will be changed in the next two weeks; one-fourth of the changes will never be implemented; you can ignore one-fourth of the problems, and the remaining one-fourth are "part of the territory."
4. Make an appointment with the principal and politely, but firmly, inform her that she has asked too much of you.
5. Talk over the problems with several colleagues.
6. Go to a psychotherapist to see if you or the school system is sick.

Once you have selected the option closest to what you think, you might discuss it with a partner. What else would you do?

Activity 25–2

DEVELOPING AN INSTRUCTIONAL THEORY

The idea of an instructional theory was introduced in chapter two. Now it might be a good idea to return to this idea. To help you develop your instructional theory, complete the following exercise.

1. What is the aim of your science teaching? What is the broad goal you would hope to achieve through your interaction with students in the science classroom?

    a. What is your primary goal?

    b. What are your secondary aims?

2. Based on the understanding of yourself, students, science, and society, what are your justifications for the goal and aims cited above?

    a. Why are these and not other aims to be the focus of science education?

    b. In a broad sense, what is to be done or not done to achieve these aims?

3. What are your conclusions about what to do, and how and when to achieve these aims?

    a. By what specific instructional methods or processes are the aims developed?

b. What is your science curriculum?

c. Is there any sequence in your instructional theory?

In sum, you should: first, state what your aims are; second, justify why these aims are important; and third, explain how you plan to achieve these aims through your science curriculum and instruction.

Activity 25–3
WHAT WOULD YOU DO—NOW?

Based on your sense of direction and flexibility, what would you do as a science teacher in these situations?

1. You are introducing a biology lesson on predator/prey relationships. The chameleons and crickets you ordered for the students to observe have not arrived.

What would you do?

2. You are teaching a physical-science lesson on energy. The class was supposed to read the chapter on energy in the book. You suddenly realize that several of the students cannot read at the level of your textbook.

What would you do?

3. During an earth-science lesson on the planets a student informs you that he has talked with a visitor from another planet—called Xerob. He describes the visitor in detail. The class is interested and starts asking the student questions.

What would you do?

4. The unit is on health, the lesson on smoking. A student tells about a person she knows who is 85 years old and very healthy. This person has smoked two packages of cigarettes a day for over sixty years. In addition, the person drinks, eats candy, and does not watch his diet.

What would you do?

Activity 25–4
IMPROVING MY SCIENCE TEACHING

What are your strengths and weaknesses? How do you think you should improve as a science teacher? Following is a self-evaluation inventory designed to provide answers to these questions. We don't know how you would like to become more effective as a science teacher. Of course, the answers to these questions vary from person to person. The inventory will provide you with insights concerning some of your own characteristics as a science teacher. The self-evaluation inventory is based on items used in a study of teacher effectiveness and later modified for the study of science teaching. Only selected items are used here.

The following statements are descriptions of various facets of science teaching. Read each of the statements carefully. Using the scale, indicate how each statement presently characterizes you as a science teacher.

5   Very characteristic of me. This is a real strength of my teaching.
4   Frequently characteristic of me. This is a good aspect of my science teaching.
3   Sometimes characteristic of me. I should evaluate this aspect of my science teaching.
2   Seldom characteristic of me. I should improve this aspect of my science teaching.
1   Never characteristic of me. I really need to improve.

As a science teacher, I:

____ 1. Am well read in science
____ 2. Have a well-organized science course
____ 3. Adjust my teaching to the class situation
____ 4. Have a good rapport with my science students
____ 5. Enjoy teaching science to students
____ 6. Have a thorough knowledge of science
____ 7. Have always planned and am prepared for science class
____ 8. Use a variety of techniques in teaching science
____ 9. Recognize the unique needs of my science students
____10. Am enthusiastic about teaching science
____11. Present science concepts that are current and relevant
____12. Recognize the need to modify daily and unit plans
____13. Facilitate different types of student activities in science
____14. Relate well with students on the individual and group level
____15. Become excited when students learn science
____16. Am well informed in science-related fields
____17. Have thought about the long-range goals of my science class
____18. Use different curriculum materials and instructional approaches to teach science
____19. Am sincere while helping my science students
____20. Make an extra effort to help students learn science
____21. Am knowledgeable concerning science-related social issues
____22. Have a continuity of course material in science
____23. Provide adequate opportunity for active work by science students
____24. Listen to student questions and ideas
____25. Am excited and energetic when teaching science

Now go back and add up your responses for the items listed below in the left column. Divide the total by 5. The result should be a number between 1 and 5 for each of the categories listed. Refer back to the five-point scale for your evaluation.

Items		Average	Category
1, 6, 11, 16, 21	=	____	Knowledge of science
2, 7, 12, 17, 22	=	____	Planning and organization
3, 8, 13, 18, 23	=	____	Teaching methods
4, 9, 14, 19, 24	=	____	Personal relations
5, 10, 15, 20, 25	=	____	Enthusiasm

Appendix

TEACHING SCIENCE ACTIVITIES

BIOLOGY

GENETIC ENGINEERING: A SPLICE OF LIFE

Overview

How do scientists create new combinations of genetic material? What are the benefits of these new combinations? Should scientists avoid or prohibit any combinations? In this activity the students will simulate the process of engineering bacteria capable of producing human growth hormone. Then they will discuss the ethical implications of genetic engineering.

Science Background

- Genetic engineering is the manipulation of a genotype to alter an organism's phenotype.
- Gene splicing is a set of processes by which scientists incorporate the DNA for a specific protein into the DNA from another cell. The host organism will express this new information.
- Ethics enters into scientific endeavors. While genetic engineering may solve a variety of problems, it nevertheless may create other problems. Consequently, scientists and nonscientists must prepare themselves to make decisions about these issues.

Student Objectives

Upon completion of this activity, the students should be able to

- Describe and simulate the processes involved in genetic engineering.
- Understand how molecular biologists use bacteria to manufacture proteins for human use.
- Support a rational point of view.

Skills

Interpretation, Analysis

Time Frame

Splicing Bits & Pieces   45 minutes

Related Disciplines

Technology, Ethics
Opening Pandora's Box   45 minutes

Materials and Advance Preparation

Splicing Bits & Pieces

Materials

- One set of colored paper clips per lab group. Each set of clips should contain:

  35 black paper clips
  27 white paper clips
  46 red paper clips
  46 green paper clips
   9 silver paper clips
- Tape, 4 small pieces per lab group

Before class

- Gather colored paper clips and divide them into sets so that each group of students has one set. You may want to store individual sets in plastic bags.

Opening Pandora's Box

Materials

- 4 index cards
- Paper, 1 sheet per student

Before class

- Prepare the 4 index cards as indicated in *Opening Pandora's Box,* step 2.
- Make a student worksheet based on the questions raised in *Opening Pandora's Box,* step 6.
- Copy the student worksheet, 1 per student.

Splicing Bits & Pieces

NOTE: This activity is for students who have a solid understanding of genetics. Students should be familiar with information transfer, DNA, RNA, and the genetic code. In addition, the students must clearly understand protein synthesis to be successful with this activity.

1. Review with your students the role of DNA in the human body. In particular, remind the students that genes code for proteins, such as hormones.
2. Sometimes people are unable to produce certain hormones. Two examples of hormone deficiencies are diabetes and human growth hormone (hGH) deficiency. To give your students a perspective on these two problems, relate the following information:

   Diabetics are unable to regulate sugar, and more than 3 million diabetics in the U.S. must receive insulin daily. Until recently, the only sources of insulin were swine and cattle pancreases; but this supply has dwindled as hog and cattle production has declined. Some diabetics develop an immune reponse to porcine or bovine insulin and so are unable to continue using it.

Children who produce an insufficient amount of hGH have extremely short stature; they may never grow more than one meter tall. About 2,500 children in the U.S. suffer from this deficiency. For many years, the only sources of hGH were sheep brains or the pituitary glands of human cadavers; it takes 500,000 sheep brains to collect 5 mg of this hormone. Pituitary glands are also very scarce, so doctors could treat only the most severely affected children. In addition, some pituitary glands came from individuals who had died of Creudzfelt-Jacob disease, a slow, degenerative brain disease caused by a virus. Because of this contamination, human cadaver pituitary glands have not been used as a source of hGH in the U.S. since May 1985.

Today, recombinant DNA technology—genetic engineering—makes it possible to produce unlimited quantities of these two hormones. Biosynthetic insulin, called Humulin, has been available since 1983. Genentech, a major commercial biotechnology firm, produces a synthetic growth hormone called Pro-tropin, which was approved for public use in 1985; and the U.S. Food & Drug Administration recently approved the marketing of another biosynthetic growth hormone called Humatrop, which is produced by Eli Lilly.

3. Define the term recombinant DNA technology for your students (see Background for the Teacher).

4. Using the information that follows, explain the basic processes of genetic engineering to your students.

To synthesize a particular substance in a new organism, a scientist must:

a. Locate the gene that codes for the production of the desired protein, such as insulin or hGH. This requires finding a specific sequence of DNA bases among the 3 billion bases that comprise the human genetic code.

b. Isolate the specific gene.

c. Insert the isolated gene into a plasmid, and ensure that the proper regulatory sequences are intact.

d. Introduce the altered plasmid to a host cell, usually a bacterium, such as *E. coli.*

e. Cultivate the *E. coli,* and produce the desired protein.

5. Divide the class into small groups and distribute a set of colored paper clips to each group. Explain to the students that they are going to simulate the steps in the recombinant DNA process. Write the following key on the board:

$$A = \text{adenine—black}$$
$$T = \text{thymine—white}$$
$$C = \text{cytosine—red}$$
$$G = \text{guanine—green}$$
$$U = \text{uracil—silver}$$

On the board, beside the key, write the 37 pairs of DNA bases listed below. This is a small section of the gene for human growth hormone, which actually has 573 pairs of DNA bases.

Partial sequence of the hGH gene:

1	2	3	4	5	6	7	8	9	10	11	12
A	A	G	C	T	T	A	T	G	G	C	T
T	T	C	G	A	A	T	A	C	C	G	A

13	14	15	16	17	18	19	20	21	22	23	24
A	C	A	G	G	C	A	T	C	G	T	C
T	G	T	C	C	G	T	A	G	C	A	G

25	26	27	28	29	30	31	32	33	34	35	36	37
C	C	G	G	A	C	G	A	A	G	C	T	T
G	G	C	C	T	G	C	T	T	C	G	A	A

6. Tell the students that this is a short piece of the hGH gene. They will use the top strand—the sense strand—of the DNA sequence to construct the complementary strand of mRNA for this sequence of the hGH gene. Remind the students to substitute uracil for thymine in the mRNA strand.

7. The mRNA strand the students create has extraneous genetic information in it called an *intron,* which scientists remove chemically. Most bacteria do not have the enzymatic systems required to remove introns. Bases 19, 20, 21, and 22 comprise the intron in this strand. Have the students remove the intron and reconnect the remaining pieces, or exons.

8. Now have the students use the 33 base mRNA strand to create a double-stranded DNA molecule for hGH. Creating this strand is a two-step process. First, the students code for a DNA strand based on the existing mRNA. Second, they create a complementary strand of DNA based on the first strand of DNA. In a lab, a scientist would use the *enzyme reverse transcriptase* to accomplish the task of copying a DNA molecule from the mRNA strand.

9. Check the students' work and then ask them to lay this representation of the hGH gene along the top of their desks.

10. Now the students need to create a paper clip model of a plasmid. Using the same color key, ask the students to create the following double-stranded DNA sequence:

1	2	3	4	5	6	7	8	9	10
G -	G -	A -	T -	C -	C -	T -	G -	A	—C
C -	C -	T -	A -	G -	G -	A -	C -	T	—G
11	12	13	14	15	16	17	18	19	20
A —C	—C	—G	—G	—A	—A	—C	—G	—T	
T —G	—G	—C	—C	—T	—T	—G	—C	—A	
21	22	23	24	25	26	27	28	29	30
C —A	—A	—G	—C	—T	—T	—C	—C	—C	
G —T	—T	—C	—G	—A	—A	—G	—G	—G	

11. Because plasmids are circular, have the students attach base 1 to base 30 in each strand of the plasmid sequence. They should mark the point of attachment with a piece of tape. Ask the students to lay the double-stranded circles on their desks. The students are now ready to recombine DNA molecules.

12. To insert the gene for hGH into the plasmid, both the hGH gene and the plasmid need "sticky ends" (complementary bases) that will attach to each other. To create these sticky ends, genetic engineers cut gene sequences with very specific restriction enzymes. These enzymes will only cut DNA in specific places, as shown below, and only if the entire sequence is present.

Ask the students which of the enzymes listed below will cut both the hGH gene and plasmid in sites that leave the hGH gene intact:

Enzyme	Cutting Site		
BAM 1	G	GATC	C
	C	CTAG	G
Hind III	A	AGCT	T
	T	TCGA	A
Hpa II	C	CG	G
	G	GC	C

13. After the students have discovered that Hind III is the only restriction enzyme that will cut the gene and the plasmid at appropriate sites, instruct them to "cut" their genes and plasmids and connect the spliced gene to the plasmid. Mark these places with tape to represent the enzyme *ligase*, which "pastes" complementary sticky ends together in nature and in the lab.

14. In a lab, scientists would next insert altered plasmids into many bacteria, which would reproduce and create identical bacteria containing altered plasmids. Because these bacteria contain altered plasmids, they are capable of producing hGH. Use the Figure to review this entire process with your students.

Opening Pandora's Box

1. Explain to your students that although scientists can easily use bacterial hosts to clone recombinant DNA and produce large amounts of a

desired protein, many difficult questions arise. Because bacteria divide so rapidly, there is virtually no limit to the synthesis of new genetic combinations. For people in need of a steady supply of insulin or human growth hormone, the products of this type of genetic engineering are invaluable. But what happens if, as in the case of hGH, a person wants to take the readily available biosynthetic growth hormone just to attain greater height? After such a large investment in research and development, the companies that manufacture the biosynthetic growth hormone might be happy to expand their market beyond hGH deficient children. Should physicians prescribe biosynthetic growth hormone to anyone who wants to be taller? Though these questions point out that in certain situations most everyone accepts genetic engineering, that is, the pro-

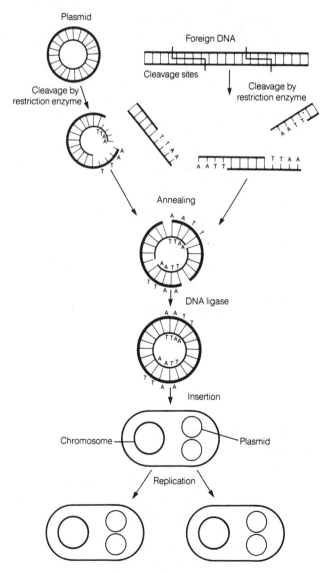

The process of genetic engineering

duction of recombinant molecules, however, many questions remain about how to regulate the resulting product.

2. Write the following viewpoints on separate index cards:

- You are the CEO of the company that developed and produced biosynthetic hGH. Your board of directors and stockholders expect this product to make a profit for the company. Even if every patient who needs hGH bought your product, the company would not recoup its investment in the development of the hormone. To whom will you market this product?

- As a pediatrician who treats children who have insufficient amounts of hGH, you are aware of the potential side effects of the biosynthetic hormone (glucose intolerance, hypertension, abnormal bone development, and enlargement of the heart, which may lead to heart failure). Some parents have asked you to prescribe hGH for a child of average height because they know that height is a desirable characteristic in our culture. What will you do?

- You are a basketball player in junior high school. You are quite good, but want to improve your chances for playing basketball in high school, in college, and maybe even professionally. If you were just a little bit taller, you would really stand out on the team. A biosynthetic growth hormone could add those centimeters, but you may develop diabetes; end up with elongated hands, feet, and chin; or even suffer heart problems. What do you think? Would you try a little hGH?

- You are the parent of a child who has an hGH deficiency. Your child has a moderate deficiency and will probably be 15–20 centimeters shorter than average when grown. Because this biosynthetic hormone is very new, no one knows what the long-term side effects may be. If your son takes biosynthetic growth hormone, he has a 50-50 chance of reaching average adult height. What will you do?

3. Divide the class into four groups and distribute one card to each group. Ask the students to discuss the hGH issue from the point of view presented on their card.

4. After each group has developed a rationale representing its view of the issue on the card, ask each group to present its issue and conclusions to the rest of the class. Do any of the groups want to reconsider their positions based on the new information?

5. Genetically altered bacteria can bear new and unforeseen genetic combinations. Release of these bacteria into the environment poses problems that concern scientists, bioethicists (people who address the ethical, legal, and public policy issues raised by the biomedical sciences), and the general public.

Explain to your students that genetic engineers are working on a variety of projects other than the two hormones already mentioned. Scientists have developed prenatal diagnostic tests that use restriction fragment length polymorphisms (RFLPs) to check for disorders, such as sickle-cell anemia, thalassemia, and hemophilia. Genetic technology has resulted in the ability to use viral vectors to carry genes as a possible treatment for metabolic disorders and has resulted in the use of recombinant interleukin-2 to treat cancer. Scientists are also developing and using techniques to improve crop yield, the nutritional value of seed crops, and the resistance of crop plants to pests, pathogens, and environmental damage. All of these techniques or products raise ethical dilemmas.

6. To encourage your students to think about these ethical issues, distribute a copy of the following questions to each student. Ask the students to answer the questions, on a separate sheet of paper, in the following manner: read the first question, think about it, and then write the answer to the question. The answer should be short and take only one minute to write. Do the same for the rest of the questions.

a. If the results of genetic technology create a real conflict between benefits and risks, what price should we be willing to pay for new knowledge?

b. Should we allow scientists to alter bacteria genetically and release them into the environment without being certain of the end result? If so, in what cases?

c. Should we allow scientists to control the evolutionary destiny of any organism? What limits, if any, should we place on scientific research?

d. Should representatives of the lay public be involved in determining the direction of genetic technology? Why or why not? How will people determine the direction of this type of scientific research?

7. After all the students have answered the questions, discuss their answers. Are there clear "right" or "wrong" answers to these questions? How do we decide what is "right" or "wrong"?

Resources for the Classroom

This activity was adapted from *Advances in Genetic Technology,* developed by BSCS, published by D.C. Heath & Co., Lexington, MA, 1988. (For more activities, including laboratory investigations, please refer to this book.)

BSCS, *Basic Genetics: A Human Approach* (Dubuque, IA: Kendall Hunt Publishing Co., 1983). (A six-week module on basic genetics for high school students.)

BSCS, *Genes and Surroundings* (Dubuque, IA: Kendall Hunt Publishing Co., 1983). (A six-week module on basic genetics for middle school students.)

The Industrial Biotechnology Association has a number of flyers and films available related to biotechnology. (Contact K. Sherrod Shim, Director of Communications, IBA, 1625 K Street, NW, Suite 1100, Washington, DC, 20006, or 202/857-0244; FAX: 202/857-0237.)

Background for the Teacher

The Sphinx, the Minotaur, and the Chimera—Greek mythology is full of such hybrid creatures. In the real world, natural barriers normally prevent the exchange of genetic information between unrelated organisms, but recombinant DNA technology has made it possible to breach genetic barriers by excising a DNA segment from one organism and joining it to a DNA segment of an unrelated species. The breaking and rejoining of DNA molecules from unrelated organisms result in recombinant DNA molecules.

Scientists use bacteria to clone recombinant DNA molecules. Some bacteria contain plasmids—small, circular, double-stranded DNA molecules that are distinct from chromosomal DNA. In the early 1970s Annie Chang and Stanley Cohen succeeded in isolating and purifying plasmid DNA molecules. These small *extrachromosomal* elements can replicate inside the bacterium and independently of the bacterial chromosome. Because they are self-replicating entities, plasmids will propagate indefinitely in the *E. coli* bacterial culture. By the same token, any foreign DNA spliced into the plasmid DNA will replicate as well. Because bacteria divide every 20 minutes, they can reproduce, within a day, billions of organisms carrying hundreds or thousands of plasmids. In this manner, foreign genes are amplified—cloned—yielding large quantities of purified genes.

Many people have concerns about genetic engineering. Even though *E. coli* is part of the normal human intestinal flora, critics of recombinant DNA technology fear that scientists might inadvertently allow *E. coli* that bear new genetic combinations to escape from the laboratory. For example, some people fear that a human could become accidentally infected with the *E. coli* strain that synthesizes human growth hormone. The hormone would pour into the intestine, unregulated by the body, upset the body's chemical balance and possibly result in death. Or they fear that someone might produce an *E. coli* strain that secretes a deadly toxin. Other concerned people think that genetic recombinants might produce adverse effects on human, animal, or plant populations.

Scientists also recognize the potential risks of genetic engineering. In 1973, concerned scientists wrote two letters that raised the question of regulating this type of research. As a result of the publication of these letters, in 1975 a group of scientists met in Asilomar, California, to discuss the risks of using recombinant DNA technology, as well as to discuss benefits and possible mechanisms for regulation. The scientists agreed to use voluntary guidelines to regulate experimentation. They decided that they could use physical containment in many experiments, such as glove boxes and laminar flow hoods, to prevent the escape of novel organisms and to protect laboratory workers. The researchers also suggested that they might genetically "cripple" cloning vectors (plasmids) and *E. coli* hosts and thus provide a form of biological containment.

Today, the Recombinant DNA Advisory Committee at the National Institute of Health must approve all genetic research funded by the federal government. Many industrial scientists voluntarily seek the approval of this committee for their work. Few other areas of scientific research are as heavily regulated as genetic engineering. Some scientists feel that this heavy amount of regulation is excessive and impedes scientific research. Others feel this amount of regulation prevents abuse. Many countries have regulations more relaxed than those in the U.S. This inequity puts the U.S. at a disadvantage in international competition. How much regulation is enough? Who should decide? What are the costs and benefits of such regulations? Clearly, there are many questions for scientists and nonscientists to answer; but only the well-informed can answer these questions.

References

M. Benjamin, et al. "Short Children, Anxious Parents: Is Growth Hormone the Answer?" *Hastings Center Report,* 14(2) (1984):13.

W. J. Brill, "Safety Concerns and Genetic Engineering in Agriculture, *Science, 227* (4685) (1985):381.

F. E. Farber, Unpublished handout from *Biology 10* (Northfield, MN: Carleton College, 1980).

Office of Technology Assessment, *Genetic Technology: A New Frontier* (Boulder, CO: Westview Press, 1982).

L. Tangley, "Engineered Organisms in the Environment? Not Yet." *BioScience, 33*(11) (1983):681.

AN INTRODUCTION TO POPULATION, RESOURCES, AND ENVIRONMENT

Overview

The aim of this activity is to develop a general understanding of the technology, economics, environmental effects and social issues related to finding and extracting resources.

Student Objectives

At the completion of this lesson the participant should be able to:

- Describe the relationship between population growth and resource use
- Define resource
- Describe the difference between reserves and resources

- Describe the role of technology, economics and environmental effects on the extraction and use of resources
- Describe the difficulties in making decisions about the distribution of limited resources

Materials

Pennies (300)

Tweezers

Toothpicks

Other items commonly available in classrooms

Riddle of lily pond

Handout of worksheets

Instructional Plan

A. Exploration

1. Use riddle to focus attention and introduce relationship between population and resources.

> There is a lily pond that has a single leaf.
> Each day the number of leaves doubles.
> On the second day there are two leaves.
> On the third day there are four leaves.
> On the fourth day there are eight leaves.
> On the thirtieth day the pond is full.
> When was the pond half full?   Set

2. Show film "World Population".
3. Purpose statement and transition to activity   Purpose
4. Explain the activity.
   - The activity simulates the exploration and extraction of earth materials needed by individuals and society.
   - Students first explore the room to assess the availability of resources (pennies).
   - Report on resources that were observed and introduce definitions. Summarize data on overhead.
   - Have the students actually "mine" the resources. Students must record the number of pennies found each minute.
   - Students must use objects to extract pennies.
   - Students will have 10–15 minutes to obtain pennies.
   - Complete a graph of the pennies found each minute.
5. Do the first exploration. Have the students spend 3 minutes looking around the room to determine how many pennies there are. (Review rules: they   Active Participation
   cannot touch, turn over, change furniture, and they cannot collect any pennies)
6. Return to groups. Have the groups report on their findings. Record observations on overhead.

B. Explanation

7. Define reserves, resources, and technology.   Information Input
8. Have the students actually "mine" the resources.   Active
9. Provide time to complete graphs.   Participation

10. Summarize and discuss resource activity.
    - What happened as their extraction of resources continued?
    - Did they find all the resources?
    - How close were the estimates of the resources?
    - What problems did they experience with time? Extraction? Location?
    - How is this activity like the actual extraction of resources?
    - What is the relationship of technology to your activity? Of economics? Of population? Of environment?
    C. Extension
11. Introduce the simulation game involving the distribution of resources.
12. Have participants complete the individual and group decisions.
13. Discuss the distribution simulation.
    - What was the basis for your individual and group decision?
    - What other information would you have requested?
    - Would you change your decisions if more units of resources were available?
    - How could more resources be obtained?
    - What lifestyle changes, price increases, environmental effects, etc. would you be willing to tolerate in order to have more resources?
D. Evaluation
14. Conclude with a discussion of the interrelationship of population, resources, and environment

Reinforcement

Transfer

Assessment

Transfer

Decision Making

Values

Personal Meaning

Closure

Definitions

Reserves: the amount of a particular resource in known locations that can be extracted at a profit with present technology and prices.

Resources: The total amount of a particular material that exists on earth.

Technology: (a) the application of science, especially to industrial or commercial objectives; (b) the entire body of methods and materials used to achieve industrial or commercial objectives; (c) the body of knowledge available to a civilization that is of use in fashioning implements, practicing manual arts and skills, and extracting or collecting resources.

Data Sheet for Distributing Resources

Your problem is to decide how to distribute resources among three groups who have requested your help. For this activity we are using the term resources to include many different things such as food, minerals, fuels, and other items needed by people. Here is the only information you have to make your decisions:

You have 300 units of resources

You presently use 200 units of resources

You can survive on 100 units of resources

Three groups want some of your resources. Here are their situations:

Group 1 —needs 250 units of resources to survive
—wants 250 units of resources

Group 2 —needs 100 units of resources to survive
—wants 200 units for survival and improvement

Group 3 —needs 50 units for survival
—wants 100 units for improvement

Group 4 —needs no units for survival
—wants 200 units for improvement

Your problem is to decide how you will distribute the resources.

Groups	1	2	3	4	5	6	7
Reserves							
Estimates of Resources							
Actual Resources							

Individual Decisions

Distribution of Resources	Group 1	Group 2	Group 3	Group 4
Reasons for Decision				

Group Decisions

Distribution of Resources	Group 1	Group 2	Group 3	Group 4
Reasons for Decision				

EVALUATING FOOD CHOICES

Overview

Students keep a record of the food they eat for one day. By means of a graph, the students evaluate their food choices. This activity is designed for middle/junior high school.

Science Background

Nutrients can be defined as the different substances in foods that function specifically to keep the body healthy. active, and growing. Some of the major nutrients needed by the body include proteins, fats, carbohydrates, vitamins, and minerals.

Protein is the body's building material. It contains nitrogen, which is necessary for all tissue building. Protein is essential for maintaining body structure, for providing substances that act as body regulators, and for producing compounds necessary for normal body functions. Milk products, meat, fish, poultry, eggs, legumes, and nuts are good sources of protein.

While protein can also provide energy for the body, *fats* and *carbohydrates* are the major food substances that provide the body with calories for heat and energy. If the body lacks sufficient amounts of fats and carbohydrates, or if there is an excess of protein in the diet, the body will use protein for heat and energy. Fats are normally consumed from margarine, butter, mayonnaise, salad dressings, and meat. Carbohydrates are found in grain products, fruit, and sugar-sweetened foods.

Although vitamins and minerals are needed in smaller quantities than are protein, fats, and carbohydrates, they remain essential to normal body functioning. Our discussion is limited to those often lacking in the diets of adolescents.

Vitamin A is important for vision. Night blindness, an inability of the eye to adjust to dim light, can result from a lack of vitamin A in the diet. Yellow, orange, and dark green vegetables, and fruits contain vitamin A (sweet potatoes, carrots, squash, spinach, broccoli, melon, apricots, and peaches).

Vitamin C contributes to the formation of a substance called collagen, which holds body tissue together and encourages healing. Vitamin C also strengthens blood vessel walls and helps the body utilize calcium in making bones and teeth. Scurvy, a disease characterized by swelling and tenderness of joints and gums, loosening of teeth, hemorrhaging, and puffiness can result from severe lack of vitamin C. Citrus fruits, broccoli, spinach, greens, potatoes, tomatoes, melon, cabbage, and strawberries contain this vitamin.

Iron is a mineral that is essential to hemoglobin, the substance of the blood that carries oxygen. Oxygen is necessary for all cells. A diet that fails to supply a sufficient amount of iron may lead to anemia. This condition is characterized by a tired and listless feeling due to a lack of energy. Although liver is a major source of iron, greens, beans, beef, pork, prunes, and raisins are also good sources.

Calcium is the bone and tooth building mineral. It forms the structure of teeth and bones and helps keep them strong. Milk products are good sources for calcium.

Major Concept

Individuals should develop eating patterns that contribute to wellness.

Student Objectives

By the end of this activity, the students should be able to:

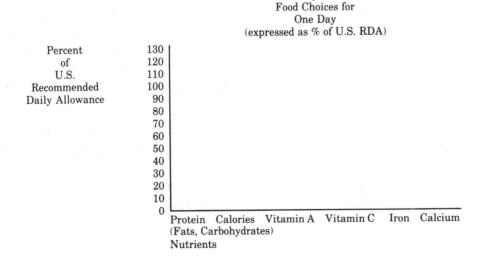

Graph of
Food Choices for
One Day
(expressed as % of U.S. RDA)

- Analyze and evaluate food choices in terms of the Recommended Daily Allowance (RDA) of protein, energy, and selected vitamins and minerals.

Materials

Comprehensive List of Foods booklet with nutritive values and percent of U.S. RDA for 139 foods, available from the National Dairy Council. Contact the office serving your area or write: National Dairy Council 630 North River Road Rosemont, IL 60018.

Vocabulary

anemia	minerals	Recommended Daily Allowance (RDA)
calories	night blindness	
carbohydrates	nutrient	
fats	proteins	scurvy
		vitamins

Procedures

1. Have the students keep a complete record of all foods eaten for one day.
2. Using the "Comprehensive List of Foods," the students should then determine the nutritive values and graph the percent of RDA that chosen foods contained. (See sample graph.)
3. Upon completion of the bar graphs, invite the students to answer the following questions:

   Is the percentage of calories (energy) in your daily diet too low, about right, or too high?

   Nutrients I need more of are_____

   Which foods could provide these nutrients?

   Foods I ate that had a lot of calories (energy) but not many other nutrients are_____

   How can I improve my diet?

THE EVOLUTION SIMULATION GAME*

Overview

The following game simulates the process of evolution. It clearly demonstrates the role of mutations, adaptations, and chance in this process. The game can also be used as an introduction to food chains, the effects of competition within an environment, the effects of pollution, or man's role in relation to environmental issues. It is designed for high school students, but with some modifications it could be played with junior high school students.

Science Background

Charles Darwin's theory of evolution states that every species on the earth is undergoing constant, gradual change controlled by natural selection. Today it is generally accepted that these changes are caused by genetic mutations. Those mutations that are harmful are weeded out by the low survival rate of their carriers. Conversely, those mutations that are beneficial gradually become more common due to the high survival rate of their carriers. Whether a given mutation is beneficial or detrimental is determined by the organism's environment: temperature, precipitation, competition, predators, and pollution.

Additional Sources

Charles Darwin, *On the Origin of Species* (Cambridge, MA: Harvard University Press, 1964).
Charles Darwin, *The Illustrated Origin of Species* abridged and introduction by Richard E. Leakey (New York: Hill and Wang, 1979).
Paul Amos Moody, *Introduction to Evolution* (New York: Harper and Row, 1970).
Ruth E. Moore, *Evolution* (New York: Time, Inc., 1964).

Major Concepts

- Mutations occur at random and their results cannot be predicted; organisms do not choose to mutate.
- Some mutations help a species adapt and survive in its environment.
- Just how helpful a mutation will be depends on the environment.
- Organisms with characteristics well suited to the environment in which they live will be able to adapt and survive.

Student Objectives

After this activity students should be able to:

- Describe the relationship between mutations and adaptations.
- Explain how natural mutations facilitate evolution.
- Describe the role the environment plays in evolution.
- Identify ways in which evolution is continuing today.

*This activity was developed and field tested by Ms. Kathy James, Carleton College, Northfield, Minnesota. It is used with her permission.

Vocabulary

Mutation

Adaptation

Materials

Handout stating rules of the game and describing the original organism.

Overheads listing the mutation for each round (1–41)

Cards stating the environmental changes (1–19)

A map of the region (see below)

Rules of the Game

All players begin as the same organism (described below) in the same geographic location (square K).

The game will be organized into rounds that represent periods of roughly one million years. These rounds will be organized as follows:

- At the beginning of each round each player picks up to two mutations from a list prepared by the teacher. The mutations for each round should be displayed on an overhead. Suggested rounds are listed below.
- Do not allow students to see the list of mutations for future rounds. Most mutations will appear in more than one round. New mutations will be added each round.
- Each mutation is permanent to the player's species and will be effective in all the following rounds.
- Any new mutation replaces any contradicting traits. These contradictions are explained in brackets [ ] after the mutation.
- Some mutations require previous mutations, which are listed in parentheses ( ) after the mutation.
- In any round, any student may choose to migrate one square in any direction as one of his mutations, but the species must have adapted to survive any changes in climate caused by the migration. (See The Region for a more detailed explanation.)
- After all mutations have been chosen, an environmental change is picked. This can be done by randomly drawing from a hat, thereby emphasizing the role of chance in evolution, or the sequence of mutations can be chosen by the teacher, allowing for the emphasis to be on the effects of specific environmental changes.
- The environmental changes only have an effect in the round in which they are chosen; no points will be gained or lost for past environmental changes.
- Students can be allowed to debate whether an environmental change was beneficial to their organism. Guidelines are included below, but these are only guidelines.

Scoring

Each student begins with five points. A score of zero represents extinction and the player is out of the game. Players attempt to survive and increase their scores.

If an environmental change is beneficial, + 1

If an environmental change is detrimental, − 1

Optional: After the first four rounds, competition may become a factor in scoring. See The Region for an explanation of the scoring if competition is included.

The Original Species: A Salamander

Color: red

Skin: moist, soft

Size: 6 inches long

Body temperature: cold blooded

Diet: Algae, swallowed whole

Reproduction: Attracts mate by smell

Mates on land

Lays eggs in shallow pools of water

Does not care for young in any way

Behavior: Does not hibernate

Low endurance—must rest after running or swimming 150 yards

Poor swimmer—is carried away by a current flowing faster than half a mile per hour

Poor jumper—can jump only one inch vertically

Moderate runner—runs at the speed of the average house cat

Rests at night in holes in the ground, under logs, or wherever it can find some shelter

General: Mute

Body and eggs absorb salts from salt water so it cannot survive in a saltwater environment

The Region

The map and descriptions of the various regions on the map allow the teacher to include competition as a factor influencing the course of evolution. After the first five rounds, if there are three or more players in a given square each player loses a point. If two players are in a square and a third player then moves in that square, making a total of three players in the square, only the player moving into the square loses a point. (The maximum limit per square will need to be increased to 3 if more than 15 students are playing.)

These migrations will force players into new environments, which are described below. Players must have adapted to survive the conditions they will encounter before moving into an environment. For example, a player cannot migrate away from the river until he can reproduce on dry land.

This aspect of the game is optional. If it is included, tell the students about the environments they will encounter in each square, an discuss the adaptations necessary to survive in each environment before the game begins.

A	E	I	M
B	F	J	N
C	G	K	O
D	H	L	P

Square A is a northern region. It is well forested, with a wide variety of trees, plants, and animals. But six months a year the ground is covered with snow, making plant life very hard to find and a fur coat a necessity. Cold-blooded animals cannot survive here, nor those who lay their eggs in water, since pools of water are scarce. Seasonal coloring, allowing an animal to be white in the winter but brown or green in the summer, is necessary here. Hibernation is also beneficial and would eliminate the need for seasonal coloring.

Squares B, E, and F are similar, but the winters are less severe. A fur coat and seasonal coloring will be helpful, but they are not a necessity.

Squares C and G are open prairie. There is little or no tree cover, but a wide variety of plants grow here. Many small birds and animals live in the grasses. Winters are cool, but snow rarely accumulates.

Square D is a desert. Days are hot and dry, but nights can be very cool. It never snows here. Water is sometimes hard to find, but desert plants are common. Some desert animals can be found here.

Squares L and P are salt water regions. Those animals whose skin is permeable to salt cannot survive here.

Squares O and N are cut off from the rest of the region by the river, so only flying predators will affect species living there. To live in this region, species must develop the ability to cross the river, which requires increased endurance and webbed feet (or three times the original endurance if webbed feet are not added).

All other squares, H, I, J and K, represent forested regions bordered by a large river. There is plenty of plant and animal life to support other forms of life. Winters are not severe; snow rarely accumulates.

Mutations

1. dryer skin
2. develops scales (1)
3. develops hair (1, 2) [cancels 4]
4. develops shell-like exterior (2) [cancels 3, 36]
5. develops brown pigment, producing reddish brown color [cancels 8, 10]
6. increases brown pigment, producing solid brown (5)
7. develops white pigment, producing spotted white [cancels 6, 10]
8. increases white pigment, producing solid white in color (7)
9. develops green pigment, producing spotted green [cancels 6, 8]
10. increases green pigment, producing solid green color (9)
11. seasonal color changes (5, 7, or 9) [cancels 12]
12. variety in pigment allowing color to change to fit environment, chameleon coloring (5, 9) [cancels 11]
13. variety in pigment so that mates are attracted by coloring (5, 7, or 9) [replaces use of scent to attract a mate so scent is lost]
14. skin becomes impermeable to salts found in salt water

Changes in Diet

15. develops small molars, allowing organism to chew plants
16. adds enzyme in the digestive track, allowing digestion of insects swallowed with the water
17. adds small canines, allowing organism to eat mice-sized rodents (16)
18. develops larger canines, allowing the organism to eat larger prey (17)
19. develops claws
20. develops a frog-line tongue, which allows the organism to catch flying insects (16)

Changes in Body Temperature and Habitat

21. becomes warm blooded (1)
22. becomes nocturnal (21)
23. builds a den/nest
24. spends part of its waking hours in trees (19)
25. nests in trees (23, 24)
26. burrows, nesting under ground (19)

Changes in Means of Reproduction

27. develops a protective covering on eggs
28. lays eggs on land (27)

29. develops pigment in egg shell which acts as a camouflage (27)
30. cares for young after eggs hatch
31. becomes a marsupial (30)
32. carries young to term (30)
33. uses voice to attract mates [replaces scent used to attract a mate]

Changes in Locomotion

34. changes in circulatory system increase endurance
35. develops webbed feet
36. leg length doubles, producing longer legs in proportion to body size, and allowing for swifter running—twice as fast as before
37. develops stronger leg muscles, allowing for greater jumping ability—twice as high as before [initial jumping ability was one inch]
38. loses limbs [cancels 35, 36, 37, 39]
39. develops fins (35) [cancels 37, 38]

Other Changes

40. increases size 50 percent (34)
41. lives in water continually (34, 35)

Environmental Changes

1. Flies begin to be seen in the area [helps 16 + 20]
2. Temperatures drop; only severe in region A, where temperatures are now consistently below freezing and snow accumulates [little effect]
3. Small green land plants become common [helps 15]
4. Worms and slugs become common [helps 16]
5. Drought: small pools dry up and the river level drops 2 feet [hurts those without 28, 31, 32]
6. A herbivorous turtle moves into the region by the river [hurts those without 15, 16, 17, or 20]
7. Rabbits begin to populate the region [helps those with 18, hurts those with 15]
8. The population of song birds in the region increases [little effect]
9. A population of freshwater carnivorous turtles moves into the river [hurts those without 28 and those with 41]
10. A population of freshwater fish that eats eggs laid in the water moves into the river [hurts those without 28 unless they also have 30, helps those with 18 that still live in or near the river]
11. A snake similar to a rattlesnake develops in the region; snakes locate their prey by warmer body temperatures [hurts those with 21 unless they have 40]
12. Hawks migrate into the region [hurts those without some form of protective coloring]
13. A weasel moves into the region; weasels locate their prey by scent [hurts those without 13 or 33; helps those with 18 and 40 four times]
14. A flood washes away regions near the river [hurts those in squares I, J, K, L, M, N, O who are without 24]
15. Sewage dumped into the river contaminates the river downstream from square J [hurts all in squares, J, K, N, O, L, P]
16. An oil spill contaminates the saltwater sea [hurts all those in squares L, O, P]
17. Prairie fire sweeps across square C [hurts those in square C without 16 and 17, helps those in square C with 16 and 17]
18. People begin to hunt species over 15 inches long [hurts those with 40 four or more times]
19. Squares I and M become a game refuge [helps all in those squares]

Tips for Playing the Game

1. Keep a simplified copy of the rules and a description of the original species where it will be visible to all the students throughout the time that the game is played. The easiest way to do this will probably be to give each student his or her own copy.
2. Have each student record his or her species evolution by writing down his or her choices of mutation and the environmental changes of each round.
3. After the first three or four rounds have been played, stop to discuss how the students' species have evolved to this point. What do they look like now? What advantages do they have that help them survive? Where can they best survive? Is there anywhere they could not survive? What additional changes might help them even more? Is it possible that evolution really happened this way?
4. Spend one full class period introducing and playing the game. Additional games/rounds can be played later with less preparation time. One round a day can be played, using the environmental changes as a means of focusing attention on the lesson topic. Or it may be useful on those days when the film you planned to show fails to come in or you did not have time to write up a lesson plan for the substitute teacher.
5. There is no limit to the number of rounds that can be played. Listed are 19 environmental changes, but these can be repeated or the list can be expanded.
6. Currently, the mutations will not allow a species to fly or walk erect. These advances involve an

incredible number of mutations. It might be a good idea to tell students this when the game begins.

7. There are no predators other than those introduced as environmental changes. Do not tell the students what types of predators these will be.

Suggested Mutation Choices

Round 1: 1, 5, 9, 15, 16, 17, 21, 27, 28, 34, 35, 40
Round 2: 7, 10, 14, 15, 16, 19, 21, 27, 29, 30, 36, 40
Round 3: 2, 3, 12, 15, 20, 22, 26, 28, 30, 33, 34, 39
Round 4: 6, 8, 11, 18, 19, 23, 29, 31, 36, 38, 39, 41

Round 5: 1, 3, 4, 5, 13, 15, 16, 24, 32, 34, 35, 36
Round 6: 2, 14, 19, 20, 21, 26, 28, 30, 33, 37, 39, 40
Round 7: 6, 7, 10, 11, 17, 18, 22, 23, 24, 32, 36, 38
Round 8: 4, 8, 9, 19, 29, 31, 34, 36, 37, 39, 40, 41
Round 9: 2, 3, 5, 13, 22, 33
Round 10: 13, 14, 35, 36, 39, 40
Round 11: 11, 14, 23, 32, 38, 39
Round 12: 3, 4, 27, 29, 40, 41
Round 13: 15, 24, 26, 30, 37, 39
Round 14: 13, 16, 22, 29, 36, 40
Round 15: 23, 26, 32, 33, 35, 41
Round 16: 4, 18, 22, 26, 40, 42
Round 17: 1, 12, 16, 34, 35, 41

USING AN IDENTIFICATION KEY

Overview

In this activity students use a simple identification key to classify several animals. The activity is designed for middle/junior high school levels. This activity can be adapted and programmed for use on a microcomputer.

Student Objectives

At the completion of this activity students should be able to:

- Use a simple identification key
- Describe the usefulness of classifying organisms
- Apply the identification key to identify an unknown organism

Materials

A variety of common organisms. The organisms should represent different phyla in the animal kingdom (see key for examples). In general organisms commonly found in life science classrooms can be used.

A key for each student or groups of students (see below).

Common references for information about organisms of different phyla.

Procedures

1. Divide the class into groups of students. The size of groups should be determined by the number and variety of organisms available.
2. Provide 3–4 organisms for each group of students.

3. Distribute and introduce the key to the students. Some of the points to make are
   - The key is made up of a series of questions that can be answered by either YES or NO.
   - The answer leads to the next question or identification of the organism.
   - Go through the key and identify one organism at a time.
4. Have the students proceed to identify their organisms.
5. The students should look up information about the organisms they have identified.
6. As a follow-up evaluation have the students go out of doors and identify an "unknown" organism.

A Classification Key

1. Does the animal have a backbone? If your answer is YES go to 1a. If it is NO, go to 2.
   1a. Does the animal have hair or fur on its body? If YES, it is a MAMMAL. If NO, go to 1b.
   1b. Does the animal have feathers? If YES, its scientific name is AVES. If NO, go to 1c.
   1c. Does the animal have smooth skin and lay its eggs in water? If YES, it is an AMPHIBIAN. If NO, go to 1d.
   1d. Does the animal have scaly skin and lay its eggs on land? If YES, it is a REPTILE. If NO, go to 1e.
   1e. Does the animal have scaly skin and lay its eggs in water? If YES, it is an OSTE-ICHTHYES. If NO, return to question 1 and check to be sure the animal has a backbone.
2. If the animal does not have a backbone begin here. Does the animal have a hard, outside covering and jointed legs? If YES, it is an ARTHRO-POD—go to 2a. If NO, go to 3.

2a. Does the animal have three pairs of legs? If YES, it is an INSECT. If NO, go to 2b.

2b. Does the animal have four pair of legs and two body sections? If YES, it is an ARACHNID. If NO, go to 2c.

2c. Does the animal have at least 5 pairs of legs and a hard covering? If YES, it is a CRUSTACEAN. If NO, go to 2d.

2d. Does the animal have many body sections with a pair of legs on each section? If YES, it is a CENTIPEDE. If NO, go to 2e.

2e. Does the animal have many body sections with 2 pairs of legs on each section? If YES, it is a MILLIPEDE. If NO, return to 2.

3. Does the animal have spines covering its skin? If YES, it is an ECHINODERM. If NO, go to 4.

4. Does the animal have a hard shell covering a soft body? If YES, it is a MOLLUSK. If NO, go to 5.

5. Does the animal have a long, wormlike body with many sections? If YES, it is an ANNELID. If NO go to 6.

6. Is your animal wormlike with a smooth tapered body? If YES, it is a NEMATODA. If NO, go to 7.

7. Does the animal have a flat ribbonlike body? If YES, it is PLATYHELMINTHES. If NO, go to 8.

8. Does the animal have tentacles around the mouth opening and a soft body? If YES, it is a COELENTERATE. If NO, go to 9.

9. Does the animal have openings, called pores, all over its body? If YES, it is a PORIFERA. If NO, go back to question 1, 2, or 3.

EFFECTS OF ACID RAIN ON SEED GERMINATION

Overview

Students investigate the effects of acid rain on seed germination by conducting an experiment with bean seeds, or locally available seed, under varying pH conditions. The estimated time for this activity is one class period to organize groups and set up the experiment. Then, take a few minutes at the start of every other class for approximately two weeks to water and measure seed growth, and to record data on individual and class groups.

Major Concepts

- Seed germination is dependent upon proper conditions of pH.
- Increases of acidity due to acid rain may inhibit seed germination and plant growth.

Student Objectives

After the activity students should be able to:

- Measure the growth of bean seed.
- Record data on an individual graph and on a class graph.
- Draw the bean seed before seed germination and each day that growth measurements are taken.
- Make a summary graph of individual graphs.
- Compare data to establish the optimum pH for the germination of a bean seed.

Materials

Petri dish

4 bean seeds (preferably seeds grown locally: alfalfa, pea, bean, etc.)

Water solutions ranging in pH from 2–7 (boiling will be necessary to drive off CO_2 and raise pH to 7)

Rain water (optional)

Absorbent paper towels

Transparent metric ruler

Graph paper

Colored chalk or magic markers

Procedures

Preparation of bean seed:

1. Assign each student a pH solution to "water" their bean seeds. A couple of students should be assigned distilled or rain water for a control. The class as a whole should represent increments on a pH scale ranging from 2–7.
2. Cut four paper discs the size of a petri dish from the absorbent paper towel.
3. Dampen the paper discs with appropriate pH or rain water solution.
4. Place two discs at the bottom of the petri dish.
5. Measure the seeds and average them.
6. Arrange seeds in the petri dish and cover with the two remaining paper discs.
7. Replace lid on petri dish and label with student name.
8. Each student should hypothesize what they believe will be the ideal pH on a piece of paper.

Preparation of Graph

1. Obtain a piece of 8 × 11 graph paper.
2. Set up graph as follows: Horizontal axis, age of seed in days; Vertical axis, length of seed in mm.

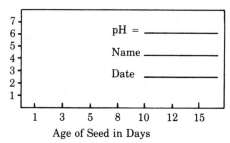

Straight Length of seed in mm.

pH = _____
Name _____
Date _____

Age of Seed in Days

Procedures for Alternate Days

The students will be taking measurements of seed growth and recording data on individual and class graphs.

- Take measurements and plotting data on individual graphs.
- Remove lid from petri dish.
- Sketch the shapes of the four seeds. Note the color of the seeds.
- Use transparent ruler to measure the straight length of seeds.
- Take the average straight line length increase and plot it on your graph. (It is important to plot the increase of seed growth because seeds are different lengths before germination takes place.)
- Make sure paper towel is still moist. If not, add more pH solution (be sure pH solutions are not mixed).
- Replace lid on petri dish.
- Construct class graph on chalkboard or large piece of white construction paper on visible wall or board and saved throughout experiment. The graph should use same layout as individual graphs.
- Assign each pH a particular color (chalk or magic marker).

- More than one student may be experimenting with the same pH solution. These students should average their results of seed length.
- Have one student representing each pH record data on the board using the code color that represents pH used. (example: a pH of 3 is represented by the color green; a pH of 7 is represented by the color purple).
- After a few recordings have been plotted, students should draw a line connecting points of same pH.

Discussion Questions

1. What appears to be the first optimal pH solution for successful seed germination and growth? The least ideal?
2. How does the local rainwater used compare to the other pH solutions used?
3. From the data expressed on the class graph, what pH do you think the rainwater has?

Evaluation

Each student should prepare a report that includes:

- Brief description and purpose of experiment
- Data collected, individual graphs, and seed drawings
- Analysis of individual class results:
  1. Ideal pH
  2. Least ideal pH
  3. Comparison of rainwater to other pH solutions
- Discussion questions: What impact on local crops might an increased acidity have? Do you think there is a reason for concern?
- A concrete example of how acid rain and its effect on seed germination could make an effect on food crops grown in the nearest agricultural area

EFFECTS OF ACID RAIN ON THE LIFE CYCLE OF FRUIT FLIES

Overview

Students investigate the effects of varying levels of acid mist on egg, larval, and pupal stages of the life cycle of *Drosophila melanogaster.* The teacher coordinates a research project for which different teams of students accumulate data on aspects of the problem. All the student teams report their results at a scientific meeting. Students are then confronted with the task of summarizing the results across the entire research effort. Finally, there is a discussion of recommendations for other experiments and recommendations based on accumulated data. Estimated time for the project is two weeks.

Science Background

The design of the activity is such that students gain some understanding of scientific investigation using the life cycle of a simple organism and the problem of acid rain.

Some of the problems related to scientific inquiry are modeled in the activity. Design of experiments, separation and control of variables, observing, graphing, and reporting data are all aspects of the activity. There is another dimension that teachers can introduce. Science is an enterprise that accumulates and evaluates new knowledge, and this is often done at scientific meetings. By having each group of students study one small part of the problem and share their results, the students can gain a better understanding of science.

The activity extends beyond the mere reporting of results. People are required to act on the best information available on a given problem. Often the information is not clear, and seldom does it provide all the answers. Students are asked to make recommendations for the control of acid rain based on the available information. Essentially, they are asked to determine harmful levels of acid precipitation for one organism. The lack of clarity of data, the fact that lower phyla organisms were studied and the weight or strength of evidence in decision making will become evident in the final stages of the activity.

Major Concepts

- The effects of logrithmic differences in acidity
- Susceptibility of different stages in the life cycle of fruit flies to acid precipitation
- Separation and control of variables in scientific experiments
- The influence of chronic low intensity changes in the environment
- Limiting factors in the life cycle
- Effects of lethal and sublethal doses of a pollutant
- Science progresses through the accumulation of information

Student Objectives

After this activity students should be able to

- Use the processes of scientific investigation, specifically to
   Design an experiment with a suitable control and single variable
   Observe changes
   Record data
   Report data to fellow students
   Analyze significance and limitations of class results
   Suggest the next logical experiment
- Use data analysis in making a recommendation on what standards should be set as tolerable limits on acid precipitation
- Use the *Drosophila* life cycle to represent organisms generally that have varying sensitivity to acid precipitation during their lives
- Describe observable effects of acid rain on organisms
- Calculate logrithmic differences in pH scale
- Identify difficulties in making decisions based on scientific information

Vocabulary

pH	Lethal dose
Life cycle stages	Control
Egg	Variable
Larva	Quantitative data
Pupa	Lethal
Adult	Sublethal
Viability	Scientific meeting

Materials

Petri dishes—5 per lab group designated as follows:

   Control with no added water

   Control with pH = 7 water (boiled and cooled) sprayed

   Experimental with assigned pH sprayed during the egg stage

   Experimental with assigned pH sprayed during the larval stage

   Experimental with assigned pH sprayed during the pupal stage

Nutrient agar prepared with standard materials

Simple grid to simplify counting

- Stock acid solutions (sulfuric or nitric) of pH 2.6, 3.6, 4.6, 5.6, and 7.0 in plastic spray bottles
- Data tables and graphs drawn by students prior to collecting data. (See examples.)

Procedures

(Note: A step by step and daily sequence are indicated)

Beginning on a Monday, spraying containers through the 13 day life cycle.

Day 0	1.	Gather 5 nutrient filled Petri dishes and label each appropriately (see materials).
	2.	Introduce a fertilized female *Drosophila* to provide eggs. Leave female in dish for 24 hours.
	3.	Prepare stock solutions and adjust sprayers to give uniform amounts of mist.
Day 1	4.	Remove female *Drosophila* and use grid to help count the number of eggs in each Petri dish. Record numbers.
	5.	Spray appropriate solutions into one control and 1st experimental Petri dish to simulate a light rain.
Days 2 & 3	6.	Repeat Step 5.
Days 4–7	7.	Spray appropriate solution into the 2nd experimental Petri dish to simulate a light rain.
Days 8–11	8.	Spray appropriate solution into the 3rd experimental Petri dish to simulate a light rain.
Day 12	9.	Count and record the number of adult *Drosophila* in each of the 5 Petri dishes.

10. Divide the number of adult *Drosophila* survivors by the original (day 0) number of eggs to obtain a percentage of survivors under your pH conditions.
11. Have the class simulate a scientific meeting at which each group will report its data and learn about the research of fellow scientists. Report data to class indicating which stage was most affected by your simulated acid rain.
12. Suggest what experiments should be done next to learn more about the effects of acid rain on organisms.

Questions, Discussion and Extension

The discussion of student work can be based on:

1. A standard lab report
2. Participation in the scientific meeting
3. Suggestions on the next steps needed to further study acid precipitation

4. Participation in an optional second set of experiments based on 3
5. Extension and elaboration of this study to the scale of a science fair project

This experimental approach could be expanded in many ways including:

1. Use other species of flora and fauna.
2. Changing a second factor such as temperature or light to test for synergistic effects.
3. Vary the amount or frequency of simulated acid precipitation.
4. Use different acids but the same pH range.
5. Observe organisms daily to note sublethal effects such as differences in activity patterns or levels of activity.
6. Expand the number of acid solutions in the range this experiment shows to be harmful. Try to more specifically pinpoint a critical or lethal concentration for each stage.

References

M. Demerec and Kaufmann, *Drosophila Guide* (Washington, DC: Carnegie Institute of Washington, 1965).

Sample Student Data Table

pH = _____

Egg #		Day 1	2	3	4	5	6	7	8	9	10	11	12		Adult #	% Surviving
			Egg			*Larva*				*Pupa*				*Adult—*		
____	Petri Dish 1															
____	2														____	____
____	3				Use X to indicate spraying schedule										____	____
____	4														____	____
____	5														____	____

Sample Class Data Table

	% Egg Survival	*% Larval Survival*	*% Pupal Survival*
pH 7			
6.6			
5.6			
4.6			
3.6			
2.6			

DIRTY WATER: WHO NEEDS IT?

Overview

Life as we know it is not possible without water. Despite its importance, water has become improperly managed, seriously depleted, and contaminated by toxic materials. In this activity, students examine the distribution of water, investigate pollutants and treatment methods, and consider their roles in the water problem, thereby recognizing that we face a frontier in maintaining this valuable resource.

Science Background

- The world's supply of water remains constant, but the supply is neither readily available for human use nor distributed uniformly.
- Specialized treatments can remove impurities and pollutants from water, but those impurities and pollutants are not removed from the earth's closed system. There is no such place as *away*.

Student Objectives

Upon completion of this activity, students will be able to

- State the percentage of water resources readily available for human use.
- Describe the steps used in water treatment and explain the results.
- Identify ways they contribute to the water pollution problem.

Skills

Observing, Investigating, Measuring, Comparing, Discussing, Evaluating

Related Disciplines

Environmental science, Life science, Mathematics, Chemistry

Time Frame

Water, Water Everywhere	15 minutes
Where is Away?	15 minutes
Pollution Solution?	45 minutes
Who, Me?	30 minutes

Materials and Advance Preparation

Water, Water Everywhere

Materials

- 7 *clear* containers—2 one-liter containers; 5 smaller containers, one of which is plastic
- 1 plate
- Overhead projector
- Masking tape
- Marking pen
- One liter of water
- Salt—34 grams
- Sand—approximately 250 ml
- Blue food coloring
- 1000 ml graduated cylinder
- One eye dropper

Before class

- Gather all materials
- Fill one small container with sand.
- Fill a one-liter container with water, add 4 drops of blue food coloring, and stir.
- Label the other 5 containers as follows:
    a one-liter container *oceans*
    a small plastic container *polar ice*
    a small container *deep ground water*
    a small container *fresh water*.
- Make a transparency of the Figure Distribution of the World's Water Supply.
- Measure and set aside 34 grams of salt.

Pollution Solution?

Materials

- Gravel, approximately 250 ml
- Sand, approximately 250 ml
- Soil, approximately 250 ml
- Salt, approximately 250 ml
- 1,000 ml beaker, 1 per lab group
- 250 ml beaker, 1 per lab group
- 500 ml beaker, 1 per lab group
- Glass stirring rod, 1 per lab group
- Granulated alum (KAl $(SO_4)^2 \cdot 12\ H_2O$), approximately 0.5 g per lab group
- Coffee filter, 1 per lab group
- Rubber bands
- Masking tape
- Household bleach (sodium hypochlorite, NaOCl), 10 ml
- Eye dropper, l per lab group
- Balance, 1 per lab group
- Tray for evaporation, 1 for the class
- Distillation setup, l for the class (optional)

Before class

- Divide the students into lab groups.
- Prepare one liter of "polluted" water for each lab group by putting approximately 25 ml each of gravel, sand, soil, and salt into one liter of tap water.
- Write the directions for water treatment on the chalkboard or on a transparency (see *Teaching Strategies*).

Where Is Away?

Materials

- All Pollution Solution materials (from completed activity above)
- Salt residue from evaporation experiment

Before class

- Complete Pollution Solution? activity. Keep water and treatment materials.
- Complete evaporation experiment. (See *Teaching Strategies* for details.)

Who, Me?

Materials

- Overhead protector

Before class

- Make a transparency of the water treatment process.

Water, Water Everywhere

The world's supply of water covers more than 70 percent of the earth's surface. Although the supply of water remains constant, it is not distributed evenly. Nearly 98 percent of the water is in the earth's oceans, where salinity makes it unavailable for many human uses. The remaining 2 percent of the earth's water is underground, or in polar ice lakes, rivers, and the atmosphere. (See Figure 1)

Perform the following class demonstration to help students visualize the distribution of the earth's water resources:

1. Display the seven containers prepared for this activity (see *Materials and Advance Preparation*).
2. Display a transparency of Figure 2. Use a graduated cylinder to distribute the one liter of water into the five empty containers according to the

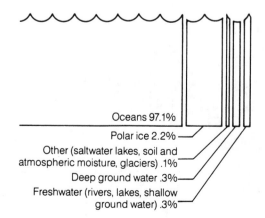

FIGURE 1
Distribution of the world's water supply

Substance	MCL*
Arsenic	0.05 mg/l
Lead	0.05 mg/l
Mercury	0.05 mg/l
Silver	0.05 mg/l
Fluoride	2.4 mg/l
Sodium	20 mg/l

*maximum contaminate level

FIGURE 2

percentages indicated in the figure. (For example, 97.1 percent of the water on the earth is found in the oceans. Because one liter contains 1000 milliliters, 97.1 percent of one liter is 971 milliliters. Therefore pour 971 milliliters into the container marked oceans.)

   NOTE: The percentages in the figure are rounded-off to facilitate this demonstration. Take care to measure accurately so you have three milliliters of water left over. Also, these percentages will vary from source to source depending on the method of calculation and the divisions used. It may be an interesting project for students to examine a variety of sources that contain data about the distribution of water.

3. After you have filled the empty containers with the appropriate amounts of water, continue with the demonstration, as follows:

- Add 34 grams of salt to the *ocean* container; this will match the salinity of the water sample with the salinity of the earth's oceans (3.5 percent).
- Place the plastic *polar ice* container in a freezer.
- Set the *other* container aside. We do not have access to this water.
- Pour the *deep ground water* into the container of sand.
- Ask the students which of the containers represents fresh water that is readily available for human use. (They should easily see that only the jar marked *fresh water* has the readily available supply.) Initiate a discussion on the limits of fresh water supplies, the problems of population distribution, and the contamination of existing supplies (refer to *Background for the Teacher*). Only a small part of this fresh water (.003 percent of the earth's total water supply) is accessible. The rest is too remote (found in Amazon or Siberian rivers) to locate, too expensive to retrieve, or too polluted to use. Hold a plate in front of the class and dramatically drop the usable portion of fresh water onto it. (Represent this portion as one drop of water from an eye dropper.)

Pollution Solution?

Faced with dwindling water resources, people have concentrated on two methods of alleviating the shortage problem. One is conservation, which includes management of toxic waste. The second method is treatment of already-contaminated water. The technology exists to purify polluted water, but economics often determines whether we use the technology. To complicate matters, the pollutants removed from the water in the purification process still exist, and handling the toxic materials creates another pollution problem.

Ask the students to work in teams of two or three and to clean a prepared sample of contaminated water as follows:

1. Fill a one-liter glass container with a well-stirred contaminated water sample (see *Materials and Advance Preparation*). Observe and record the water's color, clarity, and particulate pollution. Stir the sample and immediately pour 250 ml of the sample into a beaker. Determine and record the density of the 250 ml sample by measuring its mass and dividing mass by volume: density = grams of material/volume of material. Set this sample aside as a control.

2. Add approximately 0.5 g of alum to the water sample. Stir with a glass stirring rod for three to five minutes. Aluminum hydroxide particles (floc) will develop.

3. Allow the water to settle for 10 to 15 minutes. Observe and record the water's color, clarity and particulate pollution.

4. Place a coffee filter over a 500 ml beaker and secure it with a rubber band or masking tape. Allow room for 250 ml of water between the bottom of the filter and the bottom of the beaker.

5. Carefully pour approximately 250 ml of the water through the filter, leaving the particles behind in the one-liter container. (Be careful not to stir up the settled particles as you pour.) Observe and record the filtered water's appearance. Determine and record the density of the 250 ml of filtered water and compare it to the density of the 250 ml control set aside in step a.

6. Add one drop of household bleach to the filtered sample and stir the solution.

7. Observe the final sample and compare its appearance to the 250 ml control set aside in step a.

8. Keep all water and treatment materials for reference in the next activity, *Where Is Away?*

Help the students identify the four steps of water treatment used in this activity: flocculation, sedimentation, filtration, and sterilization. See Figure 3 below for an illustration of a water treatment process. Different treatment plants use different processes. One important process that students did not encounter in *Pollution Solution?* is biological treatment, during which microorganisms digest certain impurities. Encourage students to find out about the water treatment processes used in their community.

Identify the "pollutants" you used to prepare the water sample: gravel, sand, dirt, and salt. These materials are actually impurities, not pollutants. In this activity these impurities represent pollutants like sewage, dissolved minerals, and toxic chemicals. Ask the students if they think the treatment methods they used removed all the pollutants. They may suggest that the salt still remains in the water, and may ask to taste the water; but they should follow the universal laboratory rule: Don't taste. Instead, ask your students how they might test for salinity without tasting. Focus their suggestions on procedures they are capable of conducting. Measuring the mass of the polluted water and comparing its density to a sample of clean water of the same volume is one option; or, using a distillation process may also be a viable method.

FIGURE 3
One example of the water treatment process

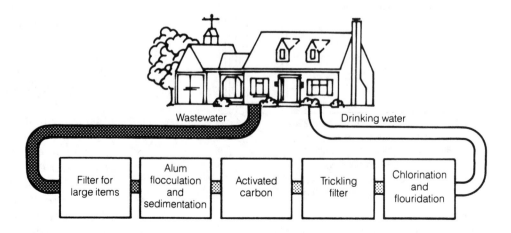

Before dismissing the students for the day, have them set up a procedure they intend to use for testing for the presence of salt, and also have them pour a small amount of the treated water into a shallow tray so that complete evaporation will have taken place before the next class meeting.

Where Is Away?

Ask students to observe the results of the evaporation of the water sample from the previous day. What do they think is there? (The residue at the bottom of the tray does contain salt.)

Display the water and treatment materials saved from the previous activity, *Pollution Solution?* Ask the students to focus on each step of the water treatment process. Did they notice that although the water became clearer with each step, the amount of waste material (flocculent debris, waste filter paper, salt residue) increased? Ask the students if they think we can depend on our current technology to remove pollutants and impurities completely from contaminated water. Can technology completely remove pollutants from the earth?

Introduce the concept of *away*. Ask students where they think *away* is. When they throw something *away*, where does it go? When a pollutant is washed *away*, where does it go? After a treatment plant has treated the water, have the impurities gone *away*? Is there really a place called *away*? If students are ready, raise the issue of ground water pollution. What happens to the ground water when pollutants are thrown *away*?

Who, Me?

With an understanding that pollution can never go *away*, your students should see that the most powerful solution to the problem of contaminated water supplies is to prevent contamination in the first place. Ask your students who they think contributes to the contamination of water supplies. Frequent answers will involve industry and agriculture. Students should be aware that, although industry and agriculture do contribute substantially to the contamination of water, individuals who use hazardous products in the home also contribute to pollution. Ask students what happens to household products that are dumped down the toilet or sink. Where is *away* in this case?

Materials are hazardous if they are toxic to living things, flammable, explosive, or corrosive. Display page 418 on an overhead projector covering up the third column, and ask the students to identify which hazardous products they have in their homes. Where are these products found?

Uncover the third column and discuss with the students the substitutes available for hazardous materials in the home. Ask students if they see any problem with using the substitutes instead of the hazardous products. Why don't more people use these safer substitutes? What are the trade-offs of using these alternatives? How would our lifestyles change if we used "elbow grease" to clean ovens and no strong chemicals? When is the trade-off worth the consequence? Can action on the household hazardous waste front make a difference in the war against contamination of water? Why or why not?

Have students write a summary of their lessons on water. Ask them to identify the current "water crisis," some of its causes, how pollution of water is measured and then treated, and how the water crisis is closer to home than they might have expected.

Resources for the Classroom

League of Women Voters. *A Hazardous Waste Primer.* Pub. No. 402 (Washington, DC.) Available from: League of Women Voters, 1730 M Street, NW, Washington, DC 20036. (A short, unbiased survey of the issue of hazardous waste.)

Concern, Inc., *Groundwater: A Community Action Guide* (Washington, DC: Concern, Inc.).

Consultant
Stephen W. Almond
Division Chemist
Halliburton Services
Oxnard, CA

Background for the Teacher

Water is a vital resource. Human beings can live almost a month without food, but cannot survive more than two or three days without water. There are five properties that make water so essential: (1) high boiling point, (2) high heat of vaporization, (3) high heat capacity, (4) lower density as a solid than as a liquid, and (5) its solvency.[1]

Water is the universal solvent. It holds and transports, in solution, nutrients that nourish plant and animal systems. Water's powerful solvency also makes it an excellent cleanser, because it dissolves and dilutes so many substances. Unfortunately, this capacity for dissolving a wide variety of substances makes water easy to pollute.

Many different things pollute water: wastes that demand oxygen (sewage, manure); disease-causing agents (bacteria, viruses); inorganic chemicals (acids, salts, metals); organic chemicals (pesticides, plastics, detergents); fertilizers (nitrates, phosphates); sediments from land erosion; radioactive substances; and heat.[2] Most of these pollutants result from human activities. Water pollution is a serious

Toxic household products

Product	Comments	Alternatives
Cleaners		
• Drain Cleaner	Contains caustic poisons	Plunger, boiling water, plumber's snake
• Oven Cleaner	Contains caustic poisons, some are carcinogenic	Salt, self-cleaning oven, "elbow grease"
• Toilet Cleaner	Contains strong acid	Mild detergent, mix of Borax and lemon juice
• Window Cleaner	Contains toxic chemical compounds, sometimes carcinogenic, may cause birth defects	Vinegar and water
• Spot Remover	Contains poisonous solvents, some are carcinogenic	Wash fabric immediately with cold water and detergent
Aerosol sprays		
• Most aerosol sprays	Contain highly toxic poisonous petroleum distillates, some are carcinogenic. Most are flammable and toxic when inhaled.	Non-aerosol Products
• Hair Spray		Setting Lotion/Gel
• Shaving Cream		Brush & Shaving Soap
• Air Fresheners		Ventilation, open bowl of fragrant spice
• Furniture Polish	Contains poisonous solvents, some are carcinogenic	Paste waxes, carnauba wax in mineral oil
Paint products		
• Paint (Oil or Alkyd)	Contains poisonous solvents, some are carcinogenic	Latex paint
• Spray Paint	Contains toxic solvents and propellants	Non-aerosol paint Mineral Oil
• Wood Finishes	Most contain harmful solvents	
• Paint Strippers	Contains poisonous solvents; some are carcinogenic	Heat gun with ventilation, hand or electric sander and wear respirator
Others		
• Moth Balls	Contain poisonous chemical compounds, may be carcinogenic	Cedar closet, store woolens in plastic
• Insect Repellent	Can be lethal if ingested	Protective clothing
• Disinfectants	Many extremely toxic	Soap, detergent, hydrogen peroxide

problem because the supply of usable water is small, the distribution is uneven, the demand for use is high, and the rate of water's replenishment is low.

Although water covers more than 70 percent of the earth, less than 1 percent is considered fresh water.[3] Because much of this fresh water is either too expensive to retrieve, too remote to reach, or too polluted to use, it turns out that only .003 percent of the earth's total water supply is available for human use.[4] This small amount of fresh water comes from both surface waters and ground water. In the United States, we draw about 75 percent of our water from lakes and rivers and 25 percent from ground water.[5] There are exceptions, however, to these average figures. For instance, the Greater New York area obtains two percent of its water from subsurface sources and 98 percent from surface sources;[6] yet Tucson,

Arizona and San Antonio, Texas are completely dependent on ground water supplies.[7]

Traditionally, water policies have been left to the states and, until recently, the federal government has been reluctant to become involved in this issue. Nevertheless, ground water issues became serious enough for the Reagan administration to acknowledge the need for limited federal action, and former Environmental Protection Agency director, Lee Thomas, urged the creation of a combined state and federal ground water program.[8]

In the United States, industry, agriculture, and our personal lifestyles depend on huge quantities of water. Per capita use is now up to 200 gallons per day.[9] This is the amount of water it takes per day to produce all the goods, grow all the food, and meet all the personal needs of each individual in the country.

In contrast, countries with comparable levels of social and economic development use far less water; for example, per capita use in Germany is 37 gallons per day; in Sweden, 54 gallons per day; and in the United Kingdom, 53 gallons per day.[10]

This high level of use in combination with the unequal distribution of resources and the pollution of water sources has made the continued availability of clean water one of the prominent environmental issues in the world. As a result, we must advance the scientific and technological frontiers that deal with water issues. In addition, people must seriously consider their roles in conserving clean water. What can we find out about water, its sources, how it cycles, and how it becomes polluted? What technological advances produce pollution? What technologies can we develop to clean up the dirty water? What is each person doing to contribute to water problems and water clean-up? How can we adjust our lifestyles to preserve our most valuable resource?

References

1. G. T. Miller, *Living in the Environment,* 2nd ed. (Belmont, CA: Wadsworth Publishing Co., 1979), p. 337.
2. Ibid, pp. 357, 359.
3. P. W. Purdom and S. H. Anderson, *Environmental Science,* 2nd ed. (Columbus, OH: Merrill Publishing Co., 1983), p. 214.
4. Miller, p. 339.
5. D. D. Chiras, *Environmental Science* (Menlo Park, CA: Benjamin/Cummings Publishing Co., 1985), p. 280.
6. L. R. Brown, et al., *State of the World 1987* (New York: W.W. Norton & Co., 1987), p. 51.
7. G. Schmitz, "Poisons Simmer in Nation's Aquifers." *The Denver Post* (9 August 1987): D-3.
8. Ibid, p. 10.
9. K. R. Sheets, "War Over Water: Crisis of the '80s." *U.S. News & World Report,* 95(18): 57.
10. P. Rogers, "The Future of Water," *The Atlantic Monthly,* 252(1) (1983): 80–92. (This article discusses water issues and discusses possible solutions.)

CHEMISTRY

QUICKIES: A COLLECTION OF CLASSROOM DEMONSTRATIONS AND DEVICES FOR TEACHING CHEMISTRY

Chemistry teachers often have a need for quick, spectacular attention-demanding illustrations or demonstrations to enhance their presentations, emphasize a principle, fix a fact, or condition the class for further learning. The following list of "Quickies" may serve these needs. They might form the nucleus for an interesting educational show before your student body, stimulating interest in chemistry through your school.

An interesting demonstration of science "magic" can be made with the "Magic Pitcher." An opaque pitcher is filled with distilled water. The contents of the pitcher are poured into a series of beakers containing a few drops of the following chemicals:

1. NH4OH
2. Phenolphthalein solution
3. H2SO4 6N
4. $BaCl_2$ supersaturated

The four beakers are filled from the pitcher, then the first two are poured back into the pitcher. The first two glasses then are refilled with "wine." The first three beakers are then poured back into the pitcher, and then all three refilled from the pitcher with "water." The four beakers are then all poured back into the pitcher, and the beakers refilled with "milk." A good line of patter, with several assistants can be worked up for this.

Surface tension phenomena may be demonstrated with simple objects. Razor blades, pins, and needles may be floated on the top of water. A small loop of thread (nylon works best) dropped on the surface of water will assume no definite shape, but a drop of detergent or soap solution dropped into the center of the loop will immediately cause it to form a circle. A matchstick floating on the surface of water will move rapidly away from a drop of soap or detergent placed near one end.

A graduated cylinder is filled about half full of water, and a cork disc is floated carefully on top of the water. The cylinder is then filled carefully with alcohol, taking care not to mix the two liquids, and the cork disc is fished off the top. A few drops of viscous lubricating oil are then dropped into the cylinder. The oil, being heavier than alcohol, drops through until it comes to the boundary of the water layer,

where the drops become almost perfectly spherical. Careful observation can also show how slowly two liquids diffuse into each other if undisturbed.

Show that the wetting property of water is increased with the addition of detergents by filling two cylinders with water, one having a detergent added. Place a piece of wool yarn on each surface and observe the time required for the wool to sink.

A glass filled with water above the rim, being held by surface tension, will float a cork in its center. In a glass only partly filled with water the cork will be pulled to the glass.

Using a fine-nozzle blow pipe prepared from a glass tube, blow small bubbles in a pan of water containing a detergent such as Tide or Joy. The bubbles will arrange themselves in patterns somewhat like molecules as they form crystals.

Light gases diffuse downward. Fill a wide mouth bottle with hydrogen. Invert it over a like bottle filled with air. While waiting for the diffusion to take place, be democratic and allow the class to vote for what they think is most likely to happen. These possibilities exist: (a) the hydrogen being lighter will remain in the top bottle; (b) the gases will mix together; (c) all the hydrogen will go to the bottom bottle; (d) most of the hydrogen will remain in the top bottle; (e) nonvoters admit they do not know what will happen. *Many* persons vote based on too few facts and too little information.

Spontaneous ignition can be effected with a half teaspoon of sodium peroxide placed on a two-inch cone of starch, sawdust, or finely chopped paper. Lay a small chip of ice on the cone. Sufficient heat and oxygen will be released by the reaction of water from the ice with the sodium peroxide to ignite the material. Kindling temperature and oxidation can be discussed following the demonstration.

Graham's law of diffusion may be demonstrated by pinning a piece of absorbent cotton to each of two corks that are fitted to an 18- to 20-mm glass tube about 44 mm long. Concentrated HCl and concentrated NH_3 solution are placed on the respective pieces of cotton and the corks inserted in opposite ends of the tube at the same time. A ring will shortly appear in the tube at the spot where the two gases meet. If the molecular weight of one of the gases is known, the other can be calculated from the respective distances the gases have traveled.

Boyle's law can be vividly demonstrated by connecting four 1-liter spherical flasks with short L-tubes connected by short pieces of rubber tubing. One of the flasks is attached to an open-end mercury manometer, and the flask at the other end of the series may be attached to a vacuum pump, a water aspirator, or a water faucet, as desired. The flasks are evacuated and the difference in levels of the mercury column noted. If one flask is clamped off from the rest of the system, allowed to fill with air, closed off, and then opened to the rest of the system, it will be noted that the height of the mercury column is only three-fourths the original height, and that therefore the pressure is one-fourth atmosphere. This can be continued to pressures above atmospheric by connecting the tube and flask to a water tap and forcing one flask full of water, at which time it will be noted that the pressure is now four-thirds atmosphere. Unless you are prepared for a shower it is not advisable to force more water than this into the system.

Gay-Lussac's law of the effect of temperature on the pressure of a gas in a closed system may be demonstrated by closing a 500-ml flask with a two-hole stopper. A thermometer that extends to near the center of the flask is pushed through one of the holes. A short piece of glass tubing connected to an open-end mercury manometer is pushed through the other hole. (It may sometimes be advisable to use a 3-hole stopper with the third hole closed by a short piece of glass tubing, a piece of rubber tubing, and a pinch clamp. This aids in leveling the mercury in the manometer before starting.) The temperature of the gas may be changed by immersing the flasks in a large container of hot water or ice water, and the difference in pressure exerted by the gas noted. You may also note that air is a very poor conductor of heat by observing how slowly the temperature changes when the temperature of the surrounding bath is changed.

Dalton's law of partial pressures may be vividly demonstrated by fitting the top of a fair-sized distilling flask with a one-hole stopper through which extends a dropping funnel. A U-tube manometer with some colored liquid in it is connected to the side-arm of the distilling flask. Some volatile liquid such as ether or chloroform is placed in the dropping funnel and a few ml of the liquid run into the flask. Since the liquid occupied only a slight part of the volume, it cannot account for the considerable rise in the manometer liquid in the U-tube. If you have equipment for sealing the volatile liquid into a thin-walled ampule, to be placed in the flask and broken after it is closed off, the demonstration can be somewhat more dramatic.

In connection with the previous experiment, you can measure rather roughly the vapor pressure of various volatile liquids by closing one end of a 12-mm x 100-cm tube and filling it with mercury. When the tube is filled, it is inverted into a shallow pan partially filled with mercury. If you now wrap a cloth dipped into hot water around the top of the tube, you will note that the level of mercury changes very little—if it has been properly filled with mercury. With a curved end dropper, now introduce a few drops of the liquid whose vapor pressure is to be measured into the bottom of the tube. The liquid will rise to the top of the tube and the mercury level will take a considerable drop. If the hot cloth is now wrapped around the top, you will note that the mercury drops much more than it did before the liquid was introduced. A cooled cloth may also be used to show an effect in the opposite direction.

EARTH SCIENCES

A PLACE IN SPACE

Overview

Without technology, the exploration of space would be impossible. As we increase the possibility that humans will one day live and work in space, we also increase the need for more sophisticated technology. In this activity, the students identify the basic needs of living things, examine a variety of self-contained biospheres designed to support life and construct a simple model of a space station. Through these experiences, the students will realize some of the challenges that scientists and engineers face when exploring the frontier of space.

Science Background

- The basic needs of living things include oxygen, carbon dioxide, water, light, food, and protection from extreme heat and cold.
- Artificial biospheres rely on technology to provide the basic needs of resident organisms.
- Engineers use scale models to help them in the design of complex systems.
- A closed system is an isolated system; neither energy nor material can pass through its boundaries.

Student Objectives

Upon completion of this activity, students will be able to

- Identify the basic needs of a living organism.
- Construct a biosphere for a simple organism such as a plant.
- Recognize different models of complex biospheres.
- Use scale models to design larger objects.

Skills

Analyzing, Discussing, Constructing models

Related Disciplines

Life science, Earth science, Physical science, Mathematics

Time Frame

Life Under Glass   45 minutes
A Human Terrarium?   45 minutes
Little Plans for Big Ideas   45 minutes

Materials and Advance Preparation

Life Under Glass

Materials

  Large potted plant

  2-liter soft-drink bottles

  1 small plant, no more than 8″ tall, for the demonstration terrarium

  Large scissors, 1 pair per lab group

  Potting soil, 10-pound bag

  Newspaper, enough to cover desks

  Seeds, 5 per student (suggested seeds: radish, marigold, alfalfa)

  500 ml beaker of water, 1 per lab group

  Duct or electrical tape, 15 cm per lab group

  Masking tape, 30 cm per lab group

Before class

- A week in advance, ask the students to bring in empty, rinsed, clear 2-liter soft-drink bottles. You will need one per student.
- Organize materials for lab groups.
- Make a soft-drink bottle terrarium using a small plant instead of seeds. This will serve as the demonstration terrarium. (See *Teaching Strategies, Life Under Glass,* step 3.)

A Human Terrarium?

Materials

  Terrarium with small plant (from Life Under Glass)

  Overhead projector

Before class

- Make transparencies of the Figures on pages 423 and 424.

Little Plans for Big Ideas

Materials

  Meter stick or metric tape measure

  Graph paper with metric divisions, 1 sheet per student

Scissors, 1 per lab group

Metric rules, 1 per student

Masking tape

Before class

• Write the dimensions of the space module on the chalkboard. (See *Teaching Strategies*, Little Plans for Big Ideas, step 2.)

Life Under Glass

1. Display a large plant and ask the students to explain what this organism needs to stay alive. List the students' responses on the chalkboard, and assist them in identifying needs that are basic to the plant's survival: minerals, water, air, and light.

2. Display the demonstration terrarium containing a small plant. Review the students' lists of basic needs. Will this plant stay alive? Why or why not? Have the class explain how each basic need of the plant is being met.

3. Divide the students into lab groups and distribute materials so students can construct terraria by doing the following:

   a. Use the large scissors to cut off the top of each plastic bottle.

   b. Separate the colored base from the rest of the bottle by tugging on it vigorously.

   c. Use the duct or electrical tape to seal the holes in the base from the inside. Do this carefully to make the base water-tight.

   d. Fill the base with soil.

   e. Add 50 ml of water to moisten the soil. *Do not overwater.* Stir the soil.

   f. Use a pencil to poke five holes in the soil, and then plant a seed in each hole. Gently cover each seed with soil.

   g. Invert the clear plastic part of the bottle to create a dome to cover the base. Use masking tape to seal the base and dome. Record names on the tape.

4. Keep the students' terraria in a warm place until the seeds germinate (two to three days), and then place the terraria in sunlight. After the majority of the seedlings are well sprouted, ask the students to evaluate the varying success of individual terraria. Have the students discuss how the basic needs of the plants are, or are not, being met. Your students may want to design and conduct experiments to test the relative importance of different factors on plant life in a terrarium.

A Human Terrarium?

1. Instruct the students to reexamine the terrarium containing the small plant. Ask the students if they think humans could live in a terrarium. Discuss the needs of humans, and list these needs on the chalkboard. Ask the students to decide which of the items listed are biological needs that are basic to the survival of humans (oxygen, light, water, food, protection from heat and cold) and which are psychological needs (companionship, entertainment, recreation). Have the class discuss how the biological needs could be met in a closed system like a terrarium.

2. Define a closed system for your students. In a closed system, the total amount of water and air remains constant. In addition, no new food or nutrients can enter the system, so food and nutrients must cycle through the system for plants and animals to use them again. The earth is a closed system, energy is the only resource that reaches the system from the outside. Sunlight is necessary to heat air and supply energy for various cycles.

3. In the Arizona desert, scientists built an artificial, closed biosphere—or a human terrarium—called Biosphere II (see Figure 1). Modeled after the biosphere of the earth (Biosphere I), Biosphere II

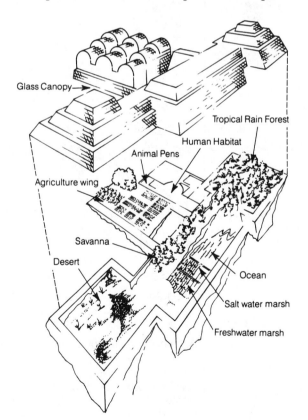

FIGURE 1
Biosphere II

was a self-supporting ecosystem containing five biomes: a savanna, a marsh, a desert, a tropical rain forest, and an ocean 35 feet deep. Four men and four women inhabited the two-acre structure for two years beginning in 1989. The $30 million project was intended to serve as a prototype for orbiting space stations or planetary outposts, and as a model for improved resource management.

Use a transparency of the Figure to present the Biosphere II project in Arizona, and discuss the project, asking the students to consider the following:

a. What were the objectives of the project? (According to the planners, there were two: to develop technology for settlements on the moon and Mars, and to improve human stewardship of earth by learning how to manage such things as human wastes.)

b. What problems would require solutions for Biosphere II to become self-sustaining? (Some suggestions are: how to seal the glass roof so that no air can escape or enter; how to cool the air temperatures, which could peak at 156° F, without using conventional methods that draw air from the outside; how to handle water purification and air quality; how to make sure there is adequate vegetation to sustain all life forms; and, how to make sure that none of the selected life forms will be a hazard to the ecosystem.)

c. What was it like to live in Biosphere II? What kind of people were appropriate to include in the group of eight Biosphereans? What skills did they need?

d. What were the social dynamics of the Biosphereans? What strains did the Biosphere-

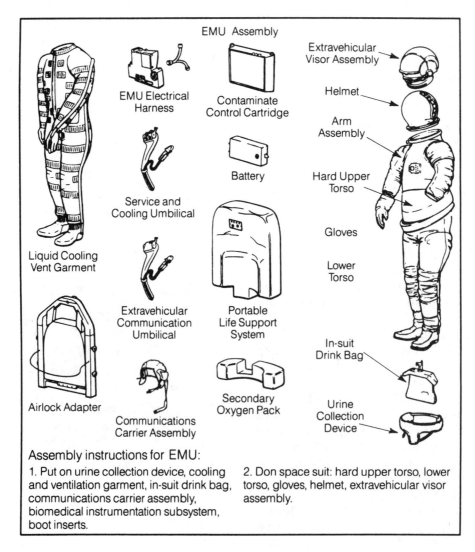

FIGURE 2
An EMU

ans encounter during their two-year stay in Biosphere II? Would the students like living for two years with seven other people in a closed system?

4. Another life-supporting biosphere model is the extravehicular mobility unit (EMU) used by astronauts in space (see Figure 2). NASA developed the EMU to enable astronauts to work in space without the support of a space craft. An attachable manned maneuvering unit (MMU) allows astronauts to work untethered in space and return safely to the spacecraft. By providing the atmospheric pressure and oxygen necessary for human life as well as insulation from the sun's heat, the EMU protects the astronaut from the hostile environment of space. The technology involved in the EMU is complex; astronauts preparing to work in space must carry all of their life-support systems with them. Use a transparency of Figure 2 to illustrate an EMU. Have the students identify the basic needs of an astronaut and describe how the EMU meets those needs.

Little Plans for Big Ideas

As we push back the frontiers of space, we must create self-supporting biospheres. Most people call these artificial biospheres space stations. In 1984, President Ronald Reagan directed NASA to develop a permanently occupied space station within a decade. Scientists once envisioned a collection of modules that would form huge, spoked wheels that would spin through space. Current U.S. plans for the station, however, describe a structure that includes four pressurized, cylindrical modules in the center of a huge supportive structure (see Figure 3). Two of these modules will provide living space, and the other two will provide a working area. The space station will house a crew of six, with replacement crews arriving every 90 days.

1. If space is available, have the students measure the dimensions of one module on the classroom floor. Instruct six people to stand within the boundaries of the module, and ask the students to imagine living in that space for 90 days at a time. Remind the students that they would have only two modules available for sleeping, eating, recreation and relaxation.

2. Currently, plans for the space station are only on paper. Because something as large as a space station is difficult to design, engineers use scale models. Scale models are small two- or three-dimensional renderings of a large object. With the advent of sophisticated computers, computer modeling has replaced paper and pencil drafting in the design of complex objects. In a scale model, the relative sizes of the parts of the model are the same as those of the larger object; all the proportions are identical. Introduce the students to the concept of a scale model. Use familiar examples, such as airplane models and architectural plans. Ask the students to make a three-dimensional scale model of one of the cylindrical modules.

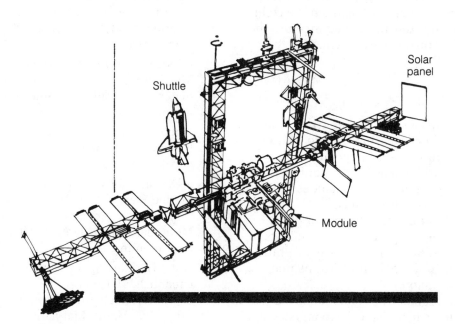

FIGURE 3
Space station construction

a. Review the dimensions with students:
   Diameter of module = 4.2 meters
   Length of module = 12.1 meters
   OPTIONAL: The module is cylindrical. In order to draw the module two-dimensionally and then roll it into a correctly scaled cylinder, ask the students to calculate the circumference of the module. Review with the students the formula for calculating the circumference of a circle from its diameter: circumference = π d. If students are not familiar with the formula for calculating the circumference, include the circumference (13.2 meters) in the dimensions.

b. Ask the students to convert the measurements of the module from meters to centimeters, using the scale of 1 cm = 1 m. In this way, one centimeter on paper will be equivalent to one meter on the module.

c. Supply each student with one sheet of graph paper with metric divisions. Ask the students to draw on the graph paper the scaled dimension they had calculated (length × circumference). The finished drawing will be a rectangle.

d. Instruct students to cut out the rectangle with scissors, and tape the two short sides together to form a cylinder. This cylinder is proportionally accurate and resembles the proposed module. Each dimension is 1/100 of the size of the real module, making the scale model, with its three dimensions, 1/1,000,000 of the size of the real module.

e. The students can use a metric ruler to check their model by measuring the diameter of the cylinder. Being careful to maintain the cylindrical form, the students should measure the diameter as approximately 4.2 cm.

Going Further

- Have the students write a letter from space, describing where they live, what they do, and how they feel about living on a space station.
- Ask the students to search their school or local libraries for science fiction that includes predictions of how humans will live in space.
- Have the students conduct research on plans for the industrialization of space. Ask the students to find out the results of various projects on shuttle flights and what industrial applications may be suited for a space station.
- Have the students draw a scale model of one room of their house. Ask them to measure the room's size and the furniture, and to draw a two-dimensional plan with all parts of the room in relative proportion.

- Have the students investigate the numerous spin-offs produced by the space program, such as teflon, velcro, and temperfoam. Information on the products is available in the library or from the U.S. Government Printing Office (address listed under *Resources for the Classroom*).
- Encourage the students to study the history of space exploration. What happened when? How did the explorations benefit life on earth? When did the first animal, man, or woman orbit the earth, walk on another planet, or travel past the moon?
- Let the students explore the accomplishments of the U.S. and Russia in space. Why is there so much competition between these nations? When have they cooperated? What other nations have active space programs?

Resources for the Classroom

N. J. Freundlich, "Biosphere," *Popular Science, 229*(6) (1986): 54–56.

G. Maranto, "Earth's First Visitors to Mars," *Discover, 8*(5) (1987): 28–43.

NASA, *NASA Facts: Waste Management.* JSC-09696 (Rev. A) (Washington, DC: USGPO, undated).

NASA, *NASA Facts: A Wardrobe for Space.* JSC-09378 (Rev. Ad.) (Washington, DC: USGPO, 1984).

J. Scobee and D. Scobee, "An Astronaut Speaks," *Science and Children, 23*(6) (reprint, March 1986).

P. Taylor, *The Kid's Whole Future Catalog.* (New York: Random House, Inc., 1982).

Government documents can be ordered from the Superintendent of Documents, U.S. Government Printing Office, Washington, DC 20402. Many fliers are free, even in bulk quantities.

A Teacher's Companion to the Space Station: A Multi-disciplinary Resource, as well as other materials, is available at the NASA Teacher Resource Centers listed below:

Alabama Space and Rocket Center
Huntsville, AL 35807
Serves Alabana.

NASA Ames Research Center
Moffett Field, CA 94035
Serves Alaska, Arizona, California, Hawaii, Idaho, Montana, Nevada, Oregon, Utah, Washington, and Wyoming.

NASA Goddard Space Flight Center
Greenbelt, MD 20771
Serves Connecticut, Delaware, District of Columbia, Maine, Maryland, Massachusetts, New Hampshire, New Jersey, New York, Pennsylvania, Rhode Island, and Vermont.

NASA Jet Propulsion Laboratory
4800 Oak Grove Drive
Pasadena, CA 91109
Serves inquiries related to space exploration and other JPL activities.

NASA Johnson Space Center
Houston, TX 77058
Serves Colorado, Kansas, Nebraska, New Mexico, North Dakota, Oklahoma, South Dakota, and Texas.

NASA Kennedy Space Center
Kennedy Space Center, FL 32899
Serves Florida, Georgia, Puerto Rico, and the Virgin Islands.

NASA Langley Research Center
Hampton, VA 23665
Serves Kentucky, North Carolina, South Carolina, Virginia, and West Virginia.

NASA Lewis Research Center
Cleveland, OH 44135
Serves Illinois, Indiana, Michigan, Minnesota, Ohio, and Wisconsin.

NASA Marshall Space Flight Center
Tranquillity Base
Huntsville, AL 35812
Serves Alabama, Arkansas, Iowa, Louisiana, Missouri, and Tennessee.

National Space Technology Laboratories
NSTL, MS 39529
Serves Mississippi.

The United States Space Foundation, 1522 Vapor Trail Drive, Colorado Springs, CO 80916, also has many teacher and student resource materials.

Background for the Teacher

Space stations orbiting earth, space travellers living in artificial, enclosed biospheres, and shuttles transporting people between earth and Mars—are these just science fiction images, or is the space program bringing us to the reality of settlements beyond earth?

NASA has been working toward the settlement of space for many years. With President Ronald Reagan's directive in 1984 to "develop a permanently manned space station—and do it within a decade,"[1] NASA was able to put form to its concepts and deadlines to its timetable. An occupied space station requires a self-supporting biosphere—a closed, complex system in which organisms support and maintain themselves. Because human survival in space requires oxygen, water, food, light, protection from temperature extremes and a shield from cosmic and solar radiation, scientists and technologists have several complex problems to solve.

The *Challenger* disaster in January 1986 changed NASA's schedule for launching a space station. Originally, NASA planned to build a station in space over the course of 18 months, taking up materials with 12 shuttle fights.[2] Because of the problems with *Challenger*, NASA decided to reduce each shuttle's cargo capacity from 65,000 pounds per launch to 40,000 pounds, thus changing the timetable for building the station. Shuttle flights will ferry the modules for living and working, and, after 11 flights, a crew of four will occupy the station.

For centuries, humans have been curious about the worlds beyond our planet. Why do we want to explore beyond the confines of earth? Why do we need to? What do we hope to accomplish?

Research in space will help answer numerous scientific questions. Aboard the space station, specialists will conduct astronomical studies, such as mapping Venus with the Magellan probe, which has high-resolution radar equipment. There is widespread interest in manufacturing in space, because the micro-gravity environment eliminates heat convection, hydrostatic pressure, sedimentation and buoyancy, and enables the fusion of mixed particles into homogeneous composites that are impossible to make on earth.[3] Private industries hope to use the space station to purify pharmaceutical and biological products, such as erythropoietin, a kidney hormone that controls the production of red blood cells. Other products include nearly flawless glass-like linings for artificial hearts that would prevent clotting, and membranes coated with antibodies that could filter the blood of an AIDS patient.[4] The computer industry hopes to improve high-speed computers by growing high-quality gallium arsenide crystals in space. Researchers also would like to develop new polymers and catalysts, to process improved fiber optics, and to create new metal alloys not produced on earth.

The scientific purpose of space travel is the pursuit of new knowledge. Scientists, however, are not the only people interested in space travel. Others also see space as an avenue to pursue their goals. The National Commission on Space has said, in its rationale for exploring and settling the solar system, that exploring the universe is a goal that will encourage increased world cooperation and will be a peaceful mission with respect for the integrity of planetary bodies and alien life forms.[5] Space is a large frontier; how and why the United States ventures into it will determine the benefits derived from its exploration.

Consultant
Victoria Duca
Director of Special Projects
U.S. Space Foundation
Colorado Springs, CO

References

1. D. A. Anderson, *Space Station*. EP-211 (Washington, DC: USGPO, undated), p. ii.
2. National Commission on Space, *Pioneering the Space Frontier* (New York: Bantam Books, Inc., 1986), p. 120.
3. Space Industries, Manufacturing facility in space cited in *The Futurist, 21*(3) (1987): 33.
4. Biddle, p. 45.
5. National Commission on Space, p. 4.

EVALUATING LABORATORY WORK: EXPERIMENT—WHY IS THE SKY BLUE? WHY IS THE SUNSET RED?

1. Have students form groups of four for this experiment.
2. Have each group follow the suggested procedure for doing the experiment.
3. As the experiment progresses, circulate among the groups and note the following: (A checklist such as found in Chapter 17 might be used.)
   a. Ability to follow directions
   b. Ability to use proper safety precautions
   c. Keeping a record of observations
   d. Working cooperatively with other members of the group
   e. Ability to form hypotheses
   f. Ability to make predictions
   g. Ability to draw conclusions from the observations and data
   h. Care in using the materials, assembly, cleanup and storage
4. What kinds of process objectives were realized in having students do this experiment? What cognitive objectives were achieved? What affective objectives?

Materials

Each group should have the following materials:

   12-inch or 14-inch rectangular aquarium (clear glass)

   Flashlight

   Concentrated sulfuric acid (H_2SO_4)

   Sodium thiosulfate: may use sodium hyposulfite (photographic fix)

   Water

   White screen or white sheet of paper

Purpose

To demonstrate the effect of the atmosphere on the sun's rays. As white light passes through the atmosphere, various colors are removed by scattering and show up in the color of the sky. Violet is removed with smallest particles; blue, with next smallest; green, with next; and so on for yellow, orange, red, etc.

Procedure

Figure 1 clarifies the procedure. Mix thiosulfate, 10 grams per gallon of water (not critical) in the aquarium. Project light through aquarium to screen. Add a few drops of concentrated sulfuric acid and stir with glass rod.

Discussion Questions

1. At the beginning, what color is the water when the flashlight shines through it? What color is the light of the flashlight when looked at directly?
2. How does the color of the water change as time goes on? How does the color of the light from the flashlight change? To what is this analogous in nature?
3. What causes the water to change color?
4. What causes the light source to change color?
5. What is the final color of the water? Why?
6. What is the final color of the light source? Why?
7. To what natural sky condition is this analogous?

Explanation

Reaction of the acid on the sodium thiosulfate releases very fine particles. Only very fine particles in the atmosphere cause the rays to scatter. This can be shown by the fact that smoke blown across a beam of light appears bluish, but chalk dust gives no coloration at all. This is because the chalk particles are too large.

The scattering effect first removes the violet and blue end of the spectrum, and later the red end as the particles grow larger. Observe the color of the "sky" water and also the color of the "sun" flashlight which remains. Color of the sun goes from white to yellow to orange to red to blackness, where it is not visible at all.

In nature the sunlight becomes redder near the horizon because the light passes through more atmosphere with larger particles when the sun is about to set.

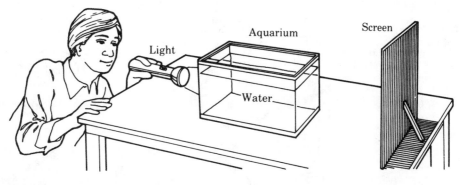

FIGURE 1

Teaching Concepts

- Light travels in waves.
- White light contains all colors.
- Short waves are scattered more than long waves.
- Short waves are scattered by smaller particles than are long waves.
- Scattering subtracts colors from a beam of white light.

- Subtracting blue from white leaves yellow; therefore, the sun appears yellow.

Additional Principle

Use a Polaroid sheet and look at the beam from the side and turn your sheet through a ninety-degree angle. Observe the fact that scattered light is polarized.

WEATHER: AIR MASSES AND FRONTS

Overview

Students observe weather reports on television over a period of a week. The concepts of air masses and fronts are then presented in a lecture-discussion format by the teacher. Weather maps are studied for the final section of the activity. Students watch weather reports on the evening news for one week. Spend one class period on lecture-discussion. This activity is for grades 6–8.

Science Background

The movement of large air masses and the influence of more localized fronts determine the majority of daily weather. An air mass is a large body of air that originates in a particular location and then moves across the earth's surface. The important characteristic of air masses is that they acquire the properties (temperature and humidity) of the region in which they originate. Air masses are either tropical or polar and either continental or maritime. The major air masses and their origins are shown in Figure 1, page 430.

Continental polar air masses are cold and dry. Maritime tropical air masses are warm and moist. Continental tropical air masses are warm and dry. Maritime polar air masses are cold and moist. The different characteristics of the air masses greatly influence local weather.

A cold front is the phrase applied to the leading edge of a cold dense air mass. Since the air is cold and dense it wedges under lighter, warmer air and forces some air up into the atmosphere. As the warm air is lifted it cools and has a reduced capacity to hold moisture. As this occurs clouds form and precipitation falls. Cold fronts are often identified by a line of storm clouds (see Figure 2).

A warm front results when warmer, lighter air pushes behind colder, denser air. The result is that warmer air moves up over the colder air producing a long area of precipitation as the warm air rises and cools. High cirrus clouds can precede the front by several days (see Figure 3).

We are influenced daily by the weather. Yet, many know little about the dynamics of this daily phenomenon. The implications of weather range from moisture for agriculture to severe weather that threatens human life.

Major Concepts

Atmospheric motion occurs on many scales.

Air masses have characteristics of the place of origin.

The interaction of warm and cold air results in different patterns of weather called fronts.

FIGURE 1
Air masses influencing the continental United States

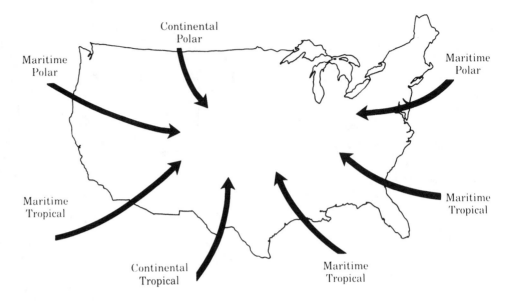

FIGURE 2
Cold front

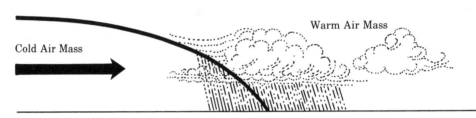

FIGURE 3
Warm front

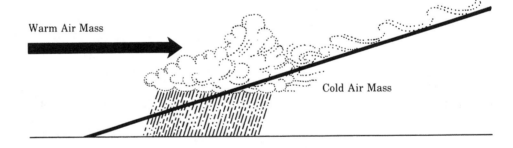

Student Objectives

At the completion of this activity the student should be able to:

- Identify a warm front
- Identify a cold front
- Describe the characteristics and influences of different air masses

Materials

Prepare overhead transparencies for Figures 1, 2, and 3.

Chalkboard

Old weather maps (from the newspaper or weather station)

Vocabulary

Cold front	Weather
Warm front	Air masses

Procedures

1. Present the concepts of air masses and fronts in a formal manner (15–20 minutes).
2. Have the students apply their observations to the presentation during a discussion period.
3. In the final section of the activity have the students look at weather maps and see if they can discover the concepts of air masses and fronts as they have actually been recorded.

Evaluation Tasks

Use Figures l, 2, and 3 without labels and have the students identify air masses and fronts.

Tell the students to observe weather forecasts for the next week and summarize their observations in terms of air masses and fronts.

Extending the Activity

Have the students look up occluded fronts and report on their characteristics.

Have a meteorologist (a local TV weather person) visit class and tell about predicting the weather.

The students can study the instruments used in recording atmospheric conditions.

THE MOON

Overview

Students make observations of the changing phases of the moon over a two month period. After a summary of their observations, the phases of the moon are demonstrated using a simple classroom demonstration.

Science Background

The moon travels around the earth in an elliptical orbit. The moon travels from west to east around the earth. (Due to the earth's rotation the moon appears to rise in the east and move toward the west.) The average distance of the moon from the earth is 384,000 kilometers (240,000 miles). The lunar month is actually 27 1/2 days; but, the earth is traveling through space in its orbit around the sun, so the time from one full moon to the next is just over 29 days. The moon rotates on its axis west to east, the same direction that it revolves around the earth. The period of rotation is exactly the period of revolution for the moon.

The moon appears larger when rising because we see it in comparison to other objects such as buildings and trees. It also appears yellow or orange when rising or setting. This is because the reflected light from the moon must pass through longer sections of the earth's atmosphere; in doing so the blue rays are reflected and scattered by dust particles. This is the same phenomenon that causes red sunsets.

As the moon travels around the earth, we see different amounts of the half of the moon that is in sunlight. During the lunar month the moon goes through a continuous change from complete darkness (new moon) to complete light (full moon) and then back to complete darkness. As the moon goes from new moon to full moon we term the phase *waxing*. The moon's change from full to new is called *waning*.

Outside of the romantic, aesthetic, and mythic qualities of the moon one of the important societal implications is that it causes tides on the earth. Tides result because the moon's pull of gravity makes a bulge in the water on the earth's side facing the moon. Tides have been proposed as one potential source of energy.

Major Concepts

Phases of the moon and lunar eclipses depend on the relative positions of the sun and moon as viewed from the earth.

The earth and moon can be thought of as a system.

Student Objectives

At the completion of this activity the student should be able to:

• Identify the phases of the moon
• Describe the phases of the moon as a relationship among the earth-moon-sun system
• Describe the cycle of lunar phases

Materials

Bulletin board calendar of two months

Duplicate of bulletin board calendar for students' notebooks

Globe

Styrofoam ball

Light source

Vocabulary

Lunar	Waning
Phases	Crescent
Waxing	

Procedures

1. Place a calendar on the bulletin board. Each day on the calendar should have a space available for one student to draw in a record of the moon as it was observed that day/night. The students should record similar observations on a daily calendar in their notebooks. Starting with a full moon is strongly recommended.

FIGURE 1
Phases of the moon—observations

Full   ¾   ½   New   ½   ¾   Full

FIGURE 2
Phases of the moon—demonstration

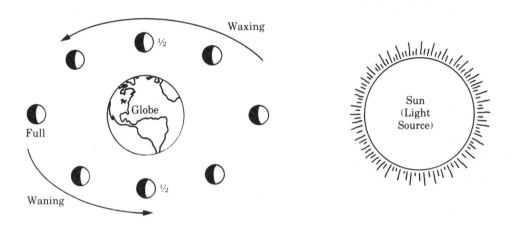

2. Continue the calendars for two full cycles of the moon. (There are 29 days from one full moon to the next.)
3. After continuing the observations for about 2 months, plan on a period of discussion in which the students summarize their observations. Use Figure 1 for the summary after the students have given their observations.
4. On a class period after the discussion of student observations plan on completing a demonstration using a light source, globe, and styrofoam ball.
5. Darken the room and place the light source in a position where it will shine on the globe. Move the styrofoam ball around the globe in such a way as to demonstrate the moon's phases (Figure 2).

Evaluation Tasks

Give the students figures similar to Figure 2 above, without the phases of the moon completed. Have them fill in the phases and label the diagram.

Set up different sun-earth-moon configurations and have the students predict the moon's phase.

Extending the Activity

This activity can be extended to show how lunar and solar eclipses occur. Usually the moon passes above or below the earth's shadow so there is not a lunar eclipses. And, the shadow projected by the moon does not cross the earth; but, when it does there is a solar eclipses along the shadow's path. These eclipses can be demonstrated and discussed with the materials and procedures of this activity. Students can also complete reports on the moon.

ASTRONOMIC DISTANCES

Overview

In this activity the students complete a scale model of astronomic distances. The goal is to have the students conceptualize the vastness of space. This activity should take two class periods.

Science Background

A light year is an astronomic measure of distance. The words "light year" as said quickly may not capture the immensity of the distance involved. Try completing the following exercise so you will have an understanding of the astronomic distance. You can have the students do the same activity. Light travels about 298,000 kilometers per second (186,000 miles per second).

$$
\begin{array}{rl}
298,0000 & \text{kilometers per second} \\
\underline{\times\,60} & \text{km per minute} \\
\underline{\times\,60} & \text{km per hour} \\
\underline{\times\,24} & \text{km per day} \\
\underline{\times\,365} & \text{km per year}
\end{array}
$$

There are some terms and symbols in the activity (see Table 1) about which students may ask. Some of these are defined for you:

Cluster—a group of stars or galaxies often identified by the constellation in which they are located

Galaxy—a group of stars

M—this stands for Messier number, a way astronomers catalogue stars

Milky Way—the galaxy in which our solar system is located

Nebula—a cloud of dust and gas

This activity should give students a new perspective relative to the earth in time and space. Our earth is small and insignificant in the scale of astronomic time and distance. Yet, our earth is the most important astronomic object as far as our existence is concerned.

Major Concepts

The average distance between stars in space is incredibly large. Stars are made of hot gases, but they differ in temperature, mass, size, luminosity, and density.

Student Objectives

At the completion of this lesson the student should be able to:

- Describe the immensity of astronomic distance
- Indicate that stars have different distances from earth
- Identify his/her location in the scale of stellar space
- Define a light year as the distance light travels in a year

Materials

Meter stick

Colored pencils

Adding machine tape (6 meter strips for each group of 2)

Vocabulary

Astronomic	Quasar
Stellar	Star
Distance	Nebula
Galaxy	

Procedures

1. Divide the students into groups of two–three.
2. Each group should have a piece of adding machine tape 6 meters long, a meter stick, and pencils.
3. Mark off a line about 5 centimeters from one end of the tape. Label this line EARTH.
4. Using the meter stick and the distances given in Table 1 plot the distances to the various stellar objects on the adding machine tape. Tell the stu-

TABLE 1
Distances to selected objects in the celestial sphere

Celestial Object	Distance in Light Years
Quasar—3c 295	4.5 billion
Hydra Cluster of Galaxies	3.9 billion
Quasar—3c 273	1.5 billion
Gemini Cluster of Galaxies	980 million
Ursa Major 1 Cluster of Galaxies	720 million
Cygenus A—radio source	500 million
Pegasus II Cluster of Galaxies	470 million
Hercules Cluster of Galaxies	340 million
Coma Cluster of Galaxies	190 million
Perseus Cluster of Galaxies	173 million
Pegasus I Cluster of Galaxies	124 million
Fornox A—radio source	60 million
Virgo Cluster of Galaxies	38 million
M49 in Virgo	11.4 million
M81	4.8 million
M31 in Andromeda	2 million
Leo II Galaxy	710 thousand
Fornox Galaxy	390 thousand
Megellanic Clouds	170 thousand
Center of Milky Way	30 thousand
Owl Nebula	12 thousand
Ring Nebula	4.5 thousand
Deneb—star	1.6 thousand
Regil—star	900 light years
Polaris—star	680 light years
Vega—star	26.5 light years
Sirius—star	8.7 light years
Alpha Centauri—star	4.3 light years
Sol—our sun	8 light minutes

dents they should start by using the scale 1 meter = 1 billion light years. (Note: When the students start plotting distances closer to the earth, millions of miles, they will find it impossible to use the scale of 1 meter = 1 billion light years. Frustration will be evident as they try to figure out how far a million is on their scale and finally how to get so many stellar objects located in such a small distance. This is the realization that is essential to the lesson. They will have to change the scale to 1 meter = 1 million light years and then they will still have difficulty with the last few distances.)

5. Discuss the problems students had with the scale 1 meter = 1 billion light years. Ask them "How did you resolve the problem?" "How does this distance make you feel in the scale of the universe?"

Evaluation Tasks

The students can use their tapes to explain the immensity of space.

Extending the Activity

The students can report on some of the stellar objects named in Table 1.

ACTIVITY FOR MIDDLE-LEVEL STUDENTS: HOW CAN HARDNESS BE USED TO IDENTIFY MINERALS?

Materials

Steel file

Copper penny

Table knife

Piece of glass

Collection of minerals

Discussion

1. What will scratch glass? Wood? A penny?
2. How can hardness be used to identify minerals?
3. A substance's resistance to scratching is called its *hardness*. If calcite scratches gypsum, which is harder? If calcite scratches both talc and gypsum, which is harder, talc or gypsum? How could you find out?

Procedure

1. Obtain a collection of minerals from a geology department. Make a list of minerals a fingernail will scratch, a file will scratch, a knife will scratch, and a copper penny will scratch. Which minerals are hardest?
2. Find out about Moh's Hardness Scale. What is the hardness of a knife blade on Moh's Scale? A penny? A steel file? A fingernail?
3. Using the hardness number of the knife blade, penny, file, and fingernail, determine the Moh number for each mineral in your collection. Record your results. Obtain a mineral from your classmate without finding out its name. Using your new knowledge, can you identify the mineral from its hardness?

Teacher's Information

Moh's Hardness Scale

1.	Talc	1.	Fingernail scratches it easily
2.	Gypsum	2.	Fingernail scratches it
3.	Calcite	3.	Penny scratches it
4.	Fluorite	4.	Knife scratches it
5.	Apatite	5.	Knife scratches it
6.	Feldspar	6.	It scratches glass
7.	Quartz	7.	It scratches glass
8.	Topaz	8.	It scratches most minerals
9.	Corundum	9.	It scratches topaz and most all minerals
10.	Diamond	10.	It scratches all other minerals

GEOLOGIC TIME

Overview

Students complete a scale model of geologic time. The primary goal of the activity is to give them a concept of the immensity of geologic time. Secondary to this, they are introduced to geologic periods and the record of life as recorded in rocks. The activity should last for two class periods.

Science Background

There are two primary methods of determining the age of materials and thus establishing a time scale. The first is an ordering of events, simply determining what happened first, second, third, and so on. In this method the dating is *relative*. The second method establishes a specific time of an organism, event, or rock stratum. This is an *absolute* method of dating materials. Geologists have used the relative method of dating materials for years. It is represented classically in the time scale constructed in this activity.

William Smith, working in the nineteenth century, is credited with formally establishing the practice of ordering geologic events. He observed that rocks revealed an orderly succession of life; that is, older species were represented in older rocks (bottom layers) and as these species disappeared from the rock record fossils of new species appeared. This is called *faunal succession*—groups of fossils succeed each other in sedimentary rock layers in such a way that the sequences of rocks are predictable. It should be noted that Smith did not develop the idea of evolution—the biological implication of his observations. He was only concerned with the fossils as chronological indicators. The method used by Smith also allowed him to correlate groups of rocks that were some distance apart. The assumption here is that similar fossils in rocks at two different locations means the rocks were deposited in the same period.

Nineteenth century geologists succeeded in ordering many formations of the world's rocks. The order was based on relative dates, since absolute dating methods had not been developed. Though there are inconsistencies and problems with this method of dating rocks it does represent a good introduction to geologic time and the record of past life and events in the rocks.

Understanding the immensity of geologic time gives students some perspective relative to our time and influence on earth. Compared to other organisms our time has been short and our impact can be viewed with mixed reactions: we probably represent the highest, most complex form of life and we have done the most to endanger our own existence and the existence of other species. It is well for students to understand the perspective of geologic time for these reasons as well as the knowledge contained about the earth's history in the rock record.

Major Concepts

- Environments can change and conserve their identities.
- Environments change because living and nonliving matter interact.
- The earth is very old, geologic time is immense.
- Interpretation of rocks and fossils provide a record of the earth's history.
- Geologic time is subdivided on the basis of natural events in the evolution of life.

Student Objectives

At the completion of this activity the student should be able to:

- Describe the immensity of geologic time.
- Relate the relative ages of some geologic events.
- Identify his/her location in the scale of geologic time.

Materials

Meter stick

Colored pencils

Adding machine tape (6 meter strips for each group of two)

Vocabulary

Geologic time (you may wish to include the names of geologic eras)

Procedures

1. Divide the students into groups of 2.
2. Each group should have a piece of adding machine tape 6 meters long, a meter stick, and a pencil.
3. Mark off a line about 5 centimeters from one end of the tape. Label this line NOW (today's date).
4. Using the meter stick and the ages given in Table 1, plot the different times on the adding machine tape. Indicate that the students should start by using the scale 1 meter = 1 billion years.
   (NOTE: As the activity progresses the students will have difficulty with the scale of 1 meter = 1 billion years. They will have to change the scale in order to include recent events on their tape. The frustration of this change and the realization of the difference between 1 year, 100 years, 1000 years, 1 million years, and 1 billion years is as much a part of the lesson as the geological peri-

ods. Let them struggle with the new scale. It may help to point out that 1 millimeter equals a million years on a scale where 1 meter equals a billion. Or, one billion = 1000 million.)

5. After the activity, discuss the problem of scale and how the students resolved it. Usually they decide to change the scale for the last meter and make 1 meter equal 1 million. Still, recent events are very hard to plot. Again, this is part of the realization of the immensity of geologic time.

Evaluation Tasks

The students can use their tapes to explain some of the earth's history. Ask the students to explain why they had trouble plotting recent events. How did they overcome the problem?

Extending the Activity

The students can do a report on one geologic period.

TABLE 1
Approximate Age in the Earth's History

1. Earth's beginning	4.5 billion years ago
2. Oldest rocks	3.3 billion years ago
3. First plants (algae)	2.0 billion years ago
4. First animal (jellyfish)	1.2 billion years ago
5. Cambrian Period (abundant fossils)	600 million years ago
6. Ordovician Period	500 million years ago
7. Silusian Period	440 million years ago
8. Devonian Period	400 million years ago
9. Mississippian Period	350 million years ago
10. Pennsylvanian Period	305 million years ago
11. First reptiles	290 million years ago
12. Permian Period	270 million years ago
13. Triassic	225 million years ago
14. First mammals	200 million years ago
15. Jurassic	180 million years ago
16. First birds	160 million years ago
17. Cretaceous Period	135 million years ago
18. Paleocene	70 million years ago
19. Eocene	60 million years ago
20. Oligocene	40 million years ago
21. Miocene	25 million years ago
22. Pliocene	11 million years ago
23. First humanlike mammals	2 million years ago
24. Pleistocene	1 million years ago
25. Humans make tools	.5 million years ago
26. Last Ice Age	10,000 years ago
27. Calendars used in Egypt	4234 B.C.
28. Pythagoras proposes theory of mountain origin	580 B.C.
29. Eratosthenes measures Earth circumference	200 B.C.
30. Mount Vesuvius eruption at Pompeii	79 A.D.
31. First U.S. satellite	1958 A.D.
32. Mount St. Helens eruption	1980 A.D.

LAB: DETERMINING THE DEPTH AND SHAPE OF THE OCEAN FLOOR

Objective

To determine the contour of a plastic ocean floor model without seeing it, using other means of observation.

Materials

1 box containing a sealed model of the ocean floor

1 metal probe

1 sheet of graph paper

5 sheets of white paper

scissors and glue

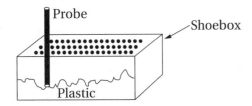

Procedures

1. With all five sheets of white paper measure down 10 cm from one edge and fold the paper at your mark.

2. (a) Place one sheet of the folded white paper on the long side of the box containing the holes in the lid, with the 10-cm section flush with the top edge of the box lid and the excess paper under the box.

   (b) Slide the paper so it is also flush with the corner of the box in which the holes begin.

   (c) Lightly tape the paper in place.

3. Notice the five rows of 10 holes in the lid of the box top.

   (a) Starting with the row closest to the paper, place the metal probe in the hole until it hits something directly below. (Make sure with each probe that the rod stays straight up and down.)

   (b) Mark the depth of the rod with your finger.

   (c) Withdraw the probe while keeping your mark and line it up on the paper 2 1/2 cm in from the corner of the box, and mark your depth of the probe on the paper by lining your mark up with the top edge of the paper. (Continue in the same way with the other nine holes, each 2.5 cm apart.)

4. Once all the depths of a row are marked, take off the paper and connect your depth marks to make a contour for the ocean floor below that row.

5. Attach another sheet of paper in the same way as before and follow the same steps for the other four rows.

6. Once all five rows have been marked on their respective pieces of paper, cut out the contours on each of the five sheets of paper.

7. Now on the flap of paper that was under the box measure back 2 cm on each of the five sheets of paper and cut off the excess.

8. The rows on the box top are approximately 2 cm apart. To create your model, glue the five contours in order 2 cm apart onto the graph paper.

9. When finished, show the teacher and have your model checked against an actual plastic sea floor model to see how close you were.

GIFTED STUDENTS

ACTIVITIES IN SCIENCE FOR GIFTED STUDENTS

Development of various talents among students requires providing for opportunities to practice these talents and abilities. Gifted students are usually quite self-reliant and resourceful. Following are several examples of activities a teacher can provide for them to give practice in self-development.

To develop organizing abilities:
- List the ways you can use a specific fact to help you.

To develop fluency and flexibility:
- Have students discuss why being fluent and flexible would be an advantage for a scientist.

To develop use of similes:
- Discuss a scientific field such as biology. Analyze science specialties in terms of similarities and differences.

To develop perception:
- Compare human sensations to animal sensations by analyzing the nervous system of each. Describe how signals are transmitted.

To develop abilities to analyze codes:
- Ask students to make a code. What codes are used in science? Why? Are there any international scientific codes?

To develop convergent production:
- Have students bring in objects of nature such as leaves, pine needles, pebbles, shells, etc., and categorize them.

To develop the ability to see trends:
- Write an invitation to inquiry.

To develop the ability to give and follow directions:
- Have students write their own directions for doing an experiment.

Plan a terrarium
Plan a garden
Plan a vegetable party
Plan a unit of study on seeds
Plan a landscaping project for trees, shrubs, and lawns

To develop divergent production:
- Have one group give oral directions to another group for performing a science experiment, testing a theory, or showing a cause and effect relationship.

To develop the ability to hypothesize:
- Answer the question, "What would happen if—?"
  There were no gravity?
  There was no action-reaction principle?
  Instead of discrete particles, matter was continuous?

To develop the ability to compare and contrast:
- Have students plan a zoo. What animals would be put together and why? What animals would definitely be kept apart and why?

To develop the ability to make decisions:
- Answer the questions
  What was the world's most important discovery and why?
  What is the best way to test a principle? Give your reasons.
  Consider different climates. Which do you prefer and why? What type of soil and crops do you prefer? Why?

To develop creativity:
- Invent new words for common objects.
- Invent new names of plants and animals. Give reasons for your choices.

CHALLENGES TO THINKING FOR GIFTED STUDENTS DISCOVERY DEMONSTRATION: BOTTLE AND KEY—PUT THE KEY IN THE BOTTLE

Procedure

1. Prepare a box as shown in Figure 1. The materials needed are listed below.

2. Demonstrate the device. Have each student look into the peephole while the teacher opens the trapdoors on the top alternately. Have students go back to their desks and try to draw a diagram of the outside and inside of the box, so that the images they see would be formed properly and in the right locations.

Materials

Two shoe boxes, cut diagonally on one end at 45° angle

Piece of window glass, cut to fit the diagonal cut of the shoe boxes

Masking tape

Black rubber tape for light seal around trap doors

Bottle of red-colored liquid

Red rubber stopper of same color as the liquid

25-watt light bulb mounted above trap door B

Small key suspended by tape from edge of opening A.

Discussion

1. What is the problem (or problems)? Is it a real problem to the students? What makes the device work? How is it built? What parts does it have?
2. What might be some explanations? It has mirrors. It is built like this (draw diagrams on the board). It has glass. (Try to select the most reasonable explanation after logical thinking.)

3. We need more information. (Let one student look the device over carefully and report the data to the class. We need accurate observations here.)
4. Draw conclusions about construction of the device. Draw conclusions about its operation.
5. Test the conclusion with something else (piece of mirror, piece of window glass, piece of one-way glass).

Explanation

The eye responds to the light having the strongest intensity.

Other Applications:

- Why do you cup your hands around your eyes to look outside at night from a lighted room?
- Some sunglasses are partially silvered mirrors. Why?
- Some rear view mirrors on cars can be adjusted when the lights from a car behind cause too much glare.
- Can you devise a way for such a mirror to work using what you have learned from this demonstration?

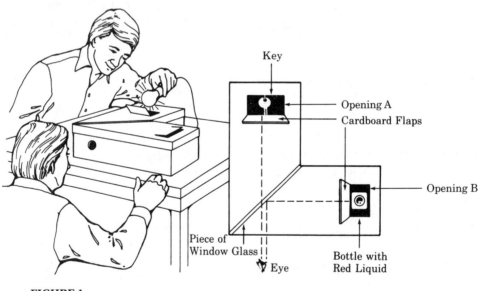

FIGURE 1
Box preparation

PHYSICS

SUPERCONDUCTIVITY: A NEW SCHOOL OF THOUGHT

Overview

In 1987, an exciting discovery piqued the interest of the scientific community: scientists synthesized new high-temperature materials that could conduct electricity with no loss of energy. This discovery marked new progress on the intellectual and technological frontiers of superconductivity. In this activity, the students will learn the scientific principles that underlie superconductivity, experience the excitement of a scientific frontier, and appreciate the political and financial implications of one of the most important scientific discoveries of the twentieth century.

Science Background

- A superconductor is a material through which an electrical current can flow without resistance.
- Resistance in a conductor causes heat; this heat occurs because free electrons collide with imperfections in the conductor's crystalline structure.
- A material can become a superconductor if, when cooled below the transition (or critical) temperature, not enough collisions with sufficient energy occur (on average) to disrupt the coherent binding of electrons that makes superconductivity possible.
- New discoveries in science often occur when scientists take a radically new approach to a problem.
- The application of scientific research does not occur independently of politics or economics.

Student Objectives

Upon completion of this activity, the students will be able to

- Explain the differences between a nonconductor (insulator), a conductor, and a superconductor.
- Describe the principles of superconductivity.
- Chronicle the history of developments in superconductivity research.
- Describe why superconductivity has excited so many scientists.
- List at least two political or economic issues related to superconductivity.

Skills

Reasoning, Understanding models, Applying information, Making decisions

Related Disciplines

Economics

Time Frame

Conducting Lessons	45 minutes
In a Class of Its Own	45 minutes

Materials and Advance Preparation

Conducting Lessons

Materials

9 volt battery, 1 per lab group

Flashlight bulb, 1 per lab group

Socket, 1 per lab group

3, 30 cm lengths of wire, 1 set per lab group

A variety of conductors and nonconductors, 1 set per lab group

Immersion heater, 1 per lab group

Styrofoam cup, 1 per lab group

Thermometer, 1 per lab group

100 ml graduated cylinder, 1 per lab group

In a Class of Its Own

Materials

Borax, 1 g per lab group

Cobalt (II) chloride or Nickel (II) chloride, .5 g per lab group

6 inch nichrome wire loop, 1 per lab group

Mortar and pestle, 1 per lab group

Bunsen burner, 1 per lab group

Dictionary

Overhead projector

Hammer

Before class

- Draw a diagram on the board to illustrate a conductivity-testing apparatus made from a battery, a bulb, a socket, and three pieces of wire.

Conducting Lessons

1. Review electrical conductivity with the students. Have each lab group assemble the conductivity

testing apparatus illustrated on the blackboard (see *Materials and Advance Preparation*), and test the conductivity of the conductors and non-conductors gathered for this activity. Next, let the students test articles of their own choosing, such as pencils, belt-buckles, or rings.

2. Explain why metals conduct electricity and other materials usually do not. Include a description, such as the following, of how a conductor differs from an insulator.

   The difference between metals (conductors) and insulators is essentially the ability of the highest energy electrons to move around the materials. In an insulator, the "energy band" containing the outer electrons is completely filled; consequently, those electrons cannot carry current. In a metal, the uppermost "energy band" is *partially* filled, enabling those electrons to carry current. Because the uppermost energy band is not filled, the electrons in a conductor can move in response to an electrical field. Although the electrons are free to roam, they cannot move from one end of a conductor to the other. Instead, they run into phonons (nuclear vibrations), impurity atoms, and other electrons, transferring kinetic energy to one another. Each collision results in resistance to the flow of current, and produces heat energy at the expense of electrical energy. (See *Background for the Teacher* for more information.)

3. Have the students perform the following experiment to determine how much heat a conductor loses. In this case, the conductor is an immersion heater—a wire with an electric current running through it.
   a. Measure 100 ml of water into a styrofoam cup.
   b. Measure and record in degrees Celsius the temperature of the water.
   c. Insert the immersion heater into the water for two minutes. Record the amount of time the heater is in the water.
   d. Remove the heater.
   e. Measure and record in degrees Celsius the temperature of the water after heating.

4. Discuss with the students the results of the experiment in terms of the model of conduction of electricity. Discuss heat loss as both a desirable and a nondesirable product of conduction.

In a Class of its Own

1. Define the term superconductivity for your students (see *Background for the Teacher*). Include a description of the differences between the free electrons of a conductor and the bound pairs of electrons in a superconductor and the way in which each conducts an electrical current. Stress that in previously known superconductors the pairing of electrons was dependent upon very low temperatures and strong electron-ion attractions. The most promising superconductors belong to a new class of ceramic materials. Although ceramics are usually thought of as insulators, there is a class of ceramics, the oxygen-defect perovskites, that are well-known to the solid state chemistry and physics communities. The metallic nature of these ceramics is due to the vacancies left by removing electrons from the uppermost energy band of the oxygen atoms. Some scientists currently think that interactions between the electrons' spins cause the pairing of electrons at higher temperatures. Recall that, at lower temperatures, the presence of ions is thought to be responsible for electron pairing (see *Background for the Teacher*).

2. Have the students work in lab groups of three or four, and prepare a ceramic material as follows:
   a. Using a mortar and pestle, grind together 1 g of borax and .5 g of Nickel (II) chloride or Copper (II) chloride.
   b. Heat a nichrome wire loop in the flame of a Bunsen burner.
   c. Dip the heated wire into the borax mixture. Be sure to get only a very small amount of the mixture on the wire. Return the wire to the flame. Repeat this process, each time picking up only a small amount of the borax mixture until the loop contains a glassy material.
   d. Observe and describe the material.

3. Discuss the appearance and physical properties of the ceramic material. Ask the students if they think it appears to be conducting or nonconducting. Ask the students to look up the definition of "ceramic" in a dictionary. Read the definition aloud: hard, brittle, electrical insulators, requires high-temperature processing, and is formed from powders. Explain to the students that it was only when scientists abandoned metals and turned to an entirely different kind of material—ceramics—that the field of superconductivity progressed. Stress that new frontiers in science often occur when scientists take a radically new approach to a problem.

4. Discuss with students the factors that currently affect the use of superconductors. Besides the extremely low temperatures required to maintain a material in a state of superconductivity, fabrication is also a problem. Ask students how they would form a ceramic material into a wire-like strand. Demonstrate the brittle nature of a ceramic by using a hammer to hit the glassy

material formed at the end of one of the student's nichrome loops. Scientists are proposing that the ceramic material be put into a thin, hollow, silver wire or into copper/nickel tubes. Even if those wires can be made, scientists are not sure that the wires will be able to carry a large enough current or have the necessary mechanical strength for some applications. The use of superconducting film in integrated circuits (computer chips) is an intriguing idea, but engineers will have to find ways to integrate the film with semiconductor technology, which cannot tolerate the high temperatures required to produce the superconducting films.

Another problem with the new materials is that they are unstable: a chunk of fired Y-Ba-CuO that is impure will dissolve completely if left in a glass of water overnight; even a pure pervoskite will eventually dissolve in water. It is not clear whether perfect crystals will react the same way, but devices made from the superconducting material may need a coating of an impermeable substance to prevent deterioration. Scientists are studying the limitations of the new ceramic materials and trying to figure out ways to make the materials easier to use. Even with the large number of scientists working on high-temperature superconductors, it will be at least five years before thin films of superconductors are in computers, and up to twenty years before superconductors are used in bulk applications, such as magnets or power lines.

5. Brainstorm potential future uses of room-temperature superconductors. Use *Background for the Teacher* as a guide. Students will be able to think of others.

Background for the Teacher

NOTE: This information reflects events in the field of superconductivity as of August 1987. The developments in this field are occurring so rapidly that by the time you read this activity, portions of this background probably are out of date. Check recent periodicals for more current information.

Early in 1987, a scientific breakthrough occurred that was so exciting it was the cover story for the May 11 issue of *Time* magazine,[1] and it generated standing-room-only crowds at the American Physical Society and the American Chemical Society meetings. What phenomenon has graduate students and Nobel Prize hopefuls alike clamoring to be involved? The answer is *superconductivity*.

Hypothetical Models

What makes a material a superconductor? To understand the currently accepted model for how superconductors work, it is helpful to look at the model for how nonsuperconductors work. These conductors are usually pictured as consisting of fixed nuclei with electrons that are essentially free to roam about the metal because the uppermost energy band is not completely filled. Electrons move in response to the

Superconductivity Time Line	
1911	Dutch physicist Heike Kamerlingh Onnes discovers superconductivity at 4K in mercury.
1950	Scientists discover alloys that keep their superconductivity in the presence of a strong magnetic field.
1960	Manufacture of large superconducting magnets becomes standardized.
1970s	Scientists discover superconductivity in polymers and organic materials. They achieve transition temperatures near 8K.
1973	Scientists discover that an alloy of niobium and germanium superconducts at 23 K.
1983	Karl Alex Mueller and Johannes Georg Bednorz begin to examine metallic oxides (ceramics) as possible superconductors.
1985	Mueller and Bednorz find superconductivity in Ba-La-CuO at 35K.
1986	Bell Labs researchers find a similar conductor at 38K.
Jan. 1987	University of Houston scientist Paul C. W. Chu finds another member of the copper oxide ceramic family, Y-Ba-CuO, superconducts at 98K.
June 1987	Researchers at the University of California, Berkeley, develop a material that retains superconducting properties at temperatures between 280 and 300 degrees Kelvin (78° F).
Aug. 1987	Colorado State University researcher Walajabad Sampath isolates bits of material that show evidence of superconductivity at room temperature—70°F.

electric field that is created when an external voltage is applied to the metal. However, the electrons are not truly "free"—they run into phonons (vibrations of the nuclei). Because of these collisions, metals have resistance to the flow of a current and they heat up when a current flows through them.

At certain temperatures, many materials become *superconductors*. It is possible for two electrons to experience an attractive force that leads to superconductivity at a given temperature (the critical temperature or T_c). This attraction is possible if a positively charged ion assists the process by "over-screening" the normal repulsion that the two electrons experience. The electrons thus form bound pairs. This leads to superconductivity because the electrons no longer behave like electrons. Normal electrons obey the Pauli Exclusion Principle, which says that no two electrons can exist in the same quantum-mechanical state; the wave functions of the electrons do not overlap. In a superconductor with bound pairs of electrons, the wave functions of the pairs overlap considerably. As a result of this overlap, all the pairs in a superconductor behave much more like a single unit; they move as one. Some collisions still take place, but they do not have sufficient energy to break up the electron pairs and the overlapping nature of the electron wave functions. Due to the overlapping nature of the electron wave function, there is no resistance, and no energy is lost through heat. Although a large number of electrons are not in a superconductive state, they do not produce heat, because they are "shorted out" by the superconducting state. This is similar to having a resistor with finite resistance and a resistor with zero resistance in a parallel circuit; the current will always take the zero resistance path, thus "shorting out" the finite resistor.

This model predicts that materials not normally thought of as good conductors will make good superconductors. A crucial aspect of the hypothesis is that electrons must be able to form bound pairs. In the superconductors known before 1986, electrons formed these bound pairs only with the help of an interaction with ions, making materials with strong electron-ion attraction good candidates. However, materials in which electrons and ions interact strongly are normally thought of as poor conductors. This led Bednorz and Mueller to study ceramics, which are normally insulators. In an interesting twist of events, however, it now appears likely that the superconductivity of the new higher temperature superconductors (23K and above) is not caused by electron-ion (phonon) interaction. Present thinking focuses on spin-mediated pairing. This means the interactions between spins cause the pairing of electrons and an ion is not necessary.[2]

Marketplace Applications

Why all the fuss over superconductors? The discovery of nitrogen-cooled superconductors could be a boon to utilities, industry, electronics, transportation, medicine, and research.[3] But one must be careful not to oversell the promise of new discoveries. All new technologies must compete with existing technologies that are continuously being improved. Present technologies produce billions of dollars of revenue, a good percentage of which corporations use to hire excellent scientists and engineers, both of whom work to extend these technologies as long as possible.

- Power companies could use superconductive transmission lines to send current hundreds of miles from a distant generating center without energy losses. Power distribution grows at a very slow rate (slightly more than one percent per year in the United States) so it may not be cost effective to use this technology in developed countries. In third world countries that do not have extensive power distribution networks in place, however, it may be very reasonable.
- Densely packed microchips made of superconductive materials would not produce heat and could be packed more closely together in a computer. This would allow for a decrease in the size of computers. These smaller computers would work faster than present machines because the signals would have less distance to travel between components.
- Trains, like the Japanese levitated train, but much simpler and less expensive to operate because of the nitrogen-cooled superconductive magnets, could fly at 300 miles per hour on a frictionless magnetic support. This application would be most important to nations without a railroad system or nations that are very dependent on public rail transportation.
- Magnetic resonance imaging (MRI) machines use powerful magnets to make images of tissues inside the body. Currently, relatively few hospitals can support the use of the helium-cooled machines, which cost about $500,000. New MRI scanners made with high temperature superconductors cooled with liquid nitrogen would be less complex and less expensive than the helium-cooled machines. This would require superconducting wire, however, which poses other difficulties.
- Physics research could benefit from the use of new superconductors in the super-magnets that constrain the flight paths of high-speed particles in particle accelerators, and safely contain the hot plasma in which nuclear fusion reactions take place.

Resources for the Classroom

B. Breathed, "Bloom County" cartoon, Sunday, 21 June 1987.

J. Gleich, "In the Trenches of Science." *The New York Times Magazine* (16 August 1987), p. 28. (An excellent review of some of the controversies and competition related to superconductivity research.)

P. Grant, "Do-It-Yourself Superconductors," *New Scientist* (30 July 1987), pp. 36–39. (This article describes a complex laboratory activity in which high school students actually made a superconductor.)

R. L. Hudson, "Scientific Saga: How Two IBM Physicists Triggered the Frenzy over Superconductors," *The Wall Street Journal* (19 August 1987), p. 1.

It is no wonder that scientists have been losing sleep over superconductivity. Leading industrial nations have recognized the potential of the new superconductors and have subsidized research in the public and private sectors. Scientists view the new superconductors in the same light as lasers and transistors.[4] Competition among institutions is great: "I'm a standard American scientist," says theoretical physicist Marvin Cohen. "My definition of science is to discover the secrets of nature—before anybody else."[5]

It is important that people realize that the first application of superconductivity is already occurring, and was unanticipated. This application is the demonstration of superconductivity in the schools. High school students have been able to create high temperature superconductors in their classrooms (see *Resources of the Classroom*). This may be the first time high school students and teachers have been able to repeat one of the great scientific findings of this century. The social impact of having emergent technological and scientific principles accessible to young scientists could renew enthusiasm for careers in science and technology.

Consultants

Paul Grant
Research Staff Member
Manager, Magnetism and Cooperative Phenomena
IBM Almaden Research Center
San Jose, CA

Joseph Serene
Research Scientist
National Science Foundation
Washington, D.C.

References

1. "Superconductors!" *Time*, *129*(19) (1987): 65–75.
2. K. A. Mueller and J. G. Bednorz, "The Discovery of a Class of High-Temperature Superconductors," *Science*, *237*(4819) (1987): 1133–1139.
3. R. Dagani, "Superconductivity: A Revolution in Electricity Is Taking Shape," *Chemical and Engineering News*, *65*(19) (1987): 8.
4. "Superconductors!" *Time*, *129*(19) (1987): 65.
5. Ibid, p. 68.

EVALUATION OF STUDENT UNDERSTANDING OF A BASIC PHYSICAL PRINCIPLE*

Each student is to be given a mimeographed sheet containing the following information:

Procedure for Part 1

1. The demonstration material is set up as indicated in Figure 1. A beaker of water is filled, and when the instructor is ready to start the demonstration, he pours water in the thistle tube labeled "X". The water will then flow from tube "Y".
2. The students are next given a mimeographed sheet resembling Figure 2 and asked to describe what they think the apparatus looks like within the can.

*This demonstration and evaluation guide was prepared by Dr. Gene F. Craven, Department of Science Education, Oregon State University, Corvallis.

3. In a few sentences, they are to explain why the water started to run and why it continues.

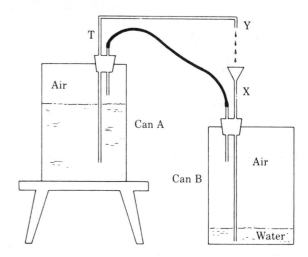

FIGURE 1

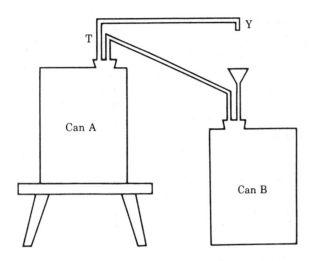

FIGURE 2

4. They are also asked to write the basic principles involved in the demonstration and how long they think the water will continue to run.

Procedure for Part 2

After students have answered the questions, they are given a copy of Figure 1 and asked to take the following test. They are to assume (1) that can "A" and can "B" are identical and (2) that all parts of the apparatus remain unchanged unless a change is specified in the statement they are considering.

Directions:

In the blank to the right of each statement place an X in the column indicating the effect which the given change would have on the rate of flow.

How would the rate at which the liquid flows from the glass tube be affected if:

	No Flow	Slower	Same Rate	Faster
1. The top of the funnel was only one-half as far above can "B" as it was in the diagram?	___	___	___	___
2. Can "B" was lowered until the top of can "B" was level with the bottom of can "A"?	___	___	___	___
3. The glass tube "T" was lengthened so that it extended twice as far above can "A"?	___	___	___	___
4. The funnel was replaced by a thistle tube extending to the same height above can "B" but having a bulb volume three times as great?	___	___	___	___
5. The tip "Y" of the glass tube from which the water is flowing was lengthened until it was level with the top of the funnel?	___	___	___	___
6. Kerosene, which is less dense than water, was used instead of water? (Neglect differences in viscosity and vapor pressure.)	___	___	___	___
7. The volume of can "B" was doubled while its height "H" remained constant?	___	___	___	___
8. The bottom of can "A" and can "B" were at the same level?	___	___	___	___
9. The funnel tube was cut off at "X" and did not extend below the stopper in can "B"?	___	___	___	___
10. The glass tube in can "B" to which the hose is fastened was extended to the bottom of the can?	___	___	___	___

Procedure for Part 3

After students have marked their papers, the instructor leads the class in discussing their answers. What types of process thinking are required in this type of demonstration?

USING A DEMONSTRATION TO MOTIVATE STUDENTS: THE DIFFUSION CLOUD CHAMBER

Procedure

1. Construct a diffusion cloud chamber as shown in Figure 1. Students can help you obtain the necessary materials and may want to participate in actual construction of the device. This is one of the best ways to motivate science students!
2. After successfully demonstrating the device, you may want to suggest other activities and extensions as followup for students who become motivated and show interest in learning more about radioactivity.
   a. What materials are radioactive?
   b. What does it mean to be radioactive?
   c. What radioactive particles are probably producing the tracks you see?
   d. What is the purpose of having dry ice on the bottom and warm water on the top of the cloud chamber?
   e. Read about radioactivity in an encyclopedia. Find out what materials are naturally radioactive.
   f. Find out about the benefits of radioactivity. Also find out about the dangers of excessive exposure to radioactivity.

Science Background

Radioactive particles traveling through a supersaturated area will cause small droplets to form by creating charged ions on which the droplets can condense.

Materials

Cylindrical glass container, with top and bottom removed

Two aluminum pie tins

Flat sheet of sponge rubber

Circular piece of black velvet

Light source—e.g., slide-projector bulb

Dry ice (small cakes several inches square)

Methyl alcohol

Glue

D.C. high-voltage source (90–200 volts) (desirable but not absolutely necessary)

Radioactive source (Old parts from luminous clock face will do)

The diffusion cloud chamber can be used to give evidence of the existence of radioactive particles such as alpha particles, beta particles, gamma rays, and cosmic particles.

A radioactive source can be obtained by taking a small fragment of a luminous dial or number of a watch or clock face which has been discarded. Also, it is possible to use a small pin coated with radioactive salt.

Setup

Suspend the radioactive source as shown about three-quarters of an inch from the velvet at the bottom. Saturate the sponge rubber with methyl alcohol and place a few drops on the black velvet. Set the whole cylinder on a cake of dry ice, which may be in chunk form or crushed. Place a little warm water in the pan on top. Shine the light directly at the source near the bottom of the container. Wait about thirty seconds for supersaturation to occur. You should be able to tell that this has happened because of the appearance of a light "snow" falling slowly in the bottom inch or so of the container. It is in this region that the cloud tracks will appear. They will occur

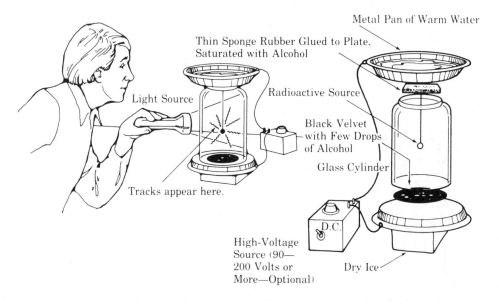

FIGURE 1
Diffusion cloud chamber

Metal Pan of Warm Water

Thin Sponge Rubber Glued to Plate, Saturated with Alcohol

Light Source

Radioactive Source

Black Velvet with Few Drops of Alcohol

Glass Cylinder

Tracks appear here.

High-Voltage Source (90–200 Volts or More—Optional)

Dry Ice

D.C.

suddenly as a streak and will then disappear by evaporation in a moment or two. A bit of persistence will bring great satisfaction in the appearance of these very fascinating cloud tracks of radioactive particles.

USING A DEMONSTRATION TO INITIATE DISCUSSION
DISCOVERY DEMONSTRATION:
THE RUBBER BAND WHEEL

Procedure

Construct the rubber band wheel as shown in Figure 1. Set up the apparatus as shown. Without explanation, shine a bright light on the wheel.

Materials

Shoe box

Cardboard wheel made of corrugated cardboard, 6 in. in diameter

Knitting needle

Four fresh rubber bands, all of equal length and thickness

Strong light source, preferably a 150-watt spotlight

Discussion

There are usually exceptions to most scientific generalizations.

Demonstrate the action of the rubber band wheel. Ask several questions to initiate discussion.

1. What do you observe?
2. What did you expect to happen?
3. What direction does the wheel turn? Is it always the same?
4. What would happen if the light came from the opposite side?
5. What would happen if the wheel were mounted in the open so light could strike all parts of it?
6. What would happen if the light were moved farther away?
7. What are some possible hypotheses or explanations?
8. Suspend a weight on a single strand of a rubber band fastened to a support. Shine the light on the rubber band. What happens to the weight?
9. How does this new information help explain the action of the rubber band wheel?

Explanation

Rubber bands in the light (heat) contract and pull the center of rotation toward the right. This makes the left side of the wheel heavier than the right side, and it turns counterclockwise.

Fact: Rubber bands under tension contract when heated, expand when cooled.

Principle: In general, solids expand when heated, contract when cooled, but rubber bands under tension are an exception.

FIGURE 1

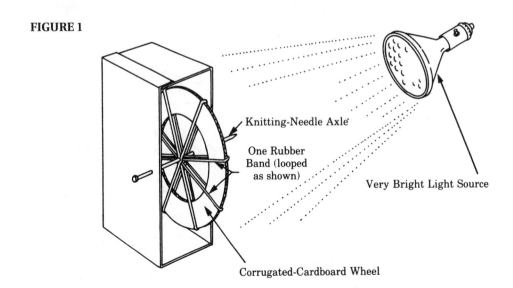

Knitting-Needle Axle

One Rubber Band (looped as shown)

Very Bright Light Source

Corrugated-Cardboard Wheel

DISCOVERY DEMONSTRATION: INQUIRING INTO FALLING BODIES

Construct the apparatus as shown in Figure 1. Demonstrate it several times. Let several students try to demonstrate it.

Materials

3-foot piece of board (1 × 2 in.)

2 small plastic cups (1-in. diam.)

Bearing ball (1-in. diam.)

Procedure

Put the ball in the cup at the end of the stick. Raise the stick to an angle of about thirty degrees. Drop the stick. The ball transfers to the other cup.

Questions

1. Why does the ball transfer to the other cup?
2. Is there a problem here? Is there anything out of the ordinary? Does it have an easy answer?
3. How did the ball get out of the first cup? Don't the ball and cup fall at the same rate of acceleration?
4. Something must be accelerating faster than gravity here. What is it? How can this happen?
5. Suppose you tossed a tumbling board over a cliff. Would all parts of it be accelerating downward at the same rate? What part of it accelerates at thirty-two feet per second per second?
6. What part of the stick in this demonstration accelerates at thirty-two feet per second per second? Where is this point?

Explanation

The cup at the end accelerates faster than thirty-two feet/sec/sec. The ball accelerates only at thirty-two ft/sec/sec. The point on the stick which accelerates at thirty-two ft/sec/sec is the "center of percussion" which is two-thirds of the way from the pivot end to the end with the cup.

1. What parts of the inquiry demonstration represented problem identification?
2. What part involved making hypotheses?
3. What part represented data-gathering?
4. What was concerned with drawing conclusions?

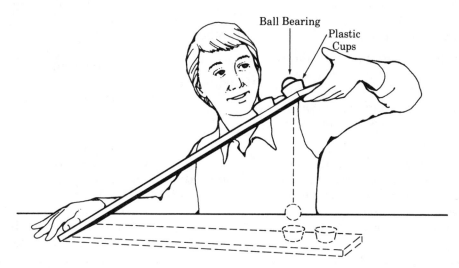

Ball Bearing · Plastic Cups · **FIGURE 1**

HOW LONG CAN YOU BOIL WATER IN A PAPER CUP?

Teacher's note: This is a junior high level inquiry lesson. Sections I through III are for the teachers only and Sections IV and V are to be duplicated for the student.

I. Concepts

· A flame is a source of radiant heat.
· Water, when heated, expands and gives off water vapor.
· Water can absorb a considerable amount of heat.
· Before a substance will burn, its kindling temperature must be reached.
· The kindling temperature is the temperature at which a substance will first start to burn.

II. Materials

Nonwaxed paper cup

Bunsen burner, propane torch, or alcohol burner

Ring stand

Ring clamp

Wire screen

III. Prelaboratory Discussion

Processes:

Hypothesizing 1. What do you think will happen to a paper cup when you try to boil water in it?

Hypothesizing 2. What do you think will happen first, the water boiling or the cup burning?

Hypothesizing 3. How do you think you could get a paper cup containing water to burn?

Designing an investigation 4. What should you do to find out?

IV. Pupil Discovery Activity

Processes:

Collecting materials 1. Obtain the following equipment: A nonwaxed paper cup, torch or burner, ring stand, ring clamp, and screen.

Designing an investigation 2. How could you use this equipment to find out if you can boil water in a paper cup?

Teacher's note: Draw a diagram on the chalkboard showing a paper cup sitting on a wire screen on a ring stand placed over a burner. The students should place the paper cup, containing not more than 5cm³ of water, on the wire screen and heat it from below with the burner.

Following directions 3. If you can think of no other ways to test your hypothesis, set up the equipment as indicated by your teacher's diagram.

Observing 4. What happens when you try to heat the water in the cup?

Inferring 5. What do you think the ring clamp and screen do to the heat from the flame?

Inferring 6. What can you say about the heat energy entering and leaving the water as you try to heat it to the boiling point?

7. Why does the water level in the cup change?

8. What effect does water in the cup have on its temperature as it is being heated?

9. Keep heating the cup until all the water is evaporated. Record your observation and conclusions.

V. Open-ended Questions

Processes:

Hypothesizing 1. If you took paper, cloth, wood, and charcoal and heated them, in what order would they start to burn? Why?

Criticizing 2. If you were going to repeat the preceding experiment, what would you do to obtain better data?

Hypothesizing 3. How would varying the amount of heat energy differ if you used a Styrofoam cup?

Hypothesizing 4. How would varying the amount of heat energy applied to the cup change the results?

Hypothesizing 5. How would the results vary if there were a different liquid in the cup such as cola, syrup, etc.?

Hypothesizing 6. In what way would the results vary if the cup were supported by a ring clamp and screen?

Designing an investigation 7. What other experiments does this investigation suggest?

HOW CAN YOU USE QUESTIONS TO SOLVE PROBLEMS? DISCOVERY DEMONSTRATION: KELVIN'S WATERDROPPER ELECTROSTATIC GENERATOR

Construct the apparatus as shown in Figure 1. Demonstrate it to the class in a slightly darkened room. Ask the following questions:

Materials

Two small juice cans

No. 2 1/2 can (reservoir)

Two short pieces of glass tubing, tapered at one end

Two 12 in. sections of rubber tubing

Coat-hanger wire shaped as shown in Figure 1

NE-2 neon lamp (0.25 watt)

Two blocks of paraffin

Blocks of wood for base and upright

Two small metal rings soldered to coat-hanger wire as shown

Procedure

Fill the reservoir can with water. By siphon action, start water flowing through each outlet tube. Adjust lower cans and rings so water falls through the rings into the cans.

Adjust spark gap so it is about one millimeter in width.

Watch the neon bulb for intermittent flashes. In a darkened room these flashes will be visible to a whole class.

Questions

1. What did you observe as the apparatus was put into operation?
2. How long did it take for the first flash?
3. How much time elapses between flashes?
4. What happens to the length of time if the gap distance is changed?

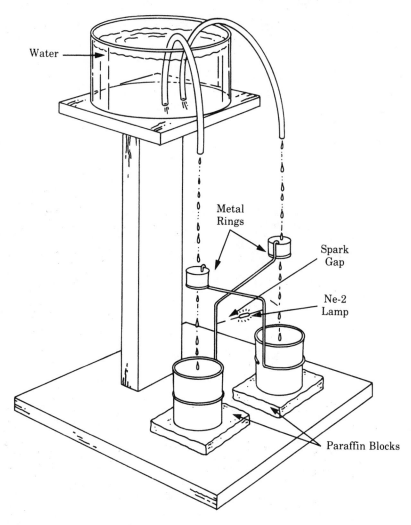

Water

Metal Rings

Spark Gap

Ne-2 Lamp

Paraffin Blocks

FIGURE 1

5. What happens when the gap is eliminated entirely?
6. What is causing the flash?
7. Where does the electricity come from?
8. What kind of charged particles are in water?
9. Suppose you were to construct an apparatus like this. Would each half of the apparatus (small can, coat-hanger wire, and metal ring) be likely to have exactly the same initial charge?
10. Suppose the side labeled A had a slightly negative charge as compared to B. What kinds of charges would be attracted to A?
11. But these charges fall into side marked B. What kind of charge do they give to B?
12. By similar action, what charge does A acquire?
13. For how long will these charge accumulations go on?
14. What is the likely charge distribution after the flash?
15. What is the complete explanation of the operation of this "water-dropper" generator?

Explanation

One side of the apparatus will have a slightly greater initial negative charge. The other side will have a slightly higher initial positive charge. This is an assumption but an extremely good one.

Ions in the water will be attracted to the metal rings differentially, with positive ions going toward the negative ring and negative ions going toward the positive ring.

But these ions do not neutralize the rings. Instead they fall through the rings and contribute to buildup of like charge in the cans.

Potential difference between the two halves of the apparatus increases until a small spark occurs at the gap. At this instant, the neon bulb flashes.

The process repeats cyclically. Widening the gap delays the discharge. Closing the gap completely prevents any build-up of potential difference. Consequently, there is no flashing.

1. How many different types of questions did you (could you) ask to arrive at an understanding of how this device operates?
2. Will simply asking the right questions finally solve the problem? What else might be needed?

PROBLEM SOLVING

AN INTRODUCTION TO SCIENTIFIC INQUIRY

Aims

To develop a fundamental understanding of, and ability to use, the methods of scientific investigation.

Student Objectives

At the completion of this lesson the student should be able to:

- Identify and state a simple problem
- Collect data relative to a simple problem
- Draw conclusions relative to data
- Form hypotheses based on observations and data
- Design a simple experiment to confirm/refute an hypothesis

Materials

Dice (or small cubes with numbers 1–6 on different sides), one die for each pair of students.

"Mystery Boxes" (small closed boxes with objects inside. Each box may contain a different object), one box for groups of 3–4 students.

Procedures

Anticipatory Set
1. Ask students to review what they think scientists do (investigate, solve problems, inquire).
2. Which goal of science is important? Why? How does the process of inquiry apply to them?

Objective and Purpose
Today's lesson is an introduction to scientific inquiry.

Instructional Input
1. *Introductory Exploration*
   Prior to your discussion place a die on each desk. Give very clear directions that they are not to touch the die.
   - A problem exists relative to the die. What is it? (Let them give their ideas.)

- Direct discussion to the identification of a problem. (What is on the bottom?)
- Focus discussion on assumptions, data, inference, etc.

2. *Explanation of Inquiry*
   - Systematic approach to problems
   - Collection of data (not assumptions)
   - Form hypothesis based on data
   - Confirm or refute hypothesis
   - Design of experiments
   - Present the information supporting your conclusion, i.e., writing a scientific paper.
   - Have students summarize the process of inquiry in terms of their observations of the die. How would they best support the case for their hypothesis of what is on the bottom, e.g., adding sides of the die, sequence of numbers, the missing number and so on. Ask them to show how they could systematically approach the problem, collect data, form hypotheses, confirm or refute hypotheses and design an experiment to support their hypothesis. Have the students write a short paper based on this activity. They should use the scientific protocol for the paper's organization.

3. *Extension of Ideas to a New Problem*
   - Present mystery box
   - Allow students to state problem, collect data, form hypothesis, design experiment and present final conclusions.

Evaluation of Objectives:
1. Present a new problem, that you have designed.
2. Have the students collect information, etc. and write a "scientific paper."
3. Evaluate the "scientific paper" and provide feedback relative to the student's understanding of the inquiry process.

TEACHING INQUIRY SKILLS

Grade Level

Junior high

Student Objectives

To gain practice in the skills of (1) measurement, (2) record-keeping, (3) graphing

Subject

Forces produced by springs

Problem

How does the length of spring depend on the force exerted on it?

Procedure

Work in pairs, or do as a student demonstration with all students recording the data and drawing the graph. Set up the spring and weights as shown in Figure 1. Add weights one at a time and check the readings each time.

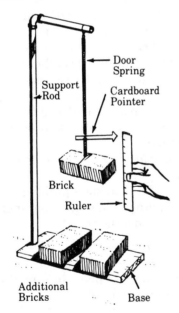

FIGURE 1
Demonstration setup

Record the results as shown in Table 1. Graph the results as shown in the graph.

Materials

Door springs

Several bricks

Ruler

String

TABLE 1

Weight (Bricks)	Stretch (cm.)
1	1.5
2	3.0
3	4.5
4	6.0

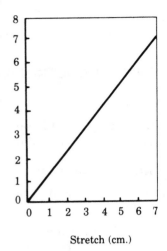

FIGURE 2
Results recorded in table and graph form

Conclusion

The change in length of a spring is directly proportional to the change in the force exerted on it—if the spring is not stretched beyond its elastic limit.

Probable Skills Developed

1. Setup and adjustment of apparatus (manipulative)
2. Observation of initial conditions and changes due to experimental factors (acquisitive)
3. Recording of data (organizational)
4. Graphing and analysis of data (organizational and communicative)
5. Drawing conclusions (organizational)

Evaluation

Can the student

1. Set up the apparatus for use?
2. Devise a plan of procedure?
3. Read a scale to the limits of its accuracy?
4. Record data in a tabular form?
5. Plot a graph?
6. Interpret a graph?
7. Draw conclusions from the experiment?
8. Recognize sources of error?
9. Report his results lucidly?

SMALL GROUP PROBLEM SOLVING

Small group discussions have the advantage of providing an atmosphere that is conducive to drawing out shy and reticent students. The setting is less threatening and the topics may be more easily controlled. Some guidelines for this variation of the discussion method follow:

1. Form groups of 3–5 persons
2. Present a problem
   a. Demonstration
   b. Story
   c. Social issue
   d. Dilemma
3. Each group appoints a spokesman
4. Allow discussion to continue 5–10 minutes
   a. Clarify the problem
   b. Suggest hypotheses for solution
   c. Discuss hypotheses
   d. Obtain consensus in the group
   e. Draw conclusions
5. Assemble as a large group
6. Spokesmen present the group conclusions
7. Discuss as a large group using guidelines discussed earlier

SCIENCE FAIR PROJECTS

MODEL OF A TORNADO VORTEX

Materials

4 posts, 1 1/2 inches × 1 1/2 inches × 16 inches

4 glass panels, 12 inches × 16 inches

2 plywood squares, 15 inches × 15 inches

2 copper tubes, 1/4-inch diameter × 6 inches long

1 heater coil, socket, and connecting electrical cord

1 plexiglass flue pipe, 10-inch diameter × 12 inches long; 1 plexiglass flue pipe, 9 1/2 inches diameter × 12 inches long

Wire rack, 10-inch diameter

1 small spotlight, socket, and connecting electrical cord

Pizza tin, 12-inch diameter

Glass or plexiglass circle, 3-inch diameter

Small metal or wooden box, 4 inches × 4 inches × 4 inches

Syringe bulb

Smoke pellets

Dry ice, 1 pound

Aluminum foil, heavy gauge

One of the most awesome spectacles in nature is a tornado. In a well-developed tornado there seems to be almost unlimited power available for destruction. Measurements of the wind velocities, pressure, and temperature changes in the heart of the tornado are often lacking because instruments are destroyed and because of the capricious and transitory nature of the storm. Placement of instruments in suitable positions for recording data is almost impossible because of the relatively small size (perhaps only one-fourth mile in diameter) and widespread area over which a tornado may occur.

The causes for this violent and spectacular phenomenon are many and varied. Tornadoes are usually formed in connection with strong cold fronts and squall lines, or with thunderstorms. The central part of the United States is particularly vulnerable, but nearly every state has experienced at least one tornado. Other continents as well, including Africa and Australia, have recorded this type of storm.

Certain conditions favor the formation of a tornado in the United States: (a) very warm, moist air near the surface of the ground, frequently moving northward from the Gulf of Mexico; (b) a cold front moving from the west or northwest toward the warm air mass, causing lifting and marked instability of the air; (c) high-velocity winds at 10,000 to 20,000 feet blowing above the cold front, frequently from west to east; and (d) warm, dry air aloft, which overlies the warm, moist air. Extreme heating by the sun on a humid summer afternoon appears to help trigger the tornado, because most tornadoes occur in late afternoon or evening.

The storm is characterized by a funnel-shaped cloud that seems to form in the overlying chaotic cloud mass and grow downward to the ground. Frequently, the portion that touches the ground is only a few hundred yards in diameter, and it consists of extremely violent winds (up to several hundred miles per hour) that pick up dust and debris, giving a visible funnel appearance. The storm generally moves in a northeasterly direction at a speed of 25 to 50 miles per hour (although there are frequent exceptions to this). The damage from the tornado comes mainly from three sources: the extremely high winds, which are strong enough to destroy most frame buildings; the sudden decrease in air pressure as the tornado passes overhead; and the drenching rain and hail that often accompany its passage.

Many investigators have attempted to study the tornado by using models and have succeeded in duplicating to some extent the appearance, if not the dynamics, of the natural storm. It is unlikely that one could actually create a tornado "in a box," but a model can be useful in examining the motions of air in a circular vortex. For example, what causes air to begin moving in a circular motion? Does the air in the vicinity of the whirling vortex get drawn into the vortex, or does it get pushed aside? Does the air within the vortex itself flow upward or downward? Why is a tornado vortex visible? Is it composed of water droplets, debris, dust, or ice crystals? The model can suggest some answers to these questions.

In an article entitled "A Tornado Model and the Fire Whirlwind" by James Miller in *Weatherwise*, the author reports some investigations with a simple vortex model. He believes that each microscopic droplet in the cloud formed in the vortex is acted upon by two forces. One is the *drag* of air spiraling toward the center. The other is the centrifugal reaction of the particles' rotation about the center. Inside the core of the vortex, the centrifugal reaction is stronger and particles are thrown outward. Outside the cloud column, air drag is stronger and particles are forced inward.

According to the model, the author hypothesizes two causes for a tornado:

1. Air must be drawn rapidly out of a region high above the earth's surface.
2. Fresh air coming in at lower levels must have some absolute rotation in the very beginning.

Since a tornado is a cyclonic storm with very low pressure at its center, air tends to rush toward the center from all sides and ascend rapidly inside the funnel. For this motion to continue, there must be some mechanism for this air to spread out or speed up and leave the vicinity when it reaches high levels. It is possible that the jet stream provides this mechanism. Recent studies on jet streams indicate that a region of divergence at high levels frequently accompanies the core of a jet stream, and this diverging air may provide the high-velocity winds that are apparently a necessary condition for tornado development.

The tornado model described here is patterned after one designed by Bellaire and Stohrer in 1963. As you construct it, keep in mind the following questions with the possibility of improving on the methods used here. Where does the tornado funnel begin—at the ground or high in the clouds? What produces the whirling action in a tornado? What is the usual direction of rotation?

Figure 1 illustrates the general appearance of the tornado chamber in action. The main chamber is an open-sided box with sliding glass panels that can be moved horizontally along the base to permit the entry of air from the sides. Smoke, admitted at two levels from a smoke generator, forms the visible vortex.

Construct the chamber from four corner posts of plywood, 1 inch by 1 inch by 16 inches long, into which have been carved grooves running the length of each post on two adjacent sides. The grooves must be sized to enclose and support the glass or plexiglass panels that will form the sides of the chamber. One post, the one that will form the left front corner of the box, should be drilled with two holes at different levels large enough to accommodate two 1/8-inch or 1/4-inch copper or steel tubes, which will admit the smoke. Nail the posts to a base of plywood, 15 inches square, into which a 10-inch hole has been cut. The base must also have grooves along the sides to accommodate the sliding panels.

Prepare a 12-inch pizza or pie tin by cutting a 3-inch hole in the bottom and gluing over it a piece of plexiglass. This small, plexiglass window will be placed over a spotlight in the working model. Nail or tape the tin over the hole in the plywood base.

The panels are 12 inches by 16 inches long, about 1 inch narrower than the sides of the box, so that slots of variable width can be opened along either the right or left sides. You will probably find plexiglass an easier material than glass to work with for this purpose. Slide the panels into place through the top opening, and paint the back panel on the outside with black enamel, or tape a piece of black construction paper over it, to enhance the visual effect of the vortex.

The top of the chamber is a sheet of plywood, like the base 15 inches square with a 10-inch hole cut into

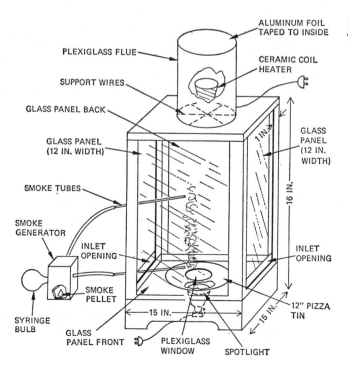

FIGURE 1
Tornado vortex chamber

PLEXIGLASS FLUE

ALUMINUM FOIL TAPED TO INSIDE

CERAMIC COIL HEATER

SUPPORT WIRES

GLASS PANEL BACK

GLASS PANEL (12 IN. WIDTH)

GLASS PANEL (12 IN. WIDTH)

SMOKE TUBES

1 IN.

16 IN.

SMOKE GENERATOR

INLET OPENING

INLET OPENING

SMOKE PELLET

15 IN.

15 IN.

12" PIZZA TIN

SYRINGE BULB

GLASS PANEL FRONT

PLEXIGLASS WINDOW

SPOTLIGHT

it for the stack. Again, grooves along the bottom sides will provide paths for the sliding panels. The plywood top can be rested on the support posts and removed as desired for access to the chamber. The draft-producing stack is made of 2 12-inch-long plexiglass tubes, one 10 inches in diameter to fit in the hole in the chamber's top, the other just big enough to fit inside the first tube. The first tube is taped to the plywood; the second is raised or lowered within the main chamber to vary the effects of the vortex. Before fitting the tubes together, glue or staple coverings of aluminum foil to the inside of both. Rig a wire rack in the bottom of the inner tube to support a ceramic heater coil.

Insert the smoke tubes through the left corner post, and attach lengths of rubber tubing. When the chamber is functioning, you can either blow cigarette smoke directly through the tubes, or run the tubes into a small, smoke-generating box. This is simply a 3-inch-square plywood box, open at one end, with holes to admit the rubber tubes. A rubber bulb syringe can be inserted through a hole in the opposite side and pressed regularly to force the smoke out the tubes. Put a burning piece of cigarette or a smoke pellet in an empty pie tin, and place the box over it.

When the chamber is completely constructed, suspend it on bricks or boxes, allowing enough of an opening beneath for the spotlight. To operate the model, fill the flat pan at the base with 1/4 inch of water, and turn on the electric heating coil in the base of the stack, and the spotlight below. The inside panels should be adjusted to allow room for air to enter in such a direction as to give a rotary motion to the rising air within the stack. For counterclockwise rotation, allow the air to enter through a 1/2-to-1-inch vertical slit on the right side of each panel, by sliding the panels to the left a short distance. Different parts of the vortex can be investigated by admitting smoke through the smoke jets. Placing a beaker of dry ice and water in a corner of the chamber produces a dense white cloud that improves the visibility of the vortex.

As you work with your tornado model, try to answer some of the following questions:

1. Can you reverse the direction of rotation of the "tornado" funnel?
2. Does the funnel descend from above or rise from below?
3. What is the rate of temperature change with height (lapse rate) from bottom to top of the chamber? You will need a series of thermometers placed at strategic locations within the chamber to answer this question, or use the thermopile described in the section on relative humidity, moving it back and forth and up and down.
4. Is a temperature inversion necessary to initiate the funnel or vortex? A temperature inversion refers to an increase of temperature with height.
5. Is this model more analogous to a waterspout or a tornado over land? In a waterspout, water drops and cloud droplets intermingle to form a visible funnel.
6. Is there a downdraft or an updraft in the center of the "tornado" funnel?
7. What is the pressure gradient from the outside of the funnel to the center? How could it be measured?
8. In what ways does the model resemble the real tornado? In what ways is it different? What about the electrical effects in a tornado? Can these be simulated? Recent theories tend toward an electrical explanation for tornadic winds. Can these be investigated?
9. Suppose a high electrical potential were placed between the pan of water and the discharge stack; for example, 200 volts D.C. at very low amperage, such as can be obtained from certain types of batteries. What would be the result? Try a potential of 100,000 volts using an electrostatic generator such as a Wimshurst static machine or Van de Graaff generator. Observe the results. Do some additional reading on the dynamics of dust whirls, tornadoes, and waterspouts in order to obtain ideas for modifying your vortex chamber and devising additional experiments.

FINDING LOCAL VARIATIONS IN RELATIVE HUMIDITY

Materials

Materials for sling psychrometer:

2 Fahrenheit thermometers ($-10°$ to $+110°$ F range)

Plywood block, 10 inches by 4 inches by 1/2 inch

6 small screws, 1/2 inch long

Wooden dowel, 1 inch diameter, 6 inches long

2 small washers

1 screw, 2 inches long

Small square of cheesecloth, 2 inches by 2 inches

If you construct the sling psychrometer described in the experiment on measuring cloud height later in this section, you will have a useful device for measuring relative humidity. If you have access to a varied topography—hills, a body of water, perhaps—you have all the raw materials for an interesting investigation in relative humidity variations. Relative humidity can be measured accurately by use of the sling psychrometer used in the experiment on measuring cloud height. The procedure is identical to that used to determine dew point. Find the dry-bulb and wet-bulb temperatures, compute the difference between them, and refer to the section of the psychrometric tables dealing with relative humidity (see Appendix B of the "Measuring Cloud Height" activity). Read downward on the left side to the dry-bulb temperature, and horizontally to the computed difference value. The relative humidity in percent is found at that point.

To study relative humidity systematically, obtain a map of the area you wish to study—or draw your own simple map—and mark on it the specific locations you can reach conveniently on a regular basis. Select a variety of sites such as a hilltop, the shore of a small body of water, a wooded area, a grassy field, a playground, an asphalt parking lot—whatever locations offer as much variety in topography, exposure, and nearness to water as possible within a workable area.

Make your observations using the sling psychrometer on a regular basis, such as at 8:00 A.M., 12:00 noon, 4:00 P.M., and 8:00 P.M., every day in each of the selected locations. Take all readings in the shade to avoid the effects of direct sunlight on the psychrometer. Note the exact time for each observation and repeat the observations at the same times for at least 10 days. At each observation, record the following information on a data sheet: location, time, date, wet-bulb degrees in Fahrenheit, dry-bulb degrees in Fahrenheit, relative humidity percent, wind direction, wind speed (est. mph), cloud cover (0 to .9), comments (precipitation, etc.).

Wind speed can be estimated accurately enough by using the Beaufort Wind Scale (Table 1).

TABLE 1
The Beaufort scale of wind force with specifications and velocity equivalents

Beaufort Number	General Description	Specifications	Velocity	
			Meters Per Sec.	Miles Per Hour
0	Calm	Smoke rises vertically	Under 0.6	Under 1
1	Light air	Wind direction shown by smoke drift but not by vanes	0.6–0.7	1–3
2	Slight	Wind felt on face; leaves rustle; ordinary vane moved by wind	0.8–3.3	4–7
3	Gentle breeze	Leaves and twigs in constant motion; wind extends light flag	3.4–5.2	8–11
4	Moderate breeze	Dust, loose paper, and small branches are moved	5.3–7.4	2–16
5	Fresh breeze	Small trees in leaf begin to sway	7.5–9.8	17–22
6	Strong breeze	Large branches in motion; whistling in wires	9.9–12.42	23–27
7	Moderate gale	Whole trees in motion	12.5–15.2	28–34
8	Fresh gale	Twigs broken off trees; progress generally impeded	15.3–18.2	35–41
9	Strong gale	Slight structural damage occurs; chimney damage	18.3–21.5	42–48
10	Whole gale	Trees uprooted; considerable structural damage	21.6–25.4	49–56
11	Storm	Very rarely experienced; widespread damage	25.5–29.0	57–67
12	Hurricane		Above 29.0	Above 67

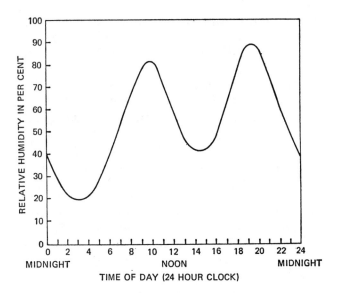

FIGURE 1
Graph showing possible daily fluctuations in relative humidity

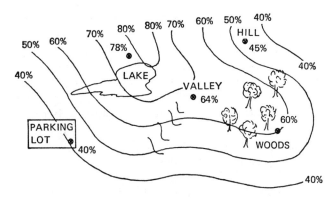

FIGURE 2
Map showing lines of equal relative humidity over varied terrain

When you have obtained data for the period of study, you can tabulate it in a variety of ways for analysis. For example, you might wish to find the average relative humidity at each location at the time of observation. Plotting these data on a graph of relative humidity versus time of day will show the daily changes that occur on a regular basis. Such a graph might look like the one in Figure 1. Or you might want to see how much fluctuation occurs in the relative humidity at a particular location over the period studied.

After you have obtained the average relative humidity at each location, plot the information on a detailed map of the area, putting down the average values obtained at each of the observation points. Draw lines of equal relative humidity on the map, as shown in Figure 2, positioning them so the individual data points fit the lines. What can you learn from such a map? Can you give any reasons for the variations in relative humidity from point to point?

Study the data obtained with respect to other factors recorded at each observation, such as cloud cover, wind speed and direction, and precipitation. Can you discover any relationships between these factors and the relative humidity? For example, in Figure 2 there is quite a difference in the relative humidity between one end of the lake and the other—from 50 percent to 80 percent. By comparing the map with a hypothetical data sheet, it might become apparent that the wind direction at the time of observation was from west to east. The air would thus pick up moisture and become more humid as it passed over the surface of the lake, explaining why the relative humidity is so much higher at the other end of the lake. Through careful coordination of all information on the contour maps and data sheets, try to obtain as much information as possible about variations in relative humidity and their causes.

MEASURING CLOUD HEIGHT

Materials

Materials for cloud height measurer
Plywood square 12 inches by 12 inches by 3/4 inch

3 screws, 3 inches long

Protractor

Magnetic compass

Plywood board 12 inches by 6 inches by 3/4 inch

Wooden stick, 12 inches by 1 inch by 1/2 inch

Metal eyelet screw, 1 inch long

Pin, 1/8-inch head

Materials for sling psychrometer
2 Fahrenheit thermometers (−10° F to +100° F range)

Plywood block, 10 inches by 4 inches by 1/2 inch

6 small screws, 1/2 inch long

Coat hanger wire, 16 inches long

Wooden dowel, 1 inch diameter, 6 inches long

2 small washers

1 screw, 2 inches long

Small square of cheesecloth, 2 inches by 2 inches

Have you ever watched cumulus clouds on a fine summer day and wondered how high they were? Perhaps you saw small planes appearing and disappearing as they flew through them, and from this concluded that the clouds were probably several thousand feet above the ground.

You'll learn here two different ways to measure cloud heights from the ground. The first method employs some basic trigonometric calculations on a theoretical triangle formed by you, at one sighting point, an associate at sighting point two, and a cloud. The second method makes use of a simple device to measure atmospheric moisture. Both systems are most successful when used to measure the heights of cumulus clouds.

According to the system of classification used by the *International Cloud Atlas*, clouds fall into four major altitude categories: Low (bases less than 6,500 feet above the ground), Middle (bases 6,500 feet to 20,000 feet above the ground), High (bases more than 20,000 feet above the ground), and clouds of Vertical Development (extending from near the ground to above 20,000 feet). Because of the difficulty of measuring angles accurately with the instruments described in the first method, your results will be best when finding the heights of clouds in the Low category, which includes cumulus and stratocumulus. Stratus clouds are more difficult to measure because of the indistinct character of the base of such clouds and the problem of locating a suitable point on which to sight.

To measure cloud heights using the method described here, you will need to enlist the aid of a helper. You will also need to construct two identical instruments for measuring angles of elevation. A diagram of the construction details is shown in Figure 1.

With a board 1 inch thick and 12 inches square as a base, secure a second board 1 inch by 6 inches by 12 inches to form the upright. Attach the upright board to the base with 1-inch screws from the bottom. Saw a notch 1 inch wide and 2 inches deep in the upright, as shown, and mount a narrow stick (1 inch by 1/2 inch by 12 inches) on a pivot inside the notch. The pivot can be a small nail hammered through the middle of the stick (6 inches from either end) and fitted into small holes drilled into the side of the notch.

Mount a small metal or plastic protractor to one side of the notch, with its center line at the same height as the pivot. A thin groove sawed vertically along one side of the upright will permit the protractor to be wedged tightly into it for support.

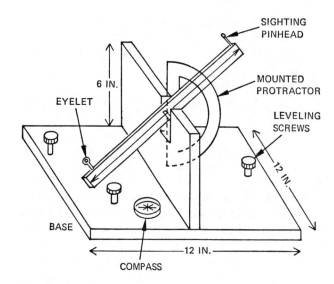

FIGURE 1
Cloud height measurer

For the leveling screws, obtain three identical 1/4-inch diameter bolts and turn them through 1/4-inch holes drilled in the base. Friction will hold them at the desired height when in use.

A small pocket compass can be set on the base of the instrument for orientation along a north–south or east–west line when cloud heights are being measured.

For sighting, insert a small pin with a 1/8-inch diameter head in the upper end of the sighting stick. At the other end, a small screw eyelet with a 1/4-inch diameter opening should be attached as shown in Figure 1.

Construct two of these instruments, and you are ready to begin taking measurements. Decide upon a base line of about 3,000 (or close to .6 mile), preferably level and unobstructed by trees or buildings. A quiet, straight country road would be ideal. If it is, in addition, oriented north–south or east–west, it will be easier to calculate angles should you decide to measure cloud directions as well as heights. The base line can be measured accurately enough by use of the odometer in a car. Check the distance by driving the car over the base line twice and averaging the results.

Or, without a car, use the speedometer on a bicycle or walk off the distance and estimate the length of the base line with an inexpensive pedometer. You may be able to set up your sighting instruments along a base line that is premeasured—for example, property boundaries for which you can ascertain the length without actual measuring. Whatever method you use, come up with as accurate an estimation of the distance as you can.

If you don't live near flat, open country or a reasonably deserted stretch of beach, you may have some trouble finding an unobstructed area in which to work. Your measurements will still work if the base line is reduced up to one half, or 1,500 feet (about 6 city blocks).

Pick a day when there are plenty of clouds from which to choose. It won't matter too much if the clouds are moving rapidly because you and your assistant will take simultaneous readings on some common point of a particular cloud moving overhead. The most convenient way to synchronize your readings is to use a walkie-talkie. If you are in the city, you might use suitably located phone booths. When you are each in position at opposite ends of the base line, you will be able to see the same cloud and confer about what point both of you will sight on.

If you do not use a walkie-talkie, it will be necessary to synchronize your watches and decide upon a specific time at which you will take your readings. If a level road is the base line, one observer can be dropped off at one end and the other can go to the point 3,000 feet away, having previously decided to measure a particular cloud at, say, the tip nearest observer one, and then both observers can immediately take their readings at the predetermined time. Or, should you be within sight of each other at opposite ends of the base line, send a prearranged signal—a large, red cloth waved at one end, for example—when the readings are to be taken.

Set the measuring instrument on an old box or other raised object, sight through the screw hole on a line with the pinhead, and note the degrees indicated on the protractor. Try to take four or five trials on the same type of cloud, and average the final results.

Following is a sample measurement made one fall day on some clouds over Denver. The diagram (Figure 2) shows the required angles and base-line measurements needed for calculation of the cloud height. The problem was solved as follows:

$P_1P_2 = 3,000$ feet
$\theta_1 = 69°; \quad \theta_1 = 82°$
*Tangent $\theta_1 = 2,605$; Tangent $\theta_2 = 7.115$

(1) $\text{Tan } \theta_1 = \dfrac{CG}{P_1G}$; $\text{Tan } \theta_2 = \dfrac{CG}{P_2G}$
(2) $CG = P_1G \text{ Tan } \theta_1$; $\quad CG = P_2G \text{ Tan } \theta_2$
(3) $P_1G \text{ Tan } \theta_1 = P_2G \text{ Tan } \theta_2$
(4) $P_1G \text{ Tan } \theta_1 = (3,000 - P_1G) \text{ Tan } \theta_2$
(5) $P_1G \text{ Tan } \theta_1 = 3,000 \text{ Tan } \theta_2 - P_1G \text{ Tan } \theta_2$
(6) $P_1G (\text{Tan } \theta_1 + \text{Tan } \theta_2) = 3,000 \text{ Tan } \theta_2$
(7) $P_1G = \dfrac{3,000 \text{ Tan } \theta_2}{\text{Tan } \theta_1 + \text{Tan } \theta_2}$
(8) $P_1G = \dfrac{(3,000) (7.115)}{2.605 + 7.115}$
(9) $P_1G = \dfrac{21,345}{9.720} = 2,196$ feet
(10) $CG = P_1G \text{ Tan } \theta_1 = (2,196) (2.605)$
(11) $CG = 5,720$ feet (height of cloud)

NOTE: The tangent of an angle is the ratio of the side opposite the angle to the side adjacent to the angle, in a right triangle. Refer to Appendix B for tangent tables.

The preceding measurements were taken on a cloud that passed directly over each of the observers. To measure the heights of clouds that do not pass directly overhead, the mathematics is a little more complicated, but it requires nothing beyond basic high school trigonometry.

In this case you will again use a base line of 3,000 feet, but it will be necessary to measure not only the elevation angles θ_1 and θ_2 to the cloud from each end of the base line but also the azimuth angles $\delta1$ and $\delta2$. Elevation angles are measured from the horizontal to the line of sight of the cloud. Azimuth angles are measured from the north–south line (or east–west line if the cloud is east or west of you) to a point on the ground directly under the cloud (see Figure 3).

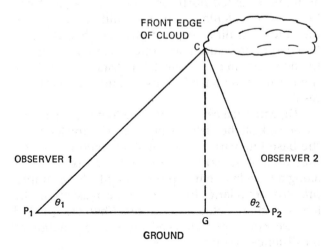

FIGURE 2
Sample cloud measurement

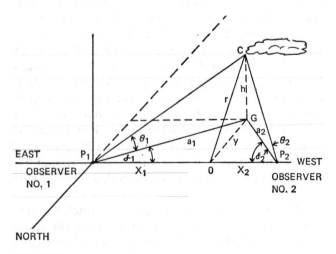

FIGURE 3
Measuring asimuth angles

To find h, the cloud height:

(1) $y = a_1 \sin \delta_1 = a_2 \sin \delta_2$

(2) $a_1 = \dfrac{y}{\sin \delta_1}$; $a_2 = \dfrac{y}{\sin \delta_2}$

(3) $y = x_1 \tan \delta_1 = x_2 = \tan \delta_2 = (3,000 - x_1) \tan \delta_2$

(4) $h = a_1 \tan \theta_1 = a_2 \tan \theta_2$

(5) Substituting,
$$h = \frac{x_1 \tan \delta_1 \tan \theta_1}{\sin \delta_1} = \frac{(3000 - x_1 \, (\tan \delta_2) \, (\tan \theta_2)}{\sin \delta_2}$$

(6) Solving for x_1,
$$\frac{3,000 - x_1}{x_1} = \frac{(\sin \delta_2) \, (\tan \delta_1) \, (\tan \theta_1)}{(\sin \delta_1) \, (\tan \delta_2) \, (\tan \theta_2)}$$

(7) $x_1 = \dfrac{3,000}{\dfrac{(\sin \delta_2) \, (\tan \delta_1) \, (\tan \theta_1)}{(\sin \delta_1) \, (\tan \delta_2) \, (\tan \theta_2)} + 1}$

(8) $h = \left[\dfrac{3,000}{\dfrac{(\sin \delta_2) \, (\tan \delta_1) \, (\tan \theta_1)}{(\sin \delta_1) \, (\tan \delta_2) \, (\tan \theta_2)} + 1} \right] \left[\dfrac{(\tan \delta_1) \, (\tan \theta_1)}{\sin \delta_1)} \right]$

To illustrate the calculation by this method of the height of a cloud that does not pass directly overhead, let:

$$\delta_1 = 30°, \ \delta_2 = 40°$$
$$\theta_1 = 45°, \ \theta_2 = 50°$$

$$h = \left[\frac{3,000 \text{ feet}}{\dfrac{(.643) \, (.577) \, (1)}{(.5) \, (.839) \, (1.192)} + 1} \right] \left[\frac{(.577) \, (1)}{(0.5)} \right]$$

$$= \frac{3,000 \text{ feet}}{1.0742} (1.154)$$

$$h = 3,223 \text{ feet}$$

Become familiar with your instruments, take a number of sightings on different kinds of cloudy days, and consider some interesting questions. How do cloud heights change with time? Do all clouds of a given type have the same base height? Do you find that cloud bases or cloud tops are more nearly the same height?

Since cumulus clouds are caused largely by convection, during which a column of moist air is rising and cooling, there is a method for finding the heights of their bases that employs dew points, or the temperature at which condensation of water vapor would begin if the air were cooled to that temperature. For the dew-point method, you will require a sling psychrometer and a set of psychrometric tables for obtaining dew points. The U.S. Government Printing Office (Washington, DC 20402) will supply a complete set of these tables; for convenience, however, an abbreviated set of psychrometric tables is included in Appendix B.

A sling psychrometer can be constructed easily from two identical, inexpensive outdoor thermometers, available in any hardware store. Carefully cut

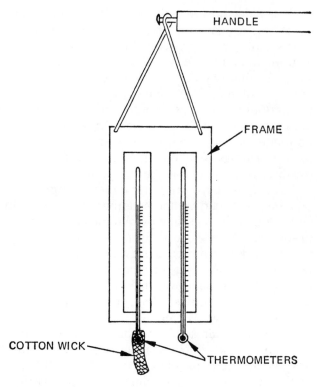

FIGURE 4
Sling psychrometer

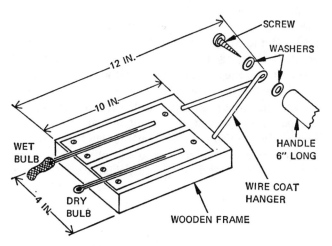

FIGURE 5
Construction details for sling psychrometer

away the lower ends of the holders so that the bulbs and about 1/4 inch of the capillaries above them are free. Mount the two thermometers side by side on a thin board (1/2 inch by 4 inches by 10 inches) as shown in Figure 4. Wrap one bulb with a small piece of cheesecloth to form a wick, and suspend the board by a coat hanger wire from a short handle (construction details are shown in Figure 5).

Pick a day on which the sky is filling with cumulus clouds to use your psychrometer. Moisten the cheesecloth wick, select a shady place, hold the instrument at arm's length and shoulder height, and swing the thermometers around the handle at a rate of about three times a second. After 1 minute, read the wet-bulb thermometer quickly and then the dry-bulb thermometer, each to the nearest 1/2 degree. Continue to swing the thermometers until two successive readings show no temperature changes, and use these readings to find the dew point.

To use the psychrometric tables, compute the difference between the temperatures of the dry bulb and wet bulb on the sling psychrometer (t − t'). On the dew-point tables, read downward on the left side to the dry-bulb temperature and horizontally across the top to the number representing the difference between the dry- and wet-bulb readings. The number found at that intersection is the dew-point temperature in degrees Fahrenheit.

To what we already know about the formation of convective clouds, such as cumulus and cumulonimbus, add an additional piece of information. The normal rate at which the dew point decreases with height above the ground is different from the dry adiabatic lapse rate, the rate at which air normally cools, without the gain or loss of any heat, as it rises and expands in the atmosphere. Consider what happens as a parcel of air is caused to rise by convection on a warm summer afternoon. As long as condensation does not occur, the temperature of the parcel will decrease by adiabatic cooling at the rate of 5.5° F per 1,000 feet of rise. At the same time, the rate at which the dew point decreases for the same rising parcel of air is 1.1° F per 1,000 feet. The temperature of the air, therefore, will decrease faster than its dew point, and after a time the two will be the same. This is illustrated in Figure 6.

Suppose a parcel of air at the ground with a temperature of 80° F and a dew point of 58° F starts to rise

in a convective cell. The difference between these two temperatures is 22 degrees. The rate at which the temperature overtakes the dew point is 4.4° F per 1,000 feet (5.5° F − 1.1° F)/1,000 feet. Thus at a height of 5,000 feet (22° F ÷ 4.4° F/1,000 feet = 5,000 feet), the two temperatures will be the same (52.5° F) and condensation will occur. This will be the base of the cumulus cloud that begins to form. Clouds will form (condensation begins) whenever the air reaches saturation or when the air reaches its dew point.

It can be seen that in this procedure we have a method for determining the height of the base of cumulus clouds. An equation that expresses the relationship used is:

$H = 227 (T_o − D_o)$, where
 H is the height sought (in feet)
 T_o is the actual Fahrenheit temperature of the air at the ground, and
 D_o is the dew-point temperature of the air at the ground.

(For the derivation of this equation, see Appendix A.)

Other questions that you might investigate with your methods of measuring cloud heights are:

1. How do various points on the base of a single cloud vary in height?
2. Does a cumulonimbus cloud grow downward as well as upward? Remember that these clouds grow because of convection and difference in air densities.
3. Can you measure the rate of ascent of a cumulonimbus cloud top? How do different cumulonimbus clouds vary in ascent rates?
4. Find the vertical thickness of a cloud by this method. Why do some cumulus or cumulonimbus clouds appear darker than others? Which permit more sunlight to come through—thin ones or thick ones?
5. From your observations, can you tell whether a growing cloud is a small cloud expanding by original water droplets moving upward and outward, or growing by new cloud material forming at the surface of the cloud, as in crystal growth? Would new cloud material form around the edges of the main cloud if conditions were right for condensation of water vapor?

Appendix A

Derivation of equation $H = 227 (T_o − D_o)$

Let H = the height of the cloud bases,
 T_o = the temperature at the ground surface,
 D_o = the dew point at the ground surface,
 T_h = the temperature at the cloud bases, and
 D_h = the dew point at the cloud bases.

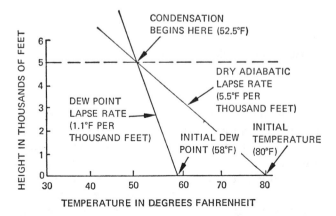

FIGURE 6

The lapse rate of temperature for a rising parcel of air is 5.5° F per 1,000 feet (adiabatic lapse rate). The lapse rate for the dew point is approximately 1.1° F per 1,000 feet. The following equations express the relationships between temperatures at the ground surface and at the cloud base, and similarly the relationships between the dew points at the ground surface and at the base of the clouds.

$$T_h = T_o - (5.5° F/1,000 \text{ feet}) H, \text{ and}$$
$$D_h = D_o - (1.1° F/1,000 \text{ feet}) H$$

Because H is the height at which condensation begins, T_h and D_h are the same temperature. Hence,

$$T_o - (5.5° F/1,000) \text{ feet } (H = D_o - (1.1° F/1,000 \text{ feet}) H$$
$$4.4 H = 1000 (T_o - D_o)$$
$$H = 227 (T_o - D_o)$$

Appendix B

Read down **TRIGONOMETRIC FUNCTIONS**

Radians	Angle	Sin	Cos	Tan	Cot	Angle	Radians
0.000	0°	0.000	1.000	0.000	∞	90°	1.571
.018	1°	.018	1.000	.018	57.29	89°	1.553
.035	2°	.035	0.999	.035	28.64	88°	1.536
.052	3°	.052	.999	.052	19.08	87°	1.518
.070	4°	.070	.998	.070	14.30	86°	1.501
.087	5°	.087	.996	.088	11.43	85°	1.484
.105	6°	.105	.995	.105	9.514	84°	1.466
.122	7°	.122	.993	.123	8.144	83°	1.449
.140	8°	.139	.990	.141	7.115	82°	1.431
.157	9°	.156	.988	.158	6.314	81°	1.414
.175	10°	.174	.985	.176	5.671	80°	1.396
.192	11°	.191	.982	.194	5.145	79°	1.379
.209	12°	.208	.978	.213	4.705	78°	1.361
.227	13°	.225	.974	.231	4.331	77°	1.344
.244	14°	.242	.970	.249	4.011	76°	1.327
.262	15°	.259	.966	.268	3.732	75°	1.309
.279	16°	.276	.961	.287	3.487	74°	1.292
.297	17°	.292	.956	.306	3.271	73°	1.274
.314	18°	.309	.951	.325	3.078	72°	1.257
.332	19°	.326	.946	.344	2.904	71°	1.239
.349	20°	.342	.940	.364	2.747	70°	1.222
.367	21°	.358	.934	.384	2.605	69°	1.204
.384	22°	.375	.927	.404	2.475	68°	1.187
.401	23°	.391	.921	.425	2.356	67°	1.169
.419	24°	.407	.914	.445	2.246	66°	1.152
.436	25°	.423	.906	.466	2.145	65°	1.135
.454	26°	.438	.899	.488	2.050	64°	1.117
.471	27°	.454	.891	.510	1.963	63°	1.100
.489	28°	.470	.883	.532	1.881	62°	1.082
.506	29°	.485	.875	.554	1.804	61°	1.065
.524	30°	.500	.866	.577	1.732	60°	1.047
.541	31°	.515	.857	.601	1.664	59°	1.030
.559	32°	.530	.848	.625	1.600	58°	1.012
.576	33°	.545	.839	.649	1.540	57°	0.995
.593	34°	.559	.829	.675	1.483	56°	.977
.611	35°	.574	.819	.700	1.428	55°	.960
.628	36°	.588	.809	.727	1.376	54°	.943
.646	37°	.602	.799	.754	1.327	53°	.925
.663	38°	.616	.788	.781	1.280	52°	.908
.681	39°	.629	.777	.810	1.235	51°	.890
.698	40°	.643	.766	.839	1.192	50°	.873
.716	41°	.656	.755	.869	1.150	49°	.855
.733	42°	.669	.743	.900	1.111	48°	.838
.751	43°	.682	.731	.933	1.072	47°	.820
.768	44°	.695	.719	.966	1.036	46°	.803
.785	45°	.707	.707	1.000	1.000	45°	.785
Radians	Angle	Cos	Sin	Cot	Tan	Angle	Radians

Read up

Relative humidity, per cent—Fahrenheit temperatures
[Pressure = 30.0 inches]

Air temperature t	Depression of wet-bulb thermometer (t − t')																				
	0.5	1.0	1.5	2.0	2.5	3.0	3.5	4.0	4.5	5.0	5.5	6.0	6.5	7.0	7.5	8.0	8.5	9.0	9.5	10.0	10.5
20	92	85	77	70	62	55	48	40	33	26	19	12	5								
21	92	85	78	71	63	56	49	42	35	28	21	15	8	1							
22	93	86	78	71	65	58	51	44	37	31	24	17	11	4							
23	93	86	79	72	66	59	52	46	39	33	26	20	14	7	1						
24	93	87	80	73	67	60	54	47	41	35	29	22	16	10	4						
25	94	87	81	74	68	62	55	49	43	37	31	25	19	13	7	1					
26	94	87	81	75	69	63	57	51	45	39	33	27	21	16	10	4					
27	94	88	82	76	70	64	58	52	47	41	35	29	24	18	13	7	2				
28	94	88	82	76	71	65	59	54	48	43	37	32	26	21	15	10	5				
29	94	88	83	77	72	66	60	55	50	44	39	34	28	23	18	13	8	3			
30	94	89	83	78	73	67	62	56	51	46	41	36	31	26	21	16	11	6	1		
31	94	89	84	78	73	68	63	58	52	47	42	37	33	28	23	18	13	8	4		
32	95	89	84	79	74	69	64	59	54	49	44	39	35	30	25	20	16	11	7	2	
33	95	90	85	80	75	70	65	60	56	51	46	41	37	32	27	23	18	14	9	5	0
34	95	90	86	81	76	71	66	62	57	52	48	43	38	34	29	25	21	16	12	8	3
35	95	91	86	81	77	72	67	63	58	54	49	45	40	36	32	27	23	19	14	10	6
36	95	91	86	82	77	73	68	64	60	55	51	46	42	38	34	29	25	21	17	13	9
37	95	91	87	83	78	74	69	65	61	57	53	48	44	40	36	31	27	23	19	15	11
38	96	91	87	83	79	75	70	66	62	58	54	50	46	42	37	33	29	25	21	17	14
39	96	92	87	83	79	75	71	67	63	59	55	51	47	43	39	35	31	27	24	20	16
40	96	92	87	83	79	75	71	68	64	60	56	52	48	45	41	37	33	29	26	22	18
41	96	92	88	84	80	76	72	69	65	61	57	54	50	46	42	39	35	31	28	24	20
42	96	92	88	85	81	77	73	69	65	62	58	55	51	47	44	40	36	33	30	26	23
43	96	92	88	85	81	77	73	70	66	63	59	55	52	48	45	42	38	35	31	28	25
44	96	93	89	85	81	78	74	71	67	63	60	56	53	49	46	43	39	36	33	30	26
45	96	93	89	86	82	78	74	71	67	64	61	57	54	51	47	44	41	38	34	31	28
46	96	93	89	86	82	79	75	72	68	65	61	58	55	52	48	45	42	39	35	32	29
47	96	93	89	86	82	79	75	72	69	66	62	59	56	53	49	46	43	40	37	34	31
48	96	93	90	86	83	79	76	73	69	66	63	60	57	54	50	47	44	41	38	35	32
49	96	93	90	86	83	80	76	73	70	67	64	61	57	54	51	48	45	42	39	36	34
50	96	93	90	87	83	80	77	74	71	67	64	61	58	55	52	49	46	43	41	38	35
51	97	94	90	87	84	81	78	75	71	68	65	62	59	56	53	50	47	45	42	39	36
52	97	94	90	87	84	81	78	75	72	69	66	63	60	57	54	51	49	46	43	40	37
53	97	94	90	87	84	81	78	75	72	69	66	63	61	58	55	52	50	47	44	41	39
54	97	94	91	88	85	82	79	76	73	70	67	64	61	59	56	53	50	48	45	42	40
55	97	94	91	88	85	82	79	76	73	70	68	65	62	59	57	54	51	49	46	43	41
56	97	94	91	88	85	82	79	76	73	71	68	65	63	60	57	55	52	50	47	44	42
57	97	94	91	88	85	82	80	77	74	71	69	66	63	61	58	55	53	50	48	45	43
58	97	94	91	88	85	83	80	77	74	72	69	66	64	61	59	56	54	51	49	46	44
59	97	94	91	89	86	83	80	78	75	72	70	67	65	62	59	57	55	52	49	47	45
60	97	94	91	89	86	83	81	78	75	73	70	68	65	63	60	58	55	53	50	48	46
61	97	94	92	89	86	84	81	78	76	73	71	68	65	63	61	58	56	54	51	49	47
62	97	94	92	89	86	84	81	79	76	74	71	69	66	64	61	59	57	55	52	50	47
63	97	95	92	89	87	84	82	79	77	74	71	69	67	64	62	60	57	55	53	50	48
64	97	95	92	90	87	84	82	79	77	74	72	70	67	65	63	60	58	56	53	51	49
65	97	95	92	90	87	85	82	80	77	75	72	70	68	66	63	61	59	56	54	52	50
66	97	95	92	90	87	85	82	80	78	75	73	71	68	66	64	61	59	57	55	53	51
67	97	95	92	90	87	85	83	80	78	75	73	71	69	66	64	62	60	58	56	53	51
68	97	95	92	90	88	85	83	80	78	76	74	71	69	67	65	62	60	58	56	54	52
69	97	95	93	90	88	85	83	81	79	76	74	72	70	67	65	63	61	59	57	55	53
70	98	95	93	90	88	86	83	81	79	77	74	72	70	68	66	64	61	59	57	55	53
71	98	95	93	90	88	86	84	81	79	77	75	72	70	68	66	64	62	60	58	56	54
72	98	95	93	91	88	86	84	82	79	77	75	73	71	69	67	65	63	61	59	57	55
73	98	95	93	91	88	86	84	82	80	78	75	73	71	69	67	65	63	61	59	57	55
74	98	95	93	91	89	86	84	82	80	78	76	64	71	69	67	65	63	61	60	58	56
75	98	96	93	91	89	86	84	82	80	78	76	74	72	70	68	66	64	62	60	58	56
76	98	96	93	91	89	87	84	82	80	78	76	74	72	70	68	66	64	62	61	59	57
77	98	96	93	91	89	87	85	83	81	79	77	74	72	71	69	67	65	63	61	59	57
78	98	96	93	91	89	87	85	83	81	79	77	75	73	71	69	67	65	63	62	60	58
79	98	96	93	91	89	87	85	83	81	79	77	75	73	71	69	68	66	64	62	60	58
80	98	96	94	91	89	87	85	83	81	79	77	75	74	72	70	68	66	64	62	61	59

Relative humidity, percent—Fahrenheit temperatures
[Pressure = 30.0 inches]

Depression of wet-bulb thermometer $(t - t')$

Air temperature t	11.0	11.5	12.0	12.5	13.0	13.5	14.0	14.5	15.0	15.5	16.0	16.5	17.0	17.5	18.0	18.5	19.0	19.5	20.0	20.5	21.0
35	2																				
36	5	1																			
37	7	3																			
38	10	6	2																		
39	12	8	5	1																	
40	15	11	7	4	0																
41	17	13	10	6	3																
42	19	16	12	9	5	2															
43	21	18	14	11	8	4	1														
44	23	20	16	13	10	7	4	0													
45	25	22	18	15	12	9	6	3													
46	26	23	20	17	14	11	8	5	3												
47	28	25	22	19	16	13	10	7	5	2											
48	29	26	23	21	18	15	12	9	7	4	1										
49	31	28	25	22	19	17	14	11	9	6	3	1									
50	32	29	27	24	21	18	16	13	10	8	5	3	0								
51	34	31	28	26	23	20	17	15	12	9	7	4	2								
52	35	32	29	27	24	22	19	17	14	11	9	6	4	1							
53	36	33	31	28	26	23	20	18	16	13	10	8	6	3	1						
54	37	35	32	29	27	24	22	20	17	15	12	10	8	5	3	1					
55	38	36	33	31	28	26	23	21	19	16	14	12	9	7	5	2	0				
56	39	37	34	32	30	27	25	22	20	18	16	13	11	9	7	4	2				
57	40	38	35	33	31	28	26	24	22	19	17	15	13	11	8	6	4	2			
58	41	39	37	34	32	30	27	25	23	21	18	16	14	12	10	8	6	3	1		
59	42	40	38	35	33	31	29	26	24	22	20	18	16	13	11	9	7	5	3	1	
60	43	41	39	37	34	32	30	28	26	23	21	19	17	15	13	11	9	7	5	3	1
61	44	42	40	38	35	33	31	29	27	25	22	20	18	16	14	12	10	8	7	5	3
62	45	43	41	39	36	34	32	30	28	26	24	22	20	18	16	14	12	10	8	6	4
63	46	44	42	40	37	35	33	31	29	27	25	23	21	19	17	15	13	11	9	8	6
64	47	45	43	41	38	36	34	32	30	28	26	24	22	20	18	16	14	13	11	9	7
65	48	46	44	41	39	37	35	33	31	29	27	25	24	22	20	18	16	14	12	11	9
66	48	46	44	42	40	38	36	34	32	30	29	27	25	23	21	19	17	16	14	12	10
67	49	47	45	43	41	39	37	35	33	31	30	28	26	24	22	20	19	17	15	13	12
68	50	48	46	44	42	40	38	36	34	32	31	29	27	25	23	21	20	18	16	15	13
69	51	49	47	45	43	41	39	37	35	33	32	30	28	26	24	23	21	19	18	16	14
70	51	49	48	46	44	42	40	38	36	34	33	31	29	27	25	24	22	20	19	17	15
71	52	50	49	47	45	43	41	39	37	35	34	32	30	28	27	25	23	22	20	19	17
72	53	51	49	47	45	43	42	40	38	36	34	33	31	29	28	26	24	23	21	19	18
73	53	51	50	48	46	44	42	41	39	37	35	34	32	30	29	27	25	24	22	21	19
74	54	52	50	48	47	45	43	41	40	38	36	34	33	31	29	28	26	25	23	21	20
75	54	53	51	49	47	45	44	42	40	39	37	35	34	32	30	29	27	26	24	23	21
76	55	53	52	50	48	46	44	43	41	40	38	36	35	33	31	30	28	27	25	24	22
77	56	54	53	52	50	48	47	45	44	42	40	39	37	35	34	32	31	29	28	26	23
78	56	54	53	51	49	47	46	44	43	41	39	38	36	34	33	31	30	28	27	25	24
79	57	55	53	51	50	48	46	45	43	42	40	38	37	35	34	32	31	29	28	26	25
80	57	55	54	52	50	49	47	45	44	42	41	39	38	36	35	33	32	30	29	27	26

$(t - t')$

t	21.5	22.0	22.5	23.0	23.5	24.0	24.5	25.0	25.5	26.0	26.5	27.0	27.5	28.0	28.5
61	1														
62	2	1													
63	4	2	0												
64	6	4	2	0											
65	7	5	4	2	0										
66	9	7	5	3	2	0									
67	10	8	7	5	3	2	0								
68	11	10	8	6	5	3	1								
69	13	11	9	8	6	5	3	1							
70	14	12	11	9	8	6	4	3	1						
71	15	13	12	10	9	7	6	4	3	1					
72	16	15	13	12	10	9	7	6	4	3	1				
73	17	16	14	13	11	10	8	7	5	4	3	1			
74	18	17	15	14	13	11	10	8	7	5	4	3	1		
75	20	18	17	15	14	12	11	9	8	7	5	4	3	1	
76	21	19	18	16	15	13	12	11	9	8	7	5	4	3	1
77	22	21	20	18	17	15	14	13	11	10	9	8	6	5	3
78	23	22	21	20	18	17	16	14	13	11	10	9	7	6	4
79	23	23	22	21	20	18	17	16	14	13	11	10	8	7	5
80	24	23	22	20	19	18	16	15	14	12	11	10	9	7	6

MEASURING CLOUD DIRECTION AND SPEED

Materials

Small table or stool, 18–24 inches high

Magnetic compass

Circular mirror, 6 inches in diameter

Plywood, 9 inches by 9 inches by 3/4 inch

3 screws, 2 inches long

Wooden dowel, 1/4 inch by 3 inches

Paper circle, 9 inches in diameter

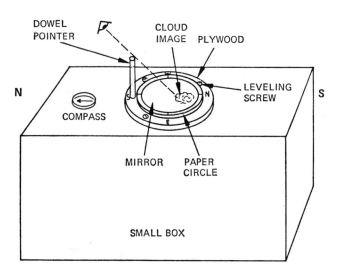

FIGURE 1
Nephoscope construction

A weather observer is interested in cloud direction and speed because of the information it gives him about winds aloft. And frequently this information is rather surprising. For example, would you expect winds a thousand feet above the ground to be exactly opposite in direction and at twice the speed of those at the ground? In fact, the average velocity of the wind does increase with height above the ground. This effect is most noticeable in the first 100 feet, the velocity generally doubling between a height of 1 1/2 feet and 33 feet, and increasing an additional 20 percent to a height of 100 feet. Such a large variation is mainly due to the reduction in frictional "drag" with increased height above the ground. Along with the increased velocity, there is usually a decrease in turbulence also, although some surface eddies can affect the air several thousands of feet above the ground, particularly in mountainous areas.

On a day when noticeable winds are present at the ground, pay particular attention to their speed and direction. Then observe the clouds drifting above you. Are they traveling in the same direction as the winds at the ground? How can you obtain a reasonably accurate measurement of their direction and speed?

An instrument used for such measurements is called a nephoscope. You can construct a simple version following the directions given here. It can be used very nicely in conjunction with the cloud height measuring techniques described earlier. As you will see, the formula for calculating speed includes cloud height. If you have become proficient in the use of the height measurer or sling psychrometer, add the nephoscope to your bag of equipment to make a complete analysis.

Obtain a circular mirror about 6 inches in diameter. Mount it on a flat piece of plywood about 9 inches in diameter, or 9 inches square, if you don't have a circular piece of wood. Glue a paper circle around the mirror and flat on the plywood surface. The circle should have a diameter of 7 1/2 inches and should be carefully marked off into 360 degrees. In other words, the calibrated paper border should be about 1 1/2 inches wide.

Glue or screw a sighting point, made of a 1/4-inch dowel 3 inches long, to the plywood at the mirror's edge, as shown in Figure 1. Mark with a felt-tip pen, lipstick, or whatever, a small dot in the center of the mirror. Finally, screw three 1/4-inch screws at three points around the plywood border. These should be long enough to extend through the base, and will be used as leveling devices when you are ready to work.

Set up the nephoscope outside on a box on reasonably level ground, and, using a small pocket compass, orient the instrument so that south on the paper circle is pointing north (see Figure 1). Bring the nephoscope to approximate level by the three adjusting screws.

To determine cloud direction, locate a cloud image at the dot in the center of the mirror. Continue watching the cloud image by sighting over the sighting point, and note the angle at which the image disappears from the edge of the mirror. This represents the wind direction at the height of the cloud observed.

To determine speed, you'll need a stopwatch or a friend with a watch with a second hand who will do the timing as you watch the image. Without either, you can always count off seconds. Time the movement of the image from the center dot to disappearance at the mirror's edge. The formula for the calculation of cloud speed is:

$$\text{Speed} = \frac{\text{cloud height (feet)} \times \text{mirror radius (inches)}}{\text{height of dowel (inches)} \times \text{time (seconds)}}$$

NOTE: If the mirror radius and dowel height are the same, the equation reduces to:

$$\text{Speed} = \frac{\text{cloud height (feet)}}{\text{time (seconds)}}$$

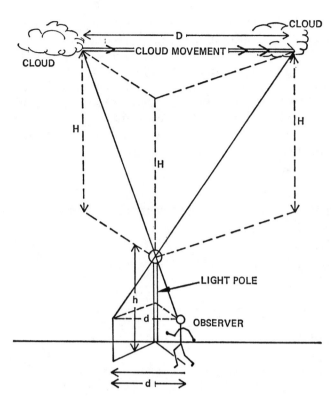

FIGURE 2
Measurements needed in direct vision nephoscope

Another way of applying the same technique to determine the speed and direction of winds at cloud level is called the *direct vision nephoscope*. In this case, you—the observer—move to keep the cloud sighted relative to a fixed point. Broken clouds at night may be sighted against the stars or moon; in the daytime, use a flagpole, light pole, or a prominent part of a building. To determine cloud direction alone, simply keep the eye stationary and watch the cloud with reference to the flagpole, or whatever you are using as your fixed point. To measure cloud velocity, it will be necessary to ascertain the time the cloud took to move through a certain angle with reference to the fixed point. Keeping the cloud sighted over the flagpole, move your position so as to keep a point on the cloud in line with the top of the pole. Drop a marker at the beginning of the observation and another at the end of a known time interval. Measure the distance you have moved during the observation and note the exact direction of movement. You will be moving in a direction opposite to that of the cloud, and you will be forming two similar triangles of which the angle points are eye level (at positions beginning and end) and pole, and cloud (at positions beginning and end) and pole (see Figure 2). Therefore,

$$\frac{D}{H} = \frac{d}{h}$$

The speed of movement of the cloud is: $V = D/t$. Substituting this in the proportion, we get:

$$V = \frac{dH}{ht,}$$

where d is the distance moved by the observer in feet,
    h is the height in feet of the pole (measured or estimated) from above the observer's eye level,
    t is the time in seconds, and
    H is the height of the clouds being measured from the top of the light pole. Because the height of the light pole is extremely small in comparison with the height of the clouds being measured, it is satisfactory to call H the height of the clouds above the ground.

Using your estimation of cloud height from the measuring techniques described in the previous section, feed your data into the formula and come up with how fast the winds at cloud level are traveling.

Some questions you might try to answer as you take measurements of speed and direction on moving clouds are:

1. Which types of clouds seem to move faster, high clouds or low clouds?
2. Can you use the nephoscope methods to obtain the rate of growth of a cumulonimbus cloud? Try it.
3. Determine the cloud direction and speed for two levels of clouds on the same day, and compute the wind shear between the two levels. Wind shear is the variation of wind speed and direction over a given vertical distance. If, for example, the lower layer of clouds had a velocity of 20 feet per second from the west, and the upper layer of clouds (say, 5,000 feet higher) had a velocity of 60 feet per second from the northwest, the wind shear could be described as 60 fps − 20 fps = 40 feet per second per 5,000 feet, or 8 feet per second per 1,000 feet, clockwise, between the lower and the upper layers of clouds. In this case, wind shear is due to the shifts in wind direction from west to northwest (clockwise), with the vertical ascent from the lower level to the upper level.
4. Observe some lenticularis clouds, such as stratocumulus lenticularis, or altocumulus lenticularis, and compute their height, speed, and direction of movement. How does the speed differ from ordinary stratocumulus or altocumulus clouds present on the same day? The lenticularis cloud is caused when air is set into vertical oscillatory motion and travels in a series of waves. If conditions are right, condensation of water vapor occurs on the rising portion of the wave, and re-evaporation occurs on the falling portion of the wave (Figure 3). As a result, a lenticular cloud may appear to remain stationary in the sky

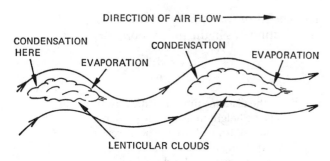

FIGURE 3
Diagram showing formation of lenticular clouds

for a period of several hours. Lenticular clouds are not uncommon in mountainous areas, where the wind currents over the mountaintops are set into wavy motion. The clouds have a distinctive appearance, resembling flat wafers or thin lenses. Frequently, several may be seen at one time, extending in a line leeward from the mountain range, or even stacked vertically, one above the other.

TECHNOLOGY

TECHNOLOGY AND THE QUALITY OF LIFE

Overview

Each student will report on a technology that he or she feels will be pivotal in improving the quality of life. Examples of such technologies in history are the wheel, the automobile, and television. Students should learn how important technology is in their lives and become familiar with careers related to significant technologies. This activity can be scheduled to occupy three to five class periods and make extensive use of library resources.

Science Background

Technology affects the way we spend our time and even the way we think. Quality of life would be somewhat different without the sophisticated technologies that we have come to depend on. Recognizing the importance of certain technologies such as computers and biotechnology will enable students to form a clearer picture of how technology interacts with our society. Career exploration may also prove useful as students learn about occupations that will be important in the future.

Innovations have often been instrumental in creating revolution in lifestyles. The wheel opened possibilities of transportation, the gun changed the nature of war, and the telegraph opened up the world to communication across thousands of miles. The common denominator in all of these technologies is that they improved the quality of life for some people in some way. In other words, these technologies have made some aspect of life easier or better.

Today, the dominant technologies include microelectronics and biotechnology. Microelectronic computers make possible efficient processing of great volumes of information. Biotechnology works wonders in replacing body parts and performing delicate surgery. Many careers are related to technologies such as these, and people with training in these areas are likely to be in demand in the future. For example, health technology careers include medical and biological researchers, laboratory technicians, and surgeons. New discoveries in all areas will probably eliminate some old jobs and create many new jobs in the next century.

Major Concepts

- Technology is an integral part of society.
- Many technologies revolutionize society by improving the quality of life.

Student Objectives

After completing this activity, students should be able to:
- recognize that technology has direct impact on our lives
- identify some technologies that are likely to prove instrumental in determining the direction that our society takes
- define quality of life
- describe the relationship between quality of life and technology

Materials

    Library resources
    Career information resources

Vocabulary

    Innovation
    Quality of Life
    Technology
    Microelectronics
    Biotechnology

Procedure

1. Have students look around the room and ask them to point out objects that illustrate the use of technology. Possible answers include computers, audiovisual materials, fluorescent lights, etc.
2. Define technology and discuss with the class what it is and how it affects all goods that are produced. Explain that sometimes a new technology may greatly affect people's lives and that this is related to the general concept of quality of life. Give examples such as the wheel, plow, electric light, etc.
3. Each student should decide on a recent innovation that he or she believes will improve the quality of life in the future. Encourage diversity in the topics. Some general topics are health, genetic engineering, food, communication, and media technologies.
4. The students should spend at least three class periods researching their topics in the library. They should concentrate on how the technology improves the quality of life and should also investigate at least one occupation related to the technology.
5. Each student should write a three-to-four-page report on his or her findings. These reports may

be handed in and evaluated or reported orally and discussed.

Extension

Find primary sources that discuss technologies of the past that have proven to be instrumental in improving the quality of many people's lives. For example, read a 1948 or 1950 article about television. How did people feel about it at the time? Did they recognize how important television would be? Lead a class discussion on this topic or have students do individual research projects on these past technologies.

Evaluation

Have students write short answers to these questions:

1. Are there any technologies that seem to be dominant today?
2. How does technology affect, for example, medical care?
3. How did the invention of the telephone, for example, improve the quality of life? Were there any tradeoffs?

USING THE MICROCOMPUTER TO MODEL SOLUTIONS TO PROBLEMS: THE COFFEE CUP PROBLEM*

How long will it take a cup of coffee to cool? Specifically, how long will it take the coffee to cool from 190 degrees to 104 degrees if it sits undisturbed at 70 degrees Fahrenheit?

We would expect the rate of cooling to change with temperature of the cup. Newton's Law of Cooling states that the rate of cooling is directly proportional to the difference in the temperature of the room and the temperature of the cup. This can be expressed as:

$$\text{Rate} = K (\text{temp. of cup} - \text{room temp.})$$

This problem can be solved by a method called *iteration*, using a small time interval as the iteration interval. For example, if the iteration length is set at 0.1 minute, the approximate cooling rate for the short interval can be calculated at 190° F. The degrees

*Peter Kelman et al., *Computers in Teaching Mathematics* (Reading, MA: Addison-Wesley Publishing Co., 1983), p. 84. Reprinted with permission.

of cooling resulting from this cooling rate approximation would then be subtracted from 190 and a new cooling rate calculated for the next 0.1 minute interval. This procedure would be repeated until the endpoint of 104 degrees is reached; the sum of the 0.1 minute intervals required to reach this point would be the approximate answer of how long it would take the coffee cup to cool to 104 degrees F.

The teacher or students could write a program like the following to perform all the calculations and print out the results.

```
10 REM . . Coffee Cooling Simulation Using
   Newton's Law
30 TE = 190
50 K = 0.09:DT = 0.1
60 PRINT "TIME", "TEMP", "CHANGE"
70 FOR T = 1 TO 200
80 TC = K* (7C − TE)
100 TE = TE + TC * DT
110 IF INT (T/5) () T/5 THEN 130
120 PRINT T/10, INT (100 * TE)/100, INT (100
    *TC)/100
130 NEXT T
```

USING MICROCOMPUTERS IN INTERDISCIPLINARY PROBLEMS

The introduction of microcomputers poses the problem of where to fit them into the curriculum. Even before the advent of this new discipline, there has been increasing demand on schools to provide coverage of new subjects: drug education, driver education, environmental studies, various ethnic studies, etc.

Now computers can help to settle some of these competing demands through meaningful interdisciplinary problem solving. While not essential for interdisciplinary activities, they can make problem solving more interesting, more realistic, and more useful to students.

The sciences are the most fertile source of problems for use of microcomputers. For example, many of the laws of physics involve the relationship between the speed of a wave, its frequency, and its wavelength. Speed (v) equals the frequency (f) times the wavelength (l), $v = f \times l$. This law involves simple multiplication or division similar to problems students do in routine problem sets.

A program for junior high students using this equation could begin by showing the definitions of speed, wavelength, and frequency. Several waves might be displayed simultaneously, with a chart showing v, f, and l. Students could change one variable, while holding the others constant and watch the change in the third. Students might then be asked to solve multiplication and division problems involving one of the variables as an unknown. The program could be written to display the results in tabular form as shown below:

This table could then be used as a basis for interdisciplinary problem solving. Some students could study sound waves, solving problems of the design of musical instruments. Others could study ocean waves, determining where to place a wave barrier to prevent wave erosion, etc.

One of the attractions of the computer as an educational tool is the relative ease with which most students can learn to write simple programs. Interdisciplinary problems provide an ideal opportunity for students to develop their own learning materials through programming.*

*Peter Keiman et al., *Computers in Teaching Mathematics* (Reading, MA: Addison-Wesley Publishing Co., 1983), p. 22. Reprinted with permission.

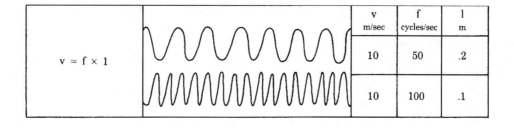

$v = f \times l$		v m/sec	f cycles/sec	l m
		10	50	.2
		10	100	.1

MATHEMATICS

STIMULATING MATHEMATICS USAGE IN SCIENCE CLASSES

The laboratory provides the opportunity for many data-gathering problems. The student may practice measuring, keeping records, and graphing. Analysis of experiments gives additional practice in using mathematics. The PSSC exercise entitled "Analysis of an Experiment" is an example. The data given in the exercise show a record of the time required to empty a can of water through a hole punched in the bottom.

TABLE 1
Amount of time to empty (in seconds)

d (in em)	h (in em)			
	30	10	4	1
1.5	73.0	43.5	26.7	13.5
2.0	41.2	23.7	15.0	7.2
3.0	18.4	10.5	6.8	3.7
5.0	6.8	3.9	2.2	1.5

Students are told to plot graphs of the data to analyze the relationships between emptying times and two other variables, diameter of the hole (d) and height of water in the can (h). Types of graphs suggested are one showing time vs. diameter for a constant height and one showing time vs. square of diameter. Graphs for different heights are also suggested. Typical questions asked in this exercise are:

1. From your curve, how accurately can you predict the time it would take to empty the same container if the diameter of the opening was 4 cm.? 8 cm.?
2. Can you write down the algebraic relation between t and d for the particular height of water used?
3. Can you find the general expression for time of flow as a function of both h and d?*

This exercise illustrates clearly how using mathematics gives a student practice in analyzing the results of an experiment and demonstrates the integral nature of mathematics in science.

Senior high school science students should learn the limitations of measurement, the sources of quantitative errors, and standards of accuracy. How accurate is a meter stick? To how many significant figures can a measurement be made? Of what value are estimated units? How accurate is a volume computation made from linear measurements which have estimated units? What are possible sources of error in an experiment? To what degree of precision are certain measurements made? How does one express the degree of precision recording data?

Knowledge of significant figures is particularly important in chemistry and physics, where physical measurements are made frequently in laboratory experiments.

*Physical Science Study Committee, *Laboratory Guide for Physics* (Boston: D.C. Heath).

MATHEMATICS CHALLENGE: USING SIMPLE MATERIALS TO FIND THE EARTH'S MAGNETIC FIELD

Obtain the necessary materials and set up the apparatus as shown in Figure 1.

Materials

Dry cell

Resistance box

Milliammeter (0–1 am. range)

Cardboard cylinder

Small sewing needle

Ten feet of No. 24 insulated copper wire

Protractor

Connecting wire

Knife switch

Terminal posts

Cellophane tape

Wood base

Construction as shown in Figure 1.

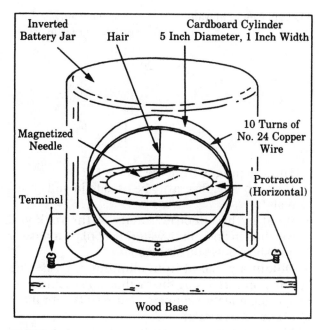

FIGURE 1

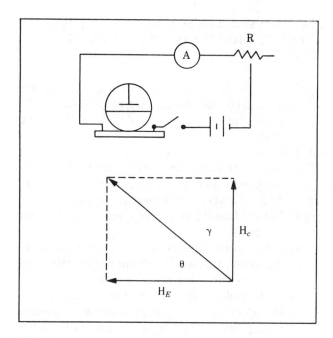

FIGURE 2

Calculations:

To find H_c, use $H_c = \dfrac{2 \pi NI}{10r}$
where

N = number of coils
I = current in amperes
r = radius of coil in cm.
H_c = magnetic field strength of coil in oersteds
H_E = magnetic field strength of earth in oersteds (to be found)

To find H_E, use $H_E = H_c \tan \gamma$ □ where $\gamma = 90° - \theta$

Experiment (see Figure 2)

Align the magnetometer so that the needle which is pointing north-south will be parallel to the base line of the protractor. Make the connections as shown and throw the knife switch. If the needle makes a full 90-degree turn, R must be increased so that the mag-

netic field H_c of the magnetometer is less strong. Adjust R so that the needle comes to rest somewhere between zero and ninety degrees. Read the milliammeter and the angular deflection of the needle (θ). Take several trials.

Your result should be in the neighborhood of 0.2 oersted for H_E at 40 degrees latitude. The values of H_E in the United States range from 0.13 oersted at Gull Island in Lake Superior to 0.28 oersted near Brownsville, Texas. The higher values are at lower latitudes because it is the *horizontal* component that is being measured.

1. Where is mathematics needed in this experiment?
2. What could you learn about the magnetic field of the earth without the use of mathematics?
3. How much more can you learn using mathematics?

MATHEMATICS IN SCIENCE: HOW WILL SPECIFIC GRAVITY HELP TO IDENTIFY MINERALS?

1. Obtain the following materials: Spring balance, string, can or jar of water, iron small object, aluminum small object, piece of glass, collection of minerals

2. Discussion:
   a. State the following: "Mary had a rock that weighed different amounts at different times. The rock has not changed in any way."
   b. What ideas do you have about how this may happen?
   c. Have you ever picked up a large rock under water and then carried it out of the water? Was it heavier in water or out of water?
   d. How could we make sure of our answer?

3. Suspend a rock on a spring balance with a length of string. Record its weight. Immerse the rock in water. Record its weight under water. How much more or less does it weigh now?

4. Specific gravity is a way to help identify minerals. Specific gravity is found by comparing the weight of a mineral in air to the amount of weight the mineral loses in water. Specific gravity may be found as illustrated in the following example:

Weight of rock in air	35 grams
Weight of rock in water	15 grams (subtract)
Loss of weight in water	20 grams

Teacher Information

The table below lists average specific gravities for common minerals.

Material	Average Specific Gravity
Pyrite	5.0
Halite	2.2 (dissolves in water)
Fluorite	3.2
Quartz	2.7
Calcite	2.7
Graphite	2.3
Galena	7.5
Hematite	5.3
Magnetite	5.2
Limonite	4.3
Talc	2.7
Mica	2.8
Gypsum	2.3
Glass	2.13–2.99
Feldspar (orthoclase)	2.6
Feldspar (plagioclase)	2.7

$$\text{Loss of weight in water } \frac{\text{Specific gravity}}{\text{Weight of rock in air}}$$

$$\begin{array}{r} 1.75 \\ 20\overline{)35} \\ \underline{20} \\ 150 \\ \underline{140} \\ 100 \\ \underline{100} \end{array}$$

The specific gravity of the rock is 1.75.
How can specific gravity be used to identify minerals?

5. What is the specific gravity of the rock you weighed in and out of water? Record your answer and show how you obtained it.

6. Obtain a piece of iron, aluminum, glass, and other objects. Using the method above, find their specific gravity. Compare your results with those of your classmates.

7. Make a list of the minerals in your collection and find the specific gravity of each. Record the specific gravity of each in a column beside the name of the mineral.

Index